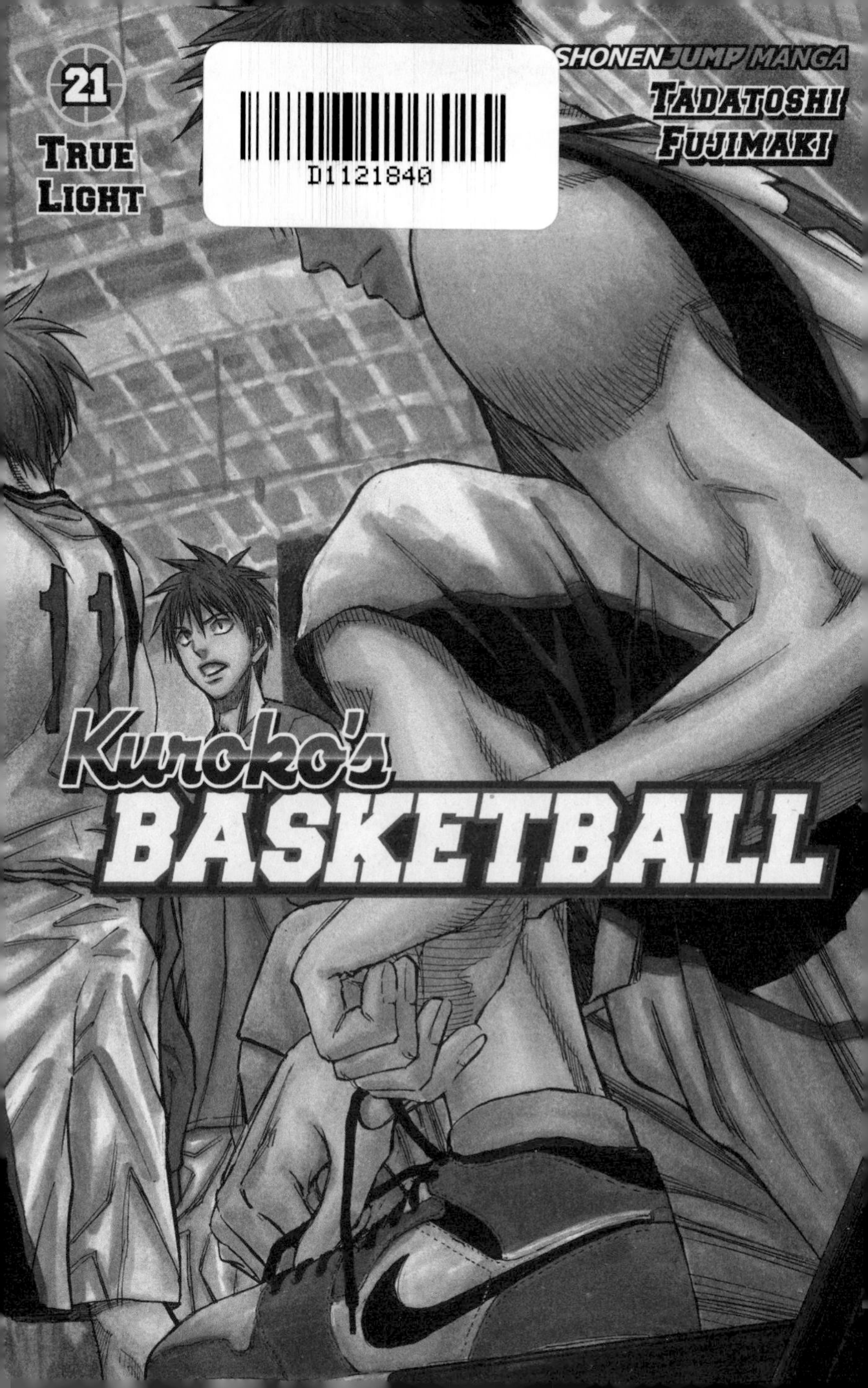
21
TRUE LIGHT
SHONEN JUMP MANGA
TADATOSHI FUJIMAKI
Kuroko's
BASKETBALL

CHARACTERS

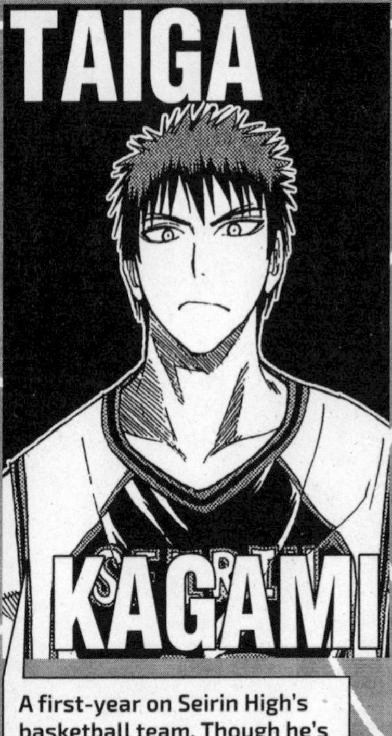
TAIGA
KAGAMI

A first-year on Seirin High's basketball team. Though he's rough around the edges, he's a gifted player with a lot of potential. His goal is to beat the Miracle Generation.

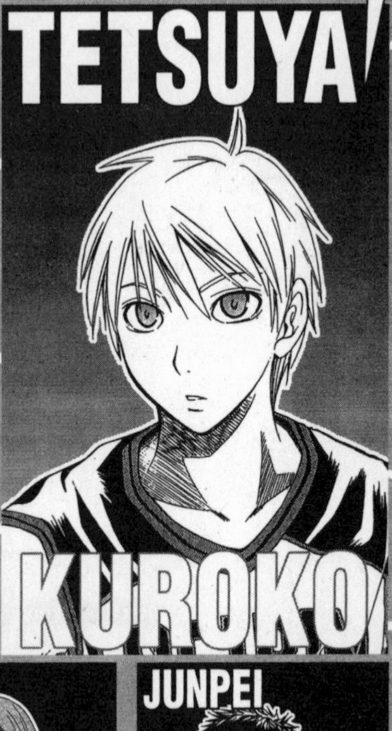
TETSUYA
KUROKO

A first-year on Seirin High's basketball team. Gifted with a natural lack of presence, he utilizes misdirection on the court to make nearly invisible passes.

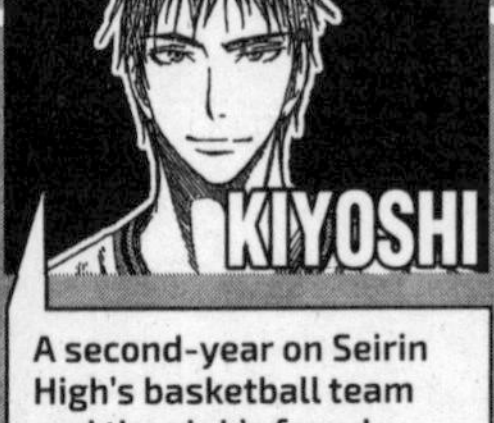
TEPPEI
KIYOSHI

A second-year on Seirin High's basketball team and the club's founder. He was hospitalized but returned shortly after Inter-High.

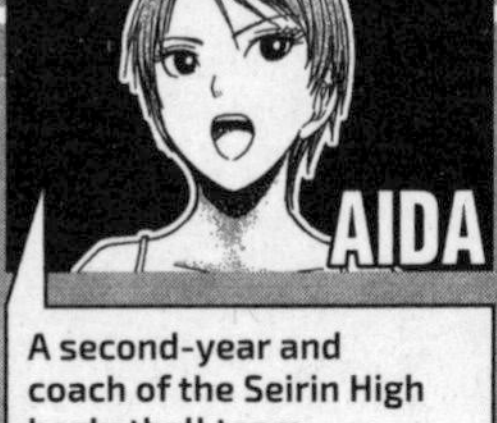
RIKO
AIDA

A second-year and coach of the Seirin High basketball team.

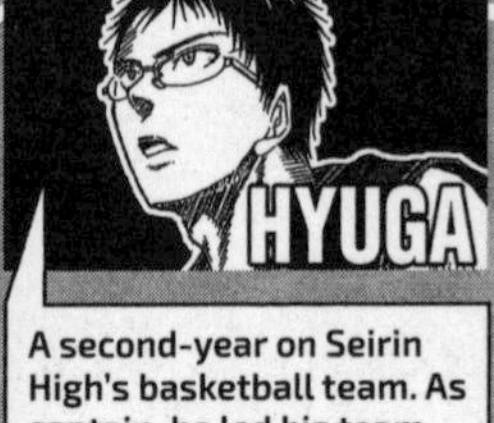
JUNPEI
HYUGA

A second-year on Seirin High's basketball team. As captain, he led his team to the Finals League last year despite only playing first-year players.

KUROKO'S BASKETBALL

RYOTA

KISE

One of the Miracle Generation. Any basketball move he sees, he can mimic in an instant.

SHINTARO

MIDORIMA

A first-year at Shutoku High, he's the top shooter of the Miracle Generation.

DAIKI

AOMINE

The ace of the Miracle Generation and Kuroko's former friend, he's now a first-year at To-oh Academy.

YUKIO

KASAMATSU

Kaijo's captain. As a second-year, his failure resulted in Kaijo's loss during the first game of Inter-High. His teammates implicitly trust him.

SEIJURO

AKASHI

Captain of the Miracle Generation during his time at Teiko Middle and the current leader of Rakuzan's ferocious team.

ATSUSHI

MURASAKIBARA

One of the Miracle Generation. A first-year on Yosen High's basketball team. He plays center, but he doesn't actually enjoy basketball all that much.

Teiko Middle School is an elite championship school whose basketball team once fielded five prodigies collectively known as "the Miracle Generation." But supporting those five was a phantom sixth man—Tetsuya Kuroko. Now Kuroko's a first-year high school student with zero presence who joins Seirin High's basketball club. Though his physical abilities and stats are well below average, Kuroko thrives on the court by making passes his opponents can't detect!

Aiming for the Winter Cup title, Seirin clashes against To-oh and Aomine in their first game of the tournament. In game four, they defeat Yosen and Murasakibara. Seirin's opponent in the semifinals is Kise and the Kaijo team that crushed Fukuda Sohgoh and former Miracle Generation member Haizaki. Meanwhile, Shutoku and Midorima take on Rakuzan and its leader Akashi!

STORY THUS FAR

TABLE OF CONTENTS

181ST QUARTER:
Present Them 007

182ND QUARTER:
That's Not Enough! 027

183RD QUARTER:
Let's Do This! 047

184TH QUARTER:
Early Bird 067

185TH QUARTER:
Can't Help but Smile 089

186TH QUARTER:
You're Up! 109

187TH QUARTER:
You've Got Teammates 129

188TH QUARTER:
Insulting 149

189TH QUARTER:
True Light 169

190TH QUARTER:
All We've Got 191

191ST QUARTER:
Plain as Day 211

192ND QUARTER:
Got Anything Else to Say? 231

193RD QUARTER:
Ain't Done Yet!! 251

194TH QUARTER:
In Order to Win 271

195TH QUARTER:
Climax! 291

196TH QUARTER:
Ain't Losing Focus 311

197TH QUARTER:
Cutting into the Lead! 331

198TH QUARTER:
This Time for Sure 351

181ST QUARTER: PRESENT THEM

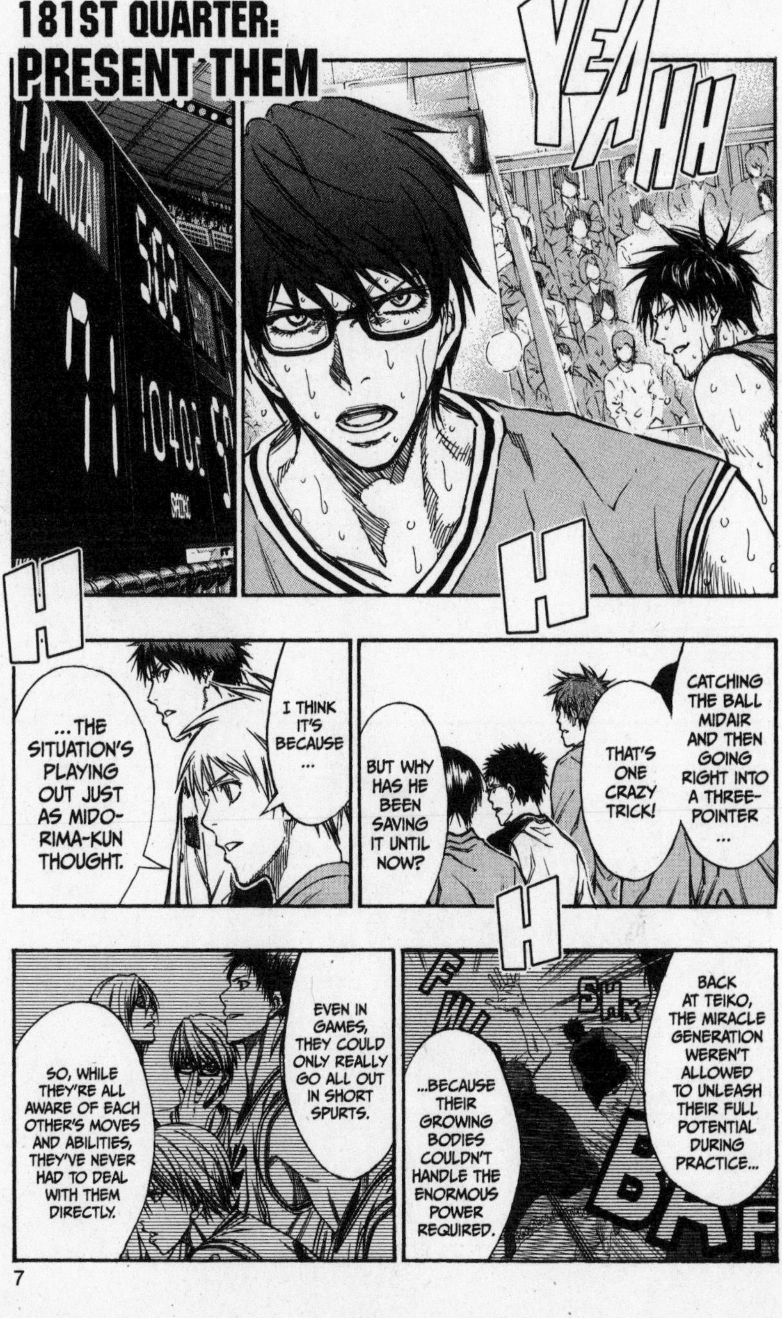
YEAHHH
H
H
CATCHING THE BALL MIDAIR AND THEN GOING RIGHT INTO A THREE-POINTER ...
THAT'S ONE CRAZY TRICK!
BUT WHY HAS HE BEEN SAVING IT UNTIL NOW?
I THINK IT'S BECAUSE ...
...THE SITUATION'S PLAYING OUT JUST AS MIDO-RIMA-KUN THOUGHT.
H
BACK AT TEIKO, THE MIRACLE GENERATION WEREN'T ALLOWED TO UNLEASH THEIR FULL POTENTIAL DURING PRACTICE...
...BECAUSE THEIR GROWING BODIES COULDN'T HANDLE THE ENORMOUS POWER REQUIRED.
EVEN IN GAMES, THEY COULD ONLY REALLY GO ALL OUT IN SHORT SPURTS.
SO, WHILE THEY'RE ALL AWARE OF EACH OTHER'S MOVES AND ABILITIES, THEY'VE NEVER HAD TO DEAL WITH THEM DIRECTLY.

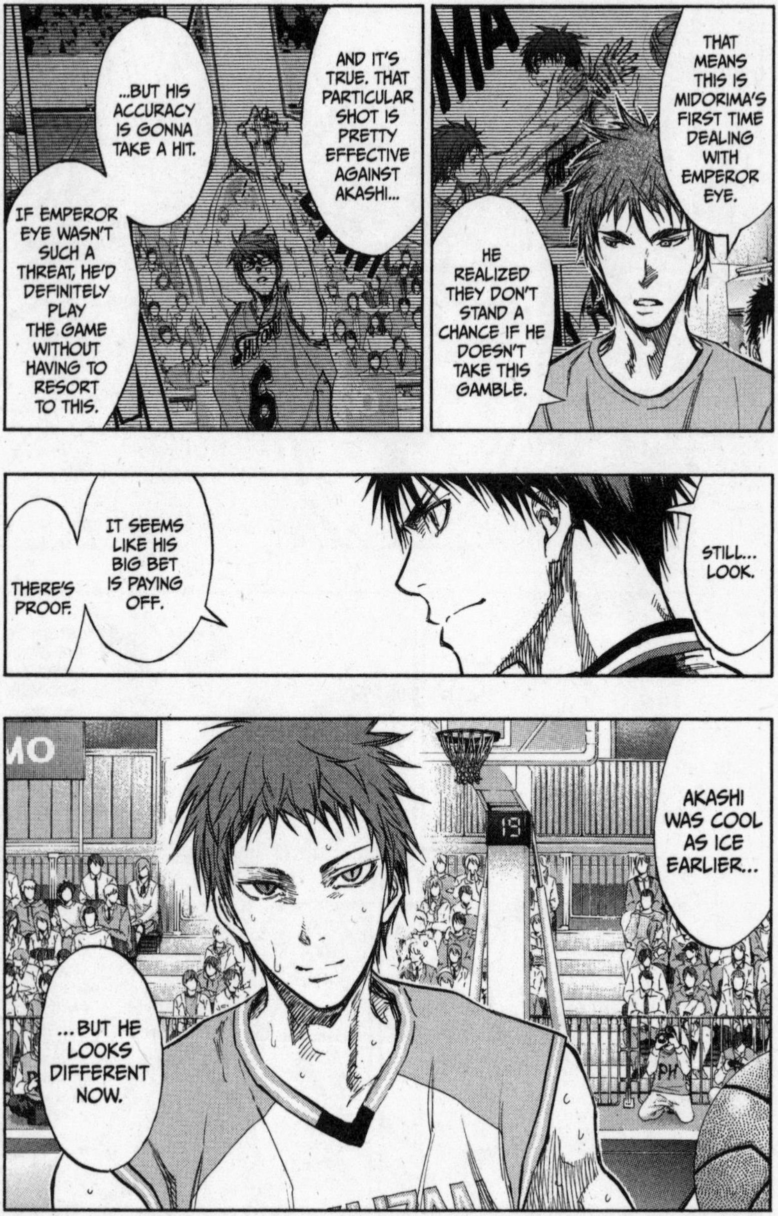
THAT MEANS THIS IS MIDORIMA'S FIRST TIME DEALING WITH EMPEROR EYE.
HE REALIZED THEY DON'T STAND A CHANCE IF HE DOESN'T TAKE THIS GAMBLE.
AND IT'S TRUE. THAT PARTICULAR SHOT IS PRETTY EFFECTIVE AGAINST AKASHI...
...BUT HIS ACCURACY IS GONNA TAKE A HIT.
IF EMPEROR EYE WASN'T SUCH A THREAT, HE'D DEFINITELY PLAY THE GAME WITHOUT HAVING TO RESORT TO THIS.
STILL... LOOK.
IT SEEMS LIKE HIS BIG BET IS PAYING OFF.
THERE'S PROOF.
AKASHI WAS COOL AS ICE EARLIER...
...BUT HE LOOKS DIFFERENT NOW.

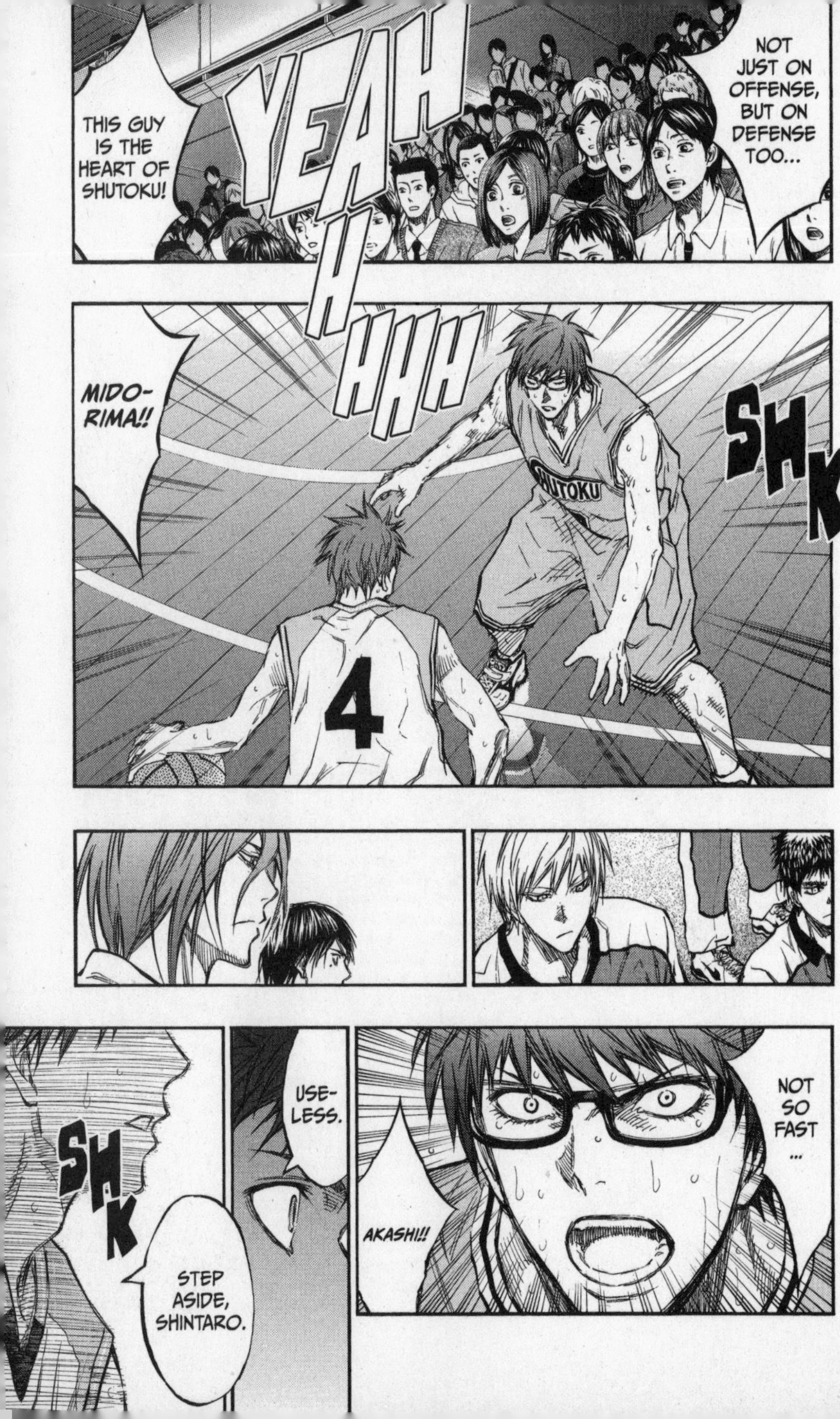
NOT JUST ON OFFENSE, BUT ON DEFENSE TOO...
YEAHHHHH
THIS GUY IS THE HEART OF SHUTOKU!
SHK
SHUTOKU
4
MIDO-RIMA!!
NOT SO FAST ...
AKASHI!!
USE-LESS.
SHK
STEP ASIDE, SHINTARO.

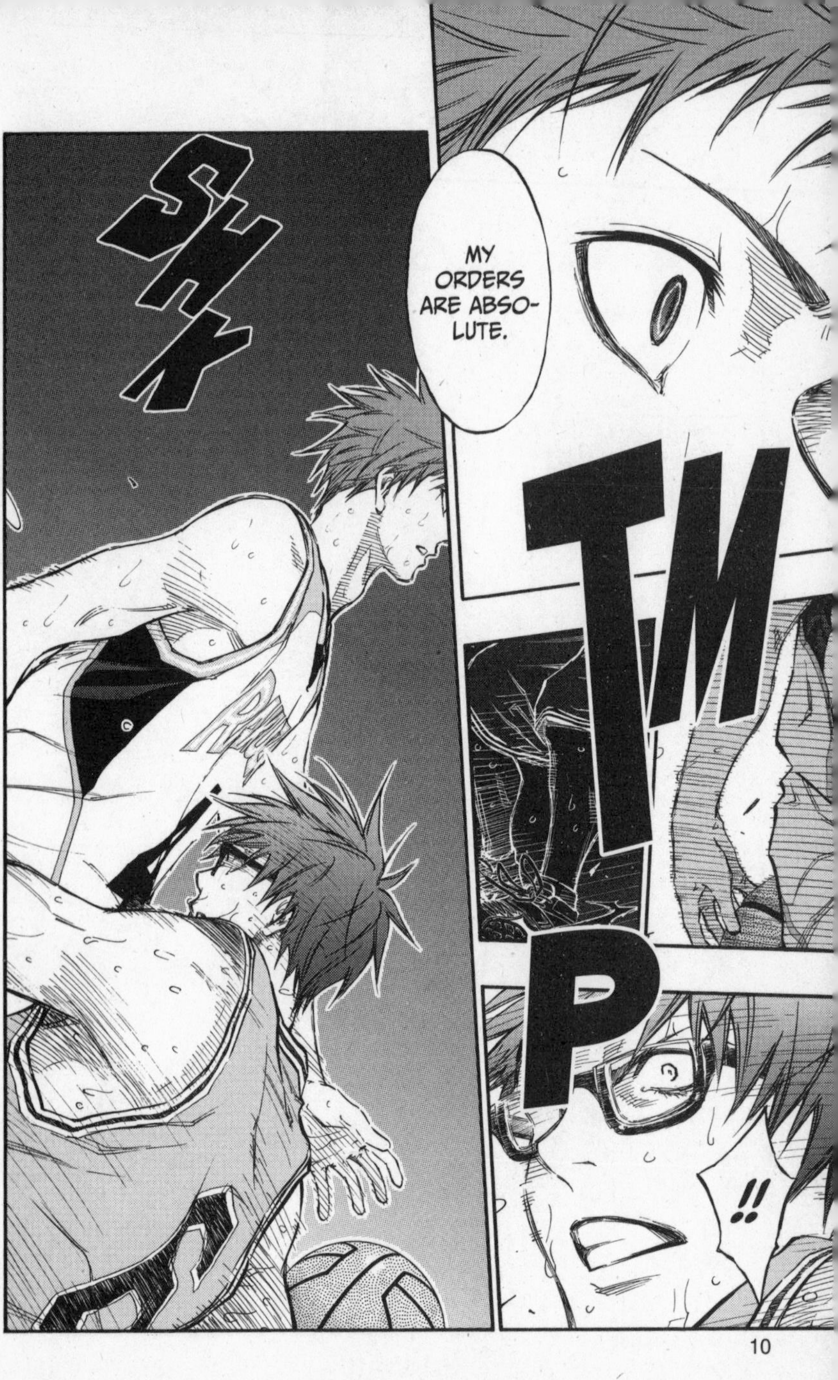
MY ORDERS ARE ABSO-LUTE.
TMP
!!
SHK

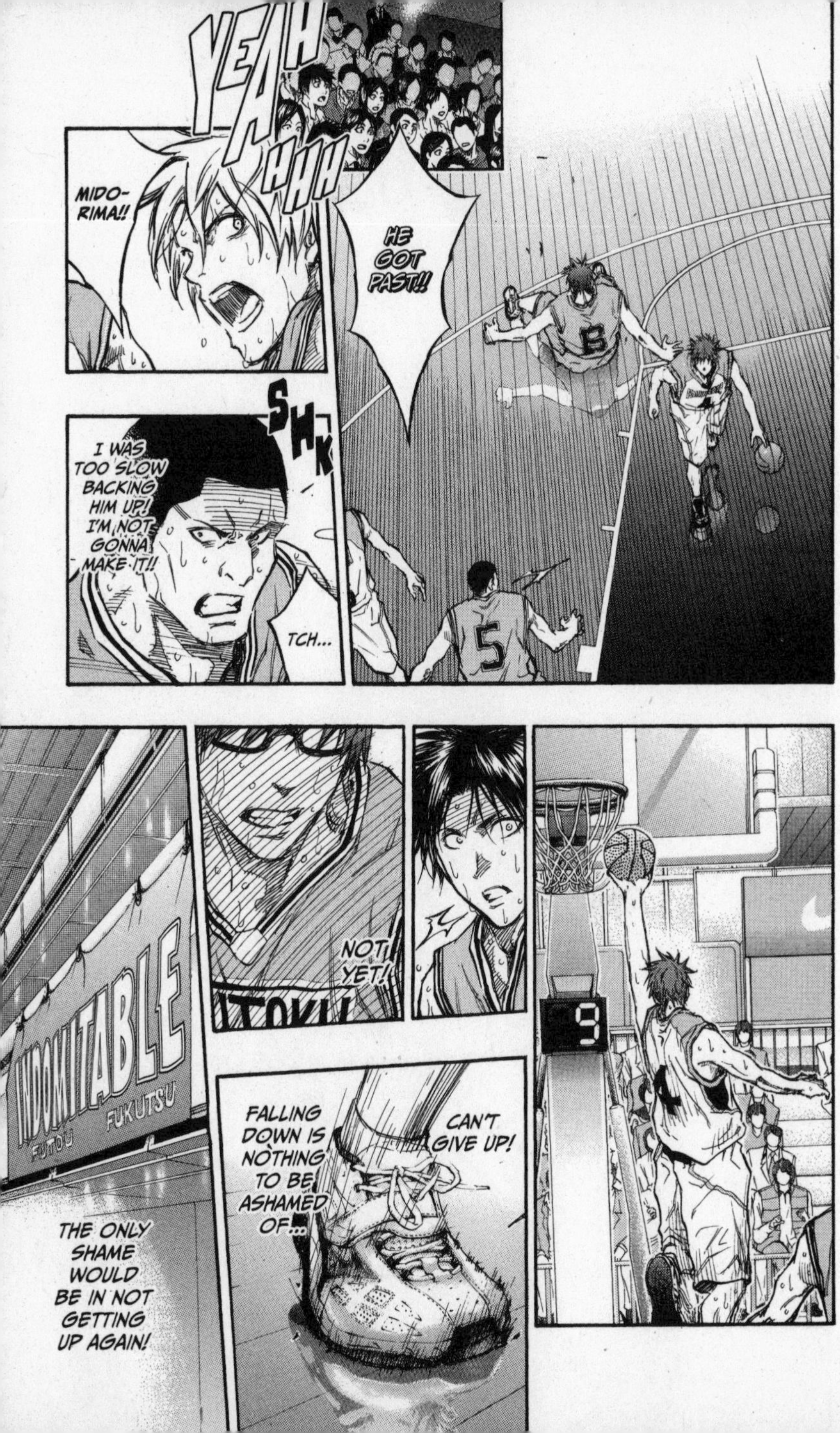
HE GOT PAST!!
TCH...
YEAHHHH
MIDO-RIMA!!
SHK
I WAS TOO SLOW BACKING HIM UP! I'M NOT GONNA MAKE IT!!
9
NOT YET!
TOKU
CAN'T GIVE UP!
FALLING DOWN IS NOTHING TO BE ASHAMED OF...
INDOMITABLE
FUTOU FUKUTSU
THE ONLY SHAME WOULD BE IN NOT GETTING UP AGAIN!

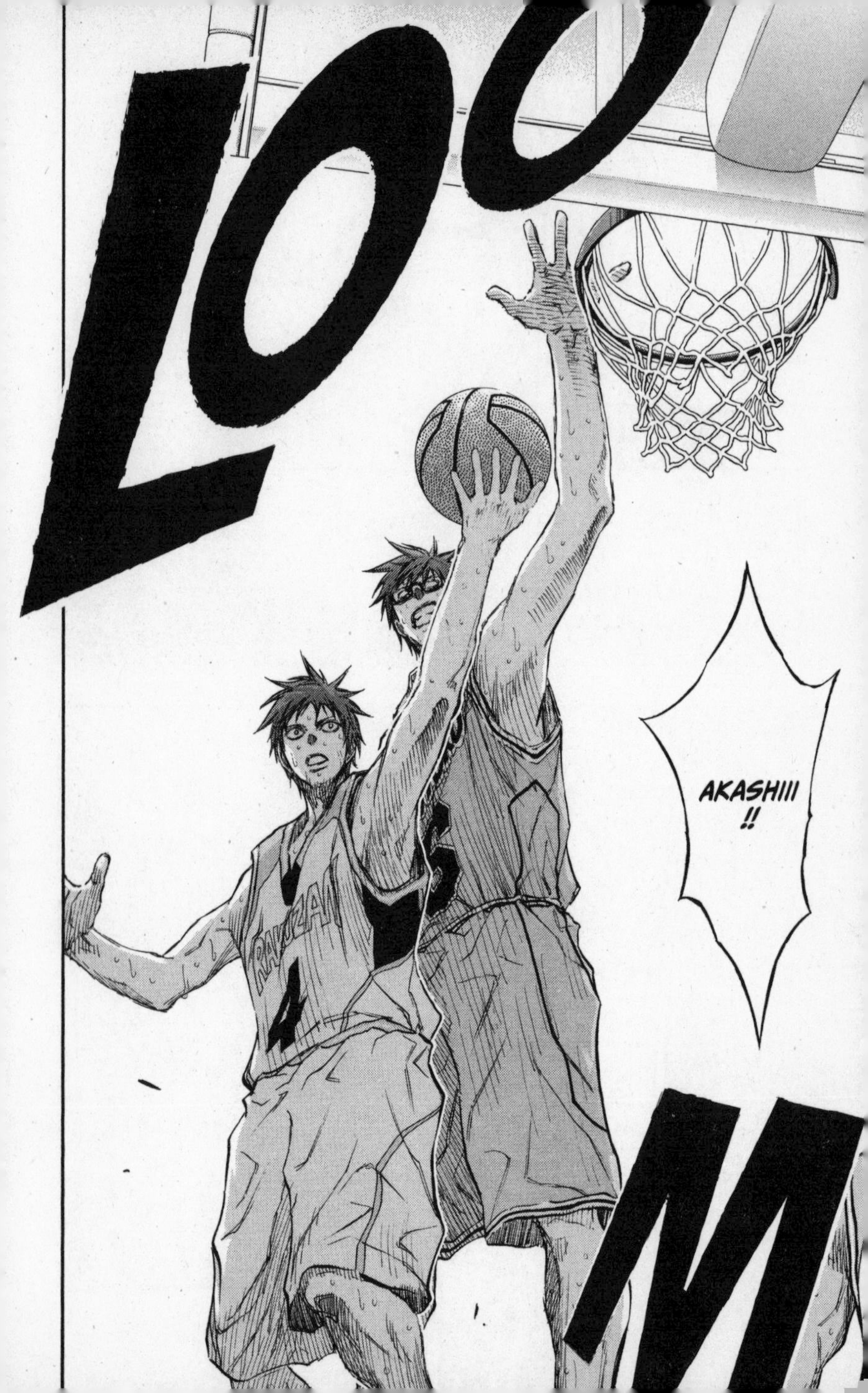
AKASHIII !!

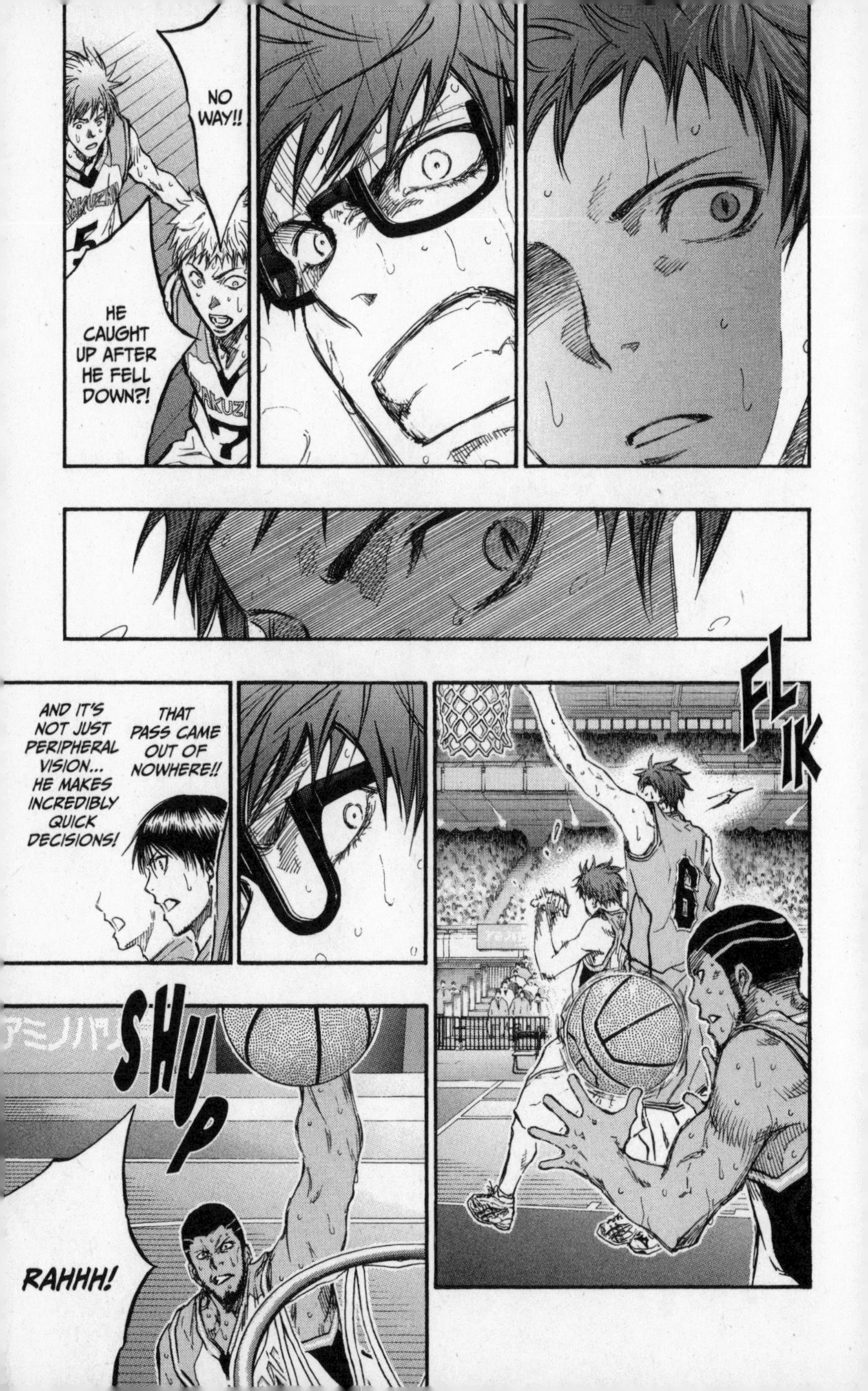
NO WAY!!
HE CAUGHT UP AFTER HE FELL DOWN?!
FLIK
THAT PASS CAME OUT OF NOWHERE!!
AND IT'S NOT JUST PERIPHERAL VISION... HE MAKES INCREDIBLY QUICK DECISIONS!
SHUP
RAHHH!

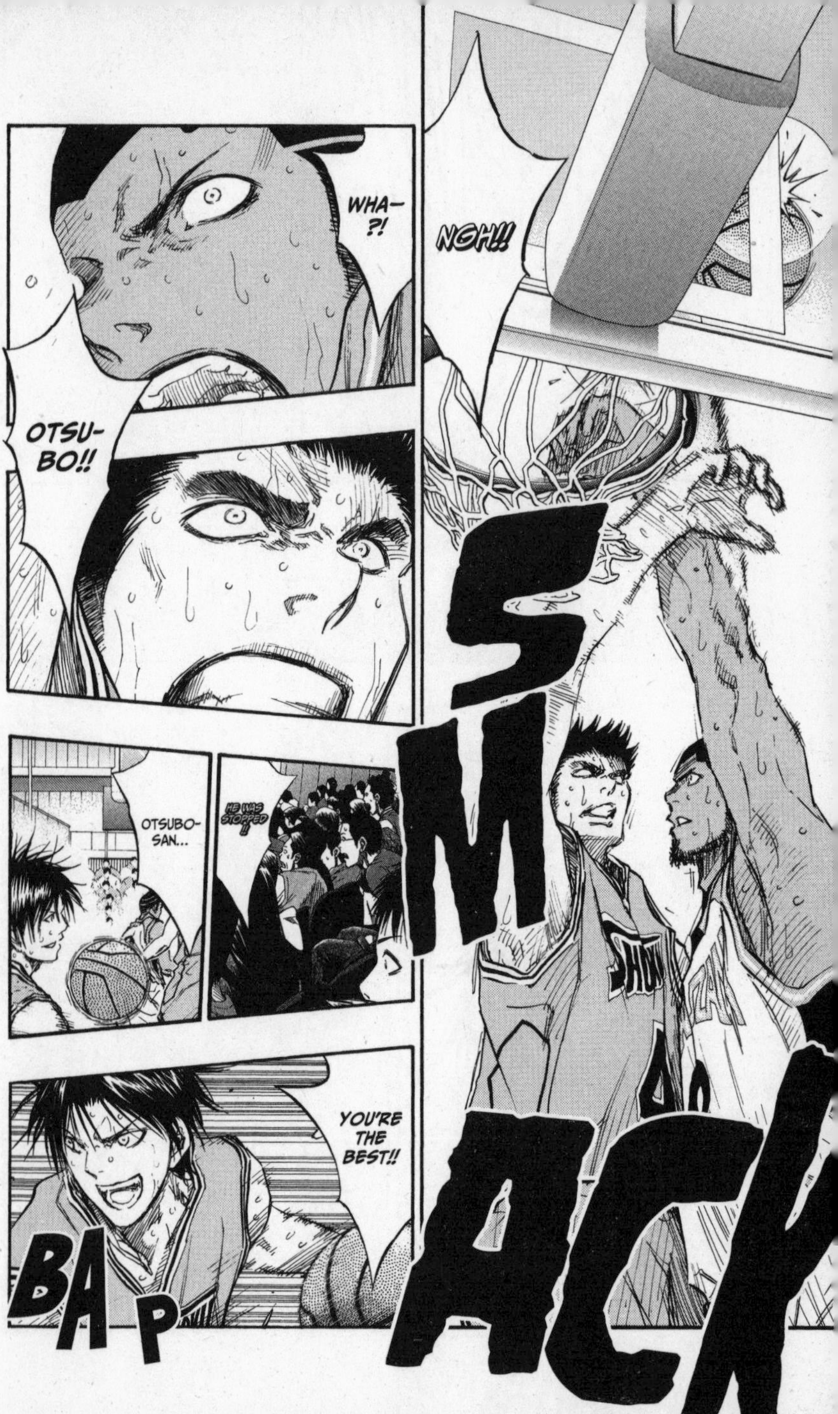
NGH!!
SMACK
WHA—?!
OTSU-BO!!
HE WAS STOPPED!!
OTSUBO-SAN...
YOU'RE THE BEST!!
BAP

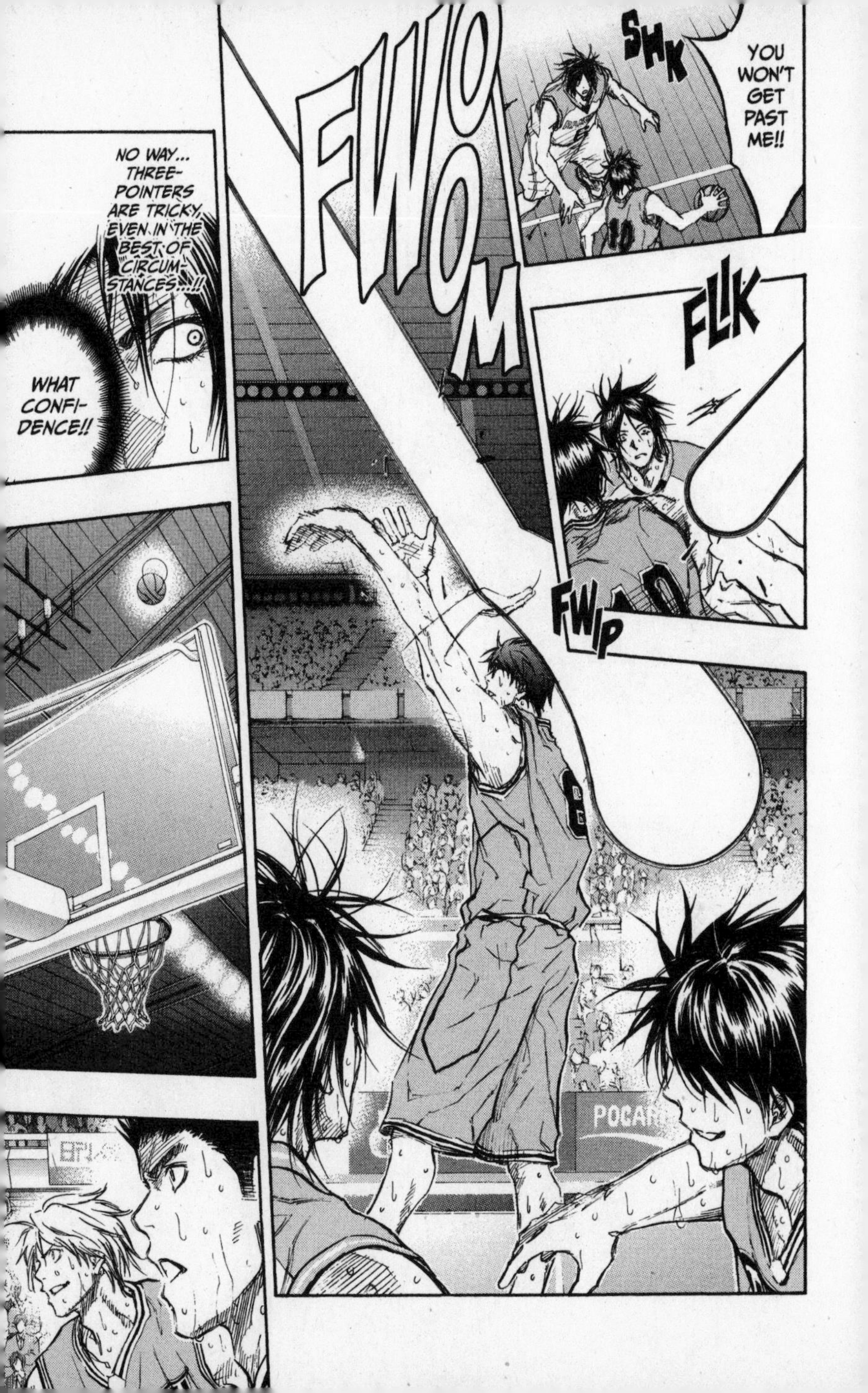
SHK
YOU WON'T GET PAST ME!!
FWOOM
FLIK
FWIP
POCARI
NO WAY... THREE-POINTERS ARE TRICKY, EVEN IN THE BEST OF CIRCUM-STANCES...!!
WHAT CONFI-DENCE!!

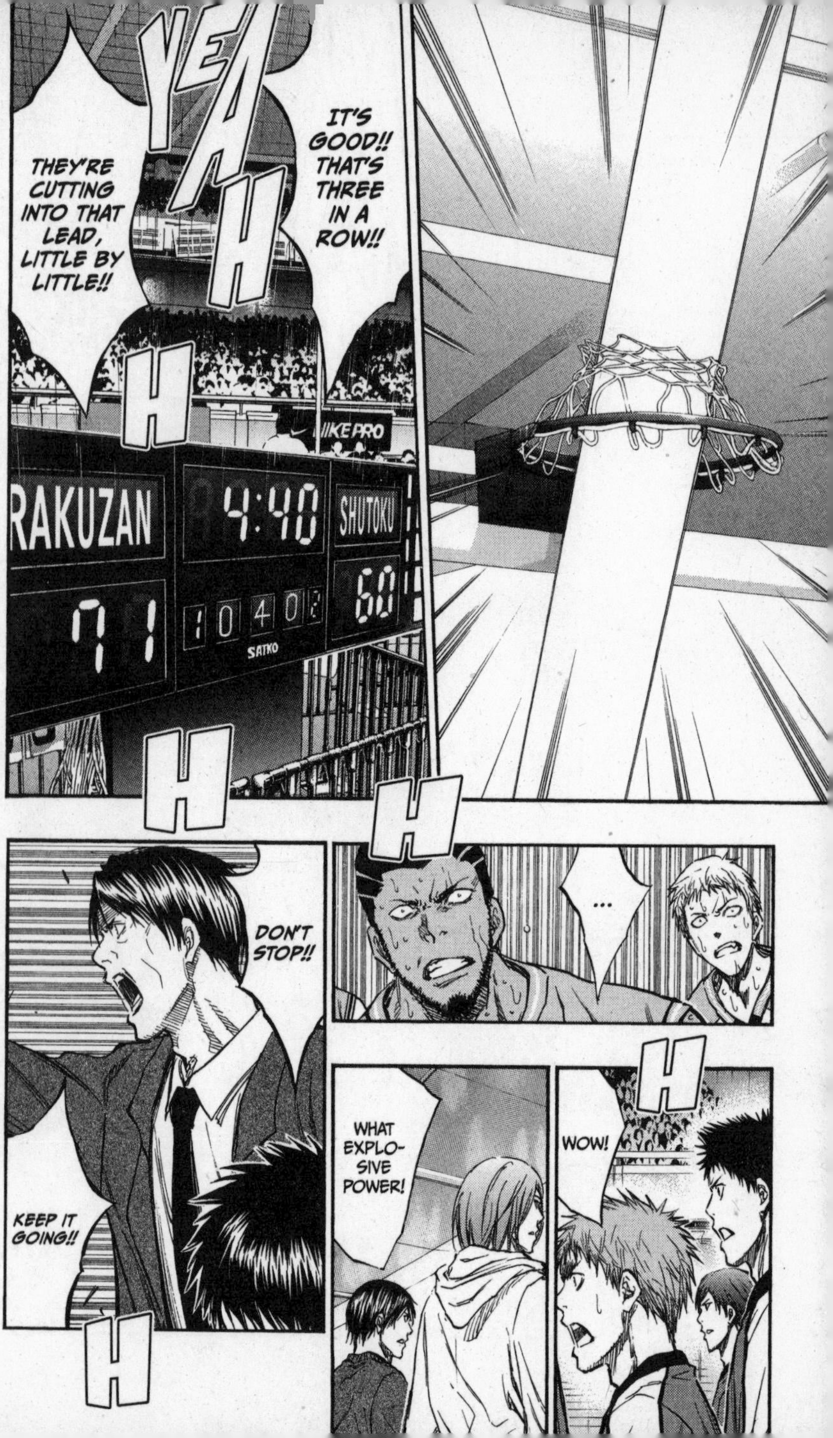
YEAHHHHHH
IT'S GOOD!! THAT'S THREE IN A ROW!!
THEY'RE CUTTING INTO THAT LEAD, LITTLE BY LITTLE!!
IKE PRO
RAKUZAN
4:40
SHUTOKU
71
60
SATKO
...
WOW!
WHAT EXPLO-SIVE POWER!
DON'T STOP!!
KEEP IT GOING!!

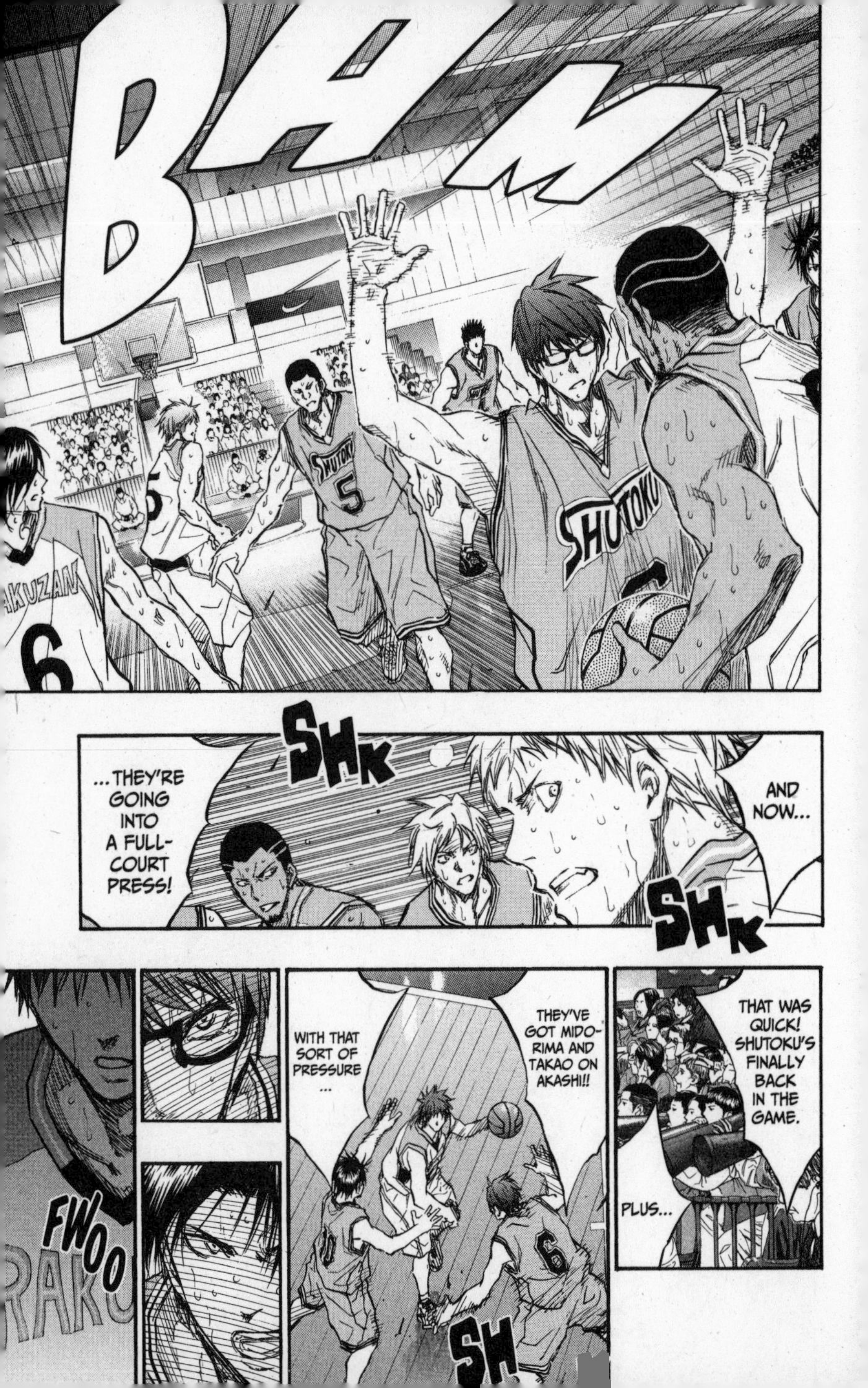
BLAM
SHUTOKU
5
SHUTOKU
6
AND NOW...
...THEY'RE GOING INTO A FULL-COURT PRESS!
SHK
SHK
THAT WAS QUICK! SHUTOKU'S FINALLY BACK IN THE GAME.
PLUS...
THEY'VE GOT MIDO-RIMA AND TAKAO ON AKASHI!!
WITH THAT SORT OF PRESSURE ...
SH
FWOO

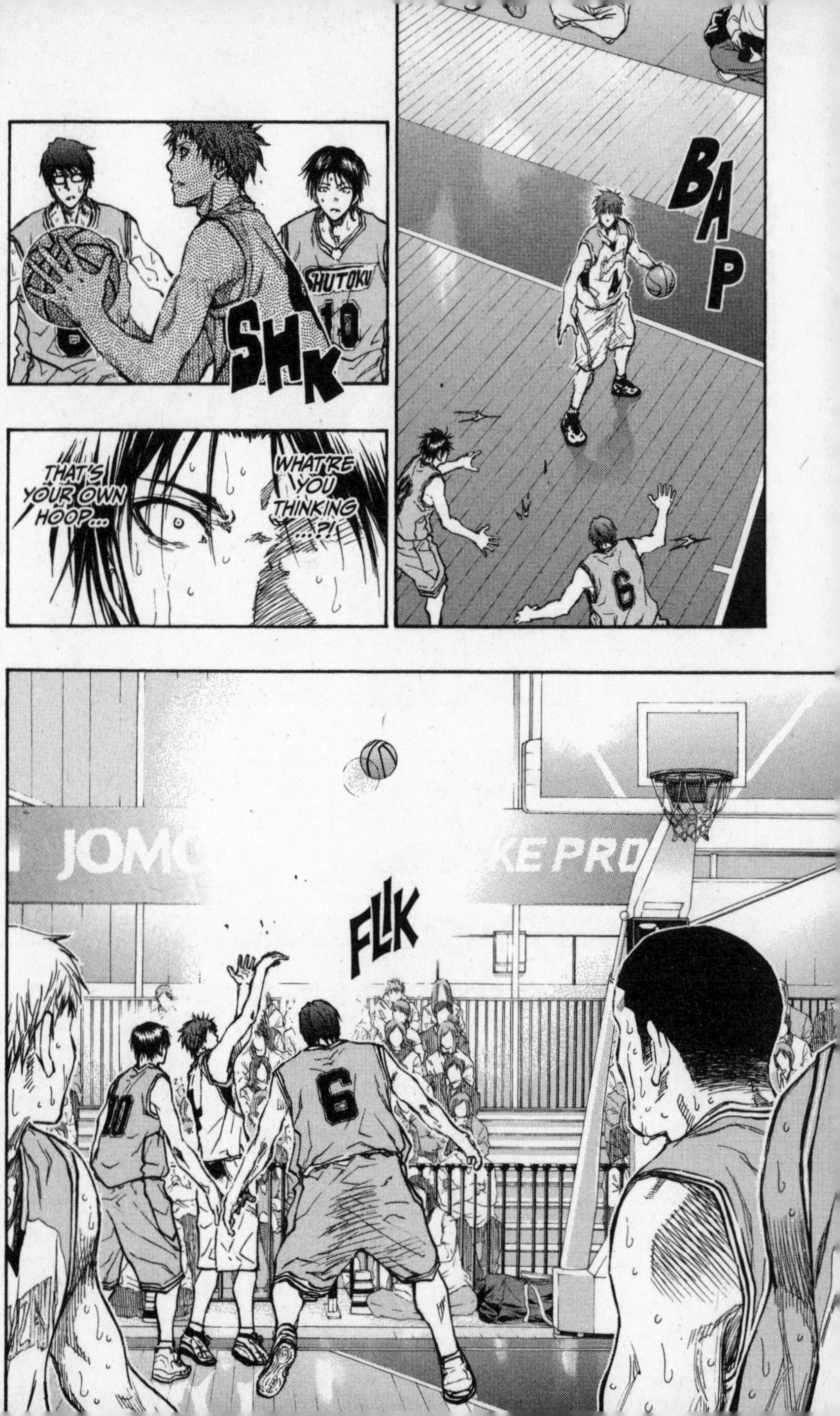
BAP
SHUTOKU
SHK
WHAT'RE YOU THINKING...?!
THAT'S YOUR OWN HOOP...
JOMO
KE PRO
FLIK

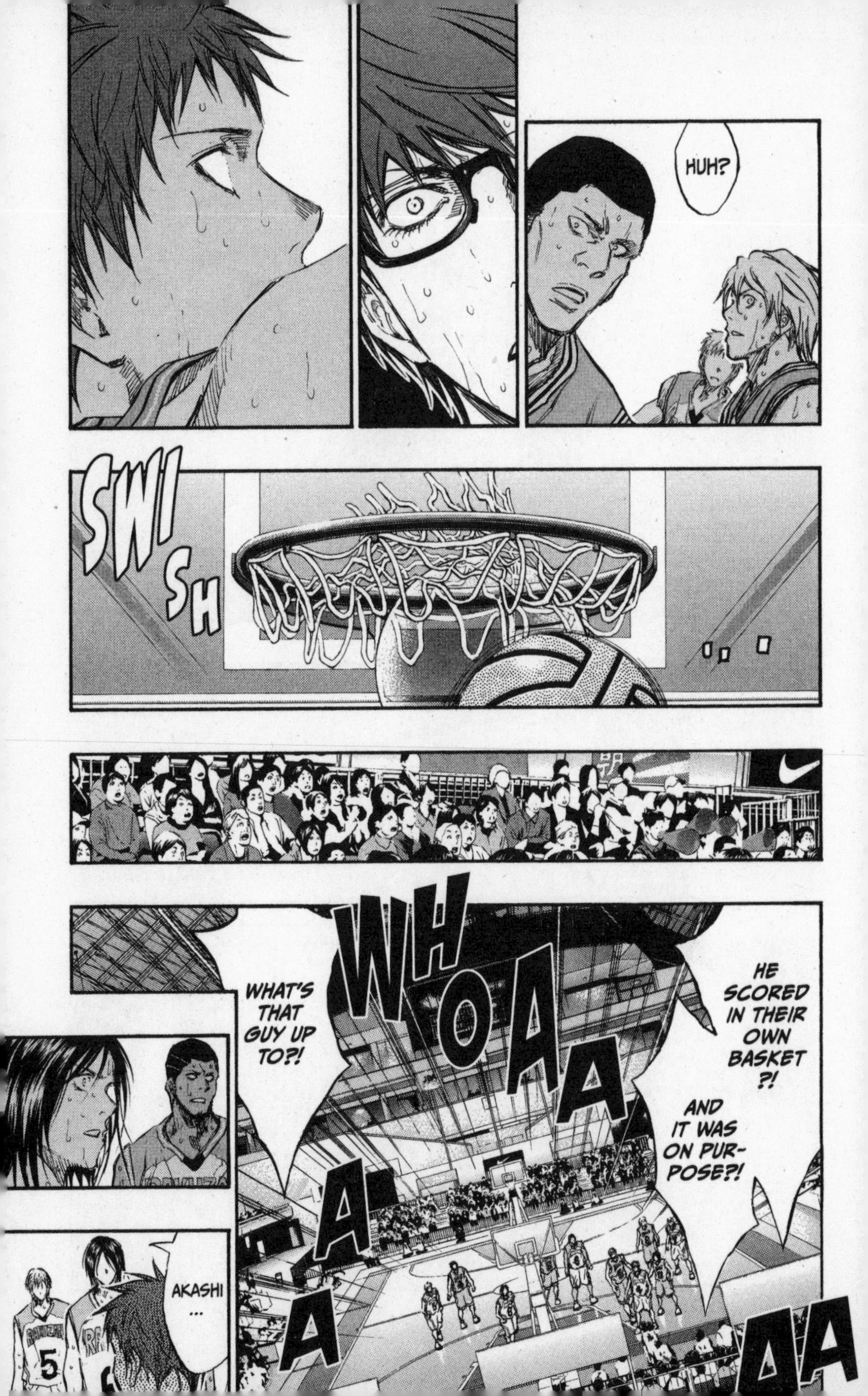
HUH?
SWISH
...
WHOAAAAAA
HE SCORED IN THEIR OWN BASKET?!
AND IT WAS ON PURPOSE?!
WHAT'S THAT GUY UP TO?!
AKASHI...

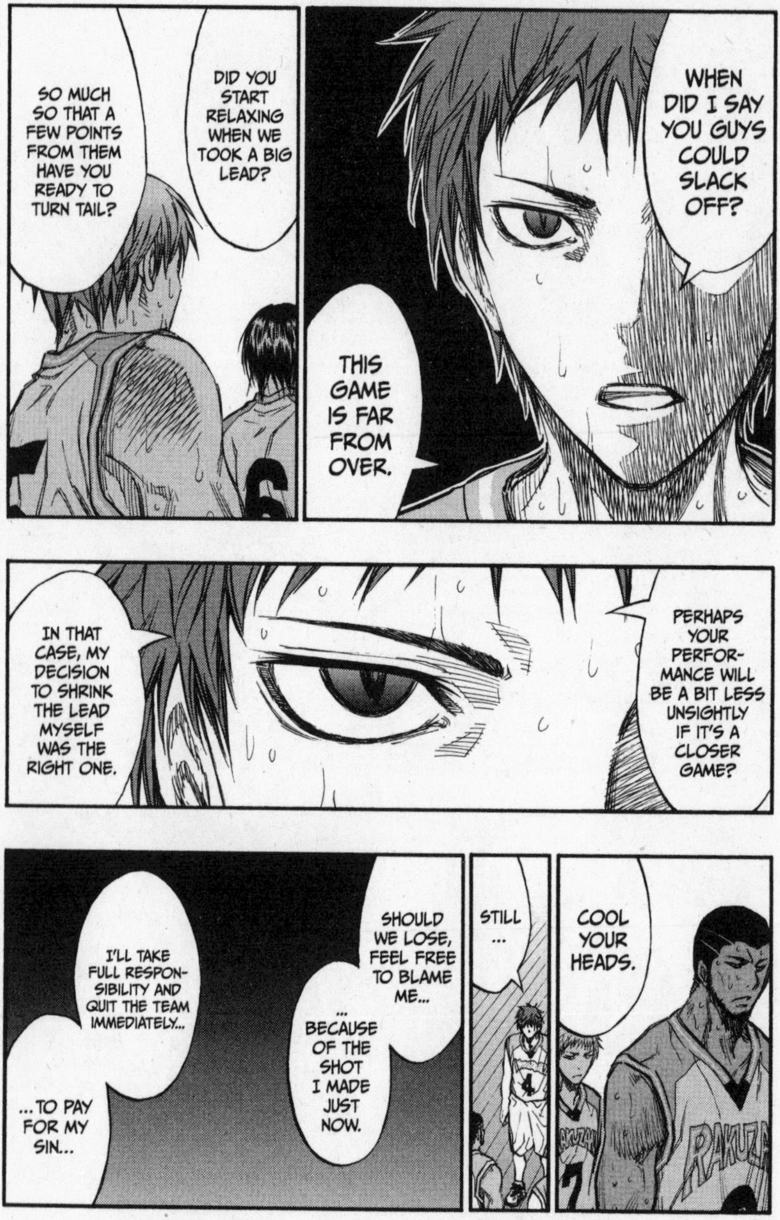
WHEN DID I SAY YOU GUYS COULD SLACK OFF?
THIS GAME IS FAR FROM OVER.
DID YOU START RELAXING WHEN WE TOOK A BIG LEAD?
SO MUCH SO THAT A FEW POINTS FROM THEM HAVE YOU READY TO TURN TAIL?
PERHAPS YOUR PERFORMANCE WILL BE A BIT LESS UNSIGHTLY IF IT'S A CLOSER GAME?
IN THAT CASE, MY DECISION TO SHRINK THE LEAD MYSELF WAS THE RIGHT ONE.
COOL YOUR HEADS.
STILL ...
SHOULD WE LOSE, FEEL FREE TO BLAME ME...
... BECAUSE OF THE SHOT I MADE JUST NOW.
I'LL TAKE FULL RESPONSIBILITY AND QUIT THE TEAM IMMEDIATELY...
...TO PAY FOR MY SIN...

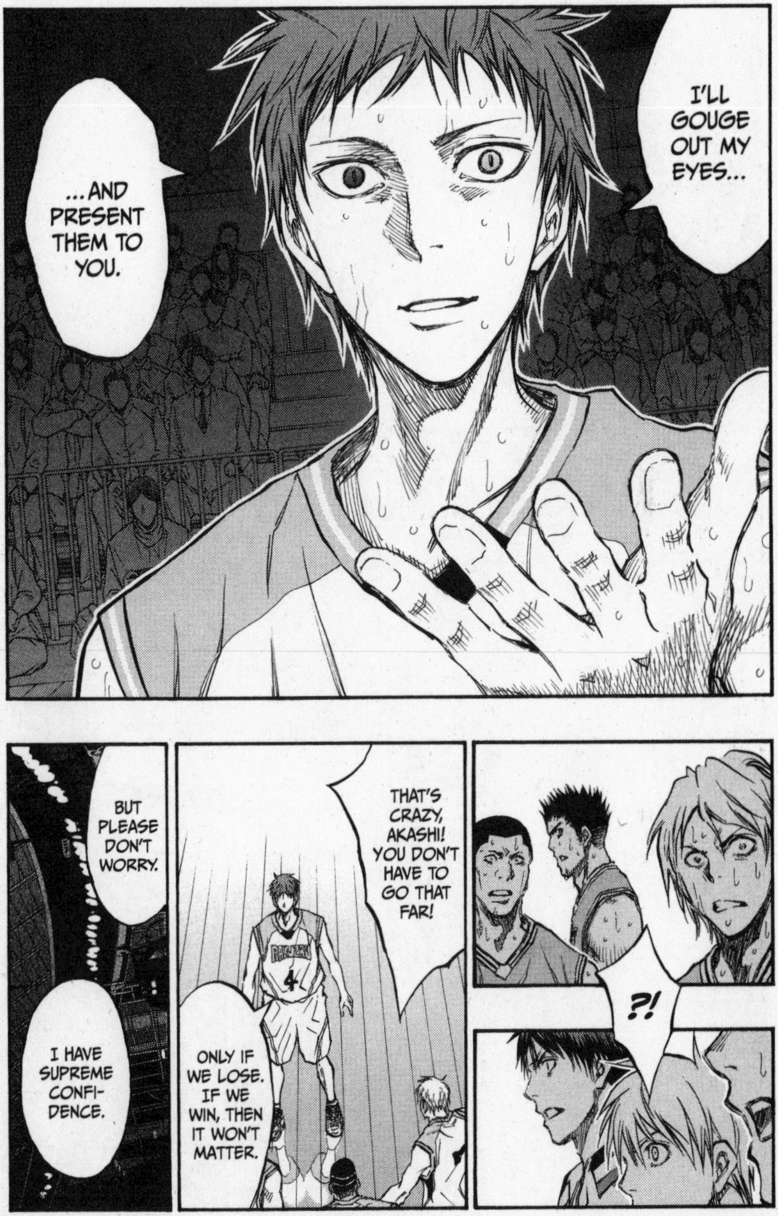
I'LL GOUGE OUT MY EYES...
...AND PRESENT THEM TO YOU.
?!
THAT'S CRAZY, AKASHI! YOU DON'T HAVE TO GO THAT FAR!
ONLY IF WE LOSE. IF WE WIN, THEN IT WON'T MATTER.
BUT PLEASE DON'T WORRY.
I HAVE SUPREME CONFI-DENCE.

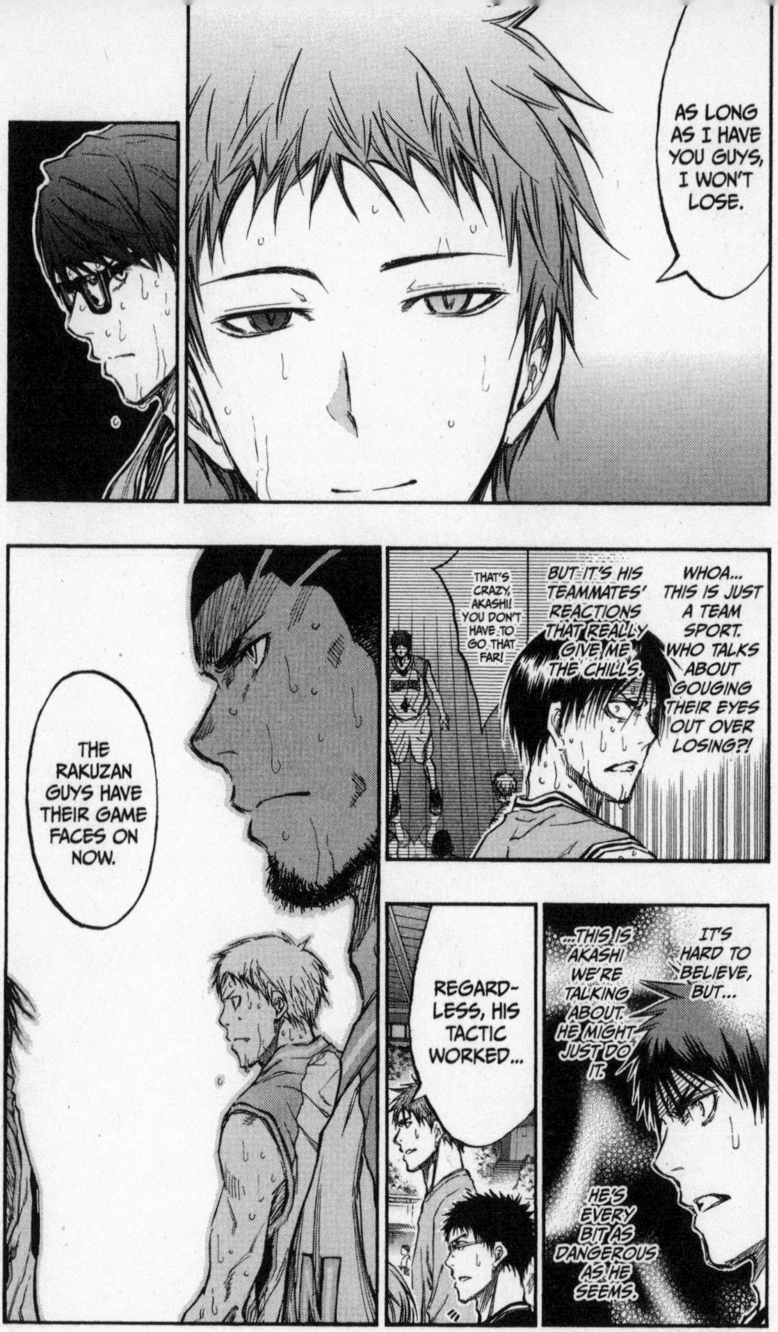

AS LONG AS I HAVE YOU GUYS, I WON'T LOSE.
WHOA... THIS IS JUST A TEAM SPORT. WHO TALKS ABOUT GOUGING THEIR EYES OUT OVER LOSING?!
BUT IT'S HIS TEAMMATES' REACTIONS THAT REALLY GIVE ME THE CHILLS.
THAT'S CRAZY, AKASHI! YOU DON'T HAVE TO GO THAT FAR!
IT'S HARD TO BELIEVE, BUT...
...THIS IS AKASHI WE'RE TALKING ABOUT. HE MIGHT JUST DO IT.
HE'S EVERY BIT AS DANGEROUS AS HE SEEMS.
REGARDLESS, HIS TACTIC WORKED...
THE RAKUZAN GUYS HAVE THEIR GAME FACES ON NOW.

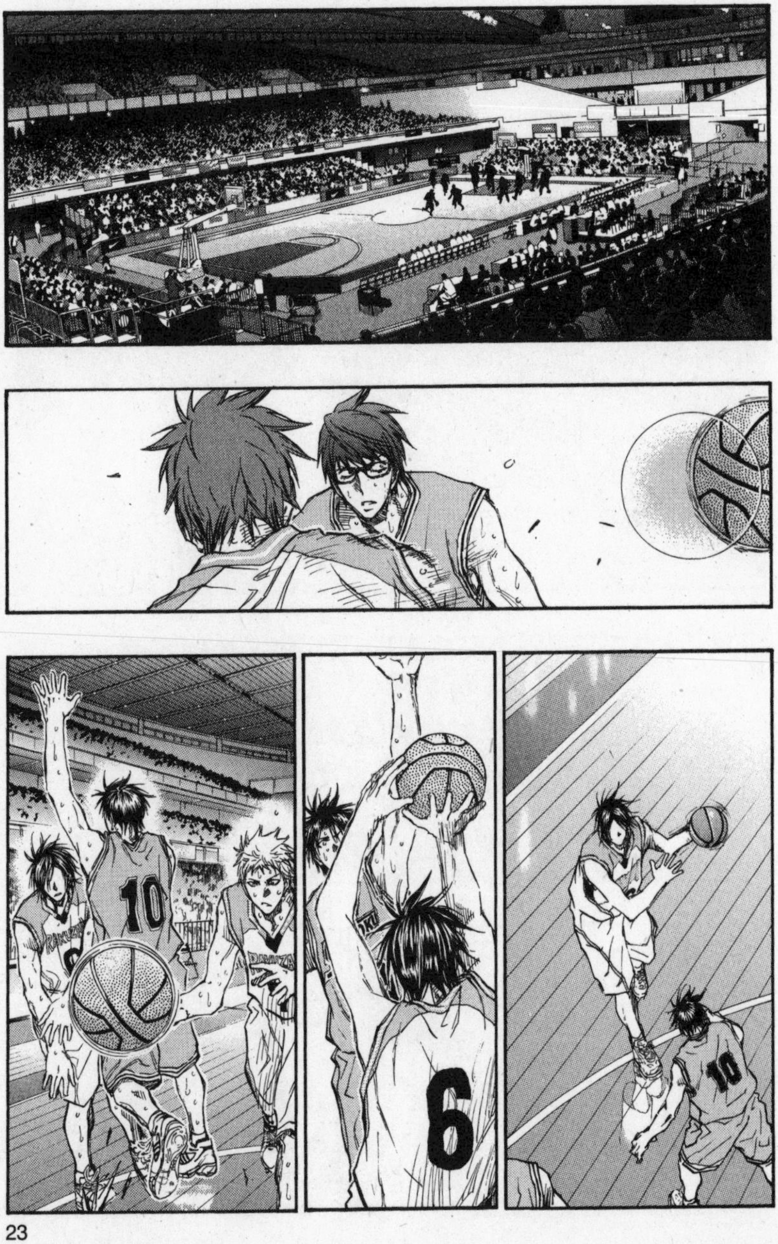

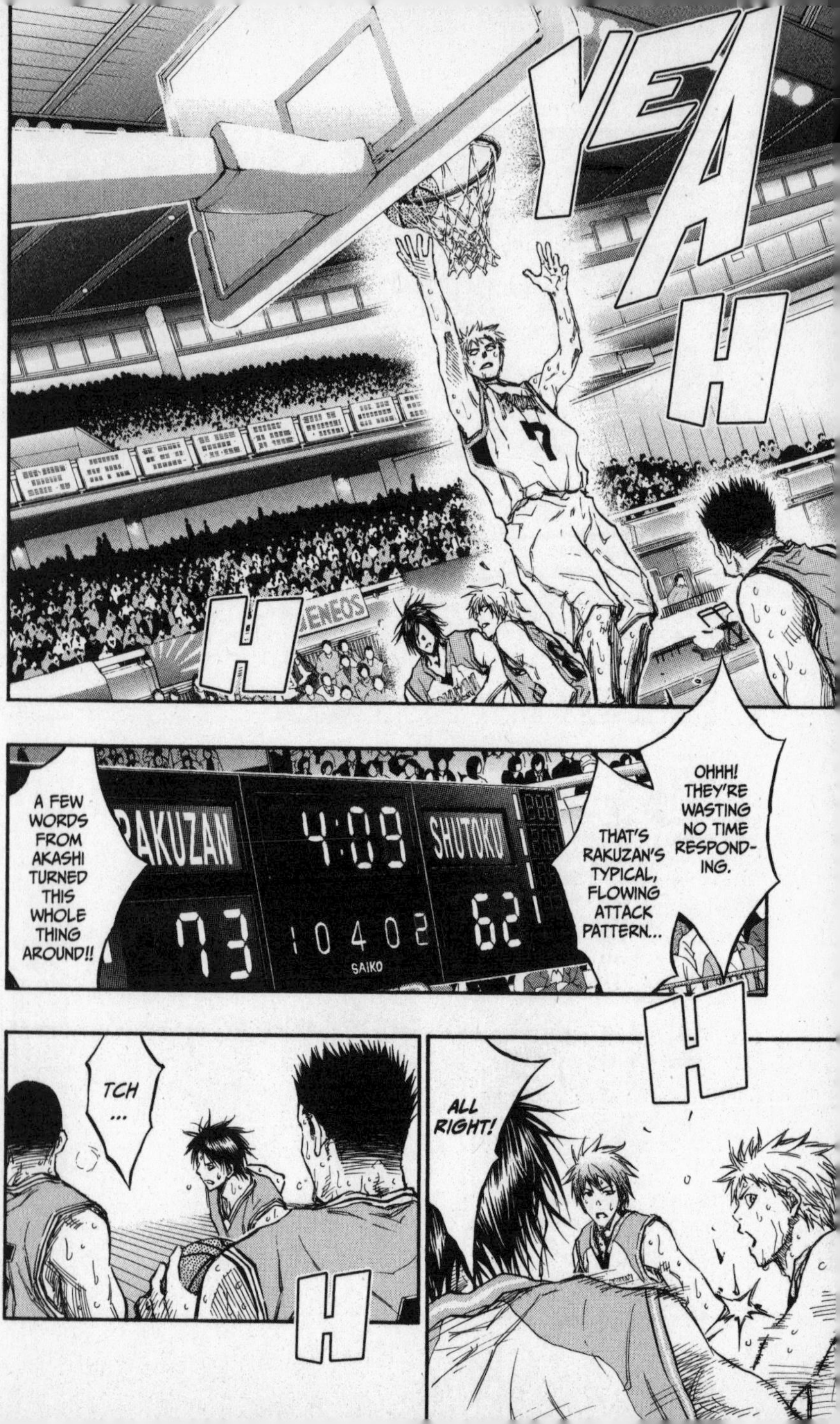
YEAAHH
H
OHHH! THEY'RE WASTING NO TIME RESPONDING.
THAT'S RAKUZAN'S TYPICAL, FLOWING ATTACK PATTERN...
A FEW WORDS FROM AKASHI TURNED THIS WHOLE THING AROUND!!
RAKUZAN
4:09
SHUTOKU
73
62
SAIKO
H
H
ALL RIGHT!
TCH...
H

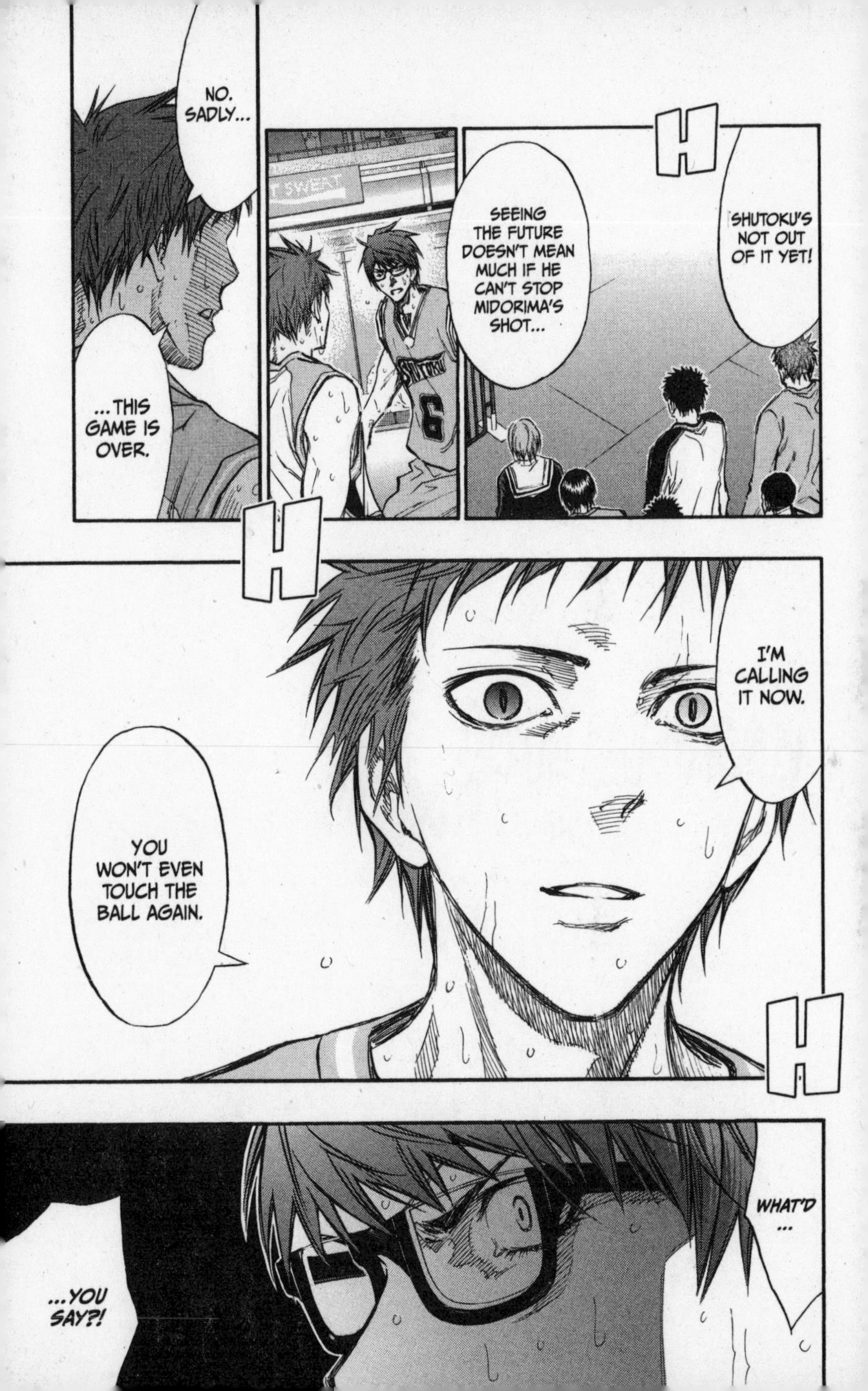
H
SHUTOKU'S NOT OUT OF IT YET!
SEEING THE FUTURE DOESN'T MEAN MUCH IF HE CAN'T STOP MIDORIMA'S SHOT...
NO. SADLY...
...THIS GAME IS OVER.
H
I'M CALLING IT NOW.
YOU WON'T EVEN TOUCH THE BALL AGAIN.
H
WHAT'D ...
...YOU SAY?!

KUROKO'S BASKETBALL BLOOPERS TAKE 2

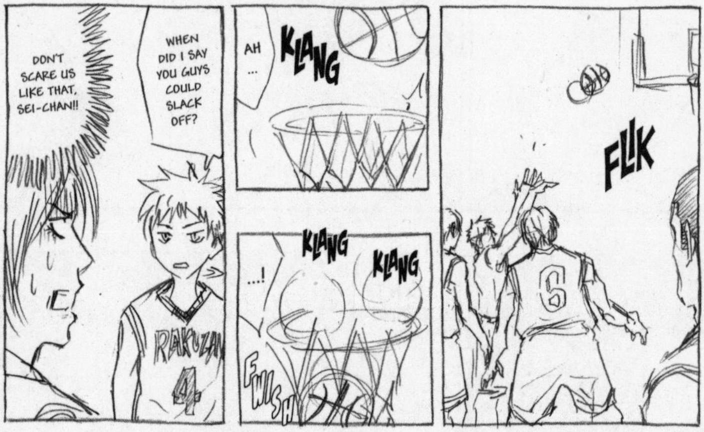
FLIK
AH ...
KLANG
...!
KLANG
KLANG
FWISH
WHEN DID I SAY YOU GUYS COULD SLACK OFF?
DON'T SCARE US LIKE THAT, SEI-CHAN!!
RAKUZAN

THERE ARE LOTS OF BLOOPERS INVOLVING AKASHI'S TOTALLY UNCOOL NEAR FAILURES.

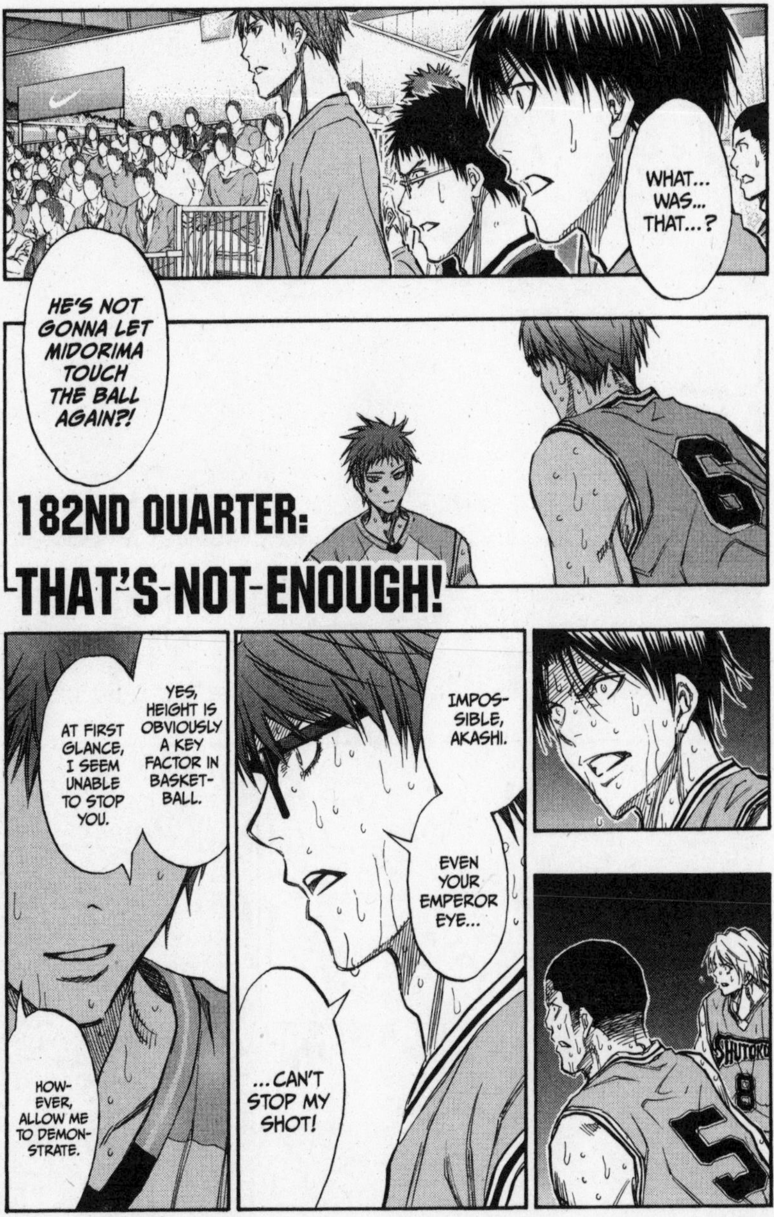
WHAT... WAS... THAT...?
HE'S NOT GONNA LET MIDORIMA TOUCH THE BALL AGAIN?!
182ND QUARTER: THAT'S NOT ENOUGH!
IMPOSSIBLE, AKASHI.
EVEN YOUR EMPEROR EYE...
...CAN'T STOP MY SHOT!
YES, HEIGHT IS OBVIOUSLY A KEY FACTOR IN BASKETBALL.
AT FIRST GLANCE, I SEEM UNABLE TO STOP YOU.
HOWEVER, ALLOW ME TO DEMONSTRATE.

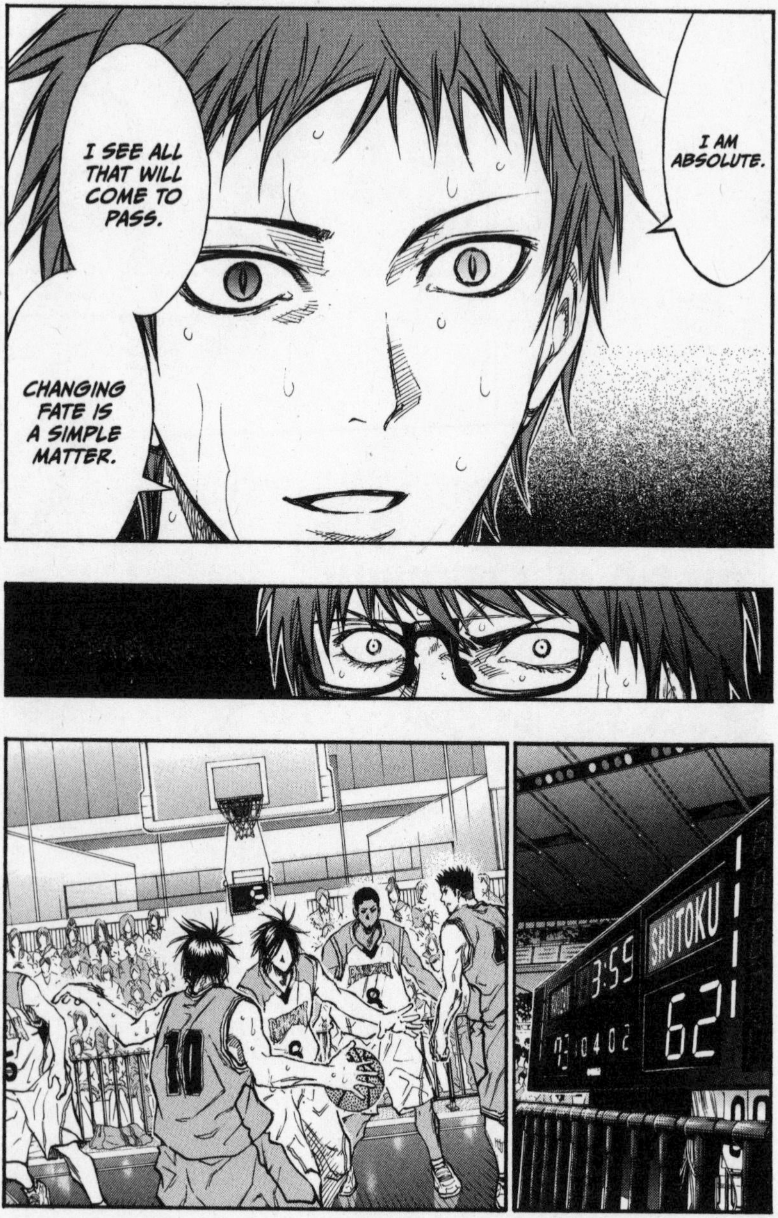
I AM ABSOLUTE.
I SEE ALL THAT WILL COME TO PASS.
CHANGING FATE IS A SIMPLE MATTER.
SHUTOKU
3:59
62

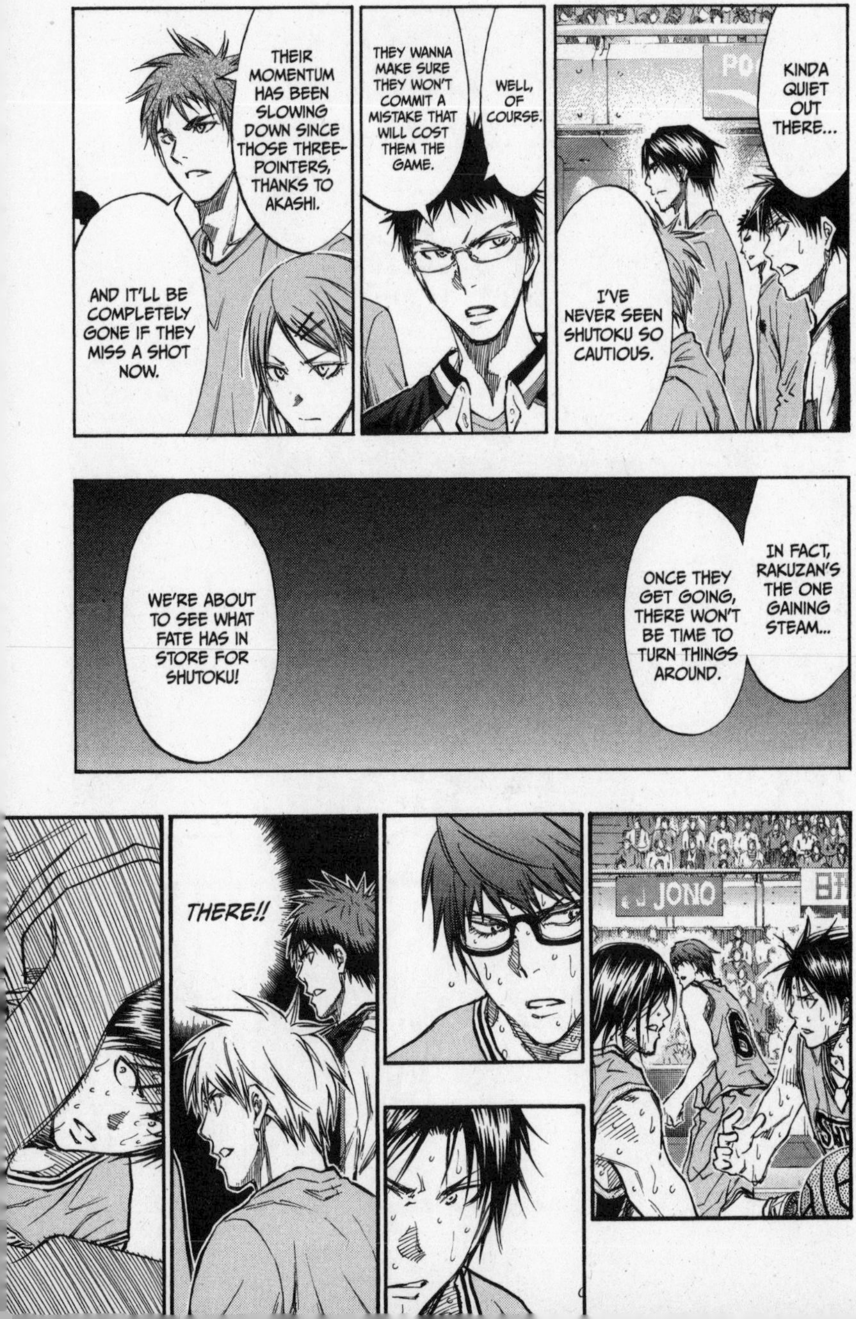
KINDA QUIET OUT THERE...
I'VE NEVER SEEN SHUTOKU SO CAUTIOUS.
WELL, OF COURSE.
THEY WANNA MAKE SURE THEY WON'T COMMIT A MISTAKE THAT WILL COST THEM THE GAME.
THEIR MOMENTUM HAS BEEN SLOWING DOWN SINCE THOSE THREE-POINTERS, THANKS TO AKASHI.
AND IT'LL BE COMPLETELY GONE IF THEY MISS A SHOT NOW.
IN FACT, RAKUZAN'S THE ONE GAINING STEAM...
ONCE THEY GET GOING, THERE WON'T BE TIME TO TURN THINGS AROUND.
WE'RE ABOUT TO SEE WHAT FATE HAS IN STORE FOR SHUTOKU!
JONO
THERE!!

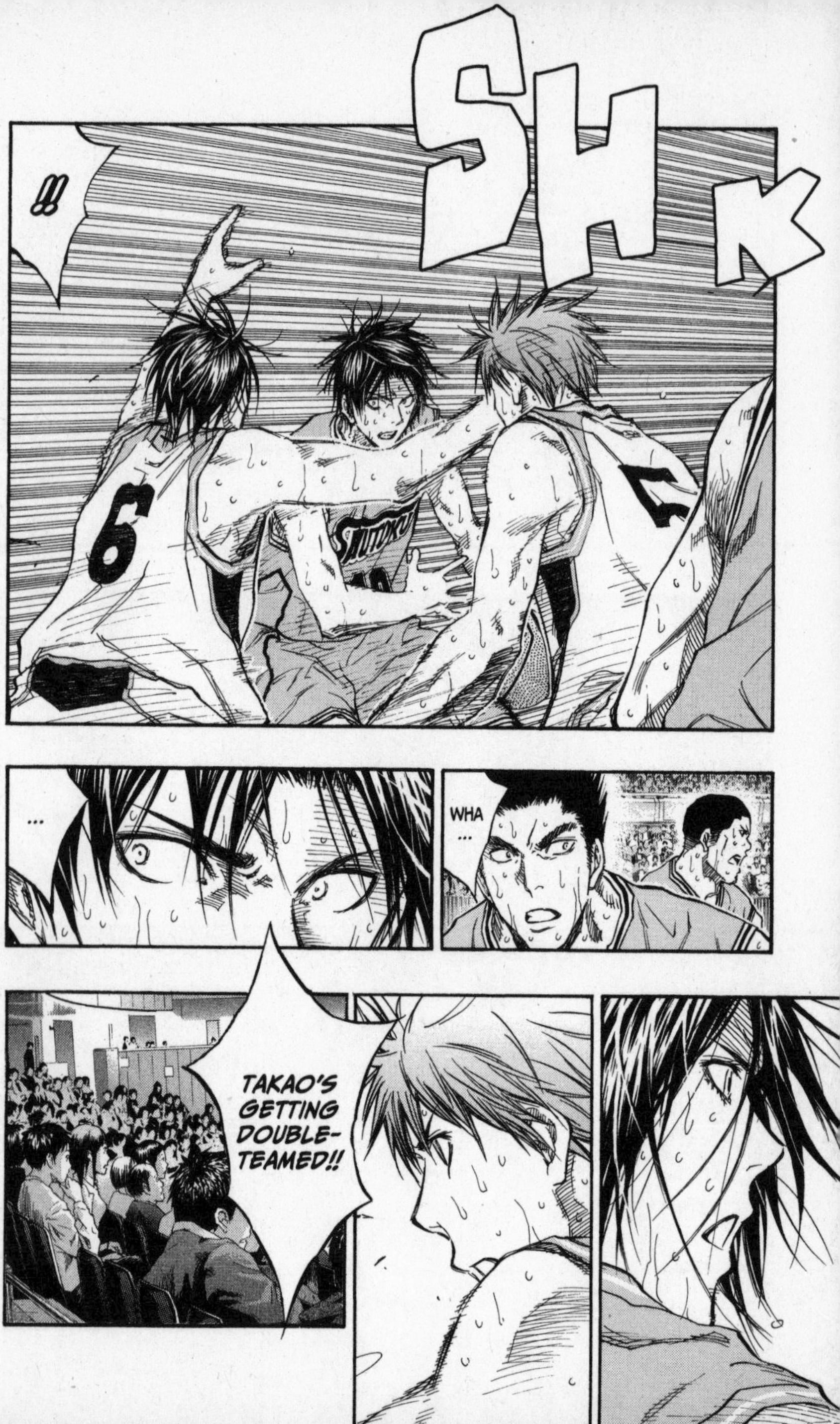
SHK
!!
WHA ...
...
TAKAO'S GETTING DOUBLE-TEAMED!!

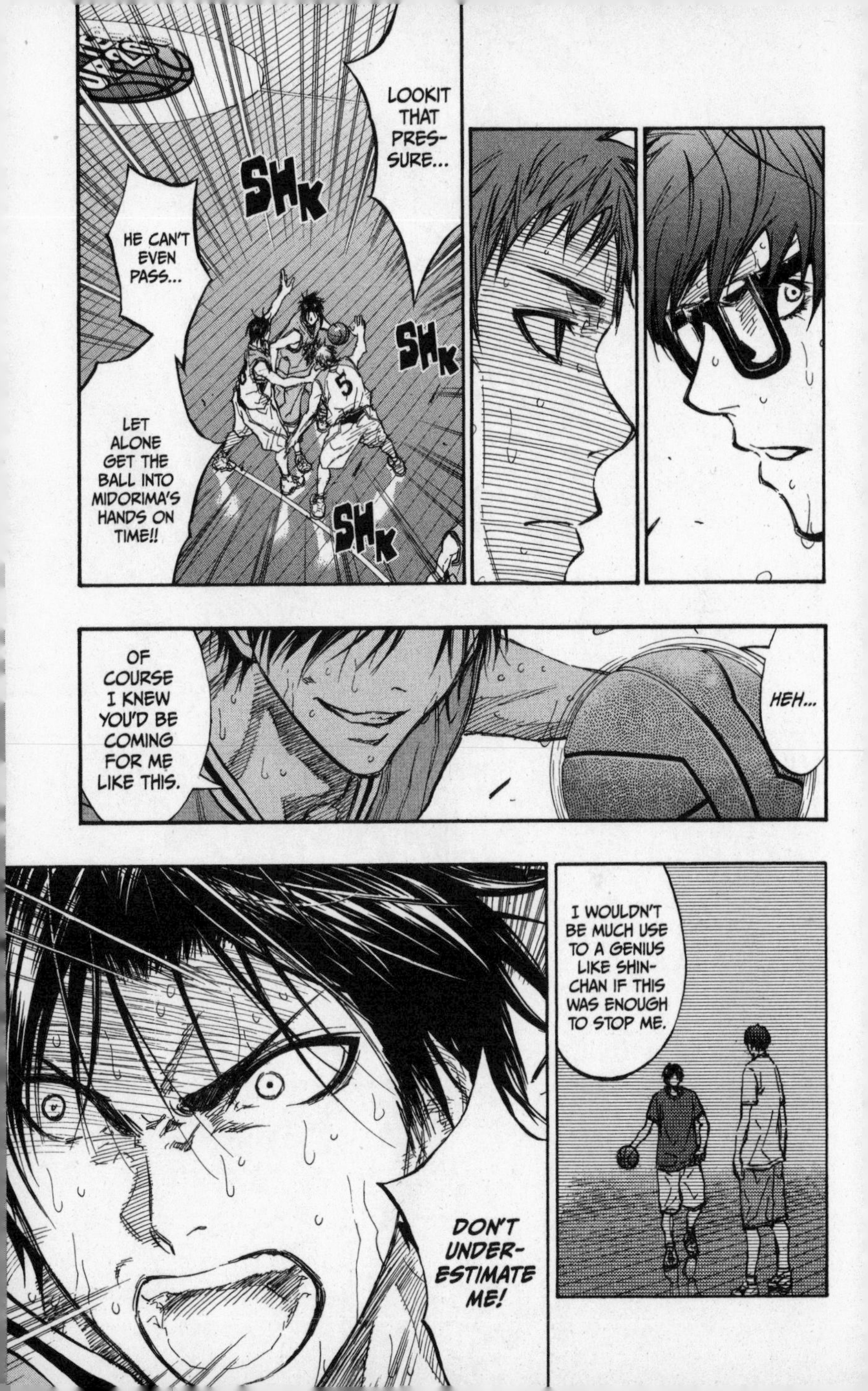
LOOKIT THAT PRES-SURE...
SHK
HE CAN'T EVEN PASS...
SHK
LET ALONE GET THE BALL INTO MIDORIMA'S HANDS ON TIME!!
SHK
HEH...
OF COURSE I KNEW YOU'D BE COMING FOR ME LIKE THIS.
I WOULDN'T BE MUCH USE TO A GENIUS LIKE SHIN-CHAN IF THIS WAS ENOUGH TO STOP ME.
DON'T UNDER-ESTIMATE ME!

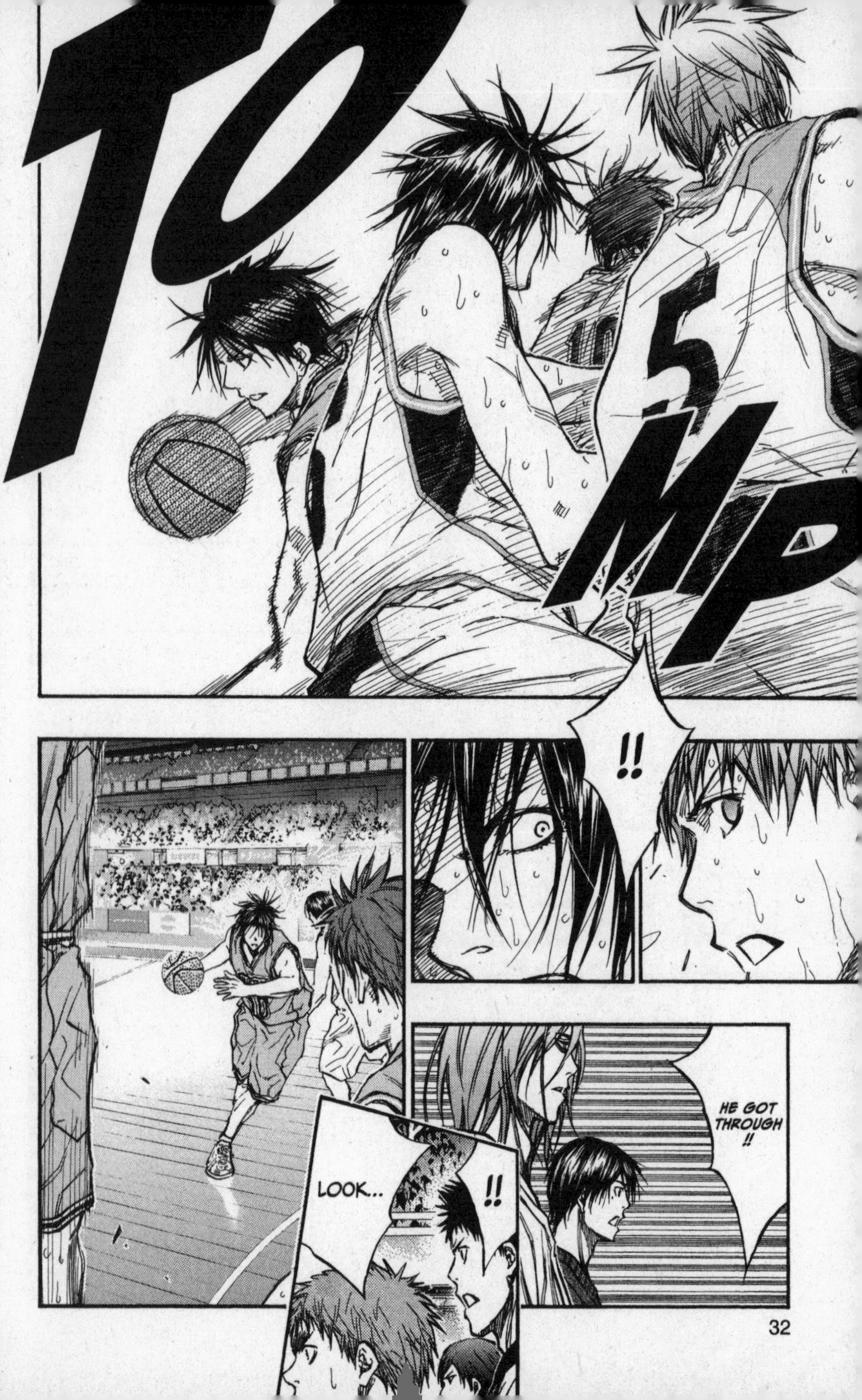
TOMP
!!
HE GOT THROUGH !!
!!
LOOK...

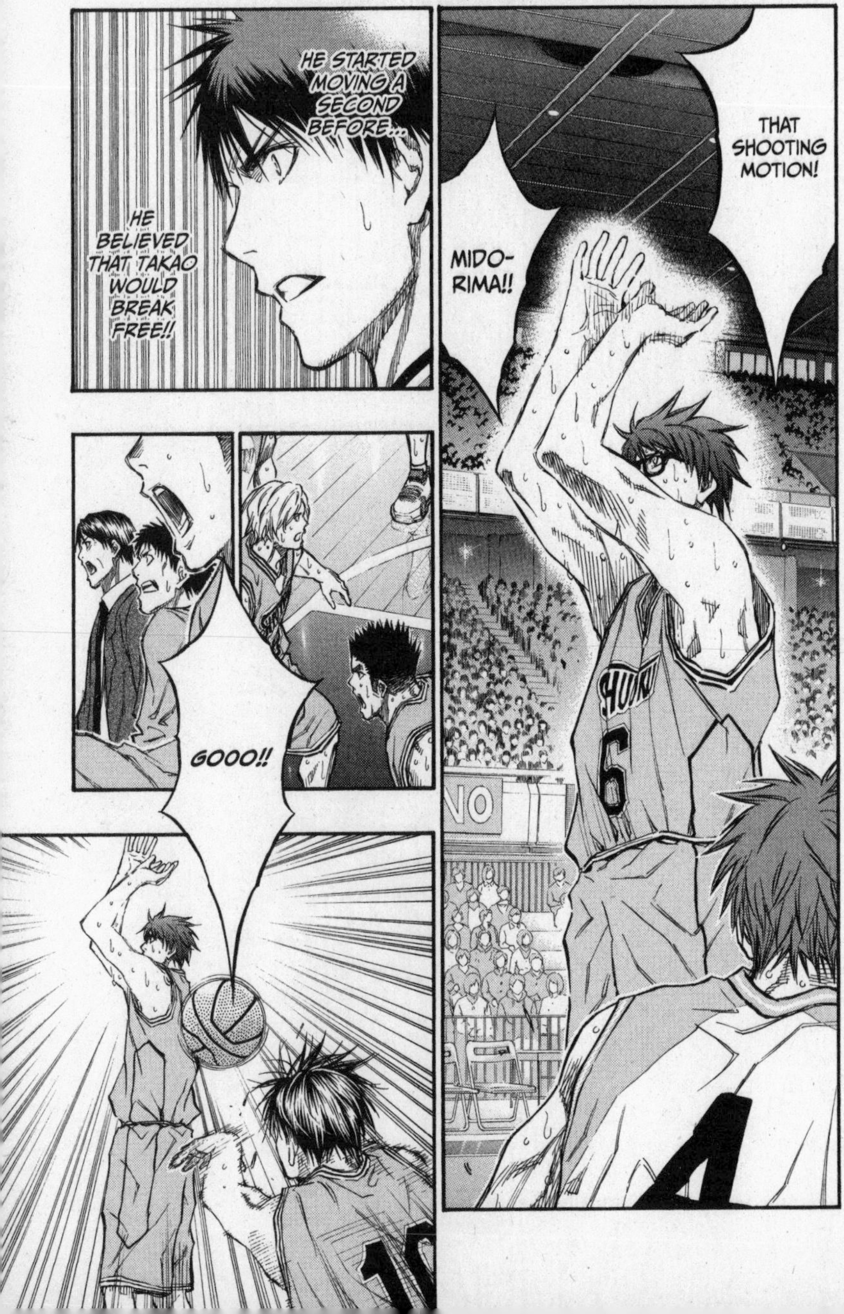
THAT SHOOTING MOTION!
MIDO-RIMA!!
HE STARTED MOVING A SECOND BEFORE...
HE BELIEVED THAT TAKAO WOULD BREAK FREE!!
GOOO!!

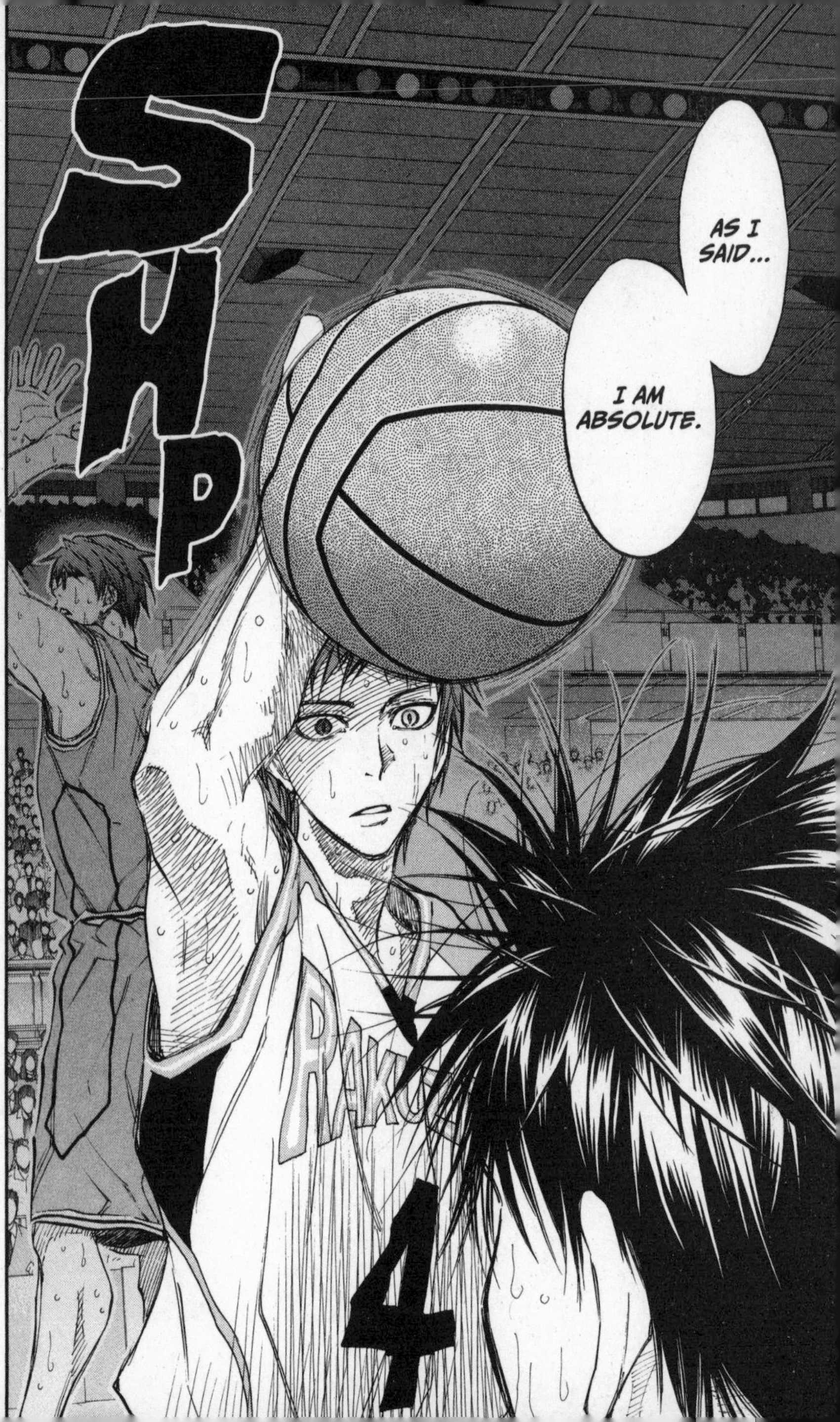
AS I SAID...
I AM ABSOLUTE.
SHP

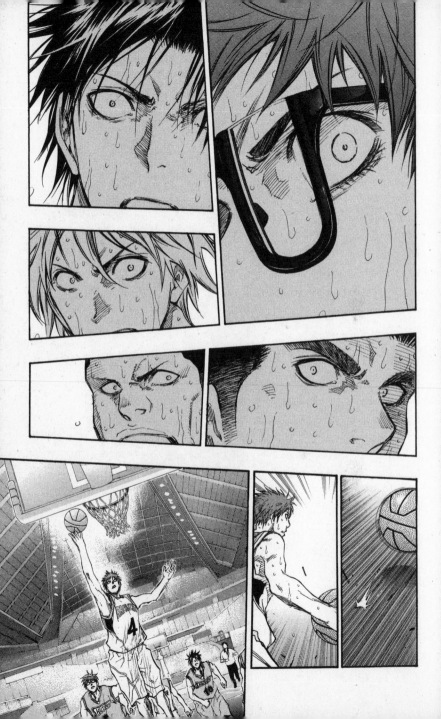

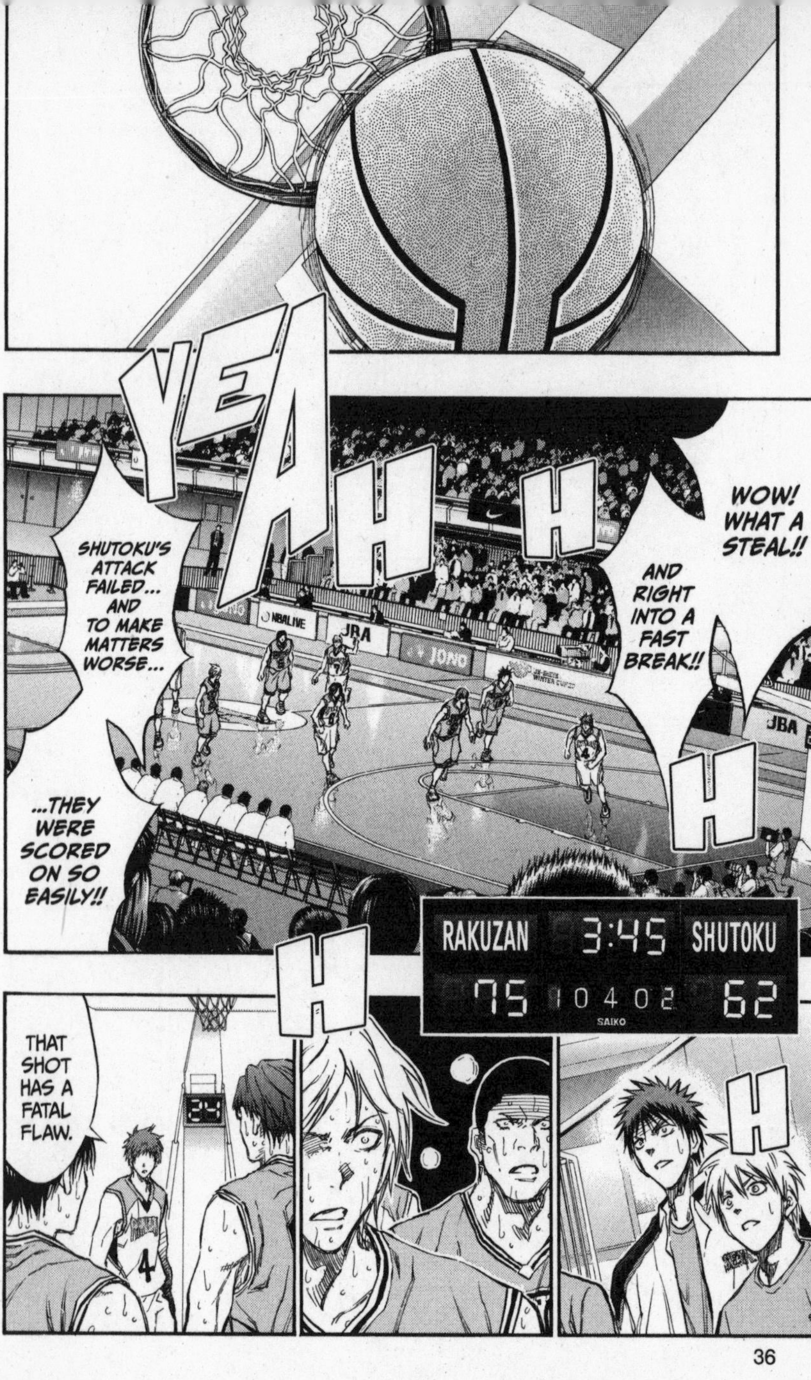
YEAHHHHH
WOW! WHAT A STEAL!!
AND RIGHT INTO A FAST BREAK!!
SHUTOKU'S ATTACK FAILED... AND TO MAKE MATTERS WORSE...
...THEY WERE SCORED ON SO EASILY!!
RAKUZAN 3:45 SHUTOKU
75 62
THAT SHOT HAS A FATAL FLAW.

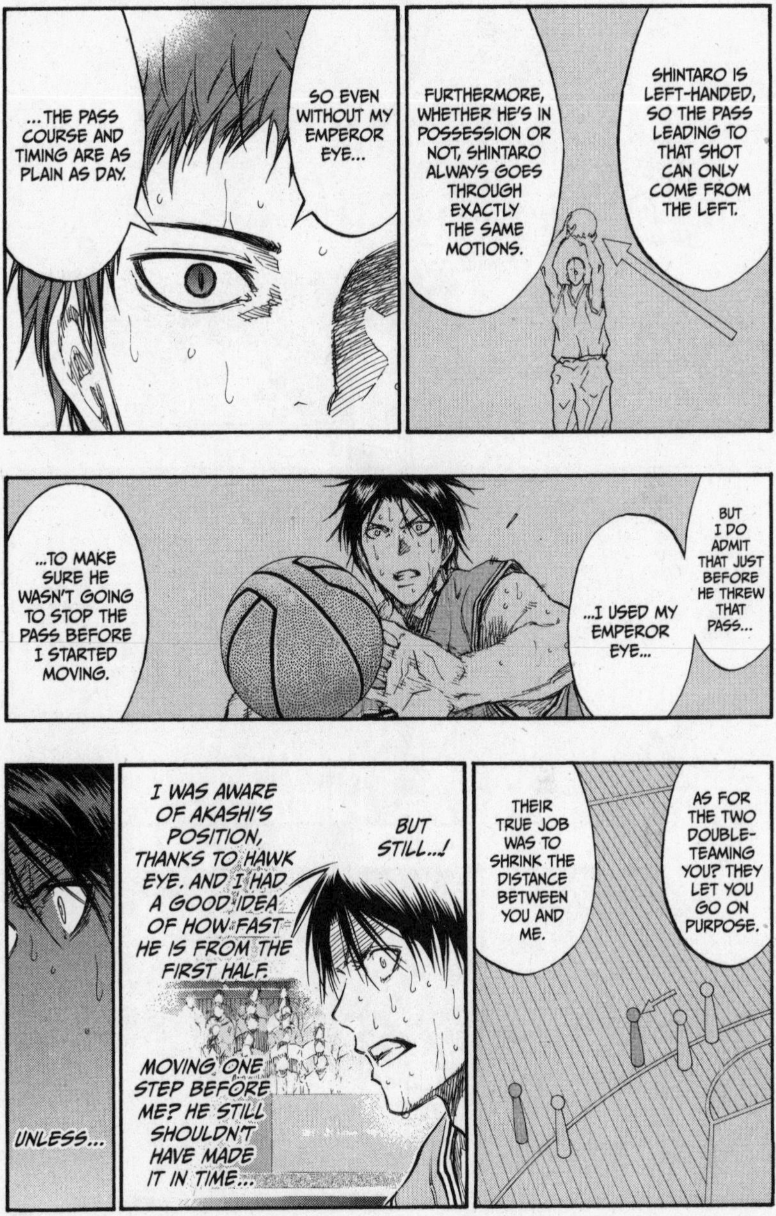
SHINTARO IS LEFT-HANDED, SO THE PASS LEADING TO THAT SHOT CAN ONLY COME FROM THE LEFT.
FURTHERMORE, WHETHER HE'S IN POSSESSION OR NOT, SHINTARO ALWAYS GOES THROUGH EXACTLY THE SAME MOTIONS.
SO EVEN WITHOUT MY EMPEROR EYE...
...THE PASS COURSE AND TIMING ARE AS PLAIN AS DAY.
BUT I DO ADMIT THAT JUST BEFORE HE THREW THAT PASS...
...I USED MY EMPEROR EYE...
...TO MAKE SURE HE WASN'T GOING TO STOP THE PASS BEFORE I STARTED MOVING.
AS FOR THE TWO DOUBLE-TEAMING YOU? THEY LET YOU GO ON PURPOSE.
THEIR TRUE JOB WAS TO SHRINK THE DISTANCE BETWEEN YOU AND ME.
BUT STILL...!
I WAS AWARE OF AKASHI'S POSITION, THANKS TO HAWK EYE. AND I HAD A GOOD IDEA OF HOW FAST HE IS FROM THE FIRST HALF.
MOVING ONE STEP BEFORE ME? HE STILL SHOULDN'T HAVE MADE IT IN TIME...
UNLESS...

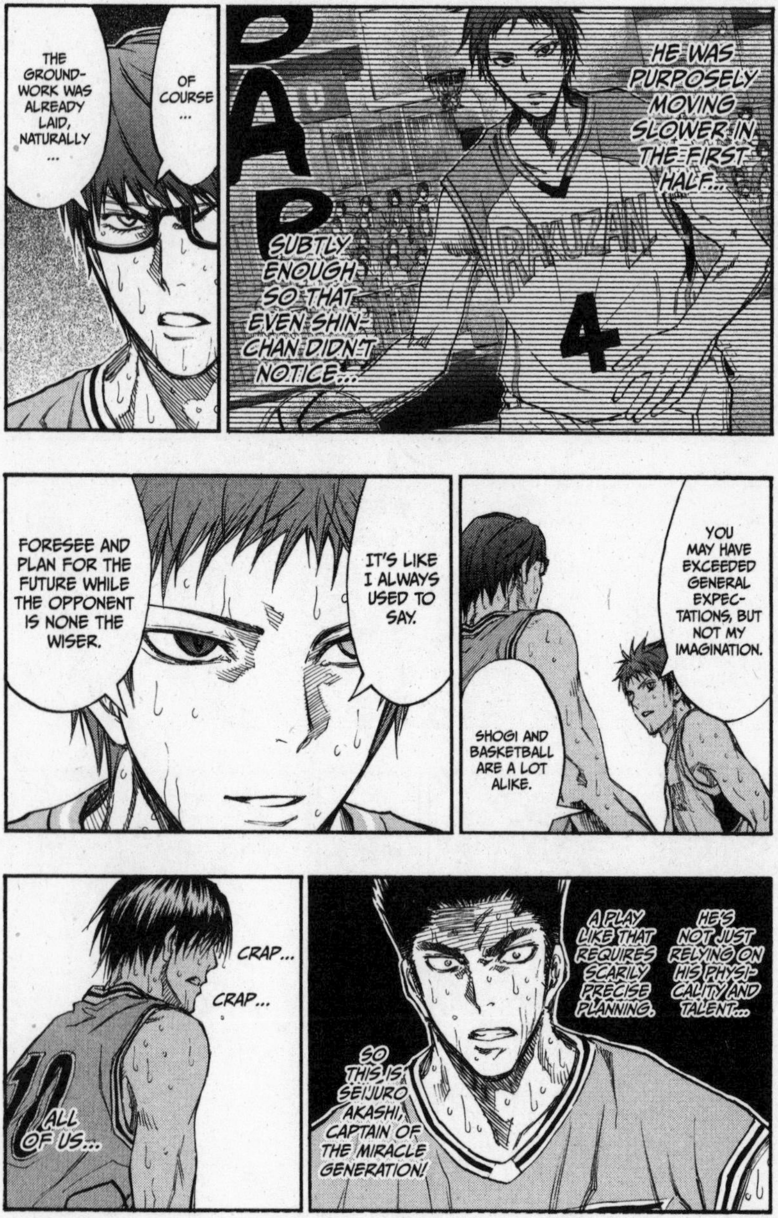
DAP
HE WAS PURPOSELY MOVING SLOWER IN THE FIRST HALF...
SUBTLY ENOUGH SO THAT EVEN SHIN-CHAN DIDN'T NOTICE...
OF COURSE ...
THE GROUND-WORK WAS ALREADY LAID, NATURALLY ...
YOU MAY HAVE EXCEEDED GENERAL EXPECTATIONS, BUT NOT MY IMAGINATION.
SHOGI AND BASKETBALL ARE A LOT ALIKE.
IT'S LIKE I ALWAYS USED TO SAY.
FORESEE AND PLAN FOR THE FUTURE WHILE THE OPPONENT IS NONE THE WISER.
HE'S NOT JUST RELYING ON HIS PHYSICALITY AND TALENT...
A PLAY LIKE THAT REQUIRES SCARILY PRECISE PLANNING.
SO THIS IS SEIJURO AKASHI, CAPTAIN OF THE MIRACLE GENERATION!
CRAP...
CRAP...
ALL OF US...

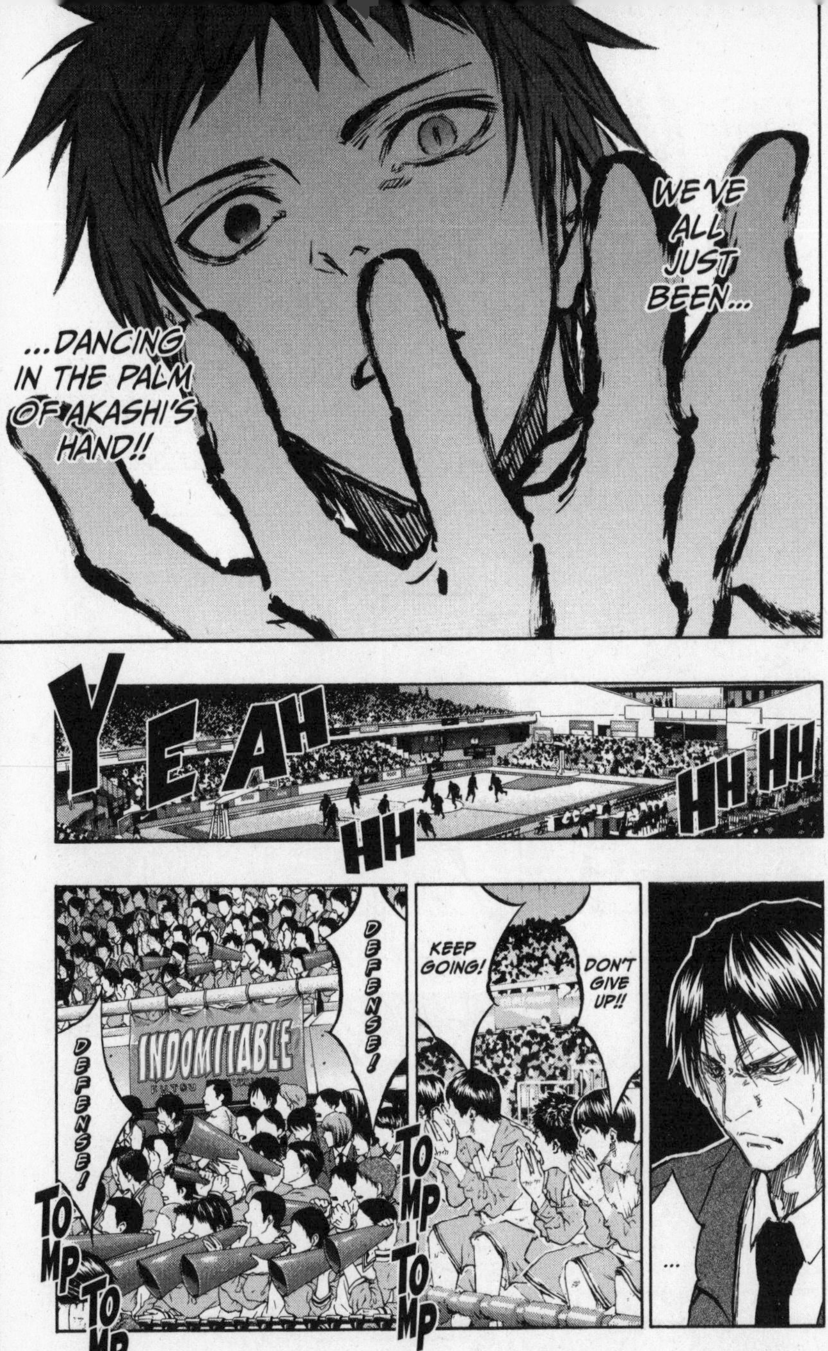
WE'VE ALL JUST BEEN...
...DANCING IN THE PALM OF AKASHI'S HAND!!
YEAH HH HH HH
...
DON'T GIVE UP!!
KEEP GOING!
TOMP TOMP
DEFENSE!
DEFENSE!
INDOMITABLE
TOMP TOMP

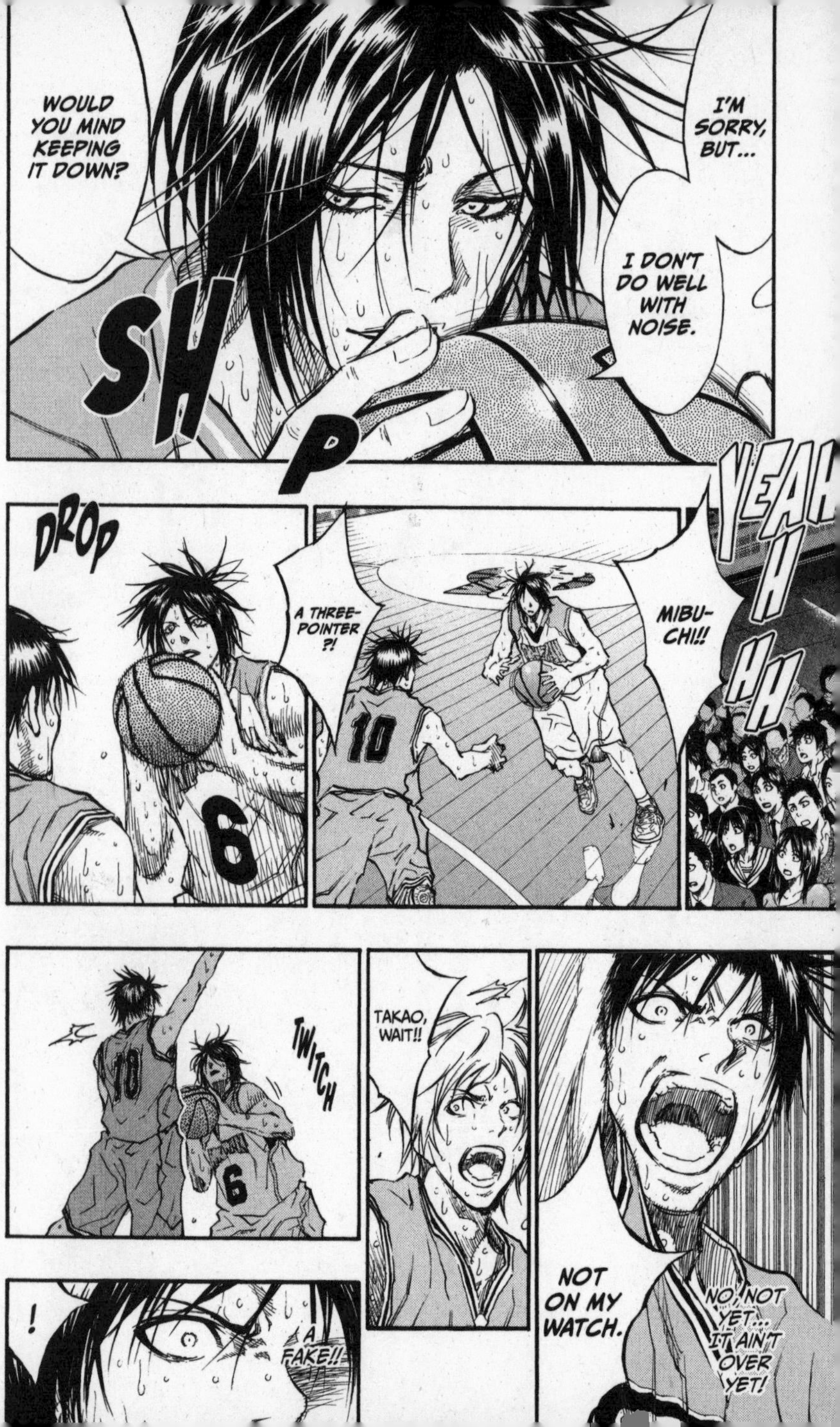
I'M SORRY, BUT...
I DON'T DO WELL WITH NOISE.
WOULD YOU MIND KEEPING IT DOWN?
SHP
YEAHHHH
MIBU-CHI!!
A THREE-POINTER?!
DROP
NO, NOT YET... IT AIN'T OVER YET!
TAKAO, WAIT!!
NOT ON MY WATCH.
TWITCH
!
A FAKE!!

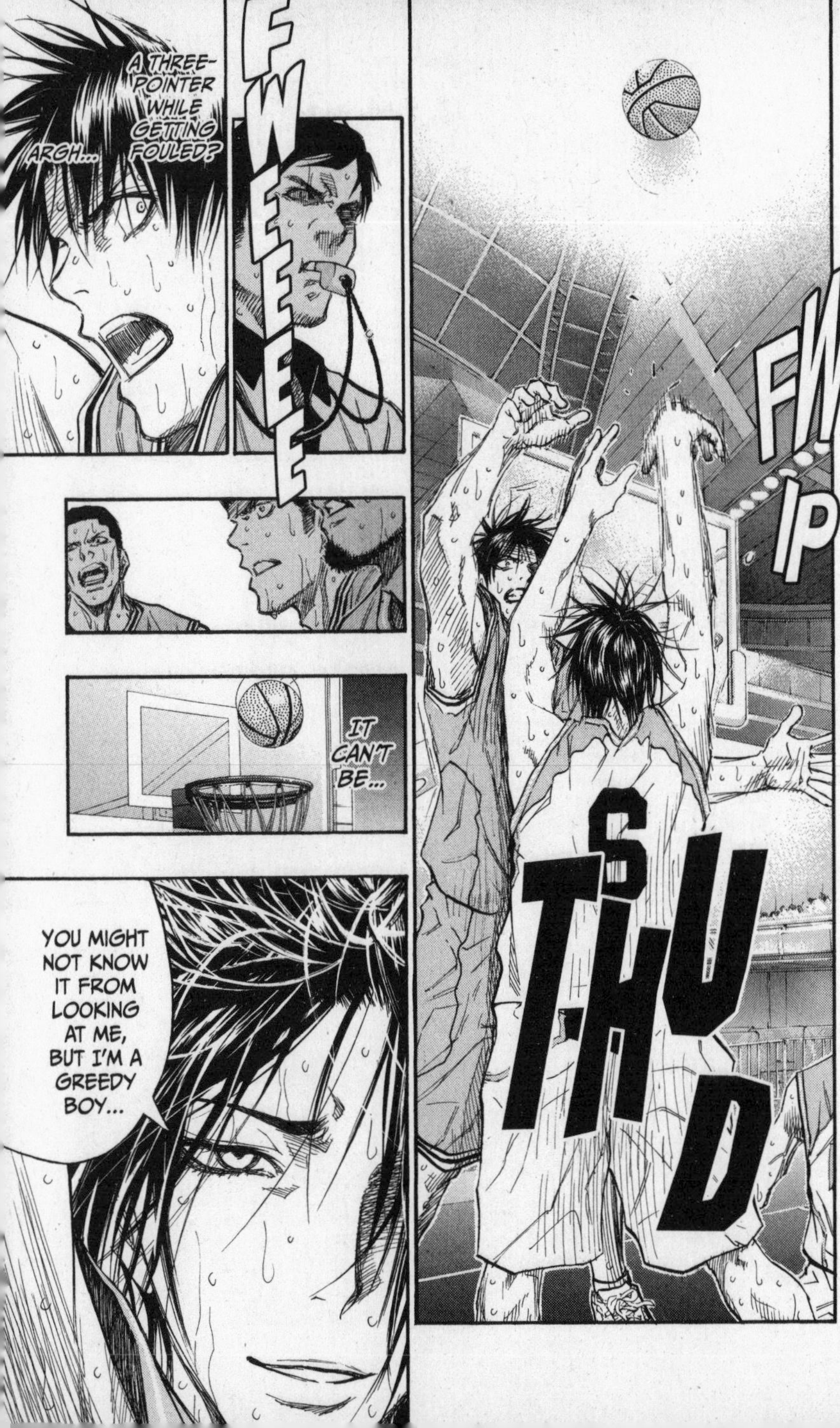

FWIP
THUD
FWEEEEE
A THREE-POINTER WHILE GETTING FOULED?
ARGH...
IT CAN'T BE...
YOU MIGHT NOT KNOW IT FROM LOOKING AT ME, BUT I'M A GREEDY BOY...

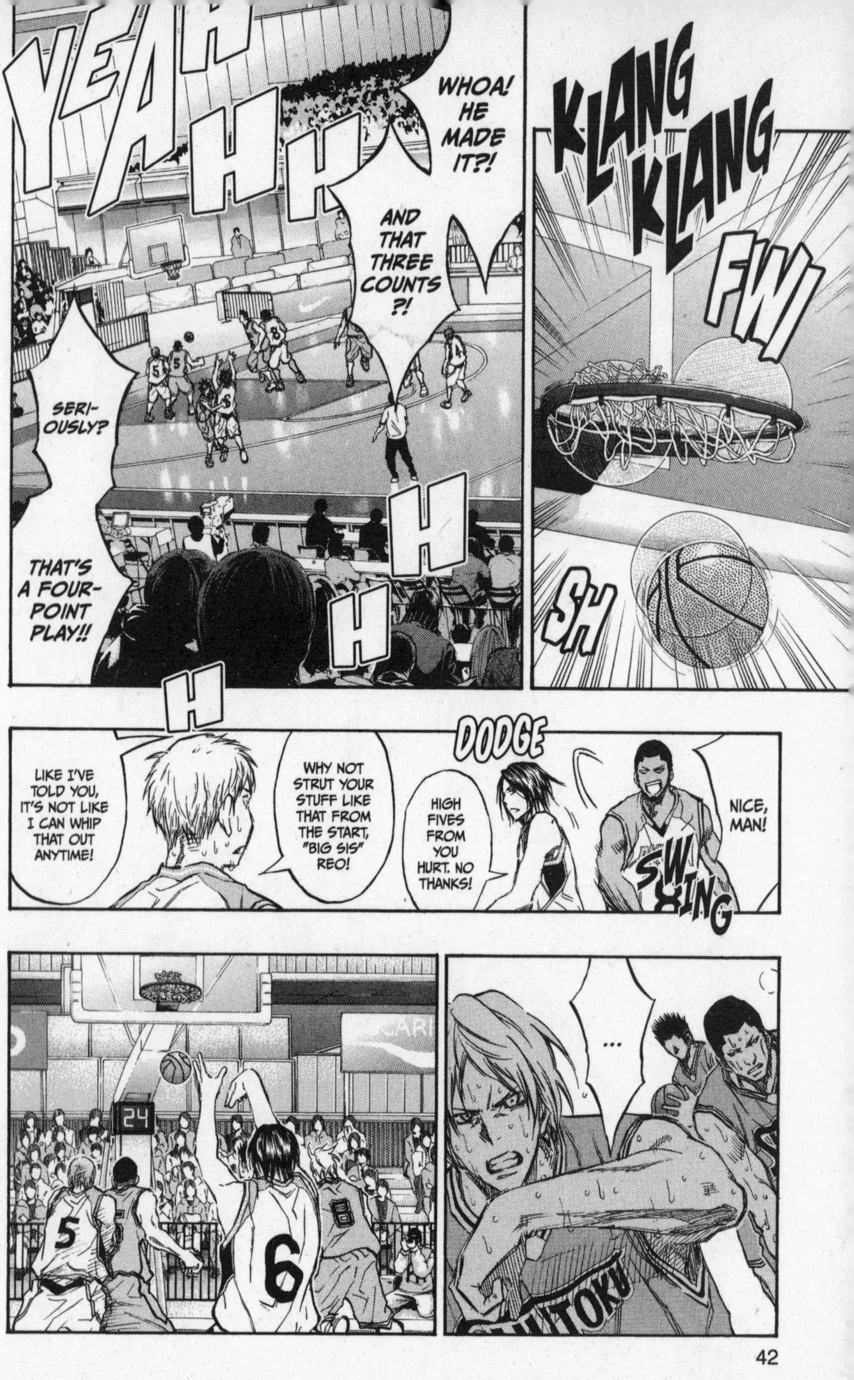
KLANG
KLANG
FWI
SH
YEAHHHH
WHOA! HE MADE IT?!
AND THAT THREE COUNTS?!
SERI-OUSLY?
THAT'S A FOUR-POINT PLAY!!
NICE, MAN!
SWING
DODGE
HIGH FIVES FROM YOU HURT. NO THANKS!
WHY NOT STRUT YOUR STUFF LIKE THAT FROM THE START, "BIG SIS" REO!
LIKE I'VE TOLD YOU, IT'S NOT LIKE I CAN WHIP THAT OUT ANYTIME!
...
24

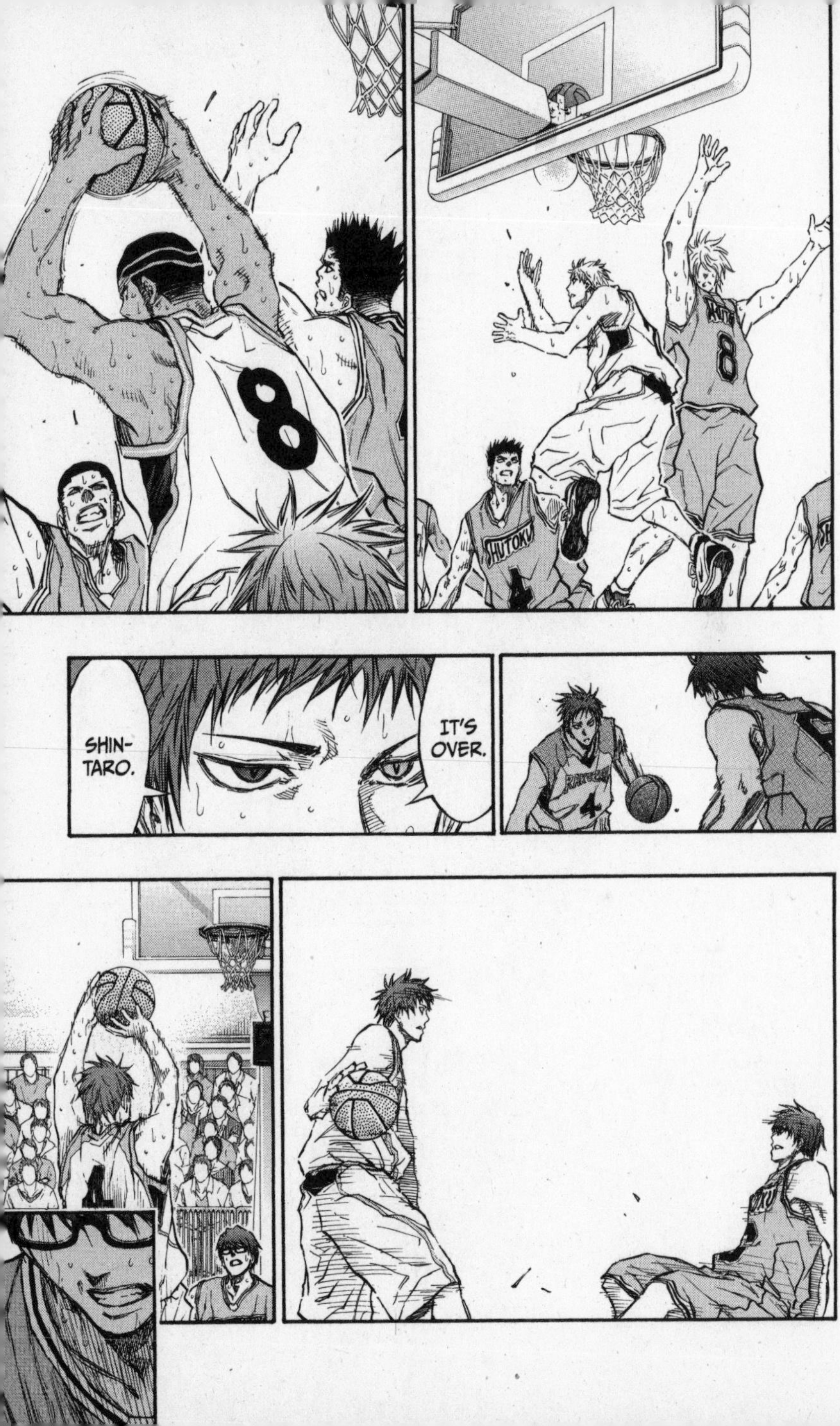
IT'S
OVER.
SHIN-
TARO.

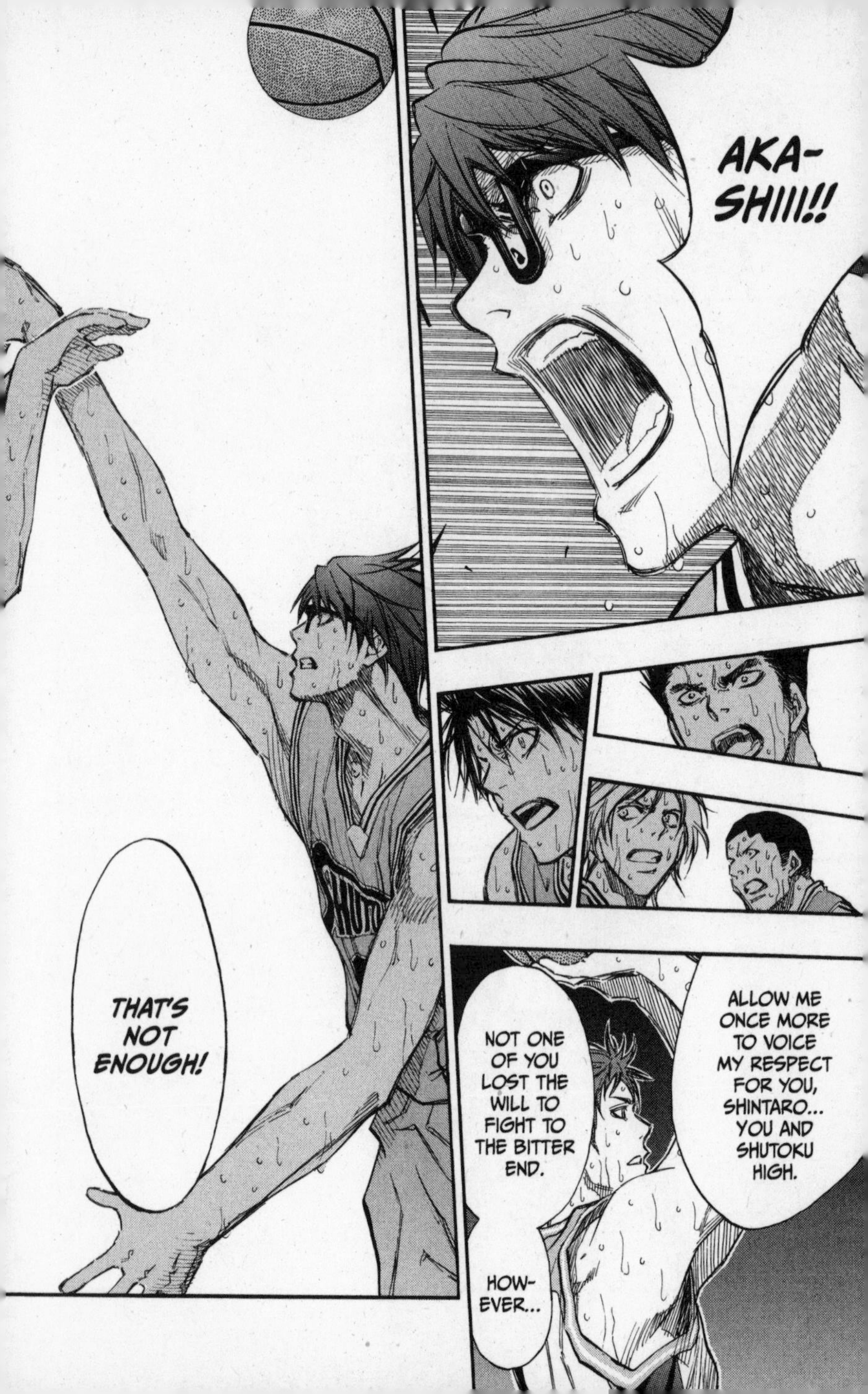
AKA-SHIII!!
ALLOW ME ONCE MORE TO VOICE MY RESPECT FOR YOU, SHINTARO... YOU AND SHUTOKU HIGH.
NOT ONE OF YOU LOST THE WILL TO FIGHT TO THE BITTER END.
HOW-EVER...
THAT'S NOT ENOUGH!

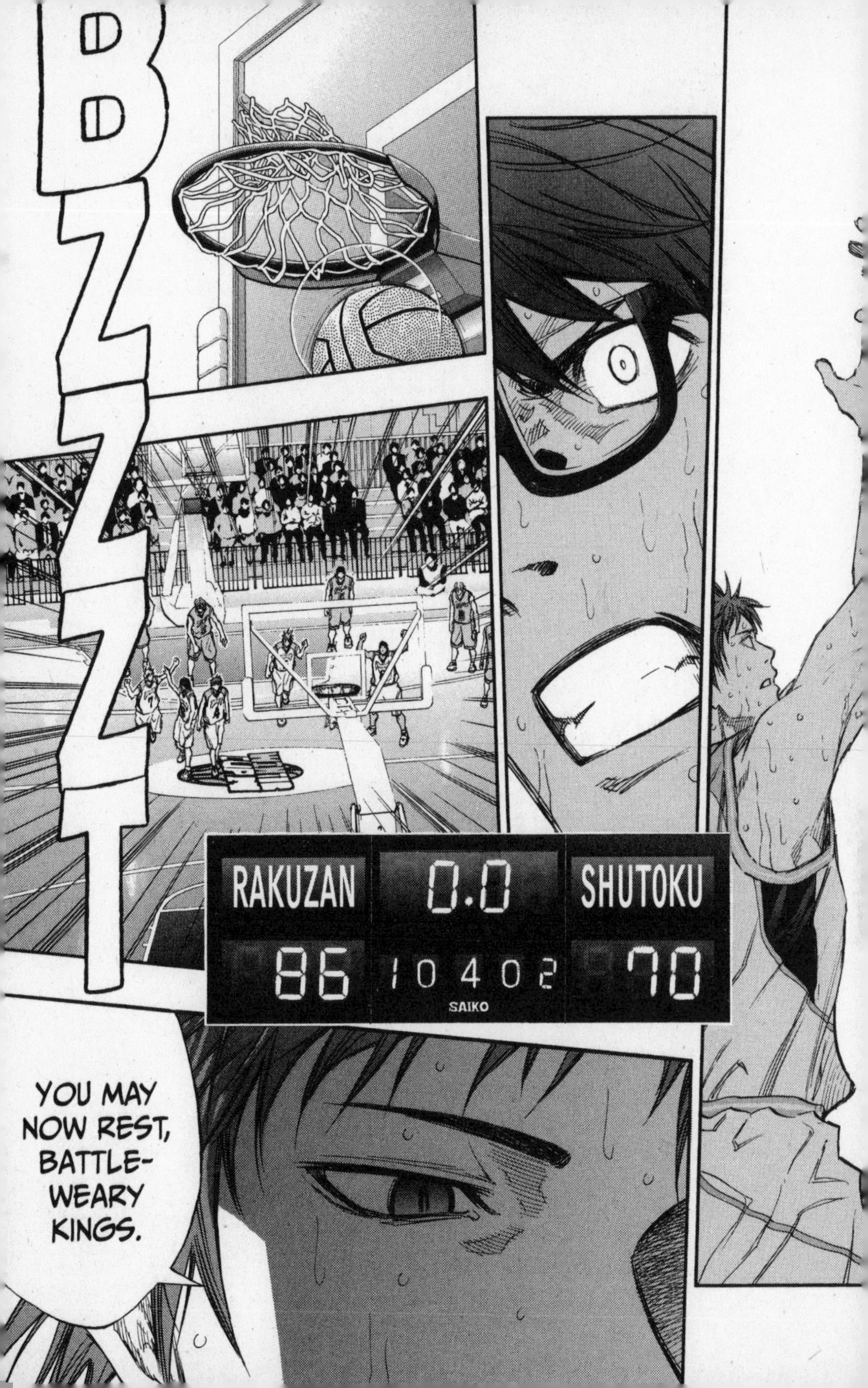
BZZZT
RAKUZAN
0.0
SHUTOKU
86
10402
70
SAIKO
YOU MAY NOW REST, BATTLE-WEARY KINGS.

KUROKO'S BASKETBALL

Q&A

(W/ HALFWAY-DECENT ANSWERS)

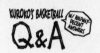

Q. **YOU KNOW THOSE PORN MAGS AND VIDEOS THAT SHOW UP NOW AND AGAIN? WHO DO THEY BELONG TO?**
(ASUNAGI from AICHI PREFECTURE)

A. HONESTLY? ALL THE BOYS ARE GUILTY OF OWNING SOME.

KUROKO'S BASKETBALL BLOOPERS

TAKE 7

HIGH FIVES FROM YOU HURT. NO THANKS!
WHY NOT STRUT YOUR STUFF LIKE THAT FROM THE START, "BIG SIS" REO!
LIKE I'VE TOLD YOU, IT'S NOT LIKE I CAN WHIP THAT OUT ANYTIME!
BESIDES, I ONLY LIKE BUMPING INTO THE CHOICEST OF BOYS!
HUH?
I WOULDN'T MIND DOING IT TO THAT SWEET THING THERE OVER AND OVER AGAIN. ♥
IS HE SERIOUS?!
SHUDDER
?!
TAKAO

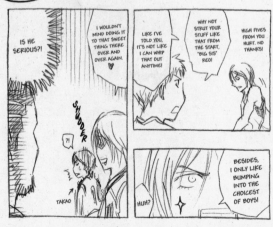

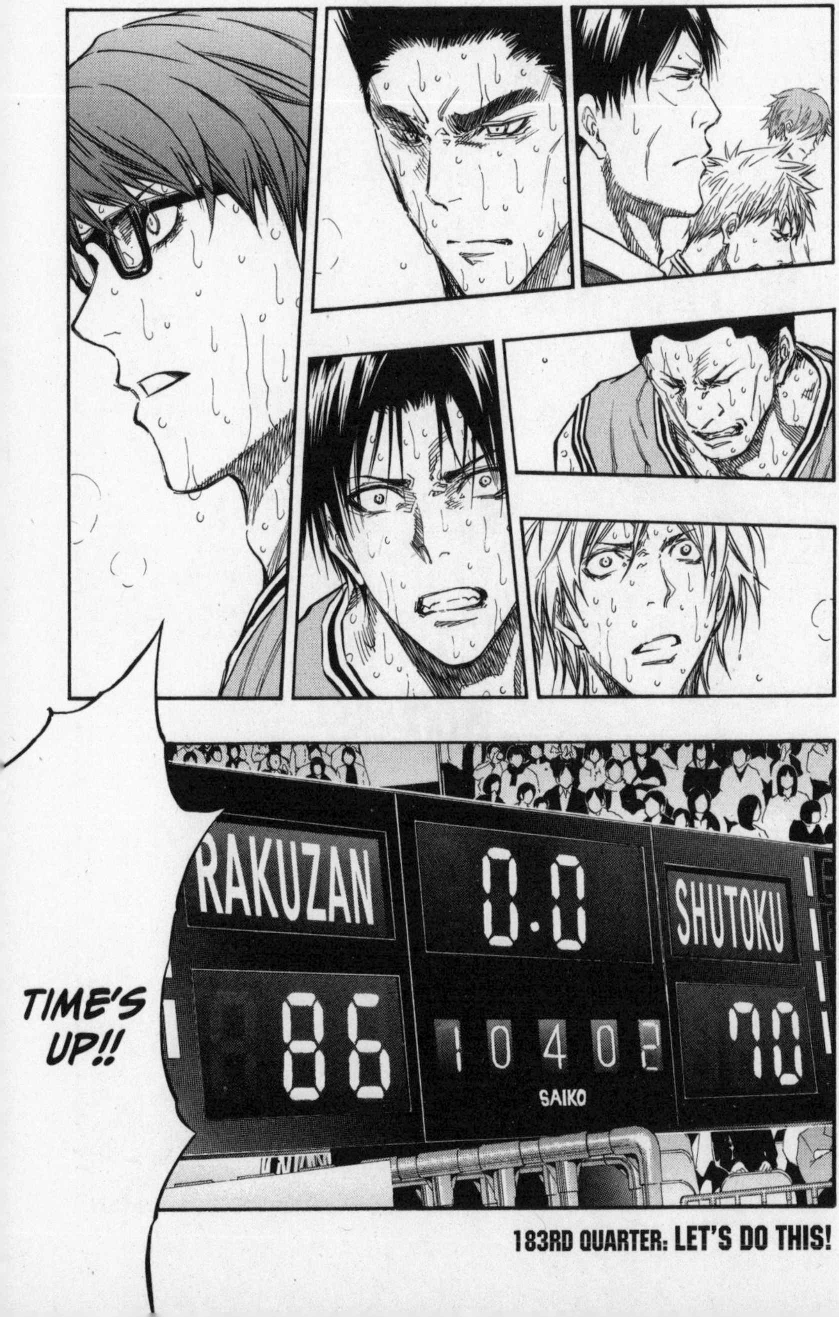
TIME'S UP!!
RAKUZAN
0.0
SHUTOKU
86
70
SAIKO

183RD QUARTER: LET'S DO THIS!

183RD QUARTER: LET'S DO THIS!

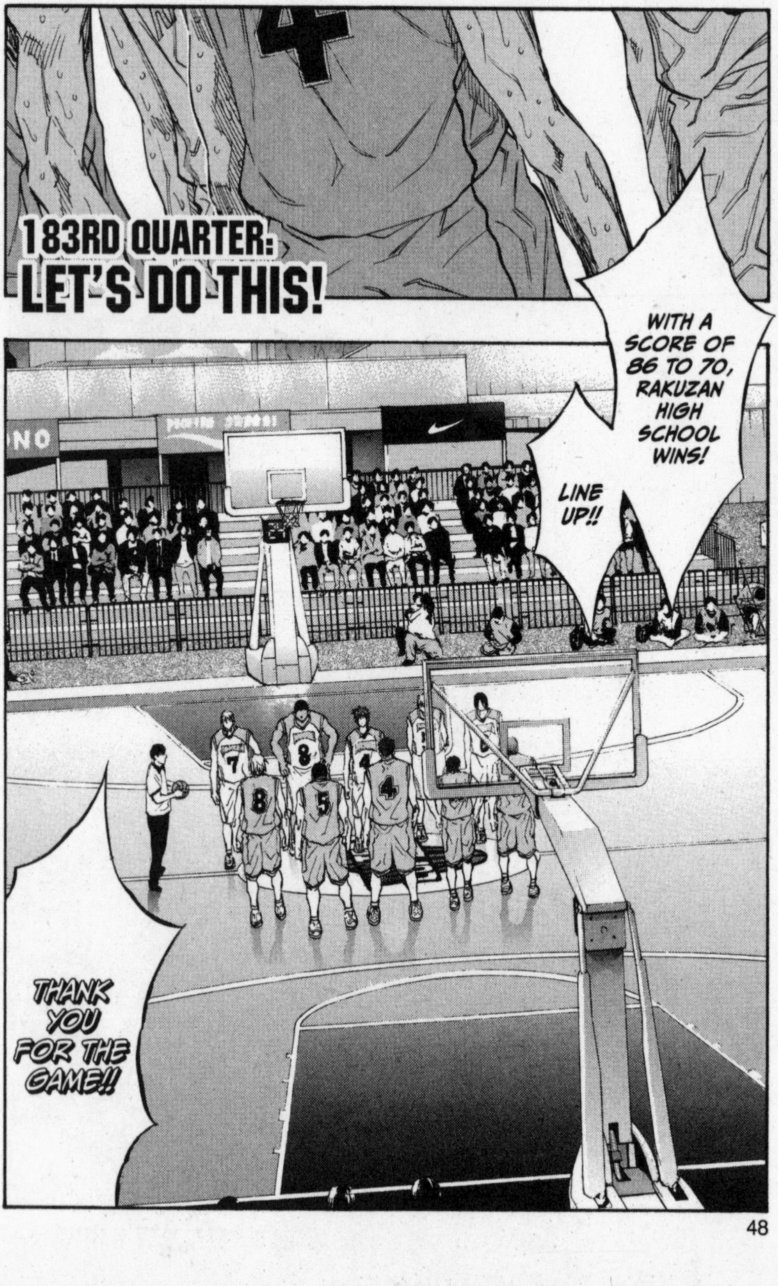
WITH A SCORE OF 86 TO 70, RAKUZAN HIGH SCHOOL WINS!
LINE UP!!
THANK YOU FOR THE GAME!!

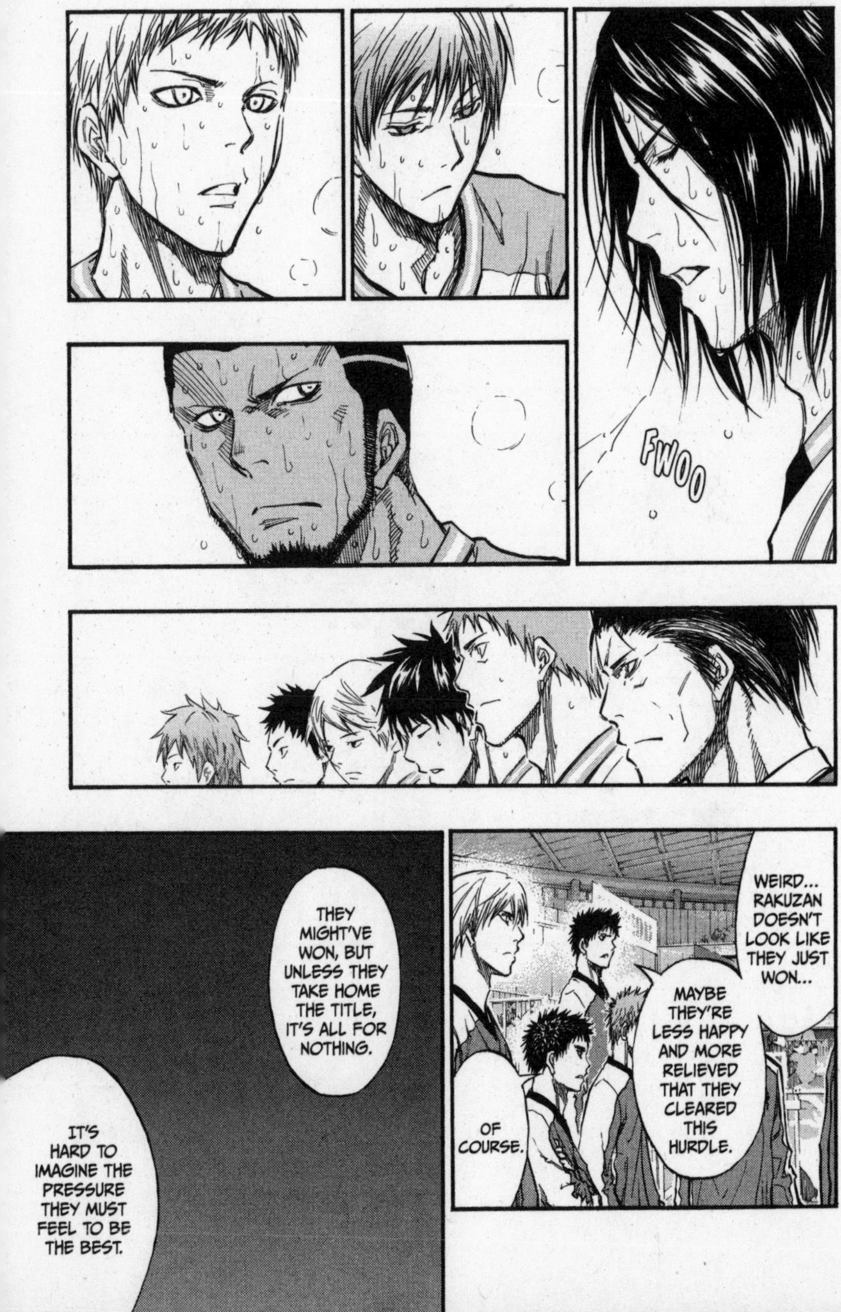
FWOO
WEIRD... RAKUZAN DOESN'T LOOK LIKE THEY JUST WON...
MAYBE THEY'RE LESS HAPPY AND MORE RELIEVED THAT THEY CLEARED THIS HURDLE.
OF COURSE.
THEY MIGHT'VE WON, BUT UNLESS THEY TAKE HOME THE TITLE, IT'S ALL FOR NOTHING.
IT'S HARD TO IMAGINE THE PRESSURE THEY MUST FEEL TO BE THE BEST.

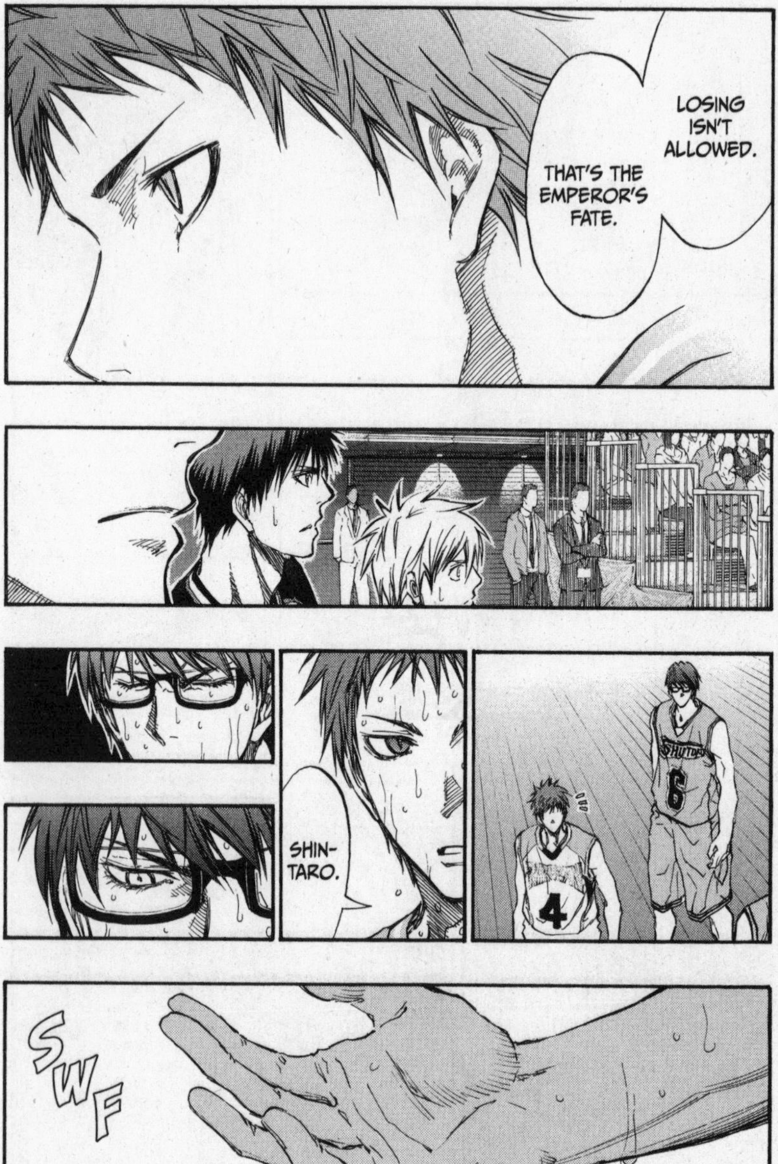
LOSING ISN'T ALLOWED.
THAT'S THE EMPEROR'S FATE.
SHIN-TARO.
SWF

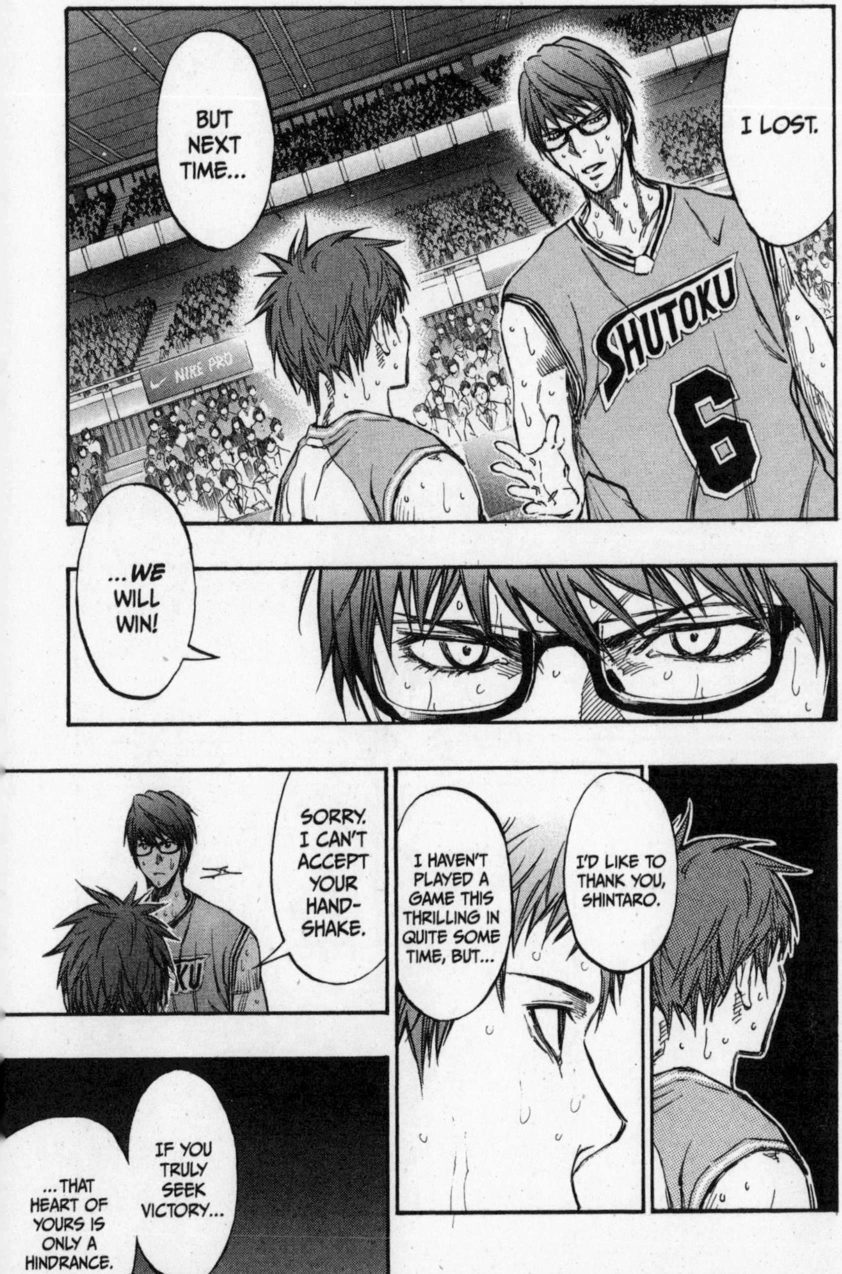
I LOST.
BUT NEXT TIME...
...WE WILL WIN!
I'D LIKE TO THANK YOU, SHINTARO.
I HAVEN'T PLAYED A GAME THIS THRILLING IN QUITE SOME TIME, BUT...
SORRY. I CAN'T ACCEPT YOUR HAND-SHAKE.
IF YOU TRULY SEEK VICTORY...
...THAT HEART OF YOURS IS ONLY A HINDRANCE.

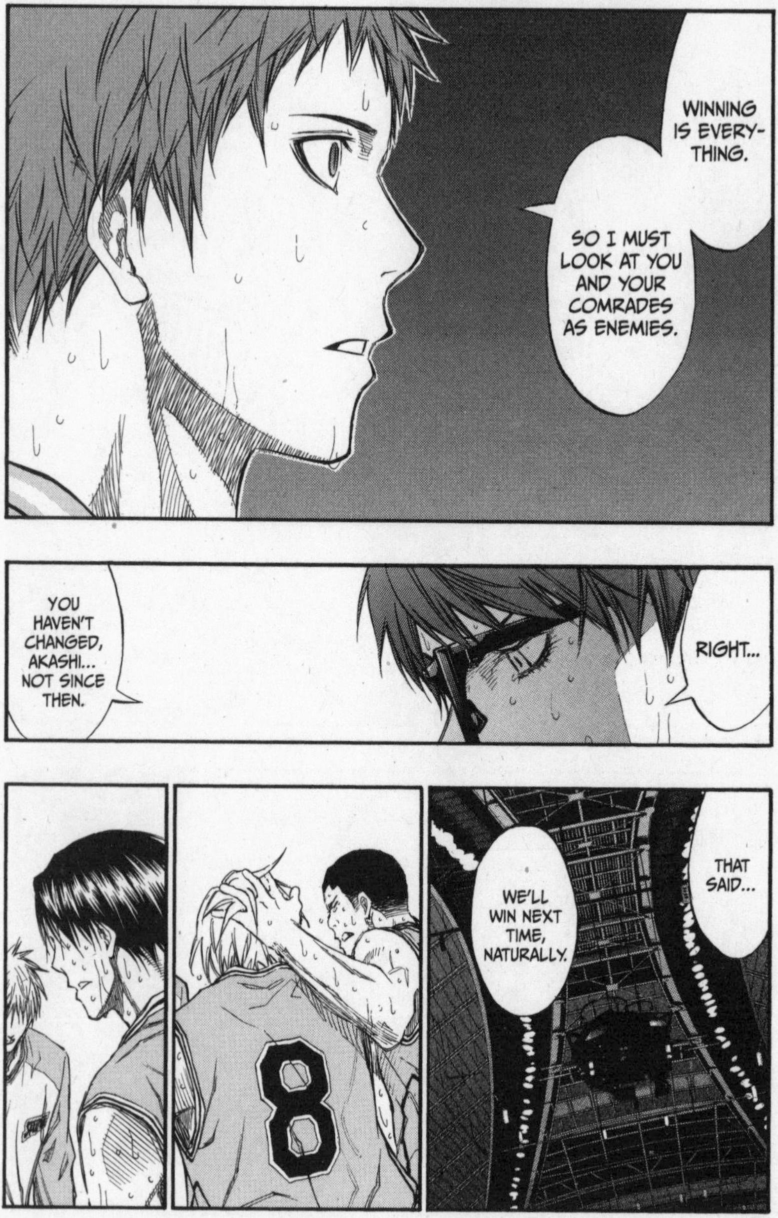
WINNING IS EVERYTHING.
SO I MUST LOOK AT YOU AND YOUR COMRADES AS ENEMIES.
RIGHT...
YOU HAVEN'T CHANGED, AKASHI... NOT SINCE THEN.
THAT SAID...
WE'LL WIN NEXT TIME, NATURALLY.

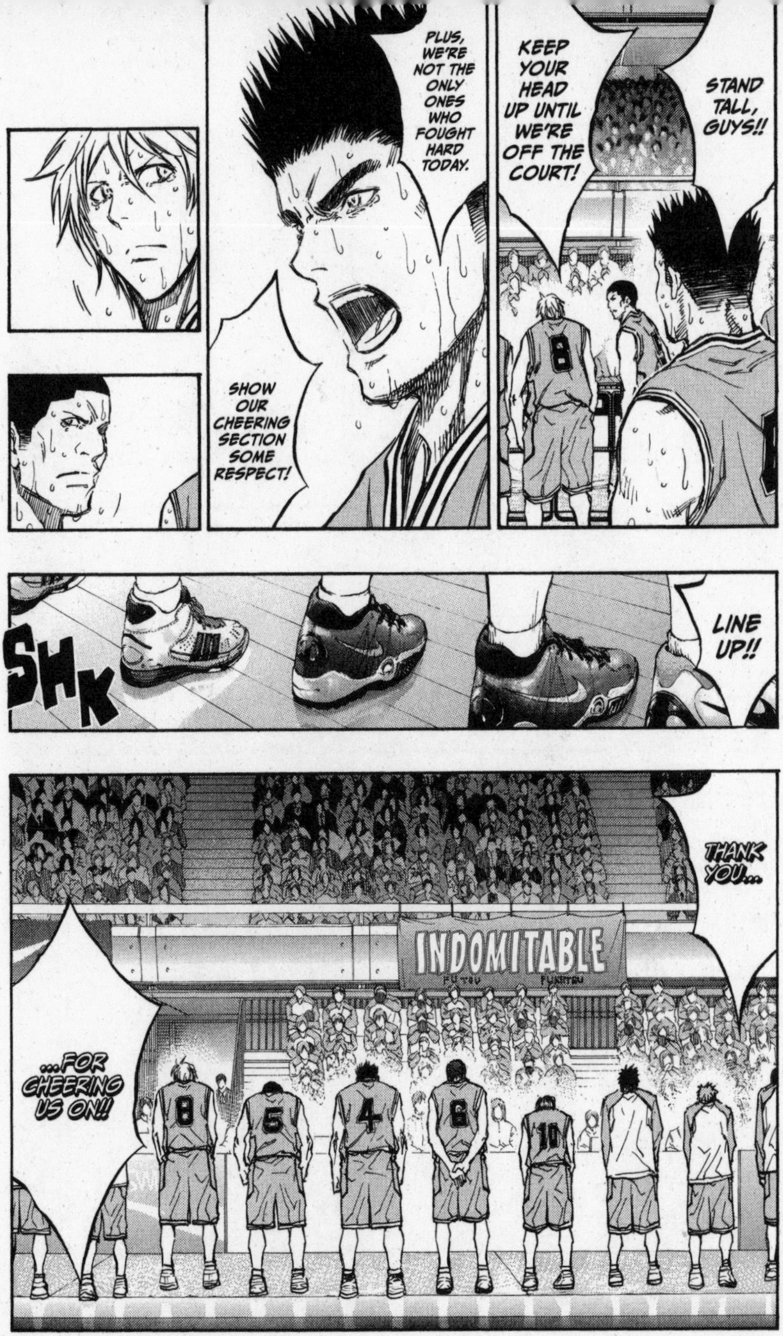
STAND TALL, GUYS!!
KEEP YOUR HEAD UP UNTIL WE'RE OFF THE COURT!
PLUS, WE'RE NOT THE ONLY ONES WHO FOUGHT HARD TODAY.
SHOW OUR CHEERING SECTION SOME RESPECT!
LINE UP!!
SHK
THANK YOU...
INDOMITABLE
...FOR CHEERING US ON!!

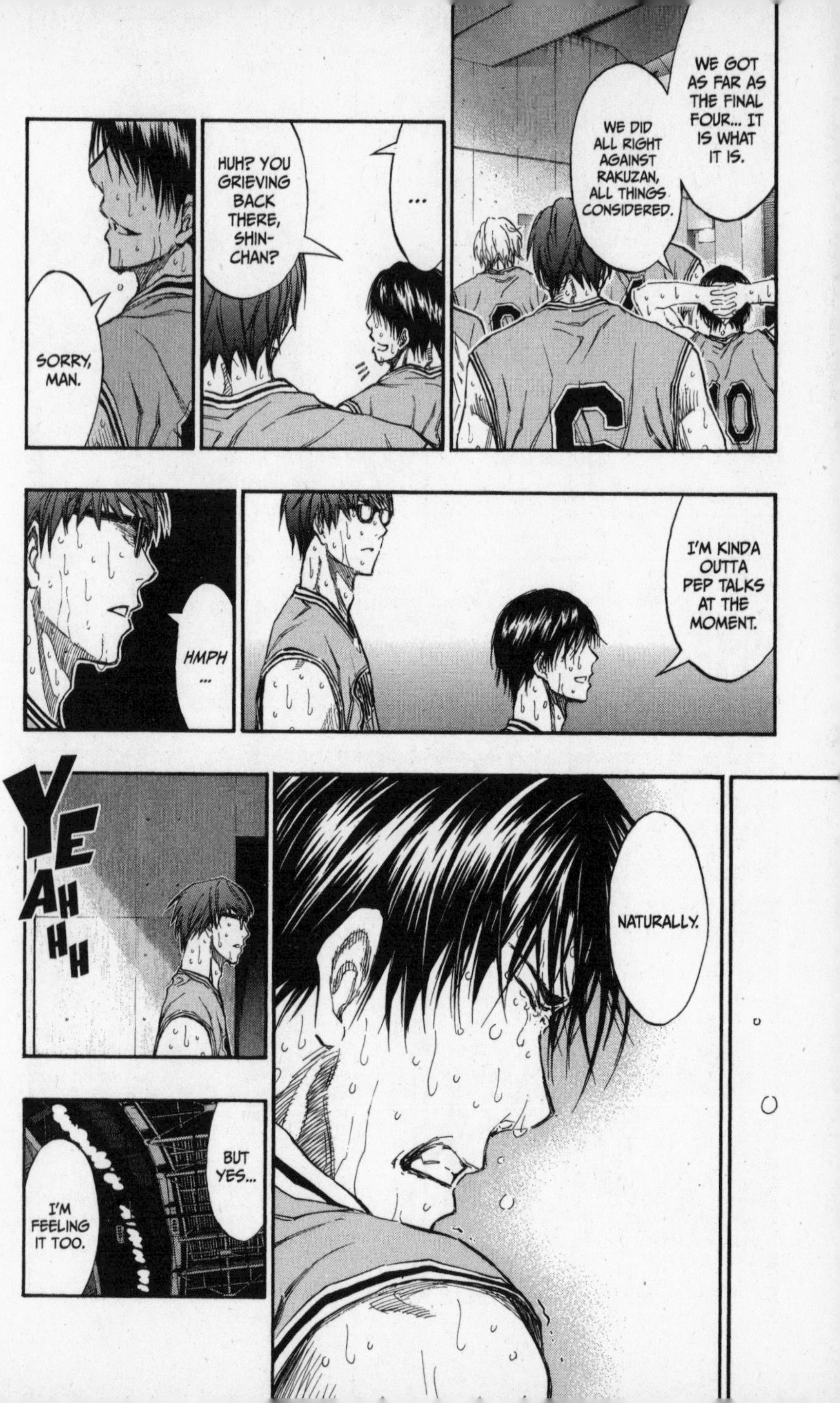
WE GOT AS FAR AS THE FINAL FOUR... IT IS WHAT IT IS.
WE DID ALL RIGHT AGAINST RAKUZAN, ALL THINGS CONSIDERED.
...
HUH? YOU GRIEVING BACK THERE, SHIN-CHAN?
SORRY, MAN.
I'M KINDA OUTTA PEP TALKS AT THE MOMENT.
HMPH ...
NATURALLY.
YEAHHH
BUT YES...
I'M FEELING IT TOO.

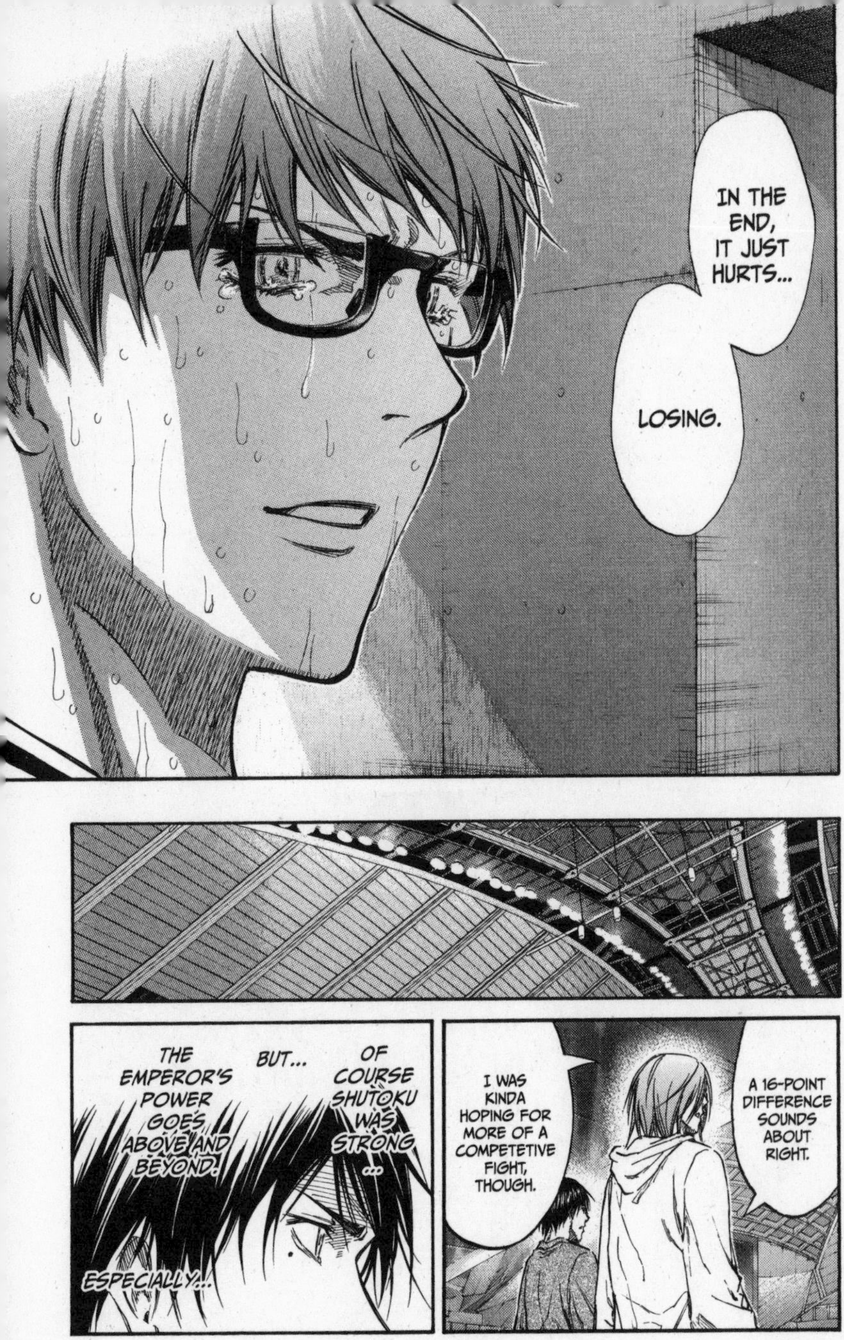
IN THE END, IT JUST HURTS...
LOSING.
A 16-POINT DIFFERENCE SOUNDS ABOUT RIGHT.
I WAS KINDA HOPING FOR MORE OF A COMPETETIVE FIGHT, THOUGH.
OF COURSE SHUTOKU WAS STRONG...
BUT...
THE EMPEROR'S POWER GOES ABOVE AND BEYOND.
ESPECIALLY...

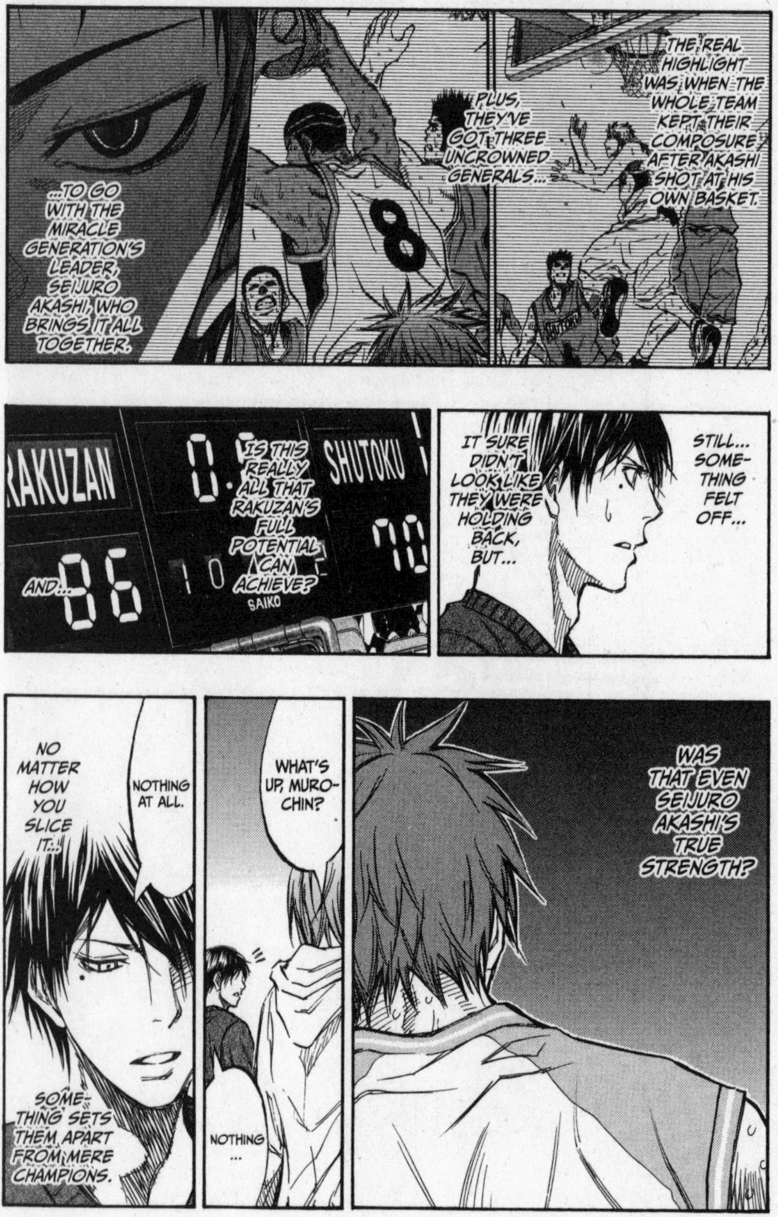
THE REAL HIGHLIGHT WAS WHEN THE WHOLE TEAM KEPT THEIR COMPOSURE AFTER AKASHI SHOT AT HIS OWN BASKET.
PLUS, THEY'VE GOT THREE UNCROWNED GENERALS...
...TO GO WITH THE MIRACLE GENERATION'S LEADER, SEIJURO AKASHI, WHO BRINGS IT ALL TOGETHER.
STILL... SOME-THING FELT OFF...
IT SURE DIDN'T LOOK LIKE THEY WERE HOLDING BACK, BUT...
IS THIS REALLY ALL THAT RAKUZAN'S FULL POTENTIAL CAN ACHIEVE?
AND...
RAKUZAN
SHUTOKU
86
SAIKO
WAS THAT EVEN SEIJURO AKASHI'S TRUE STRENGTH?
WHAT'S UP, MURO-CHIN?
NOTHING...
NOTHING AT ALL.
NO MATTER HOW YOU SLICE IT...
SOME-THING SETS THEM APART FROM MERE CHAMPIONS.

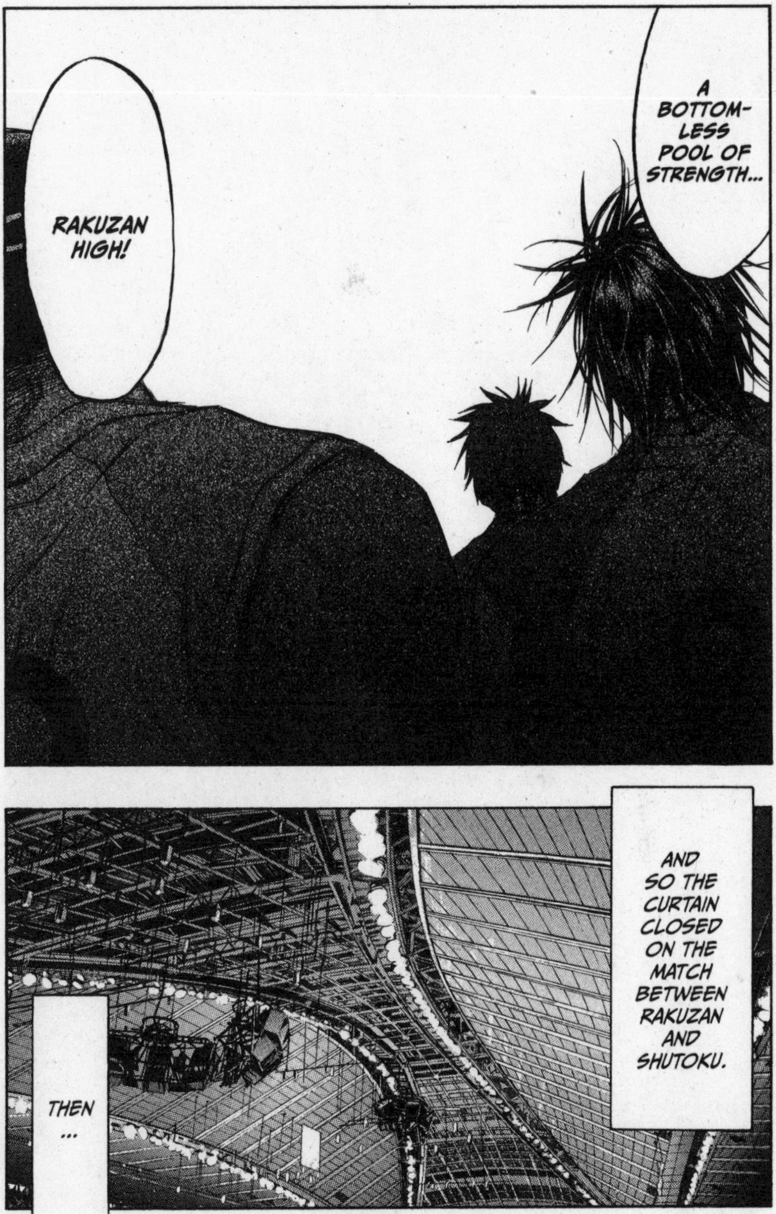
A BOTTOM-LESS POOL OF STRENGTH...
RAKUZAN HIGH!
AND SO THE CURTAIN CLOSED ON THE MATCH BETWEEN RAKUZAN AND SHUTOKU.
THEN ...

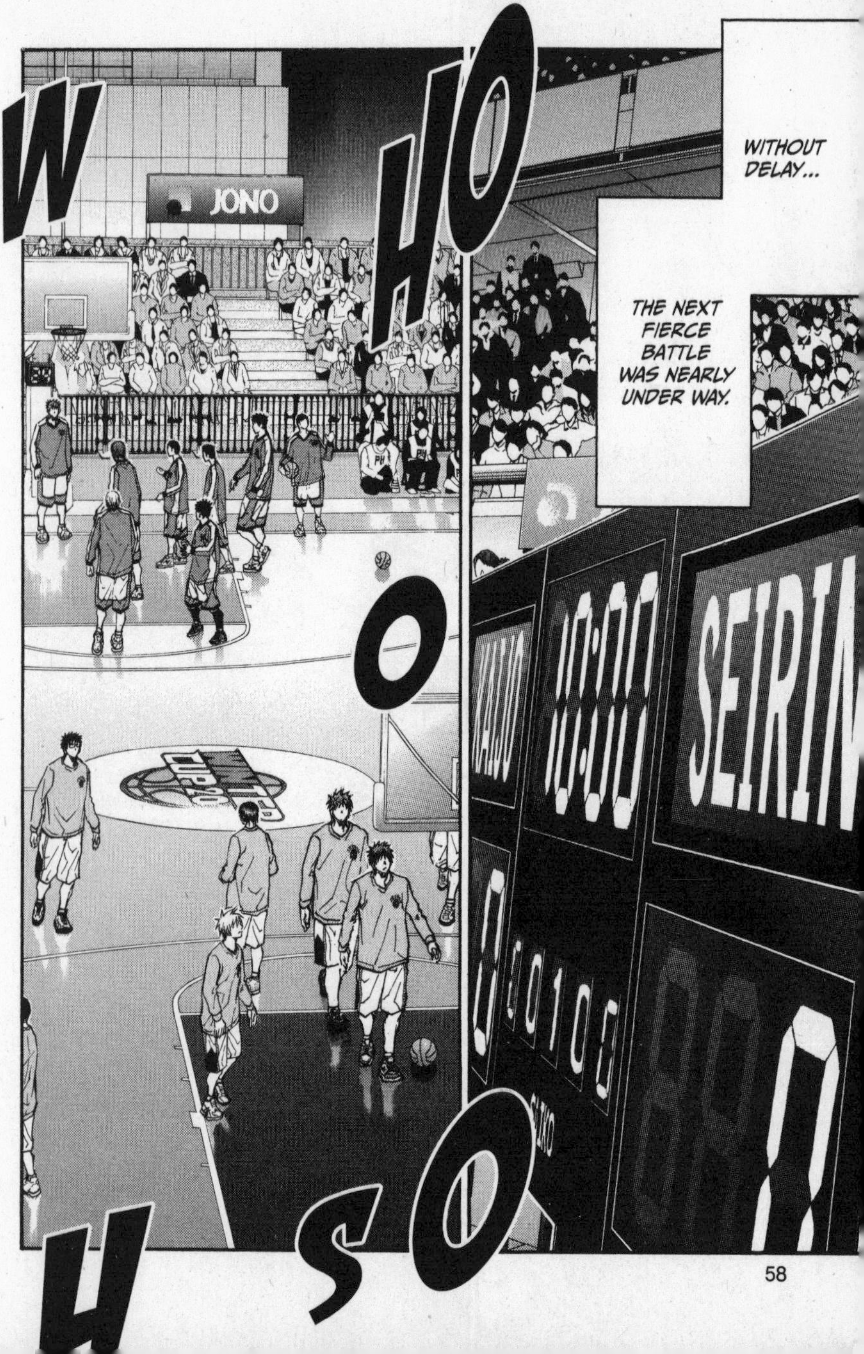
WITHOUT DELAY...
THE NEXT FIERCE BATTLE WAS NEARLY UNDER WAY.
WHOOOOSH
JONO
SEIRIN
10:00

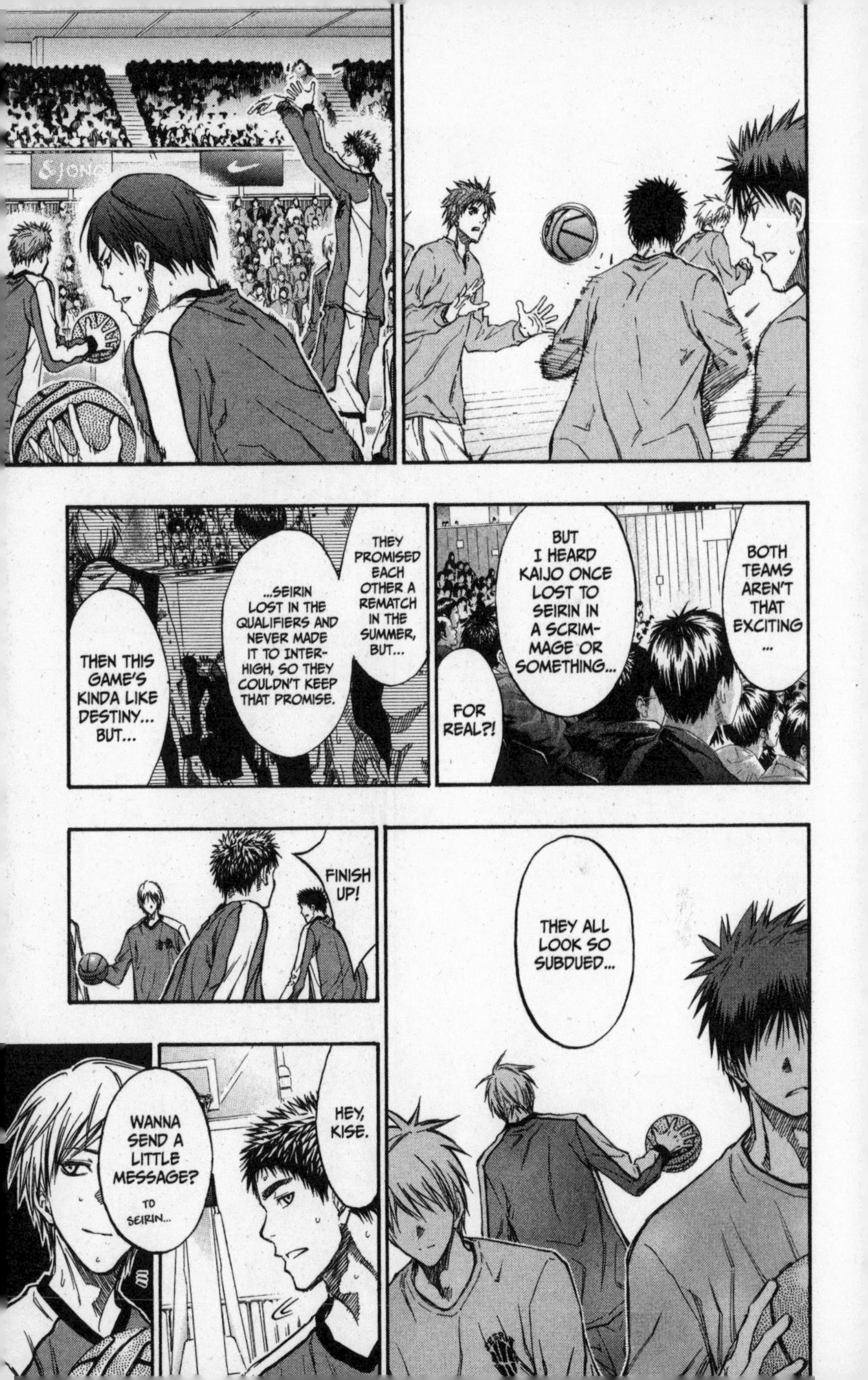
BOTH TEAMS AREN'T THAT EXCITING...
BUT I HEARD KAIJO ONCE LOST TO SEIRIN IN A SCRIM-MAGE OR SOMETHING...
FOR REAL?!
THEY PROMISED EACH OTHER A REMATCH IN THE SUMMER, BUT...
...SEIRIN LOST IN THE QUALIFIERS AND NEVER MADE IT TO INTER-HIGH, SO THEY COULDN'T KEEP THAT PROMISE.
THEN THIS GAME'S KINDA LIKE DESTINY... BUT...
THEY ALL LOOK SO SUBDUED...
FINISH UP!
HEY, KISE.
WANNA SEND A LITTLE MESSAGE?
TO SEIRIN...

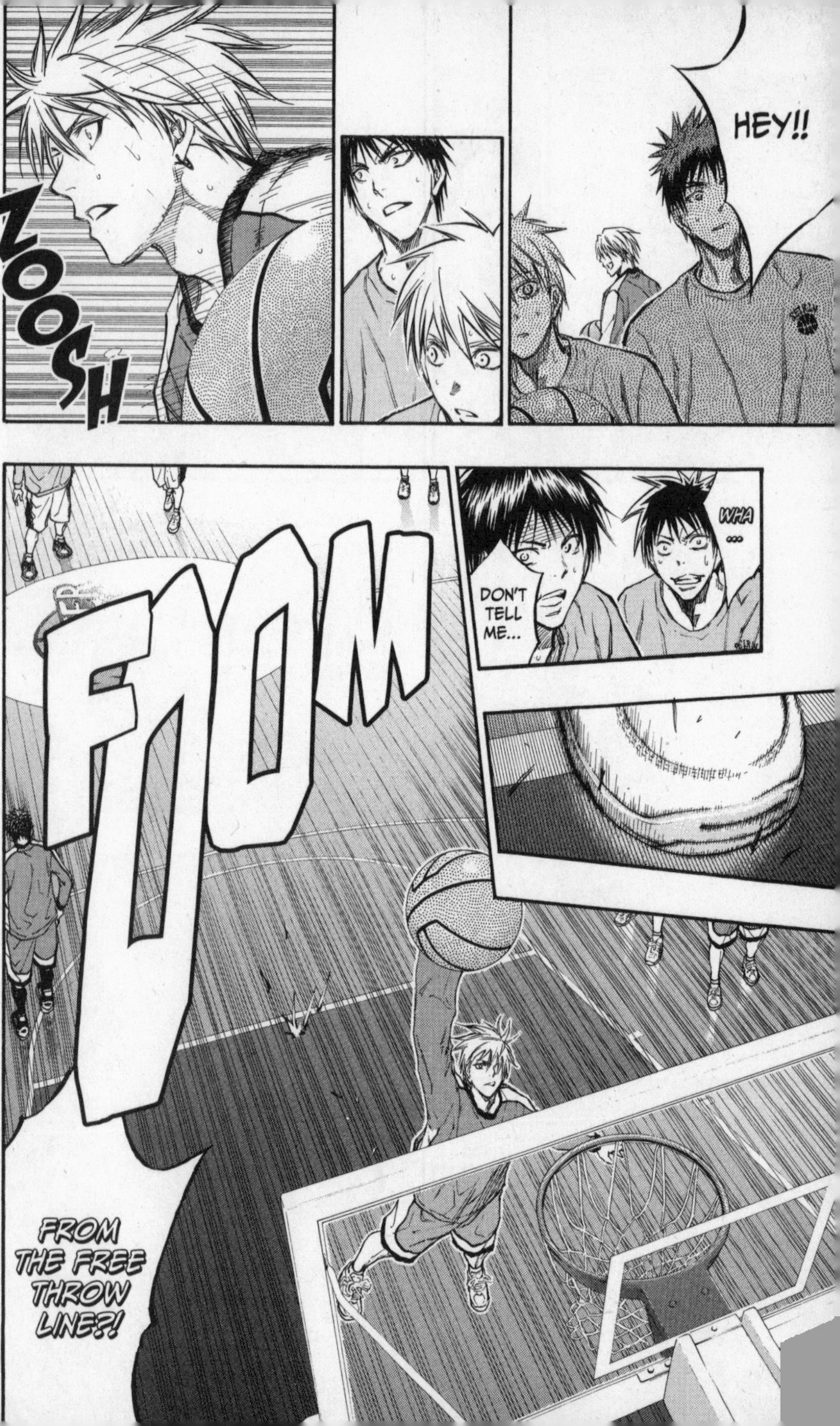
HEY!!
ZOOSH
WHA...
DON'T TELL ME...
FWOM
FROM THE FREE THROW LINE?!

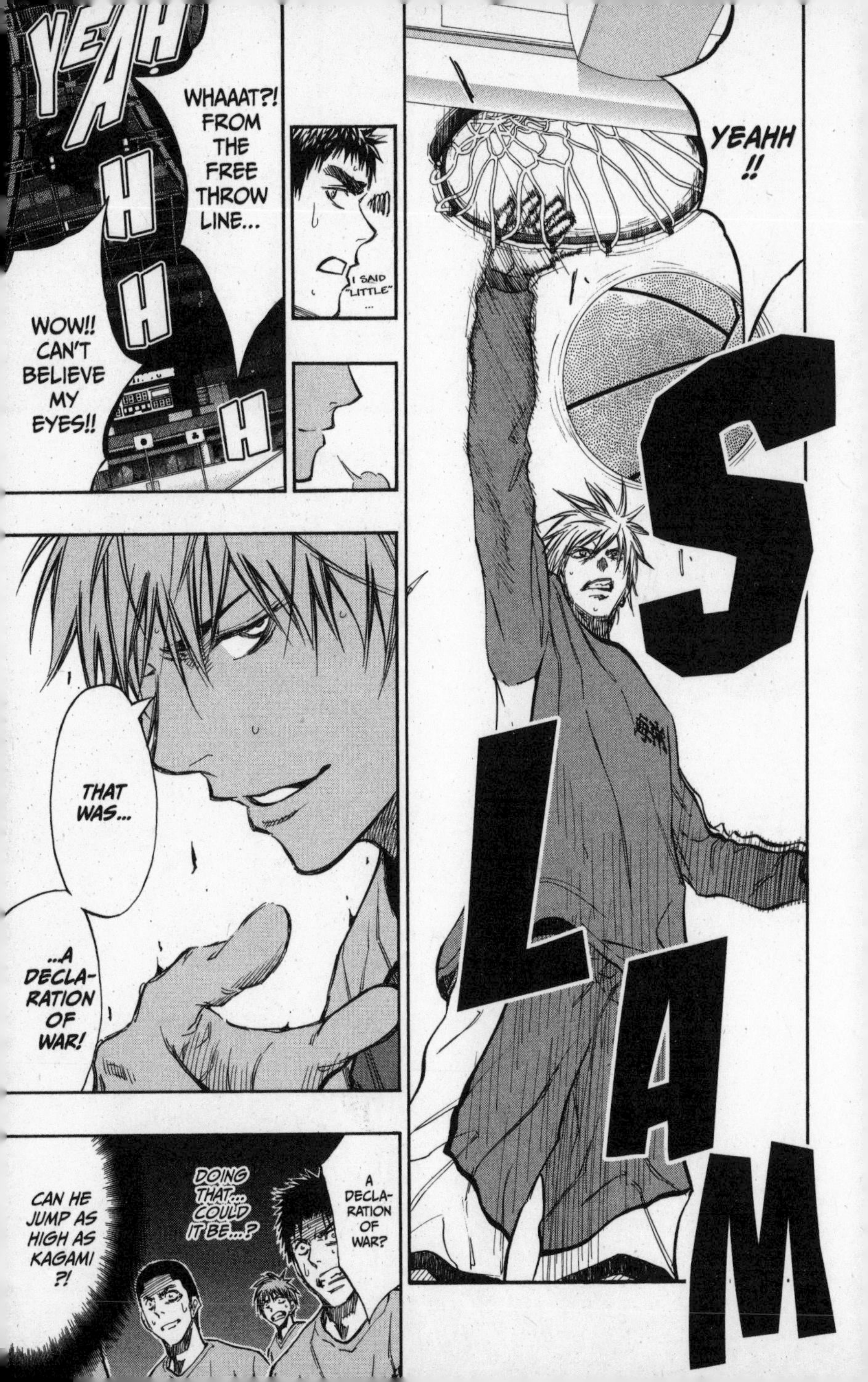
YEAHH!!
SLAM
I SAID "LITTLE"...
YEAHHHH
WHAAAT?! FROM THE FREE THROW LINE...
WOW!! CAN'T BELIEVE MY EYES!!
THAT WAS...
...A DECLARA-TION OF WAR!
A DECLA-RATION OF WAR?
DOING THAT... COULD IT BE...?
CAN HE JUMP AS HIGH AS KAGAMI?!

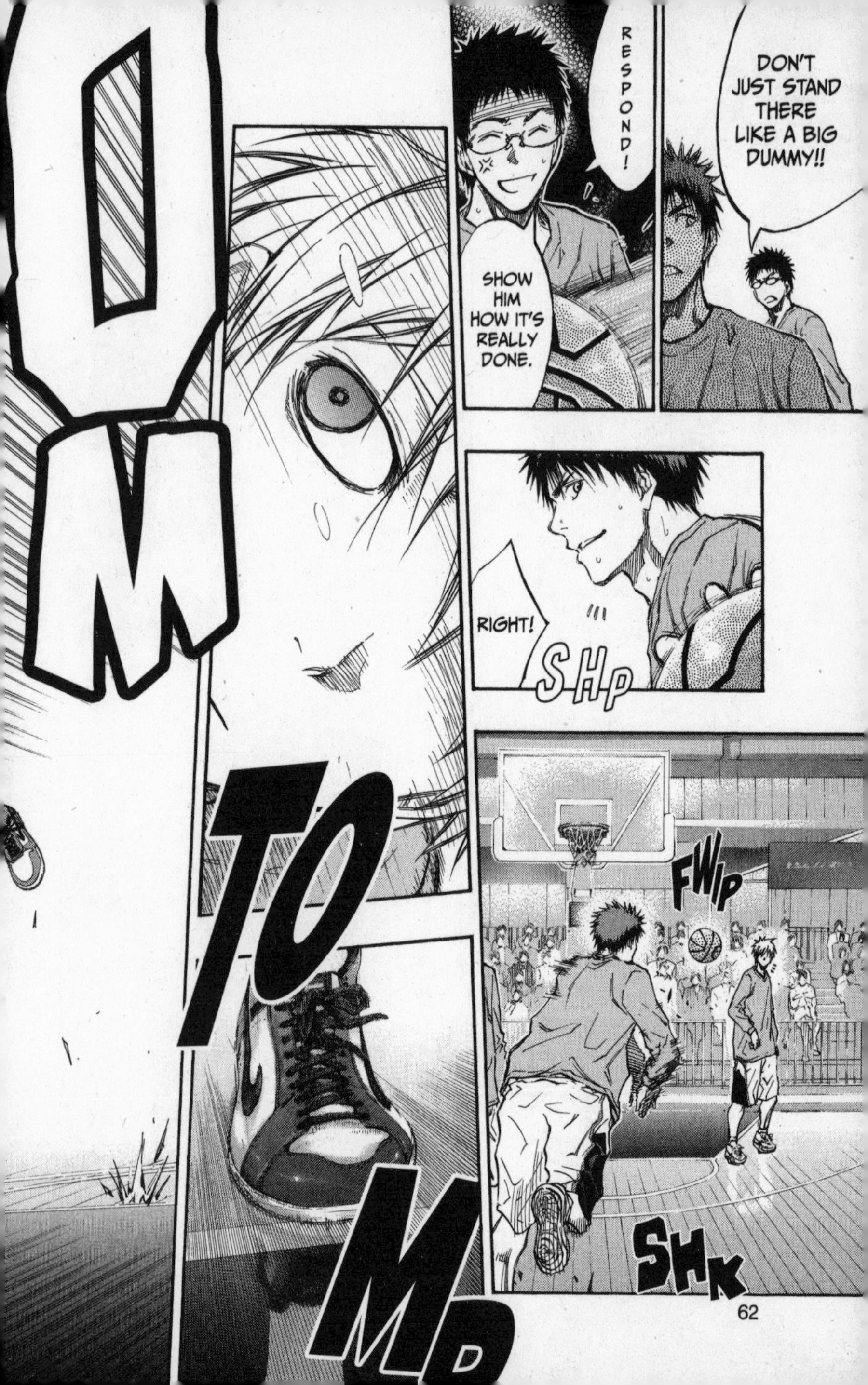
DON'T JUST STAND THERE LIKE A BIG DUMMY!!
RESPOND!
SHOW HIM HOW IT'S REALLY DONE.
RIGHT!
SHP
FWIP
SHK
IM
TOMP

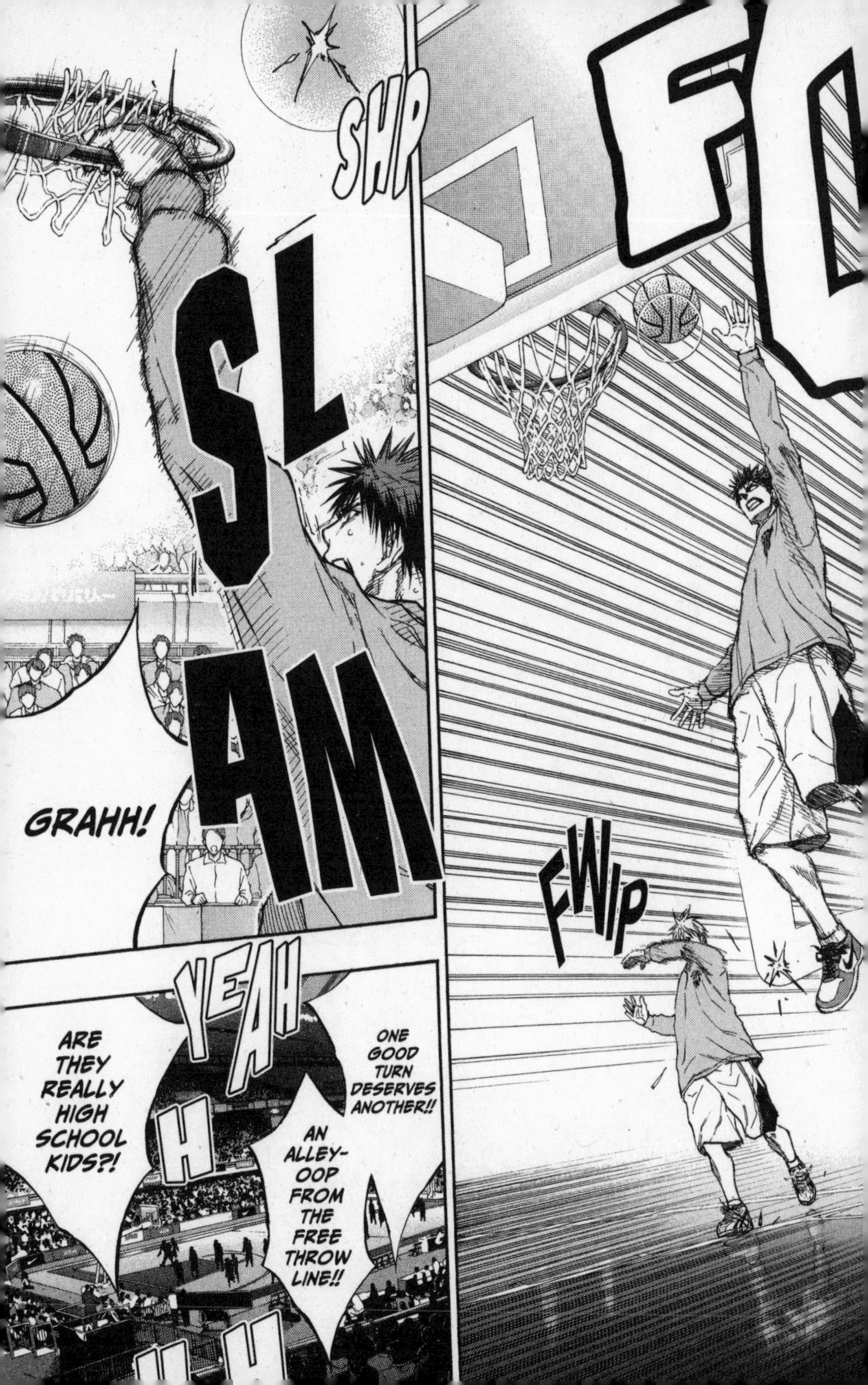
FWIP
SHP
SLAM
GRAHH!
YEAH
ONE GOOD TURN DESERVES ANOTHER!!
AN ALLEY-OOP FROM THE FREE THROW LINE!!
ARE THEY REALLY HIGH SCHOOL KIDS?!

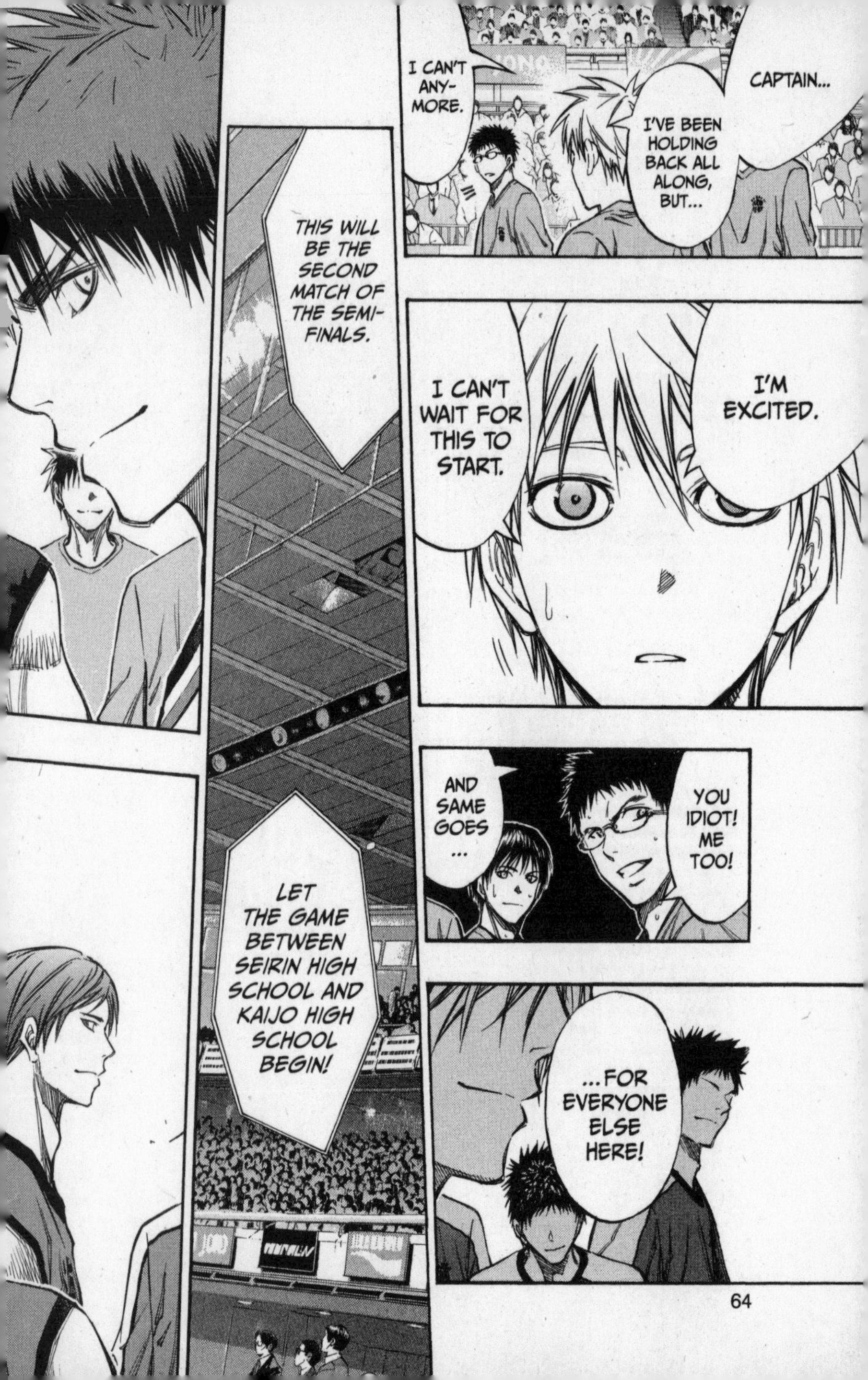
CAPTAIN...
I'VE BEEN HOLDING BACK ALL ALONG, BUT...
I CAN'T ANYMORE.
I'M EXCITED.
I CAN'T WAIT FOR THIS TO START.
YOU IDIOT! ME TOO!
AND SAME GOES ...
...FOR EVERYONE ELSE HERE!
THIS WILL BE THE SECOND MATCH OF THE SEMI-FINALS.
LET THE GAME BETWEEN SEIRIN HIGH SCHOOL AND KAIJO HIGH SCHOOL BEGIN!

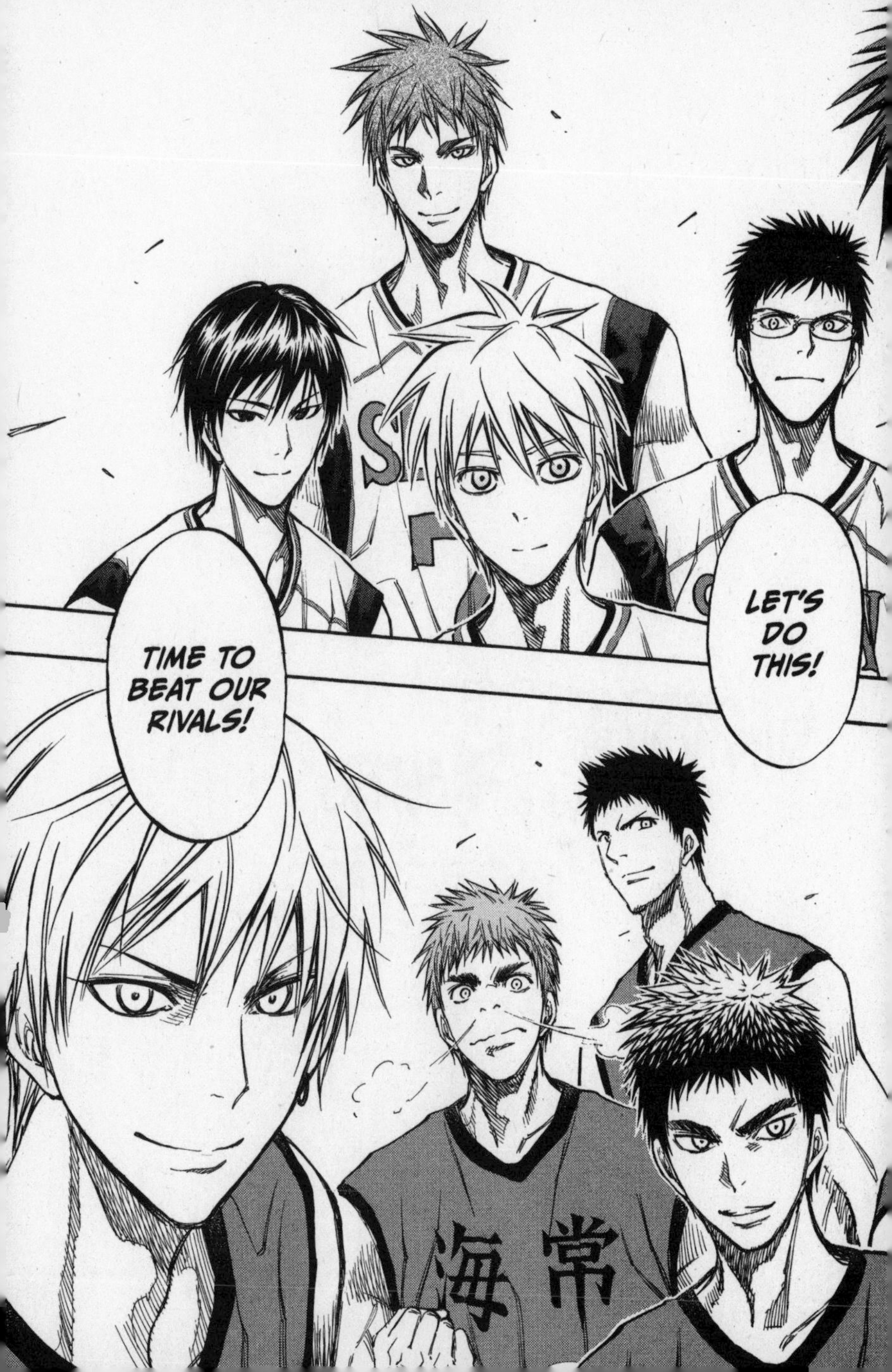
LET'S DO THIS!
TIME TO BEAT OUR RIVALS!
海常

KUROKO'S BASKETBALL BLOOPERS

TAKE 6

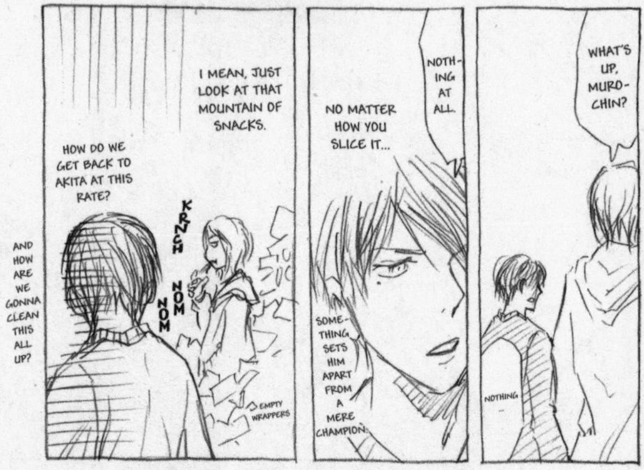
WHAT'S UP, MURO-CHIN?
NOTHING.
NOTHING AT ALL.
NO MATTER HOW YOU SLICE IT...
SOMETHING SETS HIM APART FROM A MERE CHAMPION.
I MEAN, JUST LOOK AT THAT MOUNTAIN OF SNACKS.
HOW DO WE GET BACK TO AKITA AT THIS RATE?
KRUNCH
NOM NOM
EMPTY WRAPPERS
AND HOW ARE WE GONNA CLEAN THIS ALL UP?

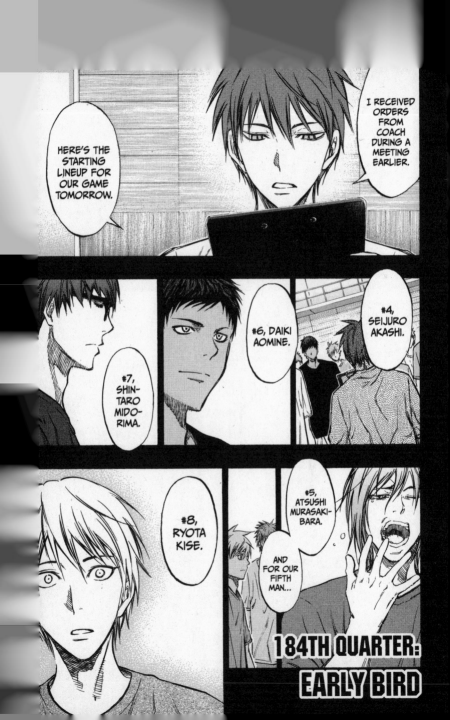

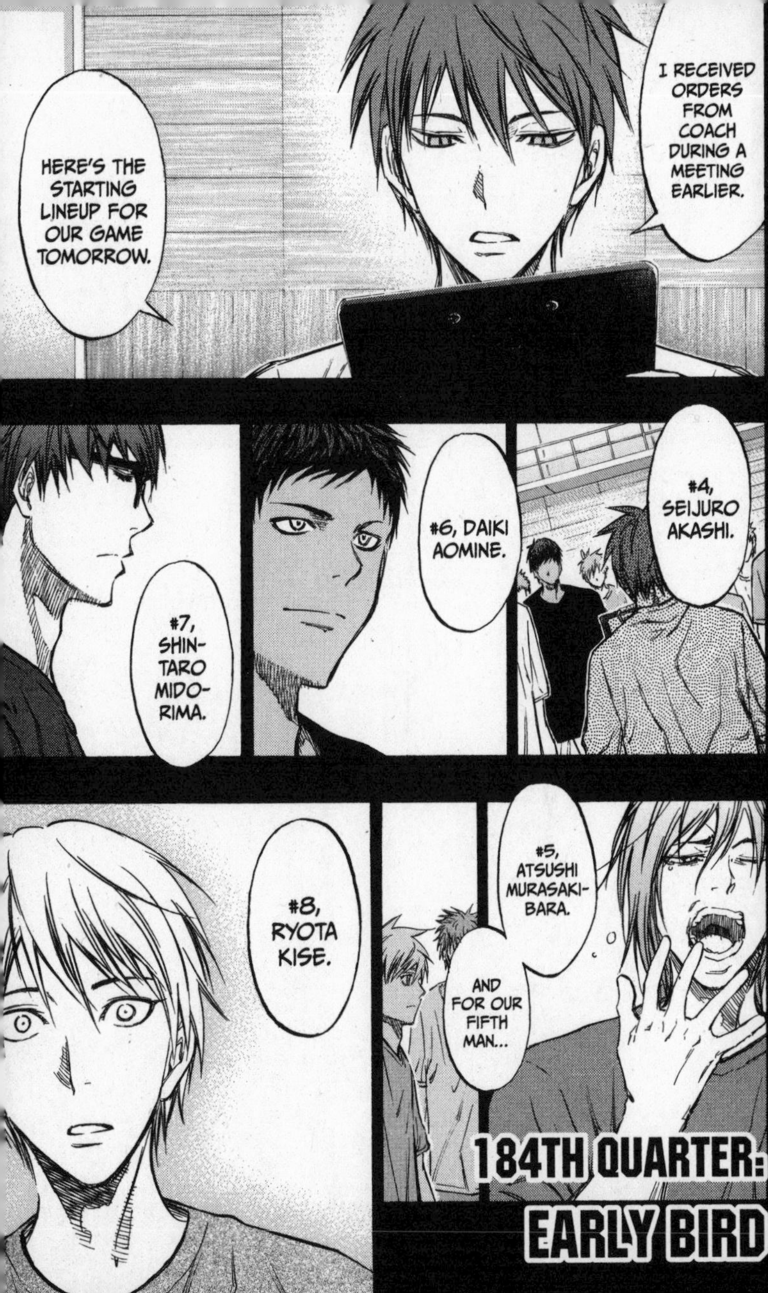
I RECEIVED ORDERS FROM COACH DURING A MEETING EARLIER.
HERE'S THE STARTING LINEUP FOR OUR GAME TOMORROW.
#4, SEIJURO AKASHI.
#6, DAIKI AOMINE.
#7, SHINTARO MIDORIMA.
#5, ATSUSHI MURASAKIBARA.
AND FOR OUR FIFTH MAN...
184TH QUARTER: EARLY BIRD
#8, RYOTA KISE.

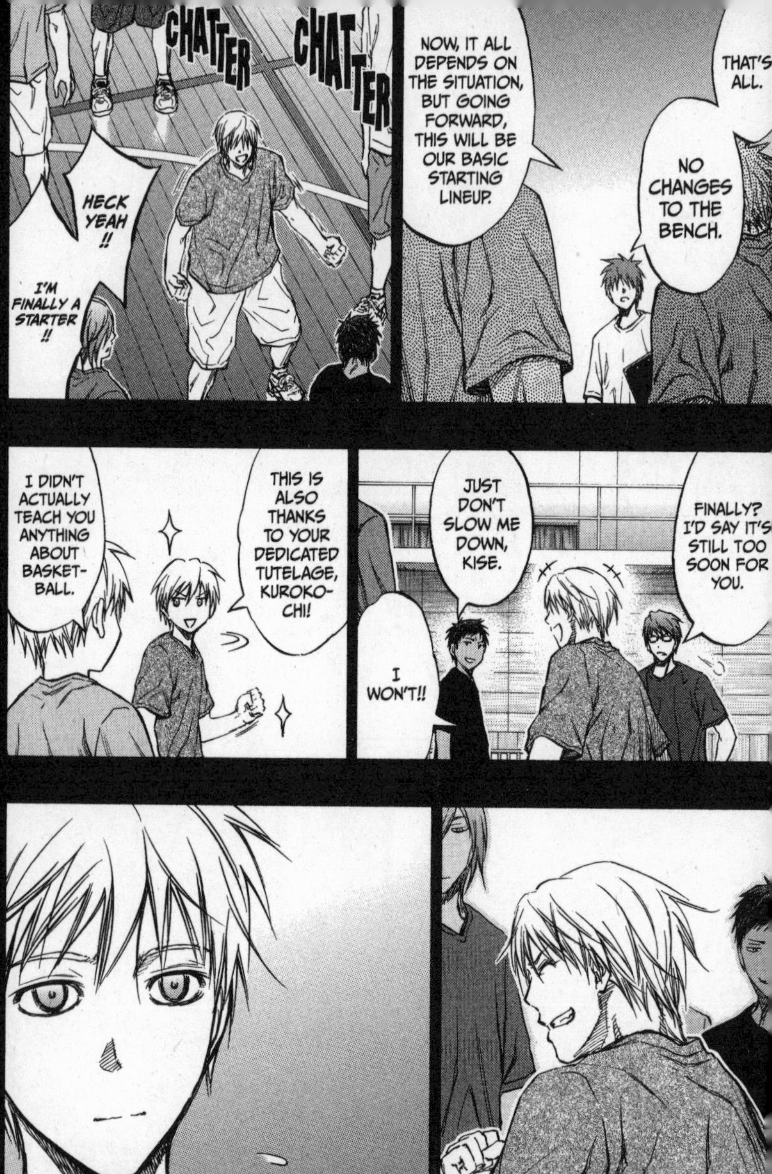
NOW, IT ALL DEPENDS ON THE SITUATION, BUT GOING FORWARD, THIS WILL BE OUR BASIC STARTING LINEUP.
NO CHANGES TO THE BENCH.
THAT'S ALL.
CHATTER
CHATTER
HECK YEAH!!
I'M FINALLY A STARTER!!
FINALLY? I'D SAY IT'S STILL TOO SOON FOR YOU.
JUST DON'T SLOW ME DOWN, KISE.
I WON'T!!
THIS IS ALSO THANKS TO YOUR DEDICATED TUTELAGE, KUROKO-CHI!
I DIDN'T ACTUALLY TEACH YOU ANYTHING ABOUT BASKET-BALL.

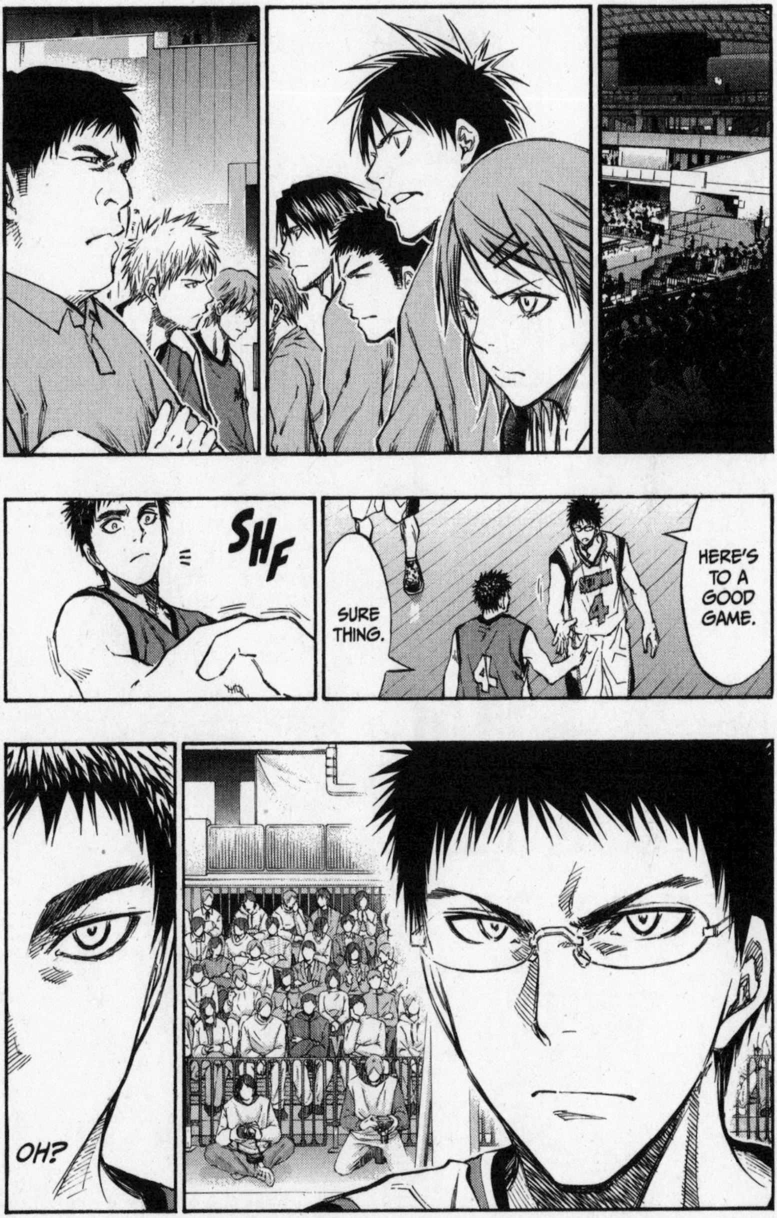
HERE'S TO A GOOD GAME.
SURE THING.
SHF
OH?

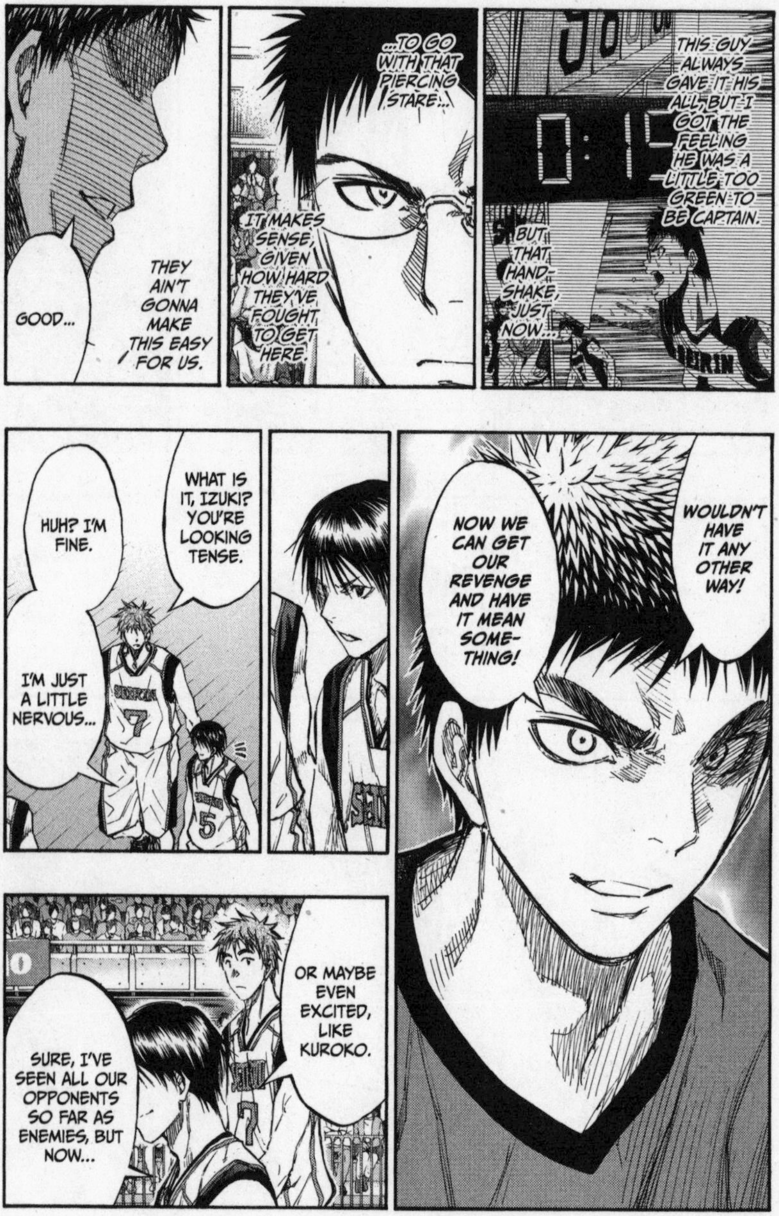
THIS GUY ALWAYS GAVE IT HIS ALL, BUT I GOT THE FEELING HE WAS A LITTLE TOO GREEN TO BE CAPTAIN.
BUT THAT HANDSHAKE, JUST NOW...
...TO GO WITH THAT PIERCING STARE...
IT MAKES SENSE, GIVEN HOW HARD THEY'VE FOUGHT TO GET HERE.
THEY AIN'T GONNA MAKE THIS EASY FOR US.
GOOD...
WOULDN'T HAVE IT ANY OTHER WAY!
NOW WE CAN GET OUR REVENGE AND HAVE IT MEAN SOMETHING!
WHAT IS IT, IZUKI? YOU'RE LOOKING TENSE.
HUH? I'M FINE.
I'M JUST A LITTLE NERVOUS...
OR MAYBE EVEN EXCITED, LIKE KUROKO.
SURE, I'VE SEEN ALL OUR OPPONENTS SO FAR AS ENEMIES, BUT NOW...

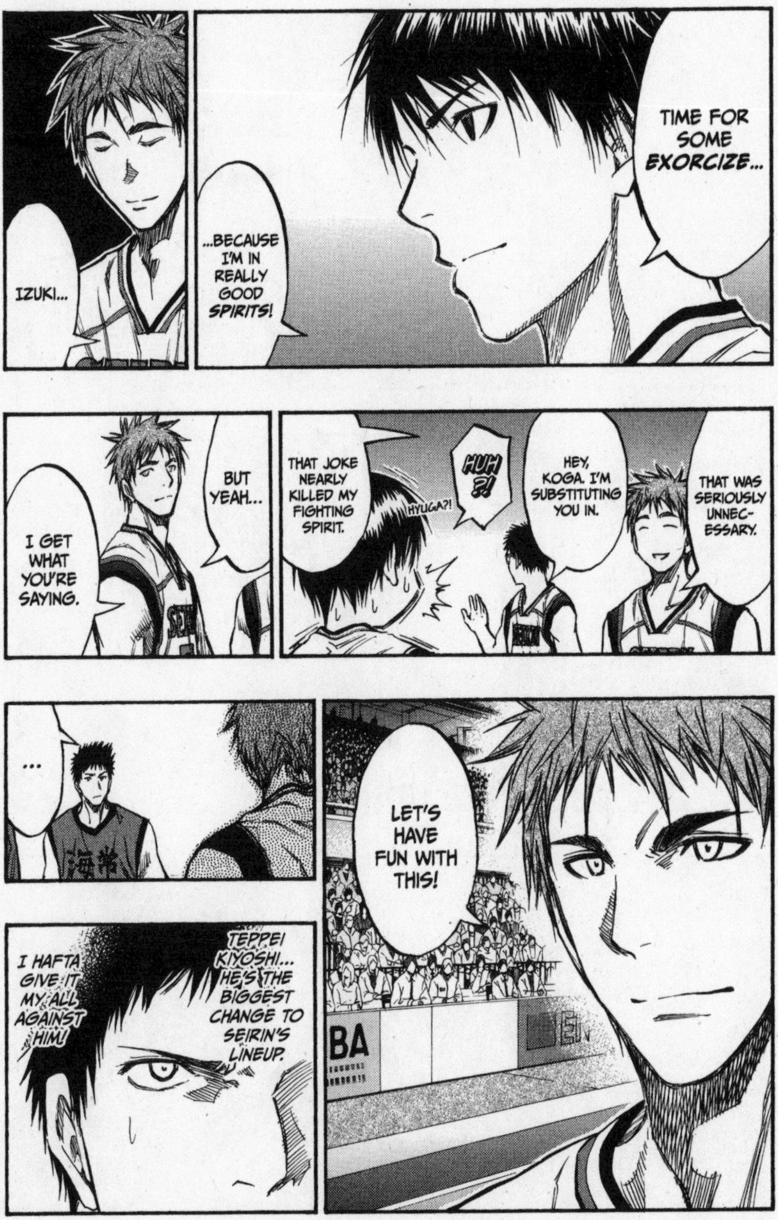
TIME FOR SOME EXORCIZE...
...BECAUSE I'M IN REALLY GOOD SPIRITS!
IZUKI...
THAT WAS SERIOUSLY UNNEC-ESSARY.
HEY, KOGA. I'M SUBSTITUTING YOU IN.
HUH?!
HYUGA?!
THAT JOKE NEARLY KILLED MY FIGHTING SPIRIT.
BUT YEAH...
I GET WHAT YOU'RE SAYING.
LET'S HAVE FUN WITH THIS!
...
TEPPEI KIYOSHI... HE'S THE BIGGEST CHANGE TO SEIRIN'S LINEUP.
I HAFTA GIVE IT MY ALL AGAINST HIM!

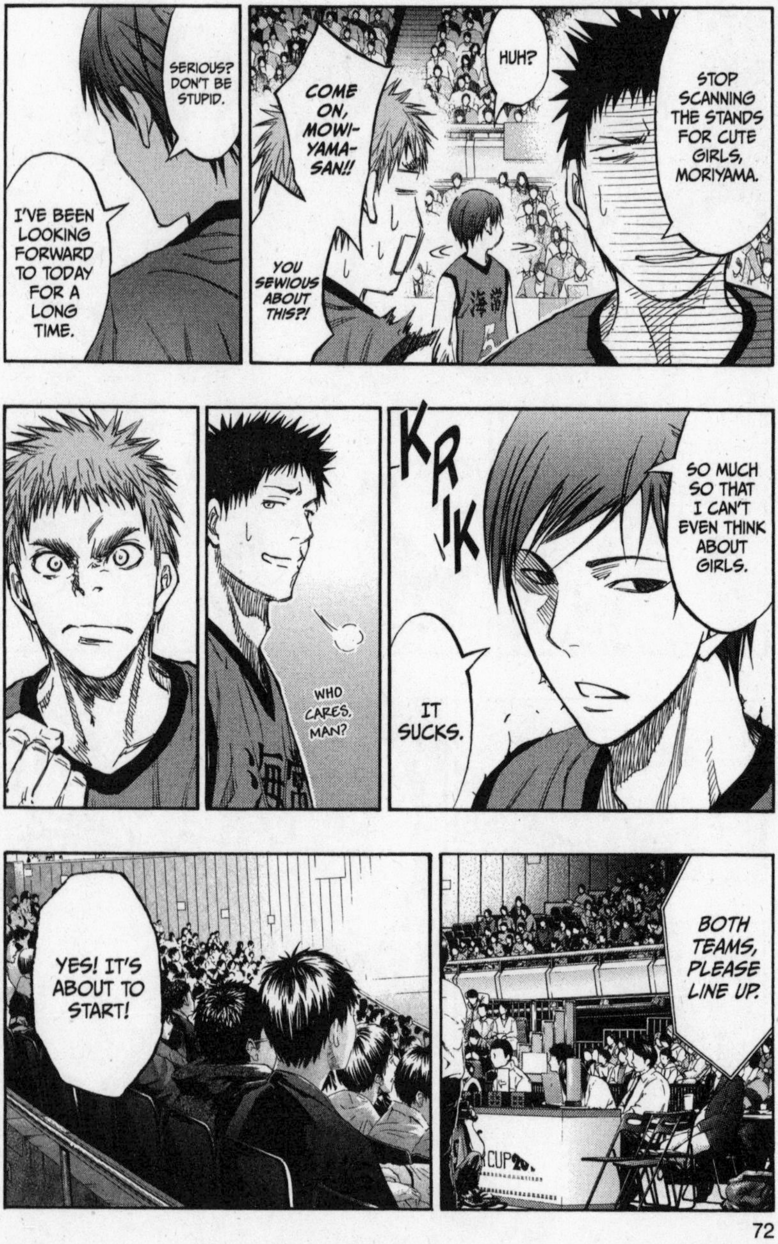
STOP SCANNING THE STANDS FOR CUTE GIRLS, MORIYAMA.
HUH?
COME ON, MOWI-YAMA-SAN!!
YOU SEWIOUS ABOUT THIS?!
SERIOUS? DON'T BE STUPID.
I'VE BEEN LOOKING FORWARD TO TODAY FOR A LONG TIME.
SO MUCH SO THAT I CAN'T EVEN THINK ABOUT GIRLS.
KRIK
IT SUCKS.
WHO CARES, MAN?
BOTH TEAMS, PLEASE LINE UP.
YES! IT'S ABOUT TO START!

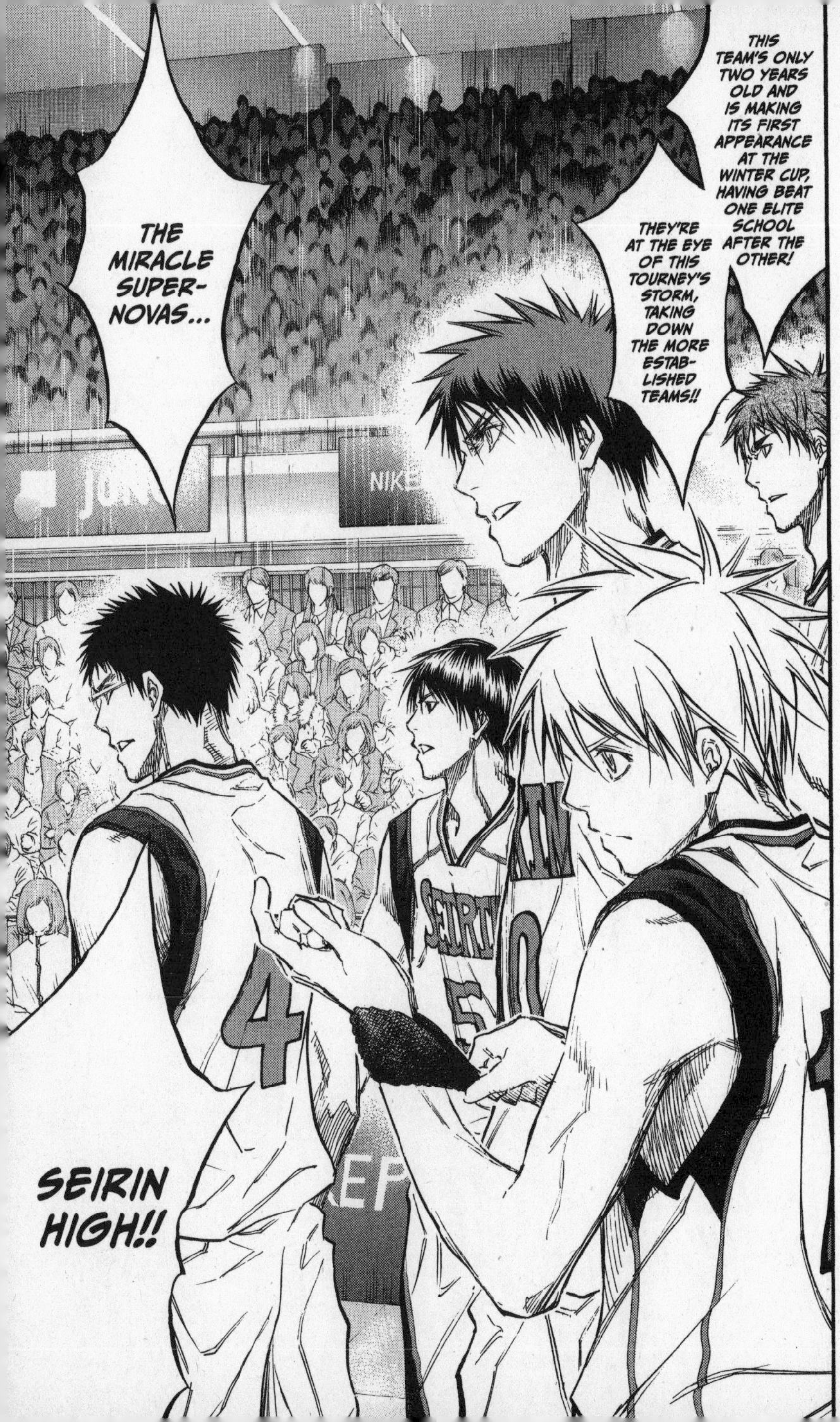
THIS TEAM'S ONLY TWO YEARS OLD AND IS MAKING ITS FIRST APPEARANCE AT THE WINTER CUP, HAVING BEAT ONE ELITE SCHOOL AFTER THE OTHER!
THEY'RE AT THE EYE OF THIS TOURNEY'S STORM, TAKING DOWN THE MORE ESTAB-LISHED TEAMS!!
THE MIRACLE SUPER-NOVAS...
NIKE
SEIRIN HIGH!!

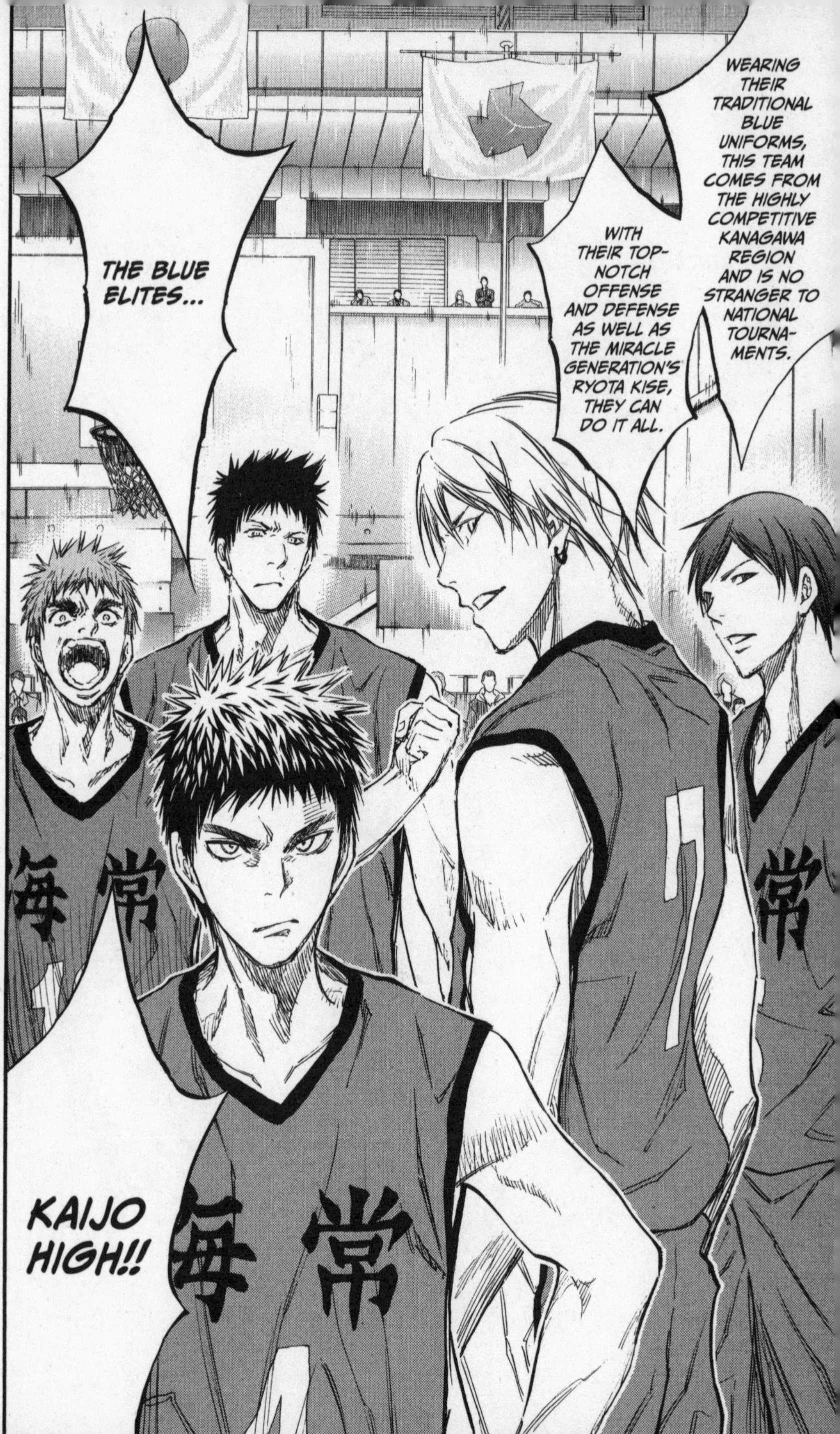
WEARING THEIR TRADITIONAL BLUE UNIFORMS, THIS TEAM COMES FROM THE HIGHLY COMPETITIVE KANAGAWA REGION AND IS NO STRANGER TO NATIONAL TOURNAMENTS.
WITH THEIR TOP-NOTCH OFFENSE AND DEFENSE AS WELL AS THE MIRACLE GENERATION'S RYOTA KISE, THEY CAN DO IT ALL.
THE BLUE ELITES...
KAIJO HIGH!!

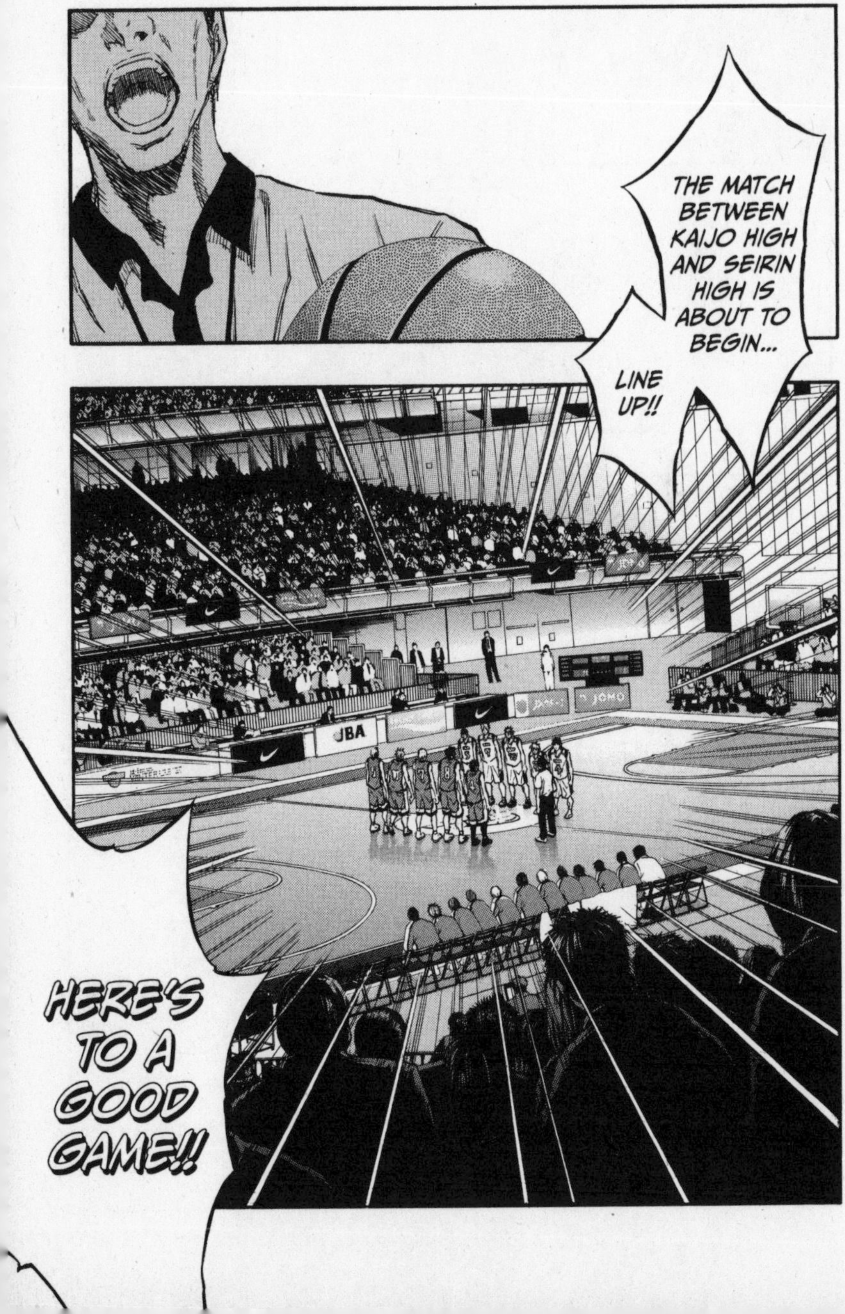
THE MATCH BETWEEN KAIJO HIGH AND SEIRIN HIGH IS ABOUT TO BEGIN...
LINE UP!!
JBA
HERE'S TO A GOOD GAME!!

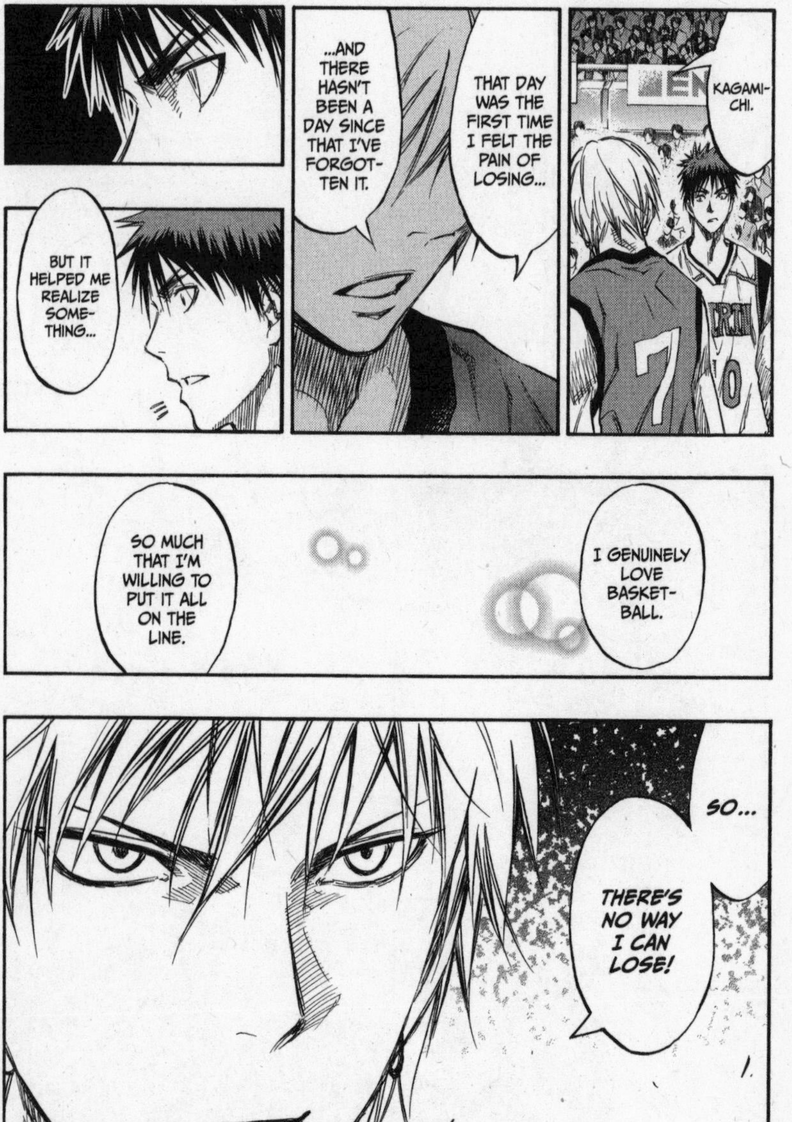
KAGAMI-CHI.
THAT DAY WAS THE FIRST TIME I FELT THE PAIN OF LOSING...
...AND THERE HASN'T BEEN A DAY SINCE THAT I'VE FORGOTTEN IT.
BUT IT HELPED ME REALIZE SOMETHING...
I GENUINELY LOVE BASKETBALL.
SO MUCH THAT I'M WILLING TO PUT IT ALL ON THE LINE.
SO...
THERE'S NO WAY I CAN LOSE!

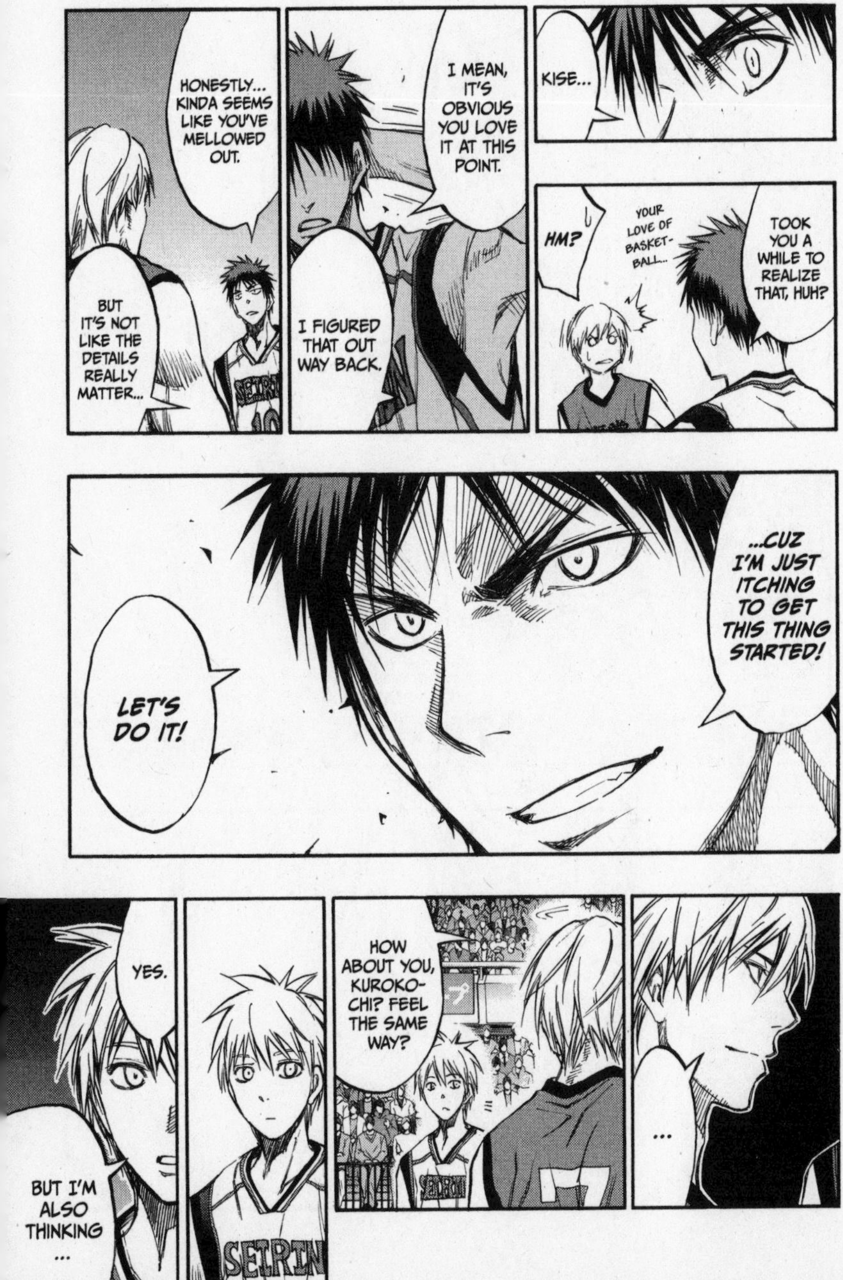
KISE...
TOOK YOU A WHILE TO REALIZE THAT, HUH?
YOUR LOVE OF BASKET-BALL...
HM?
I MEAN, IT'S OBVIOUS YOU LOVE IT AT THIS POINT.
I FIGURED THAT OUT WAY BACK.
HONESTLY... KINDA SEEMS LIKE YOU'VE MELLOWED OUT.
BUT IT'S NOT LIKE THE DETAILS REALLY MATTER...
...CUZ I'M JUST ITCHING TO GET THIS THING STARTED!
LET'S DO IT!
...
HOW ABOUT YOU, KUROKO-CHI? FEEL THE SAME WAY?
YES.
BUT I'M ALSO THINKING ...

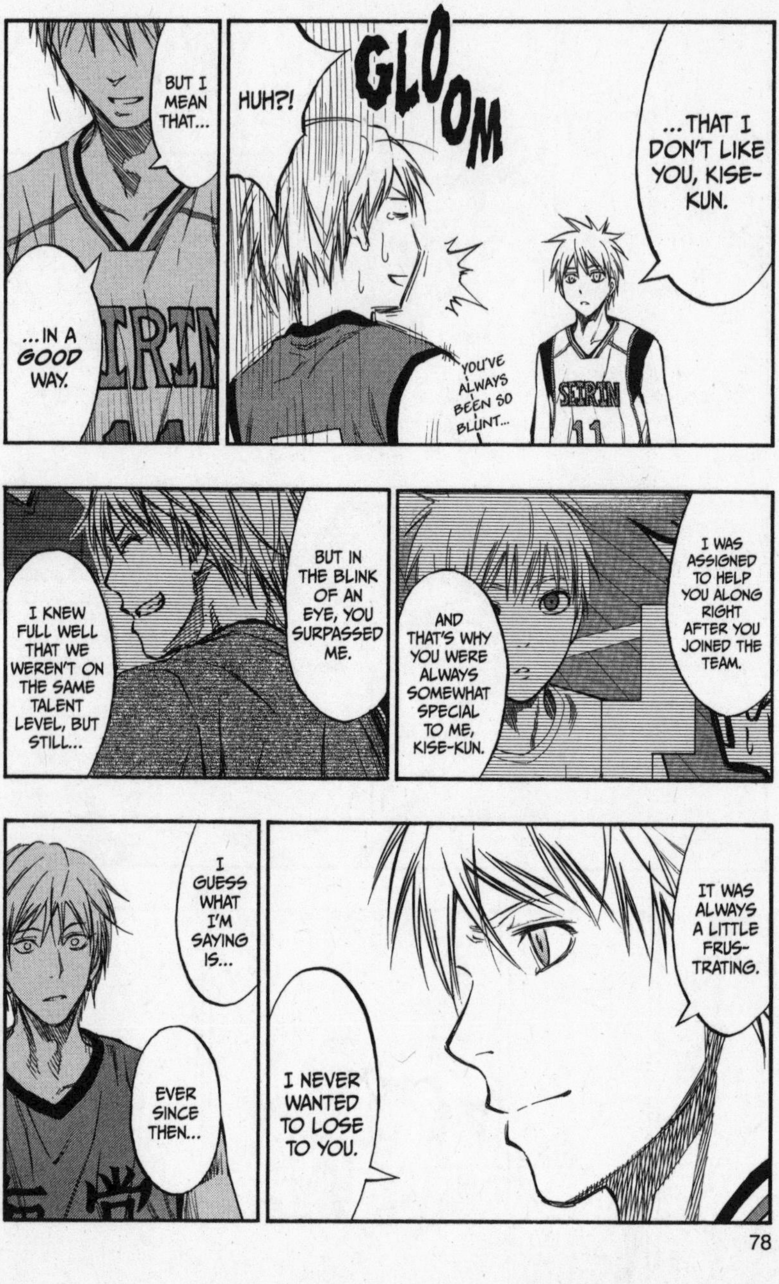
...THAT I DON'T LIKE YOU, KISE-KUN.
GLOOM
HUH?!
YOU'VE ALWAYS BEEN SO BLUNT...
BUT I MEAN THAT...
...IN A GOOD WAY.
I WAS ASSIGNED TO HELP YOU ALONG RIGHT AFTER YOU JOINED THE TEAM.
AND THAT'S WHY YOU WERE ALWAYS SOMEWHAT SPECIAL TO ME, KISE-KUN.
BUT IN THE BLINK OF AN EYE, YOU SURPASSED ME.
I KNEW FULL WELL THAT WE WEREN'T ON THE SAME TALENT LEVEL, BUT STILL...
IT WAS ALWAYS A LITTLE FRUS-TRATING.
I NEVER WANTED TO LOSE TO YOU.
I GUESS WHAT I'M SAYING IS...
EVER SINCE THEN...

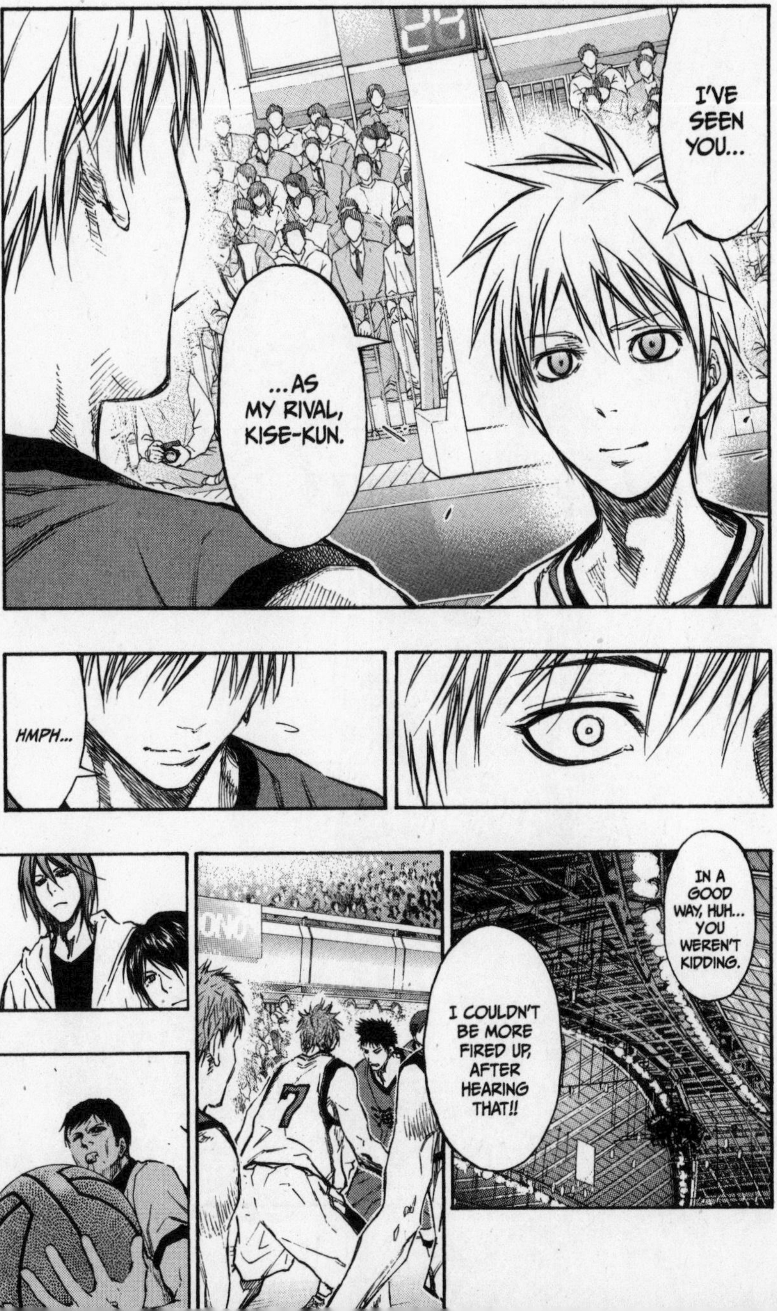
I'VE SEEN YOU...
...AS MY RIVAL, KISE-KUN.
HMPH...
IN A GOOD WAY, HUH... YOU WEREN'T KIDDING.
I COULDN'T BE MORE FIRED UP, AFTER HEARING THAT!!

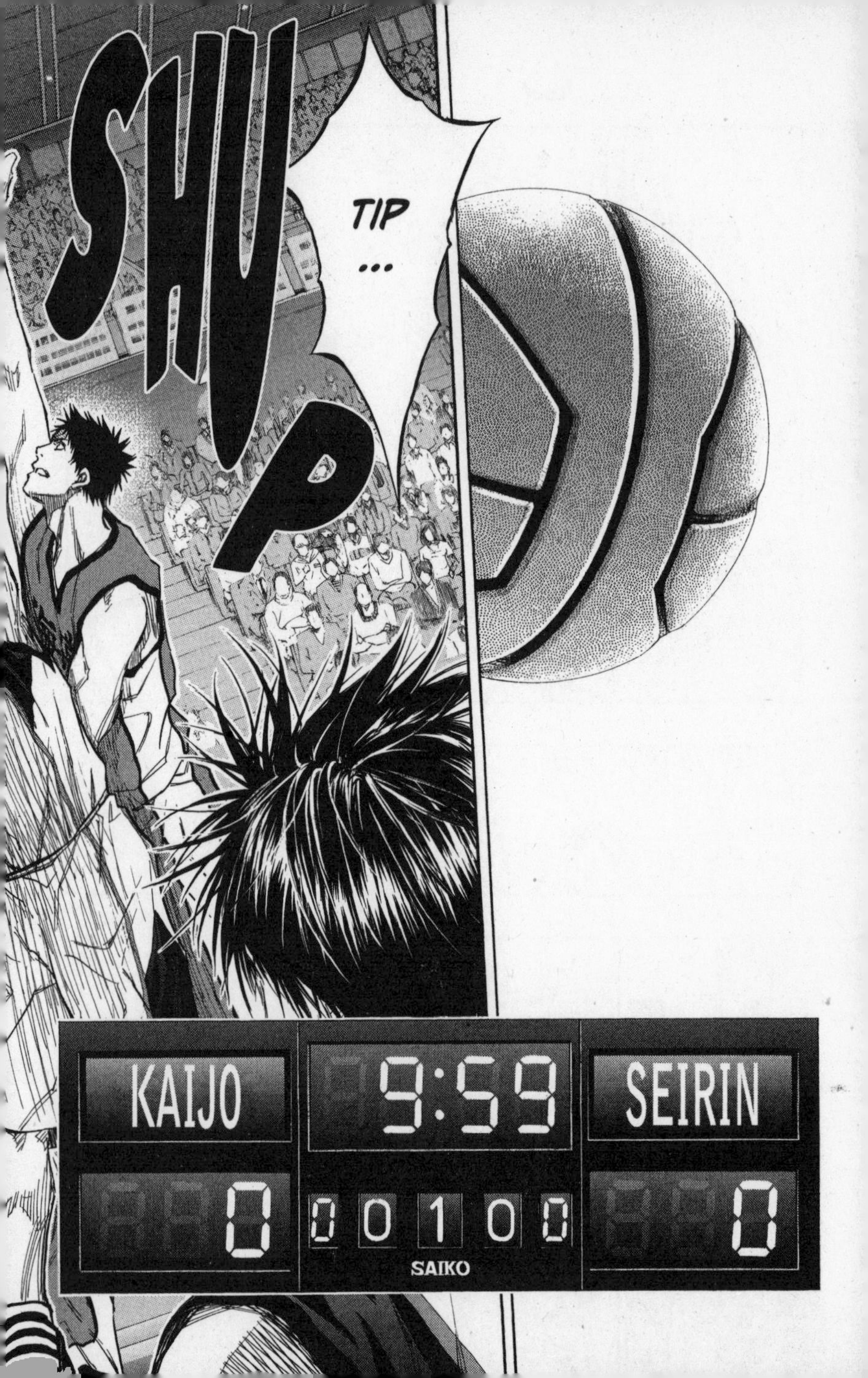
SHUP
TIP ...
KAIJO
9:59
SEIRIN
0
0
SAIKO

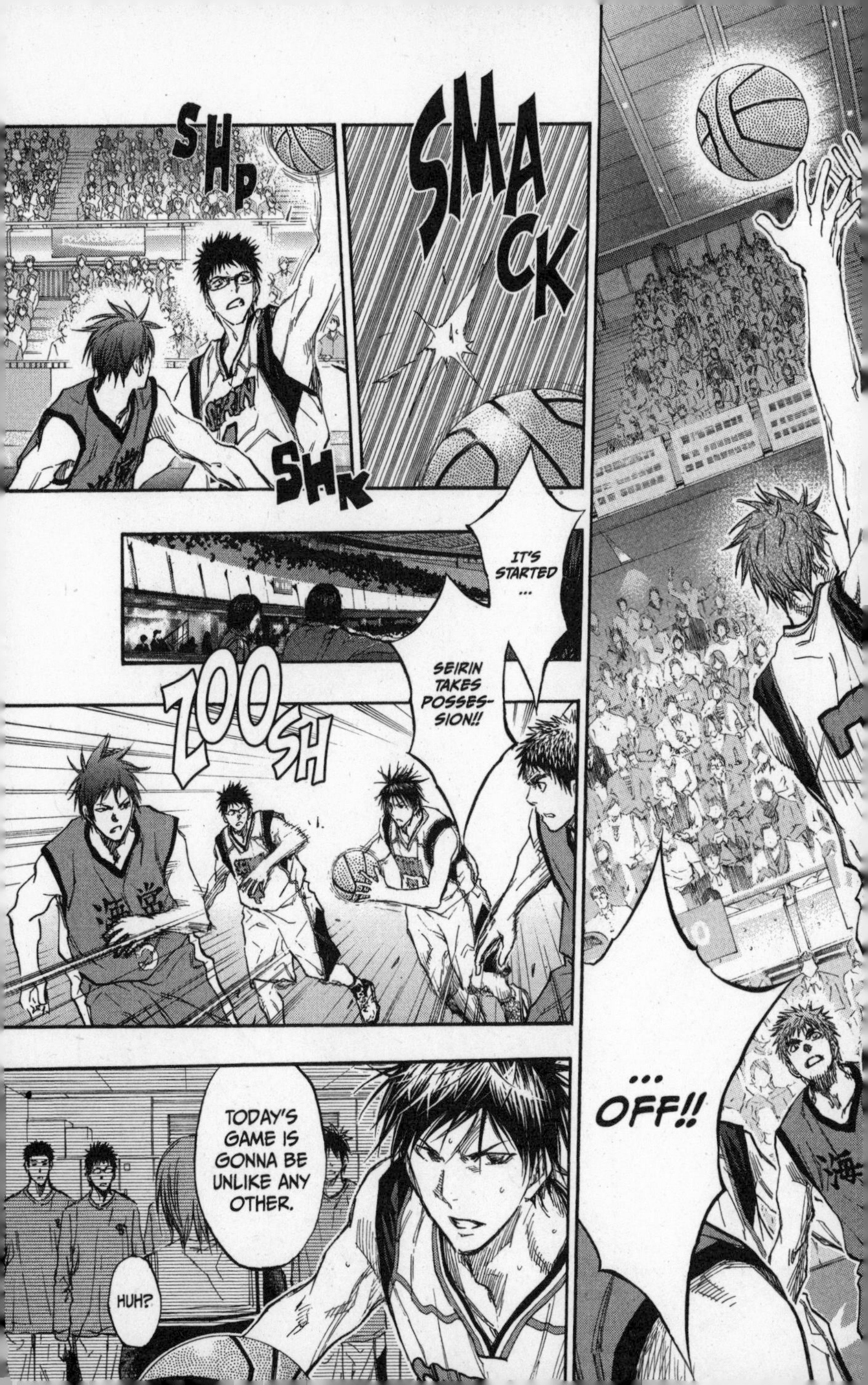
...OFF!!
SMACK
SHP
SHK
IT'S STARTED ...
SEIRIN TAKES POSSES-SION!!
ZOOSH
TODAY'S GAME IS GONNA BE UNLIKE ANY OTHER.
HUH?

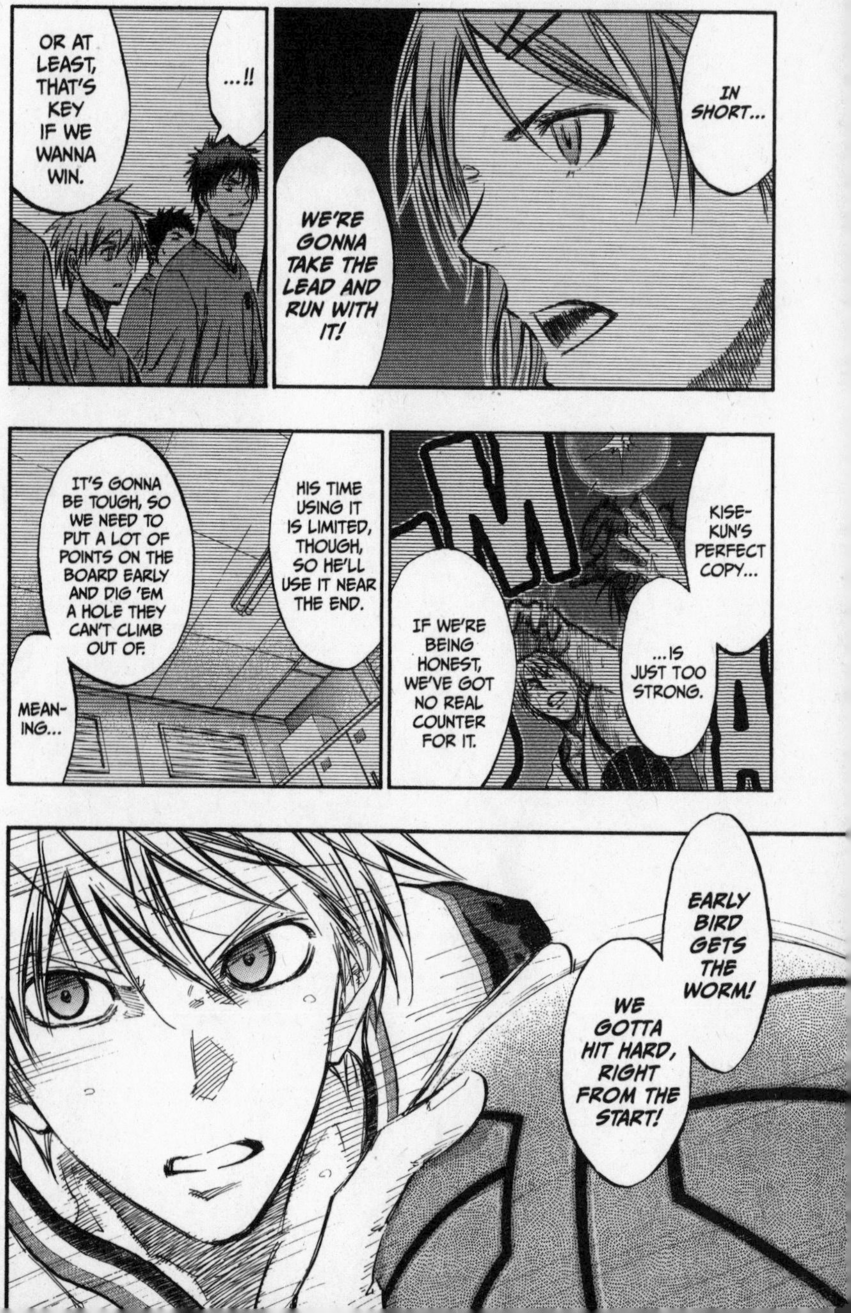
IN SHORT...
WE'RE GONNA TAKE THE LEAD AND RUN WITH IT!
...!!
OR AT LEAST, THAT'S KEY IF WE WANNA WIN.
KISE-KUN'S PERFECT COPY...
...IS JUST TOO STRONG.
IF WE'RE BEING HONEST, WE'VE GOT NO REAL COUNTER FOR IT.
HIS TIME USING IT IS LIMITED, THOUGH, SO HE'LL USE IT NEAR THE END.
IT'S GONNA BE TOUGH, SO WE NEED TO PUT A LOT OF POINTS ON THE BOARD EARLY AND DIG 'EM A HOLE THEY CAN'T CLIMB OUT OF.
MEANING...
EARLY BIRD GETS THE WORM!
WE GOTTA HIT HARD, RIGHT FROM THE START!

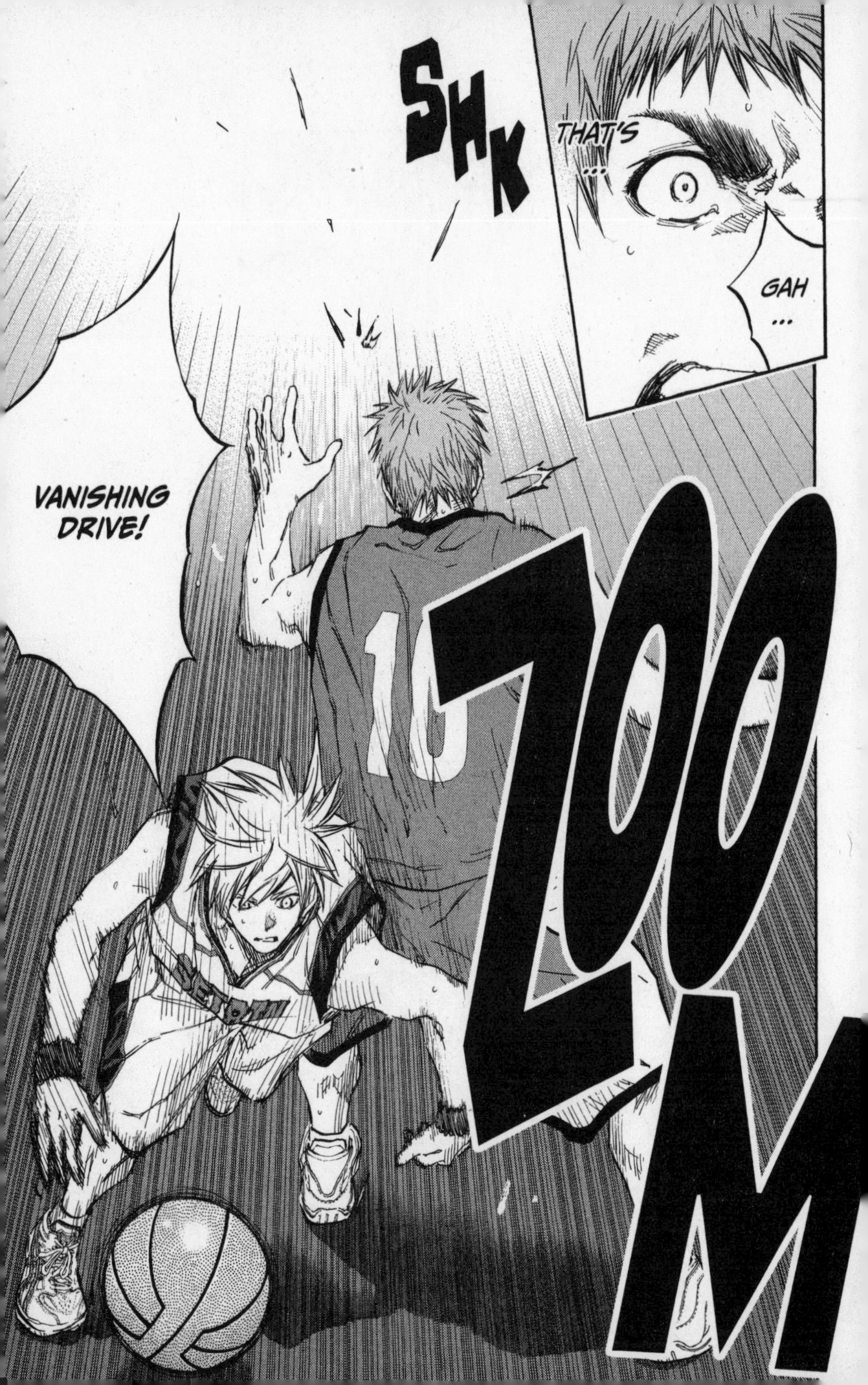
SHK
THAT'S ...
GAH ...
VANISHING DRIVE!
ZOOM

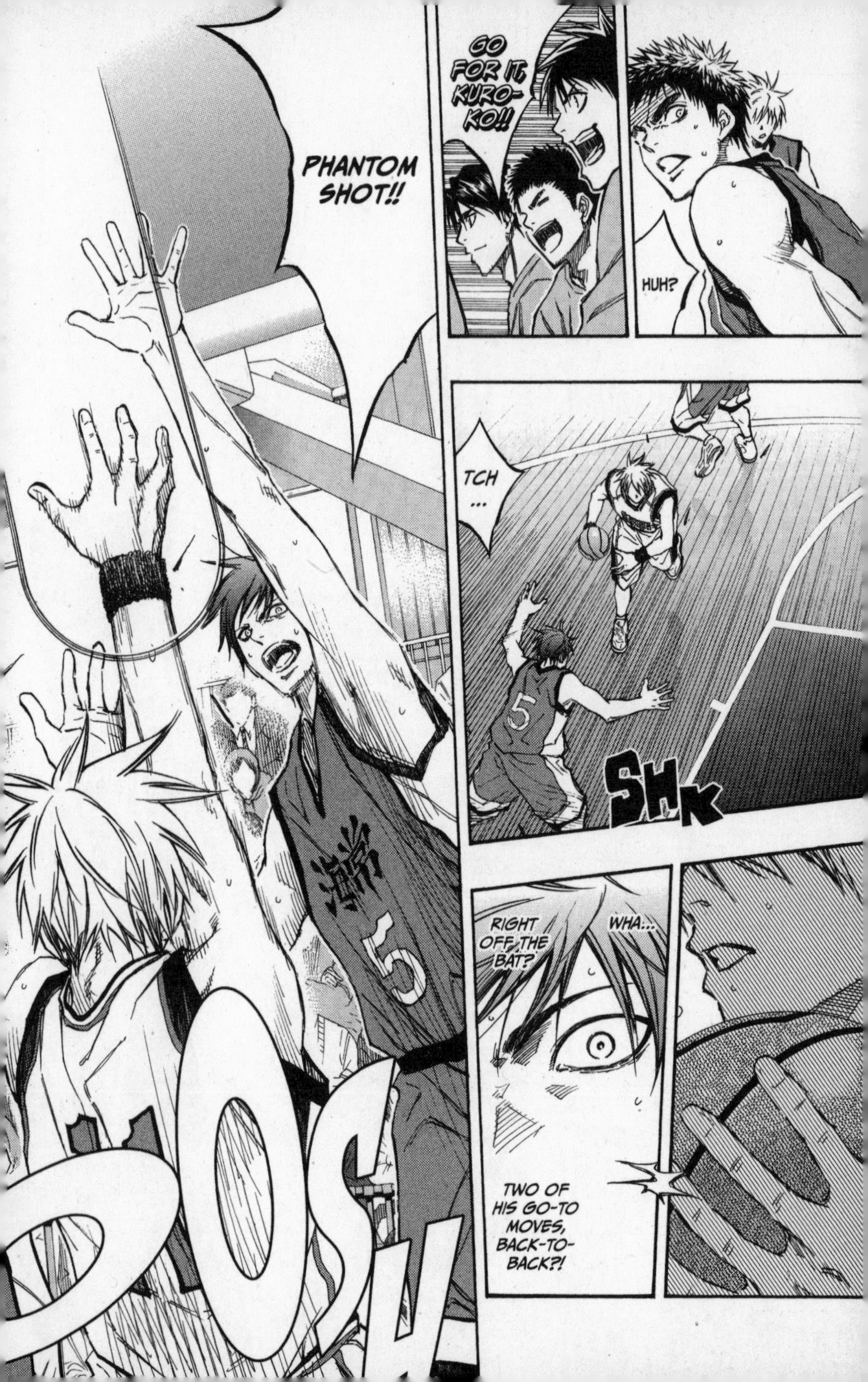
HUH?
GO FOR IT, KURO-KO!!
TCH ...
SHK
WHA...
RIGHT OFF THE BAT?
TWO OF HIS GO-TO MOVES, BACK-TO-BACK?!
PHANTOM SHOT!!

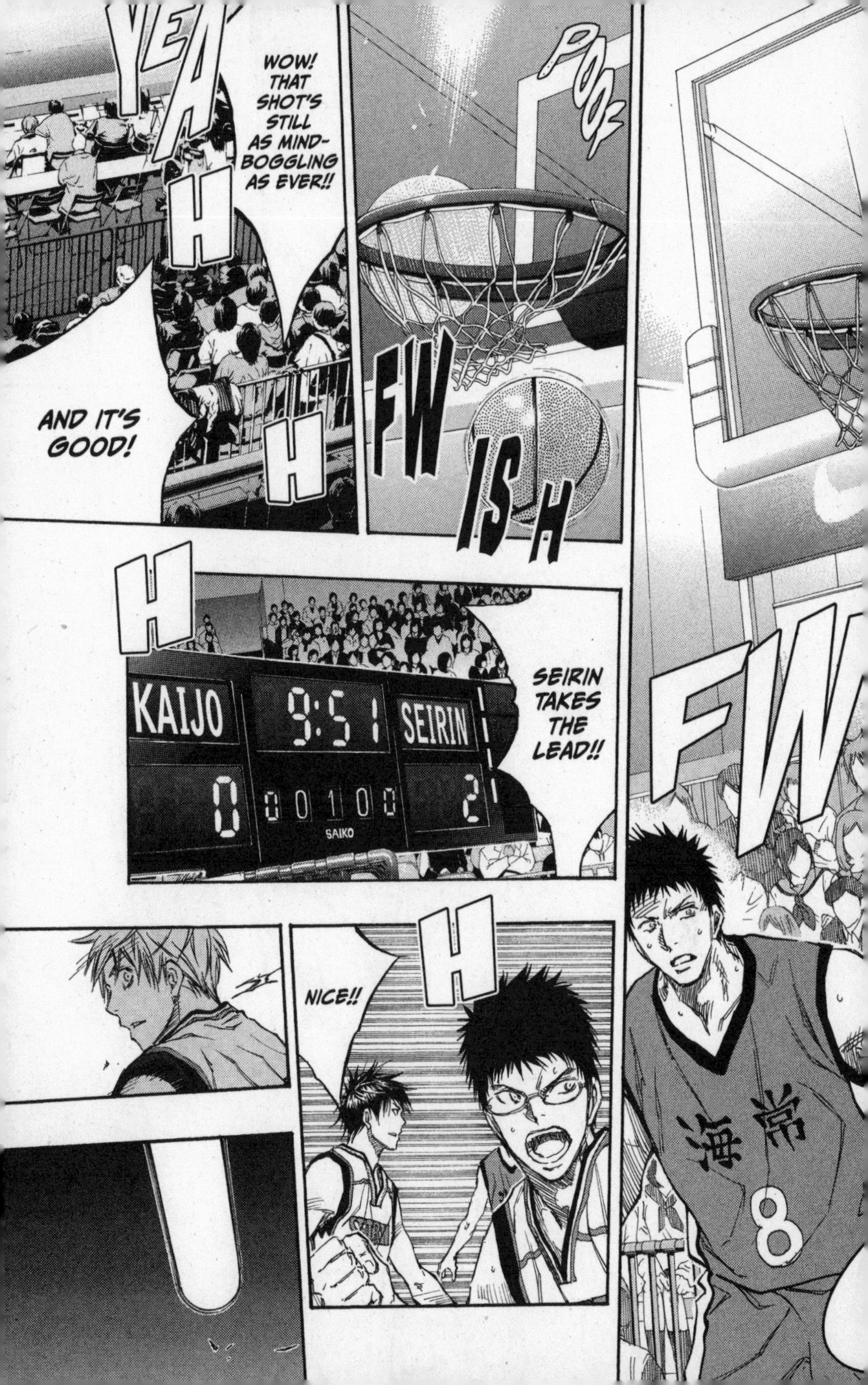
FW
POOF
FW
IS
H
YEA
H
H
WOW! THAT SHOT'S STILL AS MIND-BOGGLING AS EVER!!
AND IT'S GOOD!
H
KAIJO
9:51
SEIRIN
0
2
SAIKO
SEIRIN TAKES THE LEAD!!
H
NICE!!
海常
8

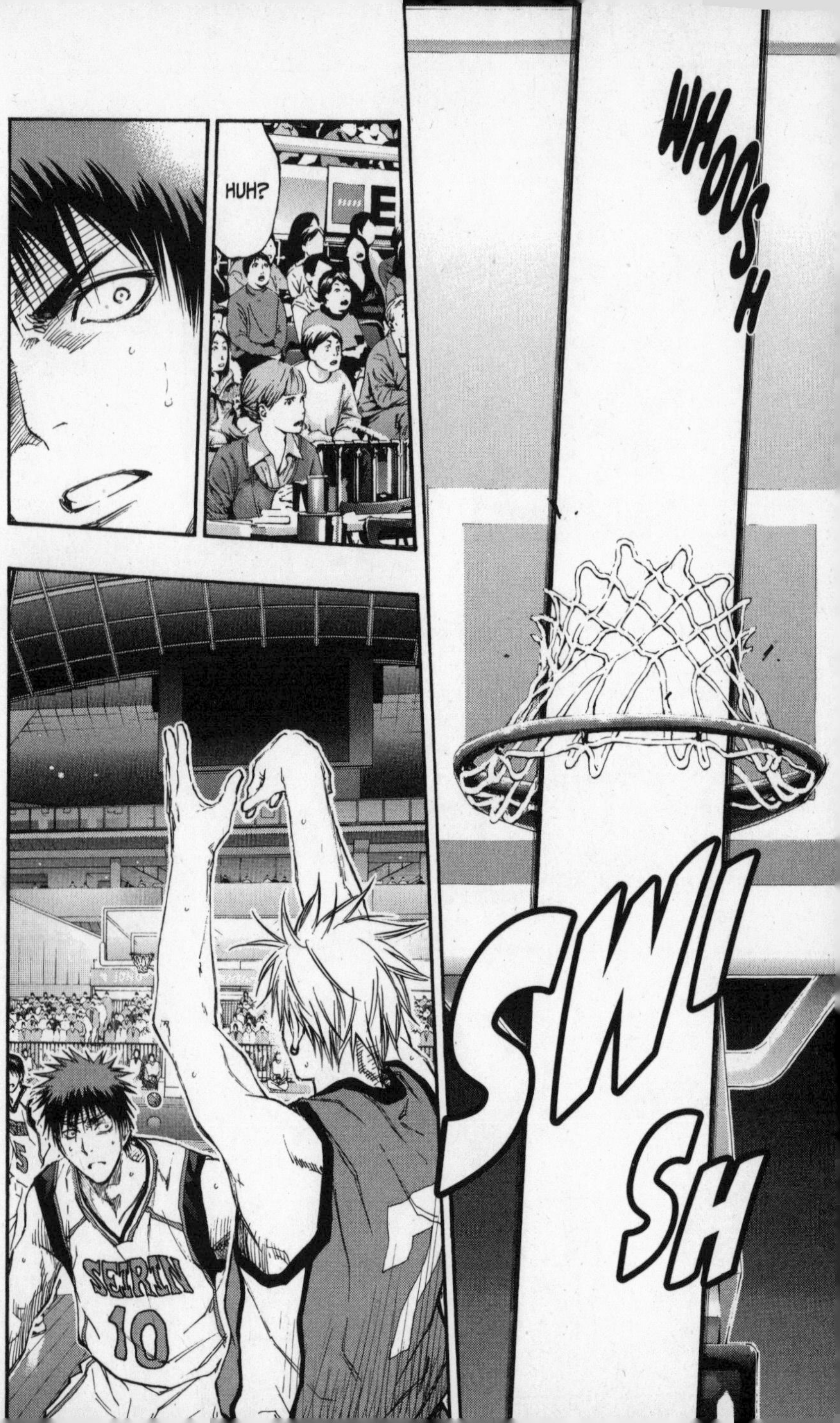
WHOOSH
SWISH
HUH?
SEIRIN
10

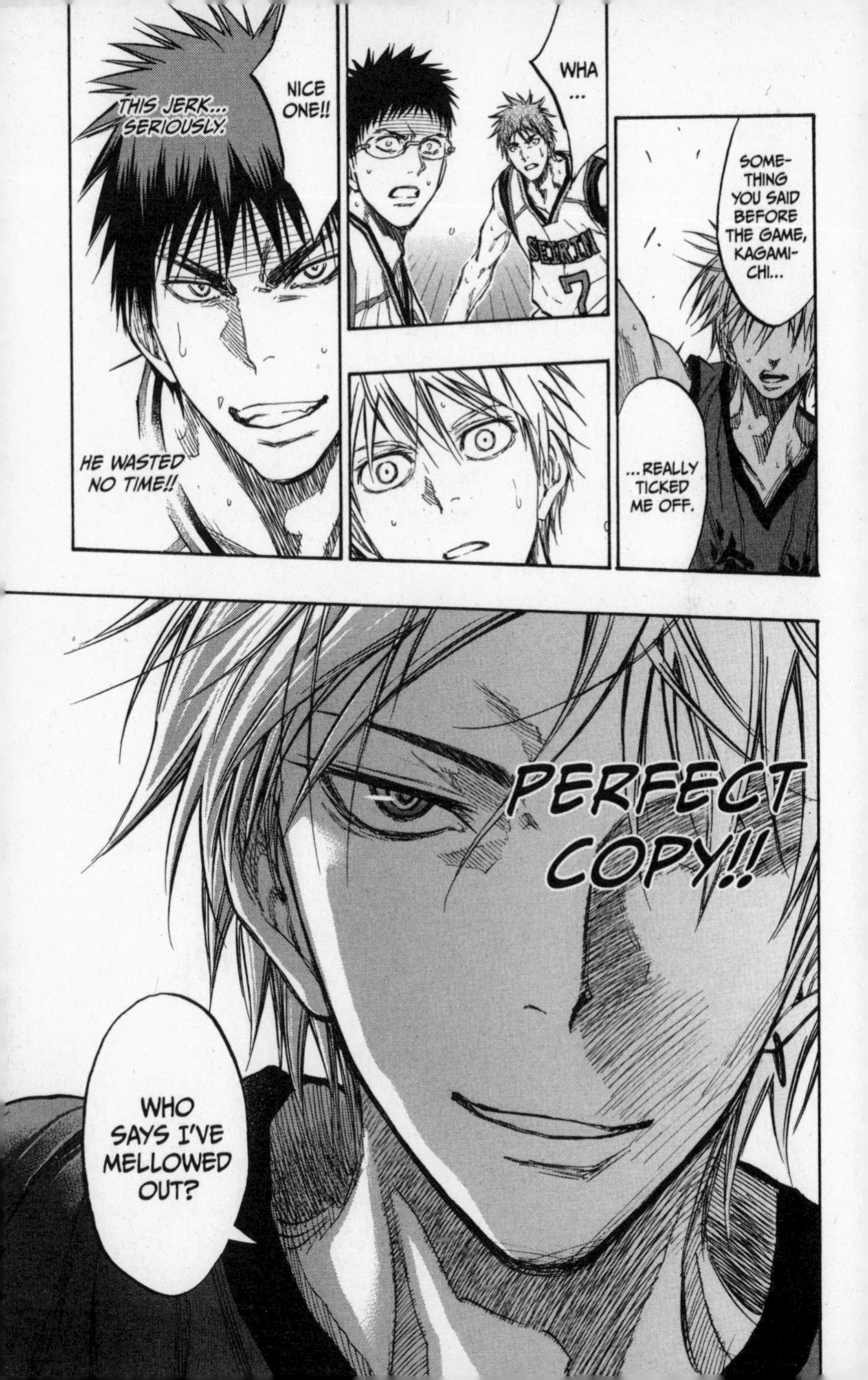
SOMETHING YOU SAID BEFORE THE GAME, KAGAMICHI...
...REALLY TICKED ME OFF.
WHA...
NICE ONE!!
THIS JERK... SERIOUSLY.
HE WASTED NO TIME!!
PERFECT COPY!!
WHO SAYS I'VE MELLOWED OUT?

KUROKO'S BASKETBALL Q&A (W/ HALFWAY-DECENT ANSWERS)

Q. PLEASE TELL US THE ACADEMIC RANKINGS OF THE MIRACLE GENERATION MEMBERS.
(POSITIVE GIRL FROM KYOTO)

A. SOMETHING LIKE THIS:
AKASHI > MIDORIMA > MURASAKIBARA > MOMOI > KUROKO > KISE = AOMINE

KUROKO'S BASKETBALL BLOOPERS TAKE 1

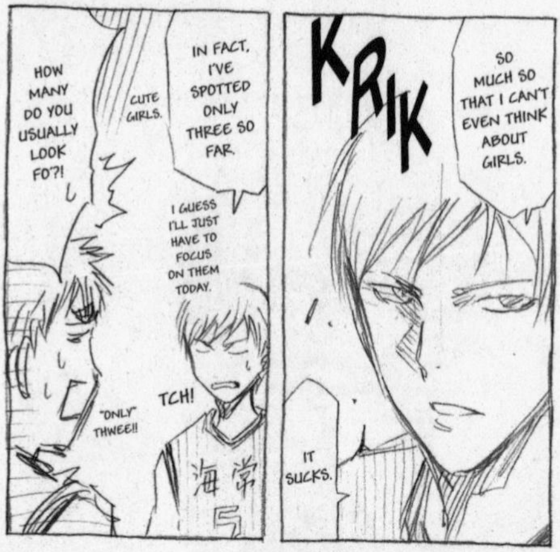
KRIK
SO MUCH SO THAT I CAN'T EVEN THINK ABOUT GIRLS.
IT SUCKS.
IN FACT, I'VE SPOTTED ONLY THREE SO FAR.
CUTE GIRLS.
HOW MANY DO YOU USUALLY LOOK FO'?!
I GUESS I'LL JUST HAVE TO FOCUS ON THEM TODAY.
TCH!
"ONLY" THWEE!!
海常
5

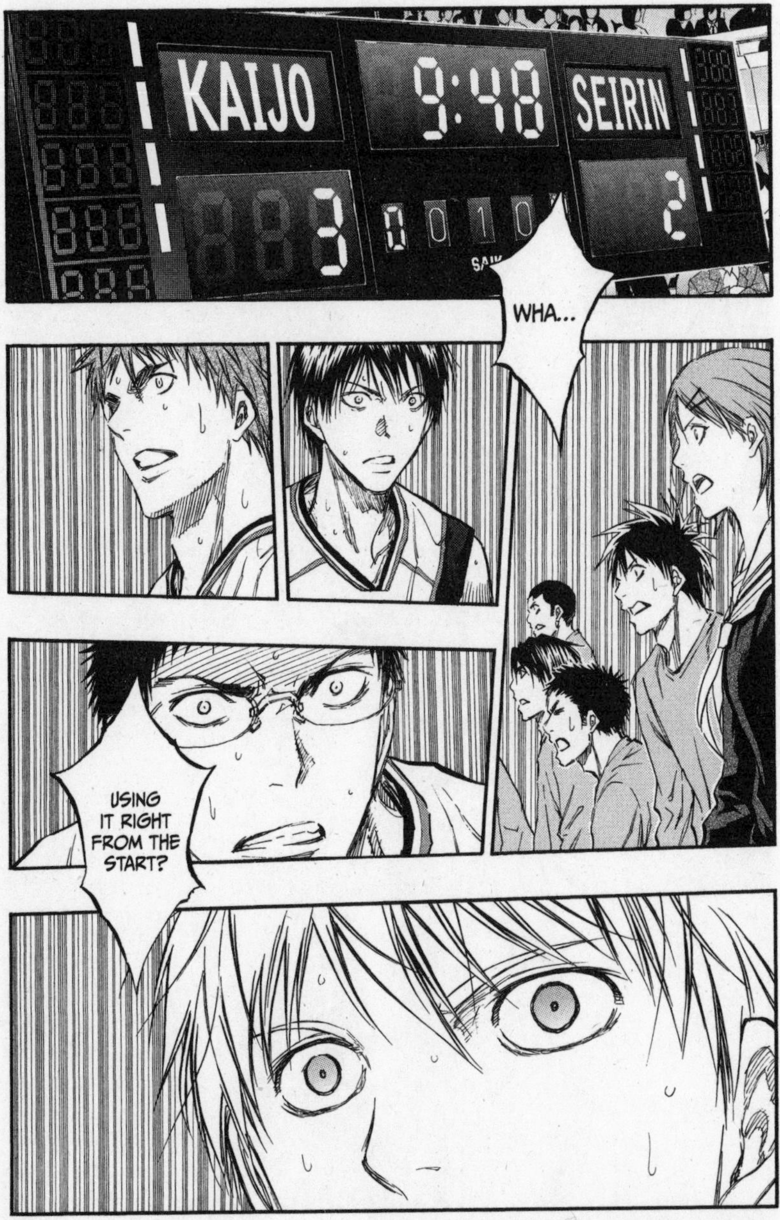
KAIJO
9:48
SEIRIN
3
2
WHA...
USING IT RIGHT FROM THE START?

185TH QUARTER: CAN'T HELP BUT SMILE

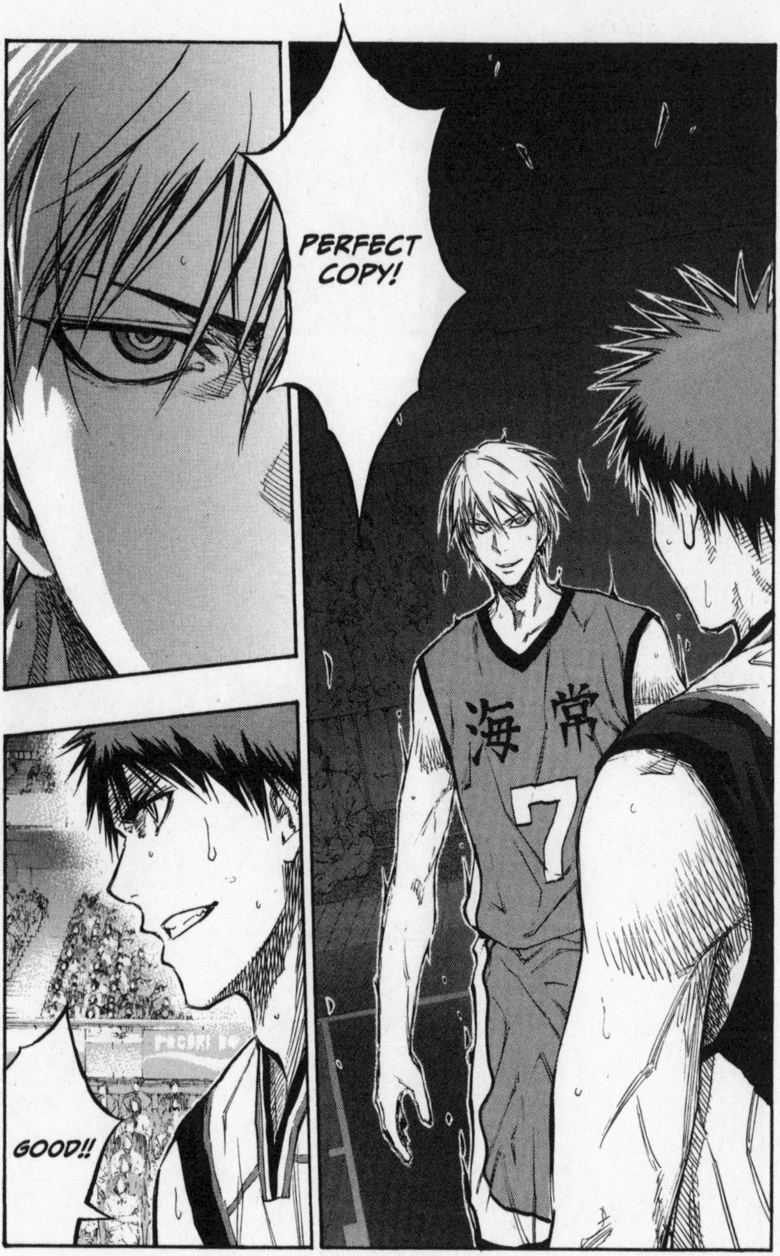
PERFECT COPY!
海常
7
GOOD!!

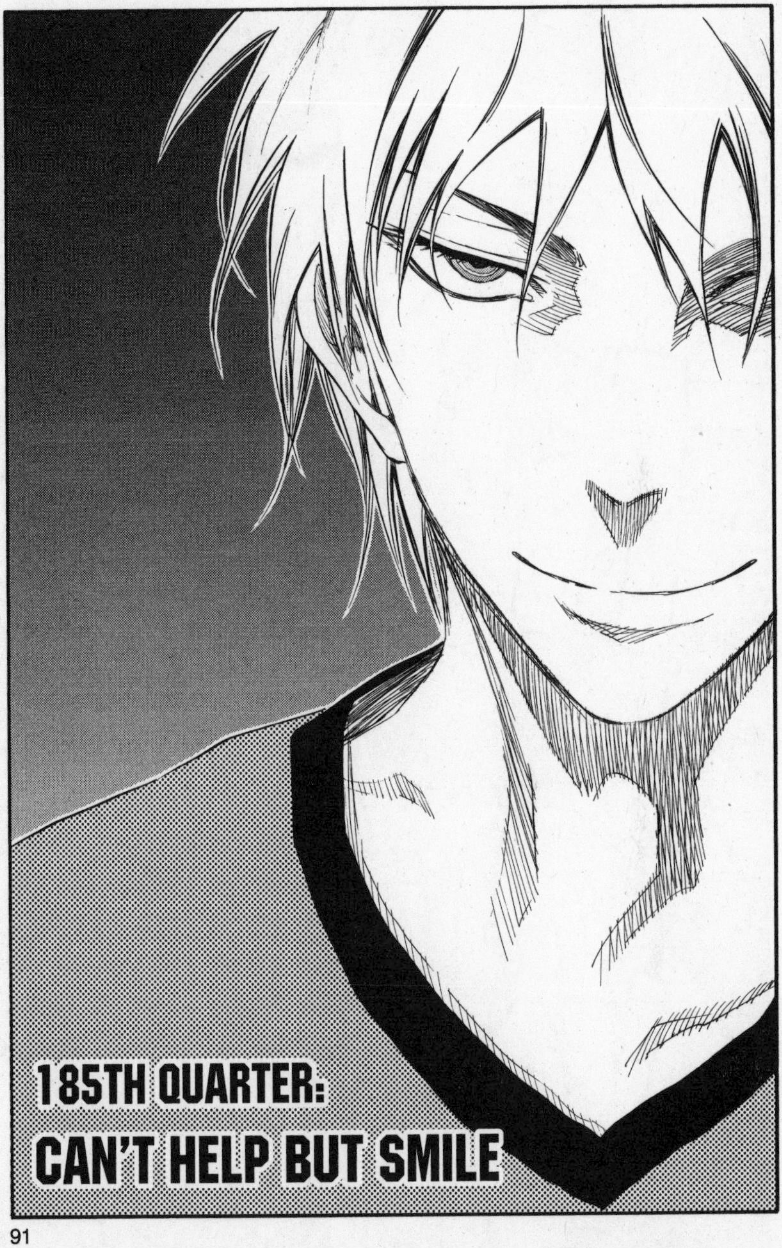
185TH QUARTER:
CAN'T HELP BUT SMILE

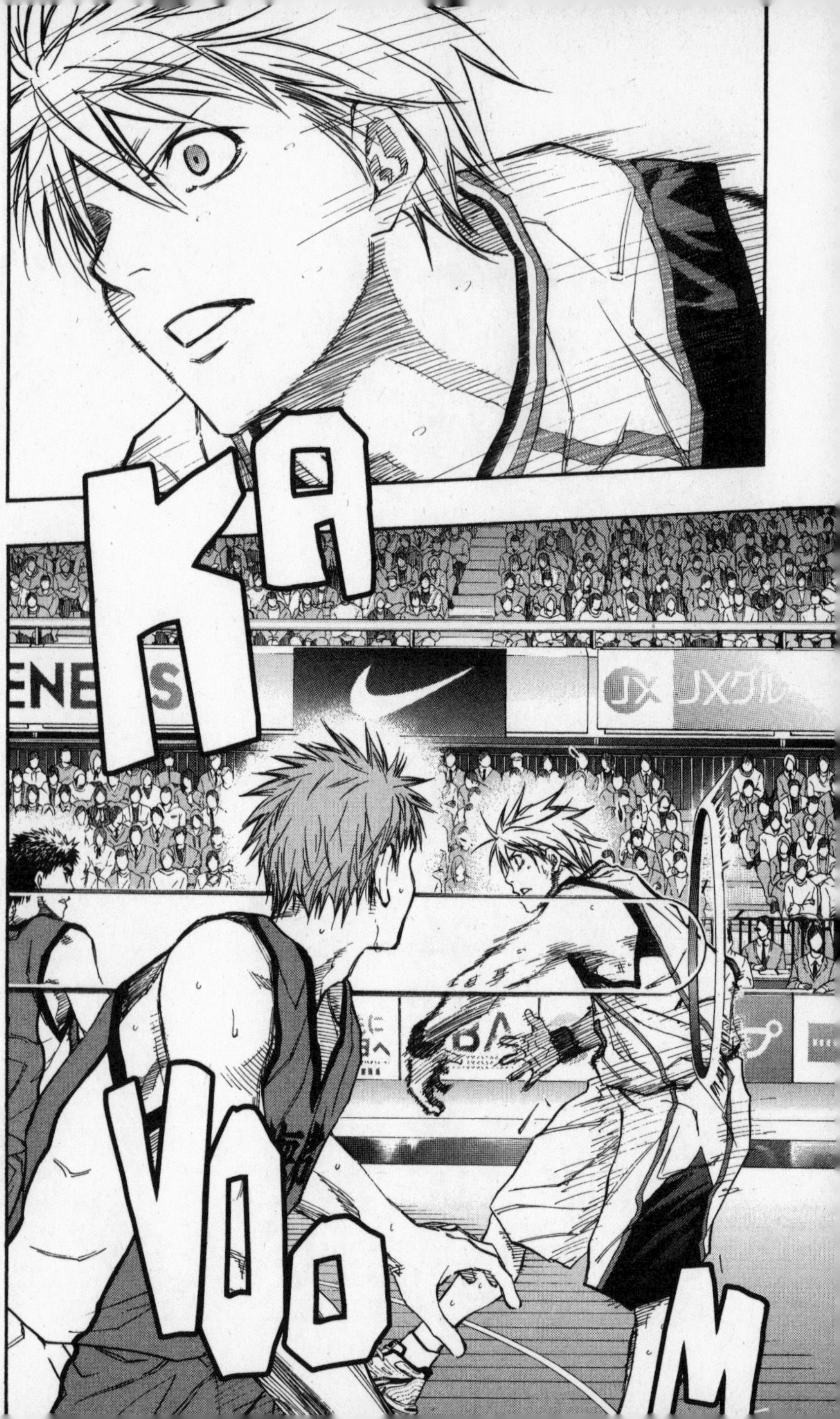
KA
VOOM

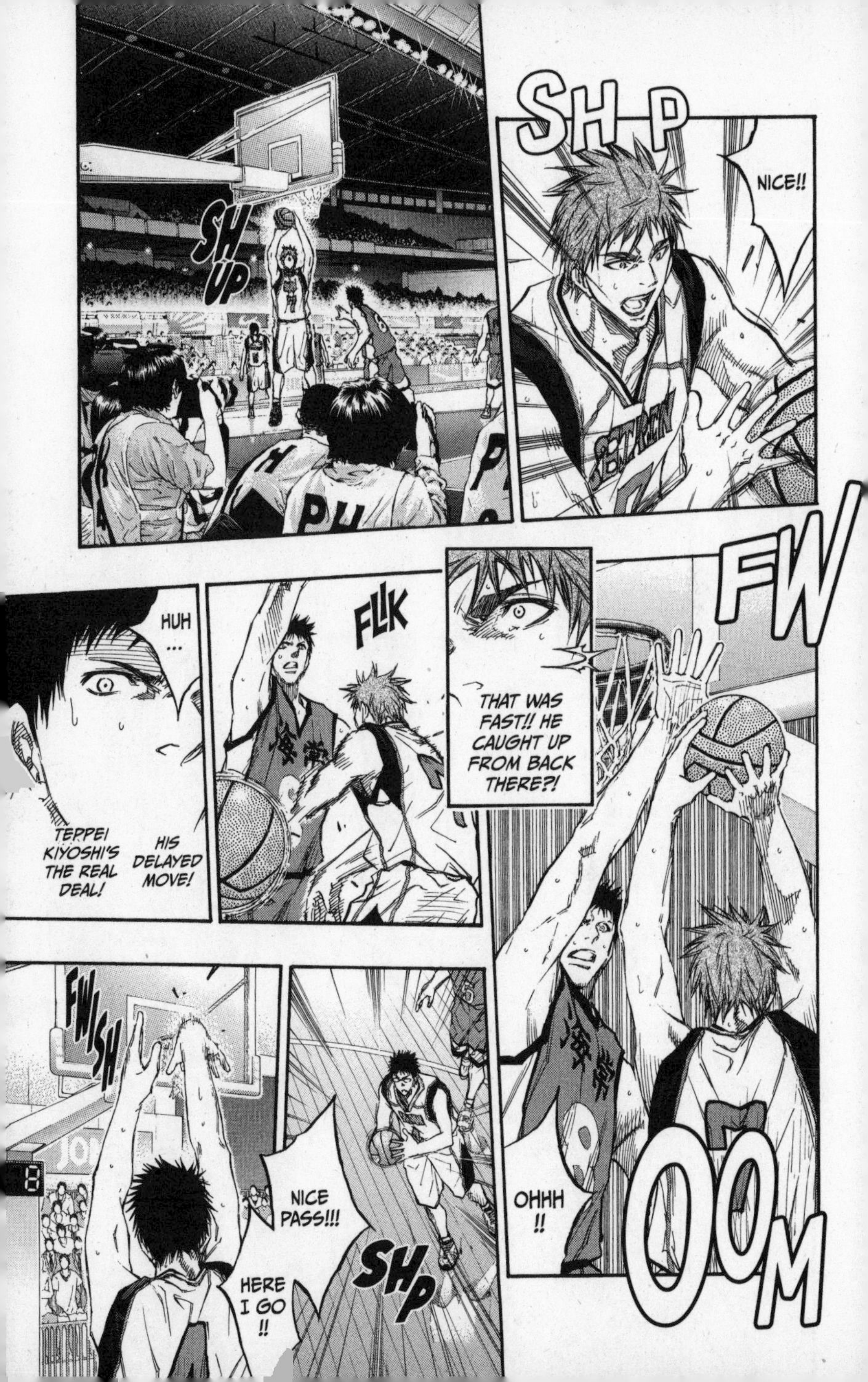
SHP
NICE!!
SHUP
FW
OHHH !!
OOOM
THAT WAS FAST!! HE CAUGHT UP FROM BACK THERE?!
FLIK
HUH ...
HIS DELAYED MOVE!
TEPPEI KIYOSHI'S THE REAL DEAL!
NICE PASS!!!
SHP
HERE I GO !!
FWISH

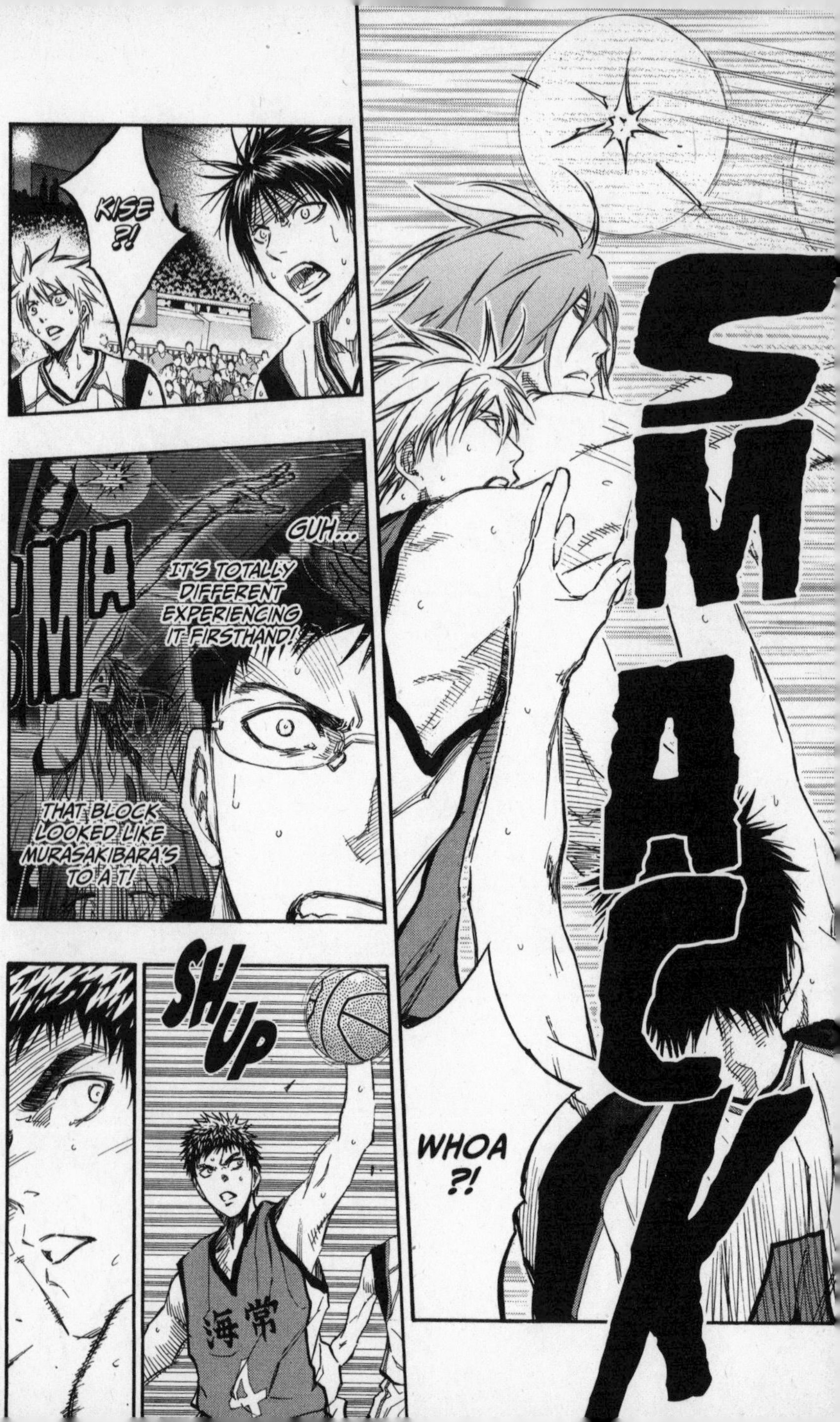
SMACK
WHOA ?!
KISE ?!
GUH...
IT'S TOTALLY DIFFERENT EXPERIENCING IT FIRSTHAND!
THAT BLOCK LOOKED LIKE MURASAKIBARA'S TO A T!
SHUP
海常

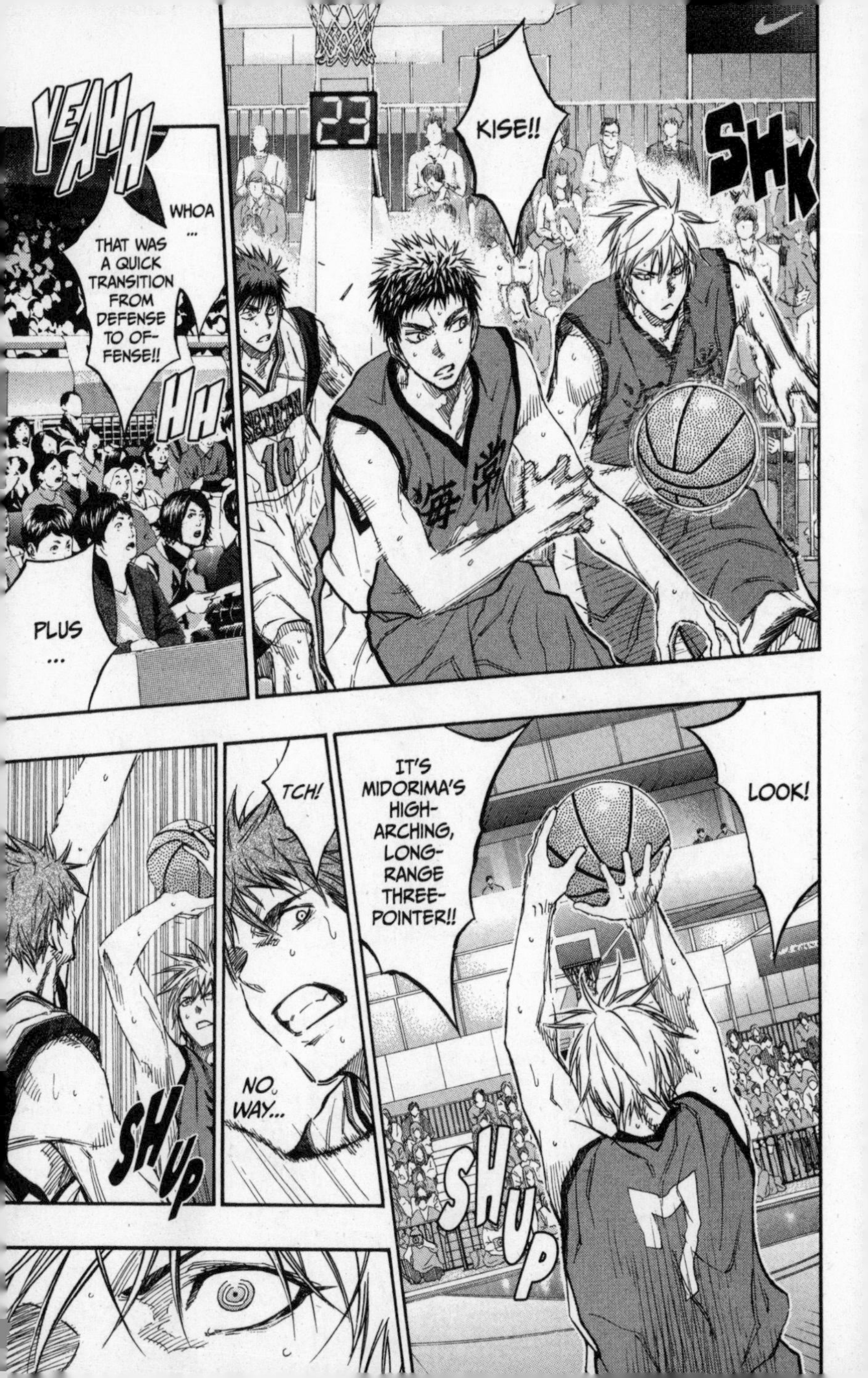
SHK
KISE!!
23
YEAHHHH
WHOA ...
THAT WAS A QUICK TRANSITION FROM DEFENSE TO OF-FENSE!!
PLUS ...
LOOK!
IT'S MIDORIMA'S HIGH-ARCHING, LONG-RANGE THREE-POINTER!!
SHUP
TCH!
NO. WAY...
SHUP

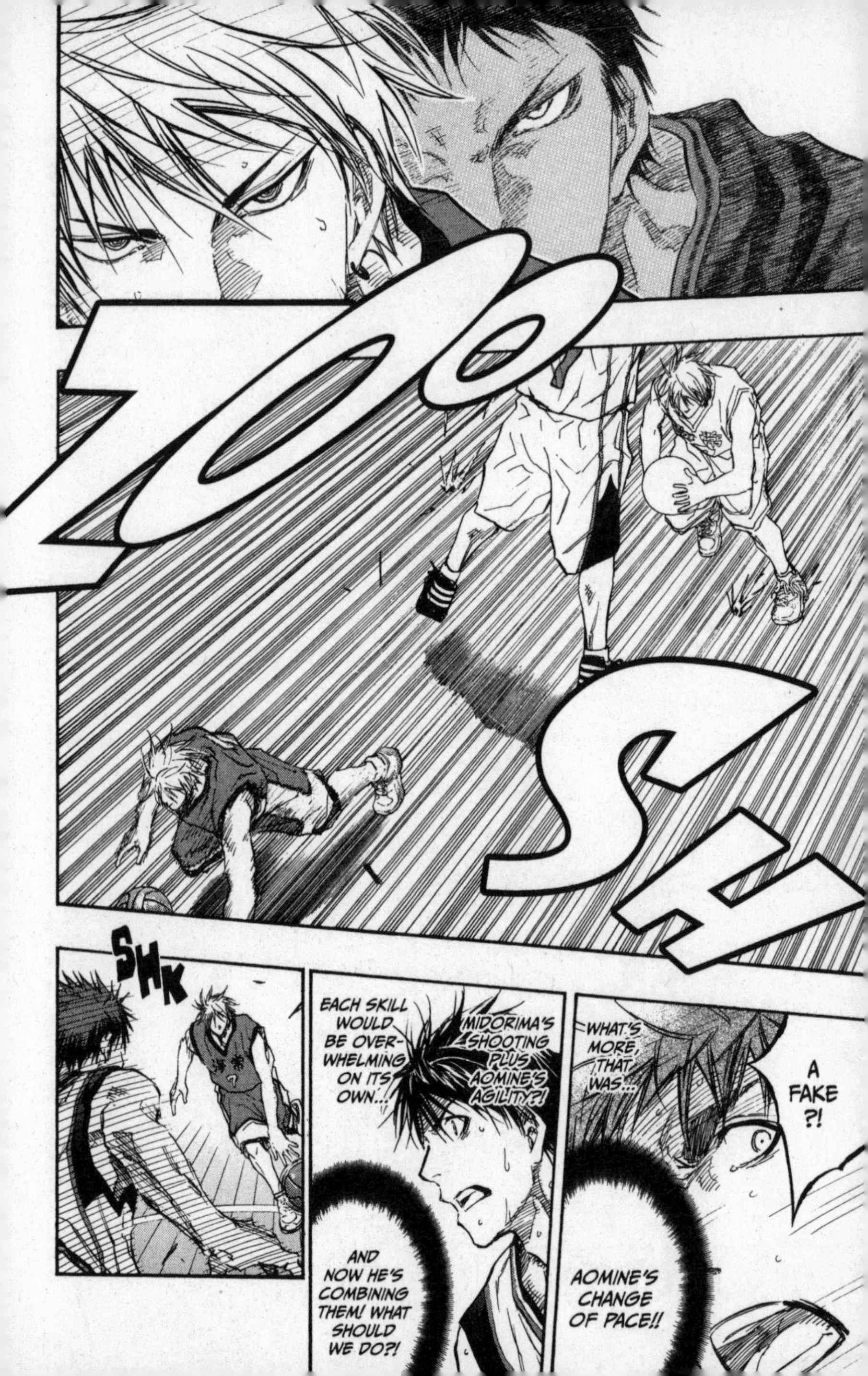
ZOO
SH
A FAKE ?!
WHAT'S MORE, THAT WAS...
AOMINE'S CHANGE OF PACE!!
MIDORIMA'S SHOOTING PLUS AOMINE'S AGILITY?!
EACH SKILL WOULD BE OVER-WHELMING ON ITS OWN...
AND NOW HE'S COMBINING THEM! WHAT SHOULD WE DO?!
SHK

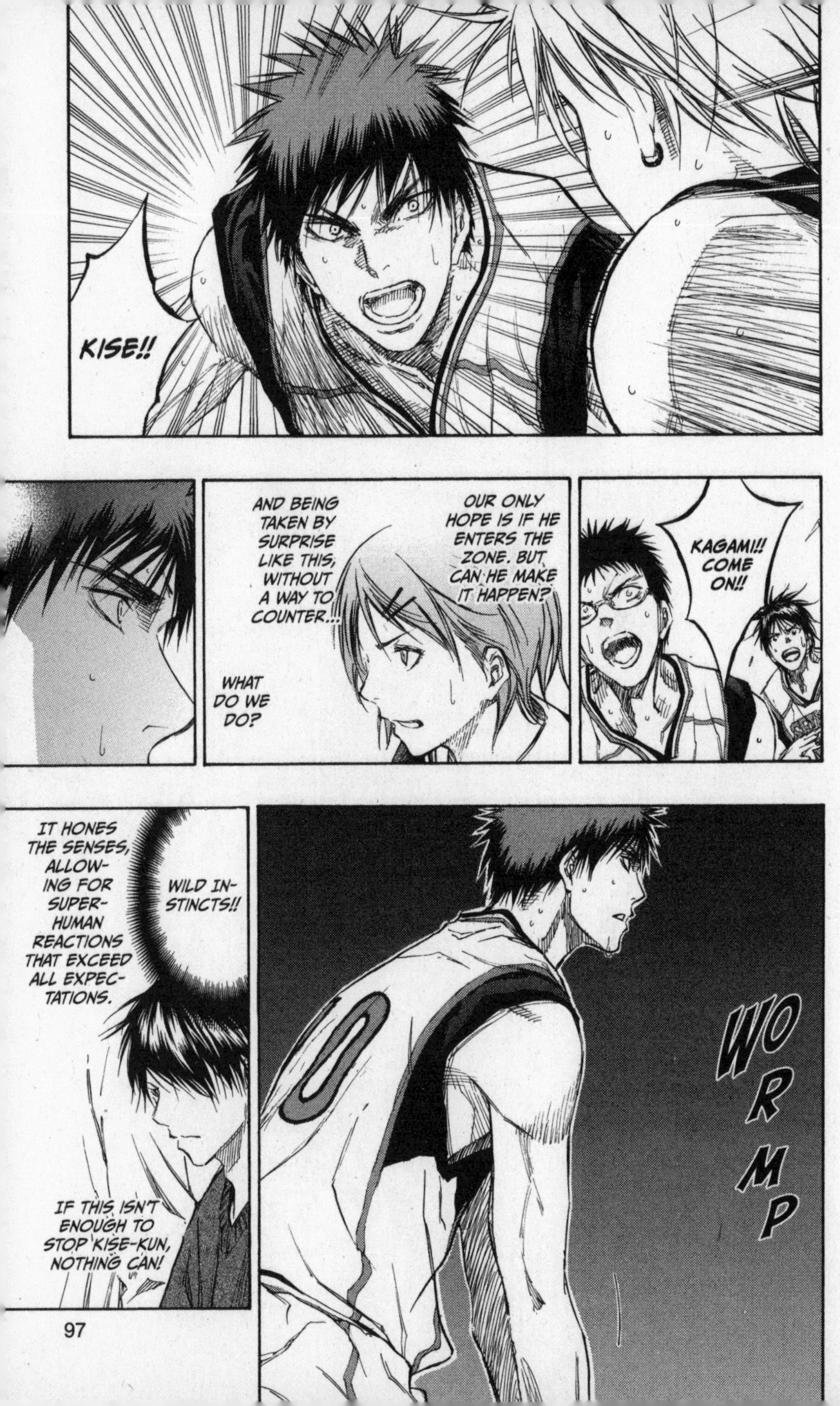
KISE!!
KAGAMI!! COME ON!!
OUR ONLY HOPE IS IF HE ENTERS THE ZONE. BUT CAN HE MAKE IT HAPPEN?
AND BEING TAKEN BY SURPRISE LIKE THIS, WITHOUT A WAY TO COUNTER...
WHAT DO WE DO?
WORMP
WILD IN-STINCTS!!
IT HONES THE SENSES, ALLOW-ING FOR SUPER-HUMAN REACTIONS THAT EXCEED ALL EXPEC-TATIONS.
IF THIS ISN'T ENOUGH TO STOP KISE-KUN, NOTHING CAN!

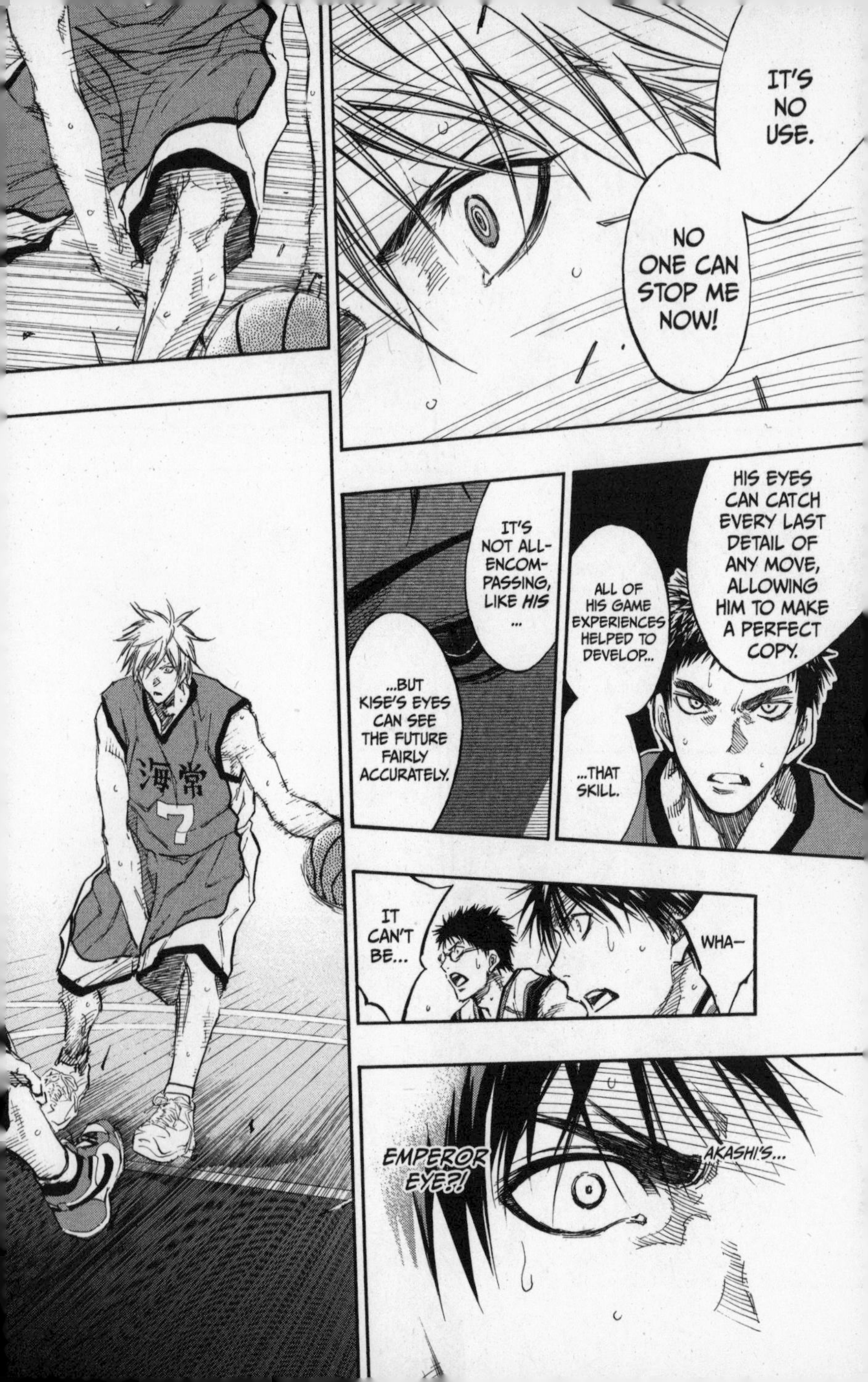
IT'S NO USE.
NO ONE CAN STOP ME NOW!
HIS EYES CAN CATCH EVERY LAST DETAIL OF ANY MOVE, ALLOWING HIM TO MAKE A PERFECT COPY.
ALL OF HIS GAME EXPERIENCES HELPED TO DEVELOP...
...THAT SKILL.
IT'S NOT ALL-ENCOMPASSING, LIKE *HIS* ...
...BUT KISE'S EYES CAN SEE THE FUTURE FAIRLY ACCURATELY.
WHA—
IT CAN'T BE...
AKASHI'S...
EMPEROR EYE?!

海常

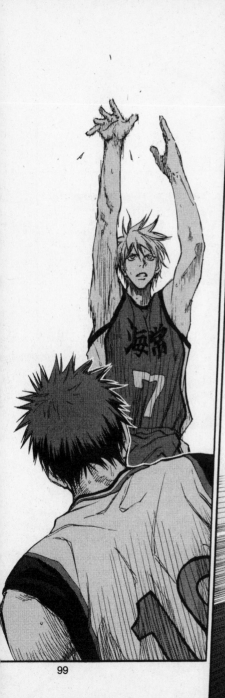

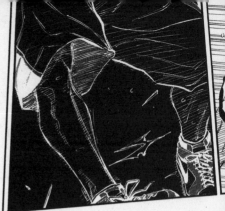

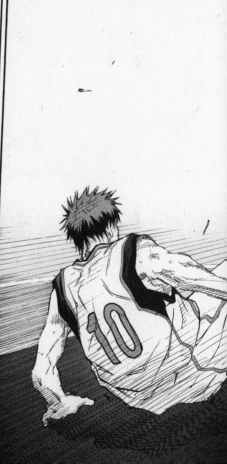

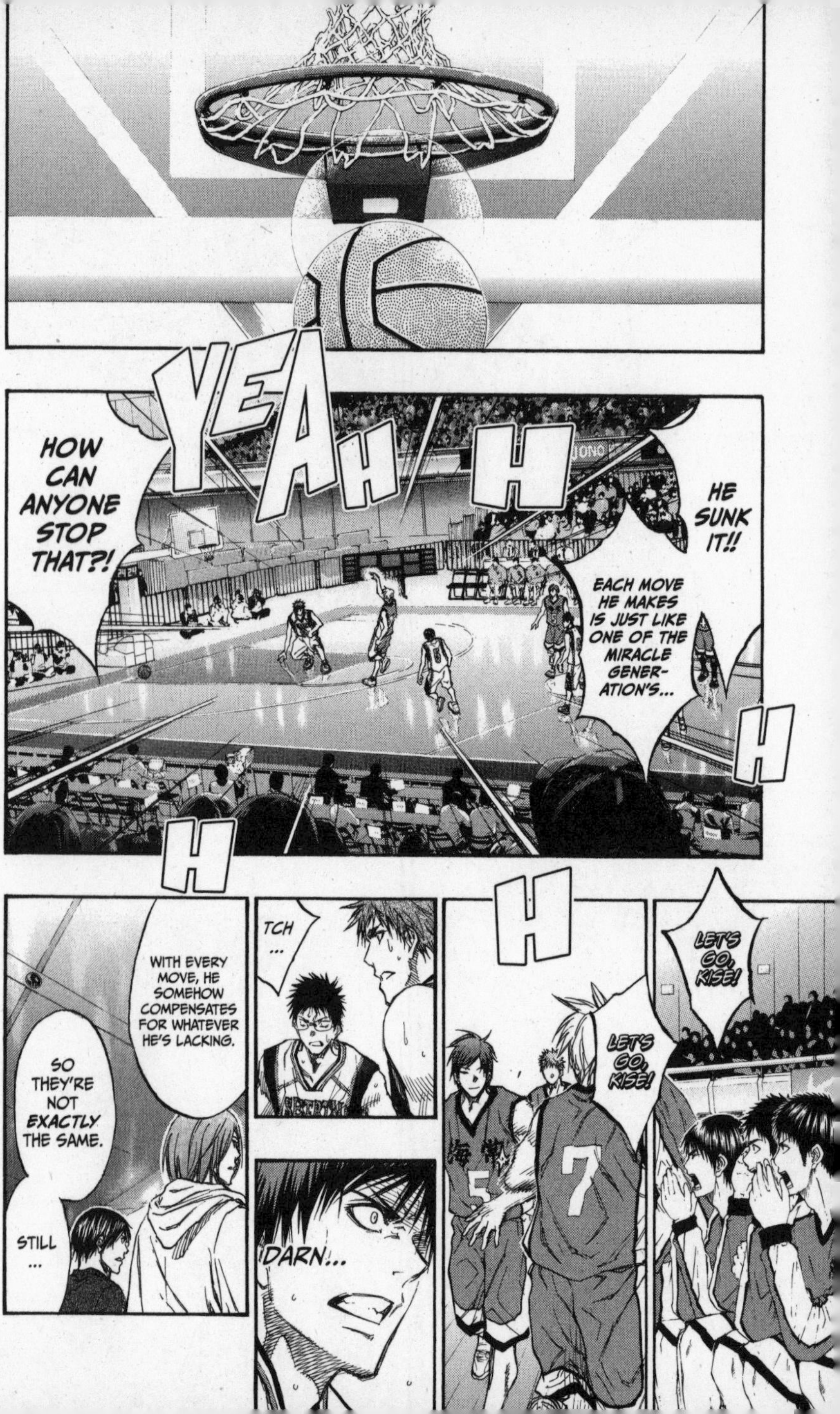
YEAHHHHH
HE SUNK IT!!
EACH MOVE HE MAKES IS JUST LIKE ONE OF THE MIRACLE GENERATION'S...
HOW CAN ANYONE STOP THAT?!
LET'S GO, KISE!
LET'S GO, KISE!
TCH...
DARN...
WITH EVERY MOVE, HE SOMEHOW COMPENSATES FOR WHATEVER HE'S LACKING.
SO THEY'RE NOT EXACTLY THE SAME.
STILL...

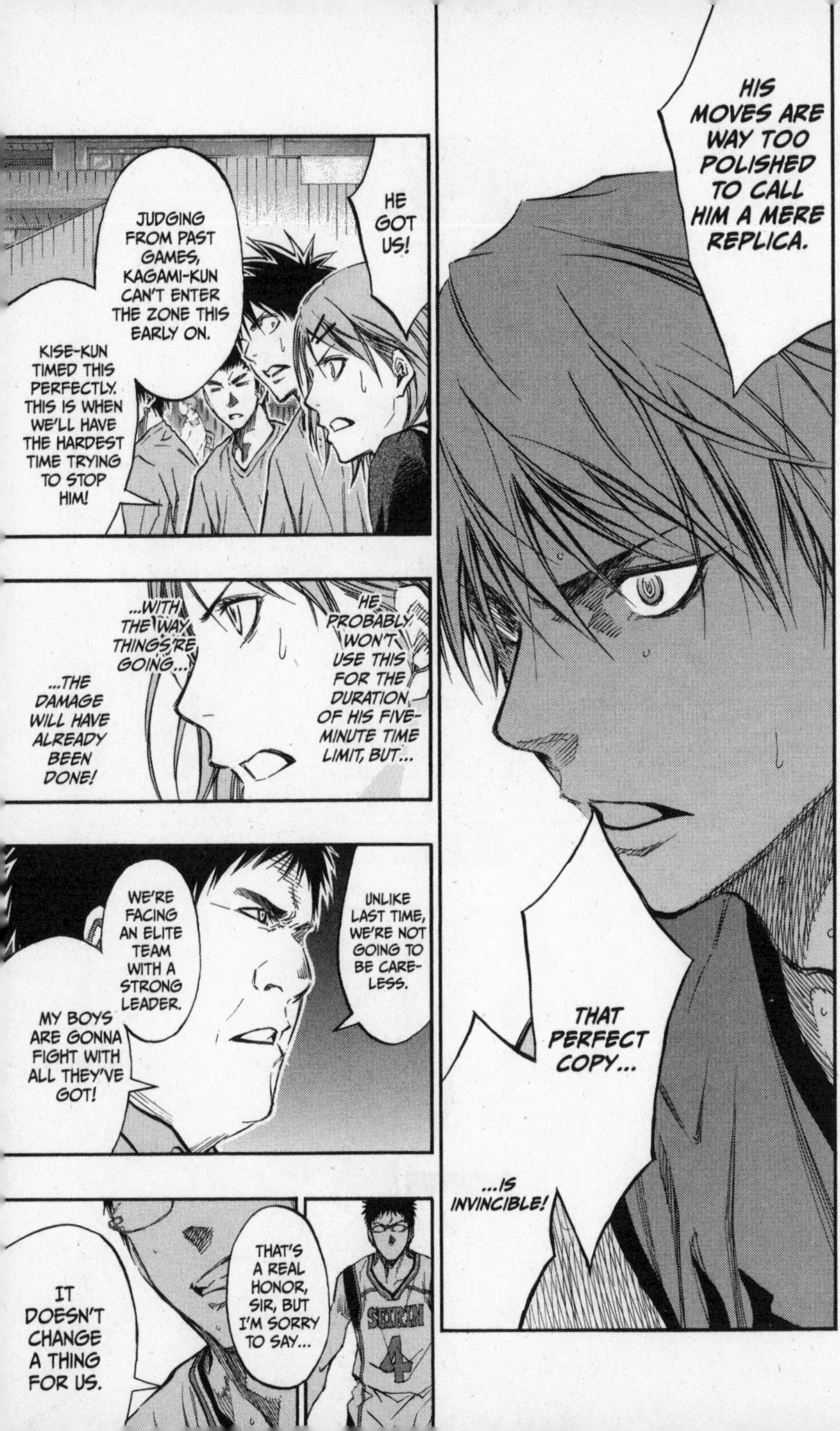
HIS MOVES ARE WAY TOO POLISHED TO CALL HIM A MERE REPLICA.
THAT PERFECT COPY...
...IS INVINCIBLE!
HE GOT US!
JUDGING FROM PAST GAMES, KAGAMI-KUN CAN'T ENTER THE ZONE THIS EARLY ON.
KISE-KUN TIMED THIS PERFECTLY. THIS IS WHEN WE'LL HAVE THE HARDEST TIME TRYING TO STOP HIM!
HE PROBABLY WON'T USE THIS FOR THE DURATION OF HIS FIVE-MINUTE TIME LIMIT, BUT...
...WITH THE WAY THINGS'RE GOING...
...THE DAMAGE WILL HAVE ALREADY BEEN DONE!
UNLIKE LAST TIME, WE'RE NOT GOING TO BE CARE-LESS.
WE'RE FACING AN ELITE TEAM WITH A STRONG LEADER.
MY BOYS ARE GONNA FIGHT WITH ALL THEY'VE GOT!
SEIRIN
4
THAT'S A REAL HONOR, SIR, BUT I'M SORRY TO SAY...
IT DOESN'T CHANGE A THING FOR US.

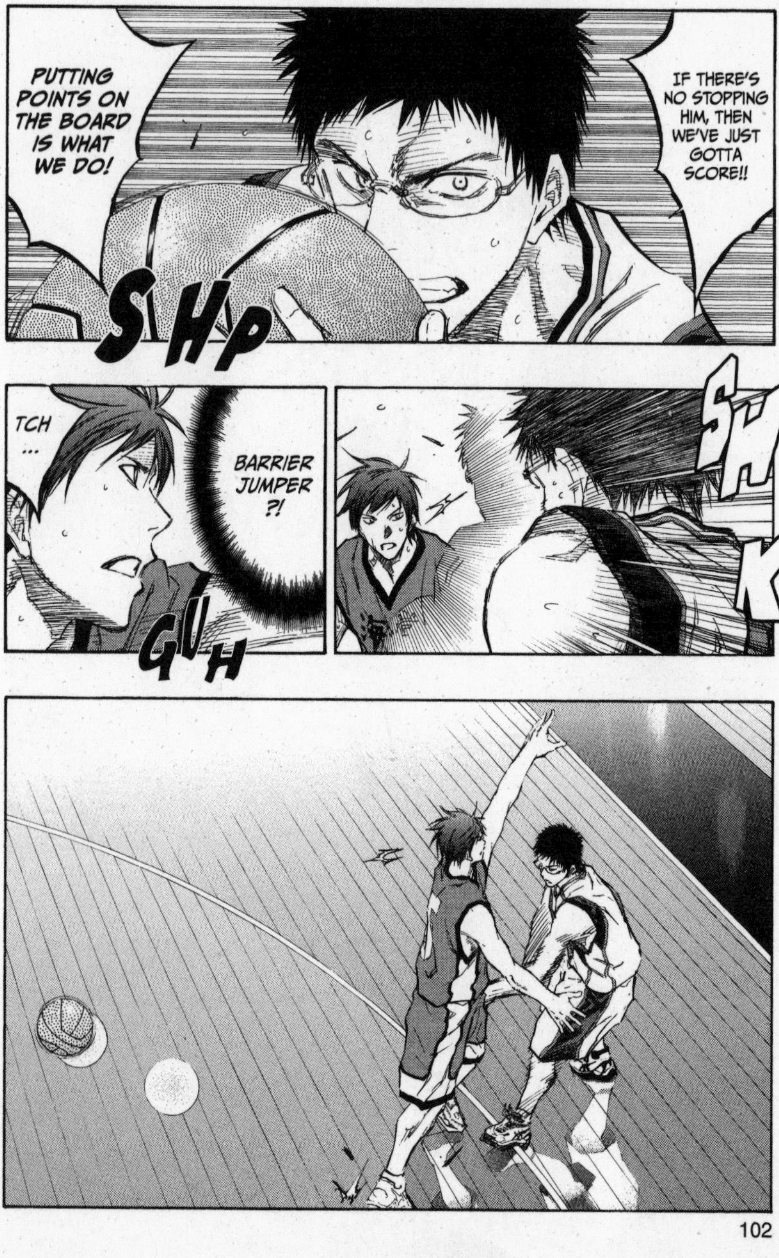
IF THERE'S NO STOPPING HIM, THEN WE'VE JUST GOTTA SCORE!!
PUTTING POINTS ON THE BOARD IS WHAT WE DO!
SHP
SHK
BARRIER JUMPER ?!
TCH ...
GUH

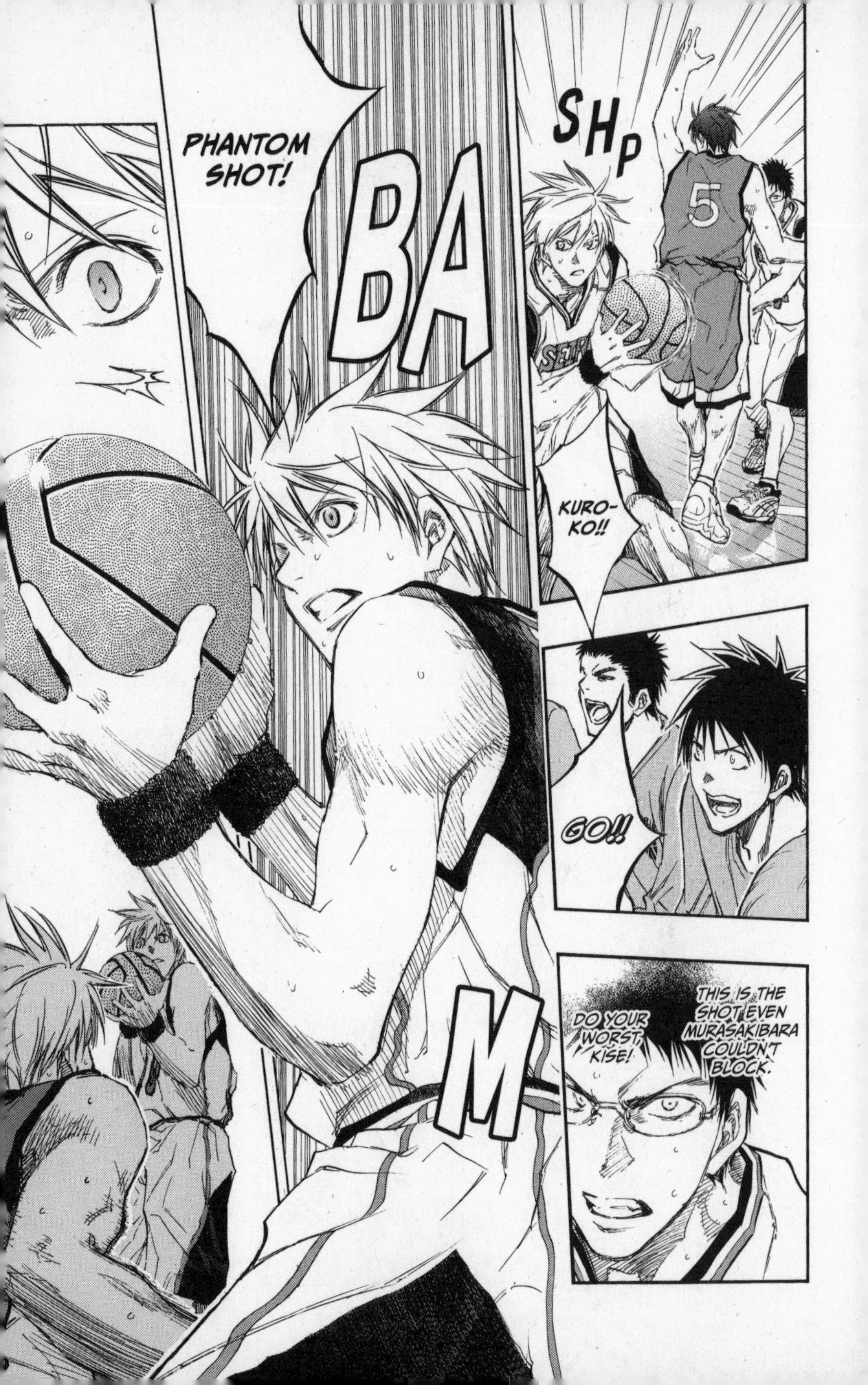
SHP
KURO-KO!!
GO!!
THIS IS THE SHOT EVEN MURASAKIBARA COULDN'T BLOCK.
DO YOUR WORST, KISE!
PHANTOM SHOT!
BA
M

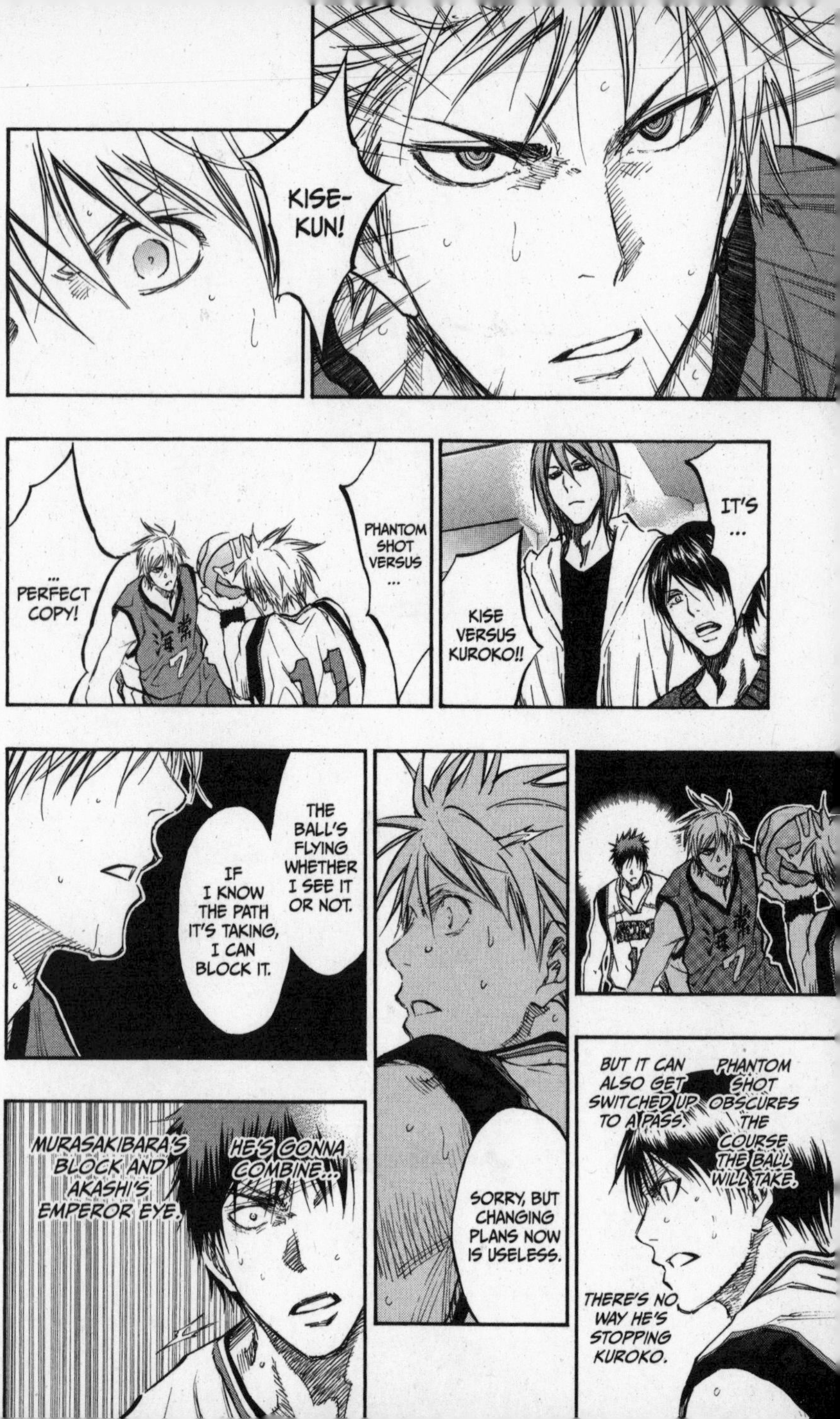
KISE-KUN!
IT'S ...
KISE VERSUS KUROKO!!
PHANTOM SHOT VERSUS ...
... PERFECT COPY!
PHANTOM SHOT OBSCURES THE COURSE THE BALL WILL TAKE.
BUT IT CAN ALSO GET SWITCHED UP TO A PASS.
THERE'S NO WAY HE'S STOPPING KUROKO.
SORRY, BUT CHANGING PLANS NOW IS USELESS.
THE BALL'S FLYING WHETHER I SEE IT OR NOT.
IF I KNOW THE PATH IT'S TAKING, I CAN BLOCK IT.
HE'S GONNA COMBINE...
MURASAKIBARA'S BLOCK AND AKASHI'S EMPEROR EYE.

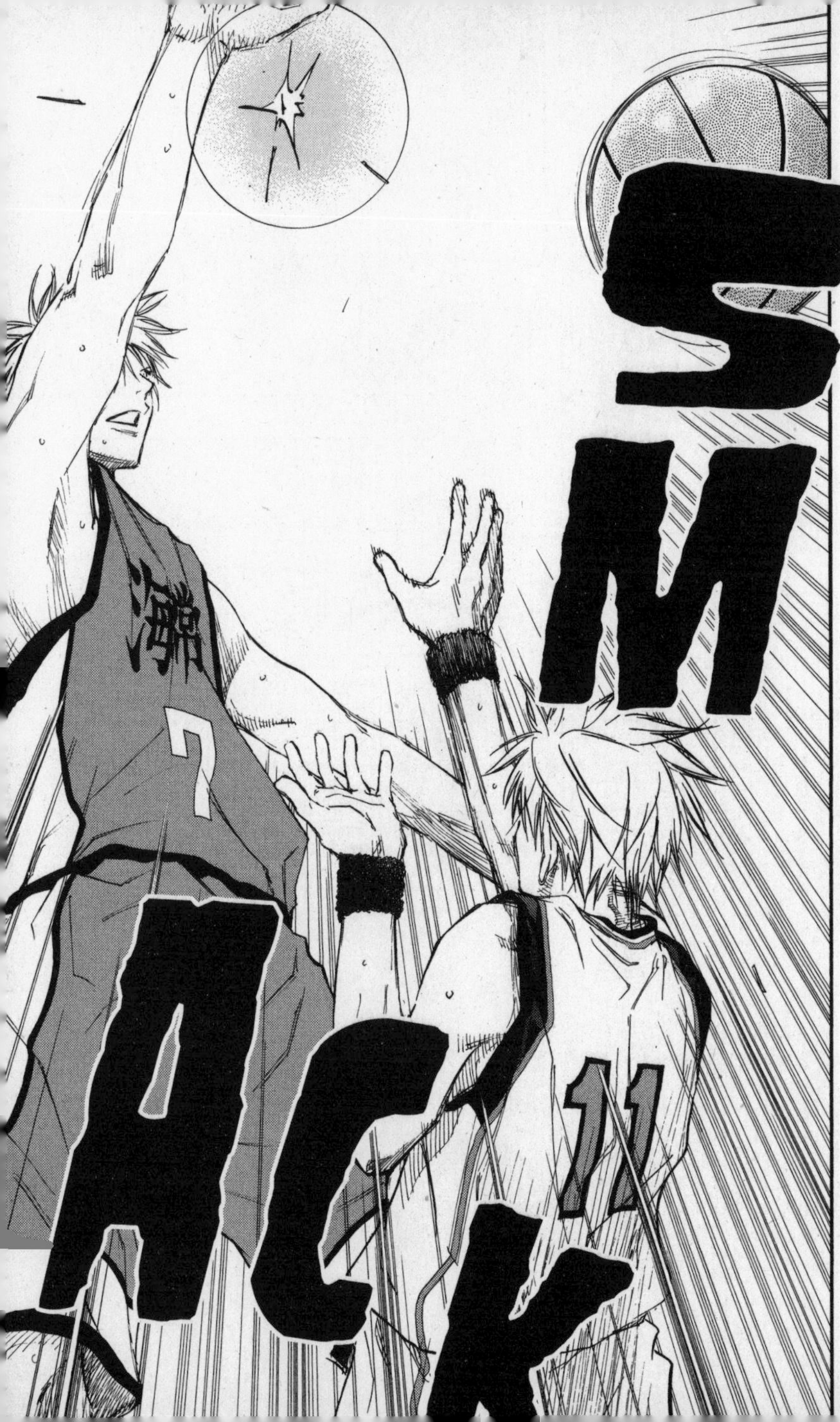
SMACK
海常
7
11

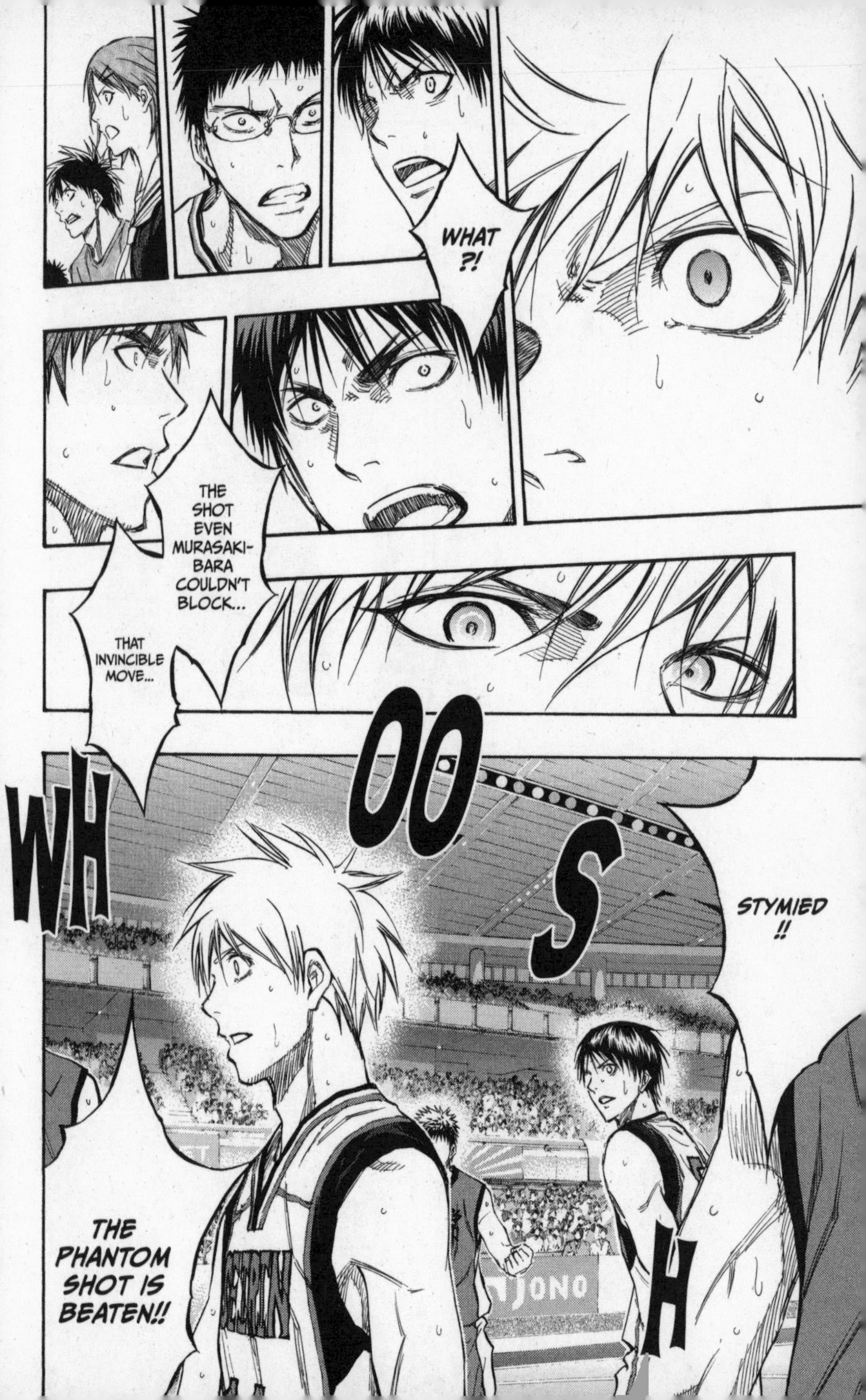
WHAT ?!
THE SHOT EVEN MURASAKIBARA COULDN'T BLOCK...
THAT INVINCIBLE MOVE...
WHOOSH
STYMIED !!
THE PHANTOM SHOT IS BEATEN!!

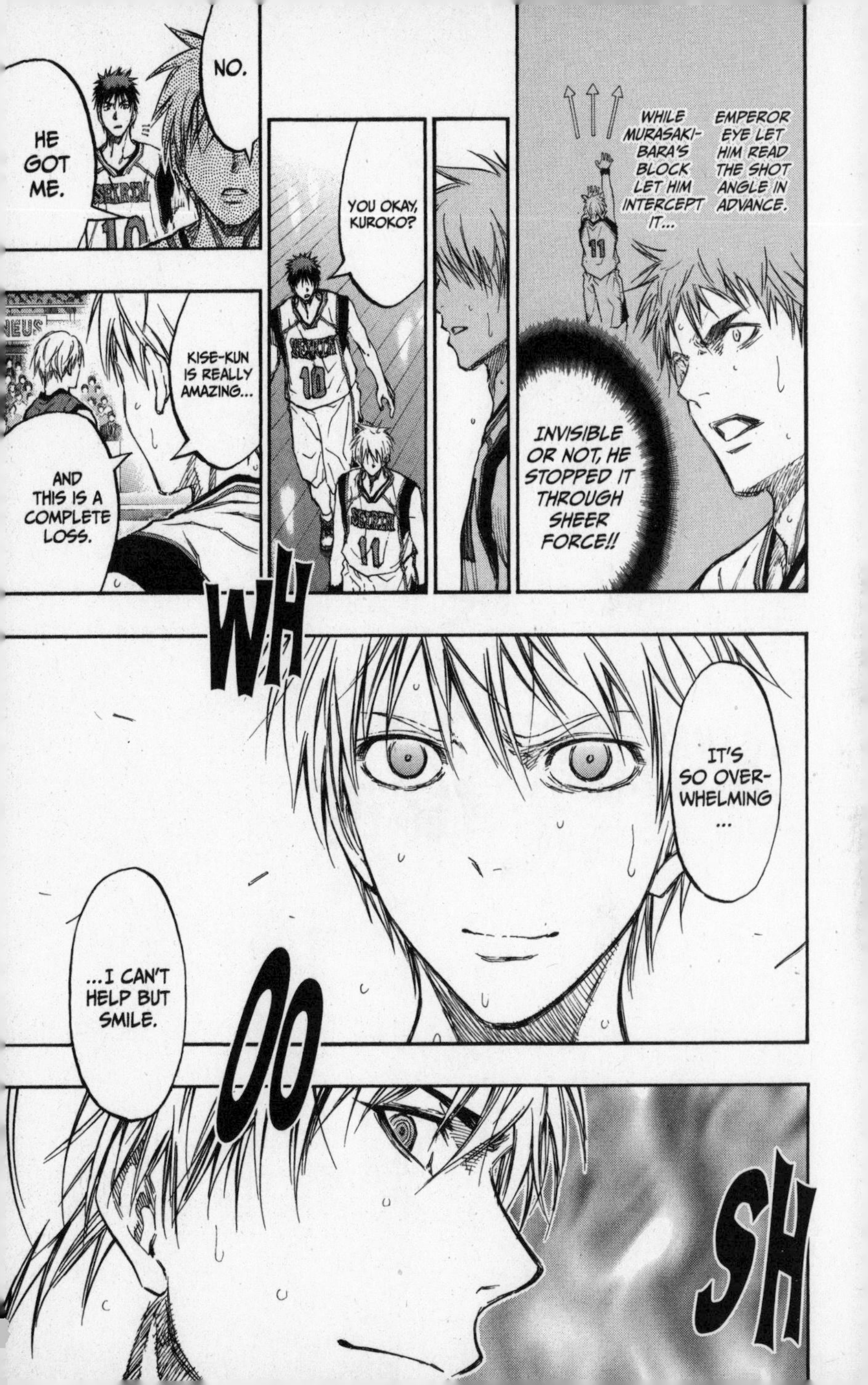
EMPEROR EYE LET HIM READ THE SHOT ANGLE IN ADVANCE.
WHILE MURASAKIBARA'S BLOCK LET HIM INTERCEPT IT...
INVISIBLE OR NOT, HE STOPPED IT THROUGH SHEER FORCE!!
YOU OKAY, KUROKO?
NO.
HE GOT ME.
KISE-KUN IS REALLY AMAZING...
AND THIS IS A COMPLETE LOSS.
WH
IT'S SO OVERWHELMING...
...I CAN'T HELP BUT SMILE.
OO
SH

KUROKO'S BASKETBALL BLOOPERS

TAKE 1

UNLIKE LAST TIME, WE'RE NOT GOING TO BE CARELESS.
WE'RE FACING AN ELITE TEAM WITH A STRONG LEADER
MY BOYS ARE GONNA FIGHT WITH ALL THEY'VE GOT!
WHAT WAS THAT?
KRIK
HEY! DIDJA HEAR THAT JUST NOW?!
THAT GUY'S GOT AN EYE FOR TALENT.
A STRONG LEADER! HE CALLED ME THAT!!
YEAH... GOOD FOR YOU, COACH.
BEAM

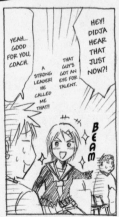

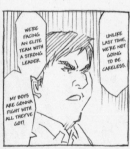

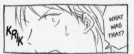

186TH QUARTER: YOU'RE UP!

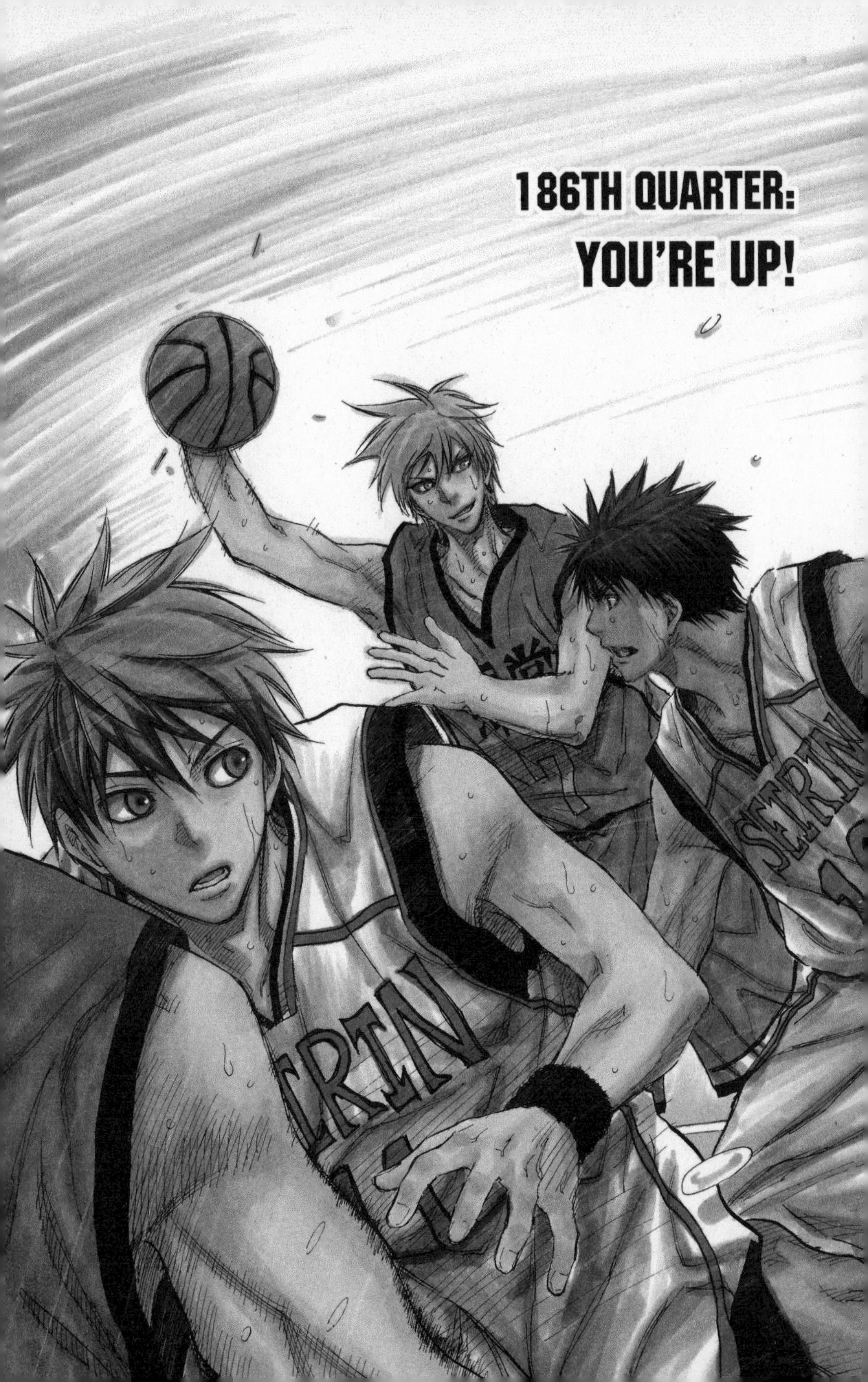

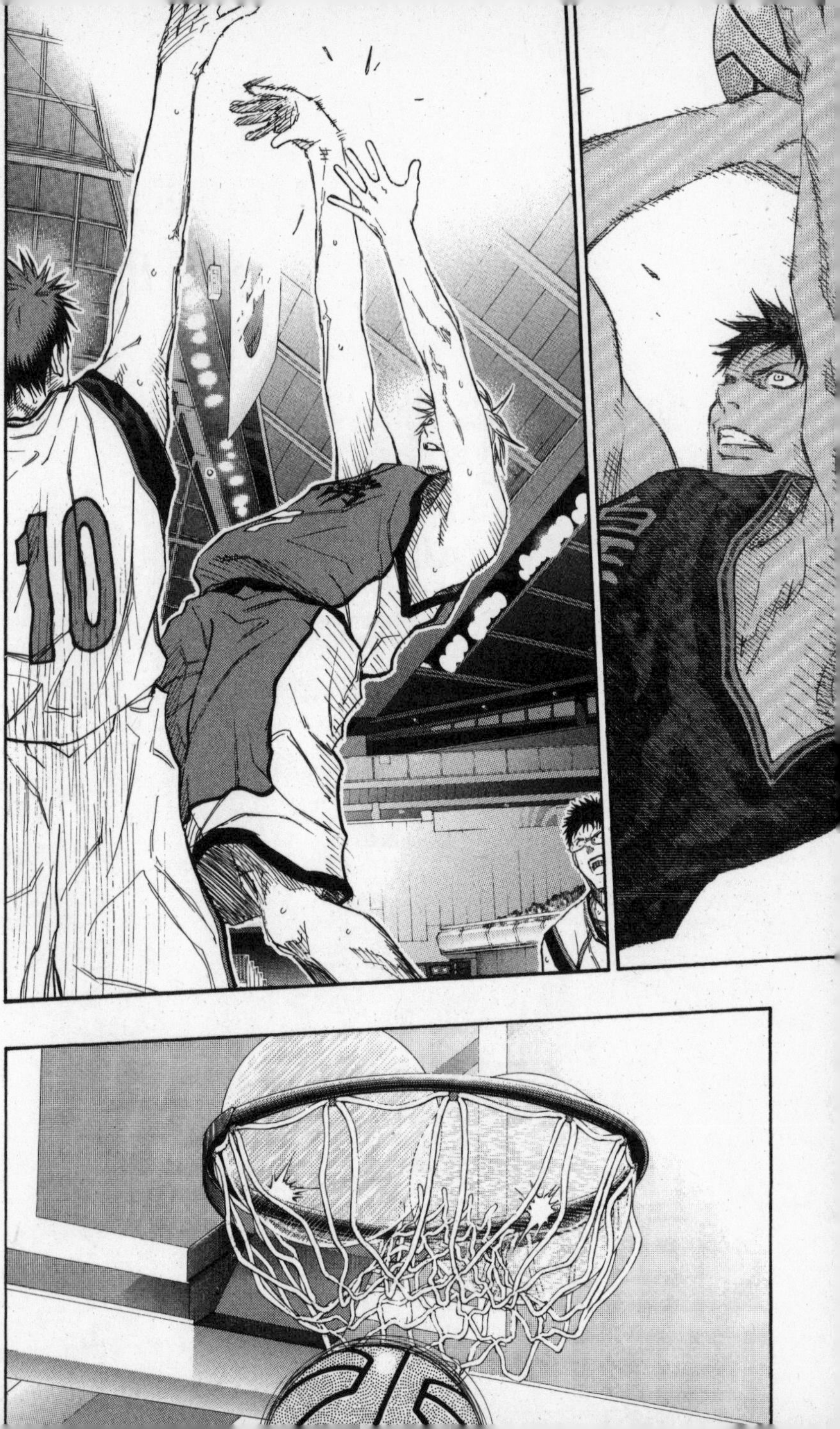

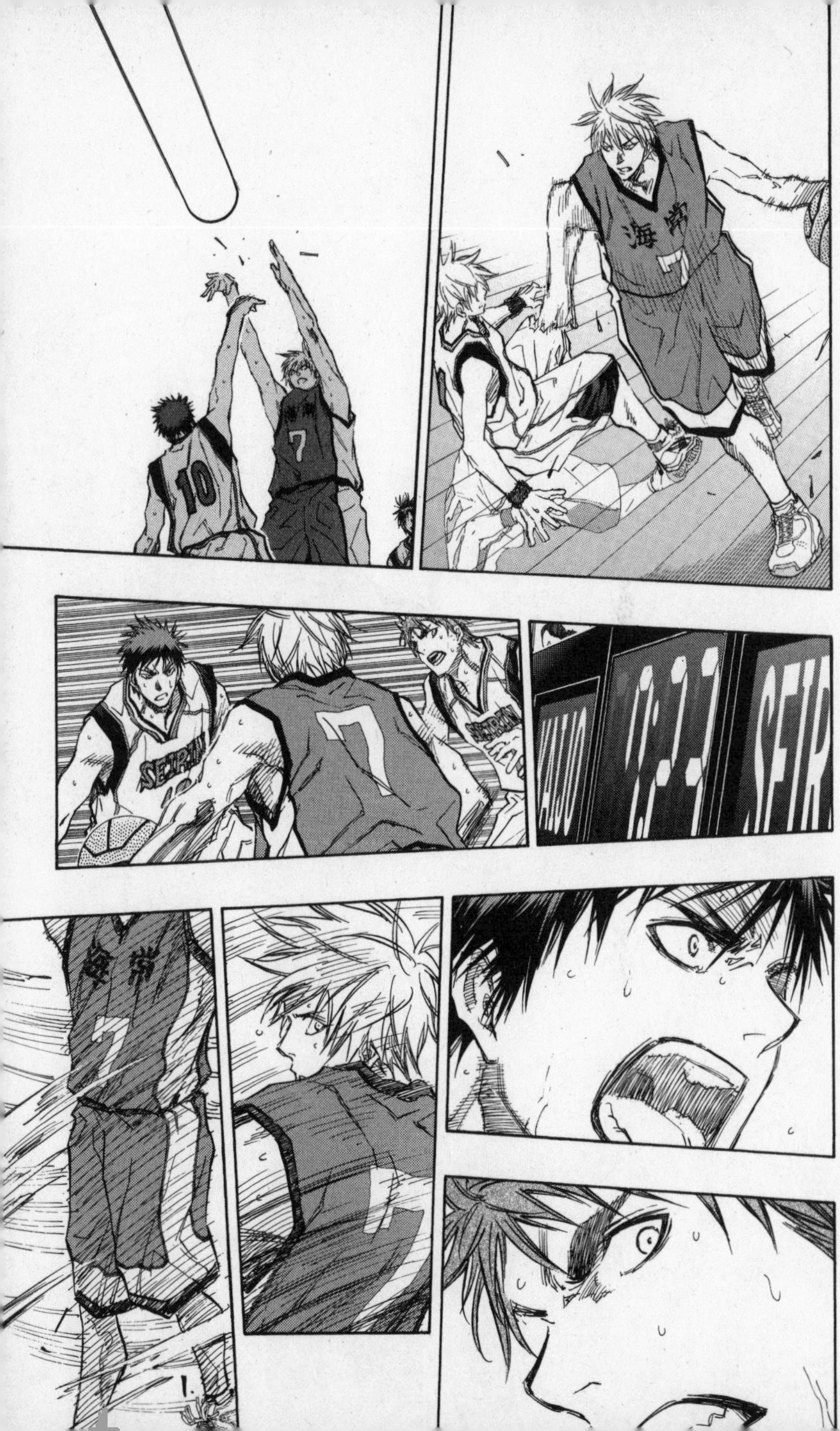

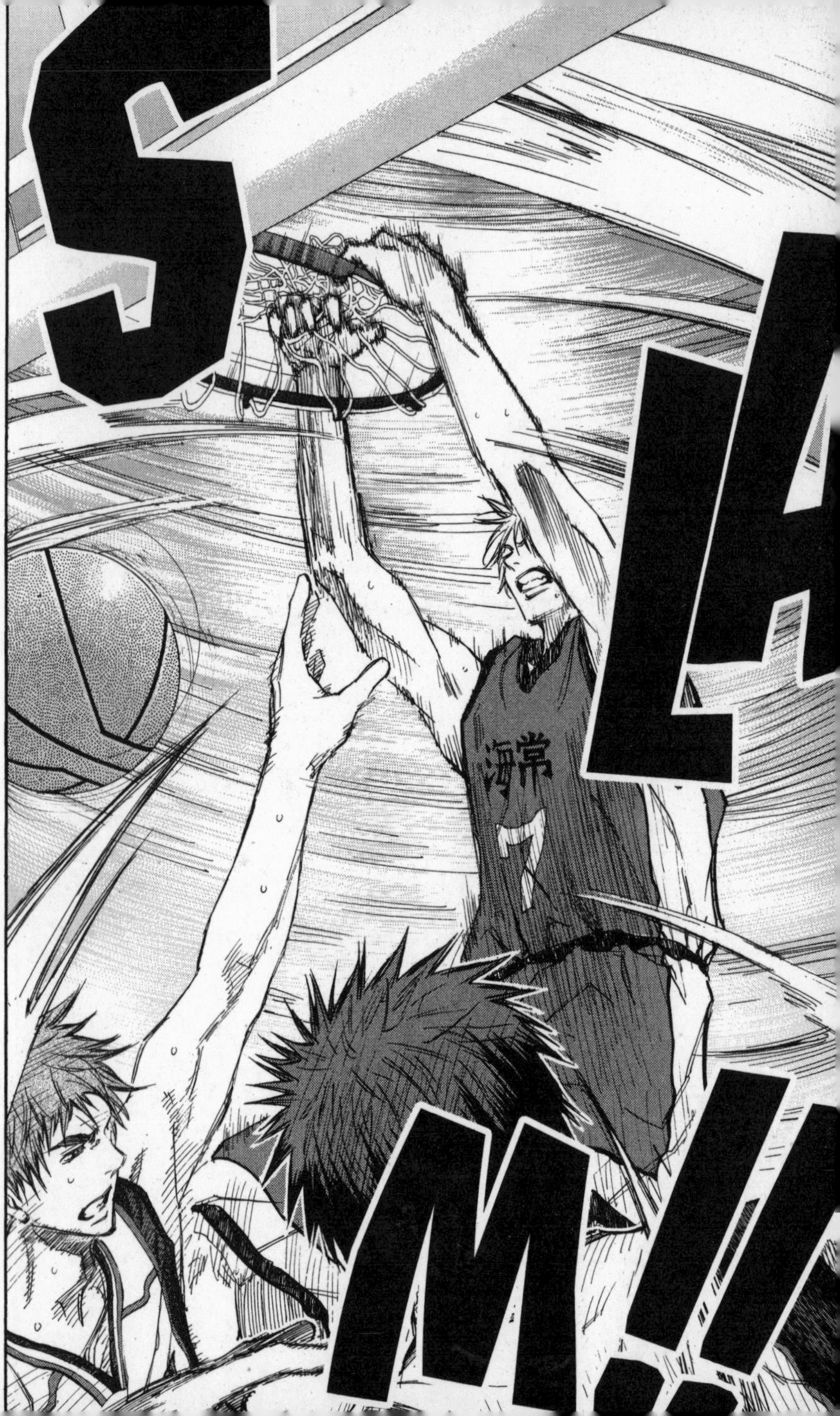
SLAM!!
海常
7

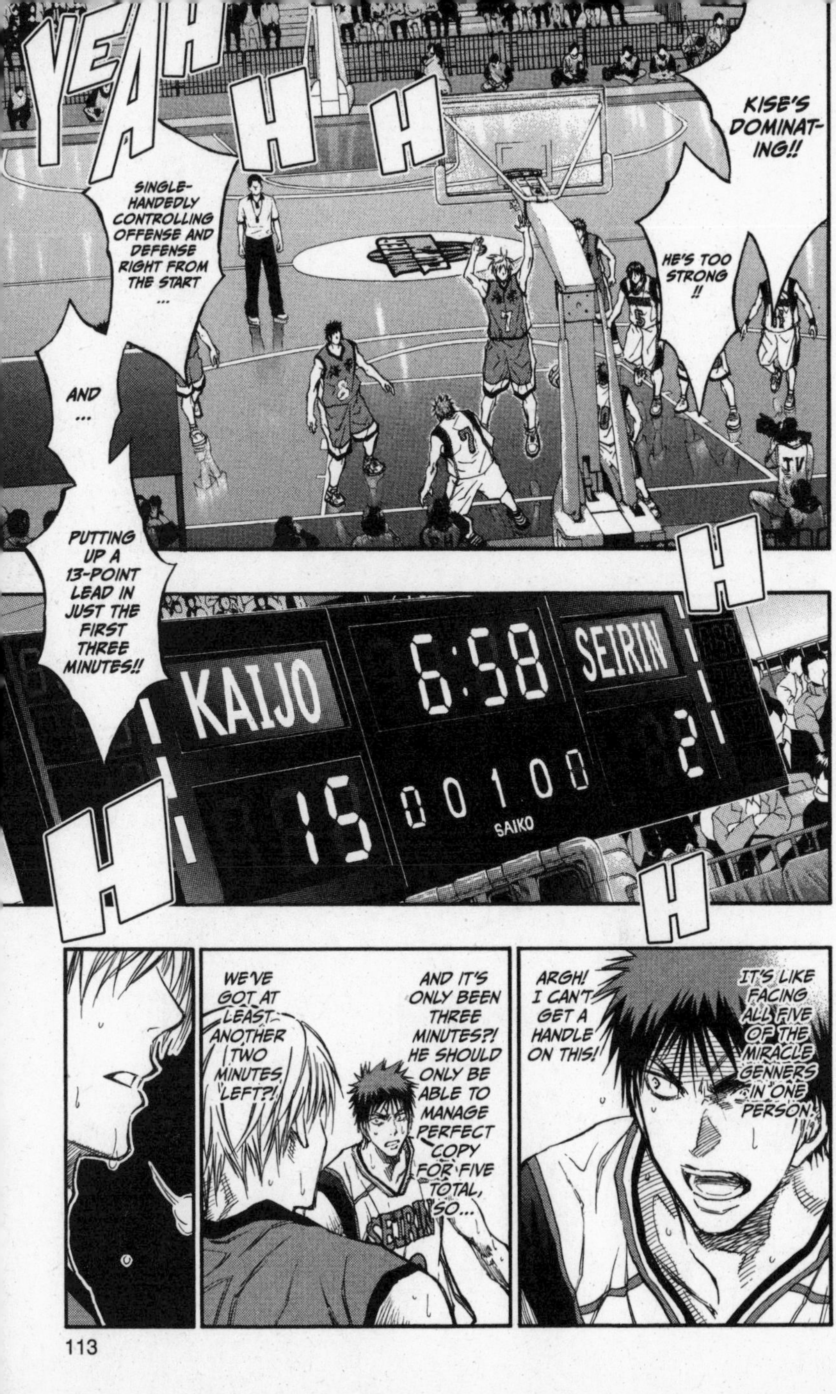
KISE'S DOMINATING!!
HE'S TOO STRONG!!
YEAH
H
H
SINGLE-HANDEDLY CONTROLLING OFFENSE AND DEFENSE RIGHT FROM THE START ...
AND ...
PUTTING UP A 13-POINT LEAD IN JUST THE FIRST THREE MINUTES!!
H
KAIJO
6:58
SEIRIN
15
00100
2
SAIKO
H
H
IT'S LIKE FACING ALL FIVE OF THE MIRACLE GENNERS IN ONE PERSON.
ARGH! I CAN'T GET A HANDLE ON THIS!
AND IT'S ONLY BEEN THREE MINUTES?! HE SHOULD ONLY BE ABLE TO MANAGE PERFECT COPY FOR FIVE TOTAL, SO...
WE'VE GOT AT LEAST ANOTHER TWO MINUTES LEFT?!
SEIRIN

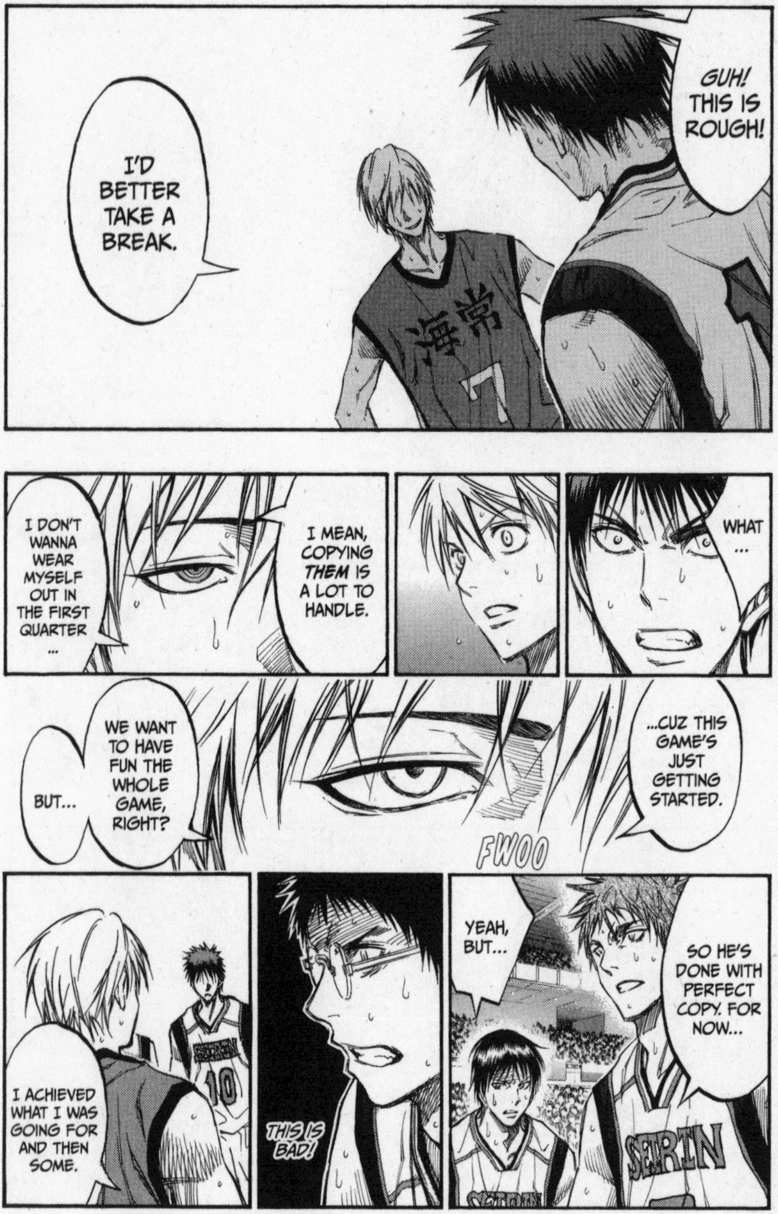
GUH! THIS IS ROUGH!
I'D BETTER TAKE A BREAK.
WHAT ...
I MEAN, COPYING *THEM* IS A LOT TO HANDLE.
I DON'T WANNA WEAR MYSELF OUT IN THE FIRST QUARTER ...
...CUZ THIS GAME'S JUST GETTING STARTED.
FWOO
WE WANT TO HAVE FUN THE WHOLE GAME, RIGHT?
BUT...
SO HE'S DONE WITH PERFECT COPY. FOR NOW...
YEAH, BUT...
THIS IS BAD!
I ACHIEVED WHAT I WAS GOING FOR AND THEN SOME.

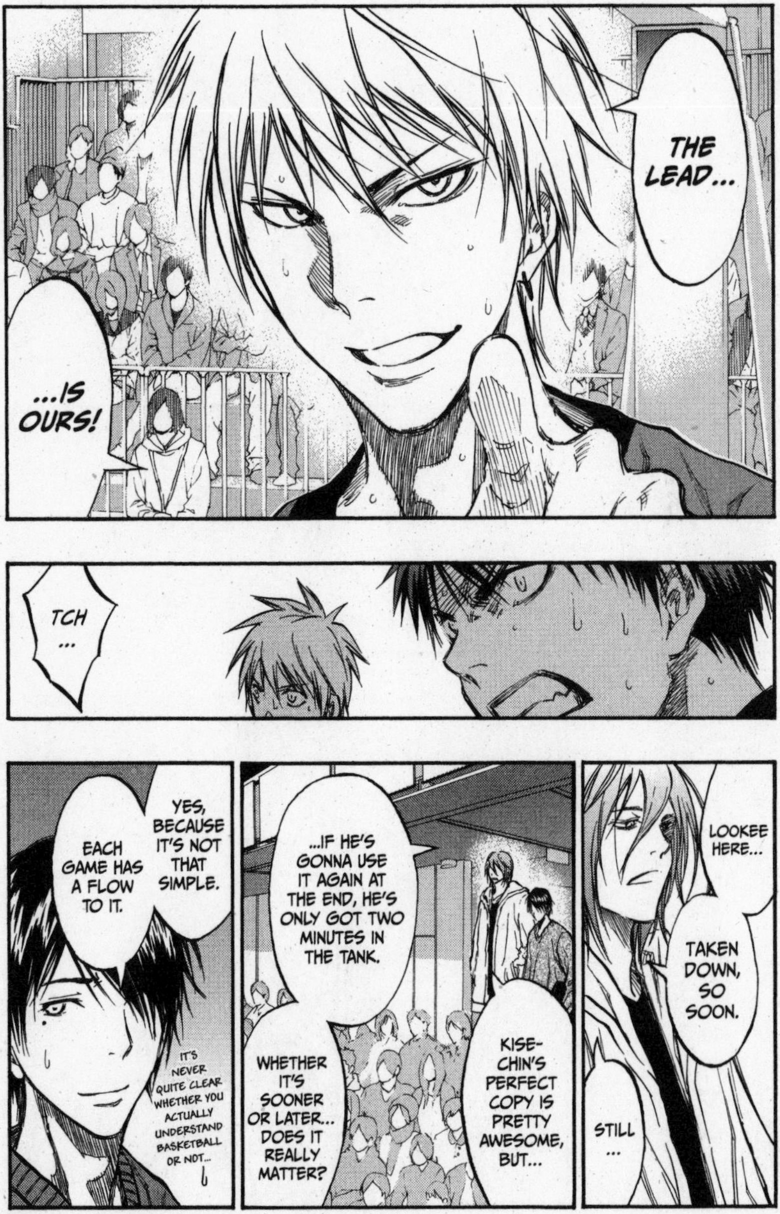
THE LEAD...
...IS OURS!
TCH ...
LOOKEE HERE...
TAKEN DOWN, SO SOON.
STILL ...
KISE-CHIN'S PERFECT COPY IS PRETTY AWESOME, BUT...
...IF HE'S GONNA USE IT AGAIN AT THE END, HE'S ONLY GOT TWO MINUTES IN THE TANK.
WHETHER IT'S SOONER OR LATER... DOES IT REALLY MATTER?
YES, BECAUSE IT'S NOT THAT SIMPLE.
EACH GAME HAS A FLOW TO IT.
IT'S NEVER QUITE CLEAR WHETHER YOU ACTUALLY UNDERSTAND BASKETBALL OR NOT...

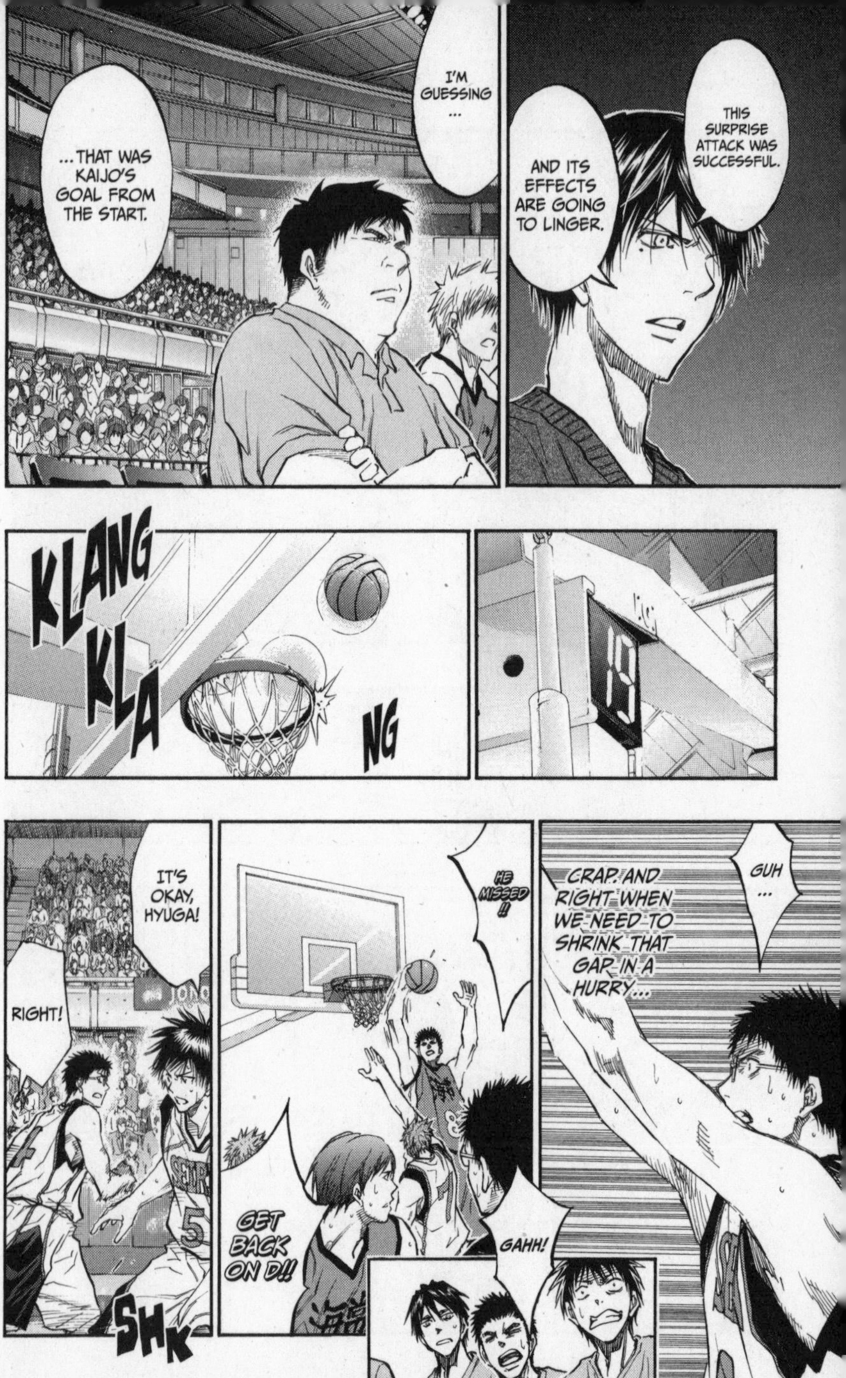
THIS SURPRISE ATTACK WAS SUCCESSFUL.
AND ITS EFFECTS ARE GOING TO LINGER.
I'M GUESSING ...
...THAT WAS KAIJO'S GOAL FROM THE START.
19
KLANG KLA NG
GUH ...
CRAP. AND RIGHT WHEN WE NEED TO SHRINK THAT GAP IN A HURRY...
GAHH!
HE MISSED !!
GET BACK ON D!!
IT'S OKAY, HYUGA!
RIGHT!
SHK

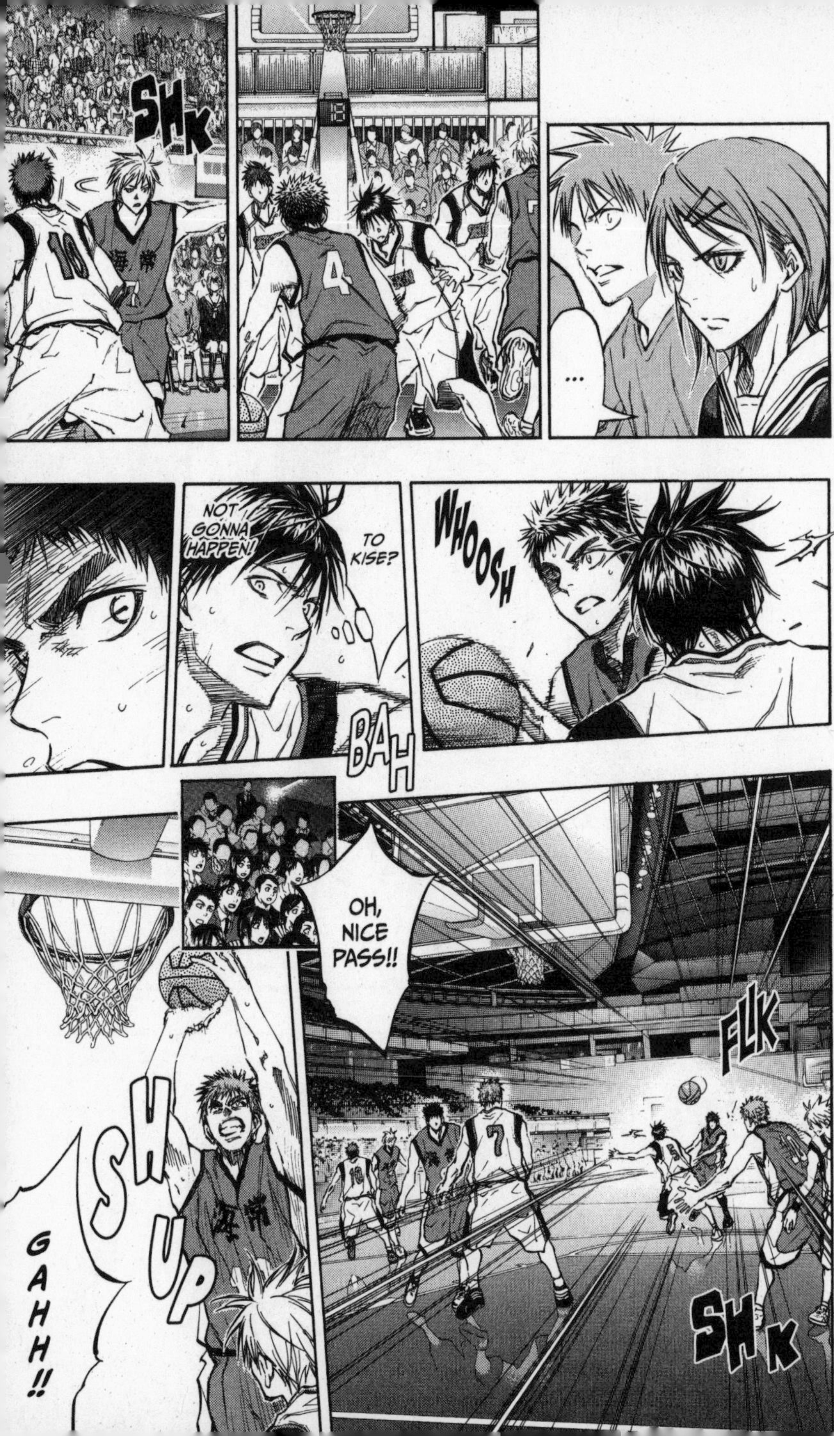
...
SHK
WHOOSH
TO KISE?
NOT GONNA HAPPEN!
BAH
OH, NICE PASS!!
FLIK
SHK
SHUP
GAHH!!

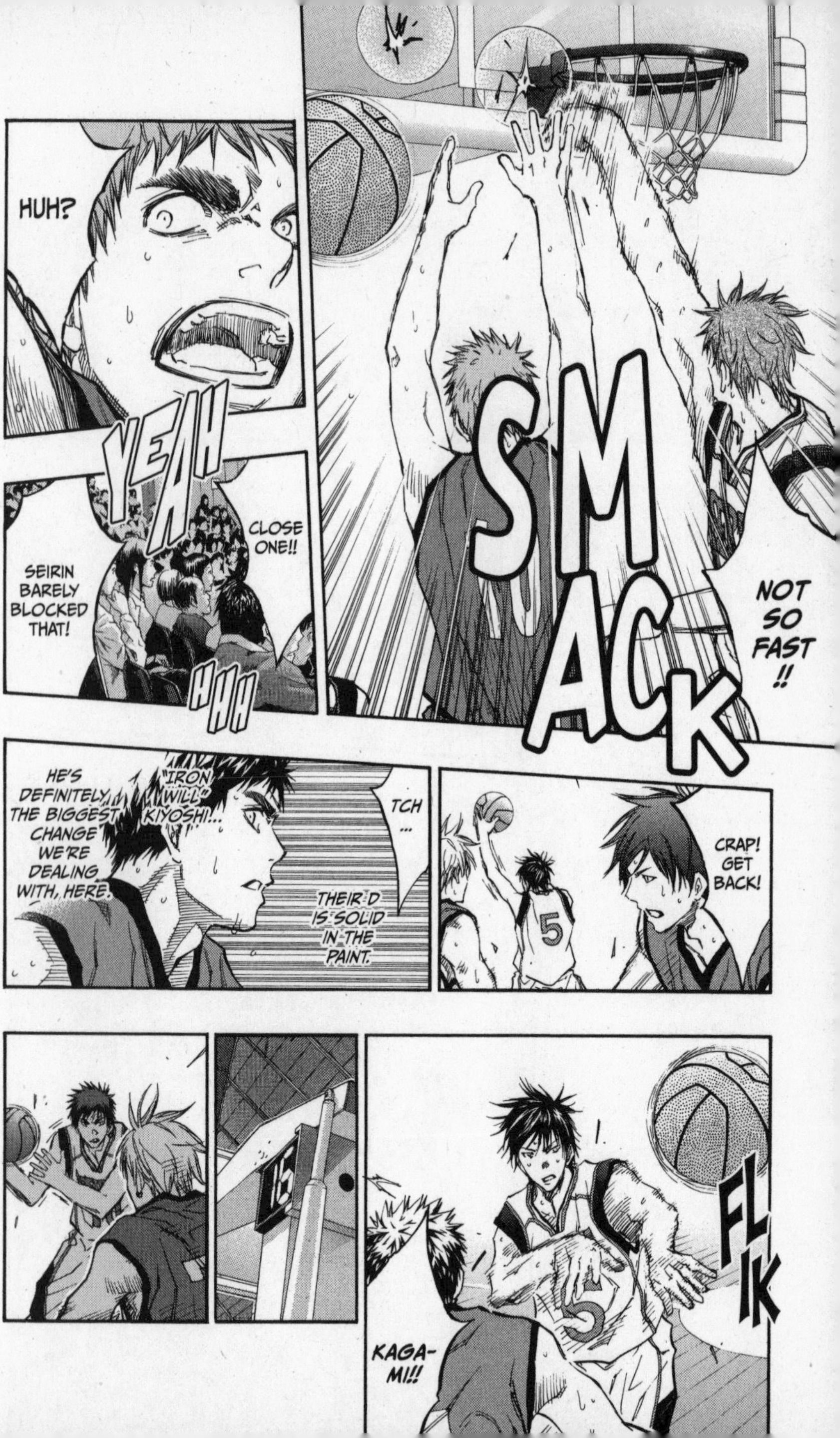

SMACK
NOT SO FAST!!
HUH?
YEAH
CLOSE ONE!!
SEIRIN BARELY BLOCKED THAT!
HHH
CRAP! GET BACK!
TCH...
THEIR D IS SOLID IN THE PAINT.
"IRON WILL" KIYOSHI...
HE'S DEFINITELY THE BIGGEST CHANGE WE'RE DEALING WITH, HERE.
FLIK
KAGAMI!!
15

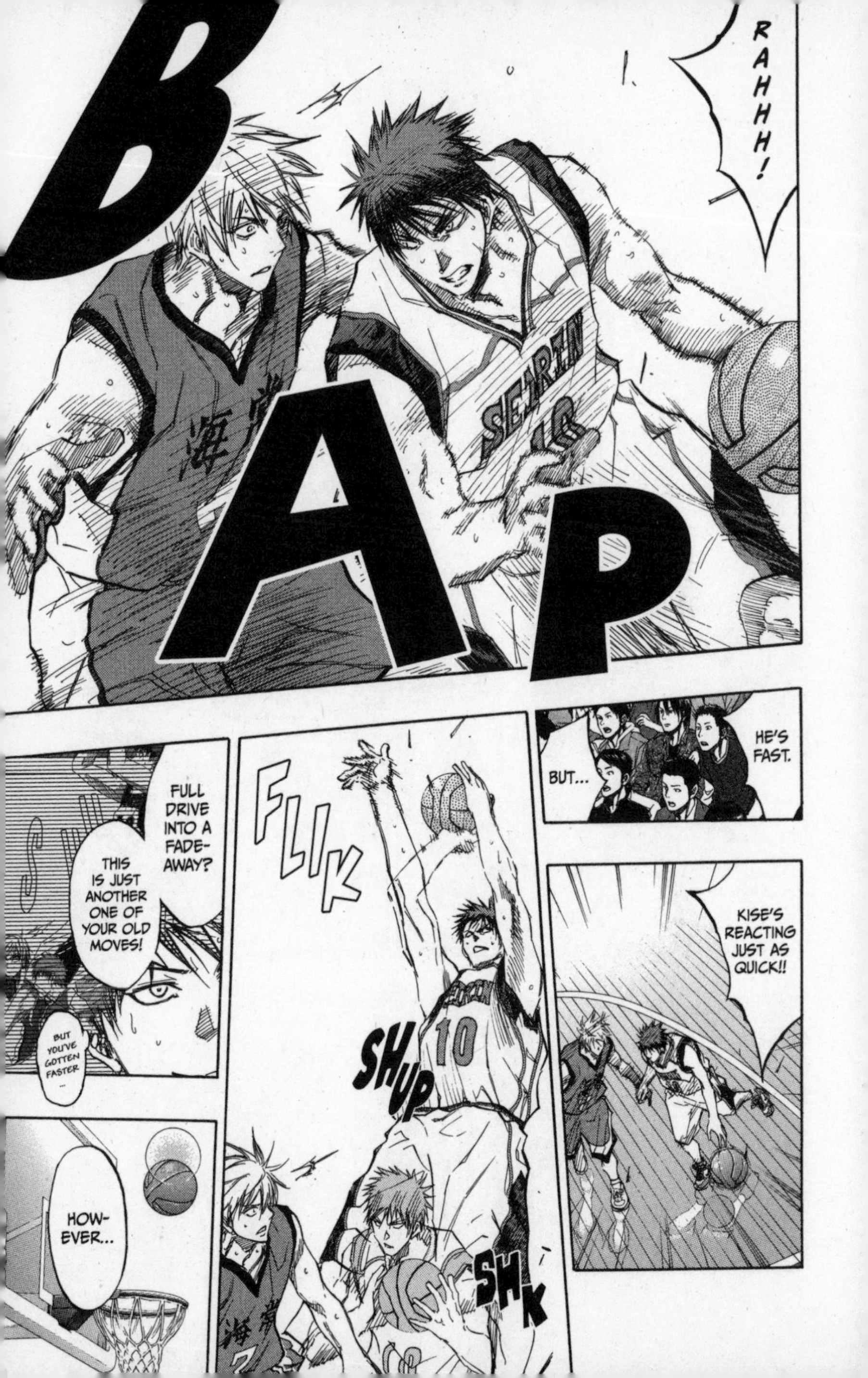
RAHHHH!
BAP
HE'S FAST.
BUT...
KISE'S REACTING JUST AS QUICK!!
FLIK
SHUP
SHK
FULL DRIVE INTO A FADE-AWAY?
THIS IS JUST ANOTHER ONE OF YOUR OLD MOVES!
BUT YOU'VE GOTTEN FASTER...
HOW-EVER...

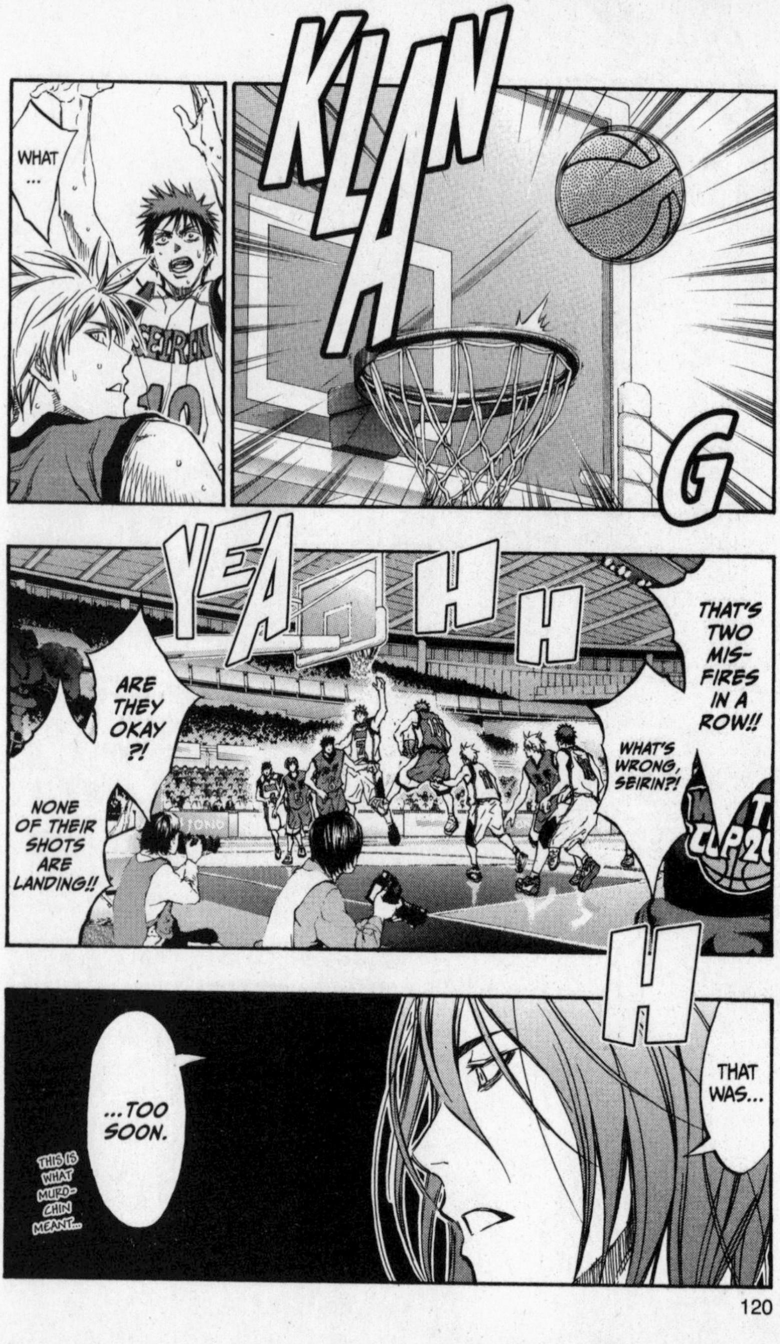
KLANG
WHAT ...
YEAHHHH
THAT'S TWO MIS-FIRES IN A ROW!!
WHAT'S WRONG, SEIRIN?!
ARE THEY OKAY ?!
NONE OF THEIR SHOTS ARE LANDING!!
THAT WAS...
...TOO SOON.
THIS IS WHAT MURO-CHIN MEANT...

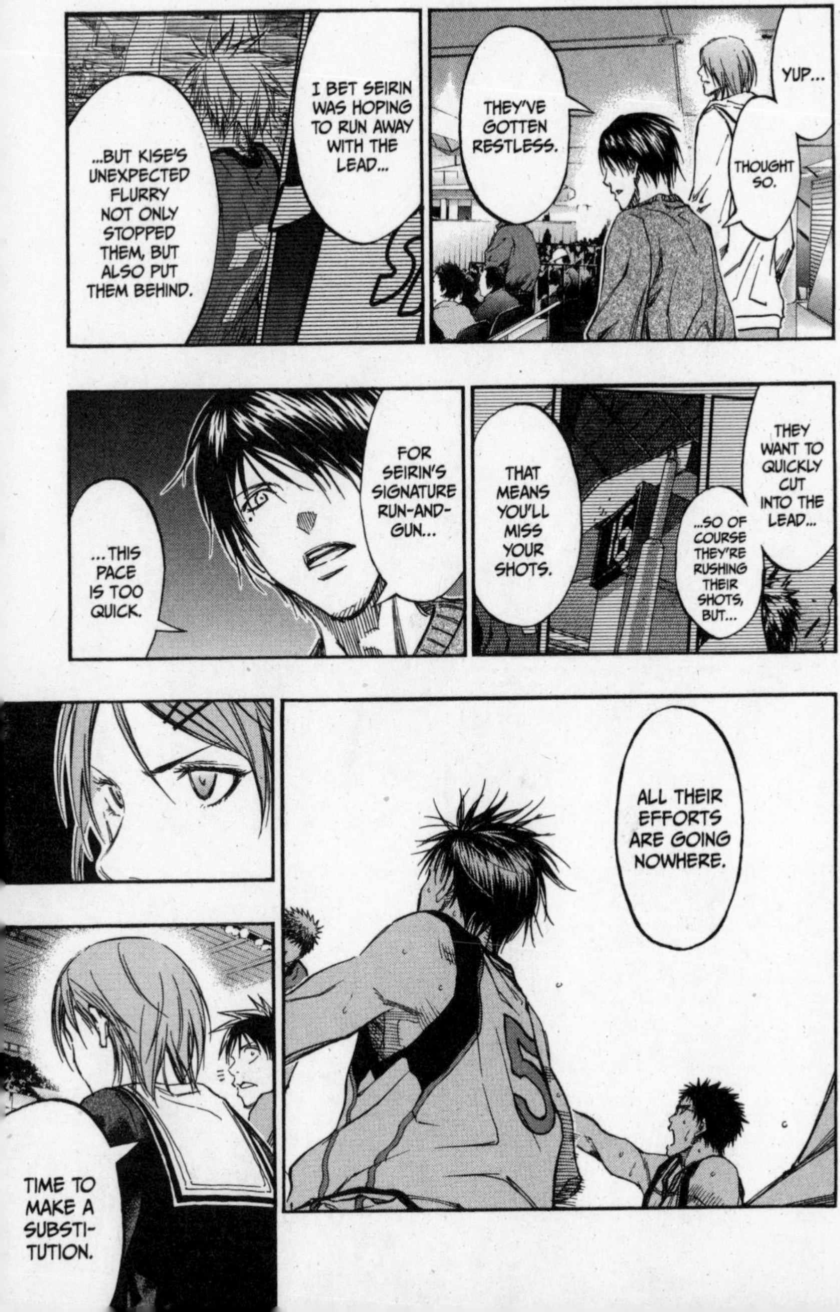
YUP...
THOUGHT SO.
THEY'VE GOTTEN RESTLESS.
I BET SEIRIN WAS HOPING TO RUN AWAY WITH THE LEAD...
...BUT KISE'S UNEXPECTED FLURRY NOT ONLY STOPPED THEM, BUT ALSO PUT THEM BEHIND.
THEY WANT TO QUICKLY CUT INTO THE LEAD...
...SO OF COURSE THEY'RE RUSHING THEIR SHOTS, BUT...
THAT MEANS YOU'LL MISS YOUR SHOTS.
FOR SEIRIN'S SIGNATURE RUN-AND-GUN...
...THIS PACE IS TOO QUICK.
ALL THEIR EFFORTS ARE GOING NOWHERE.
TIME TO MAKE A SUBSTI-TUTION.

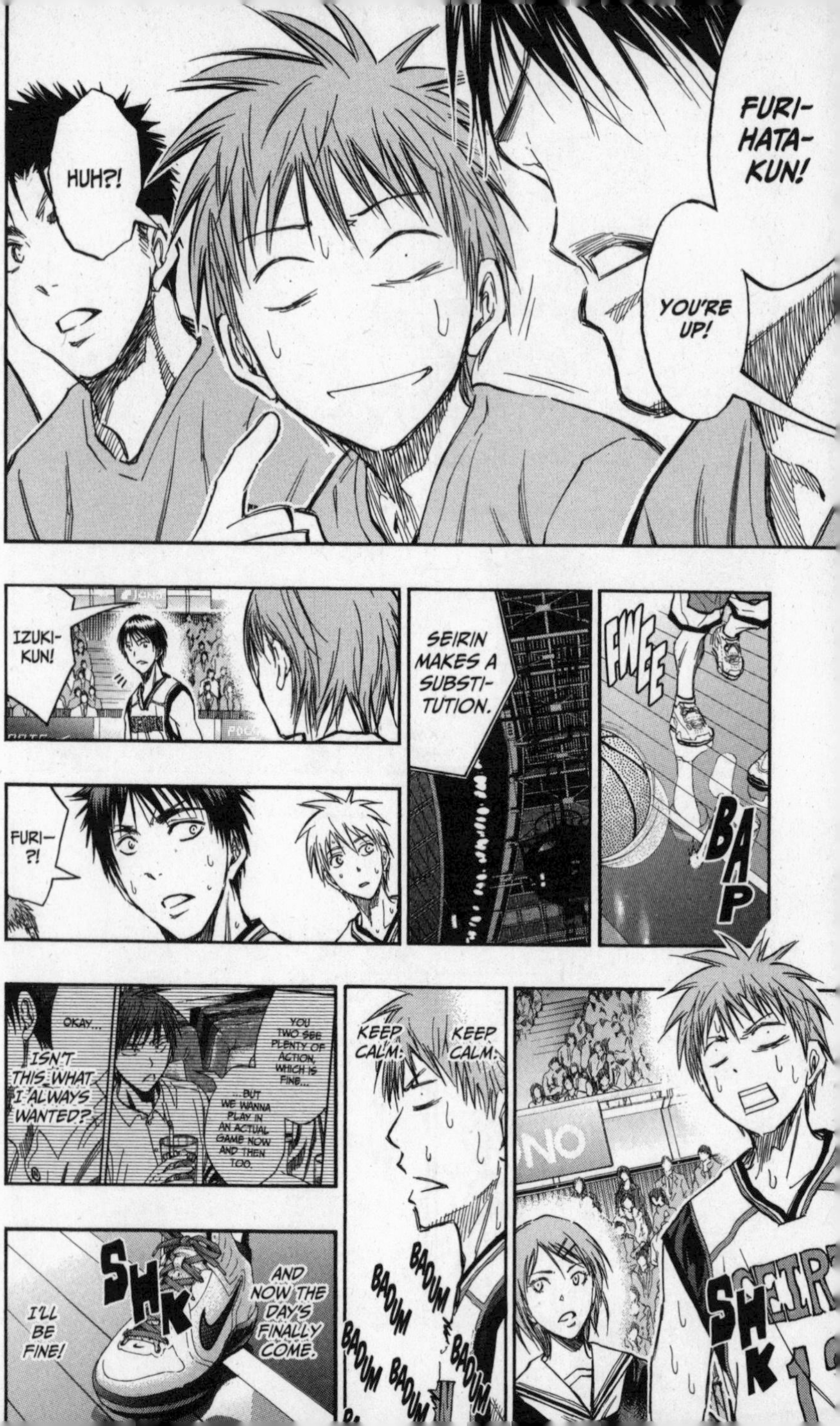
FURI-HATA-KUN!
YOU'RE UP!
HUH?!
FWEE
BAP
SEIRIN MAKES A SUBSTI-TUTION.
IZUKI-KUN!
FURI-?!
SHK
KEEP CALM.
KEEP CALM.
BADUM BADUM BADUM BADUM BADUM BADUM BADUM BADUM
YOU TWO SEE PLENTY OF ACTION, WHICH IS FINE...
...BUT WE WANNA PLAY IN AN ACTUAL GAME NOW AND THEN TOO.
OKAY...
ISN'T THIS WHAT I ALWAYS WANTED?
AND NOW THE DAY'S FINALLY COME.
SHK
I'LL BE FINE!

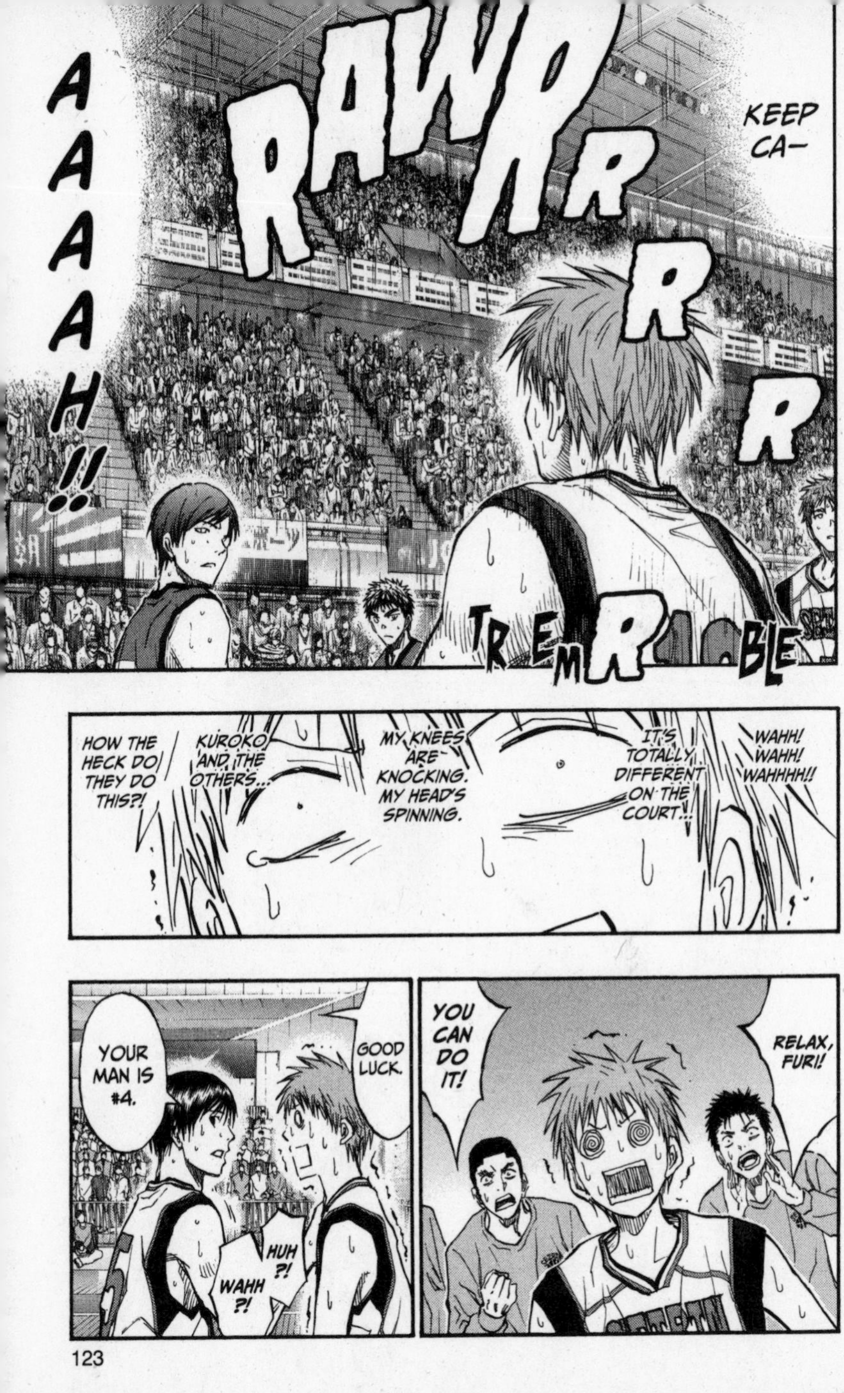
KEEP CA—
RAWRRRR
AAAAAH!!
TREMRRBLE
WAHH! WAHH! WAHHHH!!
IT'S TOTALLY DIFFERENT ON THE COURT...
MY KNEES ARE KNOCKING. MY HEAD'S SPINNING.
KUROKO AND THE OTHERS...
HOW THE HECK DO THEY DO THIS?!
RELAX, FURI!
YOU CAN DO IT!
GOOD LUCK.
YOUR MAN IS #4.
HUH?!
WAHH?!

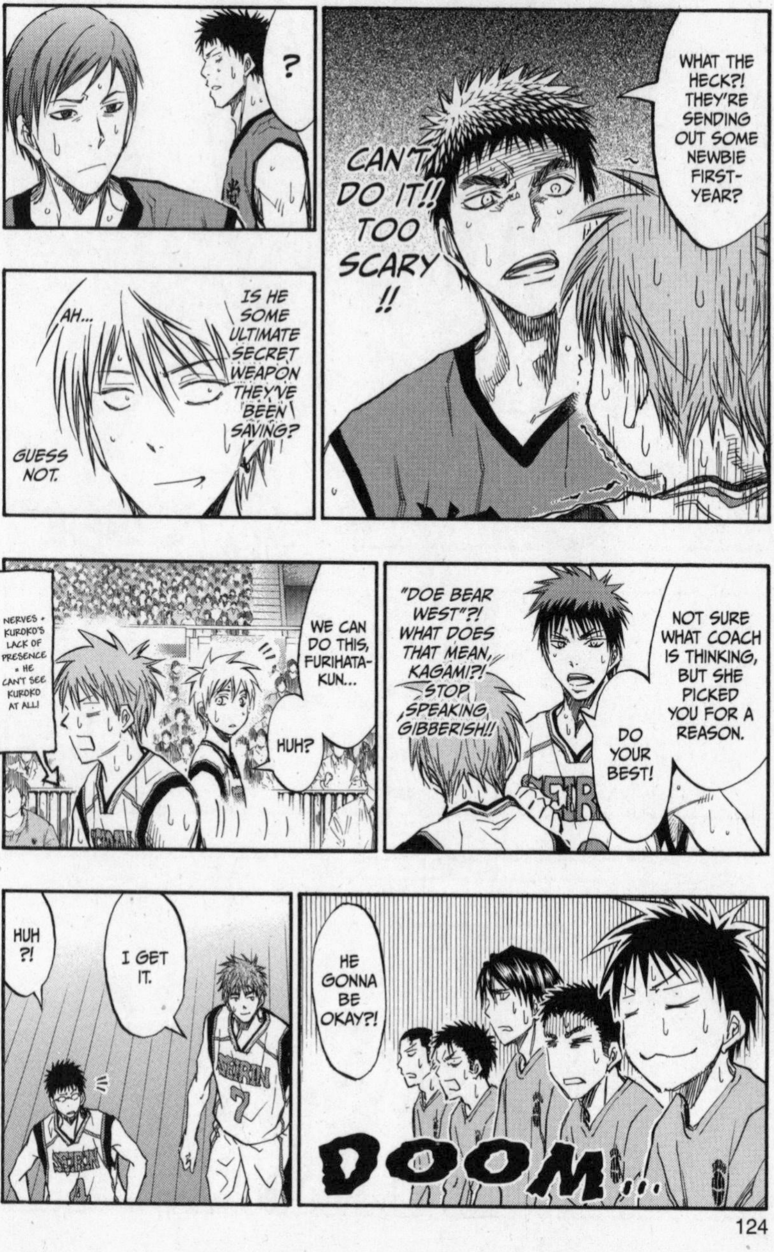
WHAT THE HECK?! THEY'RE SENDING OUT SOME NEWBIE FIRST-YEAR?
CAN'T DO IT!! TOO SCARY!!
?
IS HE SOME ULTIMATE SECRET WEAPON THEY'VE BEEN SAVING?
AH...
GUESS NOT.
NOT SURE WHAT COACH IS THINKING, BUT SHE PICKED YOU FOR A REASON.
DO YOUR BEST!
"DOE BEAR WEST"?! WHAT DOES THAT MEAN, KAGAMI?! STOP SPEAKING GIBBERISH!!
WE CAN DO THIS, FURIHATA-KUN...
HUH?
NERVES + KUROKO'S LACK OF PRESENCE = HE CAN'T SEE KUROKO AT ALL!
HE GONNA BE OKAY?!
DOOM...
I GET IT.
HUH?!

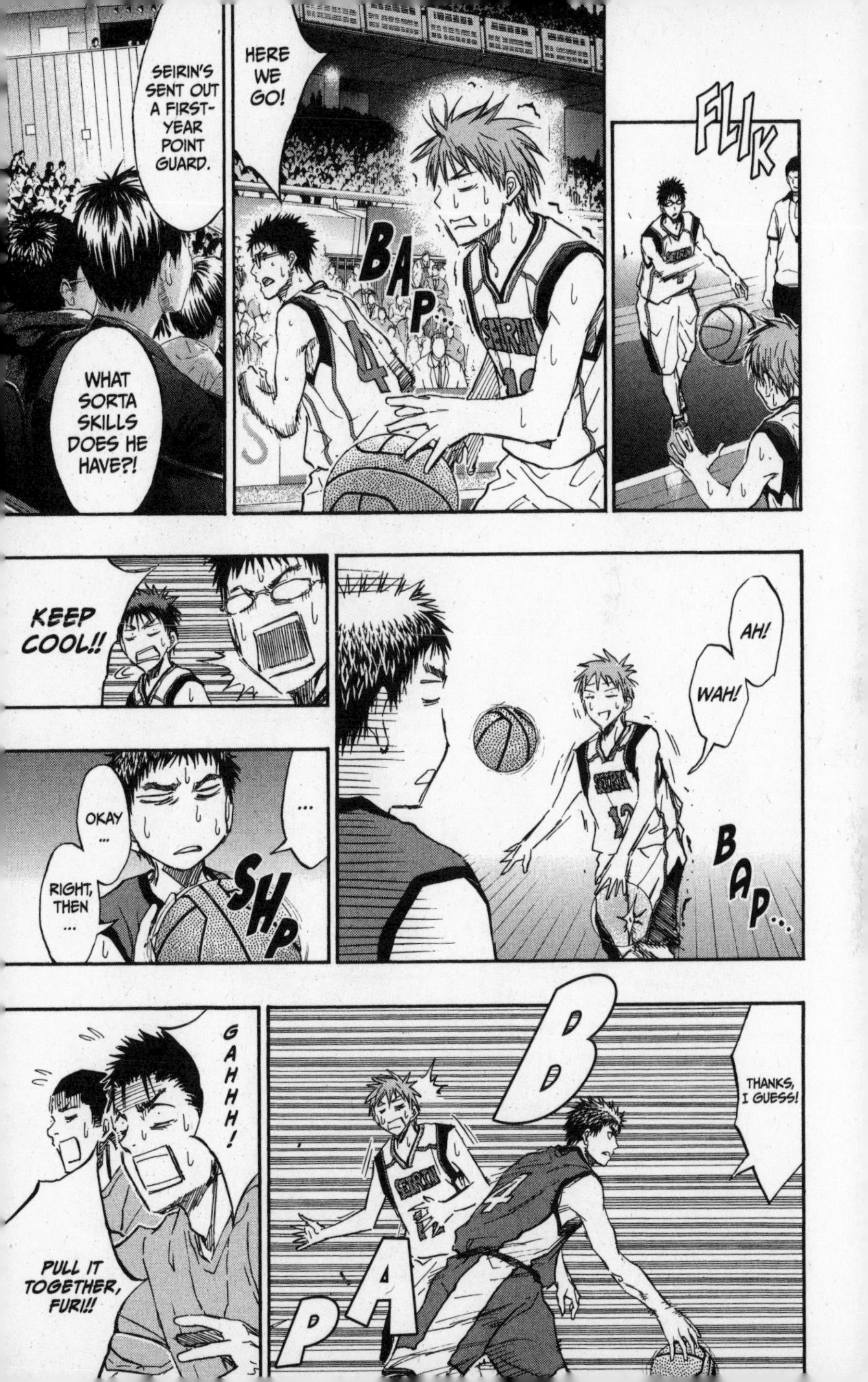
FLIK
HERE WE GO!
BAP...
SEIRIN'S SENT OUT A FIRST-YEAR POINT GUARD.
WHAT SORTA SKILLS DOES HE HAVE?!
AH!
WAH!
BAP...
KEEP COOL!!
...
OKAY ...
RIGHT, THEN ...
SHP
THANKS, I GUESS!
BAP
GAHHHH!
PULL IT TOGETHER, FURI!!

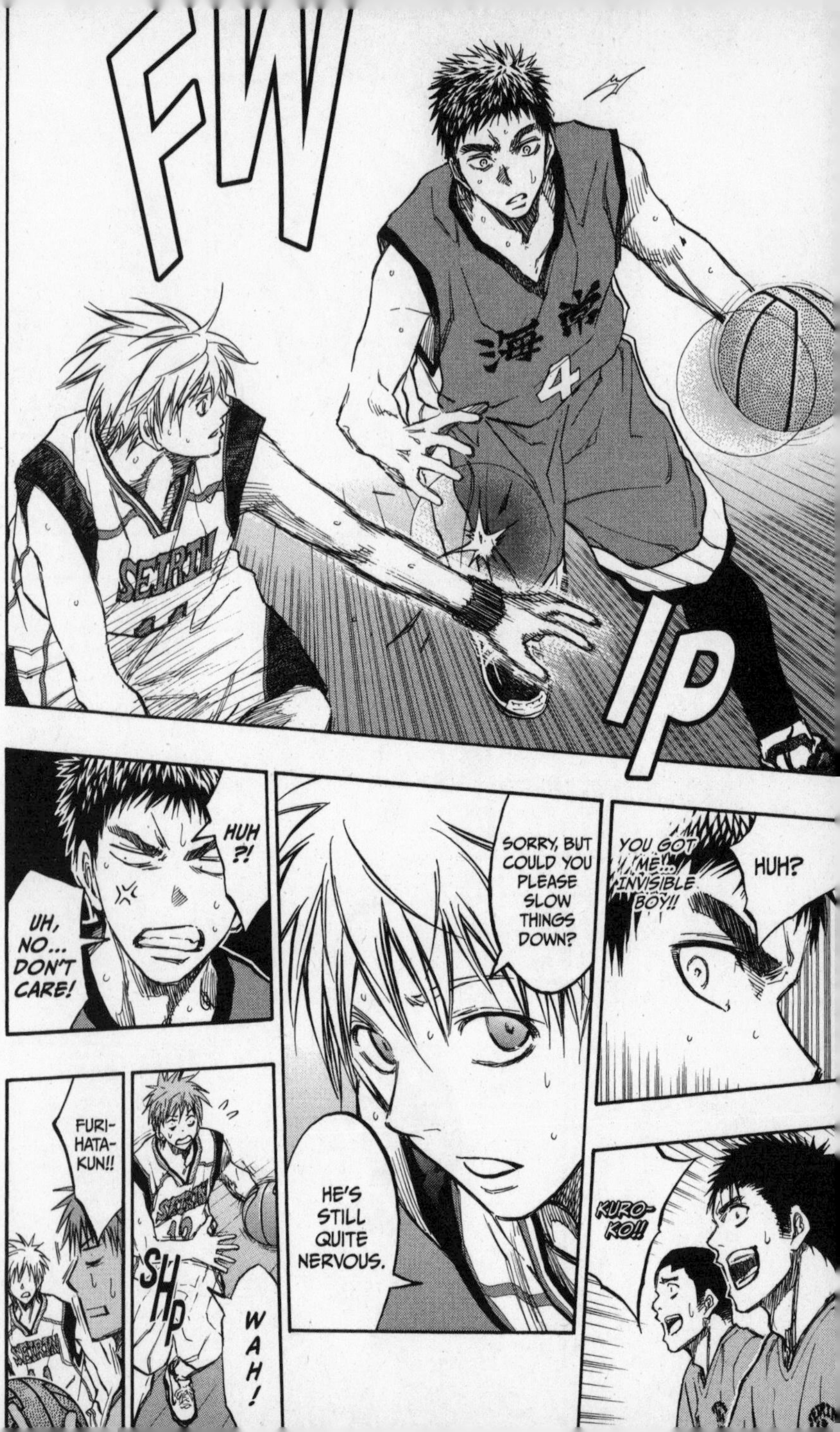
FW
IP
HUH?
YOU GOT ME... INVISIBLE BOY!!
KURO-KO!!
SORRY, BUT COULD YOU PLEASE SLOW THINGS DOWN?
HE'S STILL QUITE NERVOUS.
HUH ?!
UH, NO... DON'T CARE!
FURI-HATA-KUN!!
SHP
WAH!

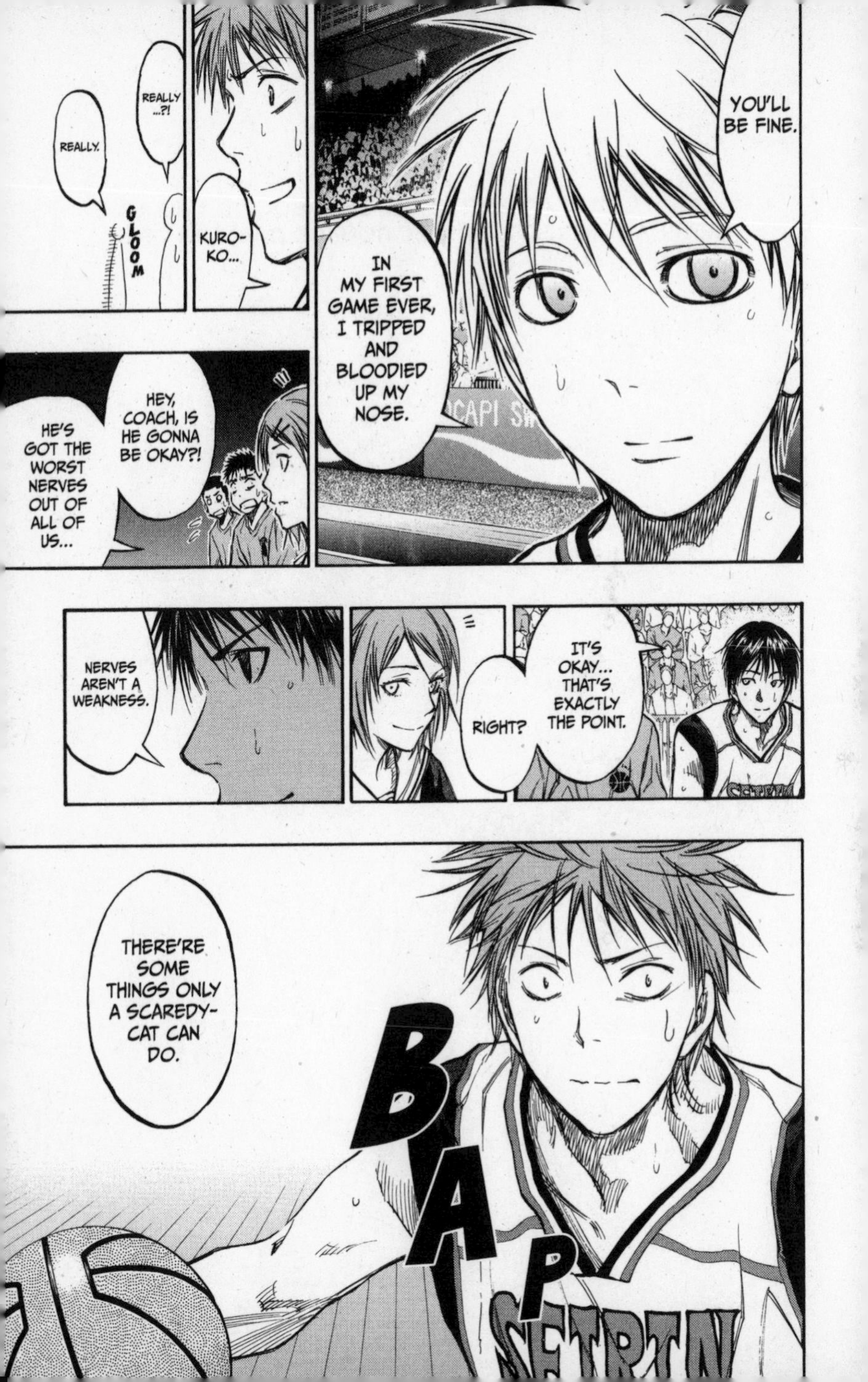

YOU'LL BE FINE.
IN MY FIRST GAME EVER, I TRIPPED AND BLOODIED UP MY NOSE.
KURO-KO...
REALLY ...?!
REALLY.
GLOOM
HEY, COACH, IS HE GONNA BE OKAY?!
HE'S GOT THE WORST NERVES OUT OF ALL OF US...
IT'S OKAY... THAT'S EXACTLY THE POINT.
RIGHT?
NERVES AREN'T A WEAKNESS.
THERE'RE SOME THINGS ONLY A SCAREDY-CAT CAN DO.
BAP

KUROKO'S BASKETBALL

Q&A

W/ HALFWAY-DECENT ANSWERS

Q. **AKASHI DIDN'T APPEAR IN THE DATA BOOK'S "MIRACLE GENERATION SECRETS" SECTION, SO CAN YOU GIVE US HIS ANSWERS?!**
(SAE from OSAKA)

A. Q1: HOW DO YOU SPEND YOUR DAYS OFF?
A: I TEND TO RIDE HORSES A LOT.

Q2: WHAT GOT YOU INTO BASKETBALL?
A: WHAT APPEALED TO ME WAS HOW THE SPORT REQUIRES BOTH INTELLIGENCE AND TECHNIQUE.

Q3: WHO IN THE MIRACLE GENERATION ARE YOU CLOSEST TO?
A: SHINTARO, PERHAPS. WE SPENT A LOT OF TIME TOGETHER RUNNING THE CLUB.

Q4: FOR THAT MATTER, WHO IN THE MIRACLE GENERATION DO YOU DISLIKE THE MOST?
A: NONE OF THEM IN PARTICULAR. IF FORCED TO SAY, DAIKI. I OFTEN WOUND UP CLASHING WITH HIS WILD SIDE.

Q5: WHAT'S YOUR FAVORITE MEMORY FROM MIDDLE SCHOOL?
A: NOTHING SPECIFIC, BUT JUST SPENDING TIME WITH THE BASKETBALL TEAM.

Q6: WHO ARE YOU CLOSEST TO ON YOUR CURRENT TEAM?
A: I WOULDN'T NECESSARILY SAY "CLOSEST," BUT I'VE HAD PLENTY OF OCCASIONS TO TALK WITH REO.

Q7: WHAT'S YOUR TYPE?
A: I PREFER REFINED, CLASSY WOMEN.

Q8: WHAT DO YOU ENJOY MOST, BESIDES BASKETBALL?
A: I RELAX BY PLAYING SHOGI. IT'S FUN WHETHER I HAVE AN OPPONENT OR NOT.

Q9: WHAT ARE YOU BAD AT?
A: NOTHING, REALLY.

Q10: WHAT IS BASKETBALL TO YOU?
A: A WAY TO IMPROVE MYSELF.

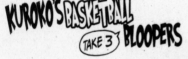

KUROKO'S BASKETBALL BLOOPERS

TAKE 3

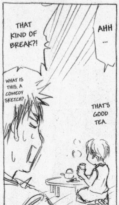

GUH! THIS IS ROUGH!
I'D BETTER TAKE A BREAK.
海常
GLUG GLUG
AHH ...
THAT KIND OF BREAK?!
WHAT IS THIS, A COMEDY SKETCH?
THAT'S GOOD TEA.

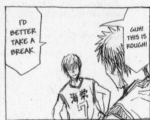

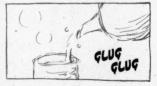

187TH QUARTER: YOU'VE GOT TEAMMATES

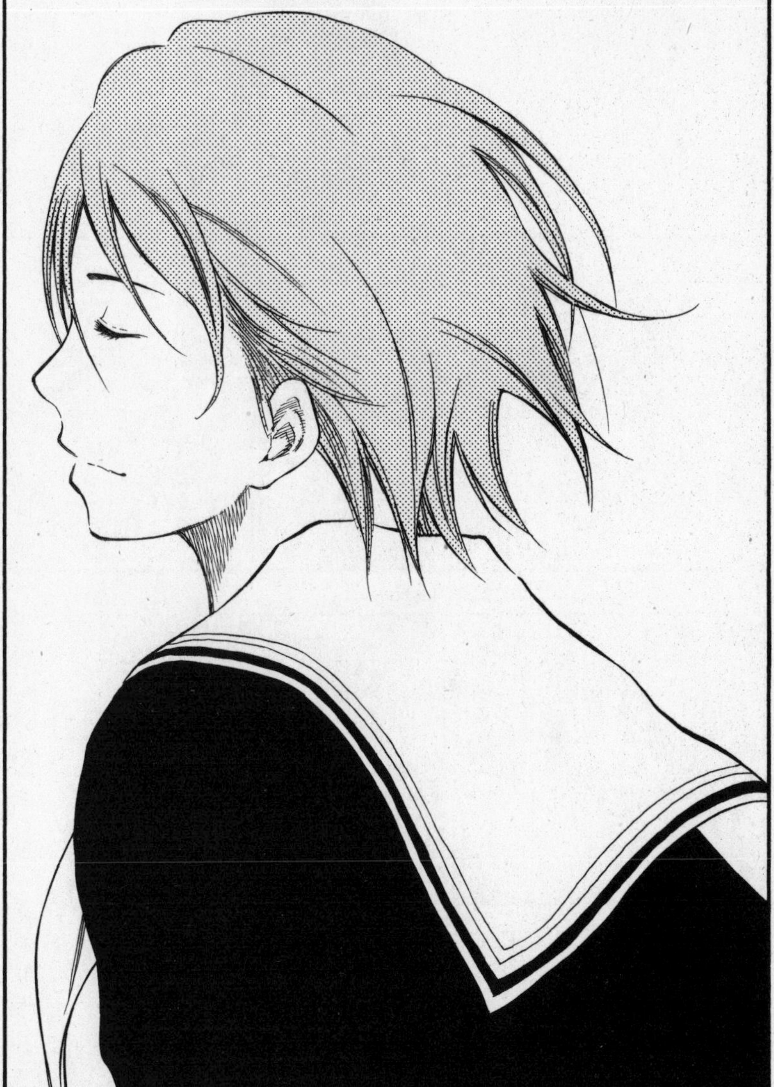

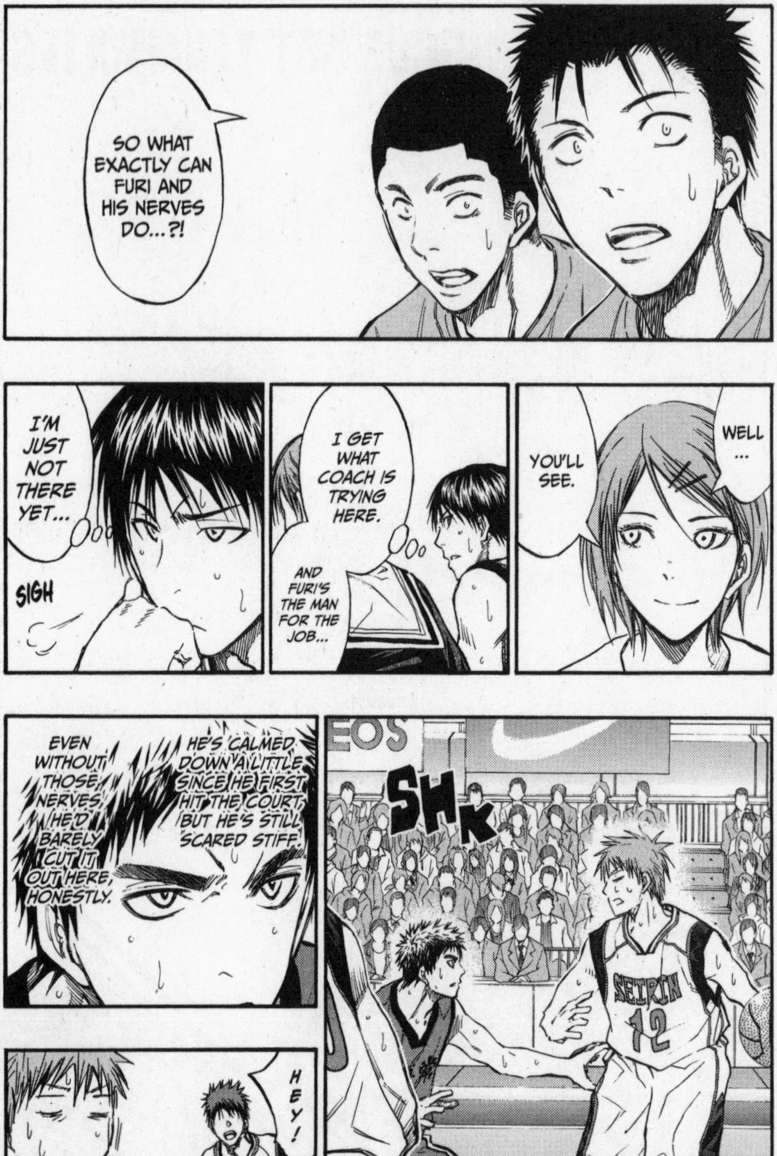
SO WHAT EXACTLY CAN FURI AND HIS NERVES DO...?!
WELL ...
YOU'LL SEE.
I GET WHAT COACH IS TRYING HERE.
AND FURI'S THE MAN FOR THE JOB...
I'M JUST NOT THERE YET...
SIGH
SHK
SEIRIN
12
HE'S CALMED DOWN A LITTLE SINCE HE FIRST HIT THE COURT, BUT HE'S STILL SCARED STIFF.
EVEN WITHOUT THOSE NERVES, HE'D BARELY CUT IT OUT HERE, HONESTLY.
HEY!

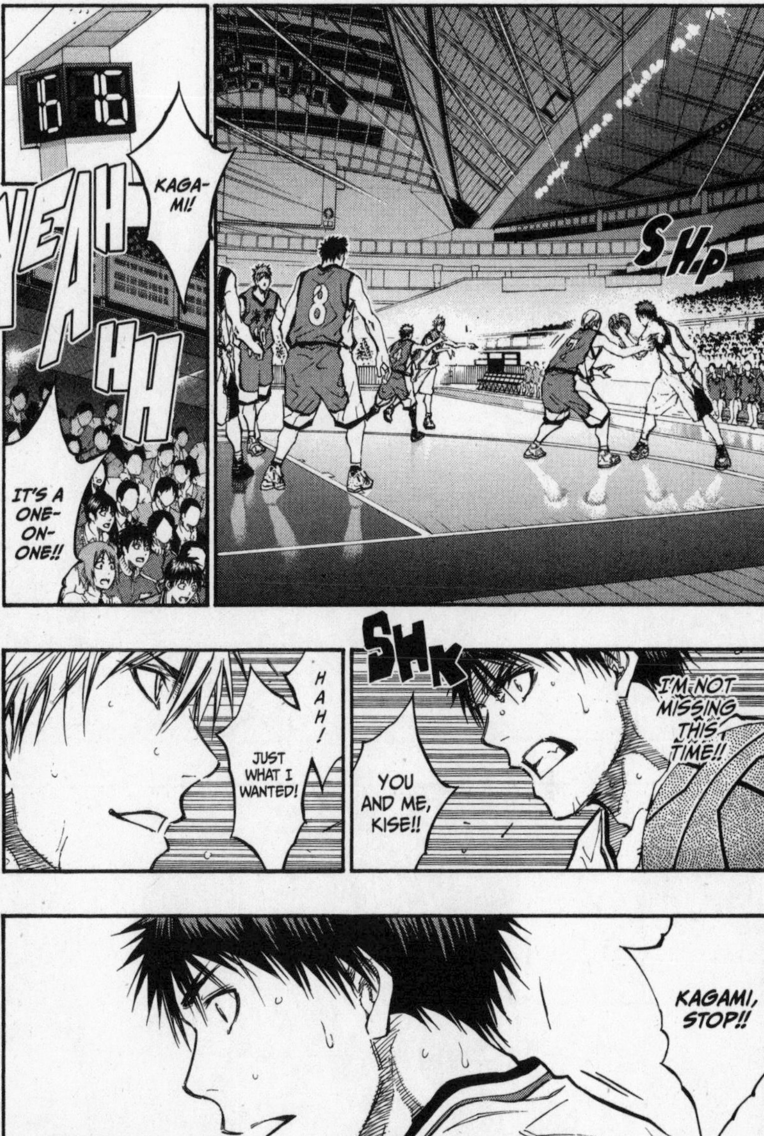
SHP
YEAHHH
KAGAMI!
IT'S A ONE-ON-ONE!!
SHK
I'M NOT MISSING THIS TIME!!
YOU AND ME, KISE!!
HAH!
JUST WHAT I WANTED!
KAGAMI, STOP!!

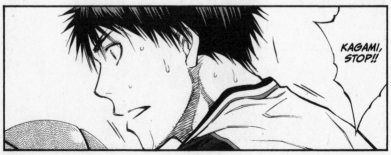

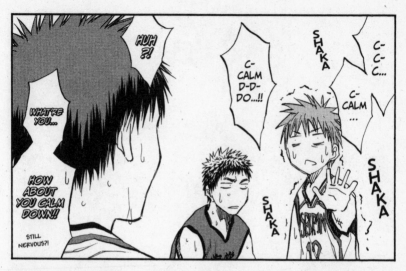

C- C- C...
SHAKA
C- CALM ...
SHAKA
C- CALM D-D- DO...!!
SHAKA
HUH ?!
WHAT'RE YOU...
HOW ABOUT YOU CALM DOWN!!
STILL NERVOUS?!
FWIP
NOT COMING AT ME?
SHUT UP. WE'RE TAKING IT BACK, FOR NOW.
HMPH ...
THIS IS...

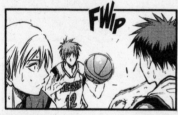

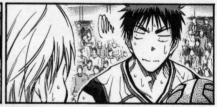

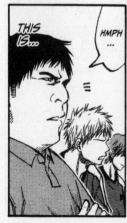

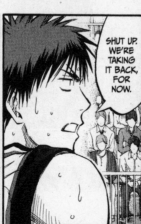

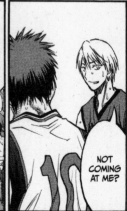

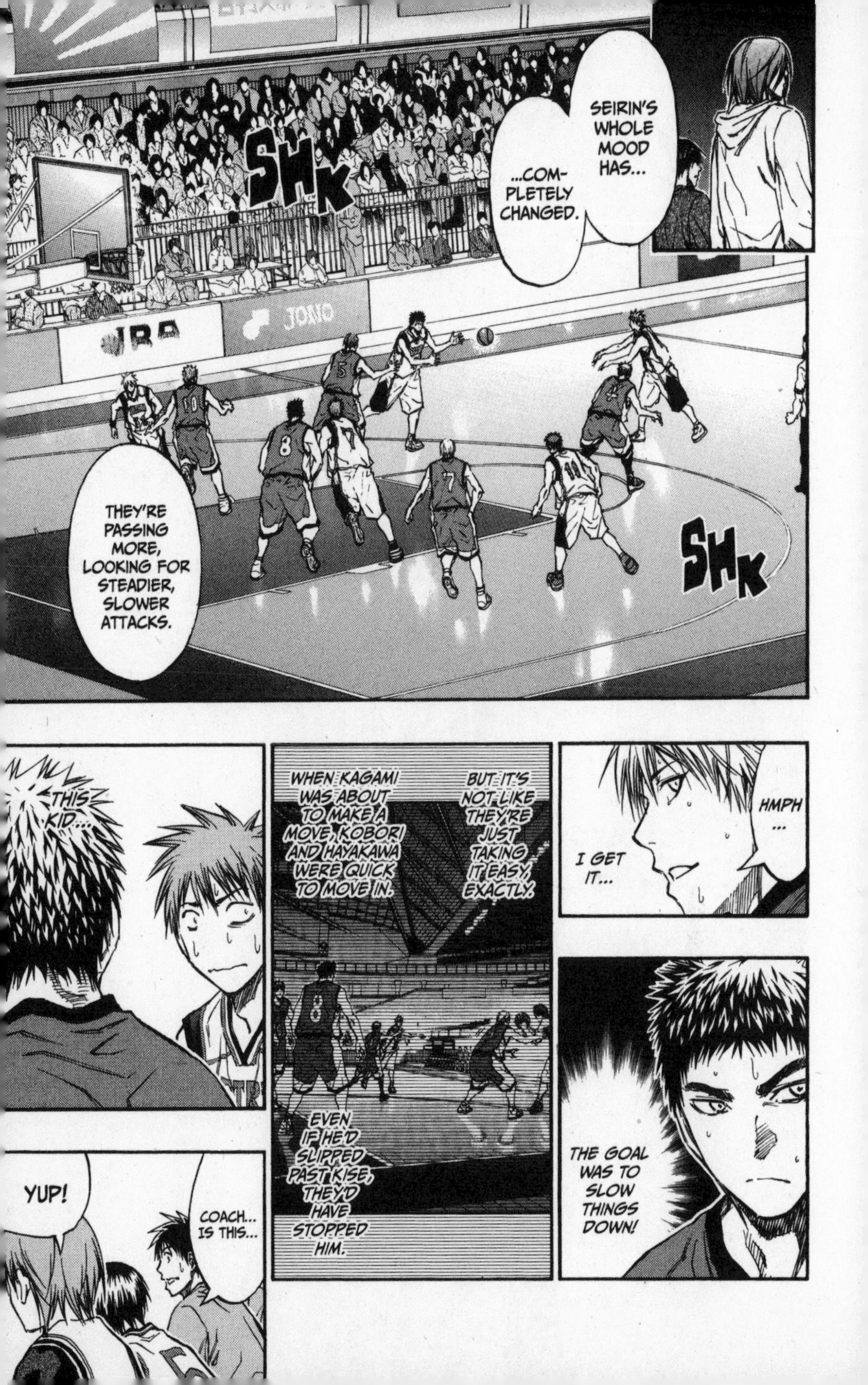
SEIRIN'S WHOLE MOOD HAS...
...COM-PLETELY CHANGED.
SHK
THEY'RE PASSING MORE, LOOKING FOR STEADIER, SLOWER ATTACKS.
SHK
HMPH...
I GET IT...
THE GOAL WAS TO SLOW THINGS DOWN!
BUT IT'S NOT LIKE THEY'RE JUST TAKING IT EASY, EXACTLY.
WHEN KAGAMI WAS ABOUT TO MAKE A MOVE, KOBORI AND HAYAKAWA WERE QUICK TO MOVE IN.
EVEN IF HE'D SLIPPED PAST KISE, THEY'D HAVE STOPPED HIM.
THIS KID...
COACH... IS THIS...
YUP!

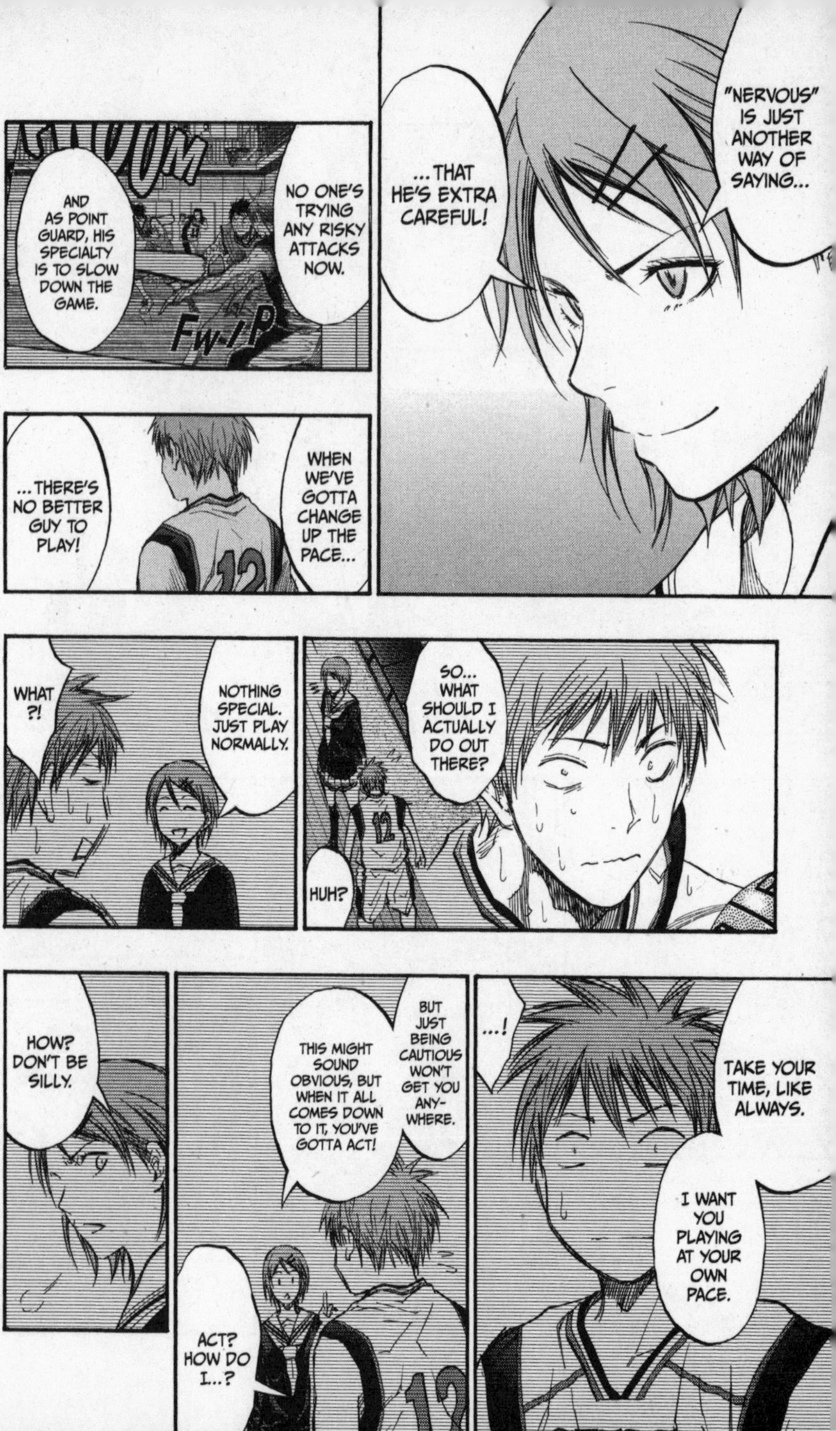
"NERVOUS" IS JUST ANOTHER WAY OF SAYING...
...THAT HE'S EXTRA CAREFUL!
NO ONE'S TRYING ANY RISKY ATTACKS NOW.
AND AS POINT GUARD, HIS SPECIALTY IS TO SLOW DOWN THE GAME.
FW-IP
WHEN WE'VE GOTTA CHANGE UP THE PACE...
...THERE'S NO BETTER GUY TO PLAY!
SO... WHAT SHOULD I ACTUALLY DO OUT THERE?
HUH?
NOTHING SPECIAL. JUST PLAY NORMALLY.
WHAT ?!
...!
TAKE YOUR TIME, LIKE ALWAYS.
I WANT YOU PLAYING AT YOUR OWN PACE.
BUT JUST BEING CAUTIOUS WON'T GET YOU ANY-WHERE.
THIS MIGHT SOUND OBVIOUS, BUT WHEN IT ALL COMES DOWN TO IT, YOU'VE GOTTA ACT!
ACT? HOW DO I...?
HOW? DON'T BE SILLY.

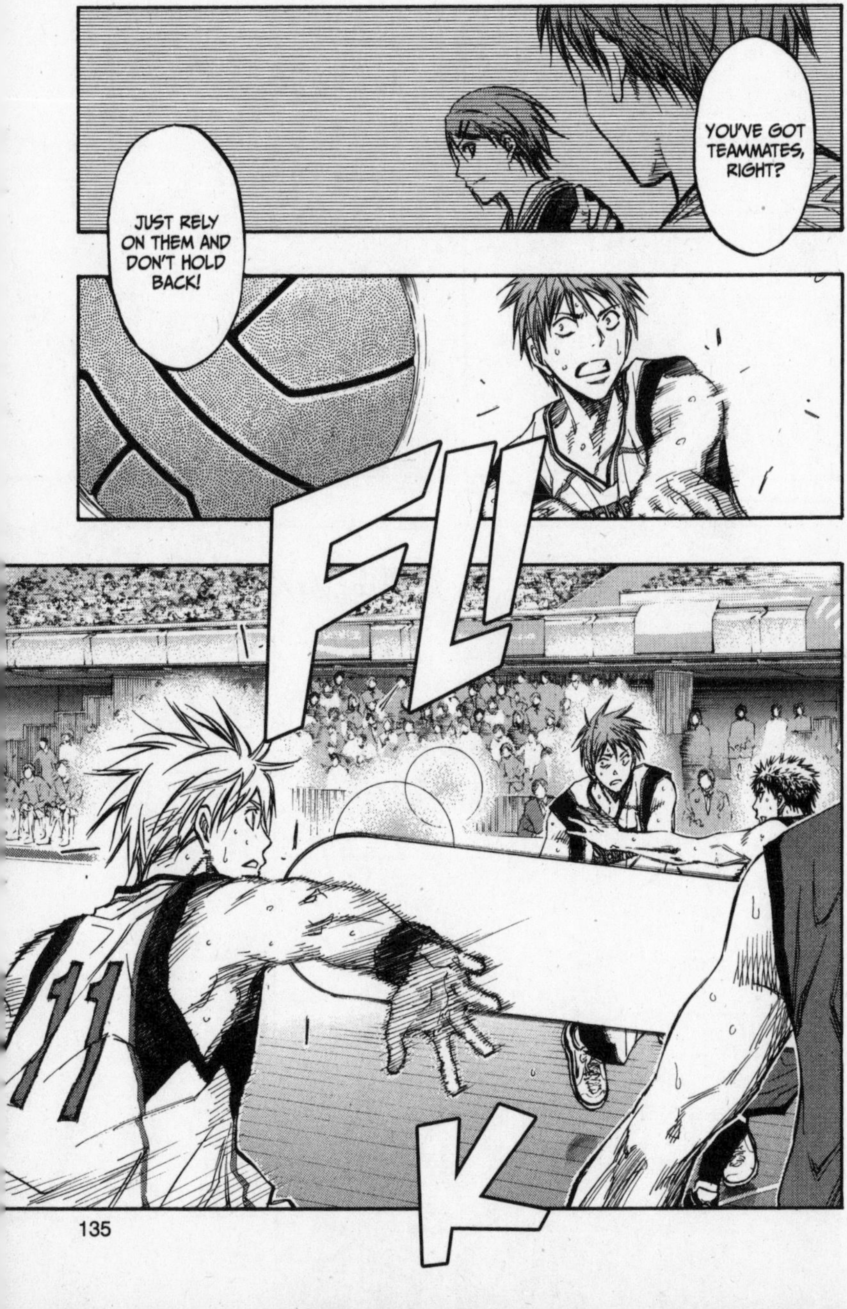
YOU'VE GOT TEAMMATES, RIGHT?
JUST RELY ON THEM AND DON'T HOLD BACK!
FLI
K

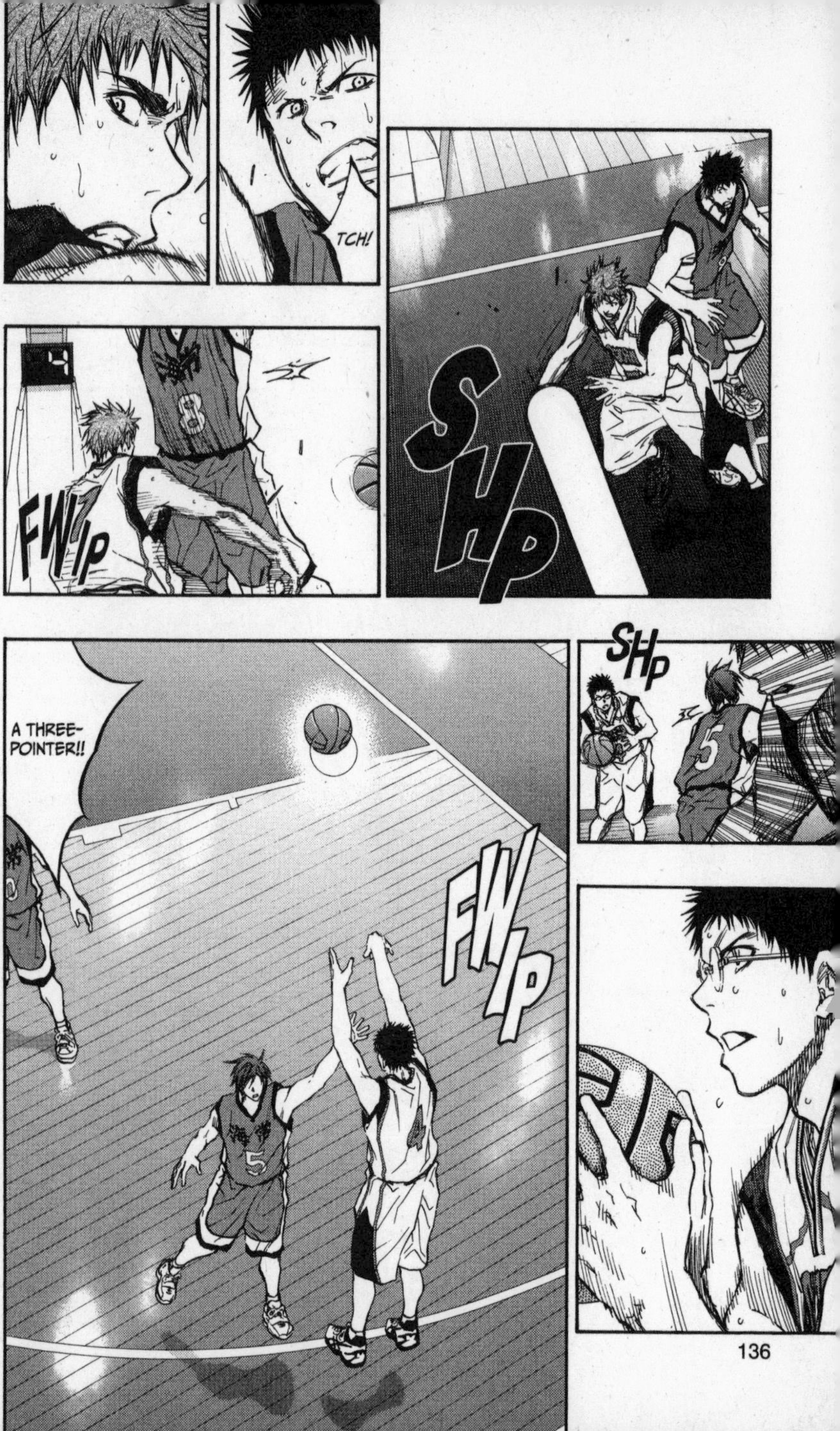
SHP
TCH!
FWIP
SHP
A THREE-POINTER!!
FWIP

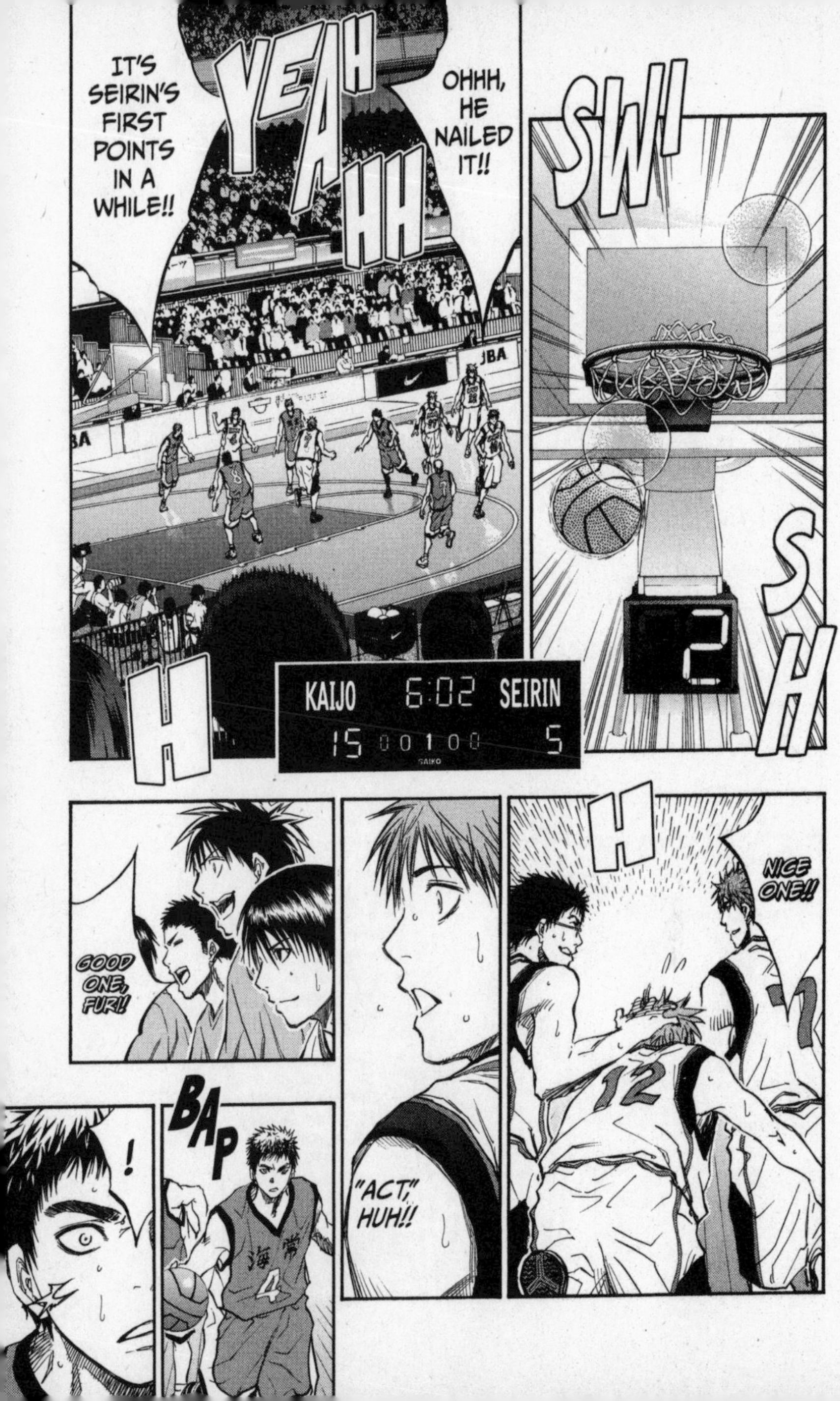
SWISH
OHHH, HE NAILED IT!!
IT'S SEIRIN'S FIRST POINTS IN A WHILE!!
YEAHHH
KAIJO 6:02 SEIRIN
15 00100 5
SAIKO
H
NICE ONE!!
"ACT," HUH!!
GOOD ONE, FURI!
BAP
!

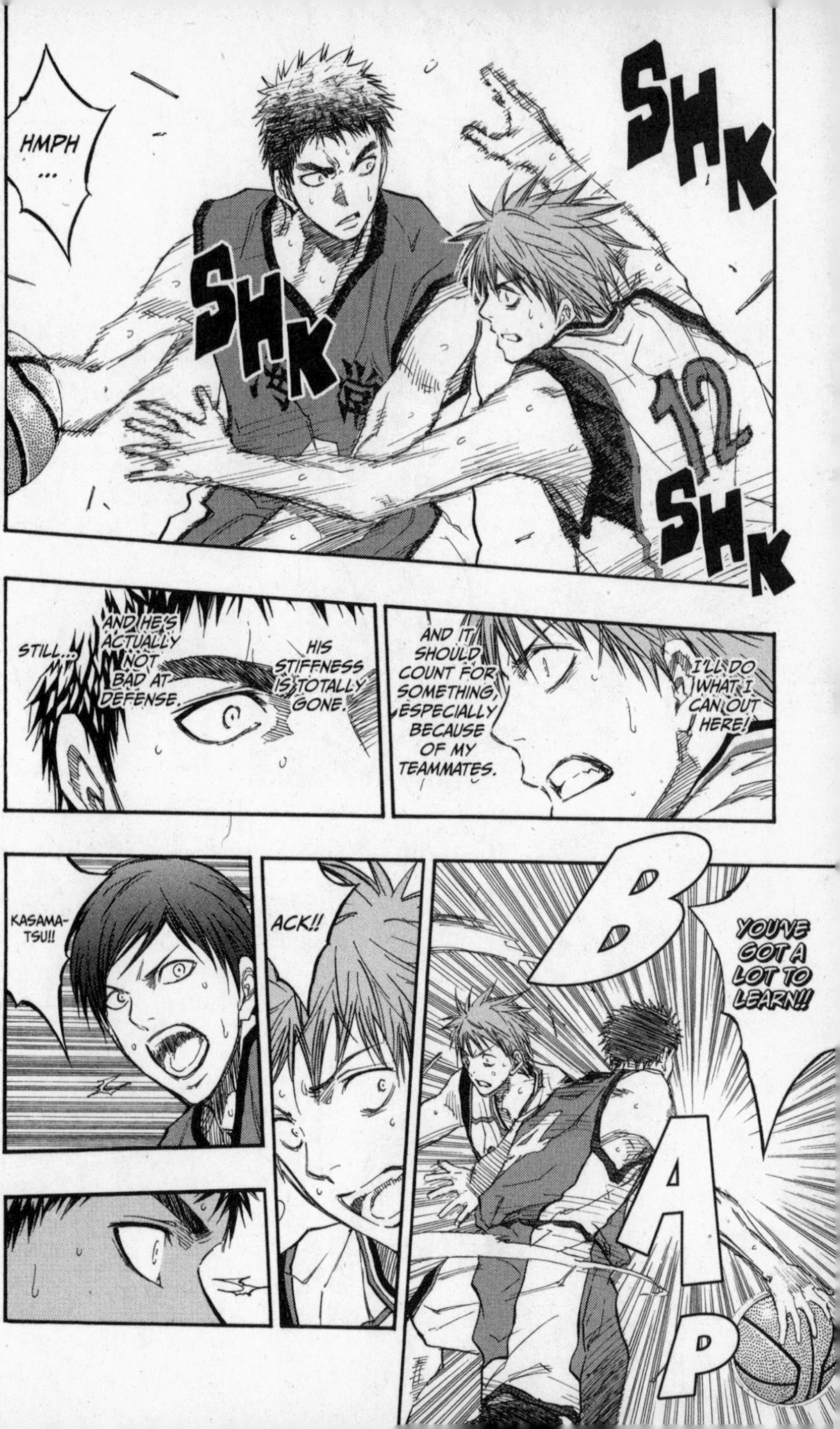
SHK
HMPH ...
SHK
SHK
I'LL DO WHAT I CAN OUT HERE!
AND IT SHOULD COUNT FOR SOMETHING, ESPECIALLY BECAUSE OF MY TEAMMATES.
HIS STIFFNESS IS TOTALLY GONE.
AND HE'S ACTUALLY NOT BAD AT DEFENSE.
STILL...
BAP
YOU'VE GOT A LOT TO LEARN!!
ACK!!
KASAMA-TSU!!

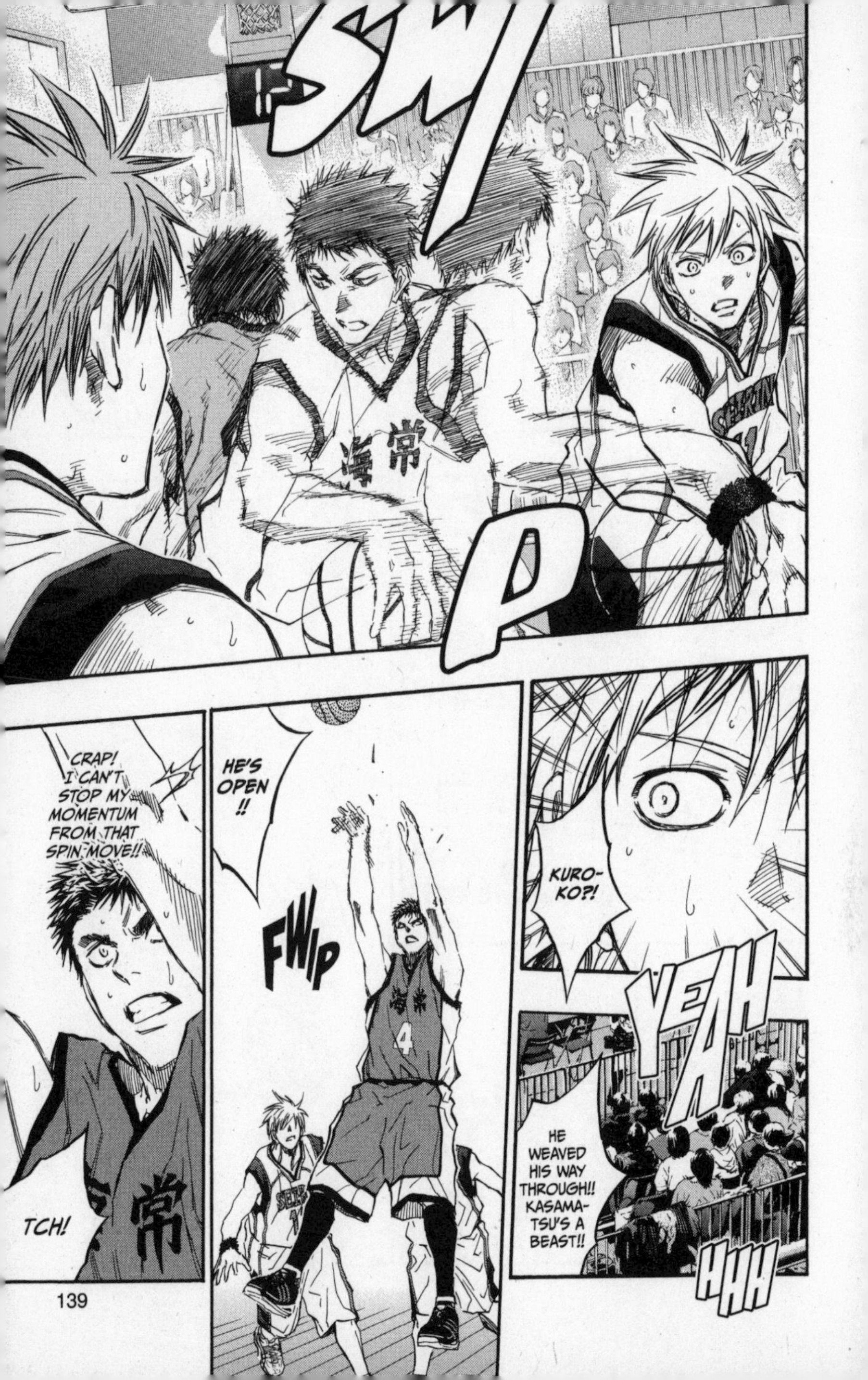
SWIP
KURO-KO?!
YEAH
HHH
HE WEAVED HIS WAY THROUGH!! KASAMATSU'S A BEAST!!
HE'S OPEN !!
FWIP
CRAP! I CAN'T STOP MY MOMENTUM FROM THAT SPIN MOVE!!
TCH!

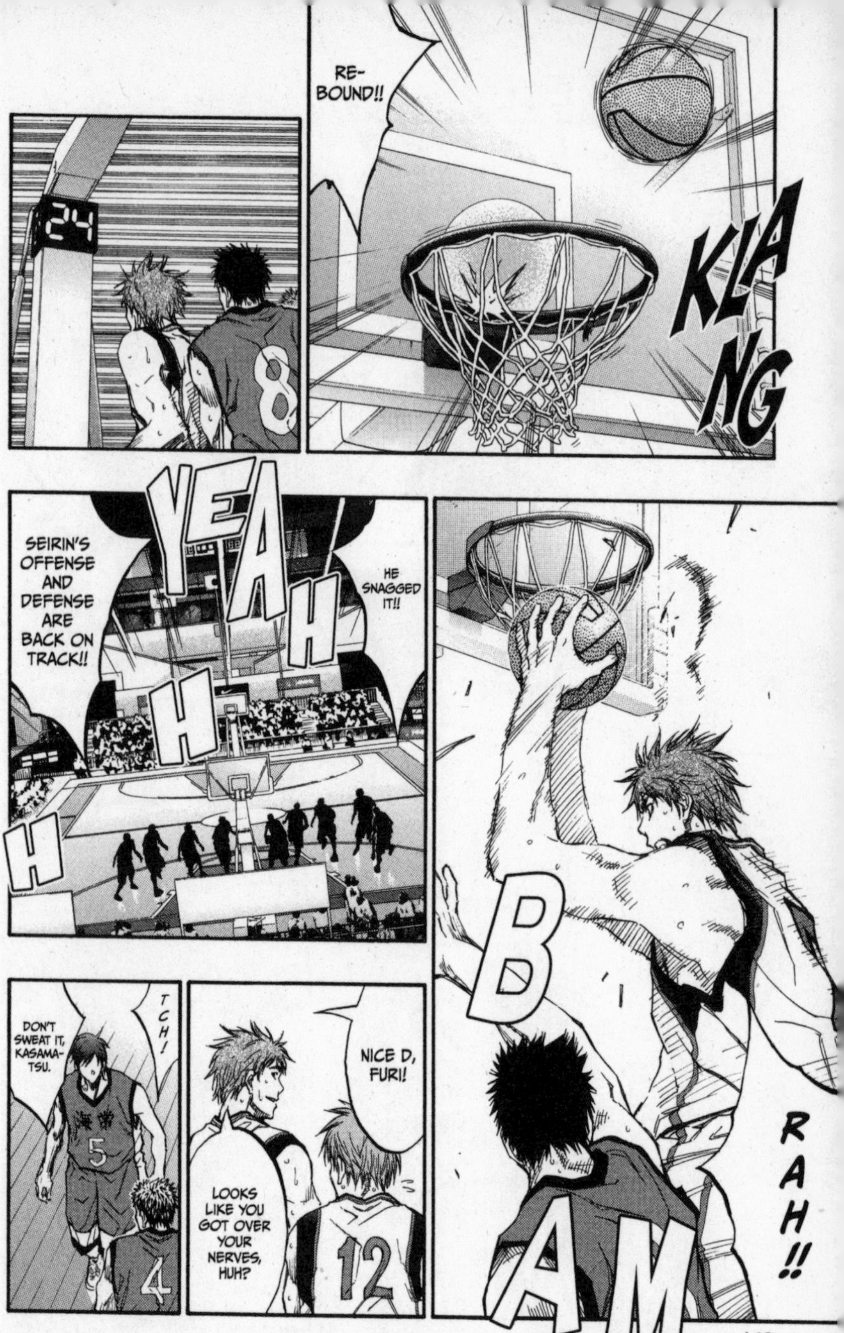

RE-BOUND!!
KLIANG
24
RAH!!
BAM
YEAHHHH
HE SNAGGED IT!!
SEIRIN'S OFFENSE AND DEFENSE ARE BACK ON TRACK!!
NICE D, FURI!
LOOKS LIKE YOU GOT OVER YOUR NERVES, HUH?
TCH!
DON'T SWEAT IT, KASAMATSU.

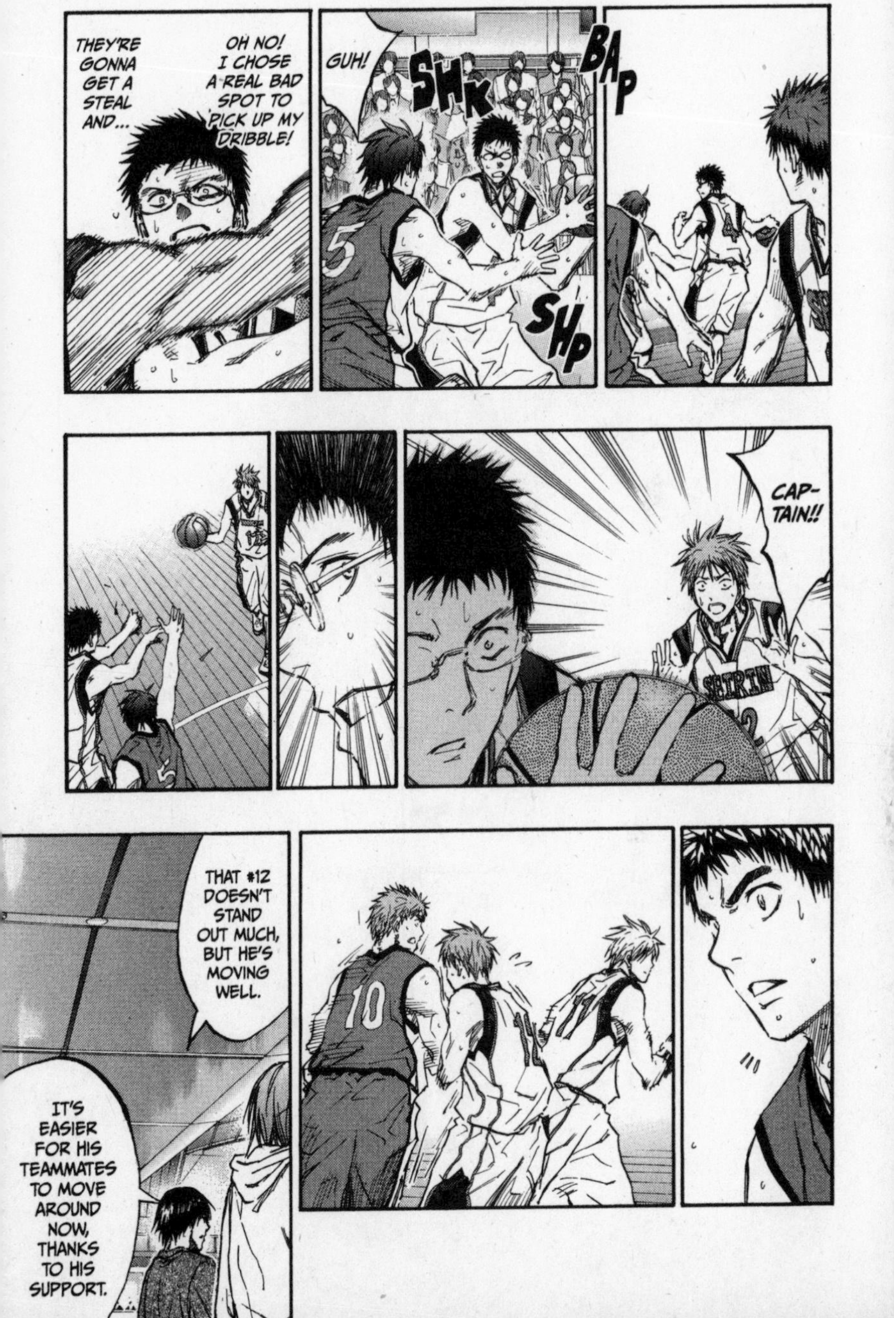
BAP
GUH!
SHK
SHP
OH NO! I CHOSE A REAL BAD SPOT TO PICK UP MY DRIBBLE!
THEY'RE GONNA GET A STEAL AND...
CAP-TAIN!!
THAT #12 DOESN'T STAND OUT MUCH, BUT HE'S MOVING WELL.
IT'S EASIER FOR HIS TEAMMATES TO MOVE AROUND NOW, THANKS TO HIS SUPPORT.

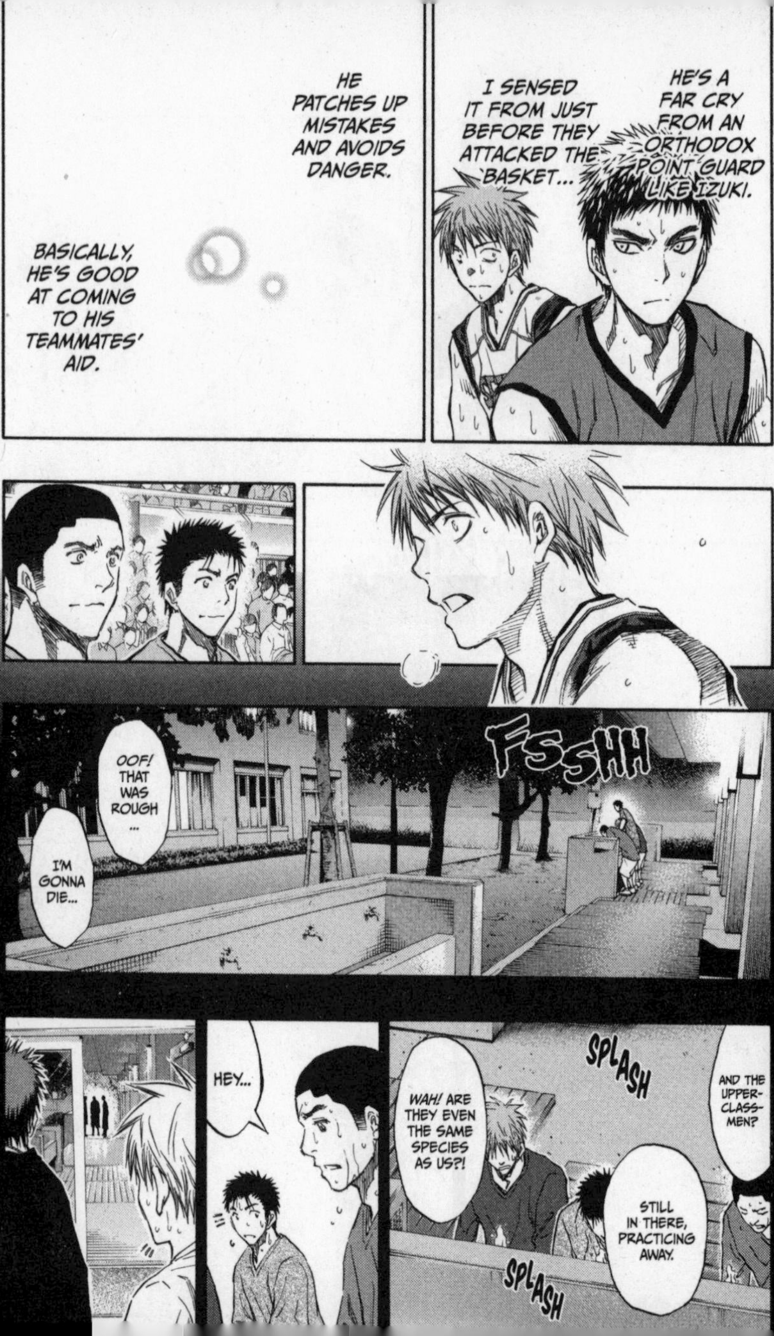
HE'S A FAR CRY FROM AN ORTHODOX POINT GUARD LIKE IZUKI.
I SENSED IT FROM JUST BEFORE THEY ATTACKED THE BASKET...
HE PATCHES UP MISTAKES AND AVOIDS DANGER.
BASICALLY, HE'S GOOD AT COMING TO HIS TEAMMATES' AID.
FSSHH
OOF! THAT WAS ROUGH...
I'M GONNA DIE...
AND THE UPPER-CLASS-MEN?
STILL IN THERE, PRACTICING AWAY.
SPLASH
WAH! ARE THEY EVEN THE SAME SPECIES AS US?!
SPLASH
HEY...

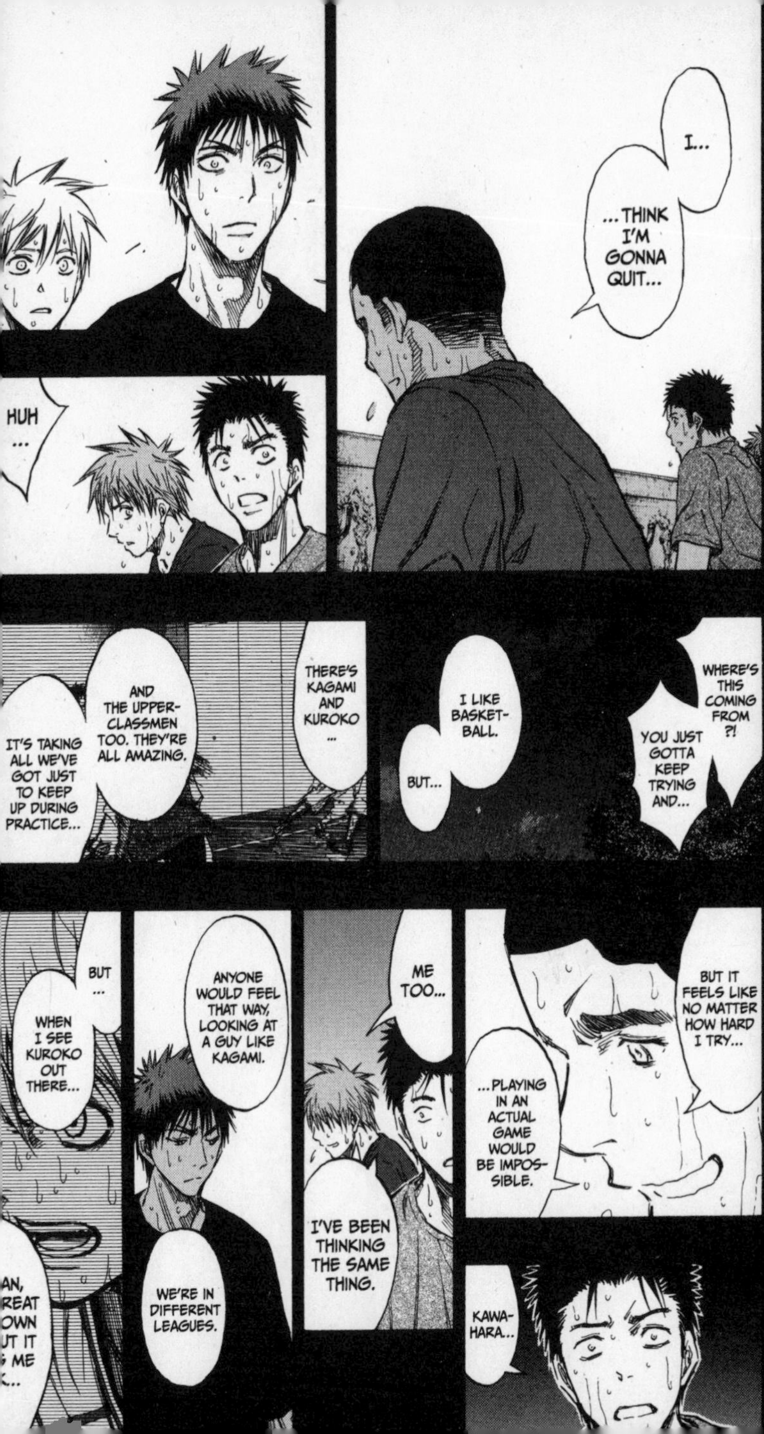
I...
...THINK I'M GONNA QUIT...
HUH ...
WHERE'S THIS COMING FROM ?!
YOU JUST GOTTA KEEP TRYING AND...
I LIKE BASKET-BALL.
BUT...
THERE'S KAGAMI AND KUROKO ...
AND THE UPPER-CLASSMEN TOO. THEY'RE ALL AMAZING.
IT'S TAKING ALL WE'VE GOT JUST TO KEEP UP DURING PRACTICE...
BUT IT FEELS LIKE NO MATTER HOW HARD I TRY...
...PLAYING IN AN ACTUAL GAME WOULD BE IMPOS-SIBLE.
KAWA-HARA...
ME TOO...
I'VE BEEN THINKING THE SAME THING.
ANYONE WOULD FEEL THAT WAY, LOOKING AT A GUY LIKE KAGAMI.
WE'RE IN DIFFERENT LEAGUES.
BUT ...
WHEN I SEE KUROKO OUT THERE...

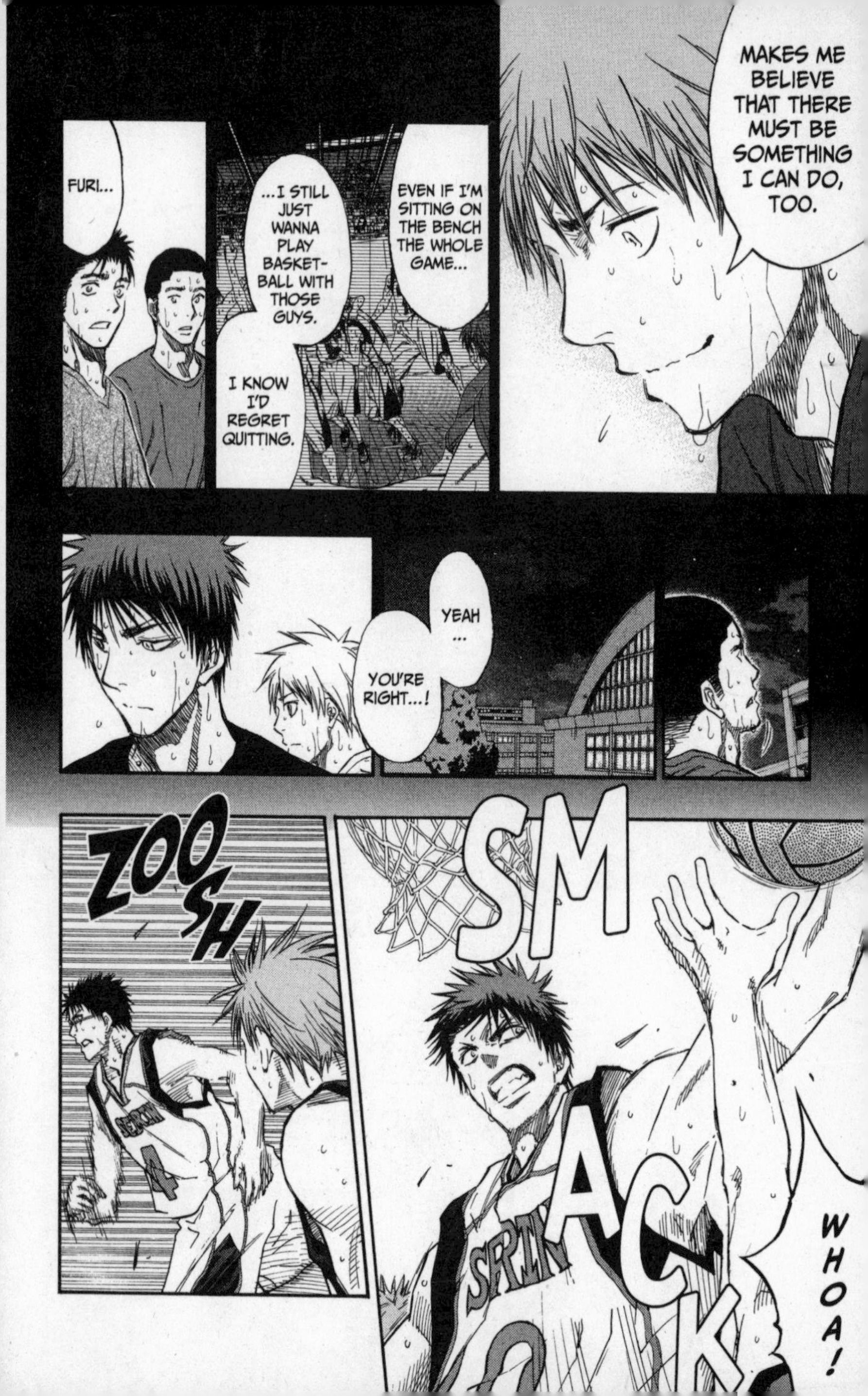
MAKES ME BELIEVE THAT THERE MUST BE SOMETHING I CAN DO, TOO.
EVEN IF I'M SITTING ON THE BENCH THE WHOLE GAME...
...I STILL JUST WANNA PLAY BASKETBALL WITH THOSE GUYS.
I KNOW I'D REGRET QUITTING.
FURI...
YEAH...
YOU'RE RIGHT...!
SMACK
WHOA!
ZOOSH

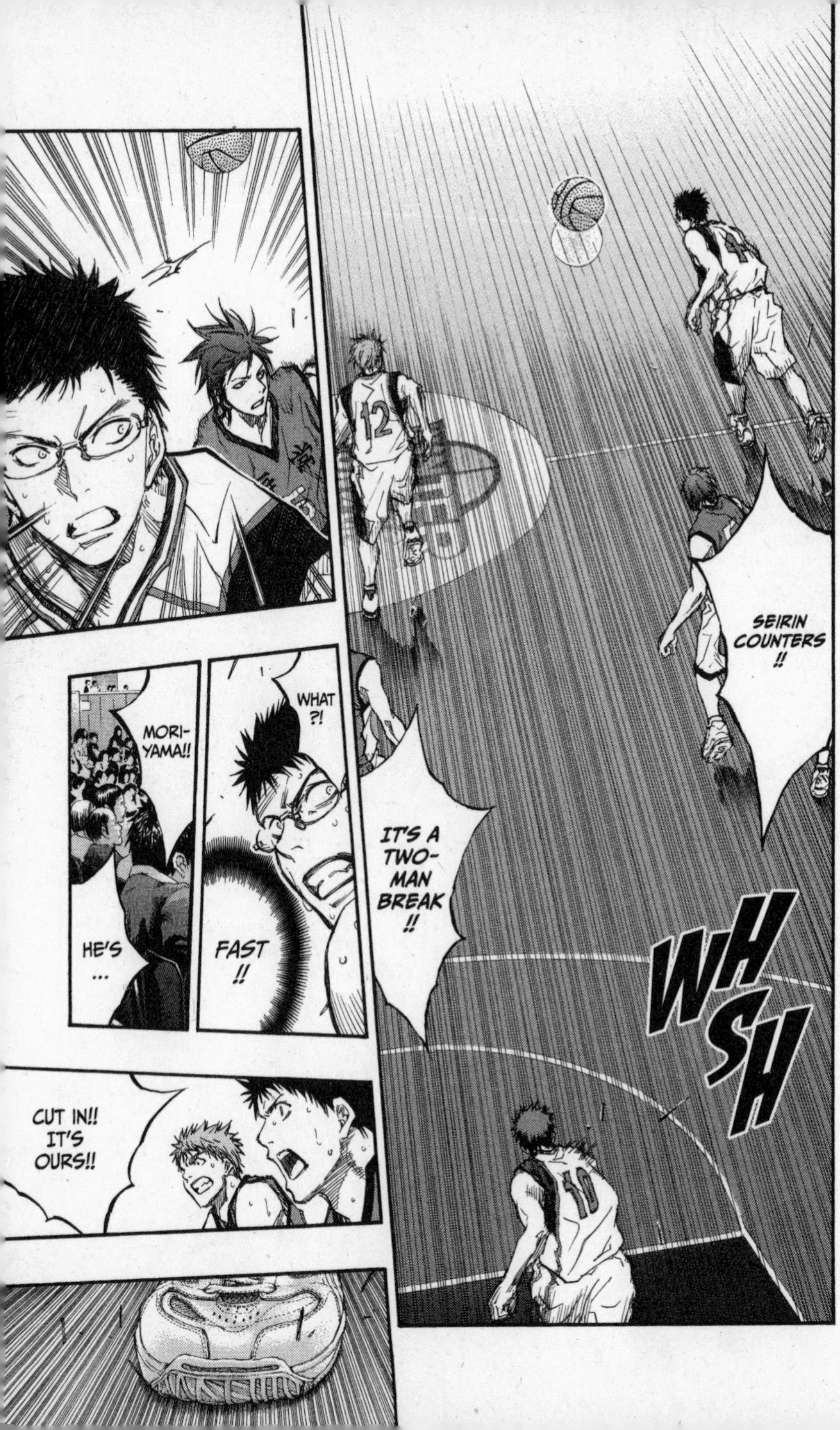
SEIRIN COUNTERS!!
IT'S A TWO-MAN BREAK!!
WHSH
WHAT?!
FAST!!
MORI-YAMA!!
HE'S...
CUT IN!! IT'S OURS!!

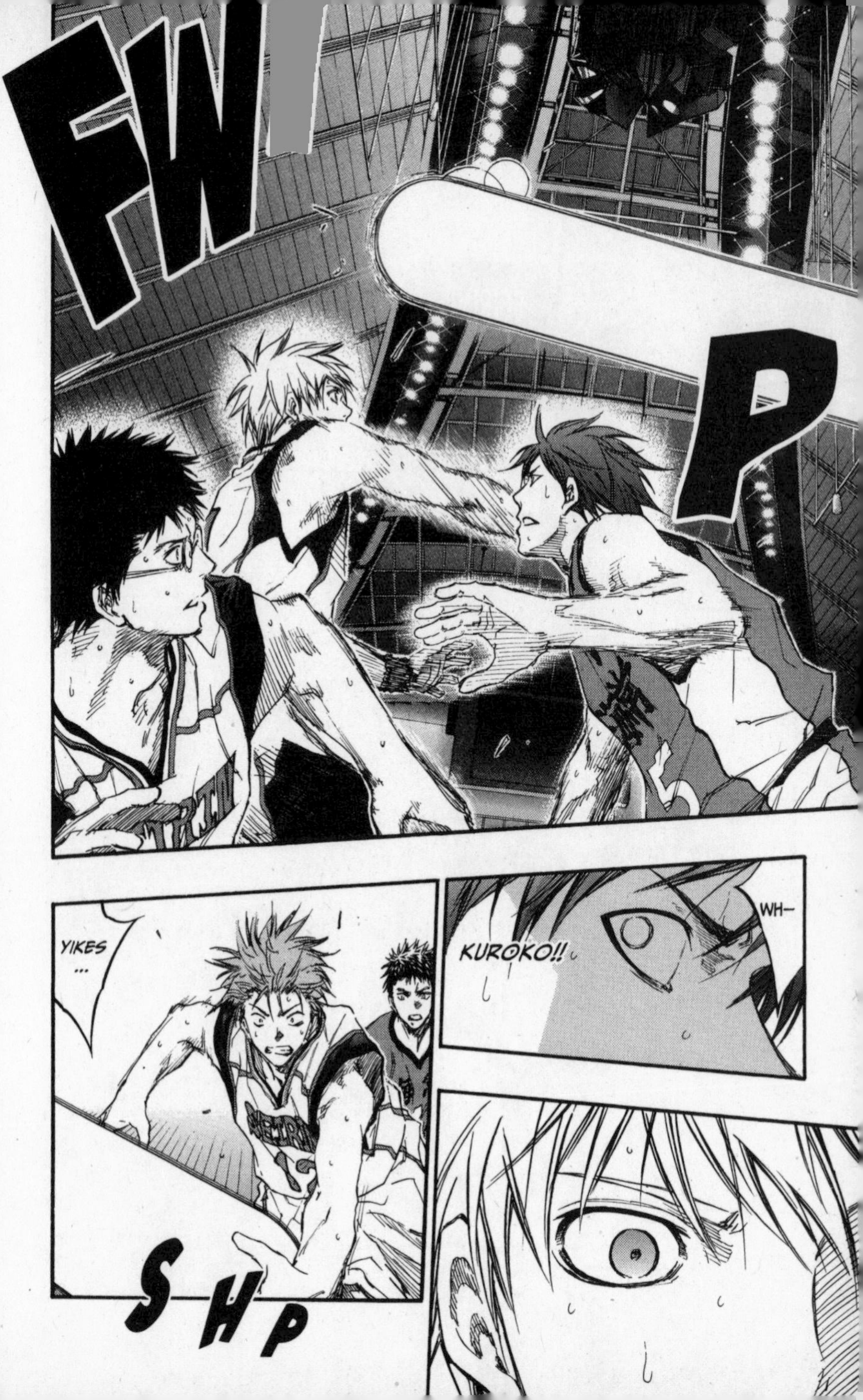
FW
P
WH—
KUROKO!!
YIKES ...
SHP

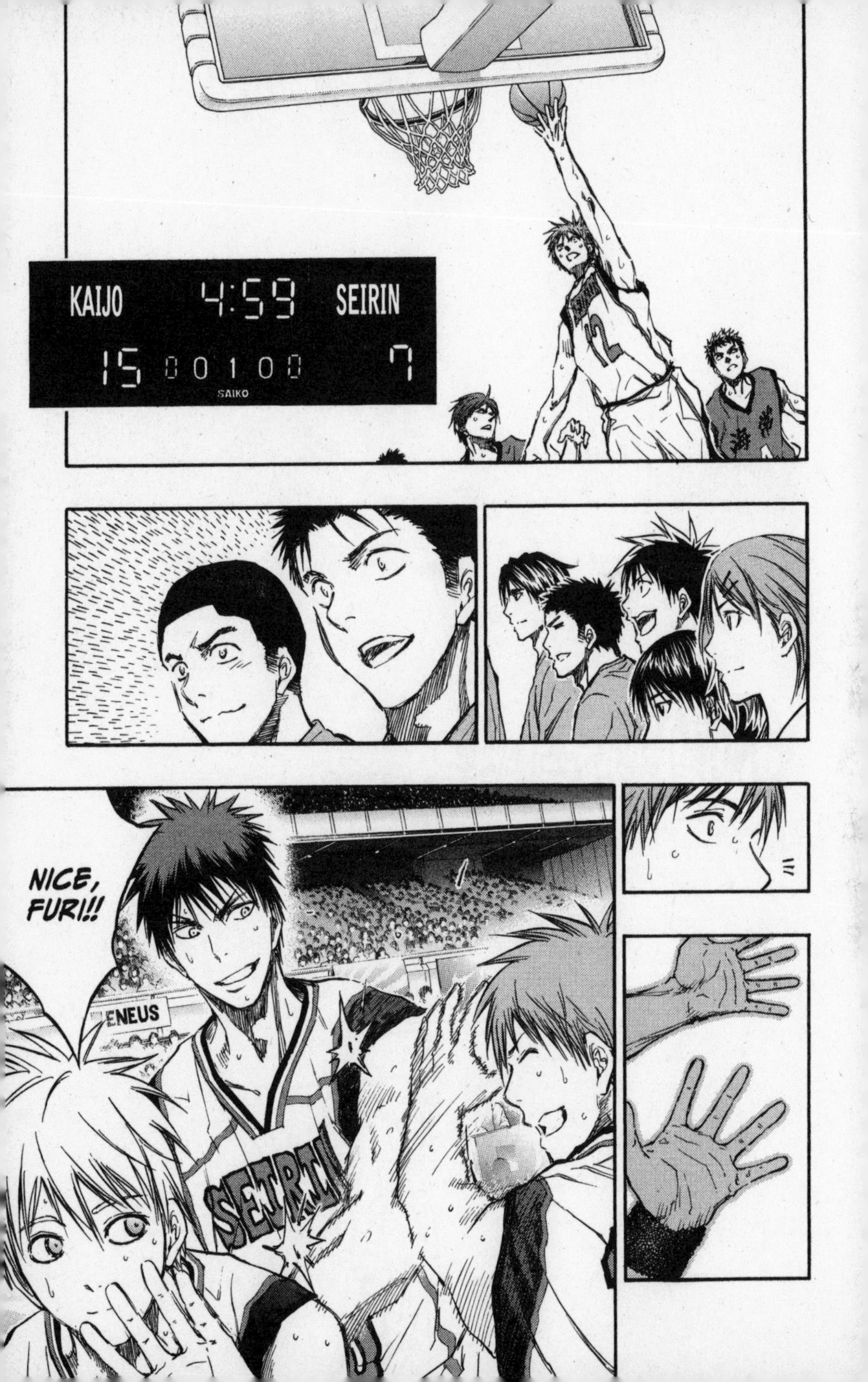
KAIJO
4:59
SEIRIN
15
00100
7
SAIKO
NICE, FURI!!
ENEUS
SEIRIN

KUROKO'S BASKETBALL BLOOPERS

TAKE 5

AND THE UPPER-CLASSMEN?
STILL IN THERE, PRACTICING AWAY.
WAH! ARE THEY EVEN THE SAME SPECIES AS US?!
HEY ...
I'M...
...THINKING OF GROWING OUT MY HAIR..
WHO...
...THE HECK...
OH...
...CARES?
SURE ...

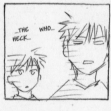

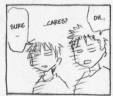

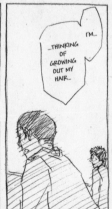

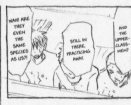

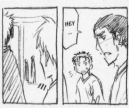

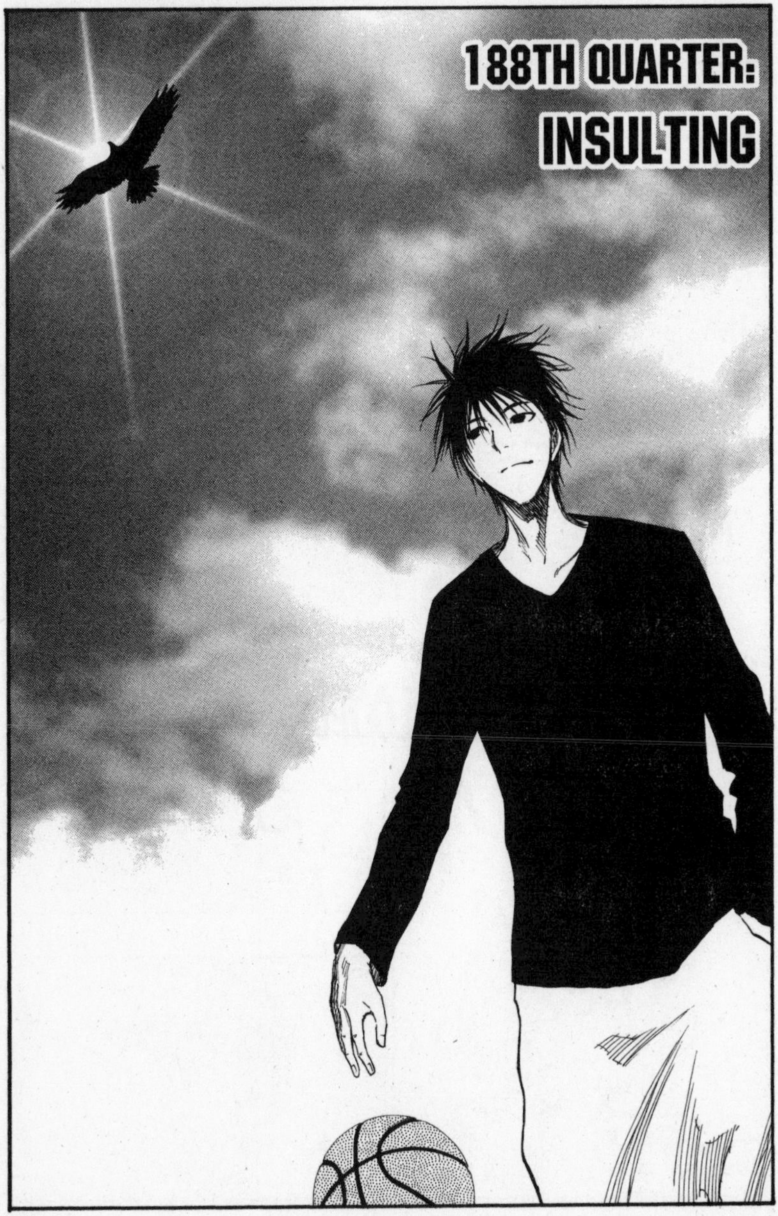
188TH QUARTER:
INSULTING

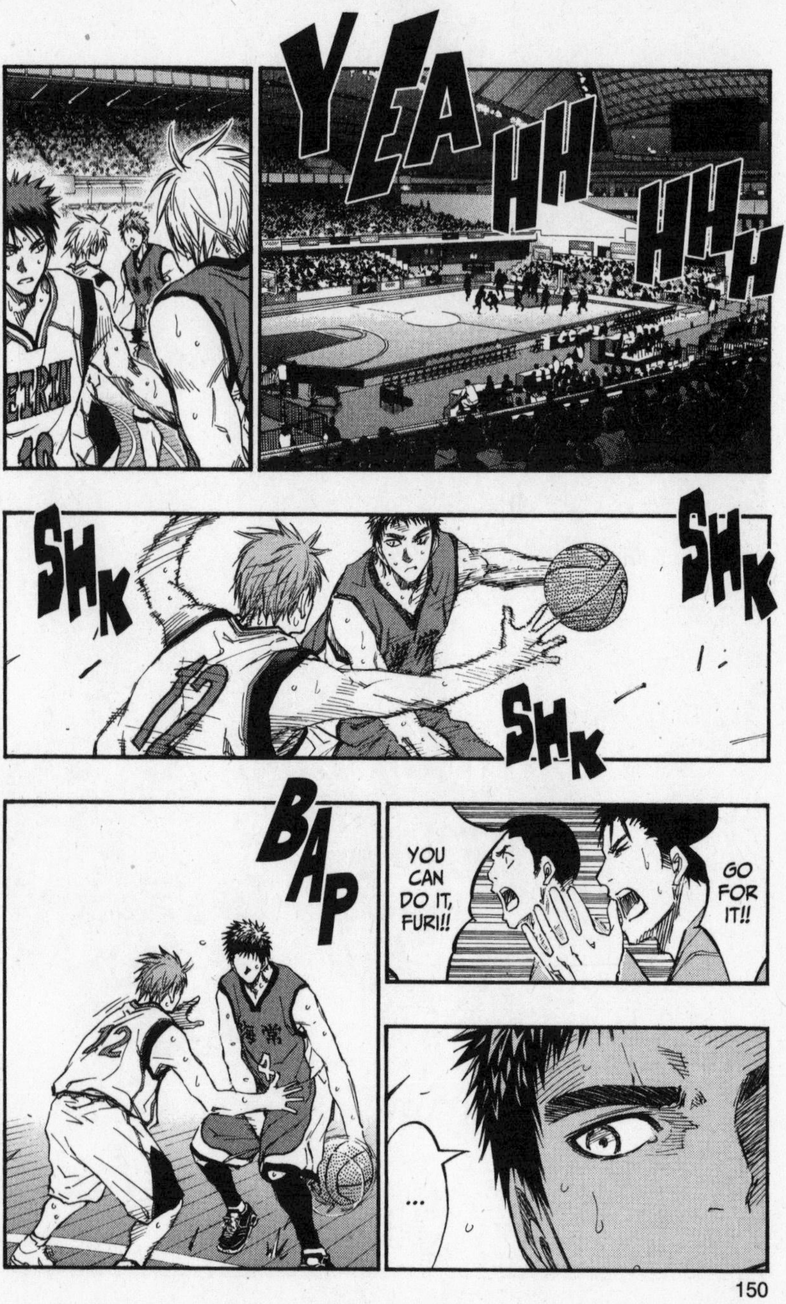
YEAHHHHH
SHK
SHK
SHK
GO FOR IT!!
YOU CAN DO IT, FURI!!
...
BAP

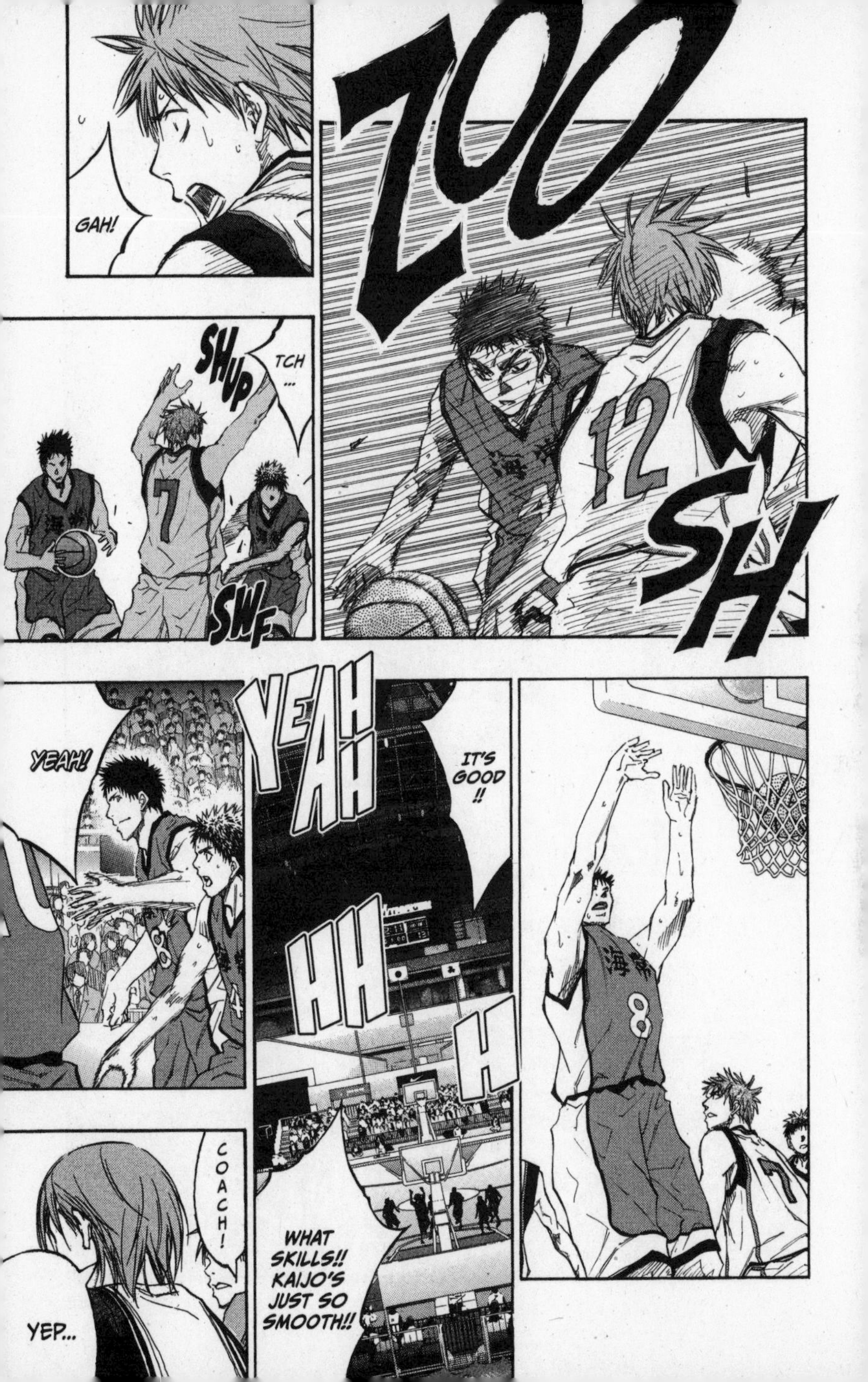
ZOO
SH
GAH!
SHUP
TCH ...
SWF
YEAH AH HHH H
IT'S GOOD !!
WHAT SKILLS!! KAIJO'S JUST SO SMOOTH!!
YEAH!
COACH!
YEP...

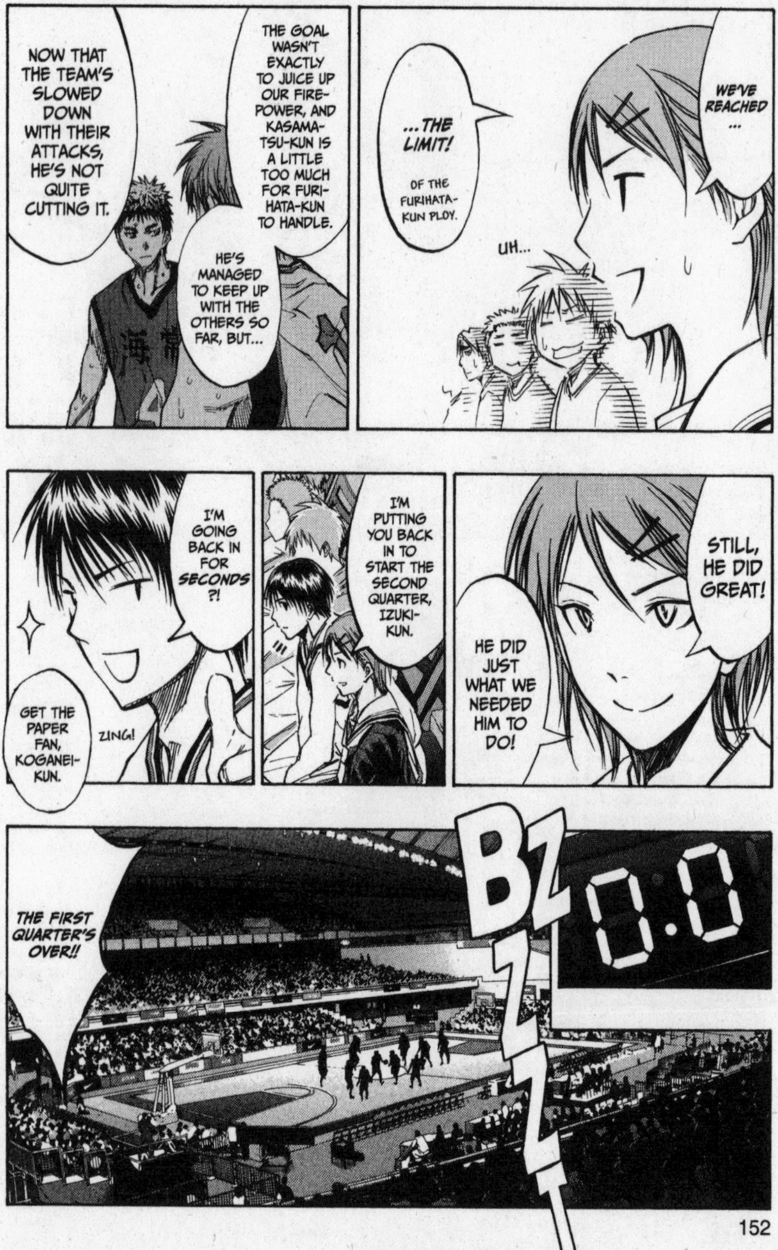
WE'VE REACHED ...
...THE LIMIT!
OF THE FURIHATA-KUN PLOY.
UH...
THE GOAL WASN'T EXACTLY TO JUICE UP OUR FIRE-POWER, AND KASAMA-TSU-KUN IS A LITTLE TOO MUCH FOR FURI-HATA-KUN TO HANDLE.
HE'S MANAGED TO KEEP UP WITH THE OTHERS SO FAR, BUT...
NOW THAT THE TEAM'S SLOWED DOWN WITH THEIR ATTACKS, HE'S NOT QUITE CUTTING IT.
STILL, HE DID GREAT!
HE DID JUST WHAT WE NEEDED HIM TO DO!
I'M PUTTING YOU BACK IN TO START THE SECOND QUARTER, IZUKI-KUN.
I'M GOING BACK IN FOR SECONDS?!
ZING!
GET THE PAPER FAN, KOGANEI-KUN.
BZZZT
0.0
THE FIRST QUARTER'S OVER!!

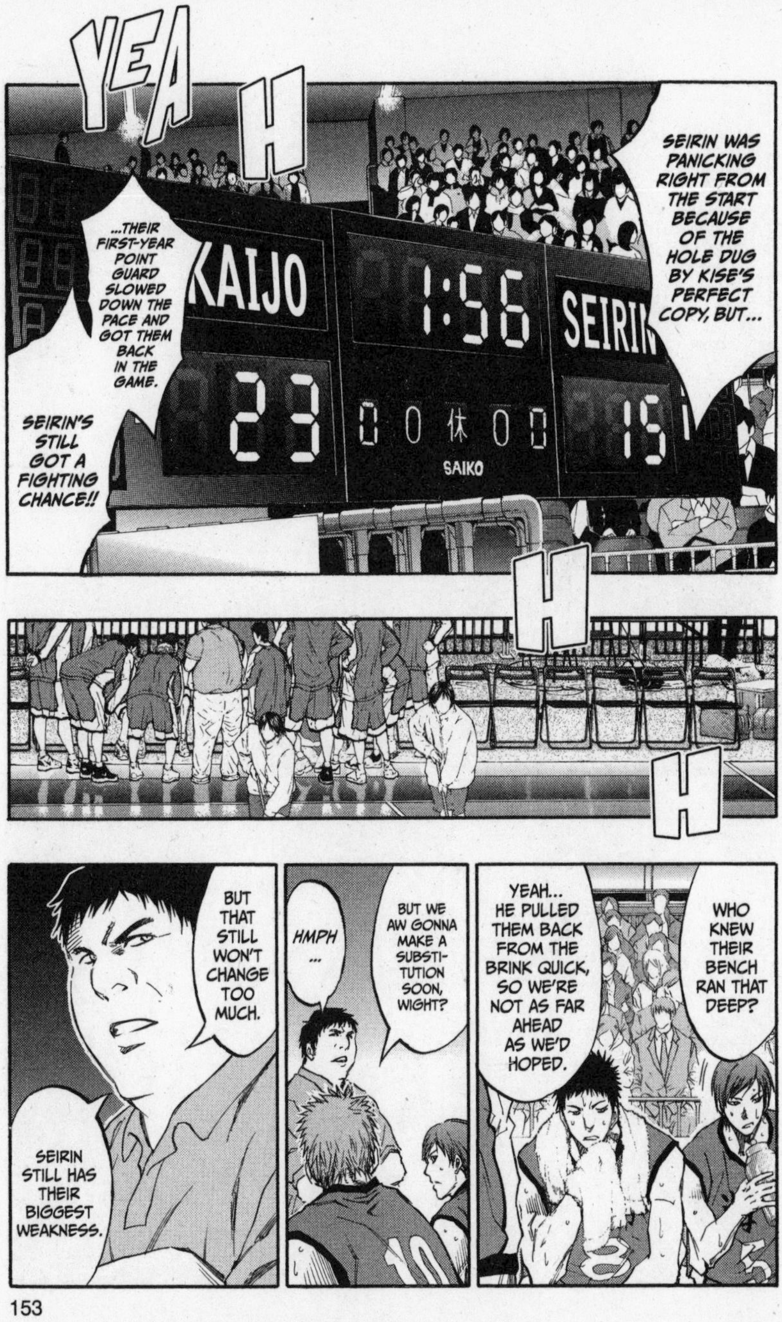
YEAHHHH
SEIRIN WAS PANICKING RIGHT FROM THE START BECAUSE OF THE HOLE DUG BY KISE'S PERFECT COPY, BUT...
...THEIR FIRST-YEAR POINT GUARD SLOWED DOWN THE PACE AND GOT THEM BACK IN THE GAME.
KAIJO
1:56
SEIRIN
23
15
SAIKO
SEIRIN'S STILL GOT A FIGHTING CHANCE!!
WHO KNEW THEIR BENCH RAN THAT DEEP?
YEAH... HE PULLED THEM BACK FROM THE BRINK QUICK, SO WE'RE NOT AS FAR AHEAD AS WE'D HOPED.
BUT WE AW GONNA MAKE A SUBSTITUTION SOON, WIGHT?
HMPH ...
BUT THAT STILL WON'T CHANGE TOO MUCH.
SEIRIN STILL HAS THEIR BIGGEST WEAKNESS.

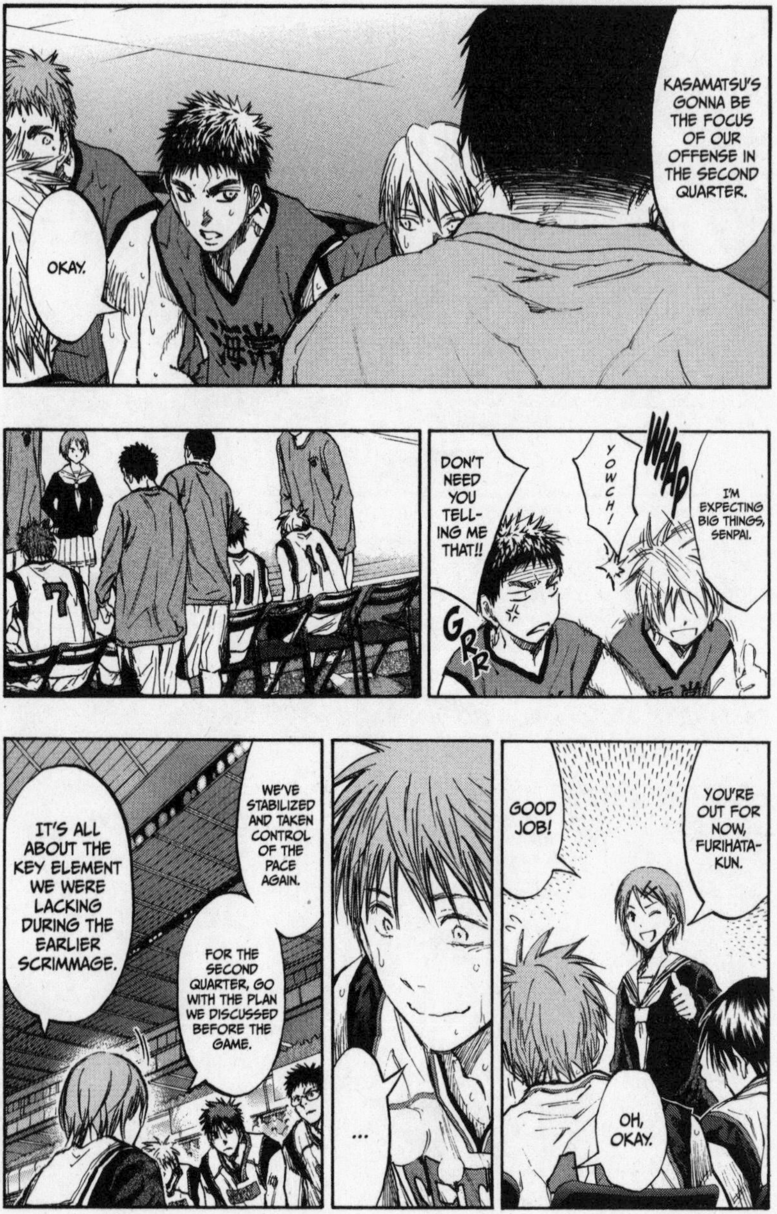
KASAMATSU'S GONNA BE THE FOCUS OF OUR OFFENSE IN THE SECOND QUARTER.
OKAY.
I'M EXPECTING BIG THINGS, SENPAI.
WHAP
YOWCH!
DON'T NEED YOU TELLING ME THAT!!
GRR
YOU'RE OUT FOR NOW, FURIHATA-KUN.
GOOD JOB!
OH, OKAY.
...
WE'VE STABILIZED AND TAKEN CONTROL OF THE PACE AGAIN.
FOR THE SECOND QUARTER, GO WITH THE PLAN WE DISCUSSED BEFORE THE GAME.
IT'S ALL ABOUT THE KEY ELEMENT WE WERE LACKING DURING THE EARLIER SCRIMMAGE.

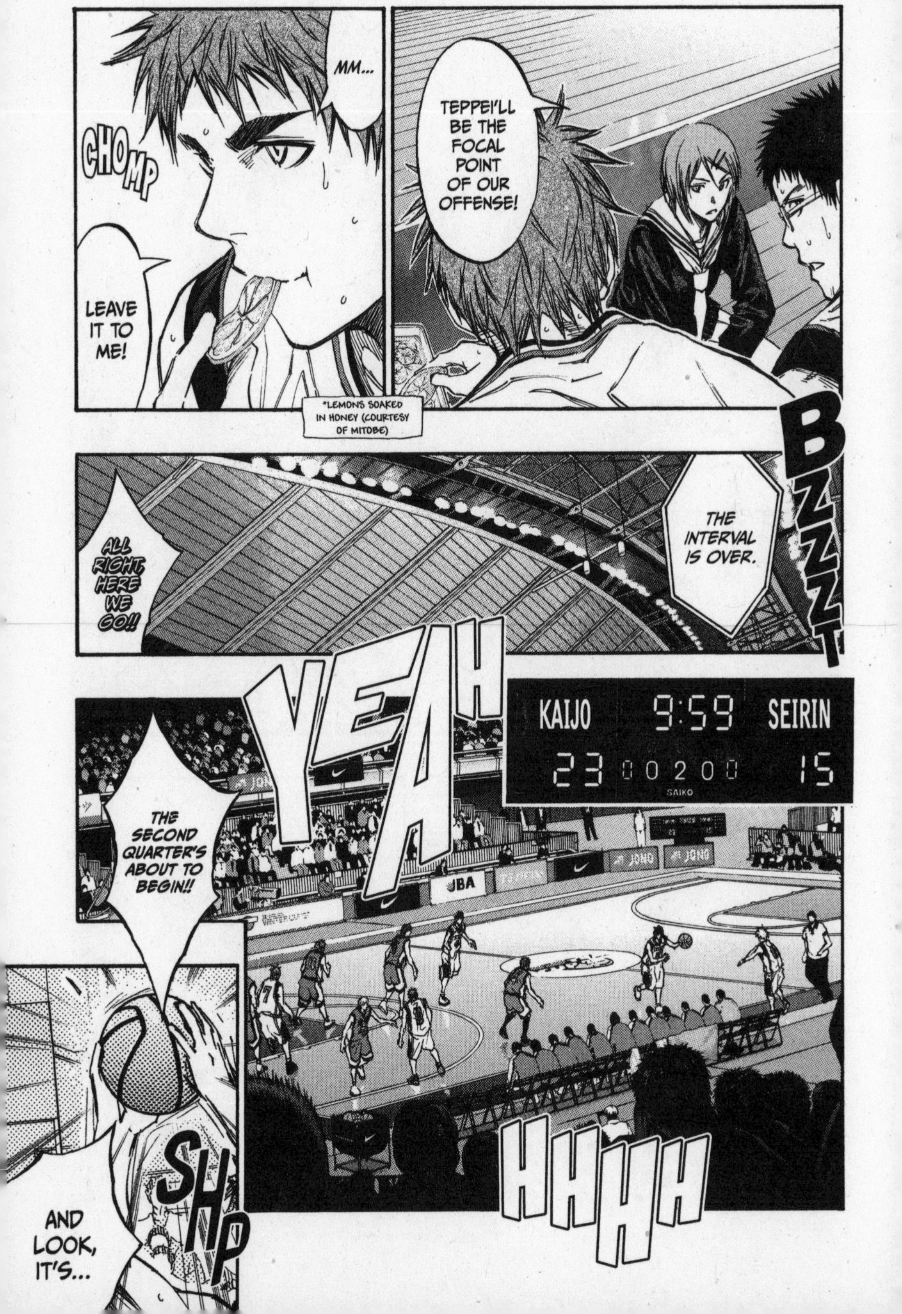
TEPPEI'LL BE THE FOCAL POINT OF OUR OFFENSE!
MM...
CHOMP
LEAVE IT TO ME!
*LEMONS SOAKED IN HONEY (COURTESY OF MITOBE)
BZZZT
THE INTERVAL IS OVER.
ALL RIGHT, HERE WE GO!!
YEAH
KAIJO 9:59 SEIRIN
23 15
SAIKO
THE SECOND QUARTER'S ABOUT TO BEGIN!!
HHHH
SHP
AND LOOK, IT'S...

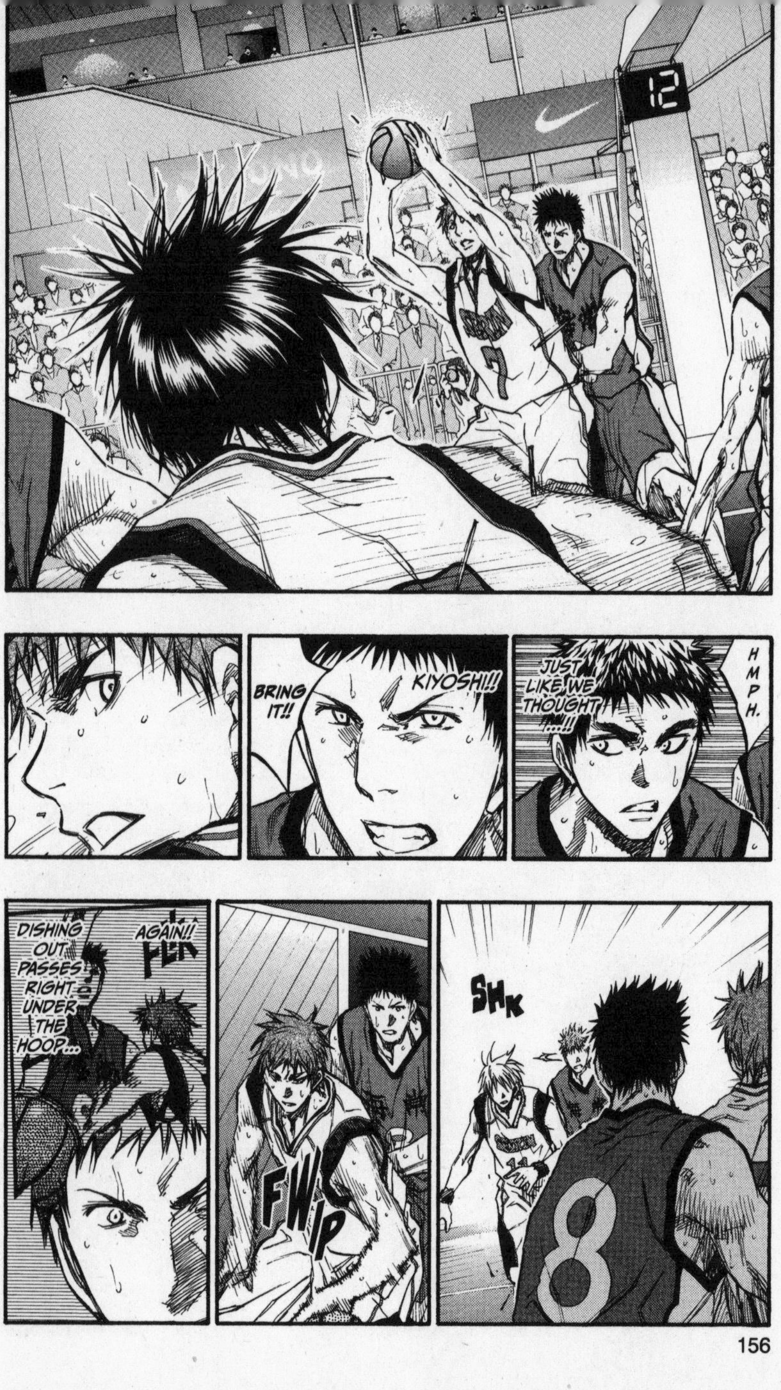
HMPH.
JUST LIKE WE THOUGHT...!!
KIYOSHI!!!
BRING IT!!
SHK
FWIP
DISHING OUT PASSES RIGHT UNDER THE HOOP...
AGAIN!!

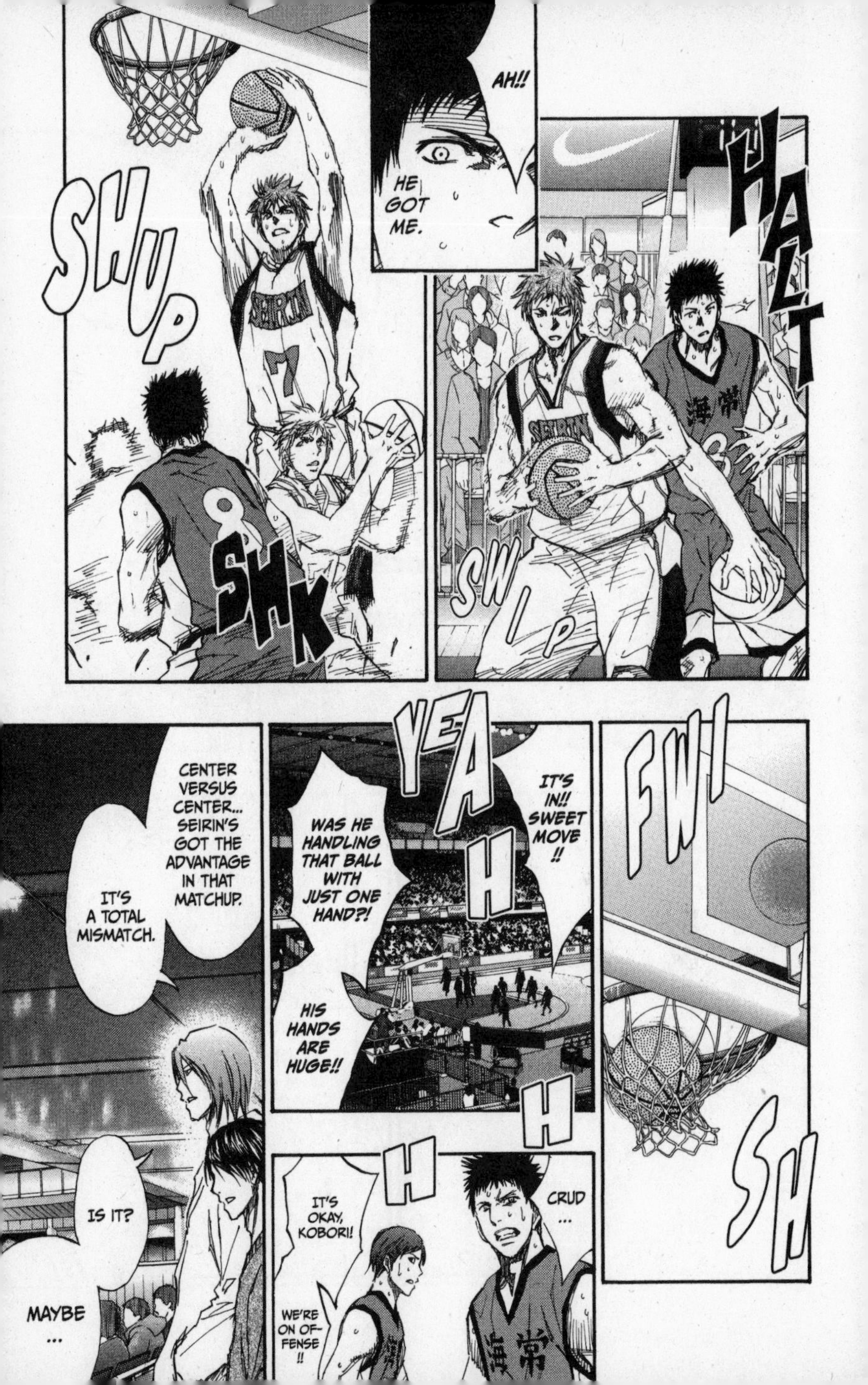
HALT
SWIP
AH!!
HE GOT ME.
SHUP
SHK
FWI
SH
YEAH
H
H
IT'S IN!! SWEET MOVE !!
WAS HE HANDLING THAT BALL WITH JUST ONE HAND?!
HIS HANDS ARE HUGE!!
CENTER VERSUS CENTER... SEIRIN'S GOT THE ADVANTAGE IN THAT MATCHUP.
IT'S A TOTAL MISMATCH.
IS IT?
MAYBE ...
CRUD ...
IT'S OKAY, KOBORI!
WE'RE ON OF-FENSE !!

...IS MORE STRAIGHT-FORWARD.

...KAIJO'S PLAN...

SHK

ONE-ON-ONE!!

...ISOLATION.

HE'S GOING INTO AN...

THEY'RE MAKING ROOM FOR KASAMATSU TO DRIVE...

WHICH MEANS...

*Isolation is when a team clears room for one player to go one-on-one against a defender.

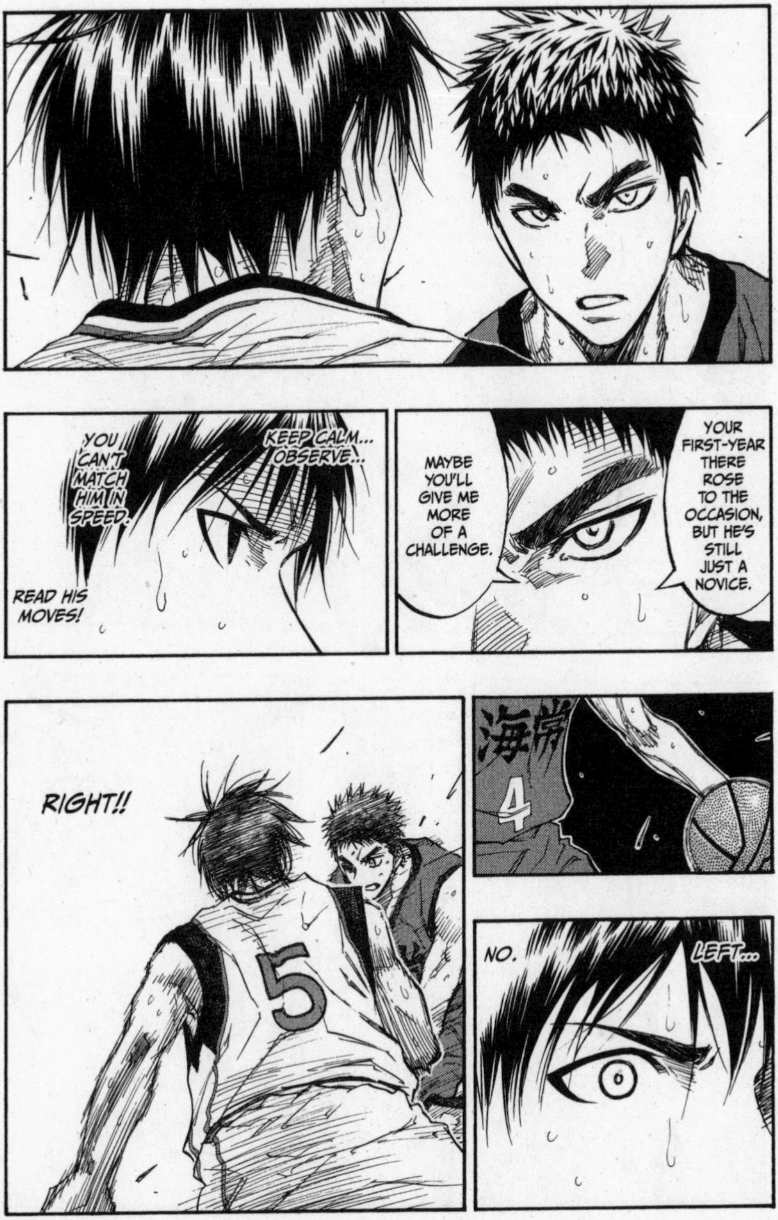
YOUR FIRST-YEAR THERE ROSE TO THE OCCASION, BUT HE'S STILL JUST A NOVICE.
MAYBE YOU'LL GIVE ME MORE OF A CHALLENGE.
KEEP CALM... OBSERVE...
YOU CAN'T MATCH HIM IN SPEED.
READ HIS MOVES!
海常
4
LEFT...
NO.
RIGHT!!
5

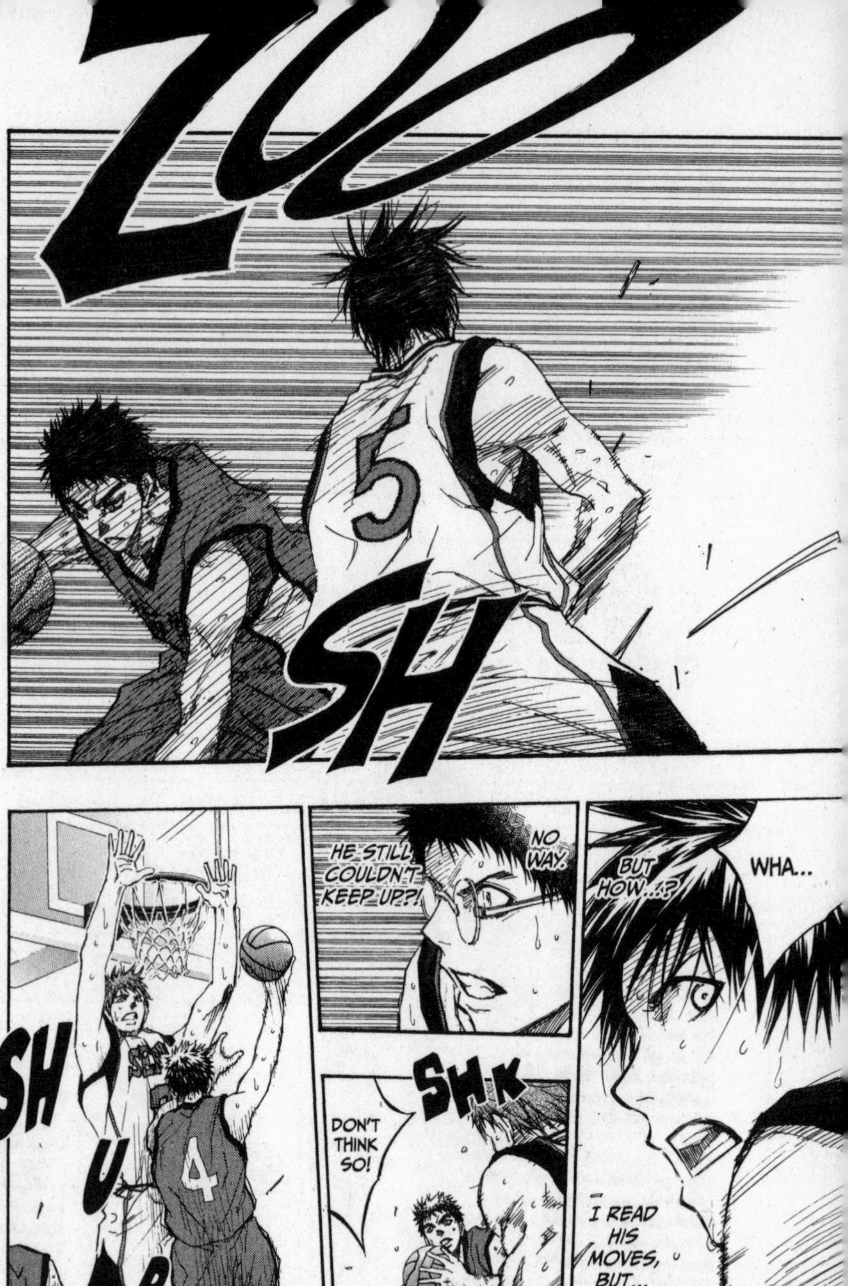
ZOO
SH
WHA...
BUT HOW...?
I READ HIS MOVES, BUT...
NO WAY.
HE STILL COULDN'T KEEP UP?!
SHK
DON'T THINK SO!
SHUP

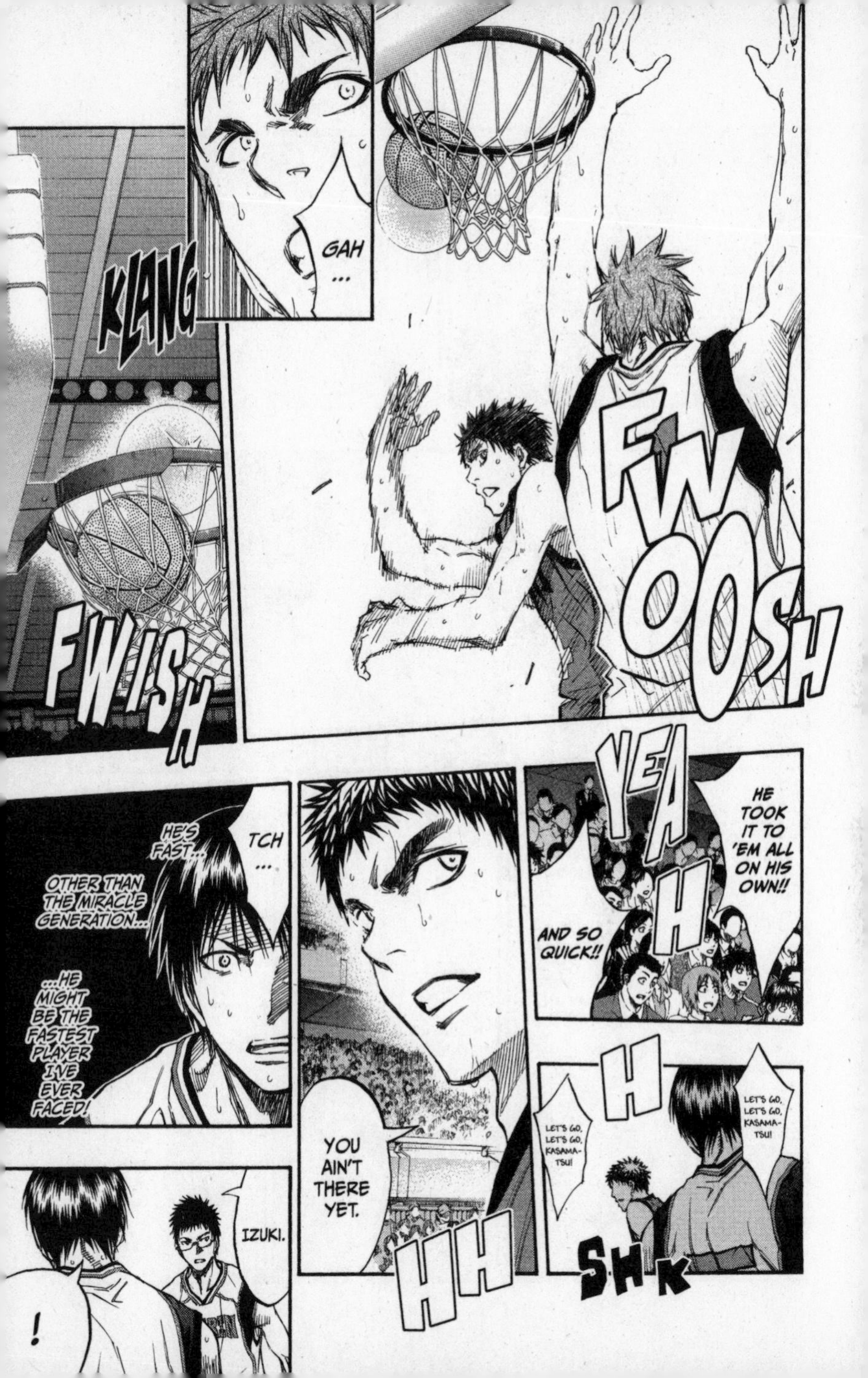
FWOOSH
GAH ...
KLANG
FWISH
YEAH
HE TOOK IT TO 'EM ALL ON HIS OWN!!
AND SO QUICK!!
H
H
LET'S GO, LET'S GO, KASAMATSU!
LET'S GO, LET'S GO, KASAMATSU!
SHK
YOU AIN'T THERE YET.
HH
TCH ...
HE'S FAST...
OTHER THAN THE MIRACLE GENERATION...
...HE MIGHT BE THE FASTEST PLAYER I'VE EVER FACED!
IZUKI.
!

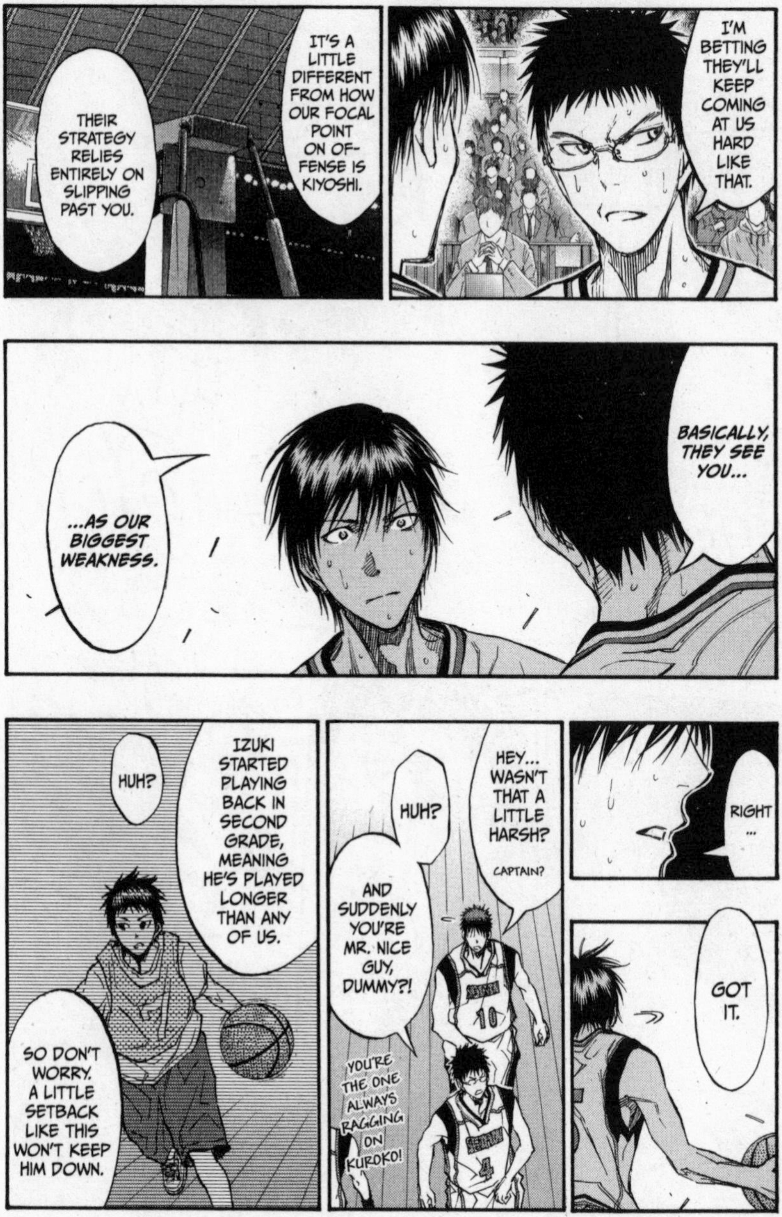
I'M BETTING THEY'LL KEEP COMING AT US HARD LIKE THAT.
IT'S A LITTLE DIFFERENT FROM HOW OUR FOCAL POINT ON OFFENSE IS KIYOSHI.
THEIR STRATEGY RELIES ENTIRELY ON SLIPPING PAST YOU.
BASICALLY, THEY SEE YOU...
...AS OUR BIGGEST WEAKNESS.
RIGHT...
GOT IT.
HEY... WASN'T THAT A LITTLE HARSH?
CAPTAIN?
HUH?
AND SUDDENLY YOU'RE MR. NICE GUY, DUMMY?!
YOU'RE THE ONE ALWAYS RAGGING ON KUROKO!
IZUKI STARTED PLAYING BACK IN SECOND GRADE, MEANING HE'S PLAYED LONGER THAN ANY OF US.
HUH?
SO DON'T WORRY. A LITTLE SETBACK LIKE THIS WON'T KEEP HIM DOWN.

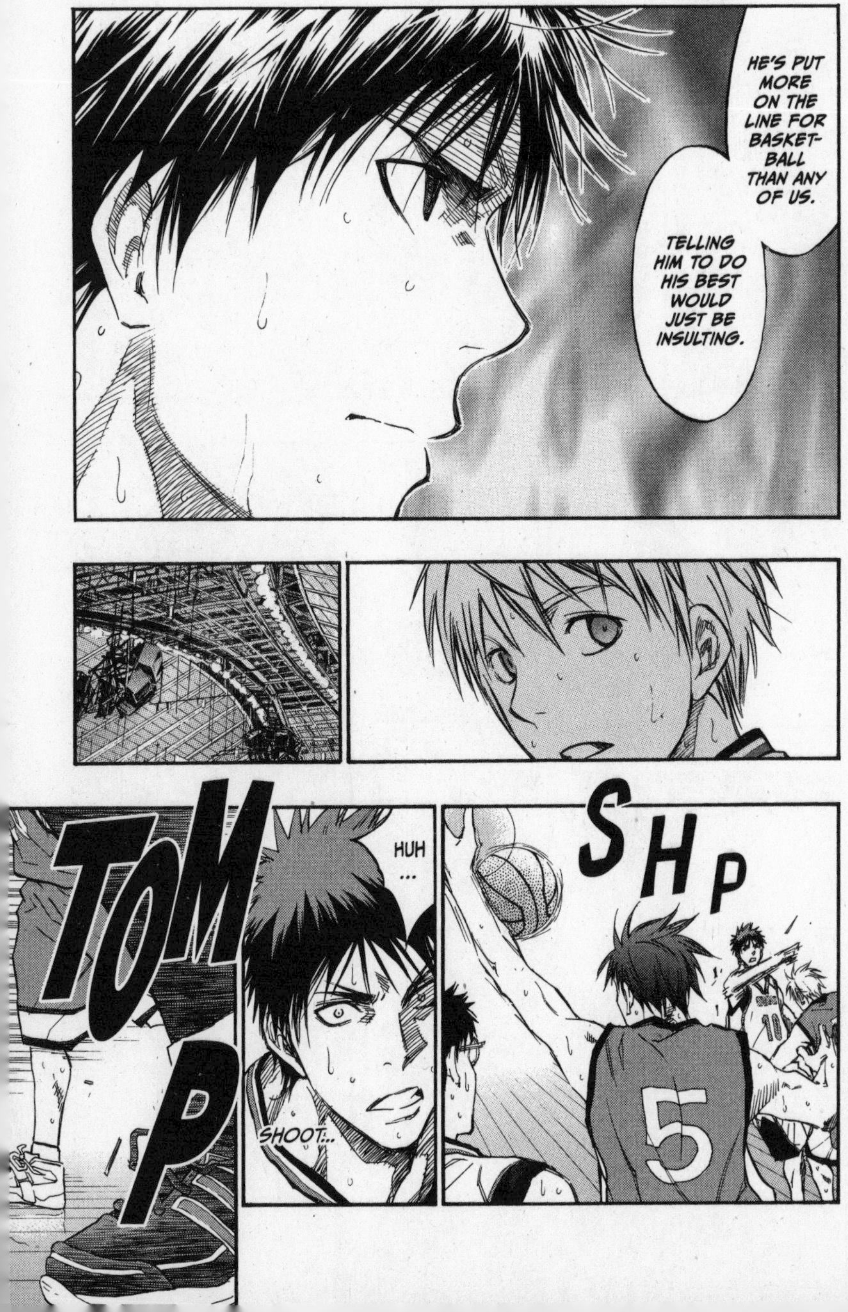
HE'S PUT MORE ON THE LINE FOR BASKET-BALL THAN ANY OF US.
TELLING HIM TO DO HIS BEST WOULD JUST BE INSULTING.
SHP
HUH ...
SHOOT...
TOMP

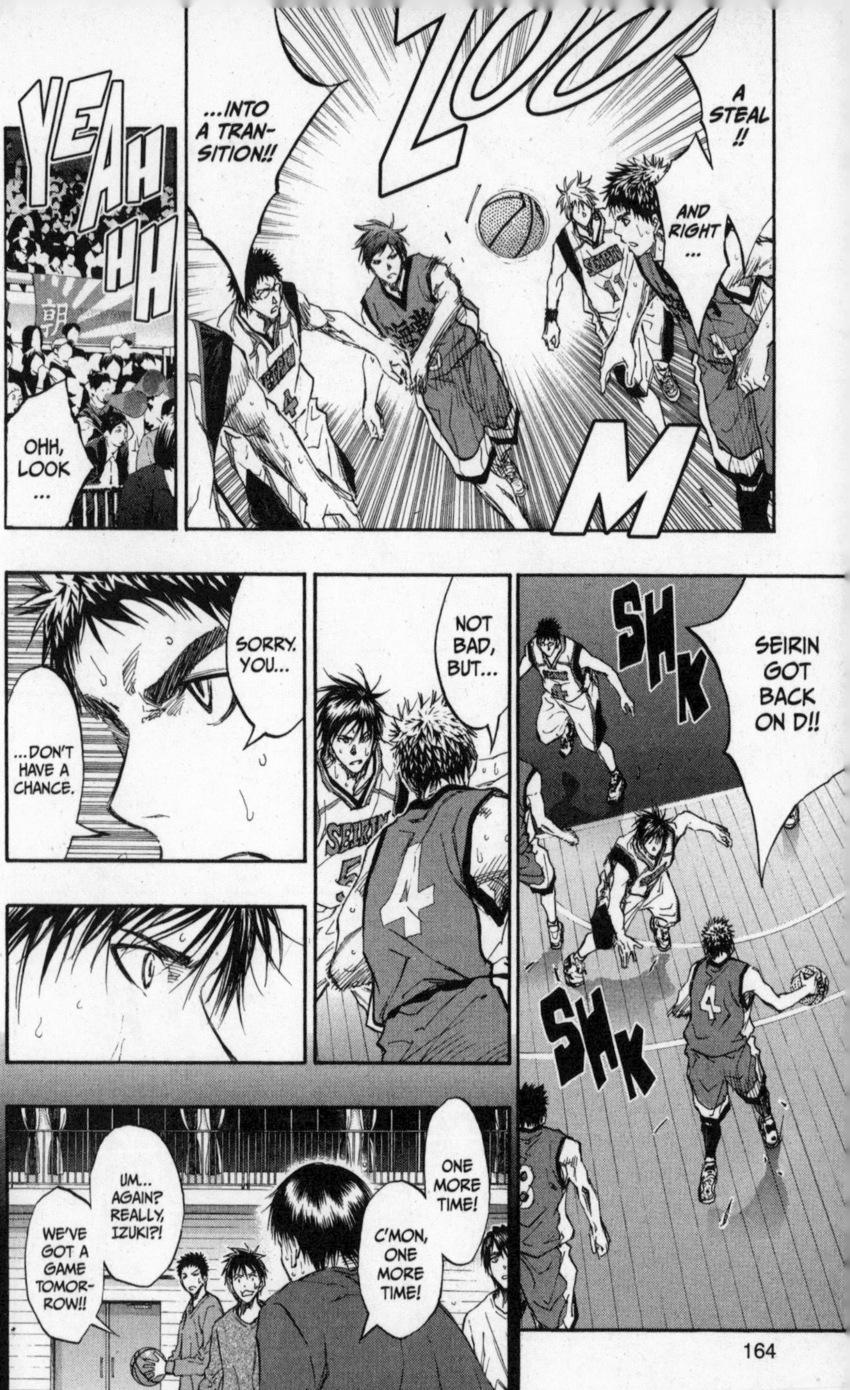
ZOOM
A STEAL!!
AND RIGHT...
...INTO A TRANSITION!!
YEAHHH
OHH, LOOK...
SHK
SEIRIN GOT BACK ON D!!
SHK
NOT BAD, BUT...
SORRY. YOU...
...DON'T HAVE A CHANCE.
ONE MORE TIME!
C'MON, ONE MORE TIME!
UM... AGAIN? REALLY, IZUKI?!
WE'VE GOT A GAME TOMORROW!!

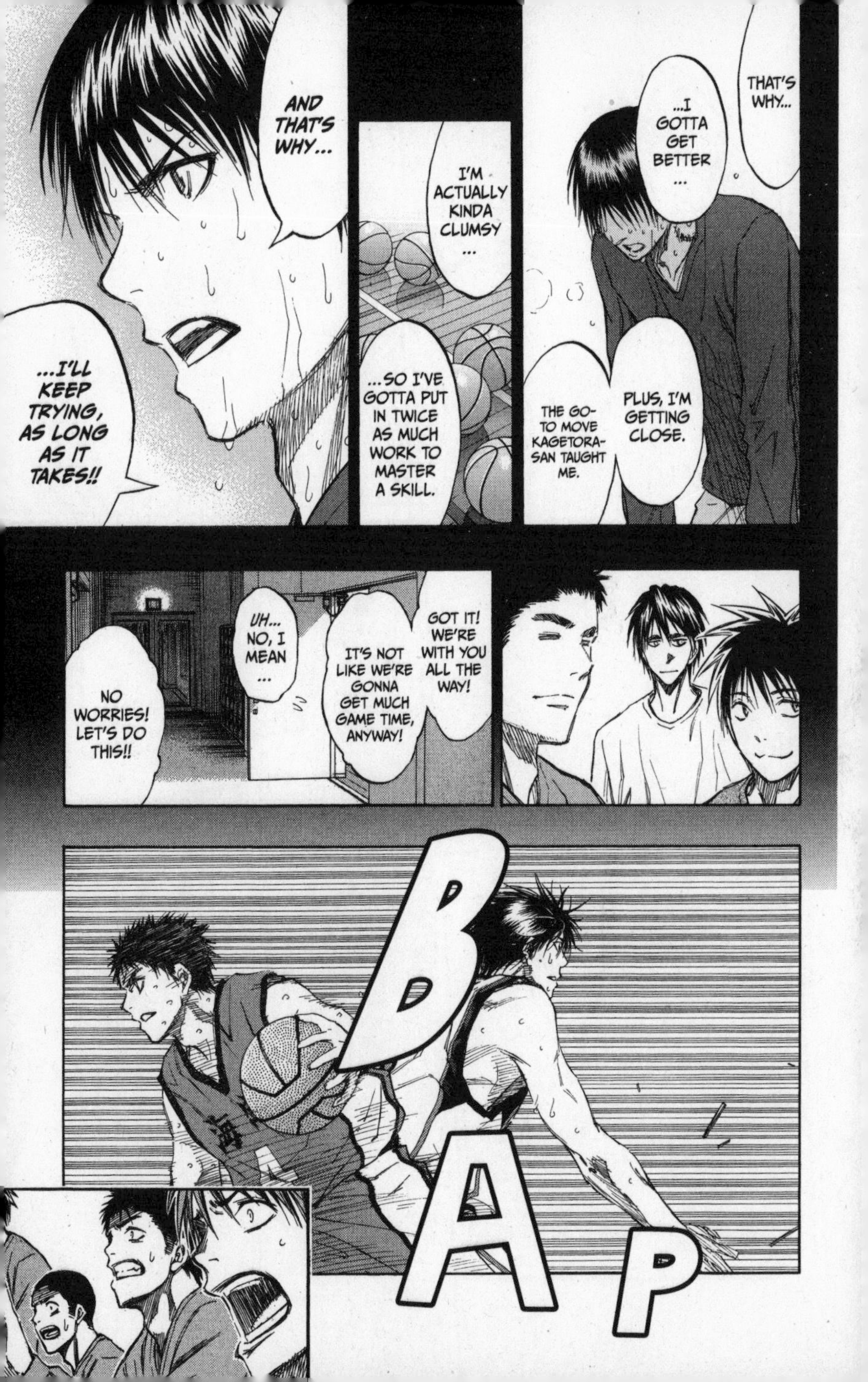
THAT'S WHY...
...I GOTTA GET BETTER ...
PLUS, I'M GETTING CLOSE.
THE GO-TO MOVE KAGETORA-SAN TAUGHT ME.
I'M ACTUALLY KINDA CLUMSY ...
...SO I'VE GOTTA PUT IN TWICE AS MUCH WORK TO MASTER A SKILL.
AND THAT'S WHY...
...I'LL KEEP TRYING, AS LONG AS IT TAKES!!
GOT IT! WE'RE WITH YOU ALL THE WAY!
IT'S NOT LIKE WE'RE GONNA GET MUCH GAME TIME, ANYWAY!
UH... NO, I MEAN ...
NO WORRIES! LET'S DO THIS!!
BAP

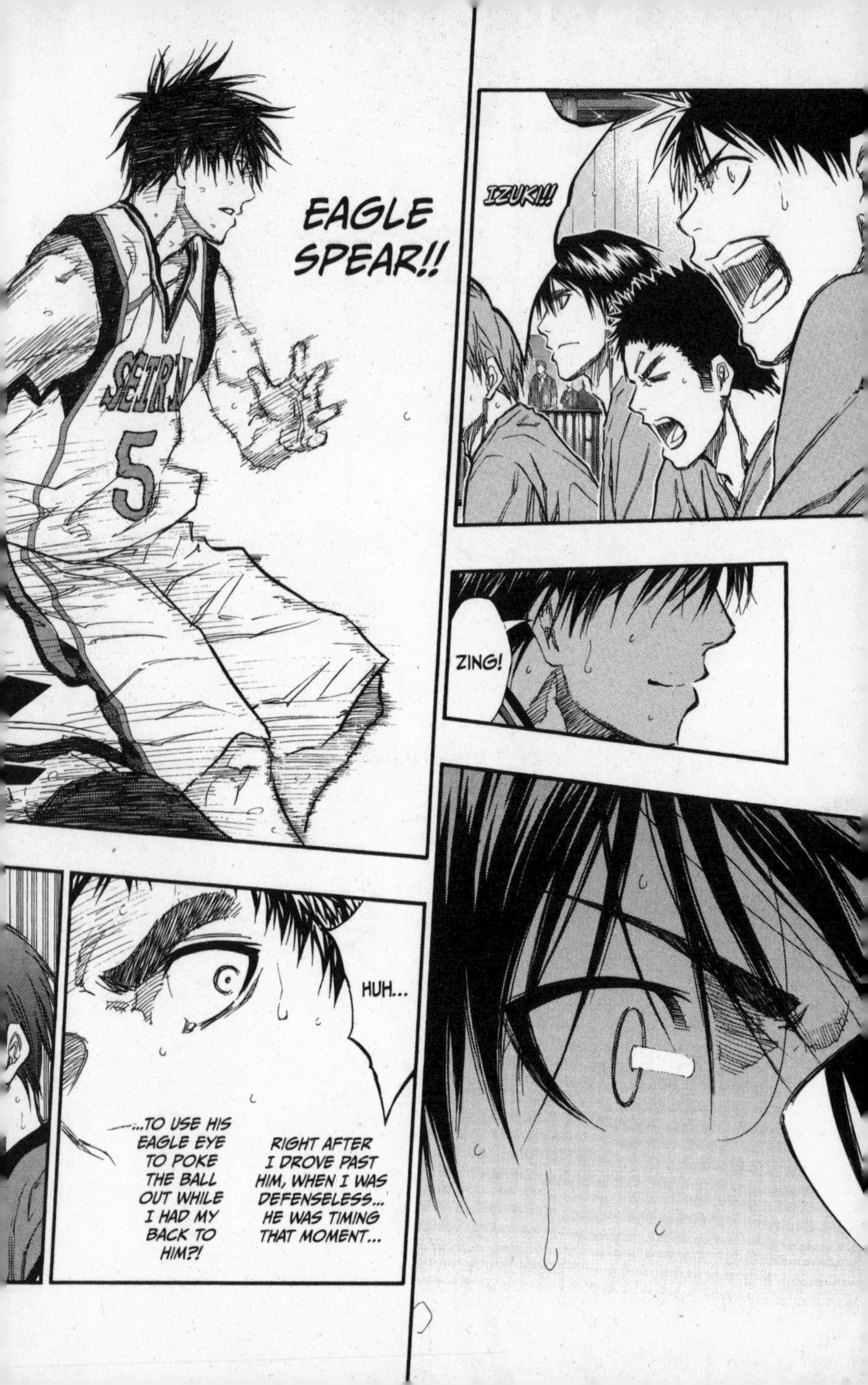
IZUKI!!
ZING!
EAGLE SPEAR!!
HUH...
RIGHT AFTER I DROVE PAST HIM, WHEN I WAS DEFENSELESS... HE WAS TIMING THAT MOMENT...
...TO USE HIS EAGLE EYE TO POKE THE BALL OUT WHILE I HAD MY BACK TO HIM?!

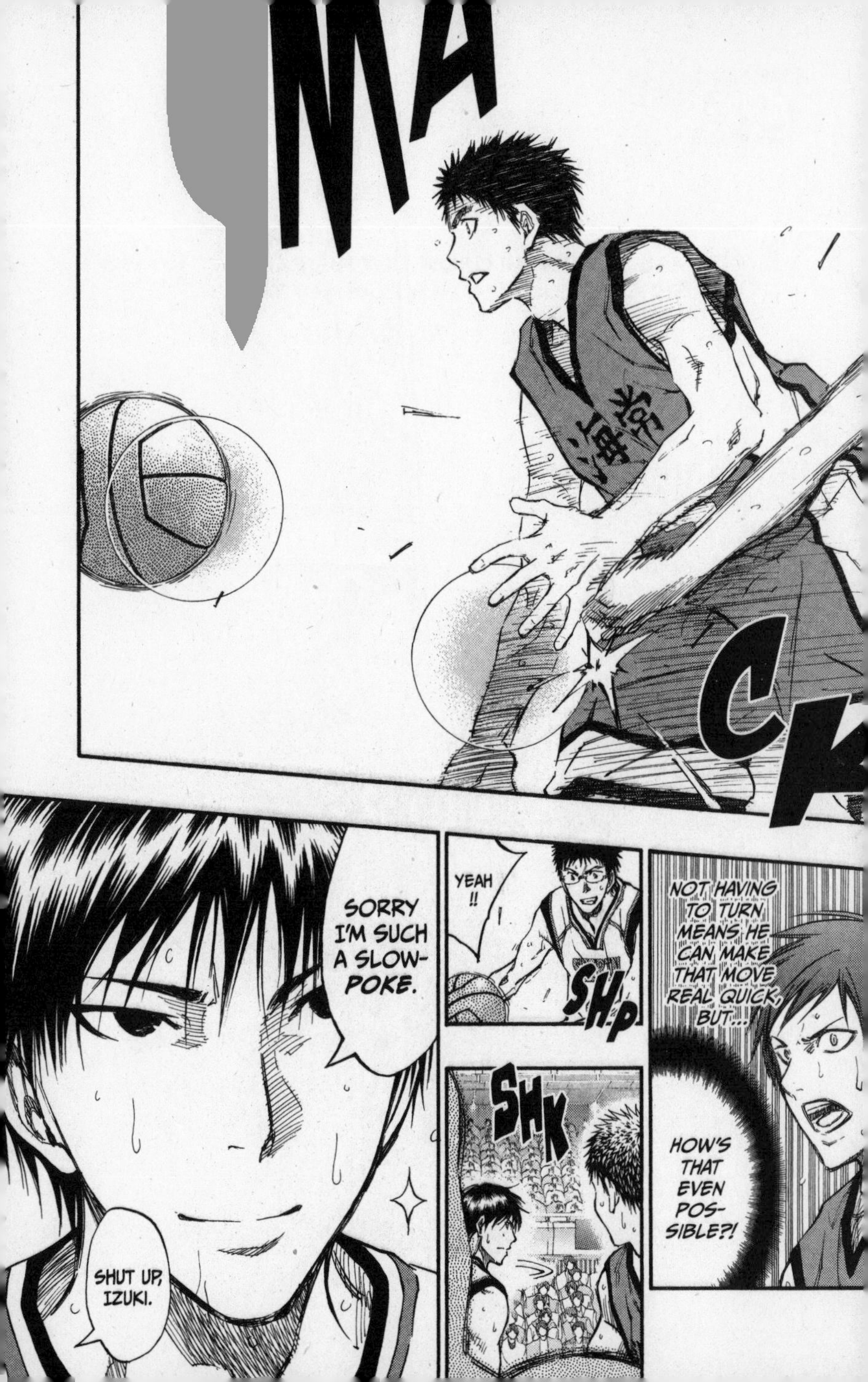

MA
CK
NOT HAVING TO TURN MEANS HE CAN MAKE THAT MOVE REAL QUICK, BUT...
HOW'S THAT EVEN POS-SIBLE?!
YEAH !!
SHP
SHK
SORRY I'M SUCH A SLOW-POKE.
SHUT UP, IZUKI.

KUROKO'S BASKETBALL Q&A

W/ HALFWAY-DECENT ANSWERS

Q. PLEASE LET AKASHI GROW OUT HIS BANGS.
(MUSHROOM MOUNTAIN RANGE from SAITAMA PREFECTURE)

A. DON'T ASK THE IMPOSSIBLE.

KUROKO'S BASKETBALL BLOOPERS

TAKE 2

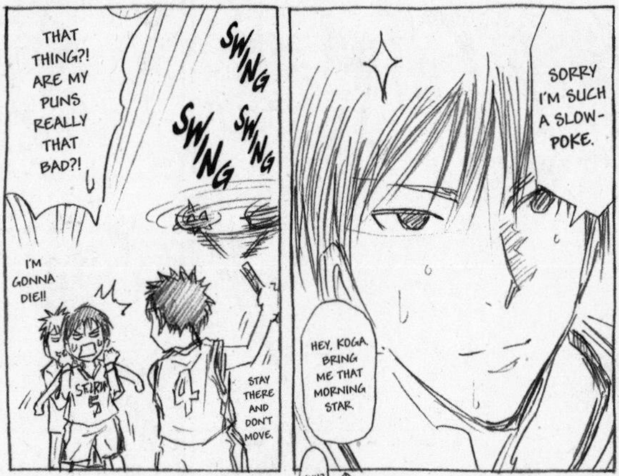
SORRY I'M SUCH A SLOW-POKE.
HEY, KOGA. BRING ME THAT MORNING STAR.
HUH?
THIS THING
THAT THING?! ARE MY PUNS REALLY THAT BAD?!
SWING
SWING
SWING
I'M GONNA DIE!!
SEIRIN
STAY THERE AND DON'T MOVE.

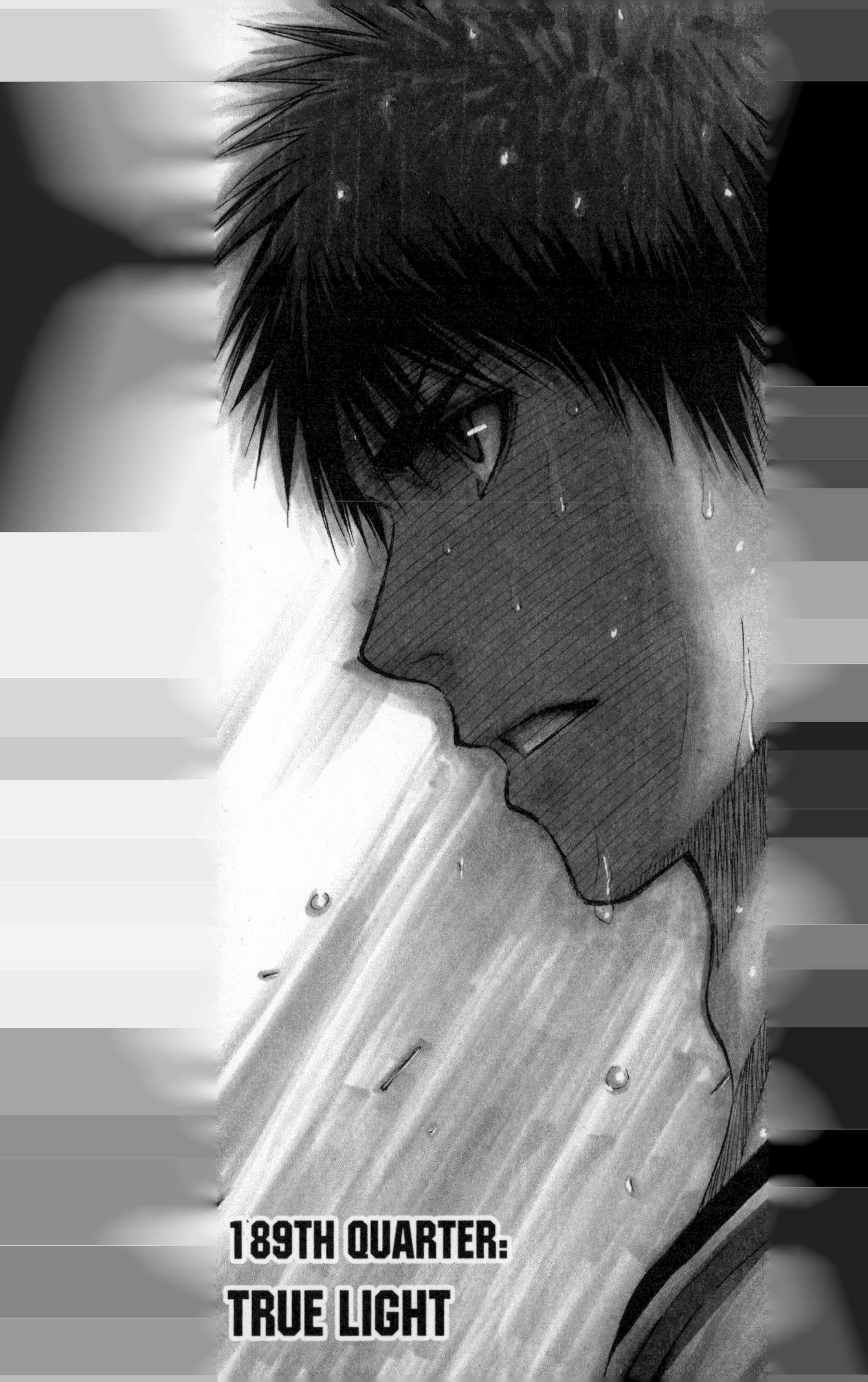
189TH QUARTER:
TRUE LIGHT

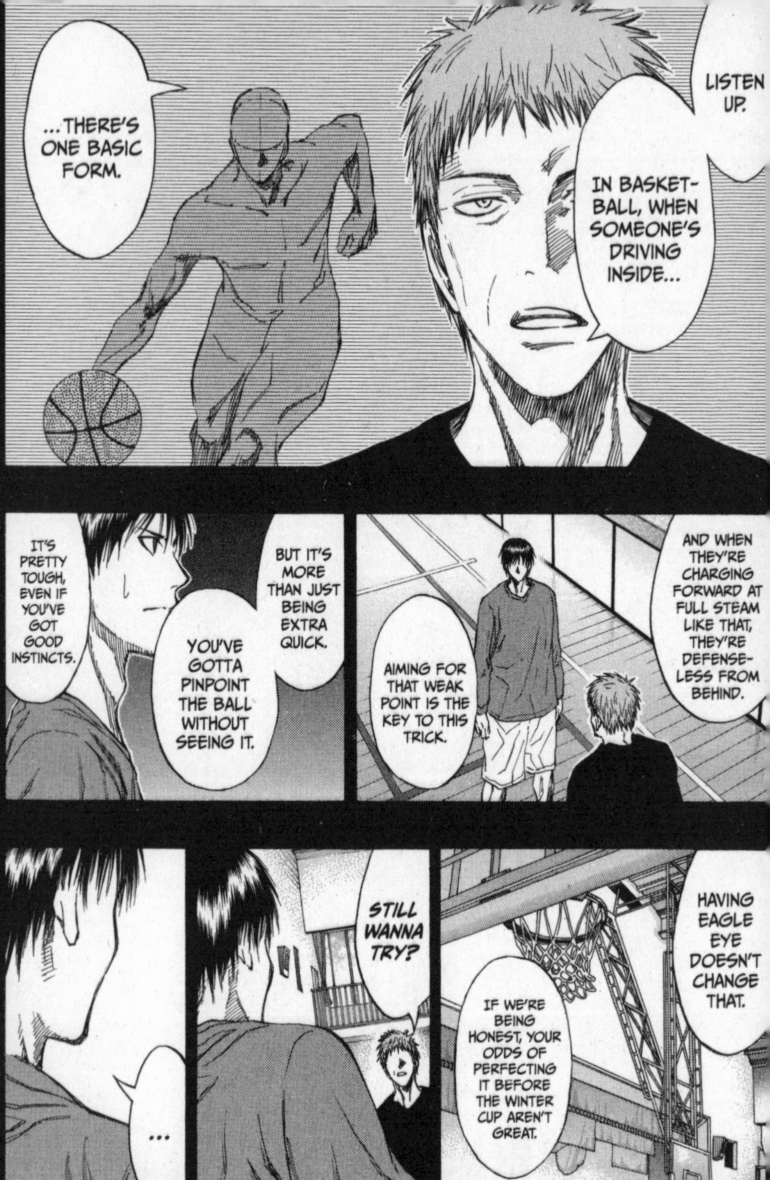
LISTEN UP.
IN BASKETBALL, WHEN SOMEONE'S DRIVING INSIDE...
...THERE'S ONE BASIC FORM.
AND WHEN THEY'RE CHARGING FORWARD AT FULL STEAM LIKE THAT, THEY'RE DEFENSELESS FROM BEHIND.
AIMING FOR THAT WEAK POINT IS THE KEY TO THIS TRICK.
BUT IT'S MORE THAN JUST BEING EXTRA QUICK.
YOU'VE GOTTA PINPOINT THE BALL WITHOUT SEEING IT.
IT'S PRETTY TOUGH, EVEN IF YOU'VE GOT GOOD INSTINCTS.
HAVING EAGLE EYE DOESN'T CHANGE THAT.
IF WE'RE BEING HONEST, YOUR ODDS OF PERFECTING IT BEFORE THE WINTER CUP AREN'T GREAT.
STILL WANNA TRY?
...

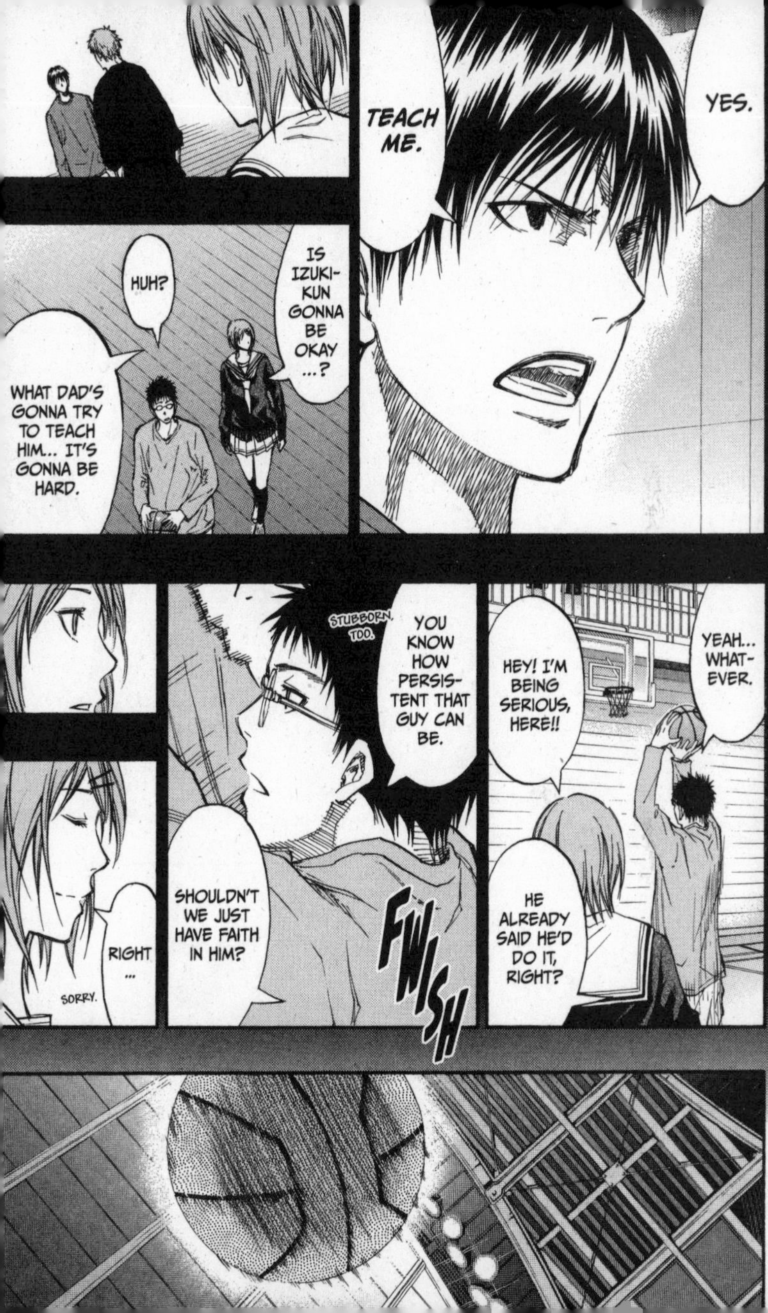
YES.
TEACH ME.
IS IZUKI-KUN GONNA BE OKAY ...?
HUH?
WHAT DAD'S GONNA TRY TO TEACH HIM... IT'S GONNA BE HARD.
YEAH... WHAT-EVER.
HEY! I'M BEING SERIOUS, HERE!!
HE ALREADY SAID HE'D DO IT, RIGHT?
YOU KNOW HOW PERSIS-TENT THAT GUY CAN BE.
STUBBORN, TOO.
SHOULDN'T WE JUST HAVE FAITH IN HIM?
RIGHT ...
SORRY.
FWISH

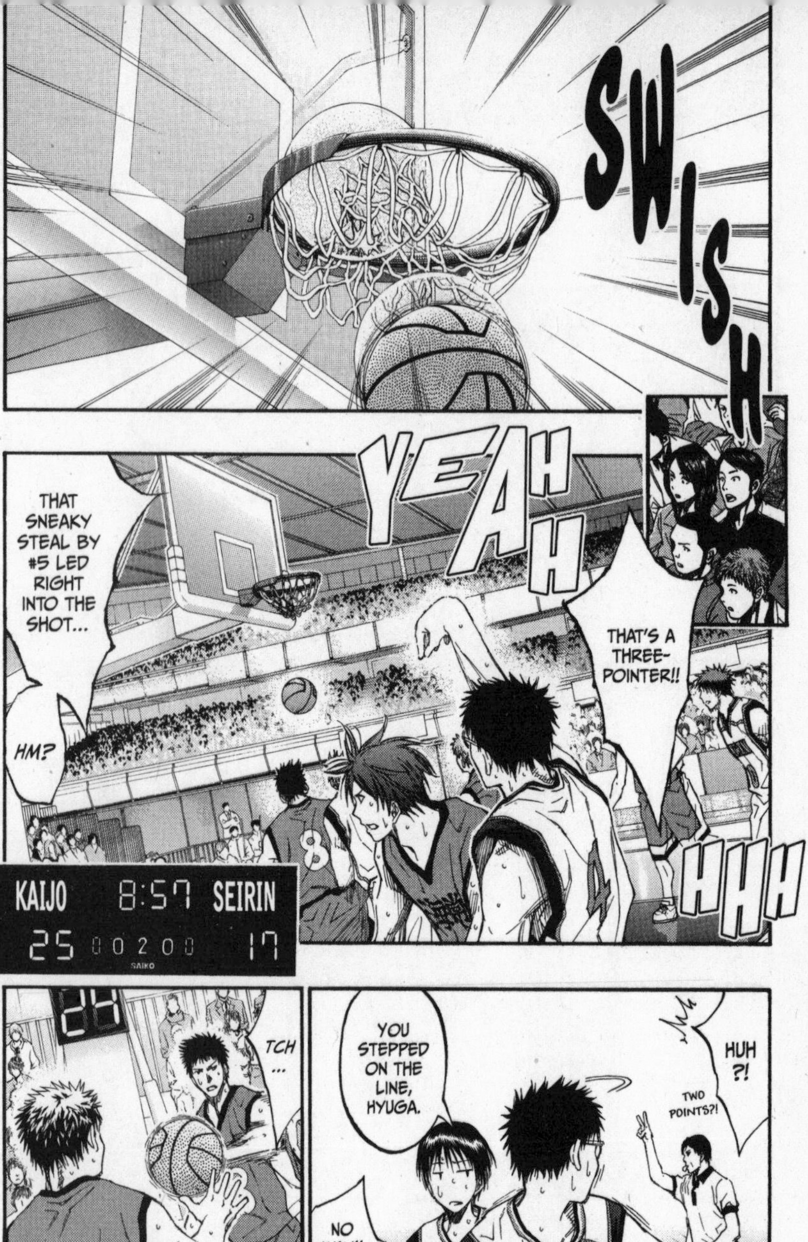
SWISH
YEAHHH
HHHH
THAT'S A THREE-POINTER!!
THAT SNEAKY STEAL BY #5 LED RIGHT INTO THE SHOT...
HM?
KAIJO 8:57 SEIRIN
25 00200 17
SAIKO
HUH?!
TWO POINTS?!
YOU STEPPED ON THE LINE, HYUGA.
NO WAY!!
WHAT A LAME MISTAKE!
SEIRIN
TCH...

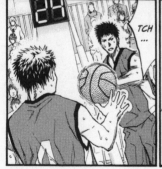

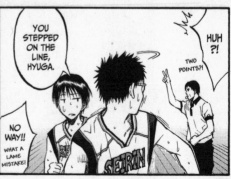

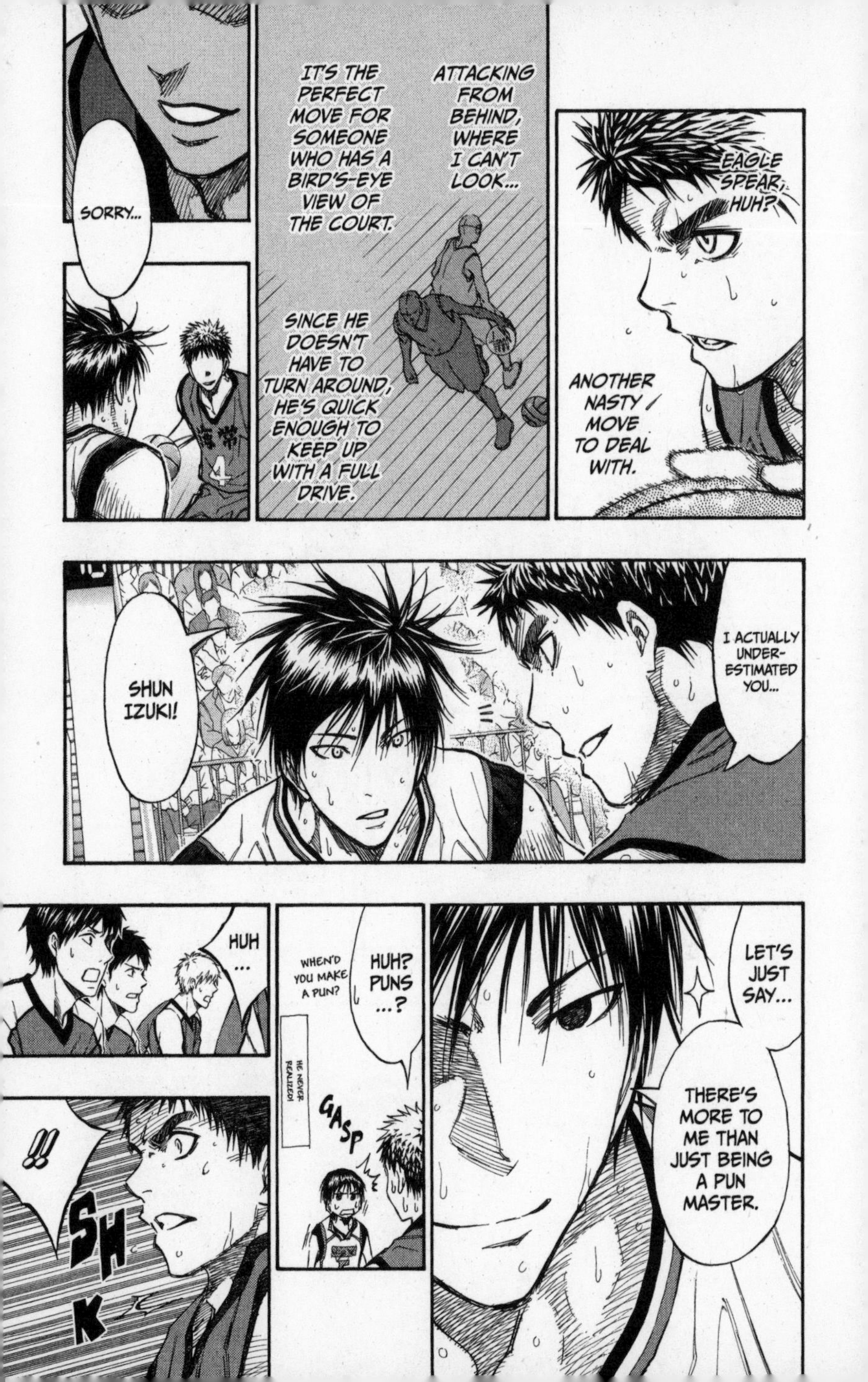
EAGLE SPEAR, HUH?
ANOTHER NASTY MOVE TO DEAL WITH.
ATTACKING FROM BEHIND, WHERE I CAN'T LOOK...
IT'S THE PERFECT MOVE FOR SOMEONE WHO HAS A BIRD'S-EYE VIEW OF THE COURT.
SINCE HE DOESN'T HAVE TO TURN AROUND, HE'S QUICK ENOUGH TO KEEP UP WITH A FULL DRIVE.
SORRY...
I ACTUALLY UNDER-ESTIMATED YOU...
SHUN IZUKI!
LET'S JUST SAY...
THERE'S MORE TO ME THAN JUST BEING A PUN MASTER.
HUH? PUNS ...?
WHEN'D YOU MAKE A PUN?
HE NEVER REALIZED!
GASP
HUH ...
!!
SHK

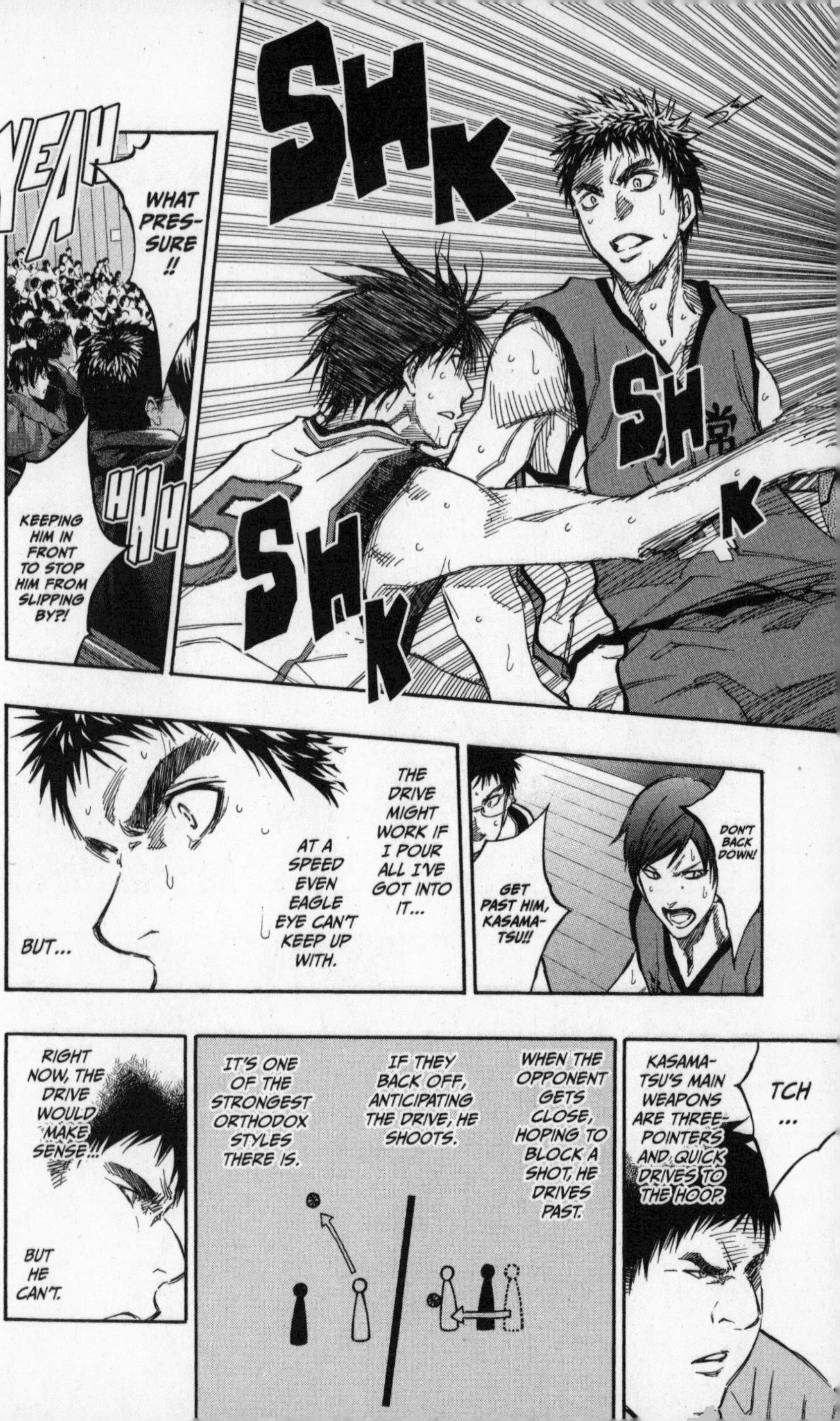
SHK
SHK
SHK
YEAH
WHAT PRESSURE!!
HHH
KEEPING HIM IN FRONT TO STOP HIM FROM SLIPPING BY?!
DON'T BACK DOWN!
GET PAST HIM, KASAMATSU!!
THE DRIVE MIGHT WORK IF I POUR ALL I'VE GOT INTO IT...
AT A SPEED EVEN EAGLE EYE CAN'T KEEP UP WITH.
BUT...
TCH...
KASAMATSU'S MAIN WEAPONS ARE THREE-POINTERS AND QUICK DRIVES TO THE HOOP.
WHEN THE OPPONENT GETS CLOSE, HOPING TO BLOCK A SHOT, HE DRIVES PAST.
IF THEY BACK OFF, ANTICIPATING THE DRIVE, HE SHOOTS.
IT'S ONE OF THE STRONGEST ORTHODOX STYLES THERE IS.
RIGHT NOW, THE DRIVE WOULD MAKE SENSE...
BUT HE CAN'T.

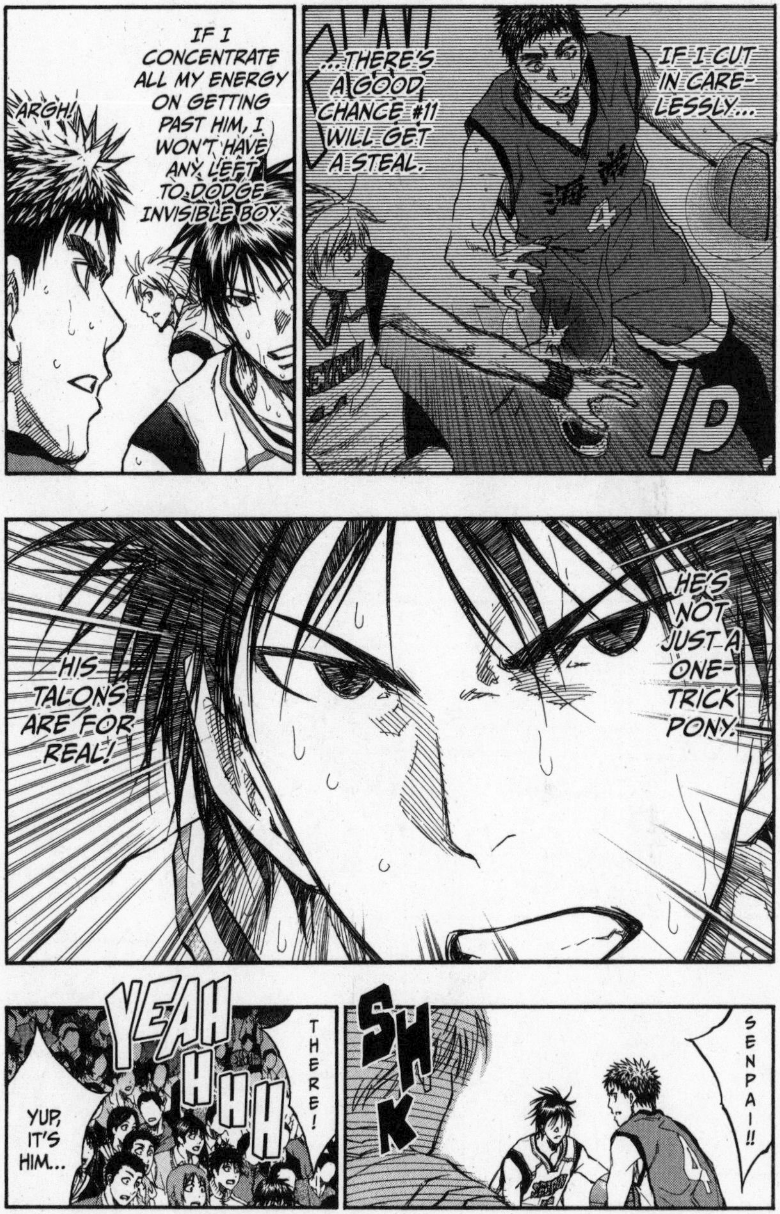
IF I CUT IN CARE-LESSLY...
...THERE'S A GOOD CHANCE #11 WILL GET A STEAL.
IP
IF I CONCENTRATE ALL MY ENERGY ON GETTING PAST HIM, I WON'T HAVE ANY LEFT TO DODGE INVISIBLE BOY.
ARGH!
HE'S NOT JUST A ONE-TRICK PONY.
HIS TALONS ARE FOR REAL!
SENPAI!!
SHK
YEAHHHHH
THERE!
YUP, IT'S HIM...

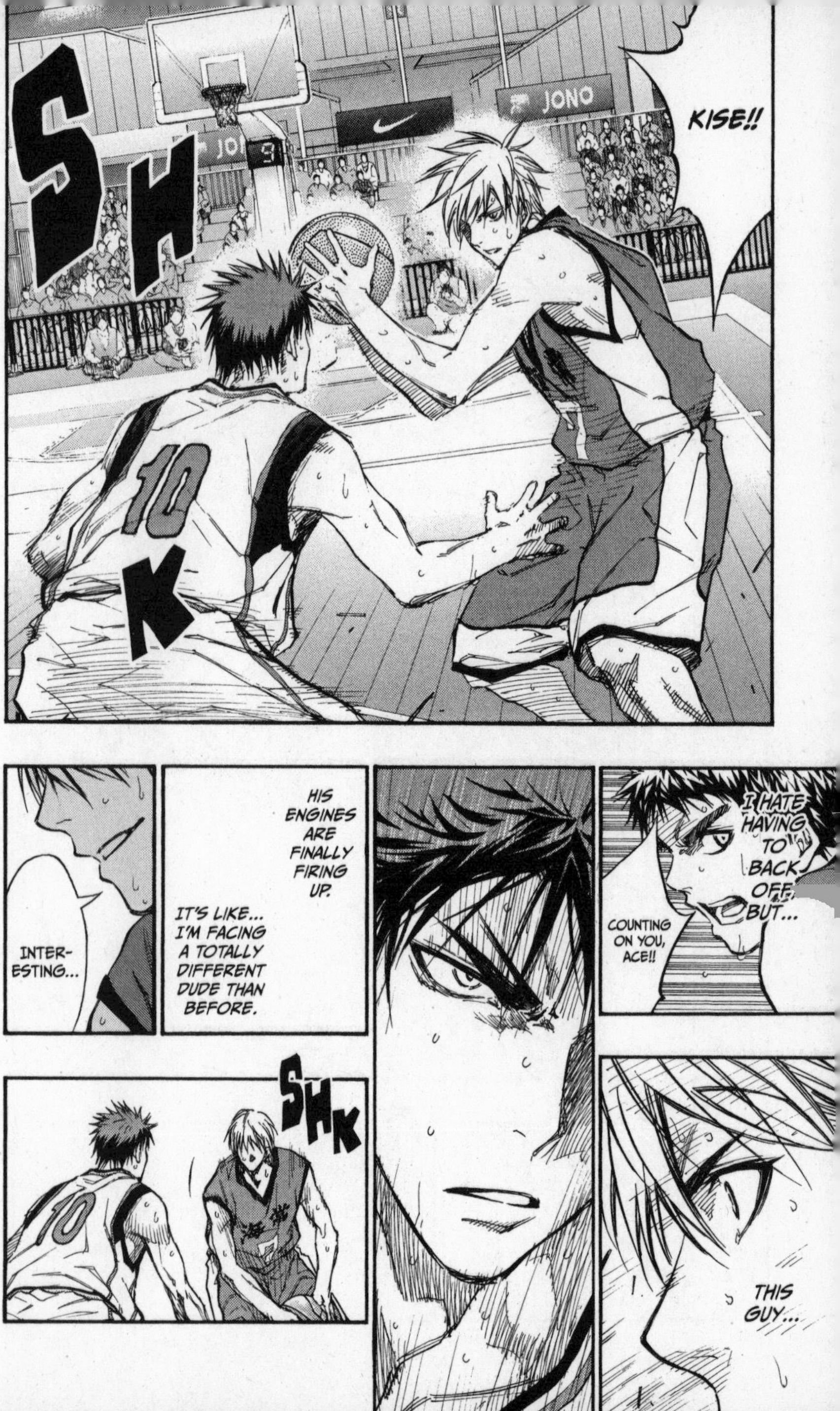
KISE!!
SH
I HATE HAVING TO BACK OFF BUT...
COUNTING ON YOU, ACE!!
THIS GUY...
HIS ENGINES ARE FINALLY FIRING UP.
IT'S LIKE... I'M FACING A TOTALLY DIFFERENT DUDE THAN BEFORE.
INTER-ESTING...
SHK

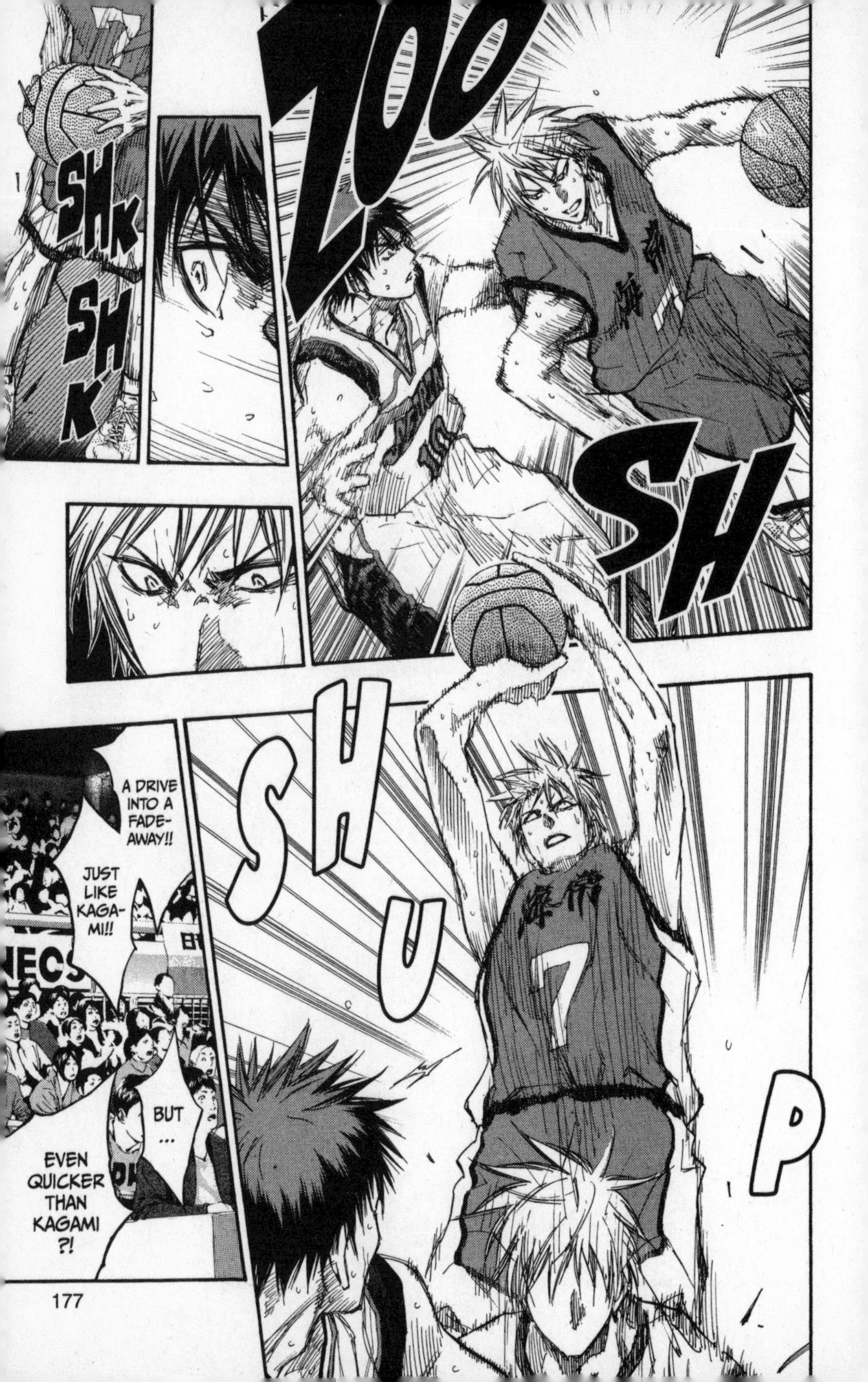
ZOOO
SH
SHK
SHK
SHUP
A DRIVE INTO A FADE-AWAY!!
JUST LIKE KAGA-MI!!
BUT ...
EVEN QUICKER THAN KAGAMI ?!

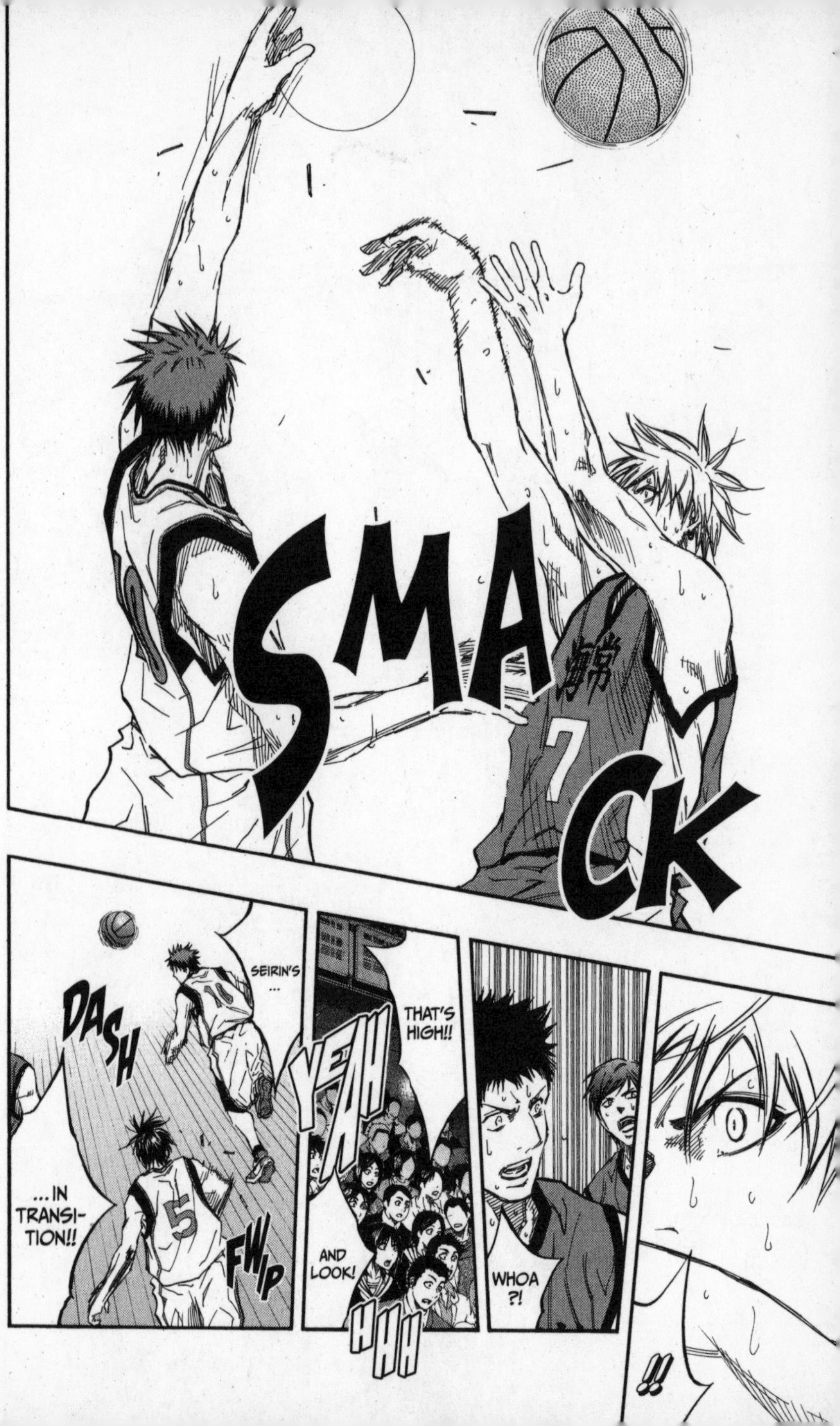
SMACK
!!
WHOA ?!
THAT'S HIGH!!
YEAHHHH
AND LOOK!
SEIRIN'S ...
DASH
...IN TRANSITION!!
FWIP

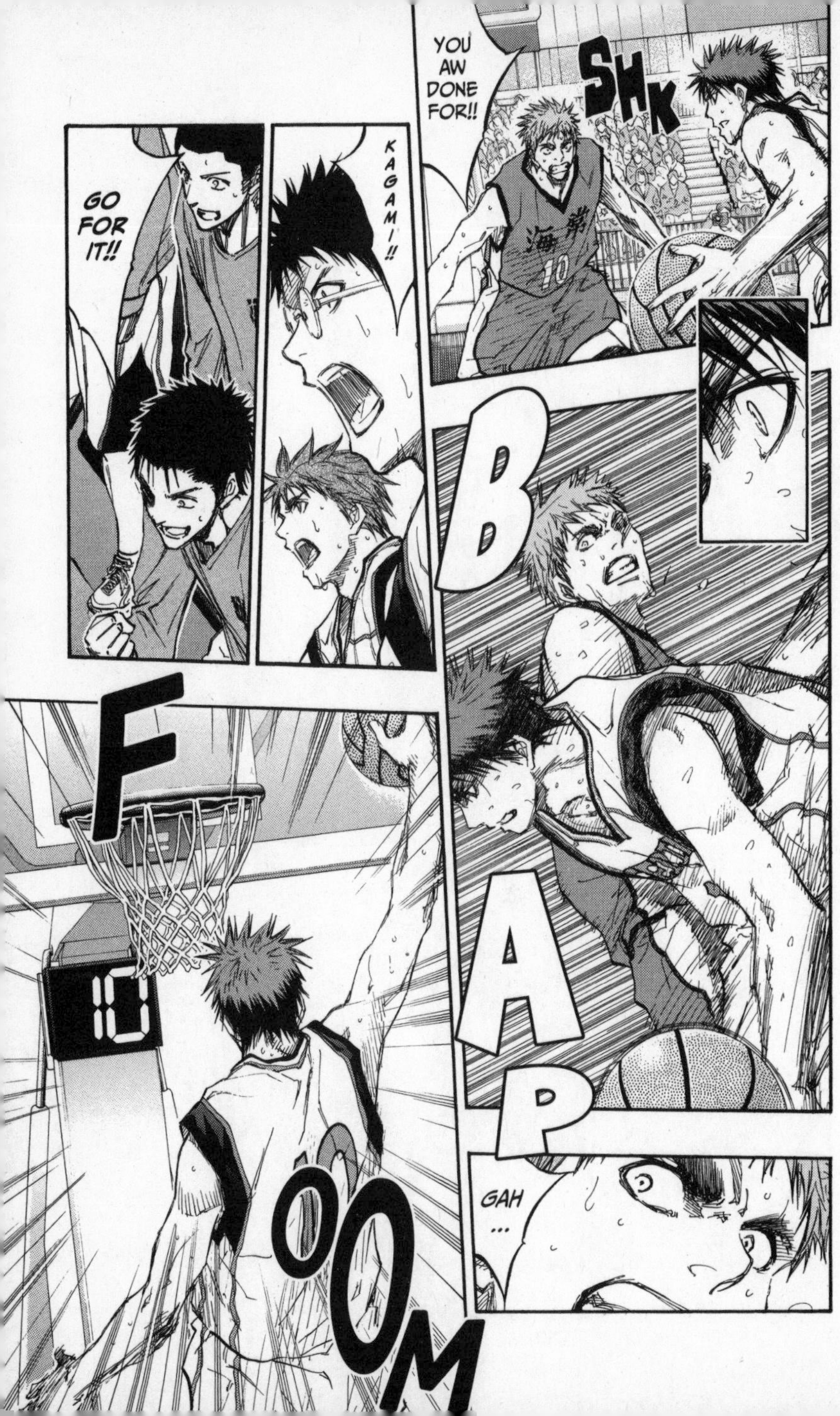
YOU AW DONE FOR!!
SHK
KAGAMI!!
GO FOR IT!!
BAP
GAH ...
FOOOM

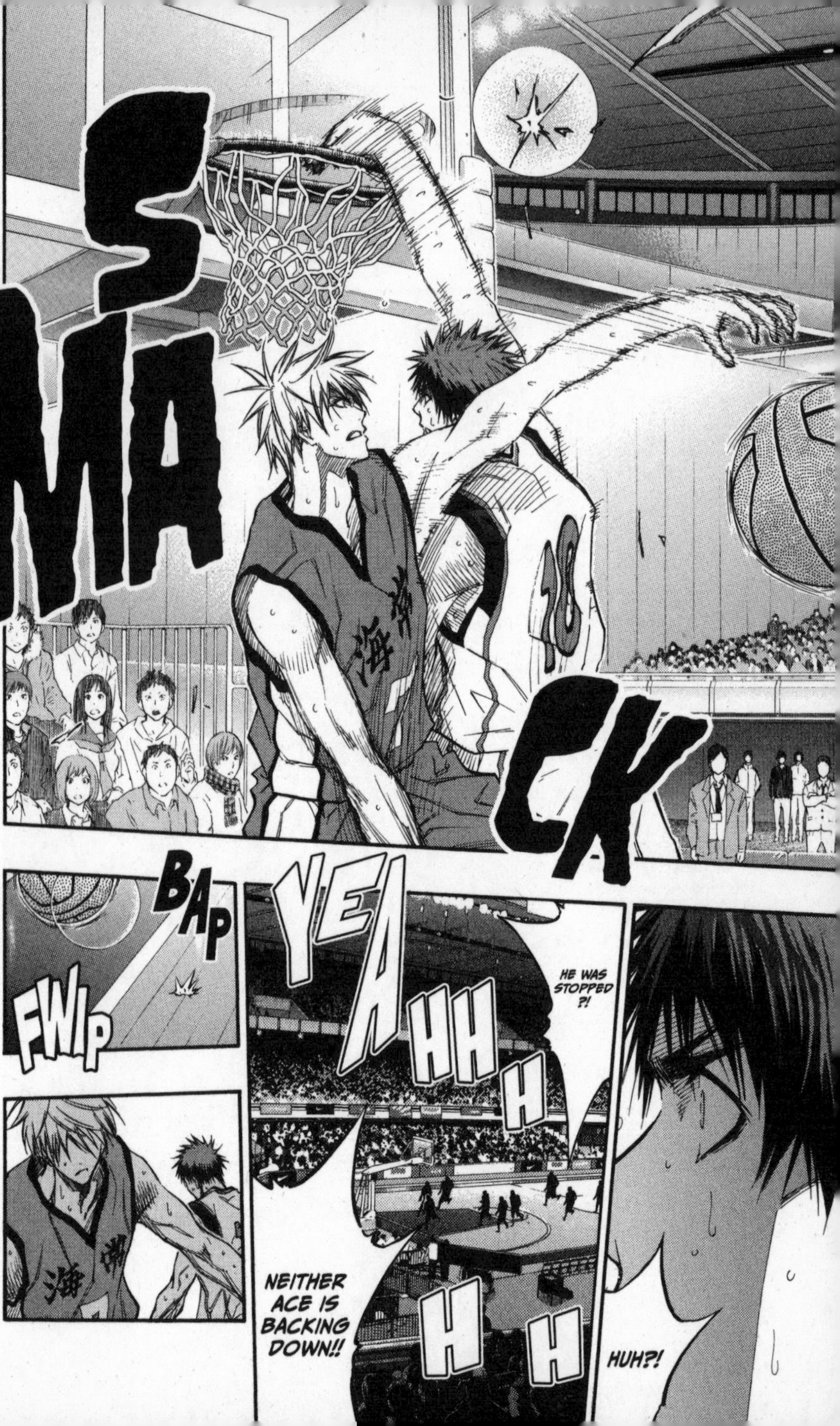
SMACK
HUH?!
HE WAS STOPPED ?!
YEAHHHHH
NEITHER ACE IS BACKING DOWN!!
BAP
FWIP

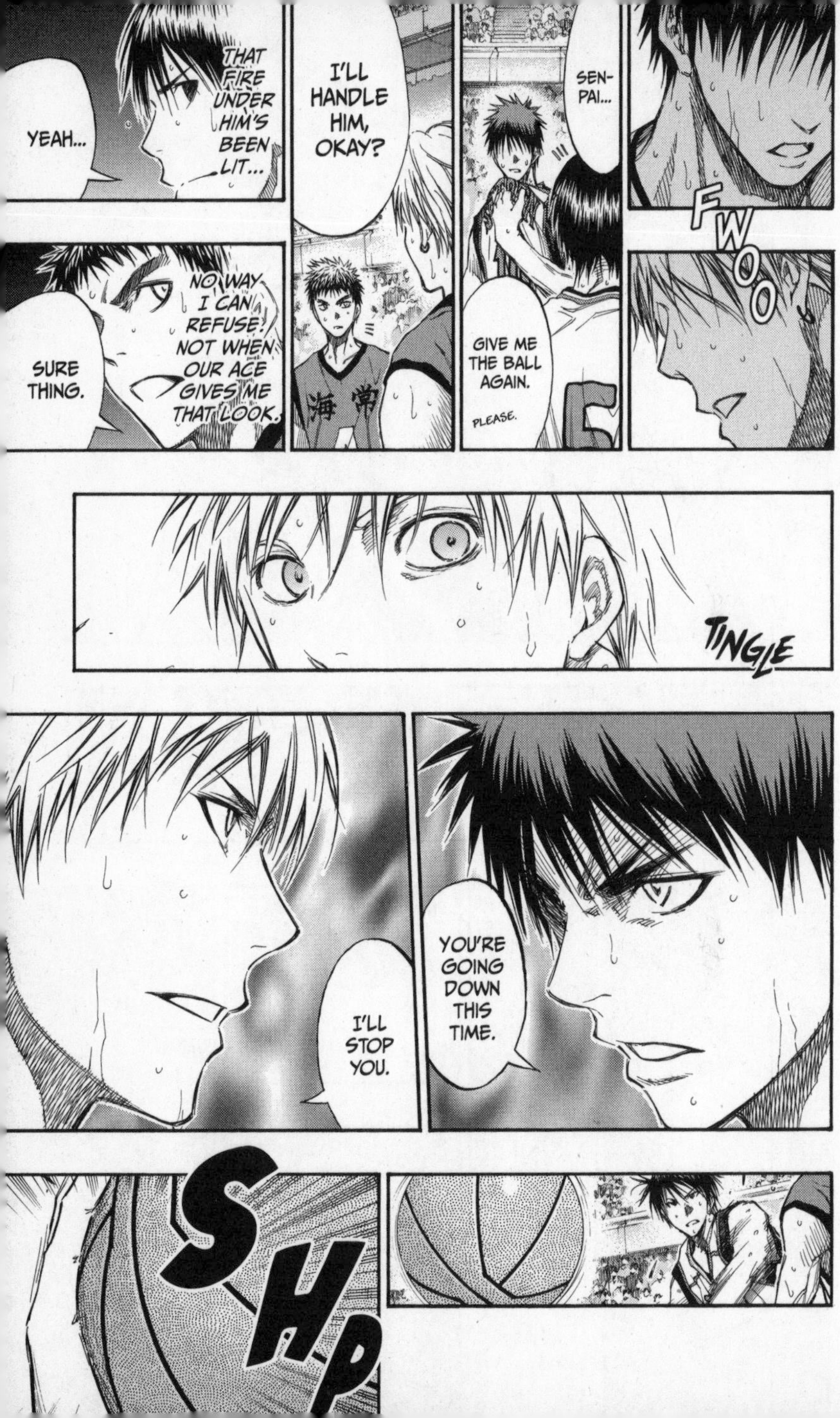
FWOO
SEN-PAI...
GIVE ME THE BALL AGAIN.
PLEASE.
I'LL HANDLE HIM, OKAY?
THAT FIRE UNDER HIM'S BEEN LIT...
YEAH...
NO WAY I CAN REFUSE! NOT WHEN OUR ACE GIVES ME THAT LOOK.
SURE THING.
TINGLE
YOU'RE GOING DOWN THIS TIME.
I'LL STOP YOU.
SHP

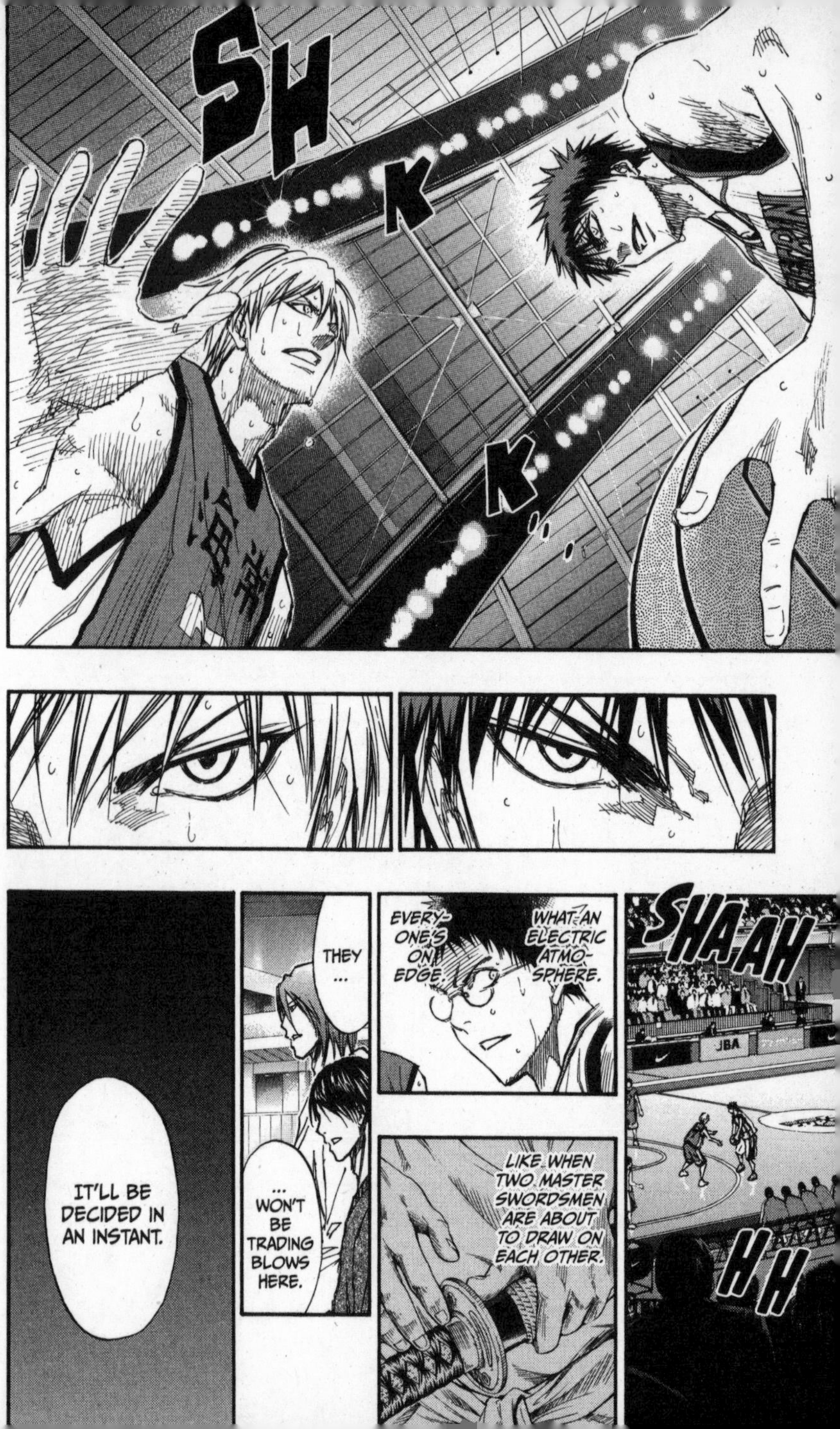
SHK
K
SHAAH
HH
WHAT AN ELECTRIC ATMOSPHERE.
EVERYONE'S ON EDGE.
LIKE WHEN TWO MASTER SWORDSMEN ARE ABOUT TO DRAW ON EACH OTHER.
THEY ...
... WON'T BE TRADING BLOWS HERE.
IT'LL BE DECIDED IN AN INSTANT.

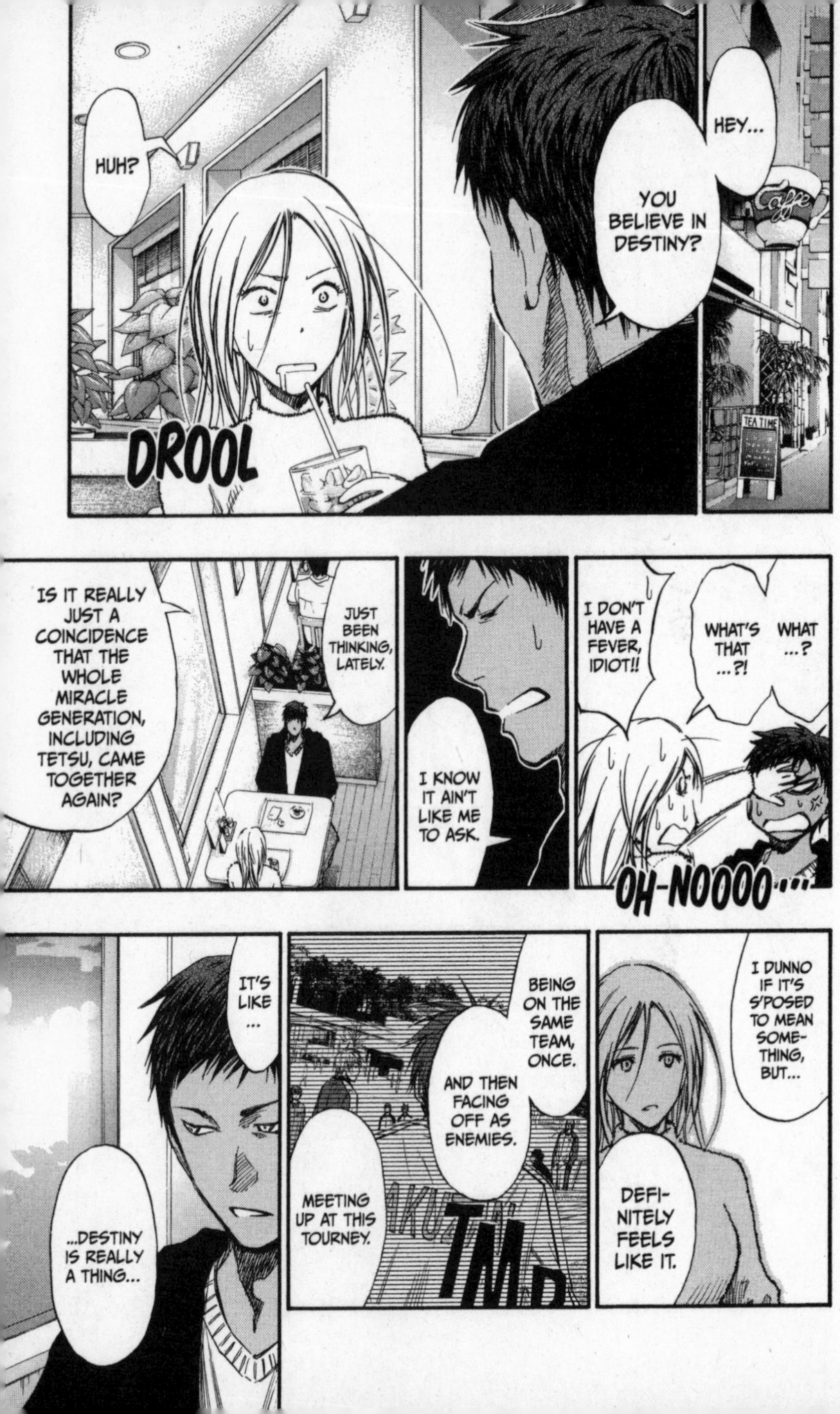
HEY...
YOU BELIEVE IN DESTINY?
HUH?
DROOL
WHAT ...?
WHAT'S THAT ...?!
I DON'T HAVE A FEVER, IDIOT!!
OH-NOOOO....
I KNOW IT AIN'T LIKE ME TO ASK.
JUST BEEN THINKING, LATELY.
IS IT REALLY JUST A COINCIDENCE THAT THE WHOLE MIRACLE GENERATION, INCLUDING TETSU, CAME TOGETHER AGAIN?
I DUNNO IF IT'S S'POSED TO MEAN SOME-THING, BUT...
DEFI-NITELY FEELS LIKE IT.
BEING ON THE SAME TEAM, ONCE.
AND THEN FACING OFF AS ENEMIES.
MEETING UP AT THIS TOURNEY.
IT'S LIKE ...
...DESTINY IS REALLY A THING...

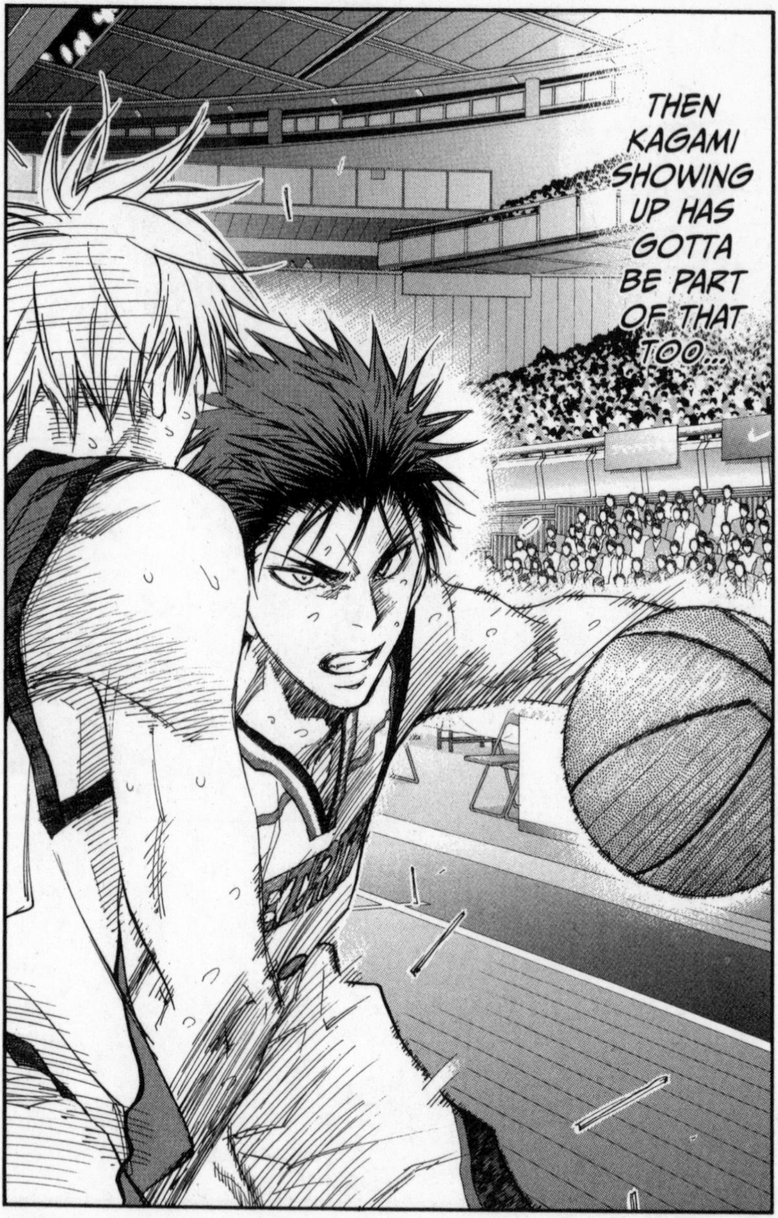
THEN KAGAMI SHOWING UP HAS GOTTA BE PART OF THAT TOO...

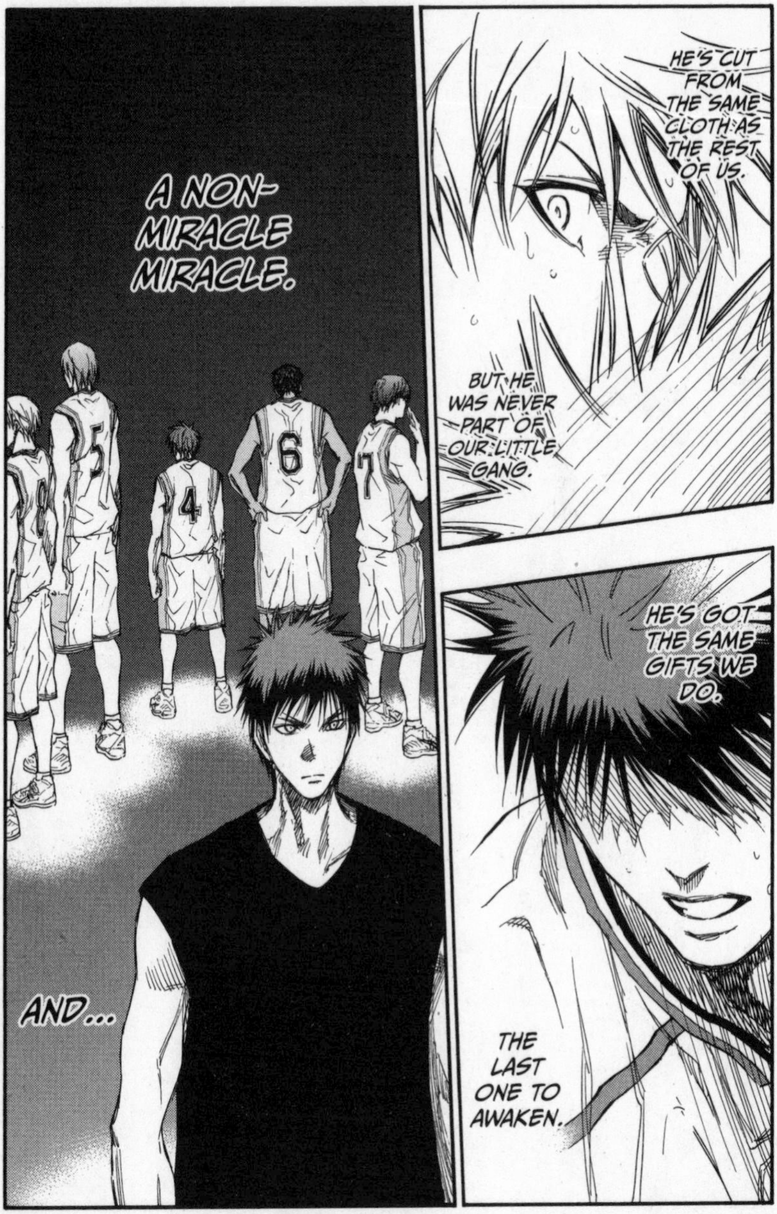
HE'S CUT FROM THE SAME CLOTH AS THE REST OF US.
BUT HE WAS NEVER PART OF OUR LITTLE GANG.
HE'S GOT THE SAME GIFTS WE DO.
THE LAST ONE TO AWAKEN.
A NON-MIRACLE MIRACLE.
AND...

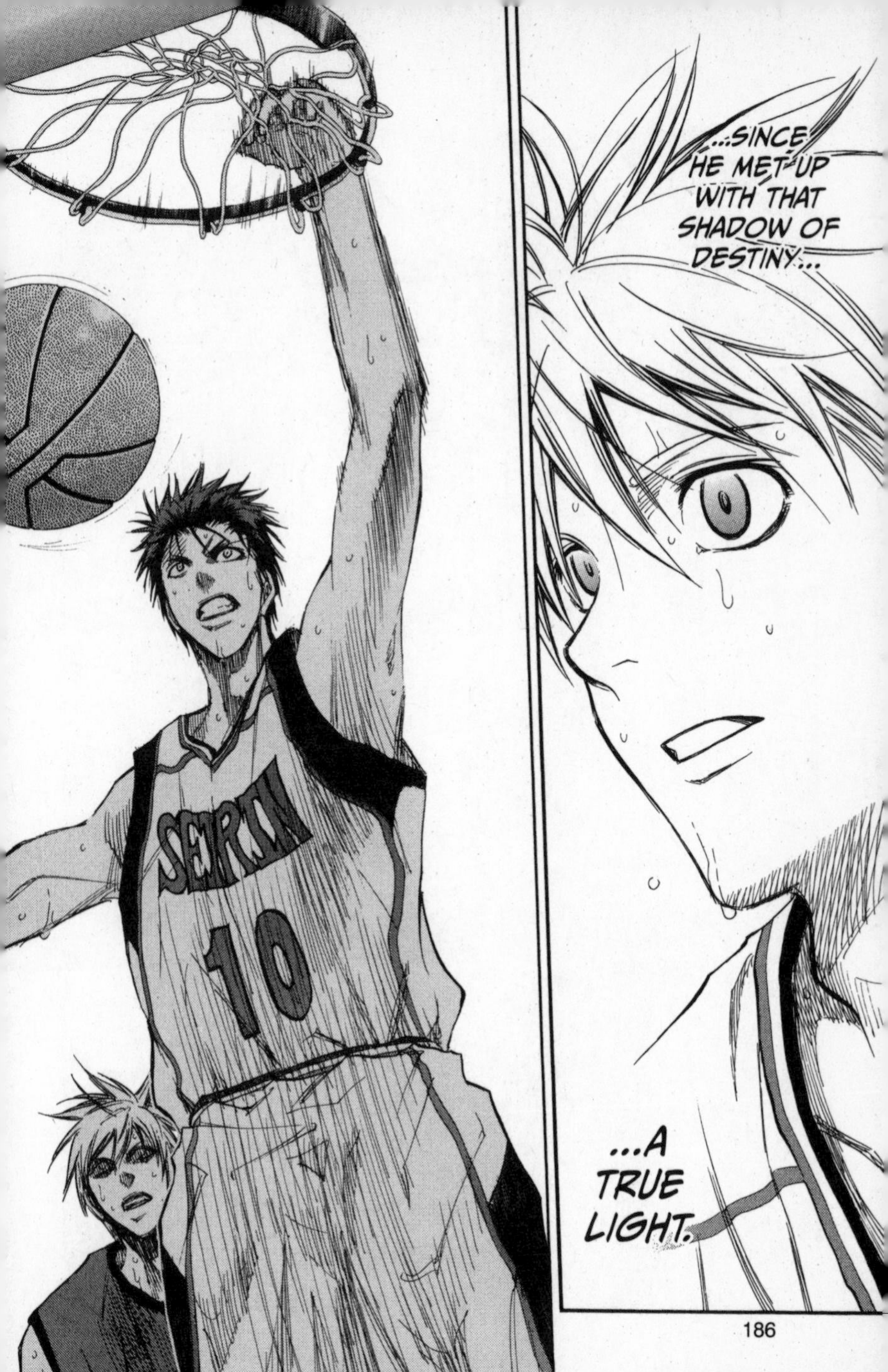
...SINCE HE MET UP WITH THAT SHADOW OF DESTINY...
...A TRUE LIGHT.

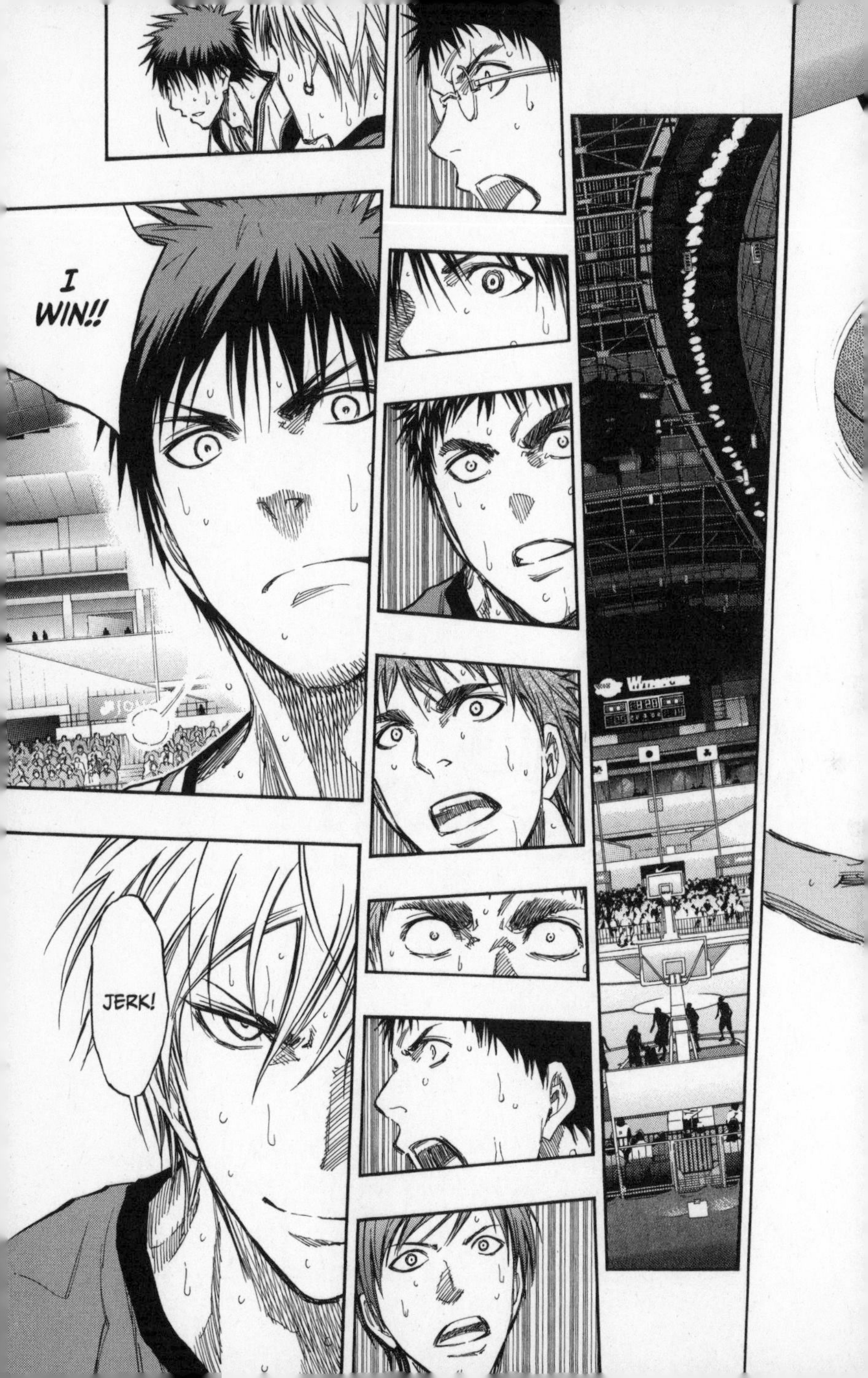
I WIN!!
JERK!

KUROKO'S BASKETBALL BLOOPERS

TAKE 2

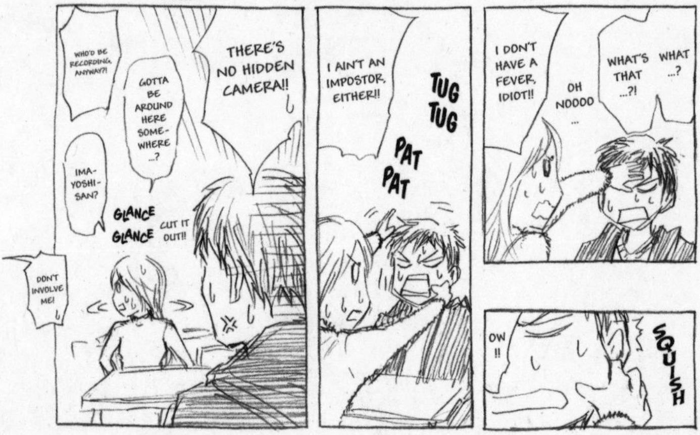

WHAT ...?
WHAT'S THAT ...?!
OH NOOOO ...
I DON'T HAVE A FEVER, IDIOT!!
SQUISH
OW !!
TUG TUG
I AIN'T AN IMPOSTOR, EITHER!!
PAT PAT
THERE'S NO HIDDEN CAMERA!!
WHO'D BE RECORDING, ANYWAY?!
GOTTA BE AROUND HERE SOME-WHERE ...?
IMA-YOSHI-SAN?
CUT IT OUT!!
GLANCE GLANCE
DON'T INVOLVE ME!

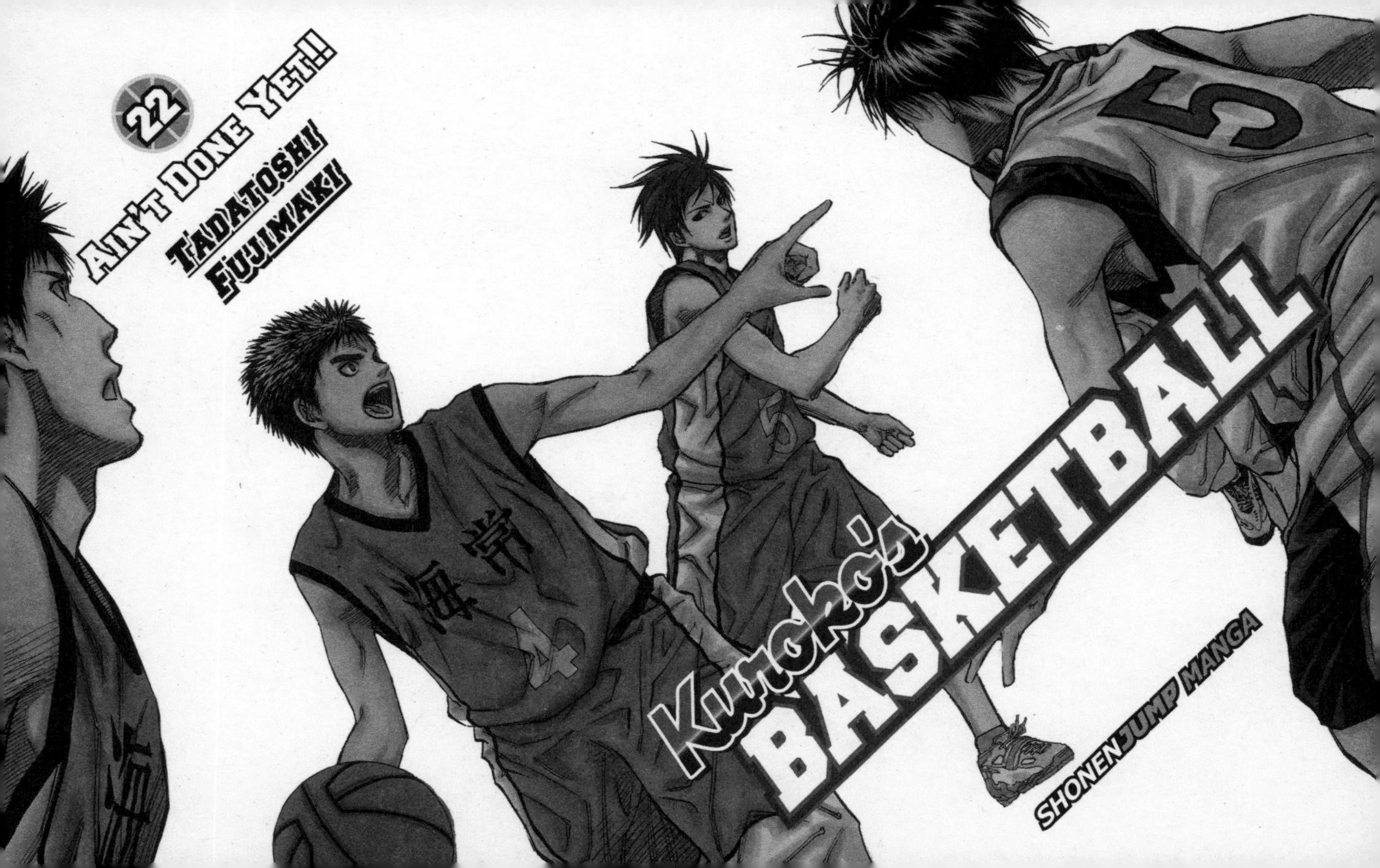
22
AIN'T DONE YET!!
TADATOSHI FUJIMAKI
Kuroko's BASKETBALL
SHONEN JUMP MANGA

TADATOSHI FUJIMAKI

When I'm not 100 percent focused (and I'm honest with myself), the things I can't write/draw are...

- Ultimate Play names.
- Boobs.
- Poetic-sounding dialogue.

—2013

190TH QUARTER: ALL WE'VE GOT

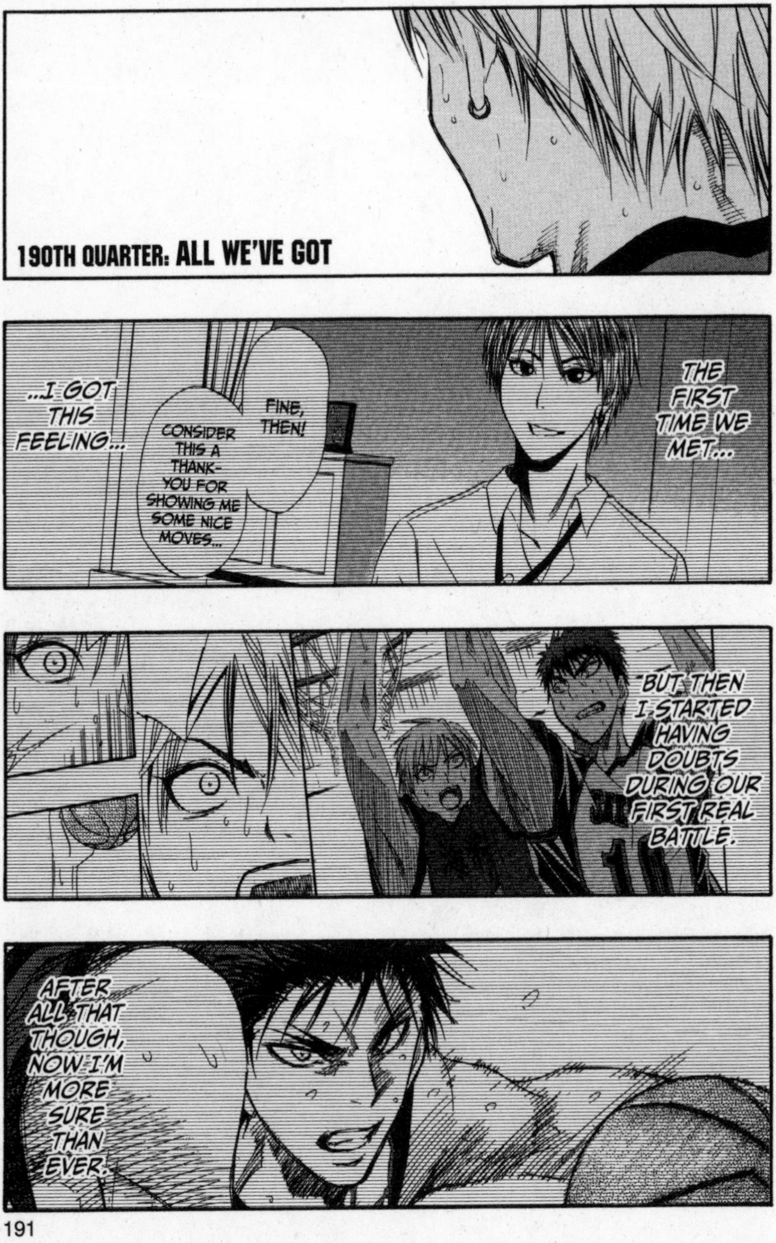
THE FIRST TIME WE MET...
FINE, THEN!
CONSIDER THIS A THANK-YOU FOR SHOWING ME SOME NICE MOVES...
...I GOT THIS FEELING...
BUT THEN I STARTED HAVING DOUBTS DURING OUR FIRST REAL BATTLE.
AFTER ALL THAT THOUGH, NOW I'M MORE SURE THAN EVER.

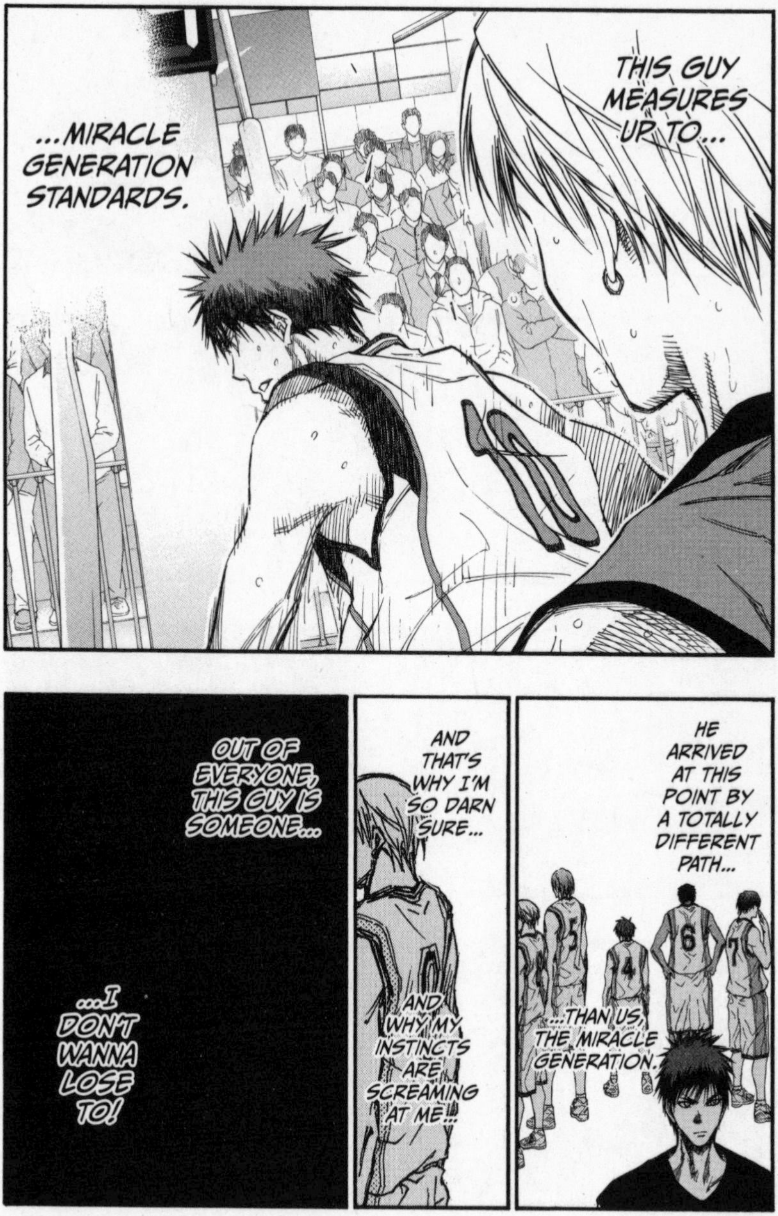
THIS GUY MEASURES UP TO...
...MIRACLE GENERATION STANDARDS.
HE ARRIVED AT THIS POINT BY A TOTALLY DIFFERENT PATH...
...THAN US, THE MIRACLE GENERATION.
AND THAT'S WHY I'M SO DARN SURE...
AND WHY MY INSTINCTS ARE SCREAMING AT ME...
OUT OF EVERYONE, THIS GUY IS SOMEONE...
...I DON'T WANNA LOSE TO!

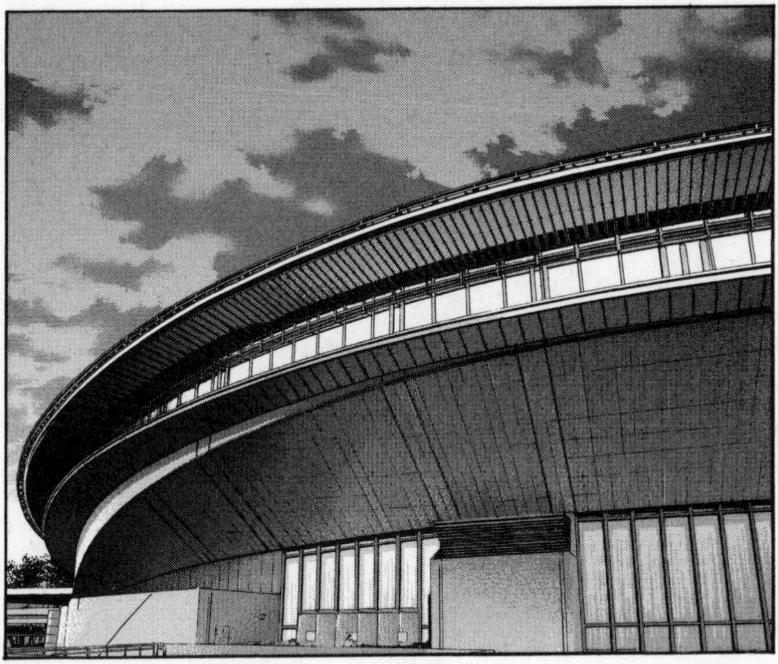

190TH QUARTER: ALL WE'VE GOT

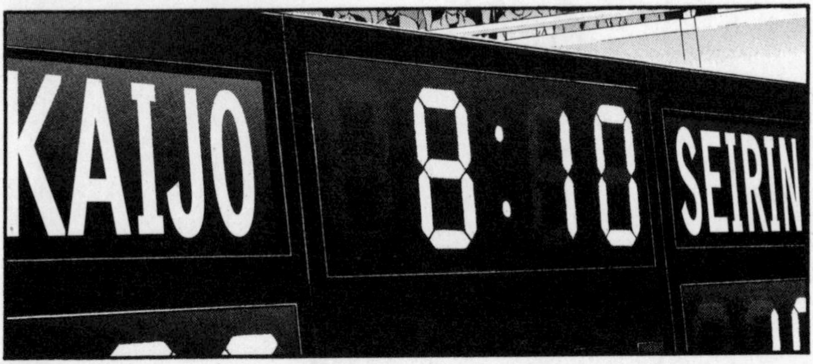
KAIJO
8 : 10
SEIRIN

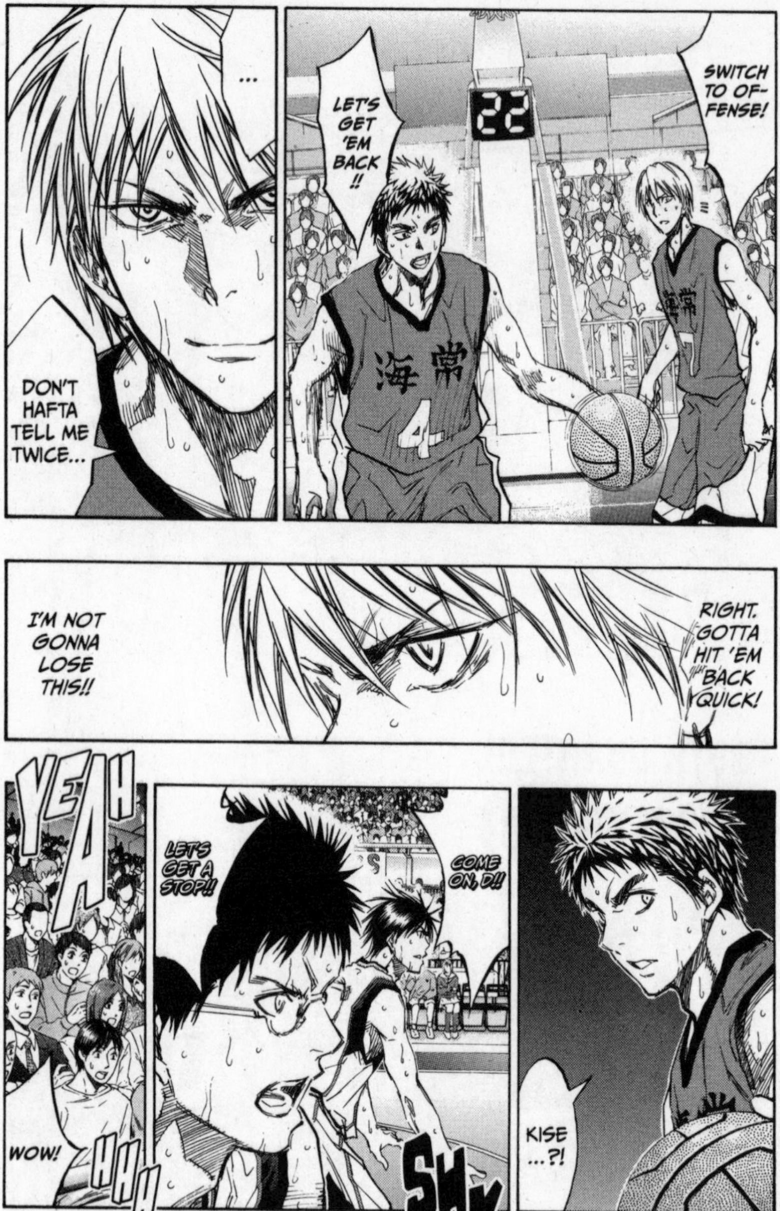
SWITCH TO OF-FENSE!
LET'S GET 'EM BACK!!
...
DON'T HAFTA TELL ME TWICE...
RIGHT. GOTTA HIT 'EM BACK QUICK!
I'M NOT GONNA LOSE THIS!!
KISE ...?!
COME ON, D!!
LET'S GET A STOP!!
SHK
YEAH HHH
WOW!

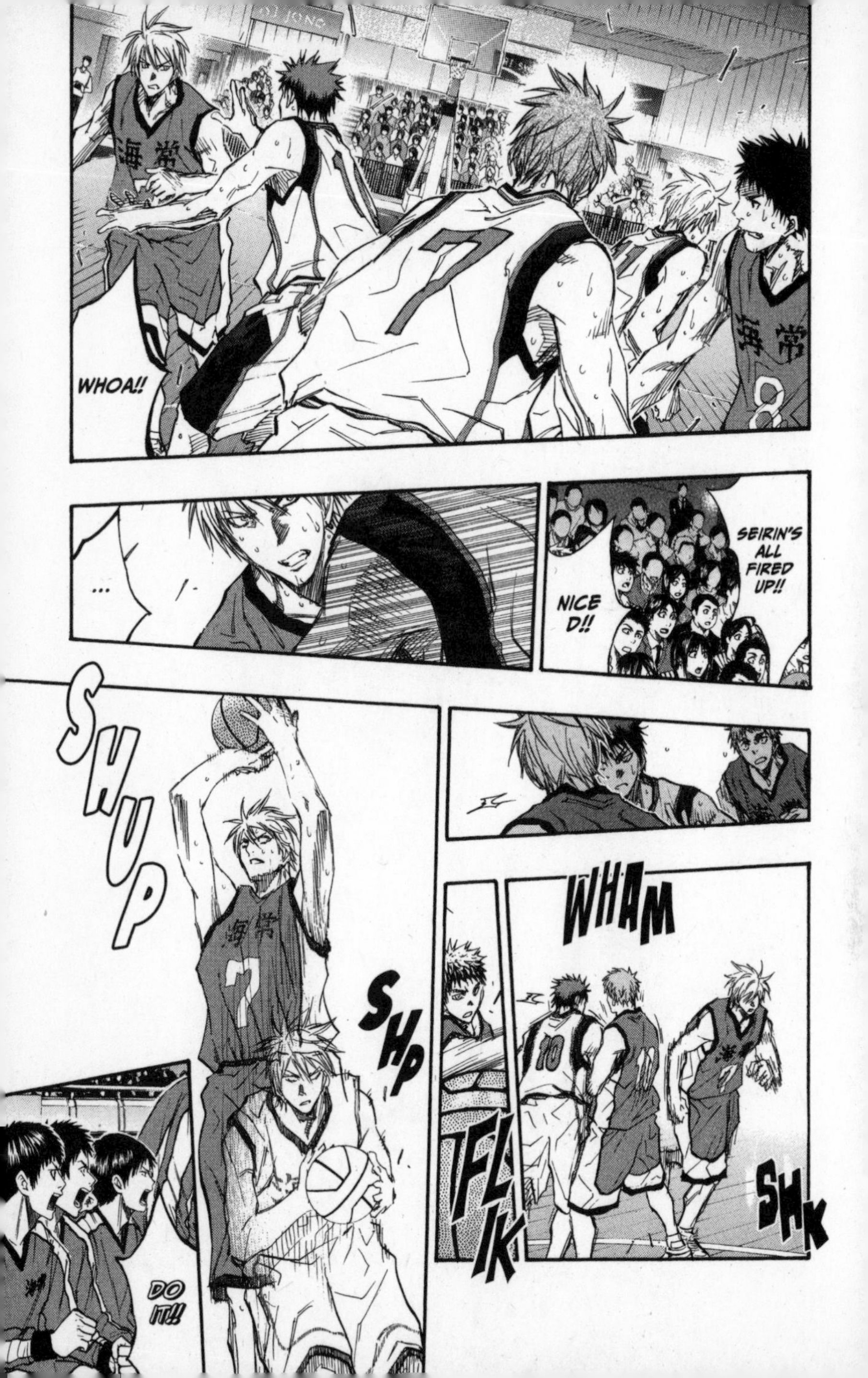
WHOA!!
SEIRIN'S ALL FIRED UP!!
NICE D!!
...
WHAM
SHK
FLIK
SHUP
SHP
DO IT!!

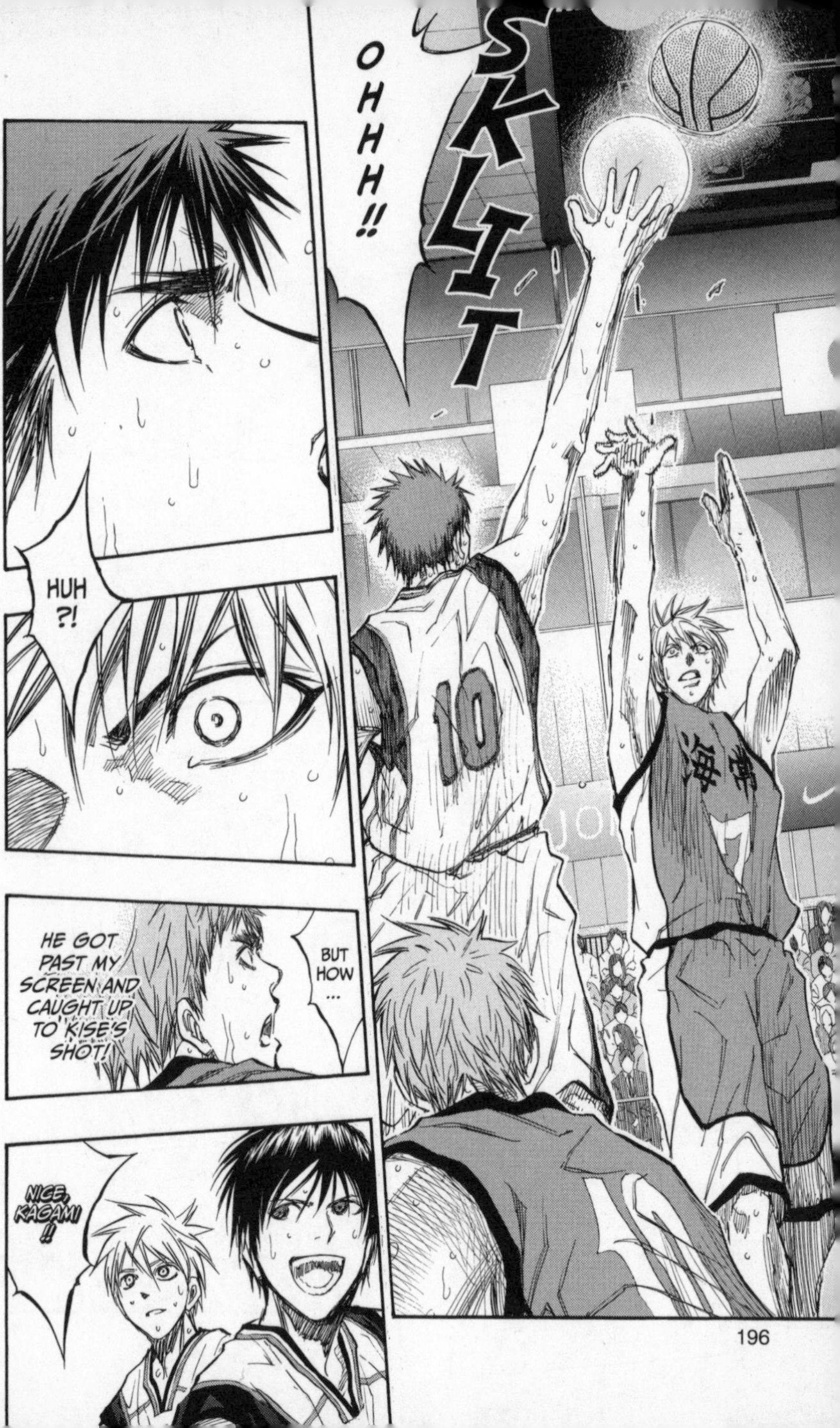
OHHHH!!
SKLIT
HUH ?!
BUT HOW ...
HE GOT PAST MY SCREEN AND CAUGHT UP TO KISE'S SHOT!
NICE, KAGAMI !!

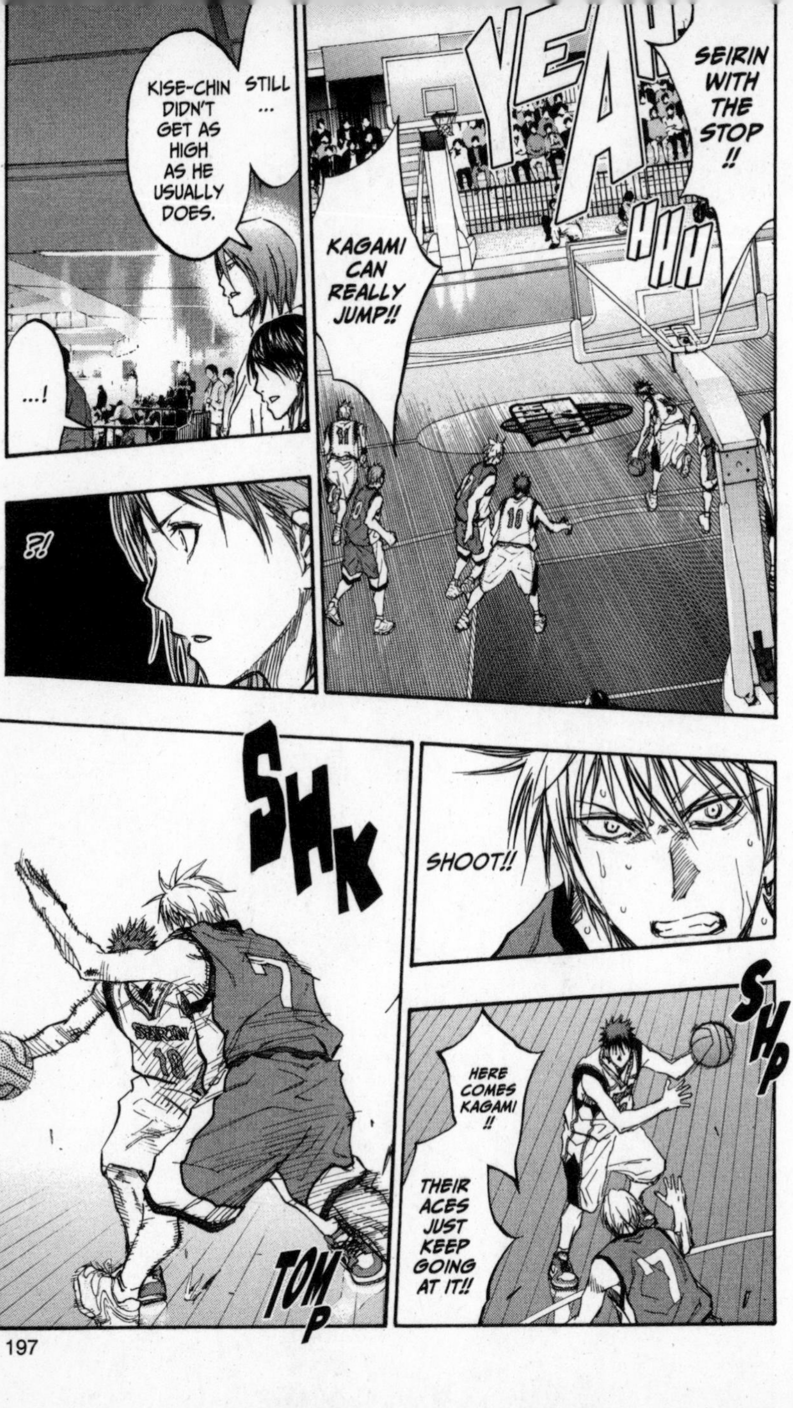
YEAAHHH
SEIRIN WITH THE STOP!!
KAGAMI CAN REALLY JUMP!!
STILL ...
KISE-CHIN DIDN'T GET AS HIGH AS HE USUALLY DOES.
...!
?!
SHOOT!!
SHP
HERE COMES KAGAMI!!
THEIR ACES JUST KEEP GOING AT IT!!
SHK
TOMP

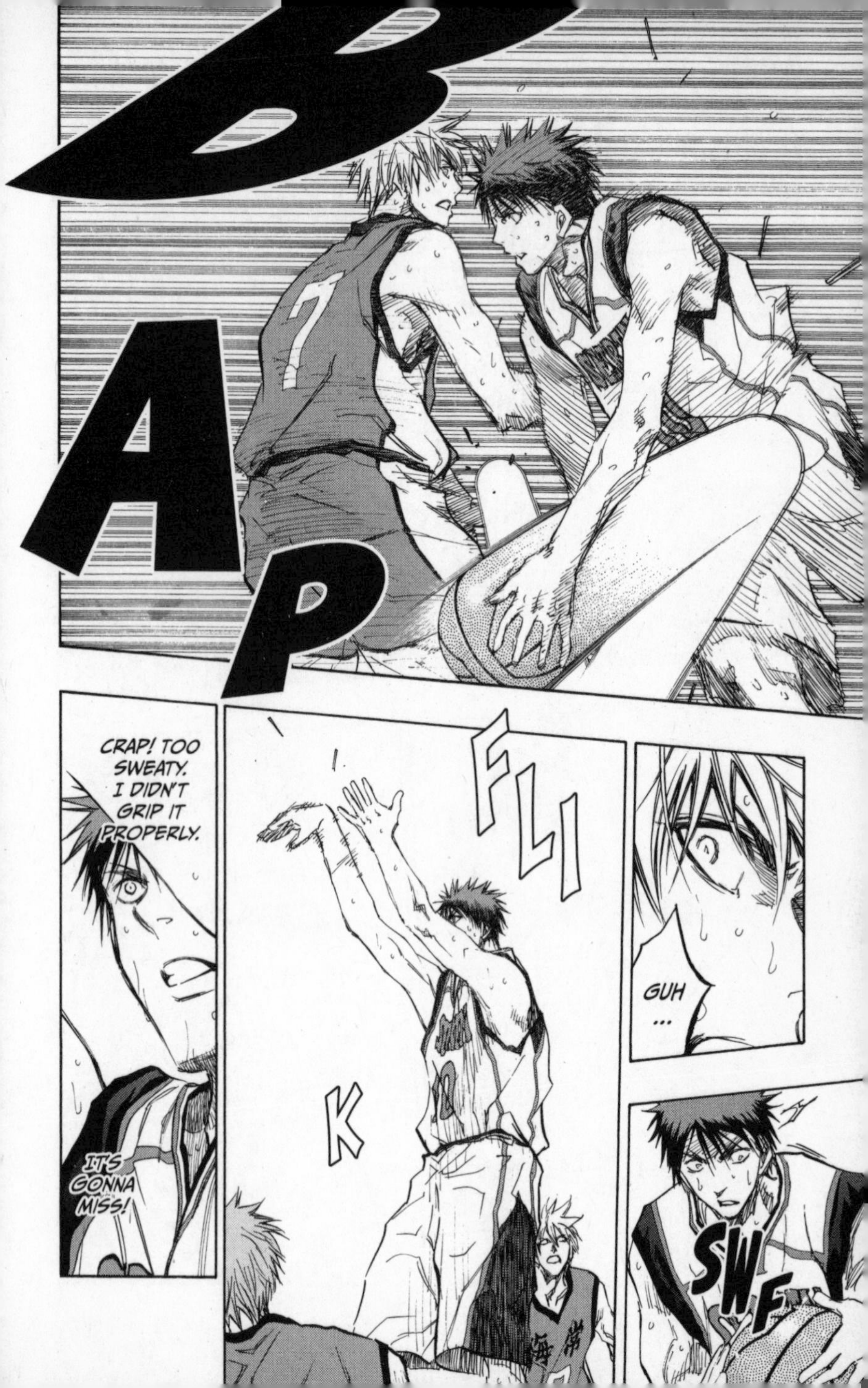
BAP
GUH ...
SWF
FLI
K
CRAP! TOO SWEATY. I DIDN'T GRIP IT PROPERLY.
IT'S GONNA MISS!

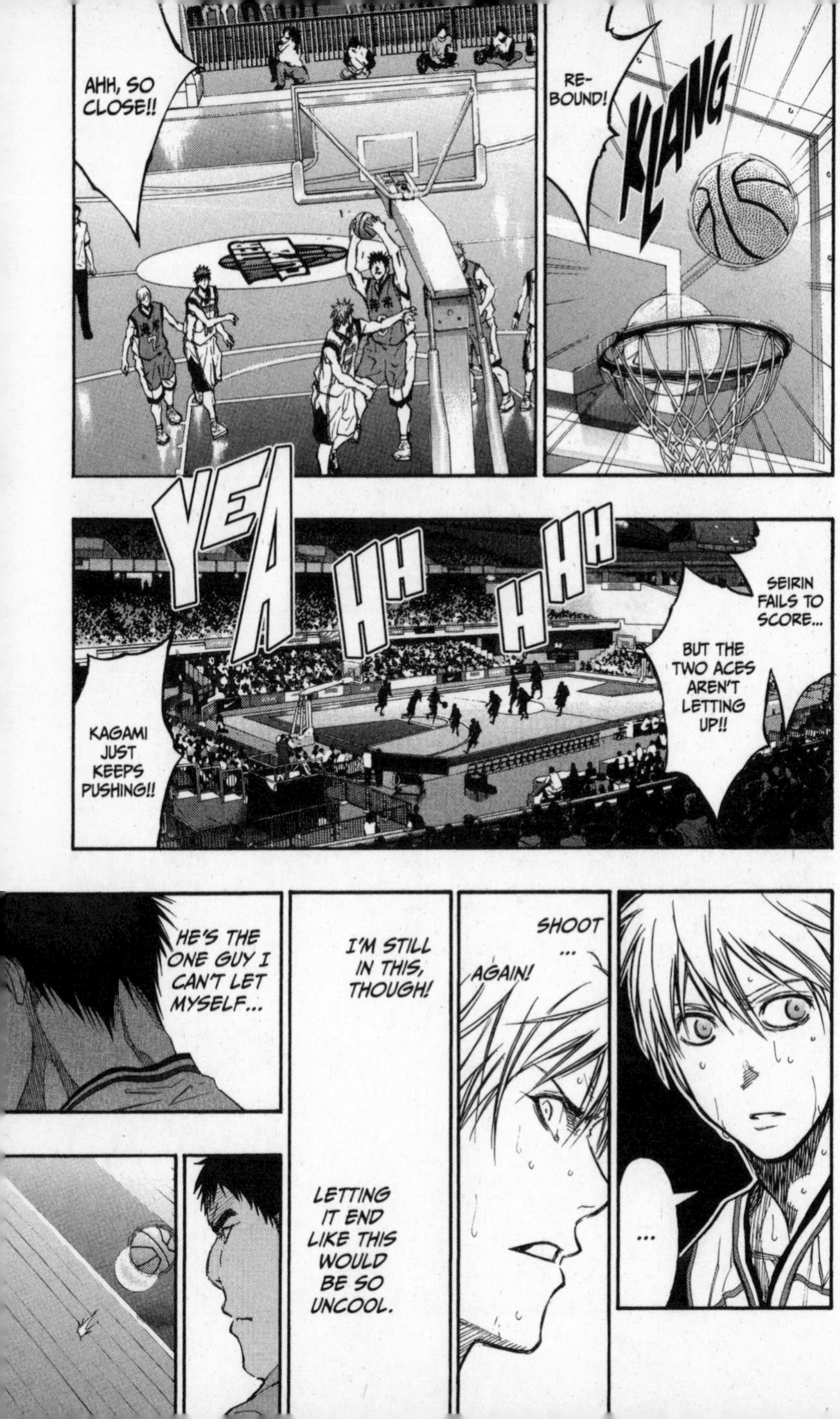
RE-BOUND!
KLANG
AHH, SO CLOSE!!
YEAHHHHH
SEIRIN FAILS TO SCORE...
BUT THE TWO ACES AREN'T LETTING UP!!
KAGAMI JUST KEEPS PUSHING!!
...
SHOOT ...
AGAIN!
I'M STILL IN THIS, THOUGH!
LETTING IT END LIKE THIS WOULD BE SO UNCOOL.
HE'S THE ONE GUY I CAN'T LET MYSELF...

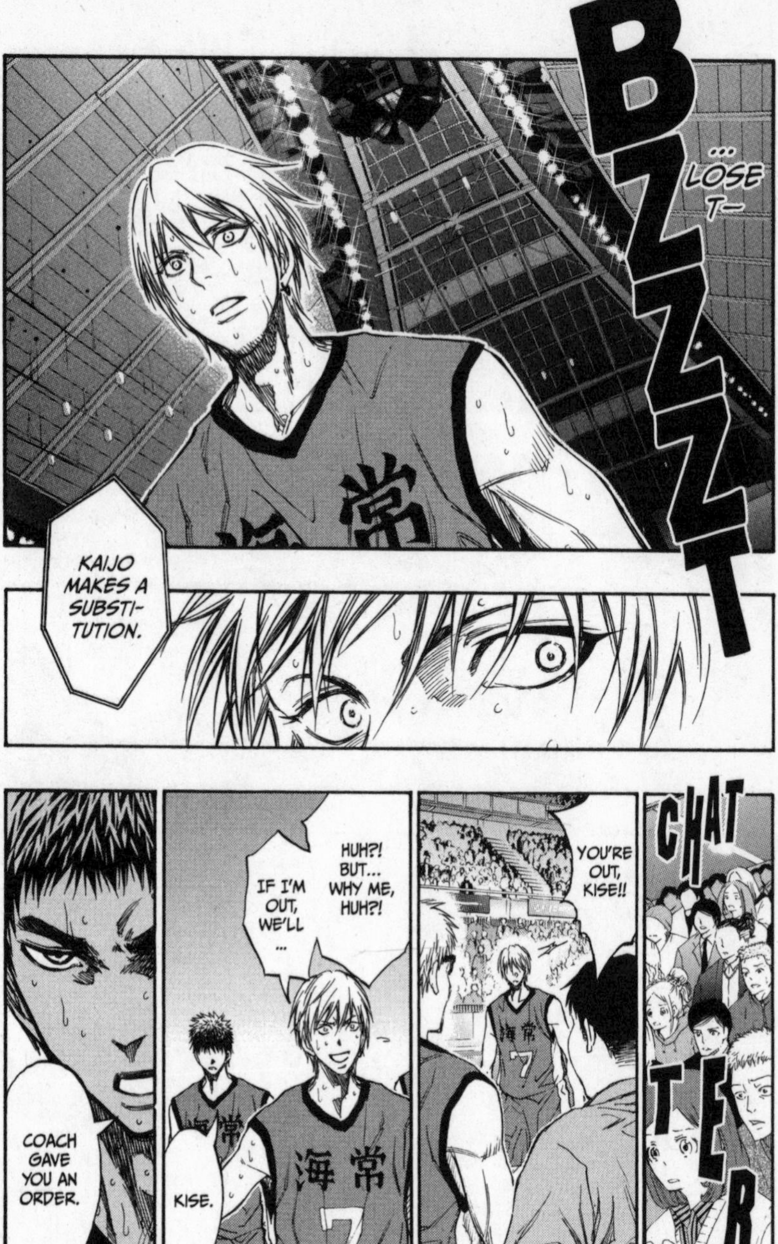
BZZZZT
...LOSE T—
KAIJO MAKES A SUBSTI-TUTION.
CHATTER
YOU'RE OUT, KISE!!
HUH?! BUT... WHY ME, HUH?!
IF I'M OUT, WE'LL ...
KISE.
COACH GAVE YOU AN ORDER.

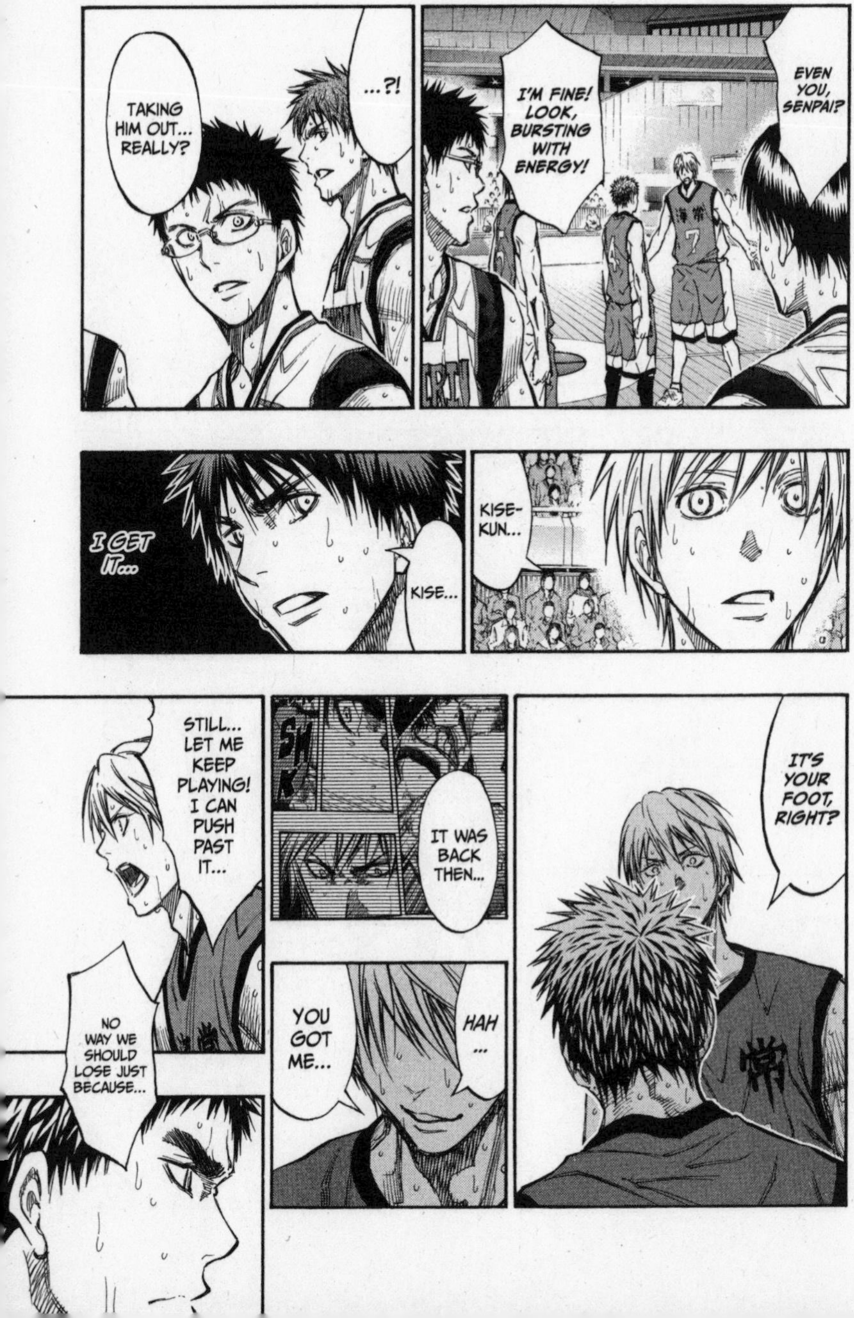
EVEN YOU, SENPAI?
I'M FINE! LOOK, BURSTING WITH ENERGY!
...?!
TAKING HIM OUT... REALLY?
KISE-KUN...
KISE...
I GET IT...
IT'S YOUR FOOT, RIGHT?
IT WAS BACK THEN...
HAH...
YOU GOT ME...
STILL... LET ME KEEP PLAYING! I CAN PUSH PAST IT...
NO WAY WE SHOULD LOSE JUST BECAUSE...

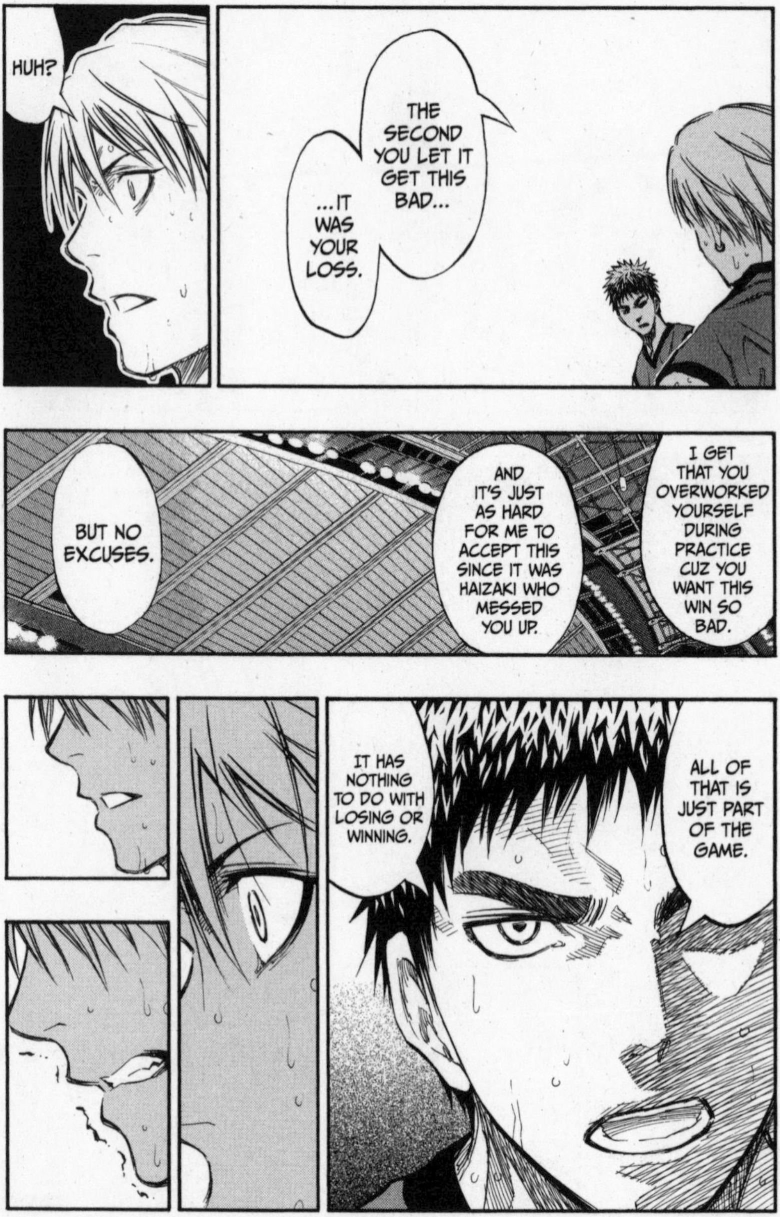
THE SECOND YOU LET IT GET THIS BAD...
...IT WAS YOUR LOSS.
HUH?
I GET THAT YOU OVERWORKED YOURSELF DURING PRACTICE CUZ YOU WANT THIS WIN SO BAD.
AND IT'S JUST AS HARD FOR ME TO ACCEPT THIS SINCE IT WAS HAIZAKI WHO MESSED YOU UP.
BUT NO EXCUSES.
ALL OF THAT IS JUST PART OF THE GAME.
IT HAS NOTHING TO DO WITH LOSING OR WINNING.

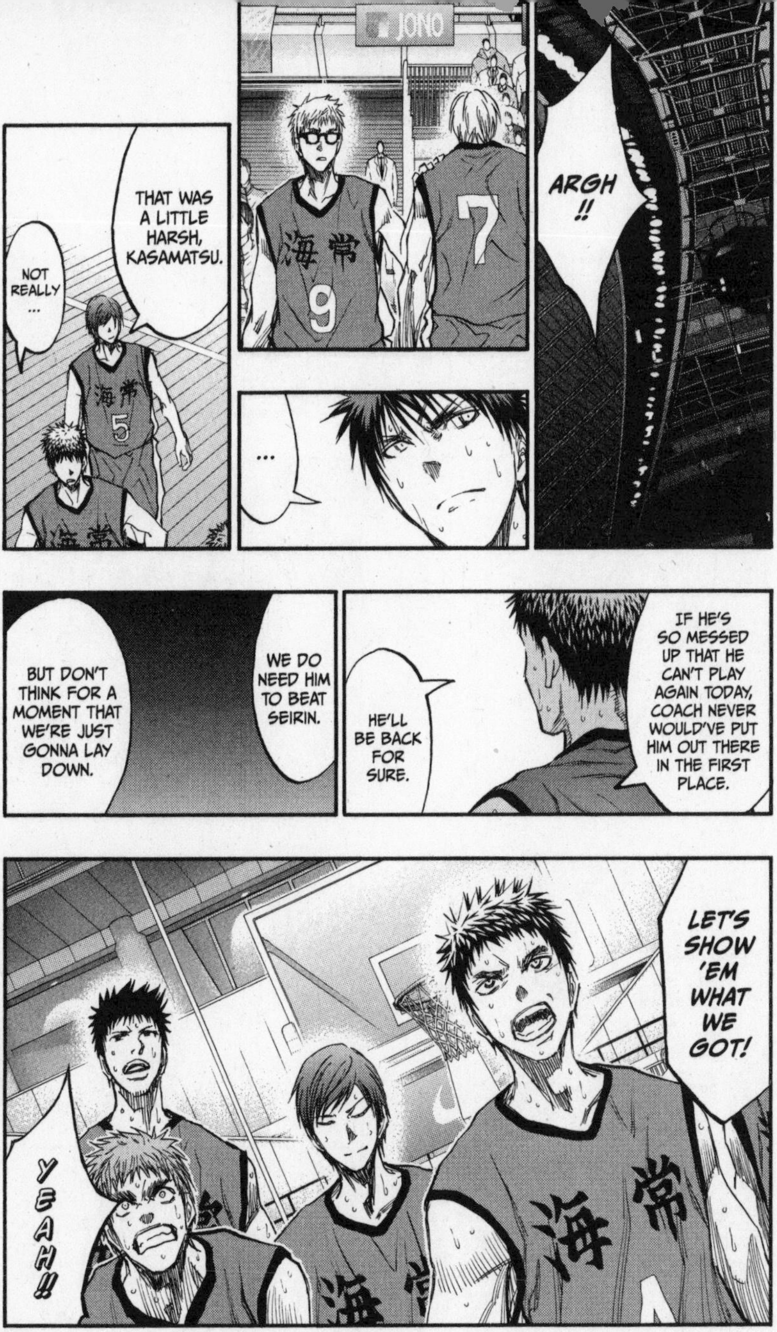
ARGH !!
JONO
...
THAT WAS A LITTLE HARSH, KASAMATSU.
NOT REALLY ...
IF HE'S SO MESSED UP THAT HE CAN'T PLAY AGAIN TODAY, COACH NEVER WOULD'VE PUT HIM OUT THERE IN THE FIRST PLACE.
HE'LL BE BACK FOR SURE.
WE DO NEED HIM TO BEAT SEIRIN.
BUT DON'T THINK FOR A MOMENT THAT WE'RE JUST GONNA LAY DOWN.
LET'S SHOW 'EM WHAT WE GOT!
YEAH!!

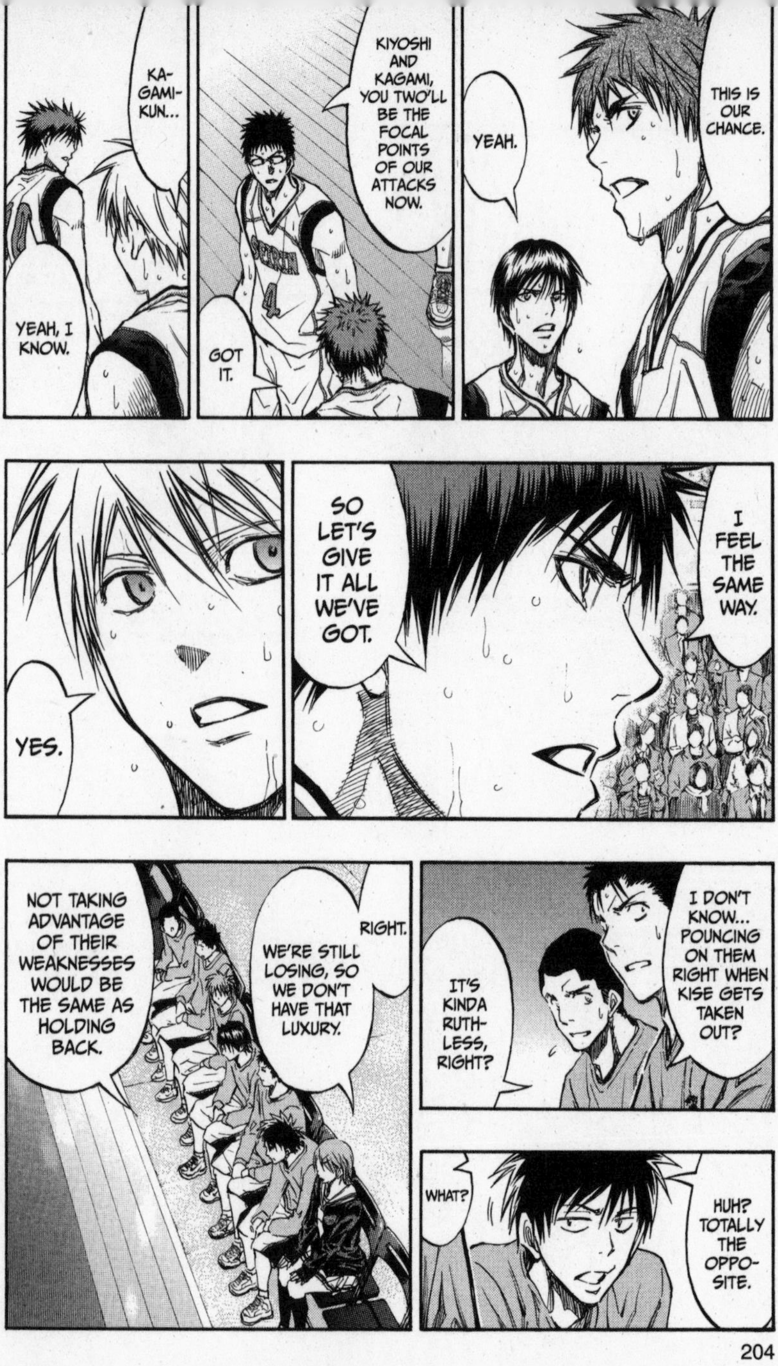
THIS IS OUR CHANCE.
YEAH.
KIYOSHI AND KAGAMI, YOU TWO'LL BE THE FOCAL POINTS OF OUR ATTACKS NOW.
GOT IT.
KA-GAMI-KUN...
YEAH, I KNOW.
I FEEL THE SAME WAY.
SO LET'S GIVE IT ALL WE'VE GOT.
YES.
I DON'T KNOW... POUNCING ON THEM RIGHT WHEN KISE GETS TAKEN OUT?
IT'S KINDA RUTH-LESS, RIGHT?
HUH? TOTALLY THE OPPO-SITE.
WHAT?
RIGHT.
WE'RE STILL LOSING, SO WE DON'T HAVE THAT LUXURY.
NOT TAKING ADVANTAGE OF THEIR WEAKNESSES WOULD BE THE SAME AS HOLDING BACK.

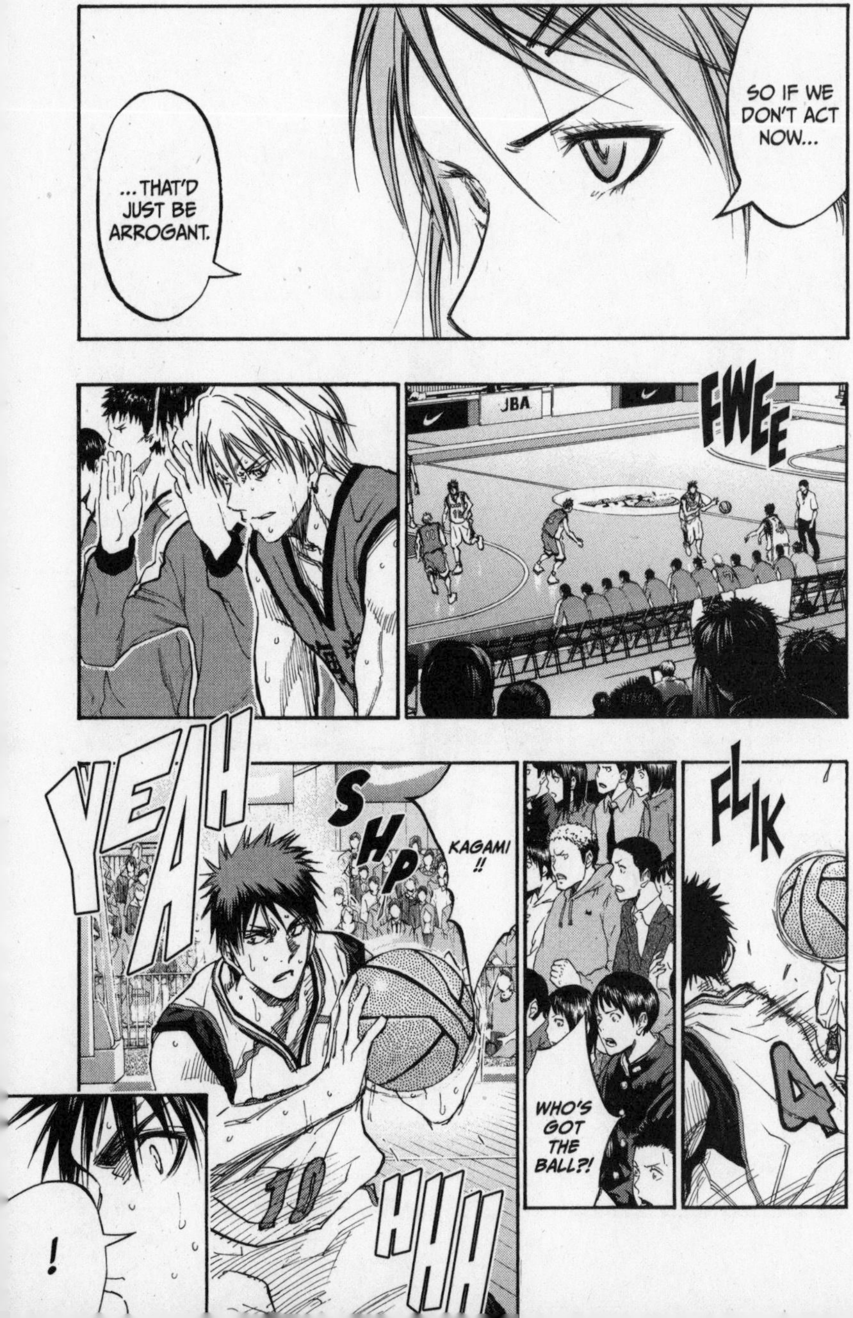
SO IF WE DON'T ACT NOW...
...THAT'D JUST BE ARROGANT.
FWEE
FLIK
WHO'S GOT THE BALL?!
SHP
KAGAMI !!
YEAH HHH
!

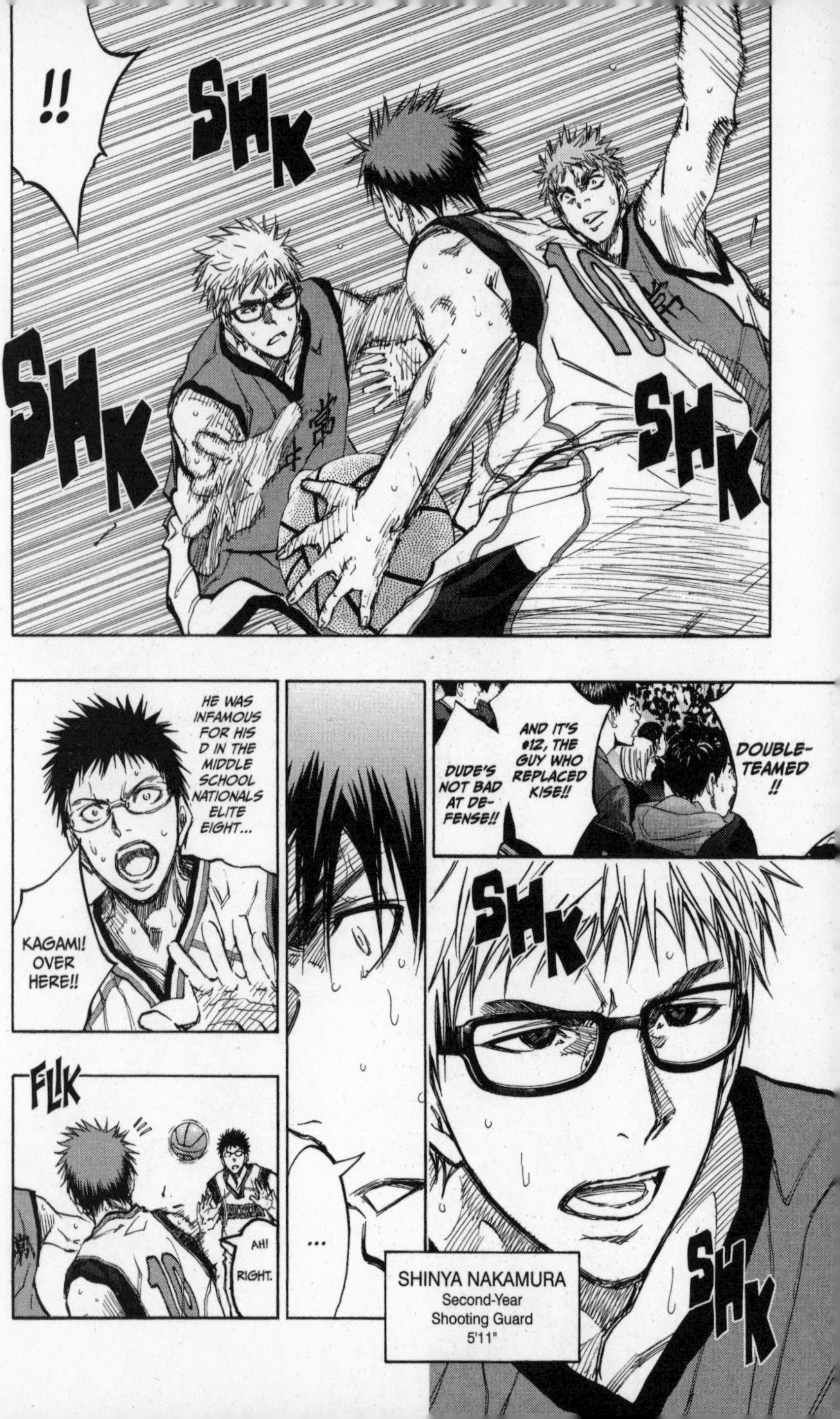
SHK
SHK
!!
SHK
DOUBLE-TEAMED!!
AND IT'S #12, THE GUY WHO REPLACED KISE!!
DUDE'S NOT BAD AT DEFENSE!!
SHK
SHK
SHINYA NAKAMURA
Second-Year
Shooting Guard
5'11"
...
HE WAS INFAMOUS FOR HIS D IN THE MIDDLE SCHOOL NATIONALS ELITE EIGHT...
KAGAMI! OVER HERE!!
FLIK
AH! RIGHT.

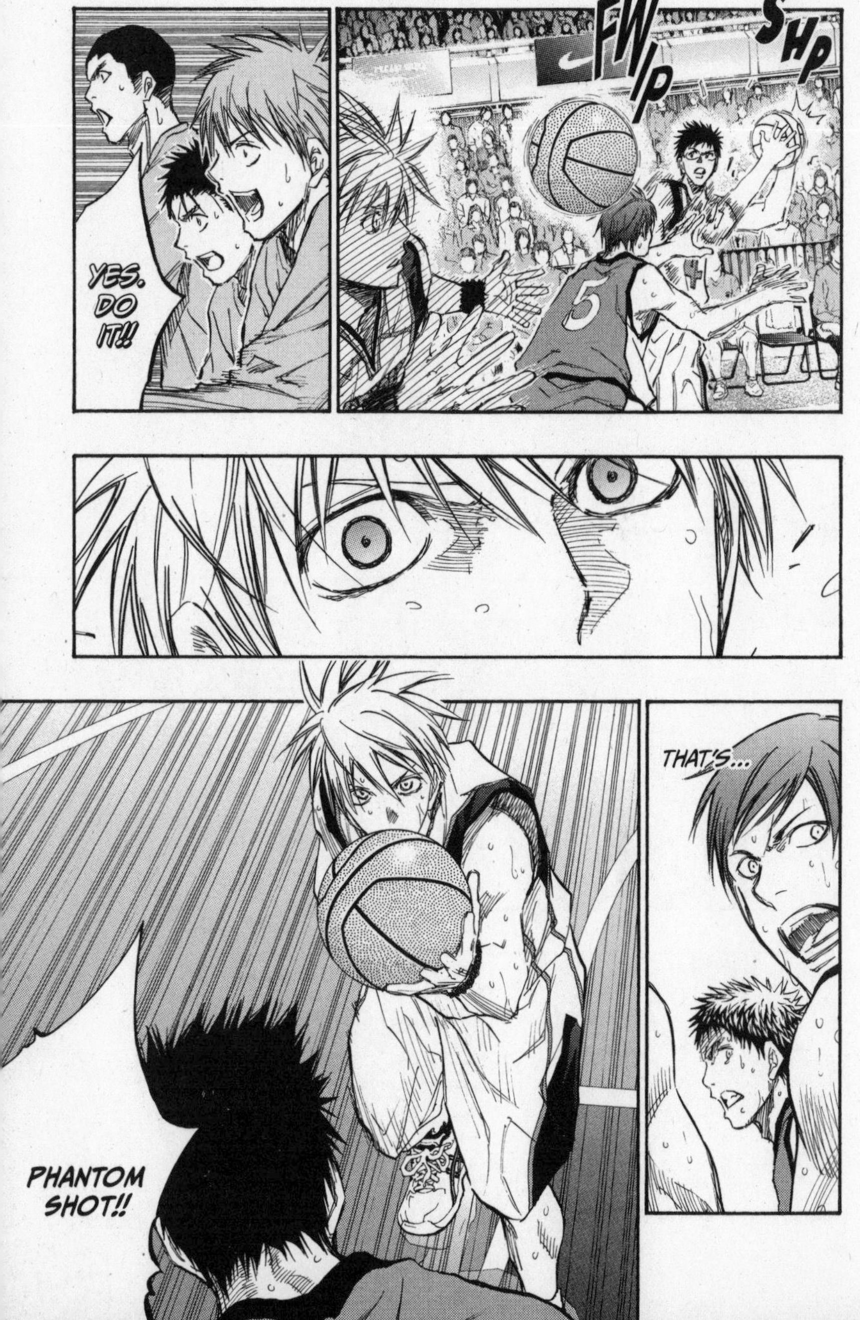
FWIP
SHP
YES. DO IT!!
THAT'S...
PHANTOM SHOT!!

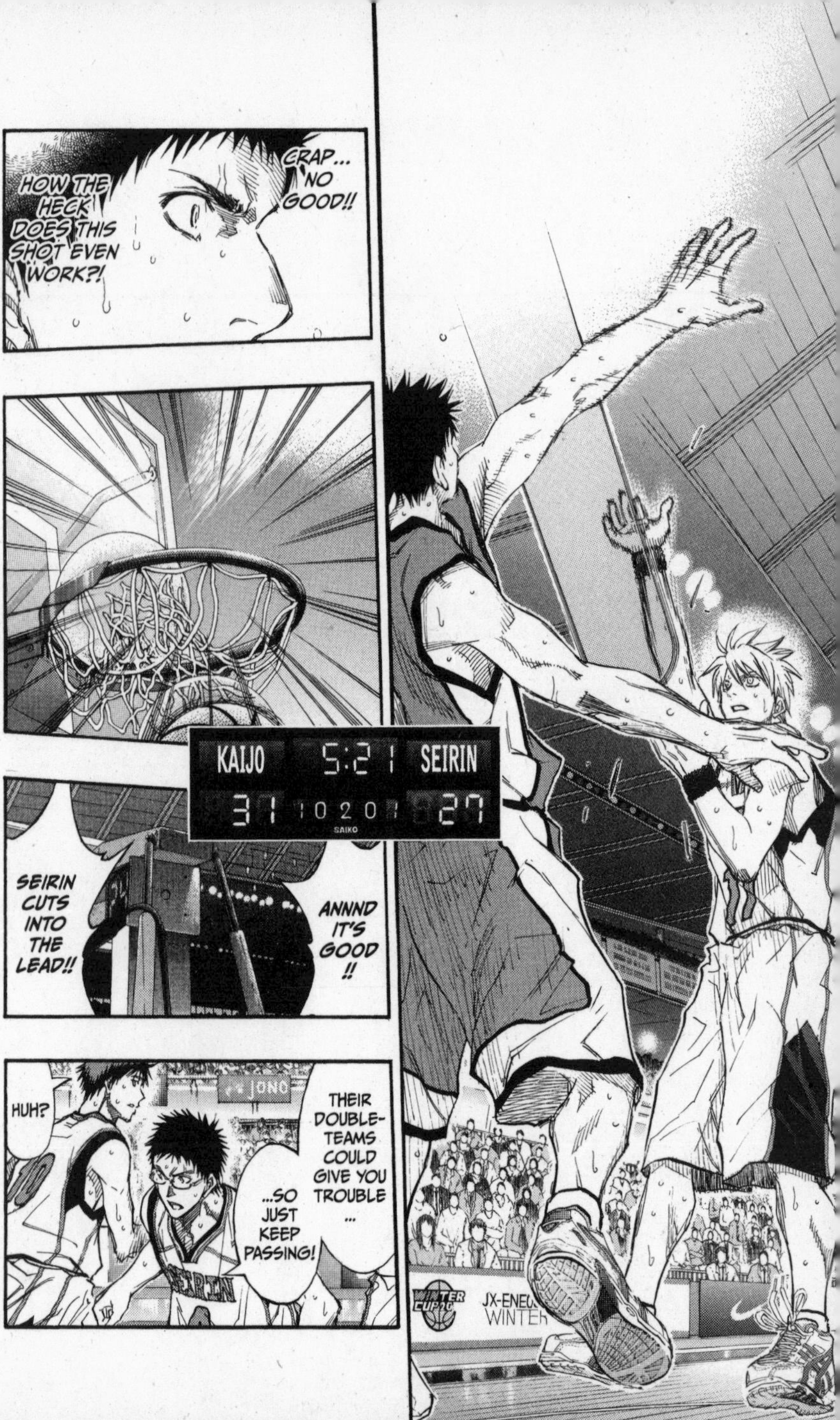
KAIJO
5:21
SEIRIN
31
27
SAIKO
CRAP... NO GOOD!!
HOW THE HECK DOES THIS SHOT EVEN WORK?!
ANNND IT'S GOOD!!
SEIRIN CUTS INTO THE LEAD!!
THEIR DOUBLE-TEAMS COULD GIVE YOU TROUBLE...
...SO JUST KEEP PASSING!
HUH?
SEIRIN
JX-ENEO
WINTER

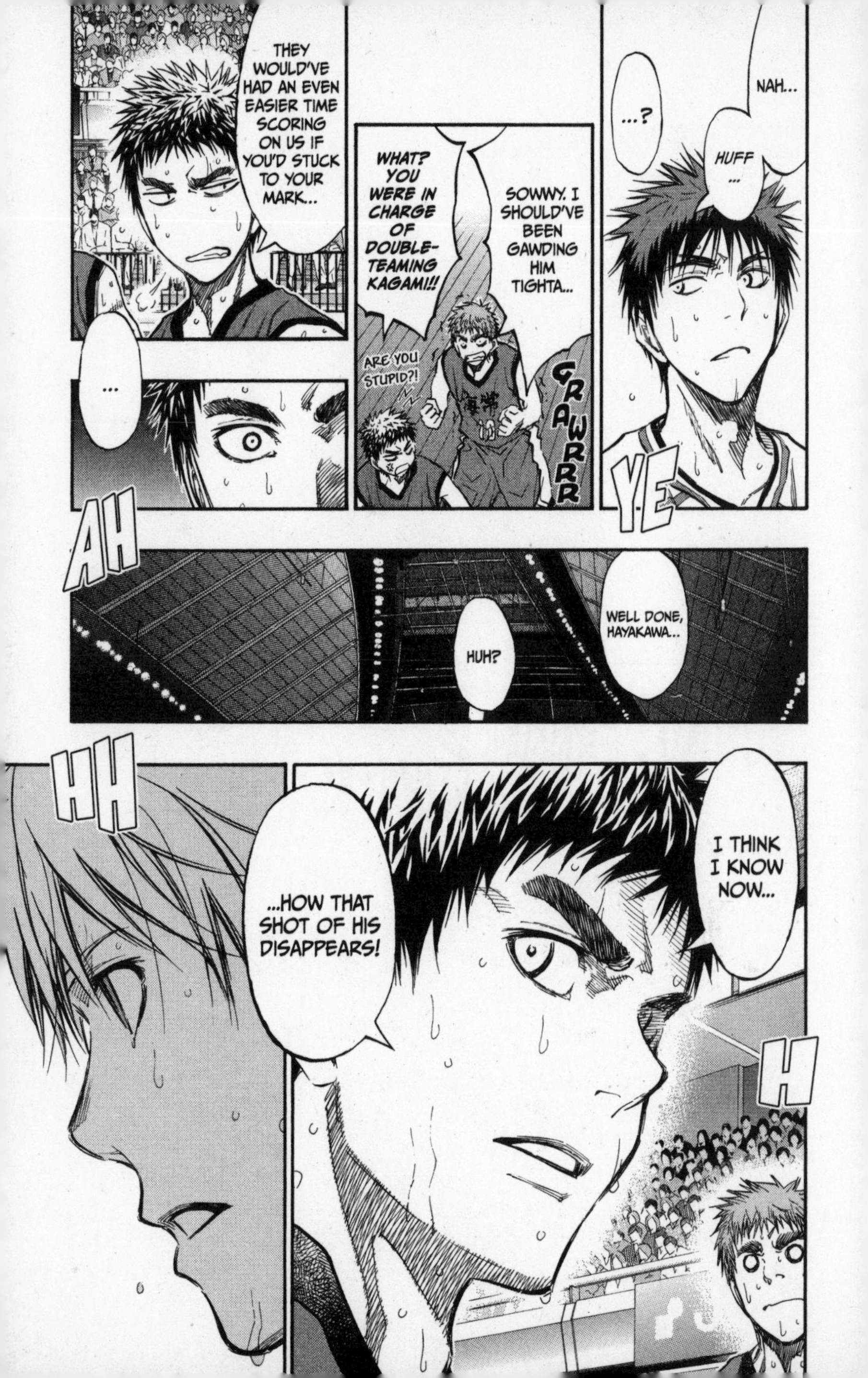
NAH...
...?
HUFF ...
YE
SOWWY. I SHOULD'VE BEEN GAWDING HIM TIGHTA...
WHAT? YOU WERE IN CHARGE OF DOUBLE-TEAMING KAGAMI!!
GRAWRRR
ARE YOU STUPID?!
THEY WOULD'VE HAD AN EVEN EASIER TIME SCORING ON US IF YOU'D STUCK TO YOUR MARK...
...
AH
WELL DONE, HAYAKAWA...
HUH?
I THINK I KNOW NOW...
...HOW THAT SHOT OF HIS DISAPPEARS!
H
HH

KUROKO'S BASKETBALL BLOOPERS

TAKE 3

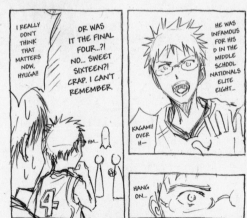

HE WAS INFAMOUS FOR HIS D IN THE MIDDLE SCHOOL NATIONALS ELITE EIGHT...
KAGAMI! OVER H—
HANG ON...
OR WAS IT THE FINAL FOUR...?! NO... SWEET SIXTEEN?! CRAP. I CAN'T REMEMBER.
I REALLY DON'T THINK THAT MATTERS NOW, HYUGA!!
HM...
...

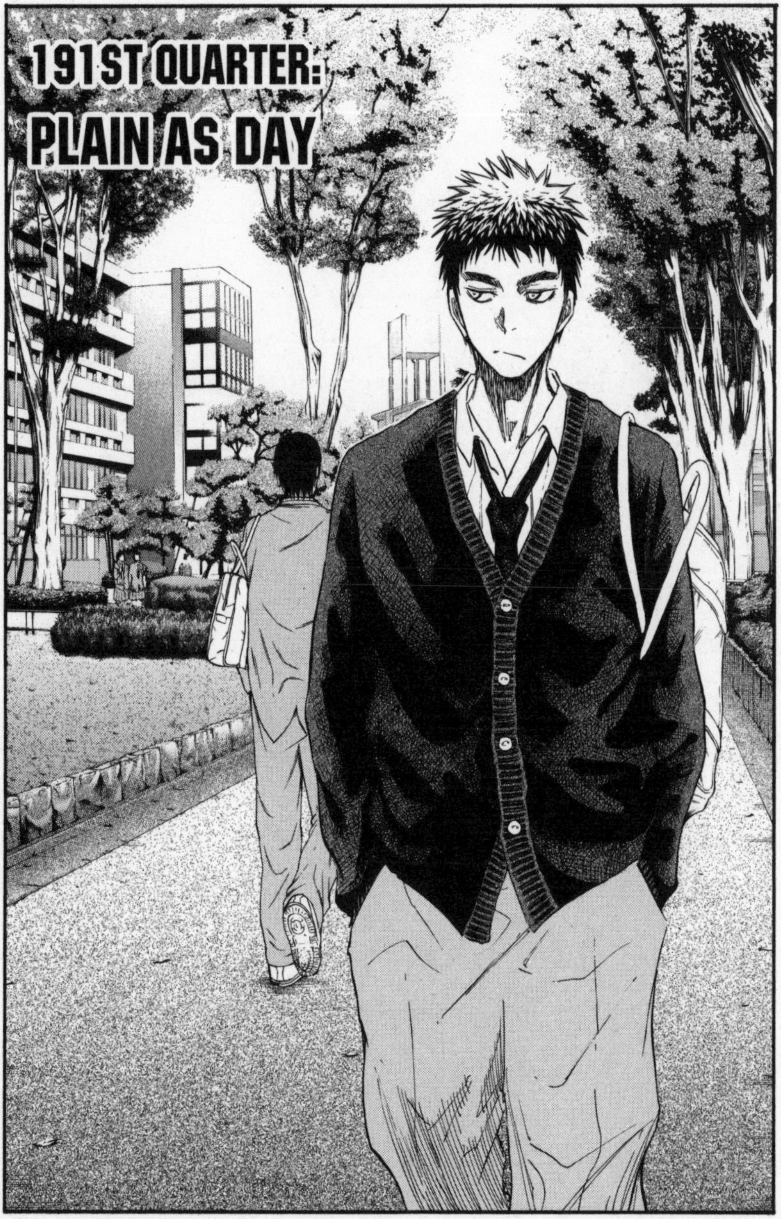
191ST QUARTER:
PLAIN AS DAY

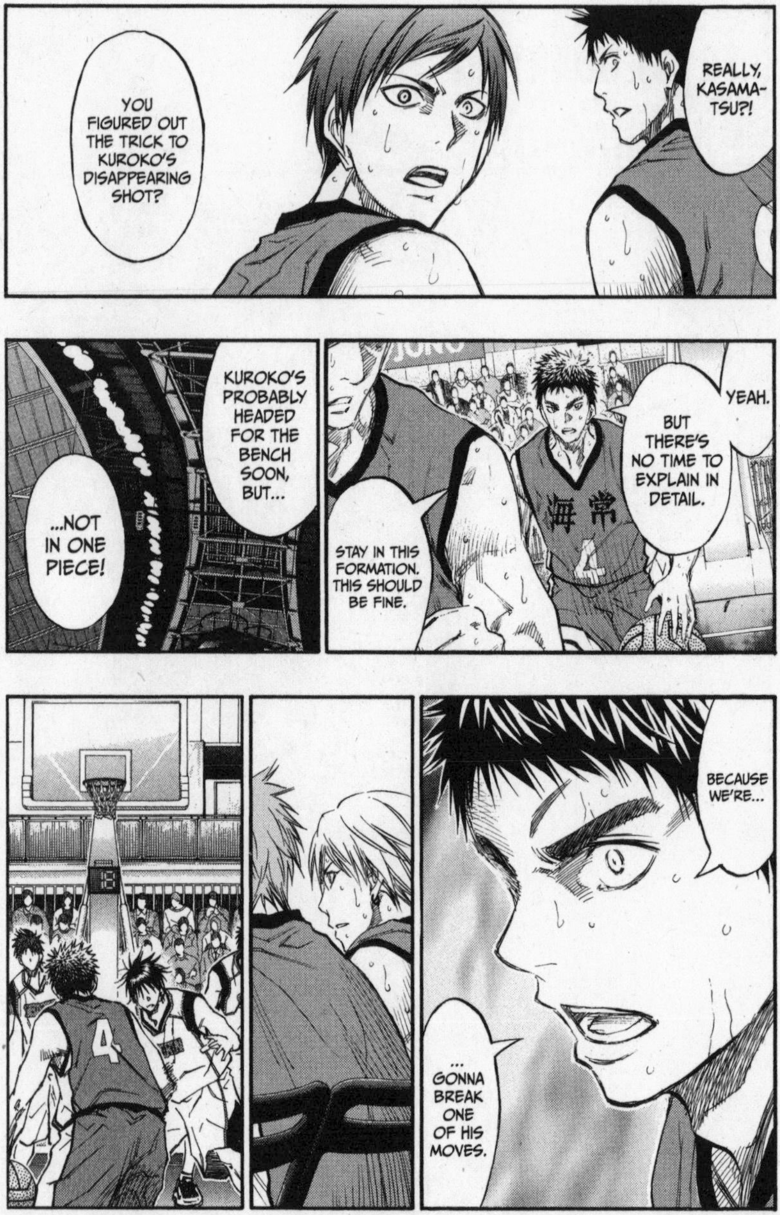
REALLY, KASAMA-TSU?!
YOU FIGURED OUT THE TRICK TO KUROKO'S DISAPPEARING SHOT?
YEAH.
BUT THERE'S NO TIME TO EXPLAIN IN DETAIL.
STAY IN THIS FORMATION. THIS SHOULD BE FINE.
KUROKO'S PROBABLY HEADED FOR THE BENCH SOON, BUT...
...NOT IN ONE PIECE!
BECAUSE WE'RE...
...GONNA BREAK ONE OF HIS MOVES.

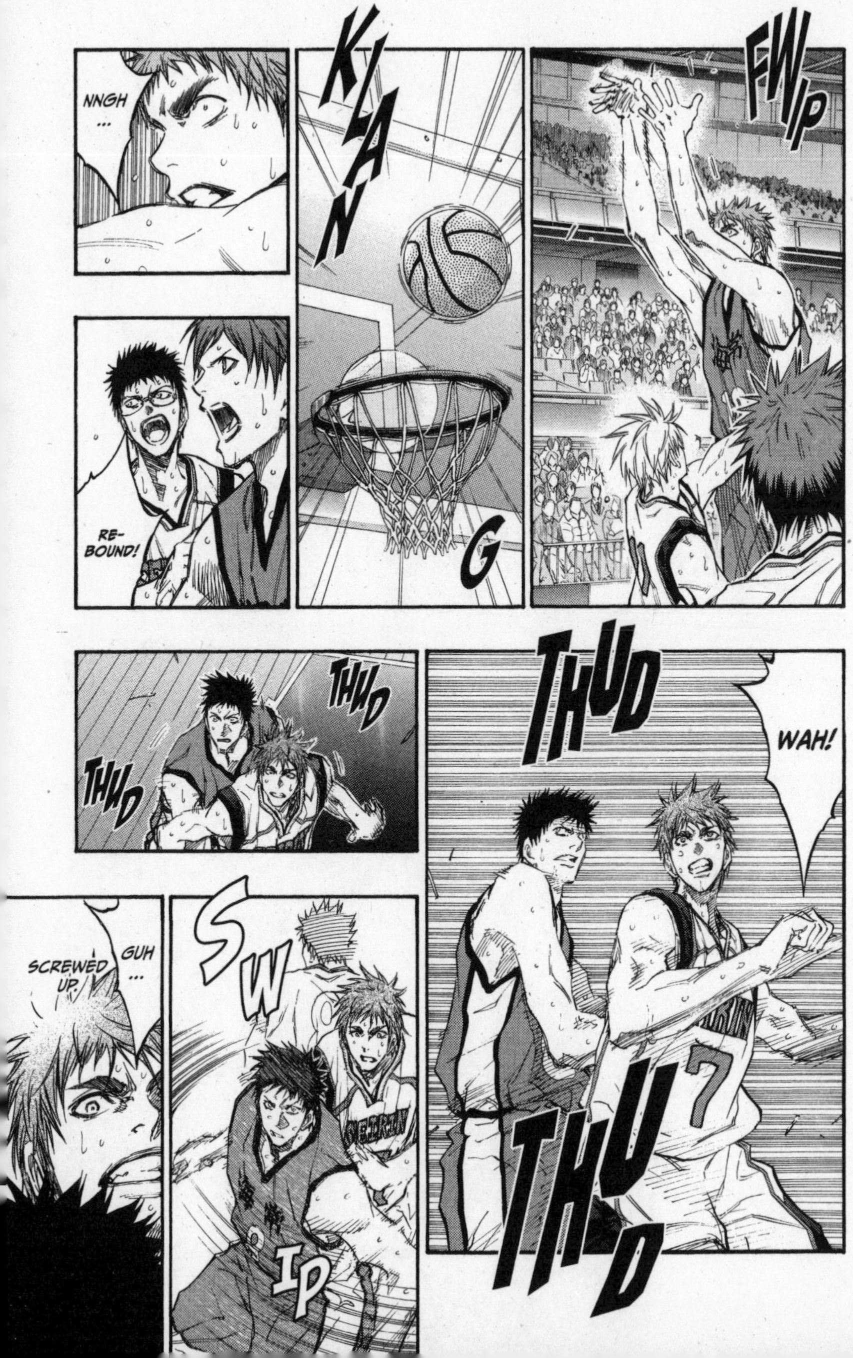
FWIP
KLANG
NNGH ...
REBOUND!
THUD
WAH!
THUD
THUD
THUD
SWIP
GUH ...
SCREWED UP.

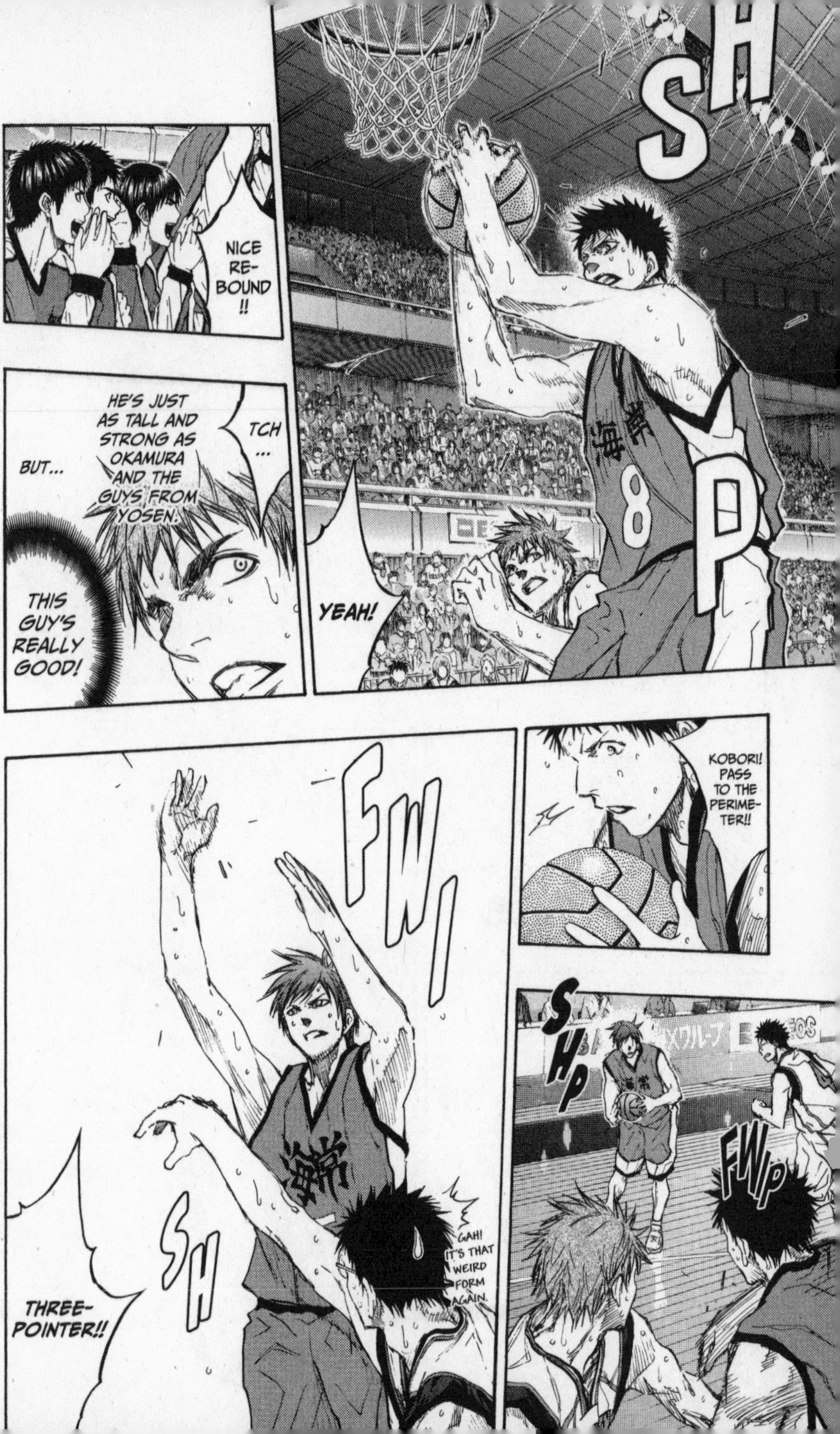
SH
YEAH!
NICE RE-BOUND!!
TCH...
HE'S JUST AS TALL AND STRONG AS OKAMURA AND THE GUYS FROM YOSEN.
BUT...
THIS GUY'S REALLY GOOD!
KOBORI! PASS TO THE PERIMETER!!
SHP
FWIP
FWI
GAH! IT'S THAT WEIRD FORM AGAIN.
SH
THREE-POINTER!!

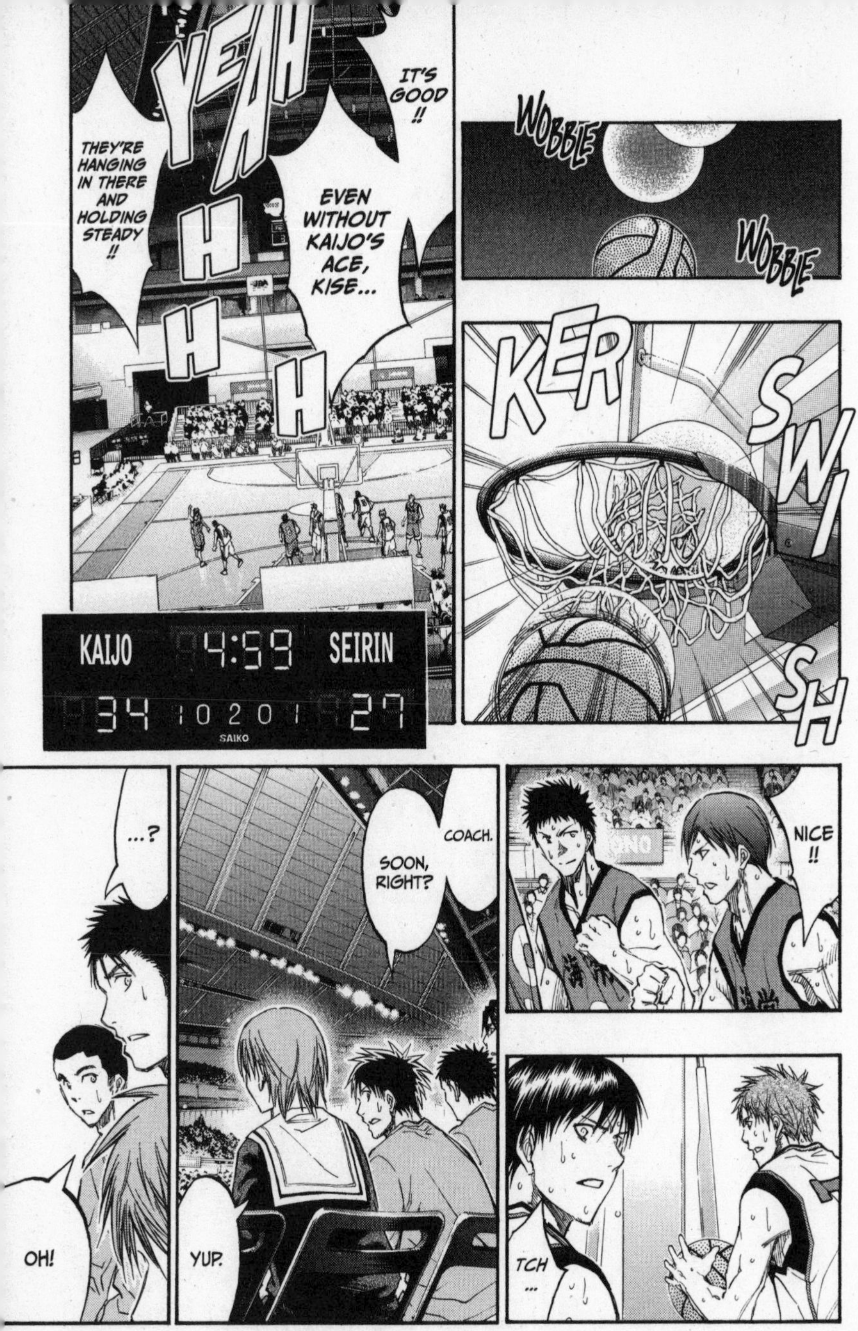
WOBBLE
WOBBLE
KER
SWISH
IT'S GOOD !!
YEAH
HHH
EVEN WITHOUT KAIJO'S ACE, KISE...
THEY'RE HANGING IN THERE AND HOLDING STEADY !!
KAIJO
4:59
SEIRIN
34
10201
27
SAIKO
NICE !!
TCH ...
COACH.
SOON, RIGHT?
YUP.
...?
OH!

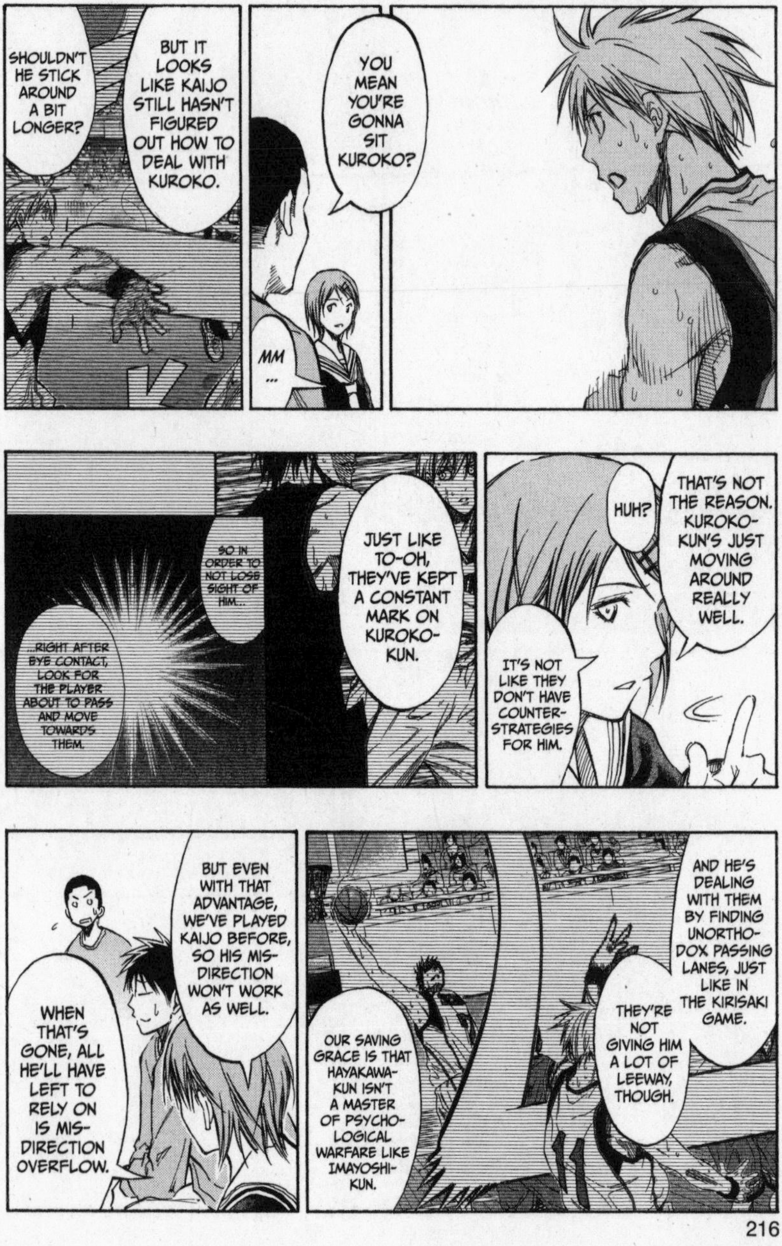
YOU MEAN YOU'RE GONNA SIT KUROKO?
MM...
BUT IT LOOKS LIKE KAIJO STILL HASN'T FIGURED OUT HOW TO DEAL WITH KUROKO.
SHOULDN'T HE STICK AROUND A BIT LONGER?
THAT'S NOT THE REASON. KUROKO-KUN'S JUST MOVING AROUND REALLY WELL.
HUH?
IT'S NOT LIKE THEY DON'T HAVE COUNTER-STRATEGIES FOR HIM.
JUST LIKE TO-OH, THEY'VE KEPT A CONSTANT MARK ON KUROKO-KUN.
SO IN ORDER TO NOT LOSE SIGHT OF HIM...
...RIGHT AFTER EYE CONTACT, LOOK FOR THE PLAYER ABOUT TO PASS AND MOVE TOWARDS THEM.
AND HE'S DEALING WITH THEM BY FINDING UNORTHODOX PASSING LANES, JUST LIKE IN THE KIRISAKI GAME.
THEY'RE NOT GIVING HIM A LOT OF LEEWAY, THOUGH.
OUR SAVING GRACE IS THAT HAYAKAWA-KUN ISN'T A MASTER OF PSYCHOLOGICAL WARFARE LIKE IMAYOSHI-KUN.
BUT EVEN WITH THAT ADVANTAGE, WE'VE PLAYED KAIJO BEFORE, SO HIS MISDIRECTION WON'T WORK AS WELL.
WHEN THAT'S GONE, ALL HE'LL HAVE LEFT TO RELY ON IS MISDIRECTION OVERFLOW.

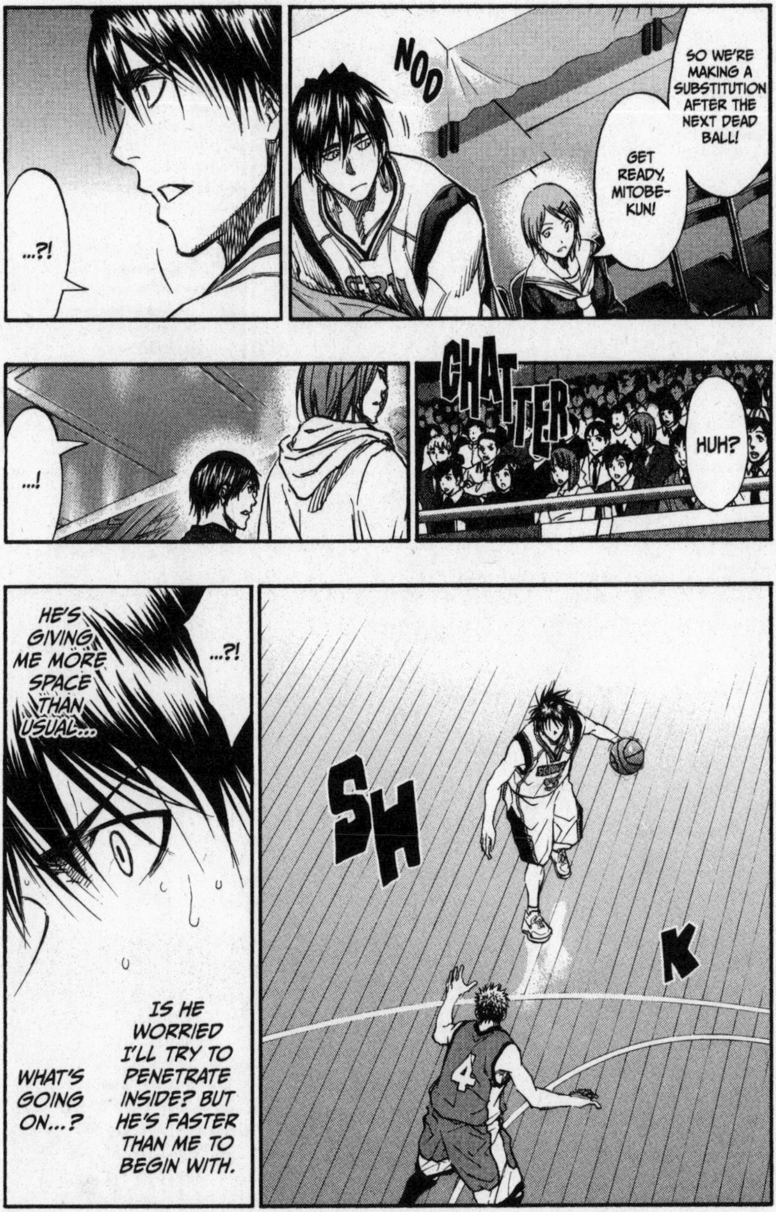
SO WE'RE MAKING A SUBSTITUTION AFTER THE NEXT DEAD BALL!
GET READY, MITOBE-KUN!
NOD
...?!
HUH?
CHATTER
...!
SH
K
...?!
HE'S GIVING ME MORE SPACE THAN USUAL...
IS HE WORRIED I'LL TRY TO PENETRATE INSIDE? BUT HE'S FASTER THAN ME TO BEGIN WITH.
WHAT'S GOING ON...?

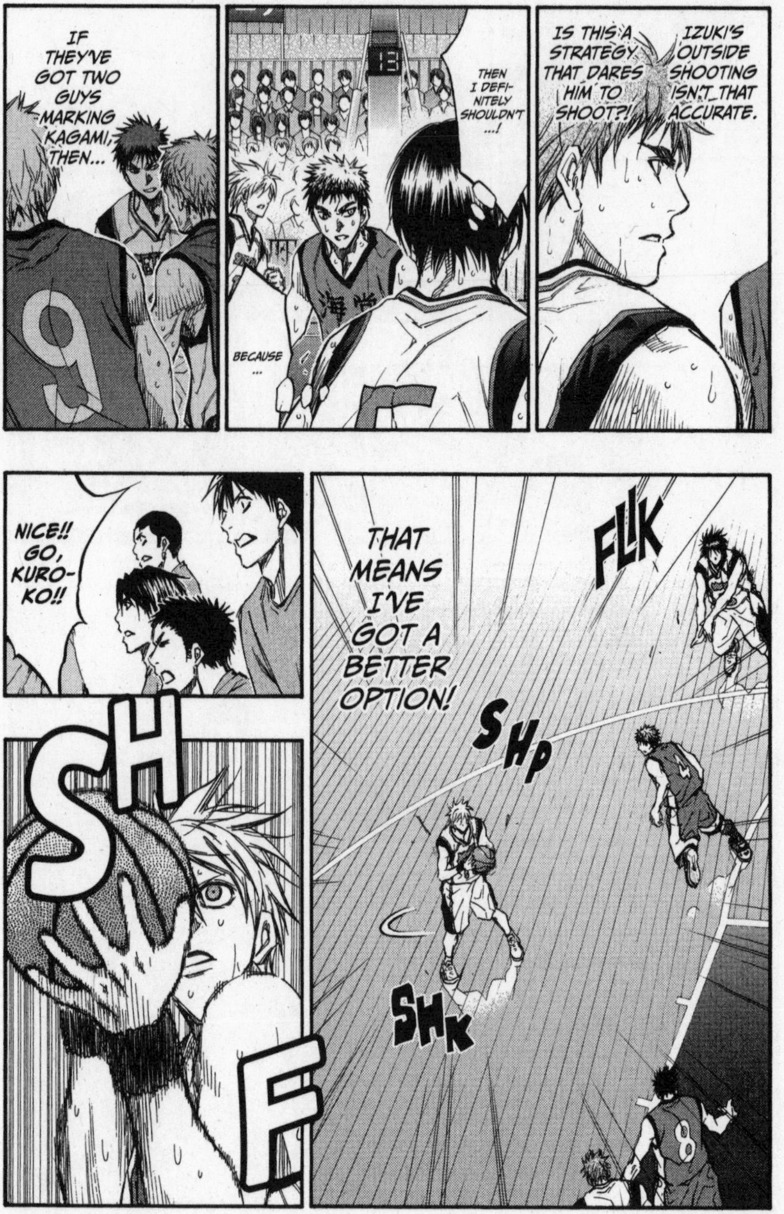
IZUKI'S OUTSIDE SHOOTING ISN'T THAT ACCURATE.
IS THIS A STRATEGY THAT DARES HIM TO SHOOT?!
THEN I DEFINITELY SHOULDN'T ...!
BECAUSE ...
IF THEY'VE GOT TWO GUYS MARKING KAGAMI, THEN...
FLIK
THAT MEANS I'VE GOT A BETTER OPTION!
SHP
SHK
NICE!! GO, KURO-KO!!
SH
F

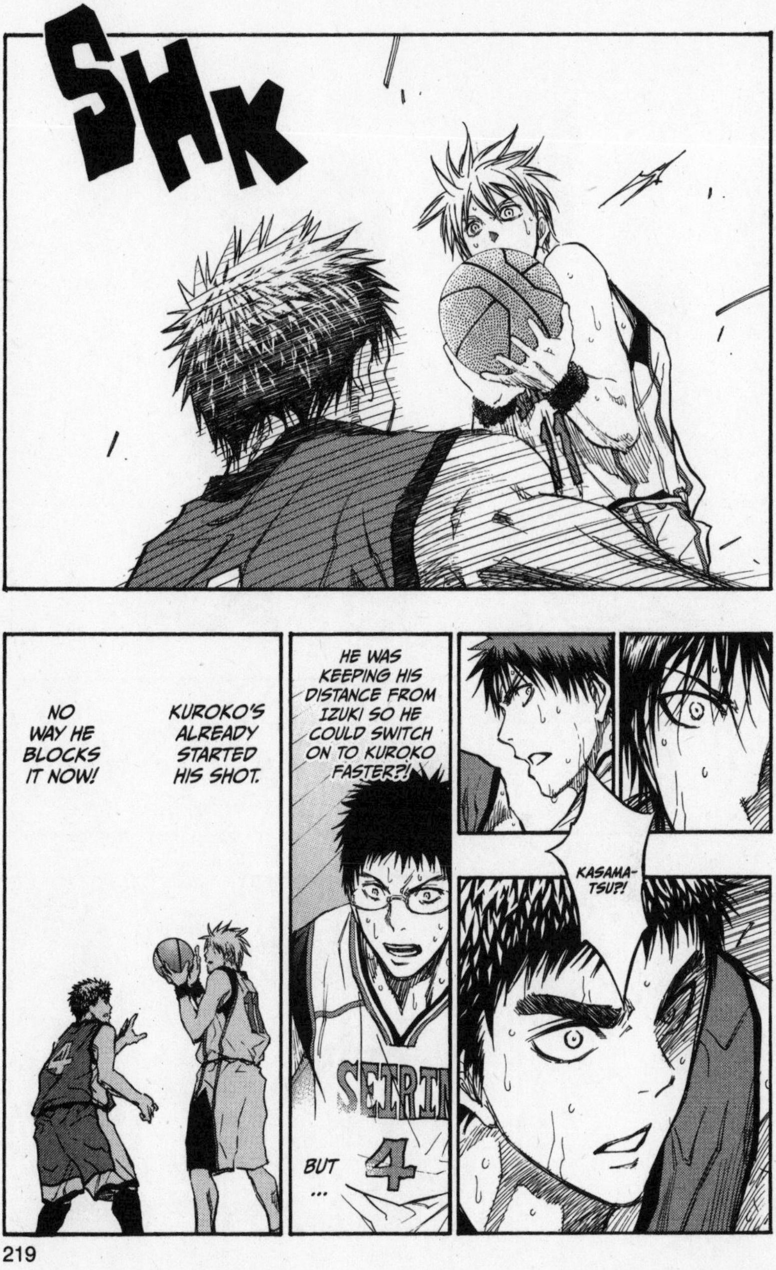
SHK
KASAMA-TSU?!
HE WAS KEEPING HIS DISTANCE FROM IZUKI SO HE COULD SWITCH ON TO KUROKO FASTER?!
BUT ...
KUROKO'S ALREADY STARTED HIS SHOT.
NO WAY HE BLOCKS IT NOW!

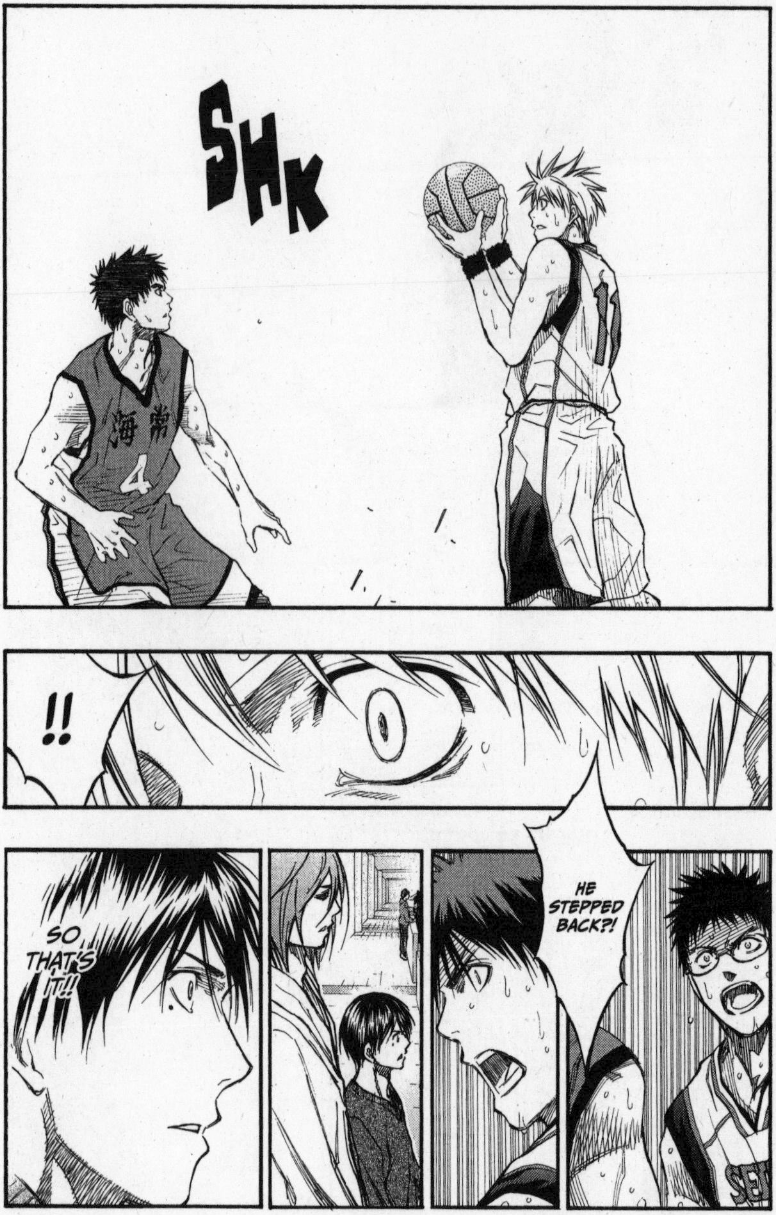
SHK
!!
HE STEPPED BACK?!
SO, THAT'S IT!!

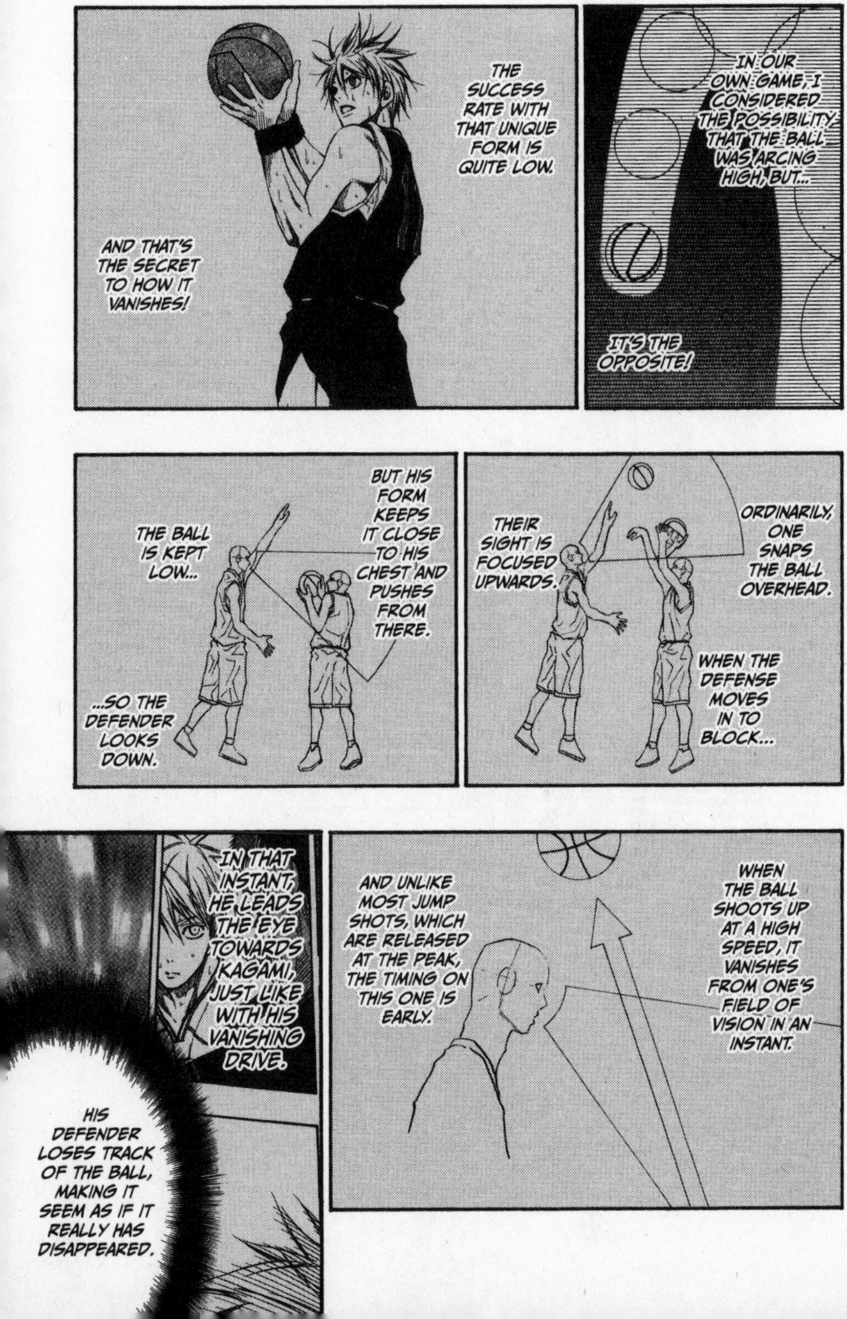
IN OUR OWN GAME, I CONSIDERED THE POSSIBILITY THAT THE BALL WAS ARCING HIGH, BUT...
IT'S THE OPPOSITE!
THE SUCCESS RATE WITH THAT UNIQUE FORM IS QUITE LOW.
AND THAT'S THE SECRET TO HOW IT VANISHES!
ORDINARILY, ONE SNAPS THE BALL OVERHEAD.
WHEN THE DEFENSE MOVES IN TO BLOCK...
THEIR SIGHT IS FOCUSED UPWARDS.
BUT HIS FORM KEEPS IT CLOSE TO HIS CHEST AND PUSHES FROM THERE.
THE BALL IS KEPT LOW...
...SO THE DEFENDER LOOKS DOWN.
WHEN THE BALL SHOOTS UP AT A HIGH SPEED, IT VANISHES FROM ONE'S FIELD OF VISION IN AN INSTANT.
AND UNLIKE MOST JUMP SHOTS, WHICH ARE RELEASED AT THE PEAK, THE TIMING ON THIS ONE IS EARLY.
IN THAT INSTANT, HE LEADS THE EYE TOWARDS KAGAMI, JUST LIKE WITH HIS VANISHING DRIVE.
HIS DEFENDER LOSES TRACK OF THE BALL, MAKING IT SEEM AS IF IT REALLY HAS DISAPPEARED.

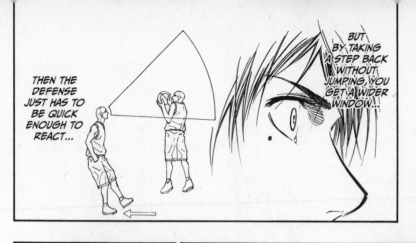

BUT BY TAKING A STEP BACK WITHOUT JUMPING, YOU GET A WIDER WINDOW...

THEN THE DEFENSE JUST HAS TO BE QUICK ENOUGH TO REACT...

IT'S AS PLAIN AS DAY.

TOM

P

SERA 11

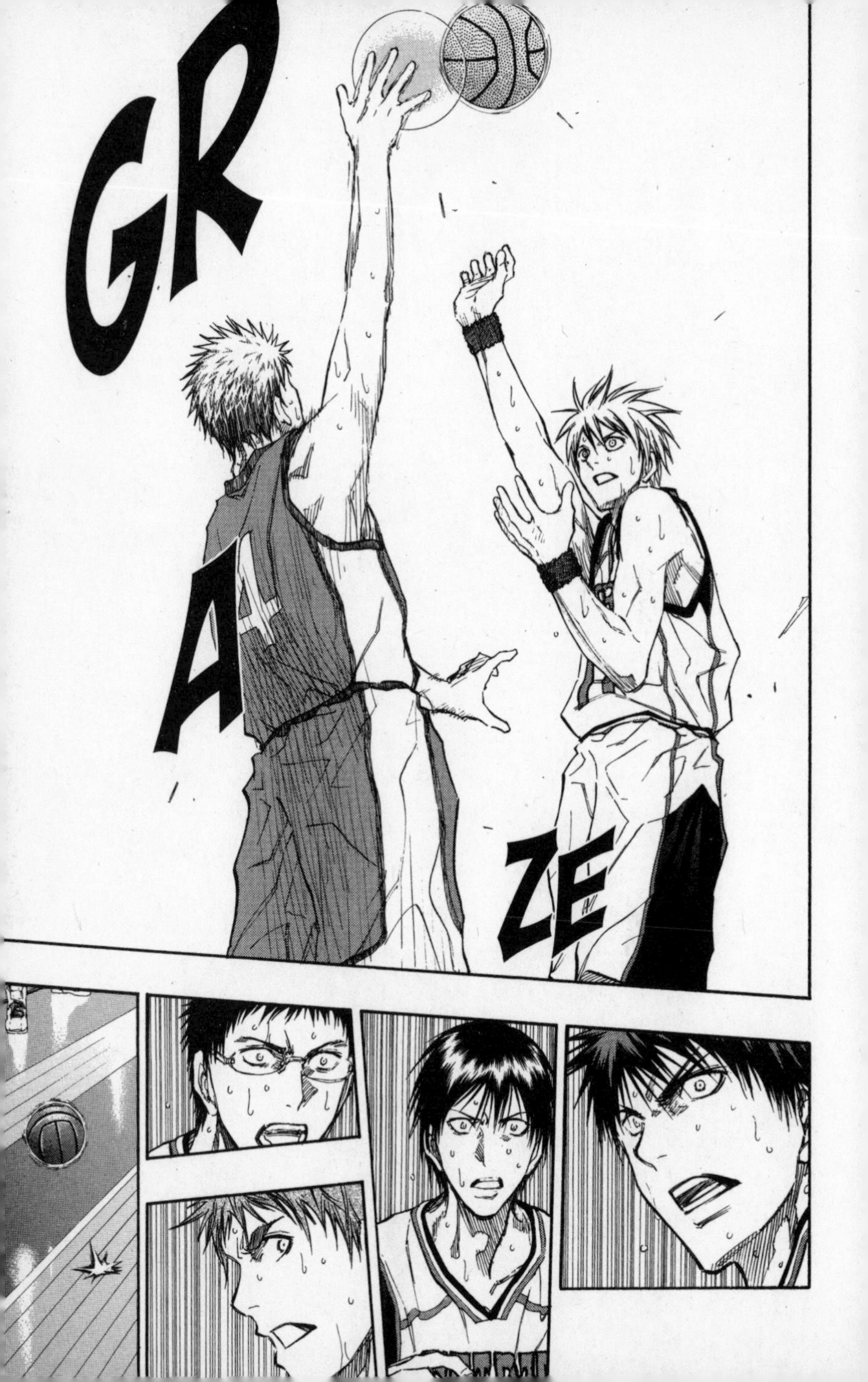
GRAZE

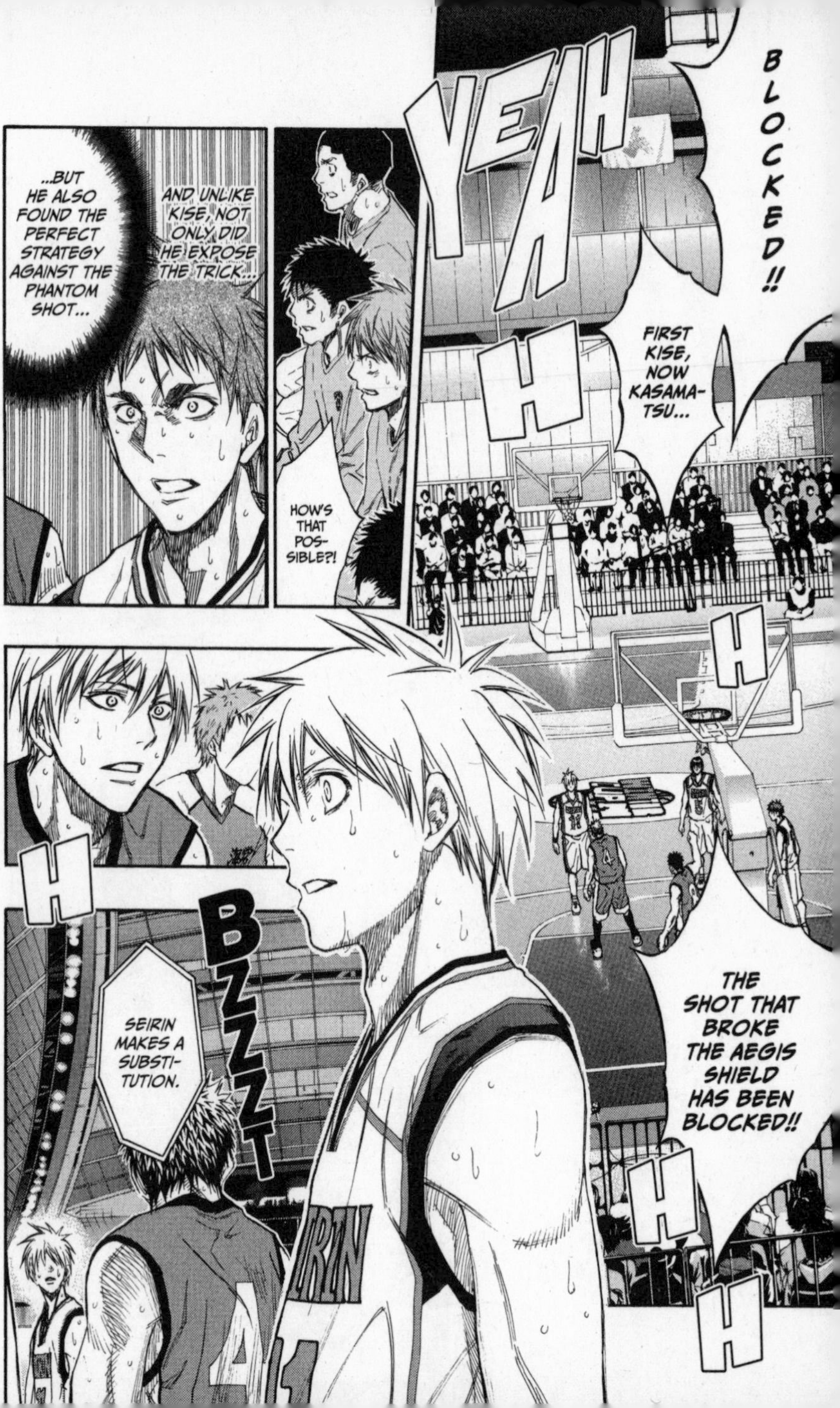
BLOCKED!!
YEAH
H
FIRST KISE, NOW KASAMATSU...
H
THE SHOT THAT BROKE THE AEGIS SHIELD HAS BEEN BLOCKED!!
H
H
H
HOW'S THAT POSSIBLE?!
AND UNLIKE KISE, NOT ONLY DID HE EXPOSE THE TRICK...
...BUT HE ALSO FOUND THE PERFECT STRATEGY AGAINST THE PHANTOM SHOT...
H
BZZZT
SEIRIN MAKES A SUBSTITUTION.

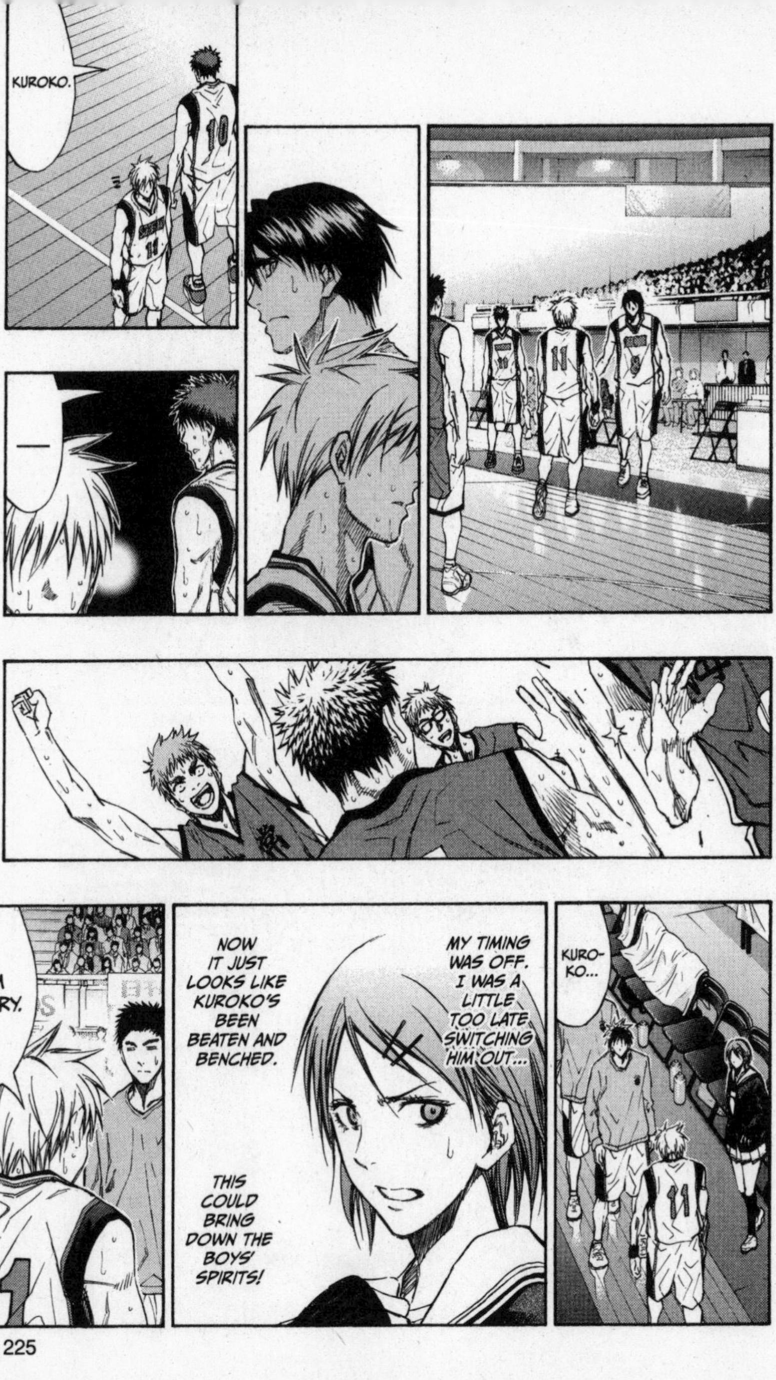
KUROKO.
—
KURO-KO...
MY TIMING WAS OFF. I WAS A LITTLE TOO LATE SWITCHING HIM OUT...
NOW IT JUST LOOKS LIKE KUROKO'S BEEN BEATEN AND BENCHED.
THIS COULD BRING DOWN THE BOYS' SPIRITS!
I'M SORRY.

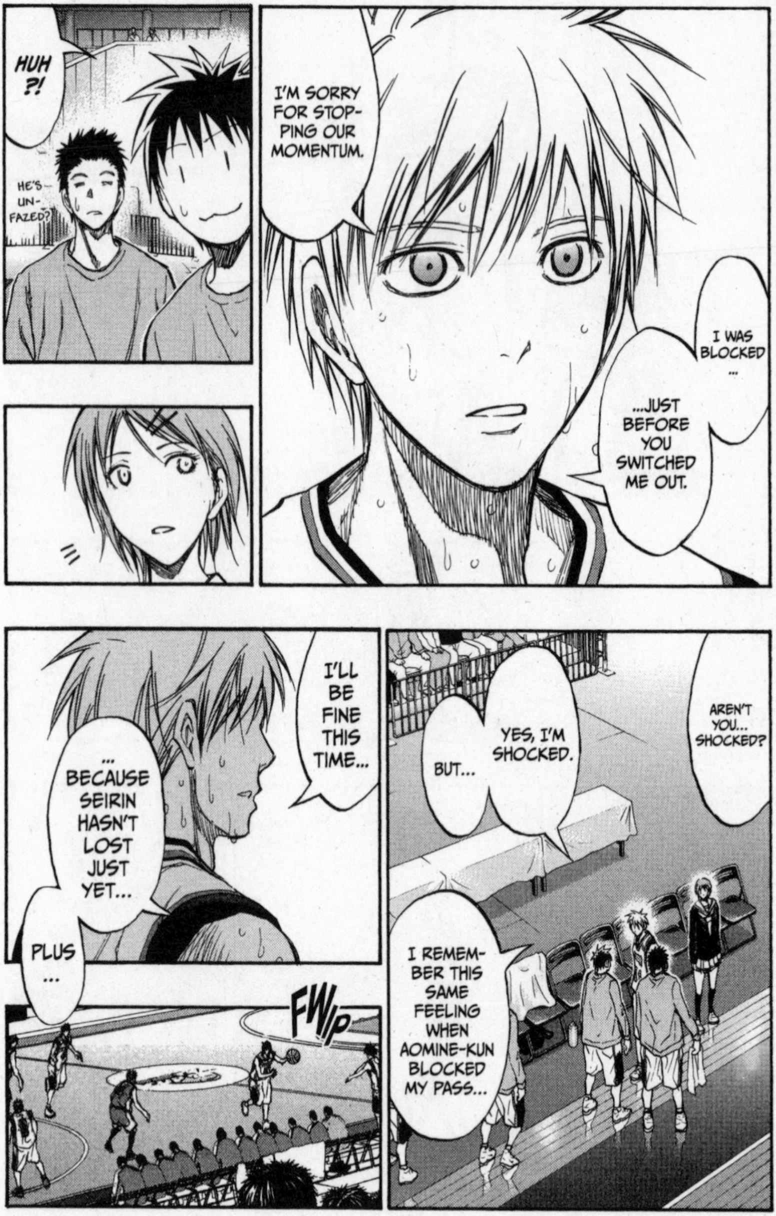
I'M SORRY FOR STOP-PING OUR MOMENTUM.
I WAS BLOCKED...
...JUST BEFORE YOU SWITCHED ME OUT.
HUH ?!
HE'S UN-FAZED?
AREN'T YOU... SHOCKED?
YES, I'M SHOCKED.
BUT...
I REMEM-BER THIS SAME FEELING WHEN AOMINE-KUN BLOCKED MY PASS...
I'LL BE FINE THIS TIME...
...BECAUSE SEIRIN HASN'T LOST JUST YET...
PLUS...
FWIP

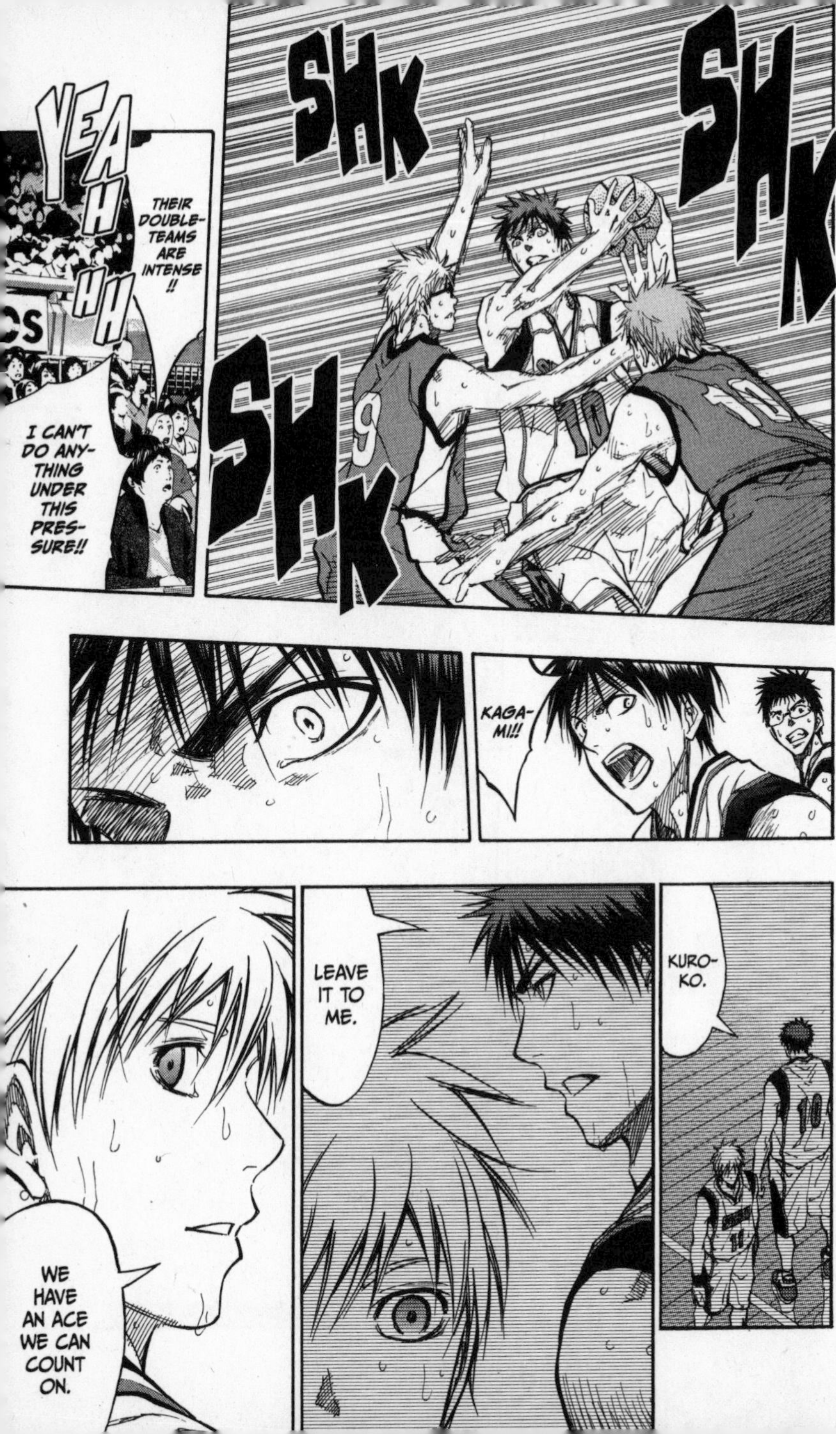
SHK
SHK
SHK
YEAHHHH
THEIR DOUBLE-TEAMS ARE INTENSE!!
I CAN'T DO ANYTHING UNDER THIS PRESSURE!!
KAGAMI!!
KURO-KO.
LEAVE IT TO ME.
WE HAVE AN ACE WE CAN COUNT ON.

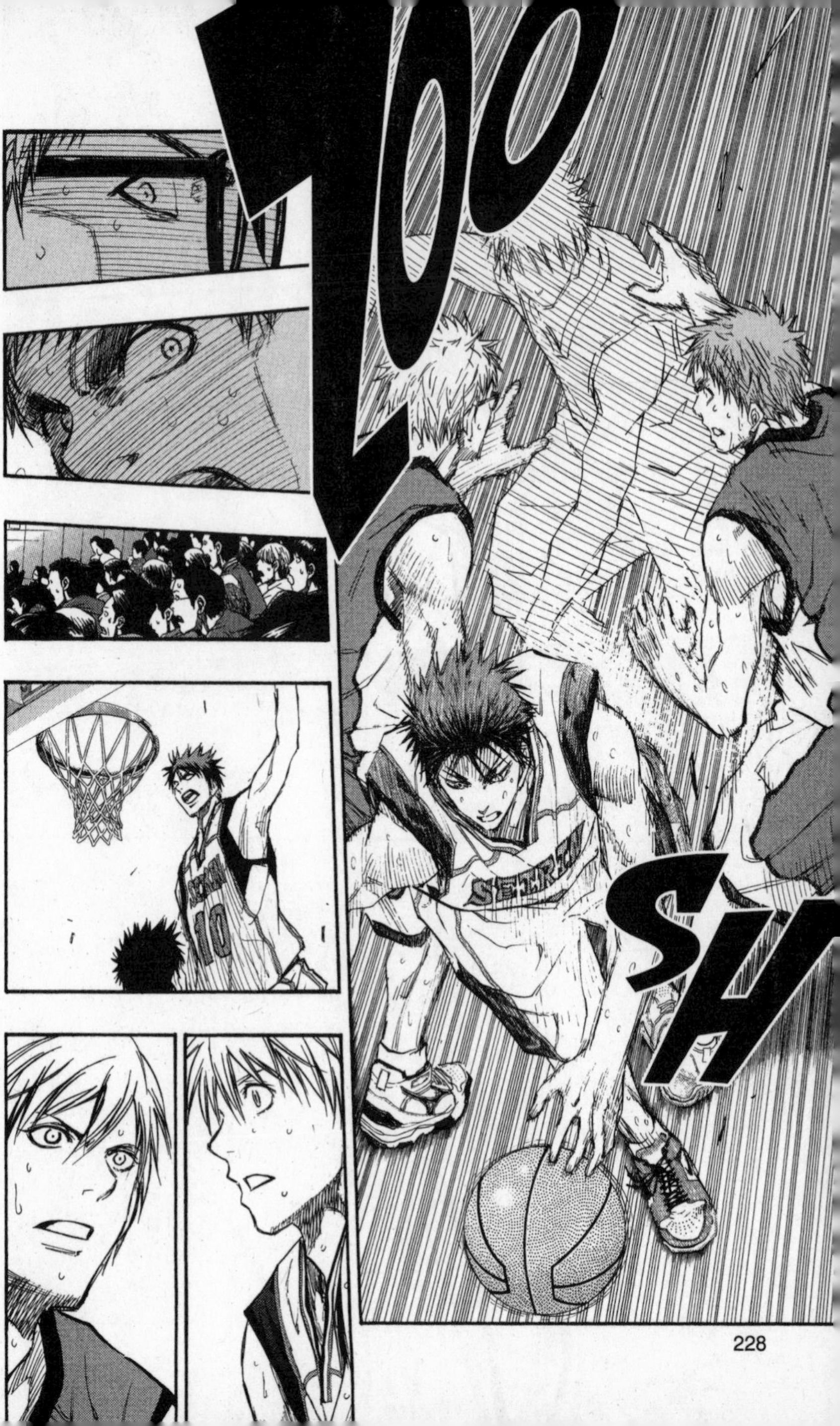
SH

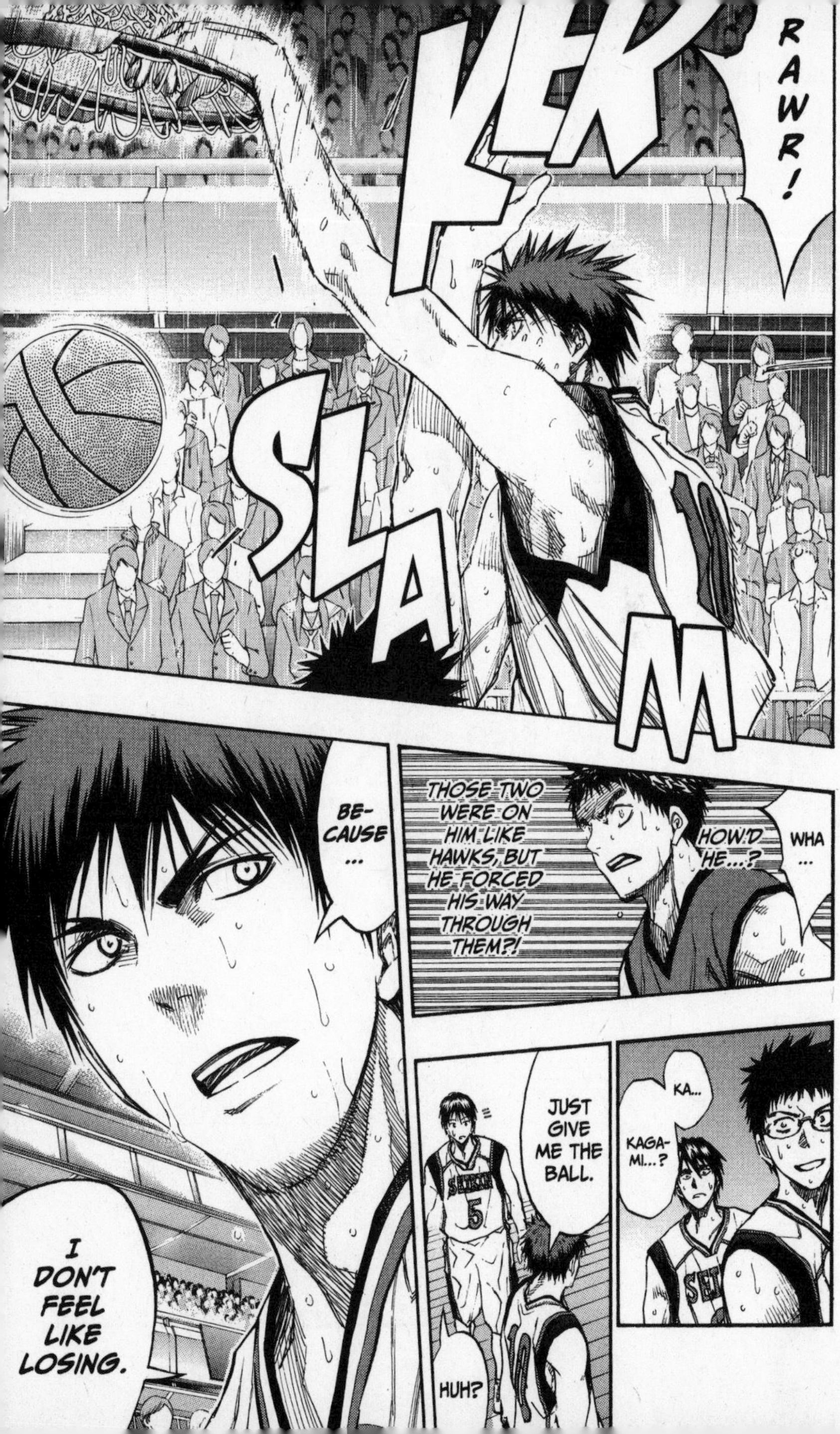
RAWR!
SLAM
WHA ...
HOW'D HE...?
THOSE TWO WERE ON HIM LIKE HAWKS, BUT HE FORCED HIS WAY THROUGH THEM?!
KA...
KAGA-MI...?
JUST GIVE ME THE BALL.
HUH?
BE-CAUSE ...
I DON'T FEEL LIKE LOSING.

KUROKO'S BASKETBALL Q&A
W/ HALFWAY-DECENT ANSWERS

Q. **IS KIYOSHI SENPAI ACTUALLY SMART? WHAT LEVEL OF ACADEMIC TESTS HAS HE PASSED?**
(TATAMI ROOM from HIROSHIMA PREFECTURE)

A. LEVELS 1 TO 5.

KUROKO'S BASKETBALL BLOOPERS
TAKE 1

KURO-KO.
YOU'RE HUNGRY ...?
NO! WRONG! WHY WOULD I SAY THAT?! IF YOU CAN'T HEAR ME, JUST TELL ME!!
KA-GA-MI
HOW MUCH OF A GLUTTON ARE YOU?

192ND QUARTER: GOT ANYTHING ELSE TO SAY?

KA...
KAGAMI...?!
AS HIS TEAMMATES, WE KNOW BETTER THAN ANYONE HOW AMAZING KAGAMI-KUN CAN BE.
BUT WE'RE STILL SHOCKED.
THIS SPEAKS TO...
...KAGAMI-KUN'S INCREDIBLE GROWTH.
THEY SAY PEOPLE DON'T JUST IMPROVE STEADILY. IT HAPPENS IN STAGES.
THAT'S DEFINITELY THE CASE HERE... HE GETS BETTER EVERY TIME HE FACES ONE OF THE MIRACLE GENNERS.
THE FIRST TIME WE MET, I COULDN'T GET A READ ON HIS POTENTIAL.
HOW FAR CAN HE REALLY GO, I WONDER?
IT MAKES HIM SUPER RELIABLE FOR SURE, BUT AT THE SAME TIME, THAT ENDLESS POTEN-TIAL...
IT'S A LITTLE...
...SCARY.

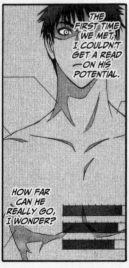

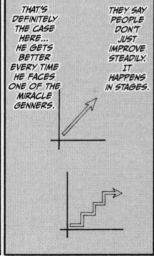

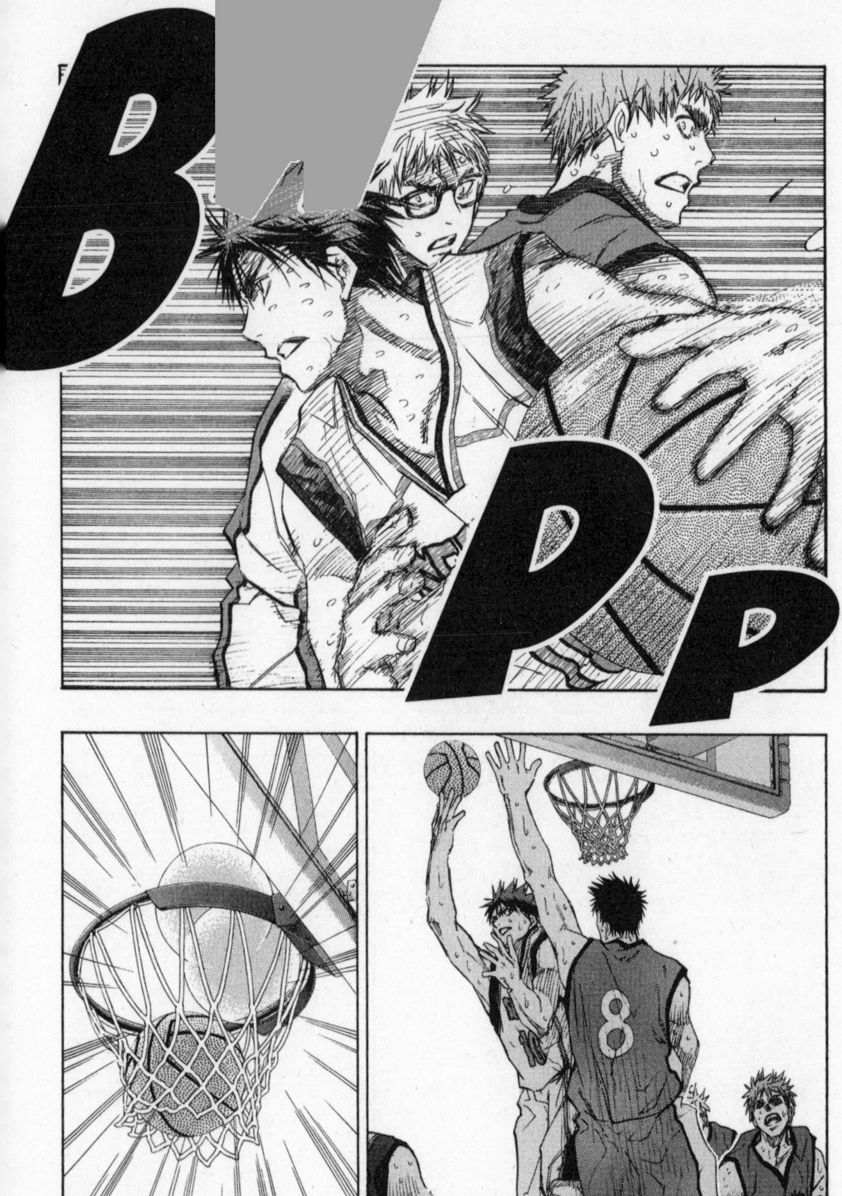
B
PP

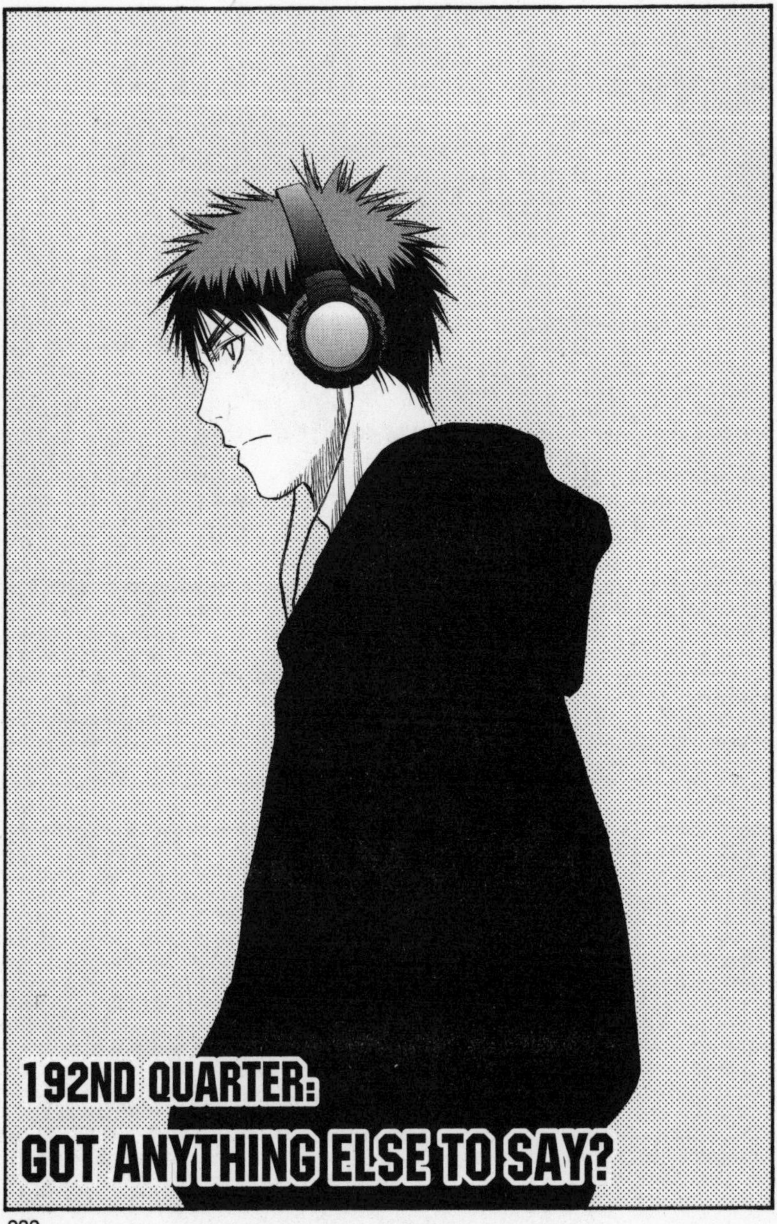
192ND QUARTER:
GOT ANYTHING ELSE TO SAY?

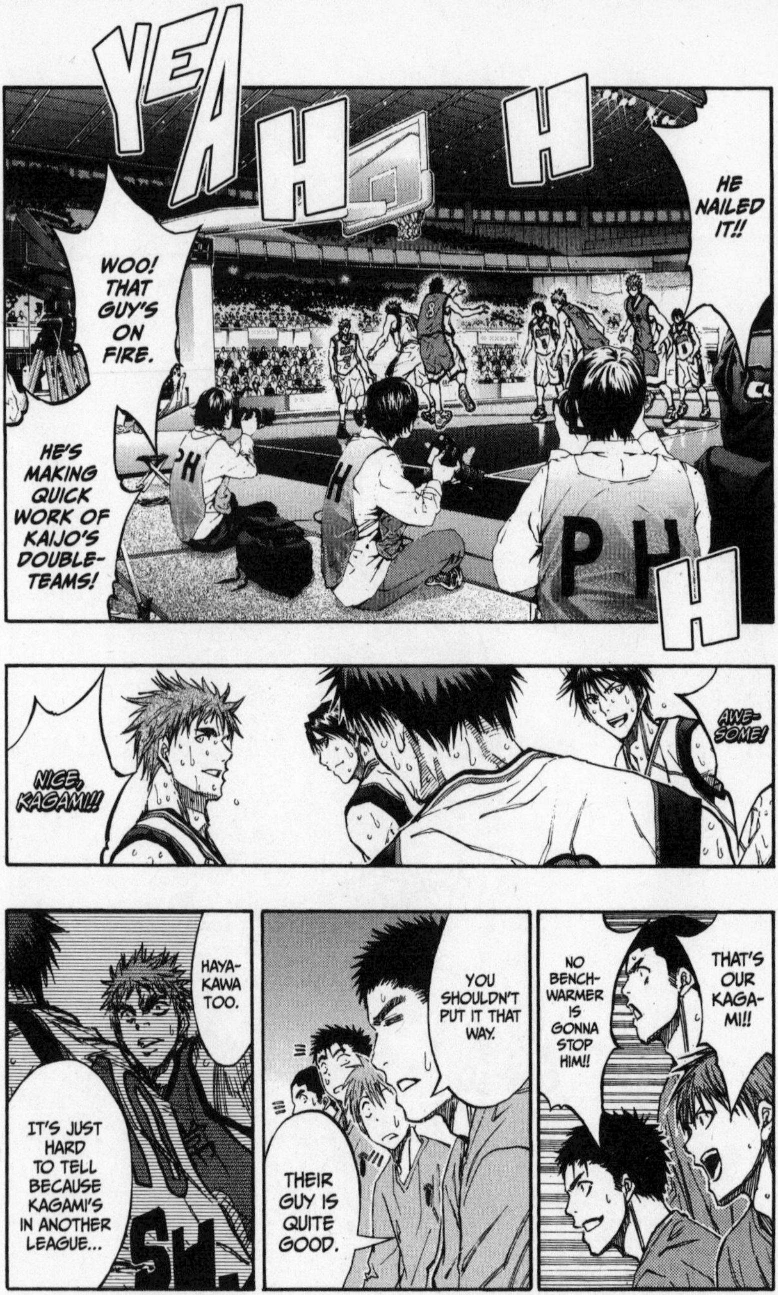
YEAHHHH
HE NAILED IT!!
WOO! THAT GUY'S ON FIRE.
HE'S MAKING QUICK WORK OF KAIJO'S DOUBLE-TEAMS!
AWE-SOME!
NICE, KAGAMI!!
THAT'S OUR KAGA-MI!!
NO BENCH-WARMER IS GONNA STOP HIM!!
YOU SHOULDN'T PUT IT THAT WAY.
THEIR GUY IS QUITE GOOD.
HAYA-KAWA TOO.
IT'S JUST HARD TO TELL BECAUSE KAGAMI'S IN ANOTHER LEAGUE...

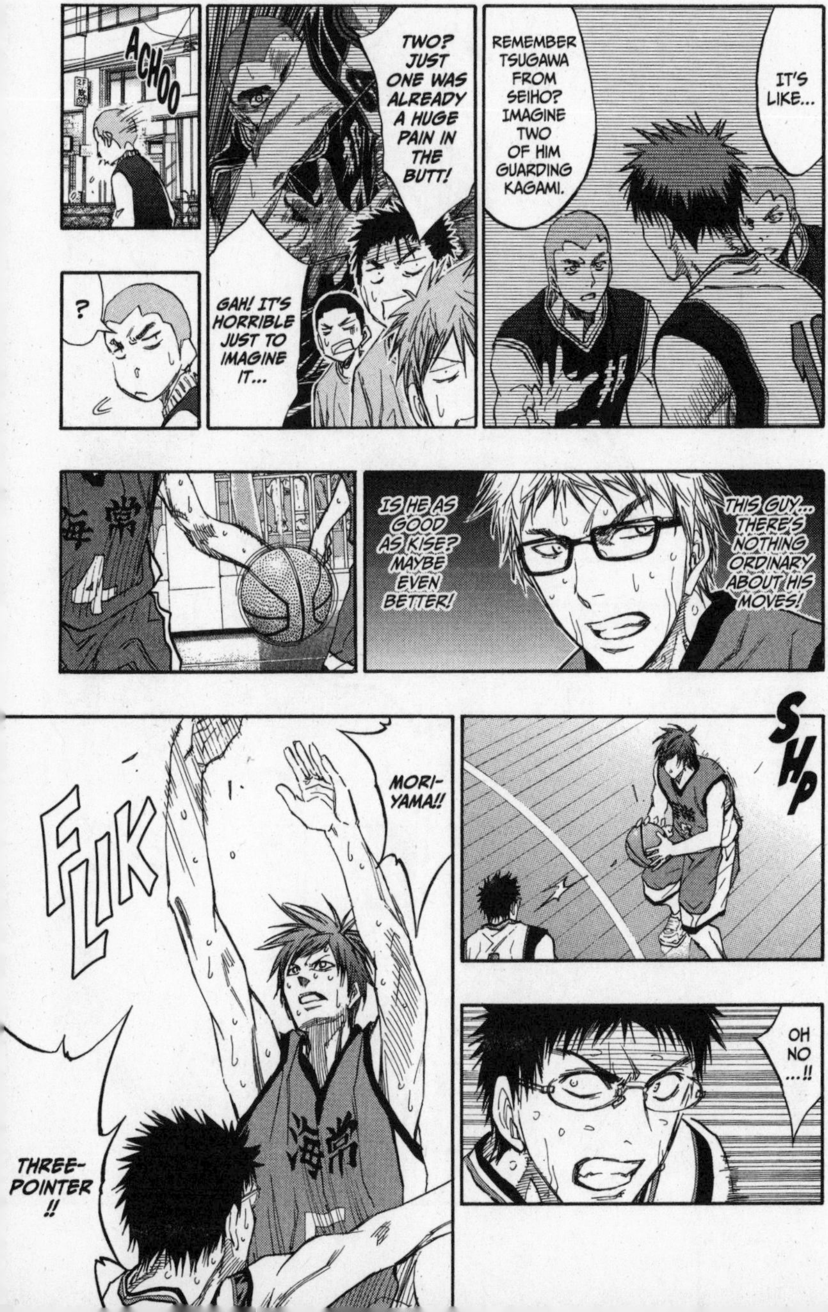
IT'S LIKE...
REMEMBER TSUGAWA FROM SEIHO? IMAGINE TWO OF HIM GUARDING KAGAMI.
TWO? JUST ONE WAS ALREADY A HUGE PAIN IN THE BUTT!
GAH! IT'S HORRIBLE JUST TO IMAGINE IT...
ACHOO
?
THIS GUY... THERE'S NOTHING ORDINARY ABOUT HIS MOVES!
IS HE AS GOOD AS KISE? MAYBE EVEN BETTER!
SHP
OH NO ...!!
MORI-YAMA!!
FLIK
THREE-POINTER !!

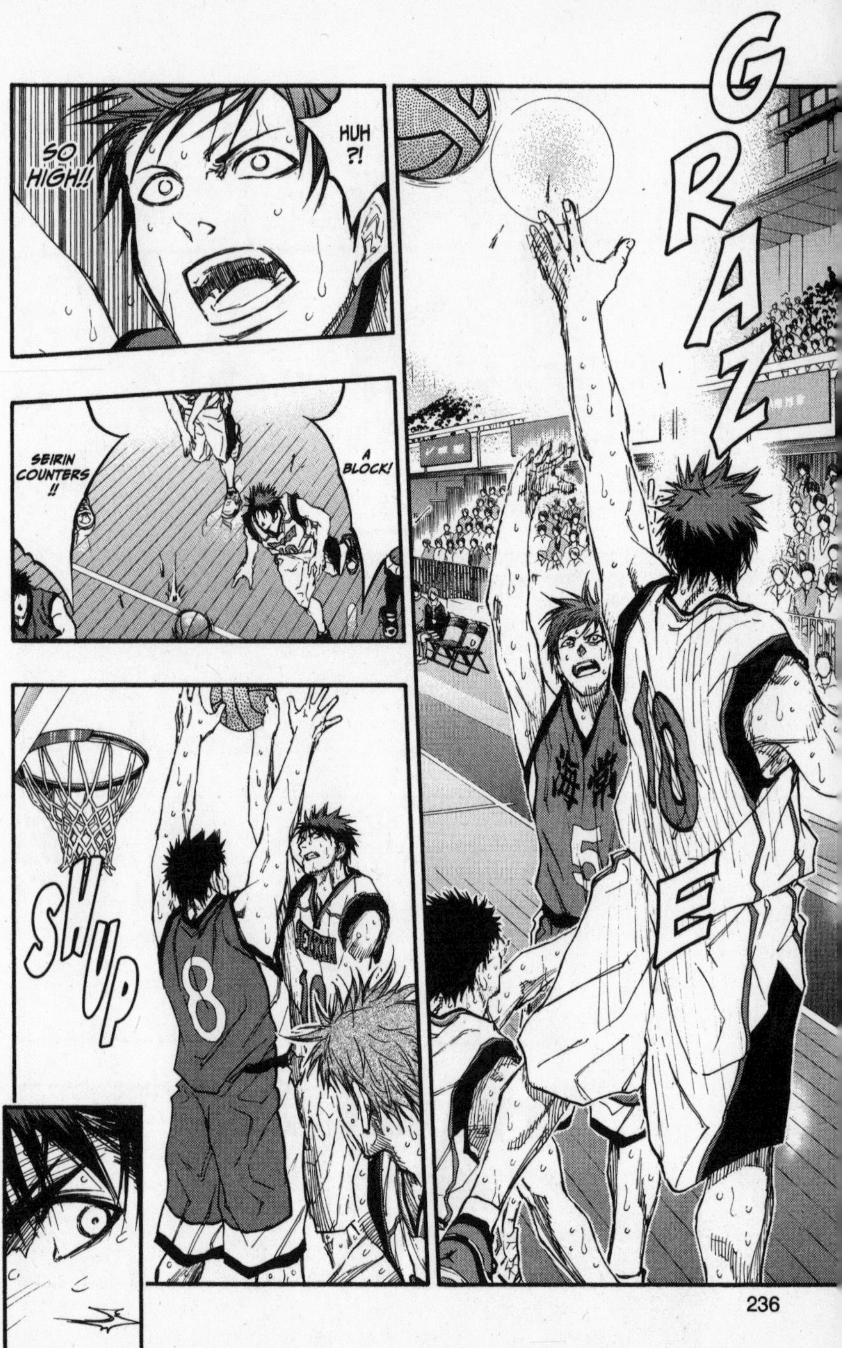
GRAZE
HUH ?!
SO HIGH!!
A BLOCK!
SEIRIN COUNTERS !!
SHUP

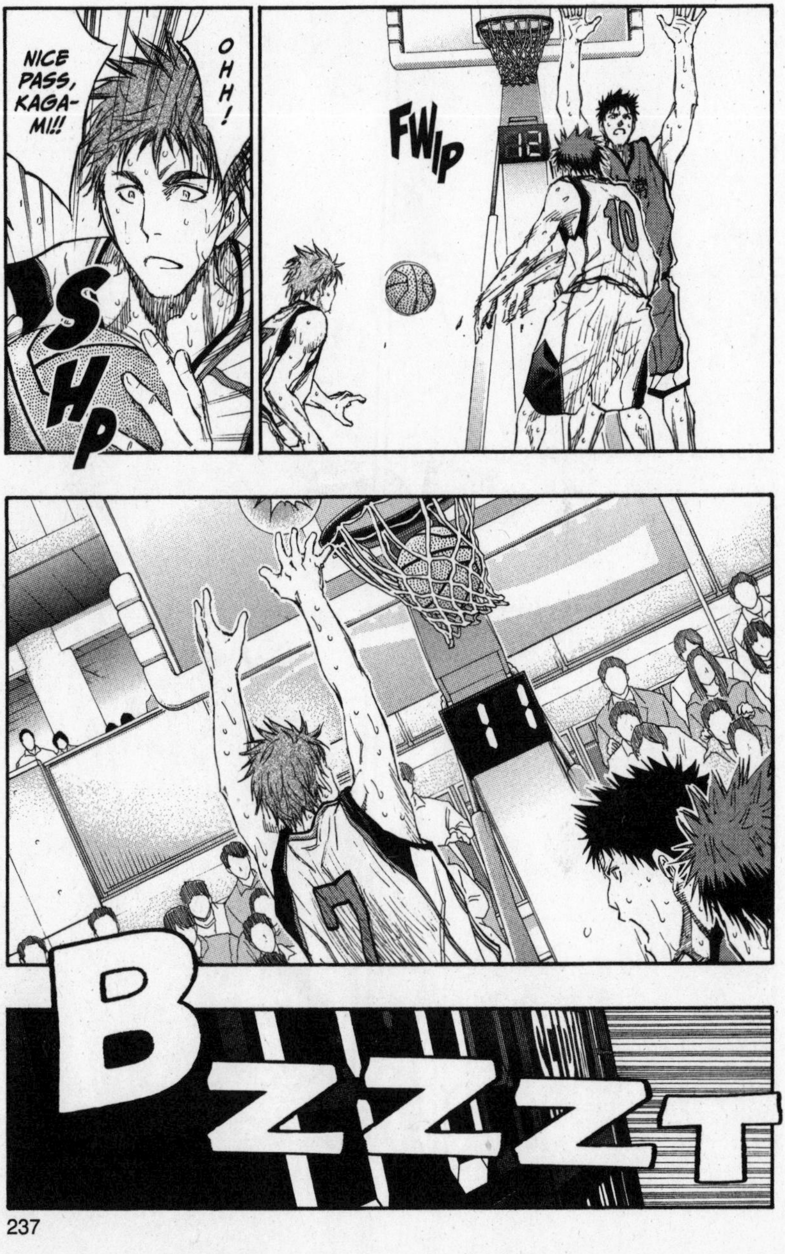
FWIP
OHH!
NICE PASS, KAGAMI!!
SHP
BZZZT

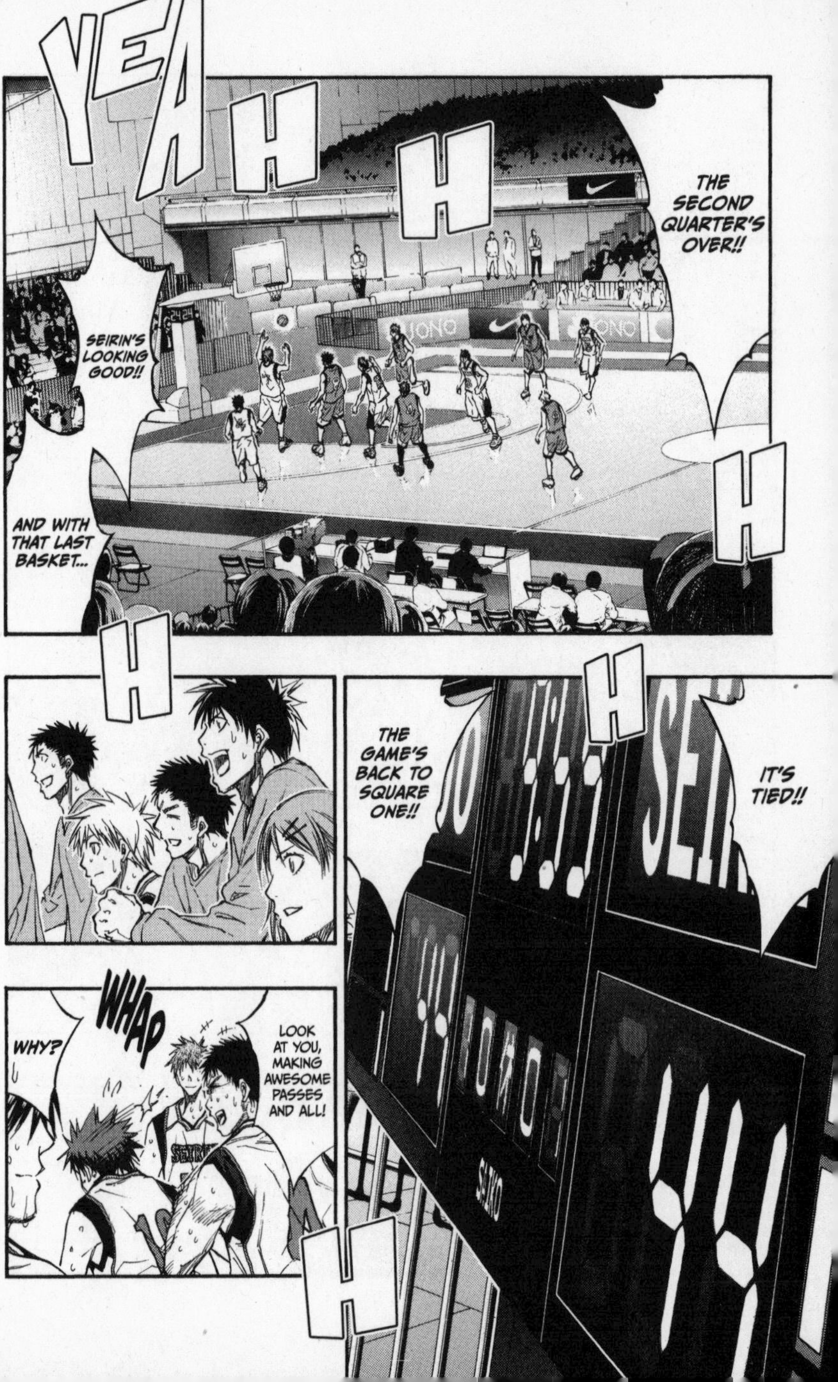
YEAHHHHHH
THE SECOND QUARTER'S OVER!!
SEIRIN'S LOOKING GOOD!!
AND WITH THAT LAST BASKET...
IT'S TIED!!
THE GAME'S BACK TO SQUARE ONE!!
LOOK AT YOU, MAKING AWESOME PASSES AND ALL!
WHAP
WHY?

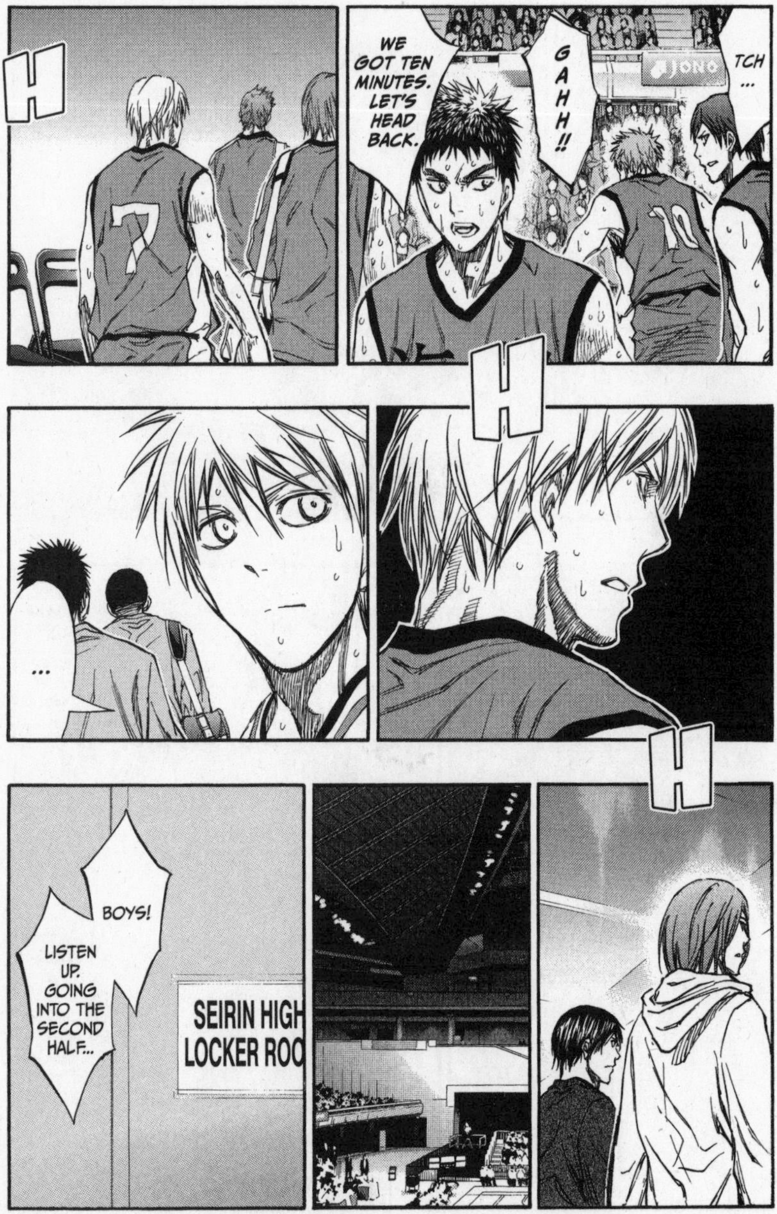
TCH ...
GAHH!!
WE GOT TEN MINUTES. LET'S HEAD BACK.
H
H
...
H
BOYS!
LISTEN UP. GOING INTO THE SECOND HALF...
SEIRIN HIGH LOCKER ROO

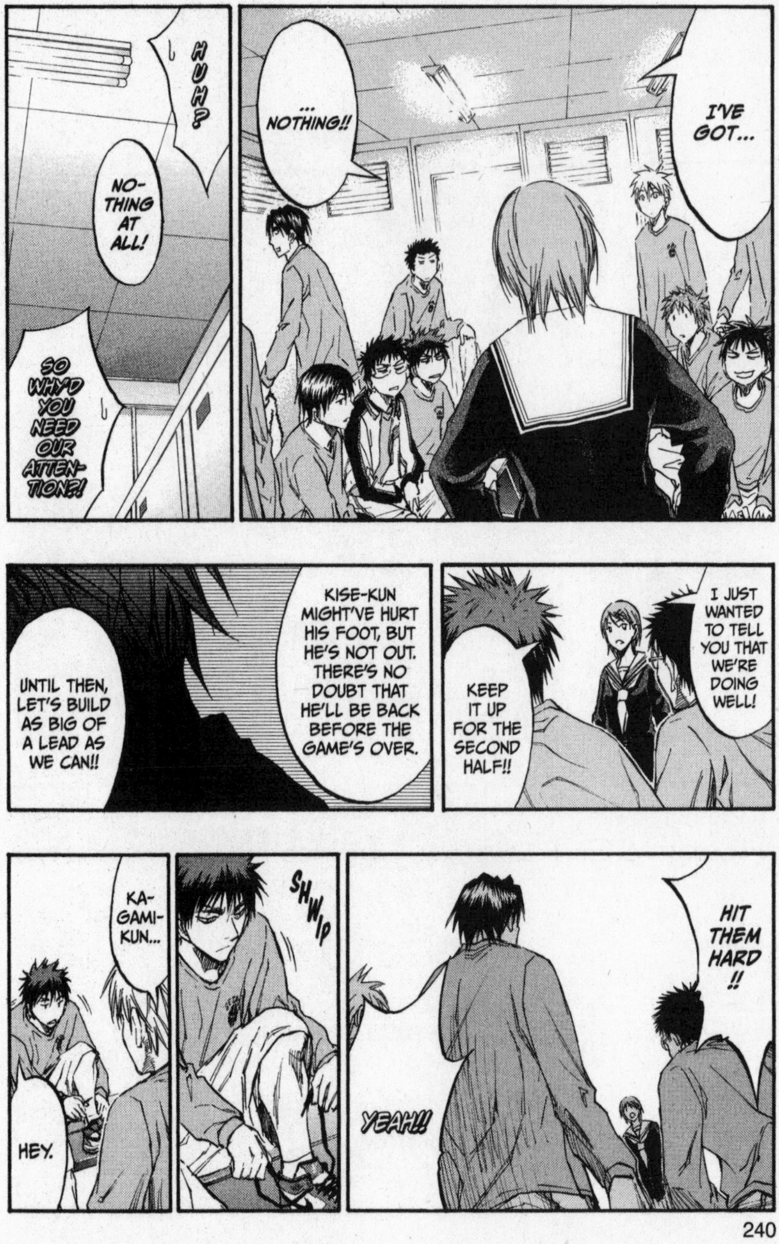

I'VE GOT...
... NOTHING!!
HUH?
NO-THING AT ALL!
SO WHY'D YOU NEED OUR ATTEN-TION?!
I JUST WANTED TO TELL YOU THAT WE'RE DOING WELL!
KEEP IT UP FOR THE SECOND HALF!!
KISE-KUN MIGHT'VE HURT HIS FOOT, BUT HE'S NOT OUT. THERE'S NO DOUBT THAT HE'LL BE BACK BEFORE THE GAME'S OVER.
UNTIL THEN, LET'S BUILD AS BIG OF A LEAD AS WE CAN!!
HIT THEM HARD !!
YEAH!!
SHWIP
KA-GAMI-KUN...
HEY.

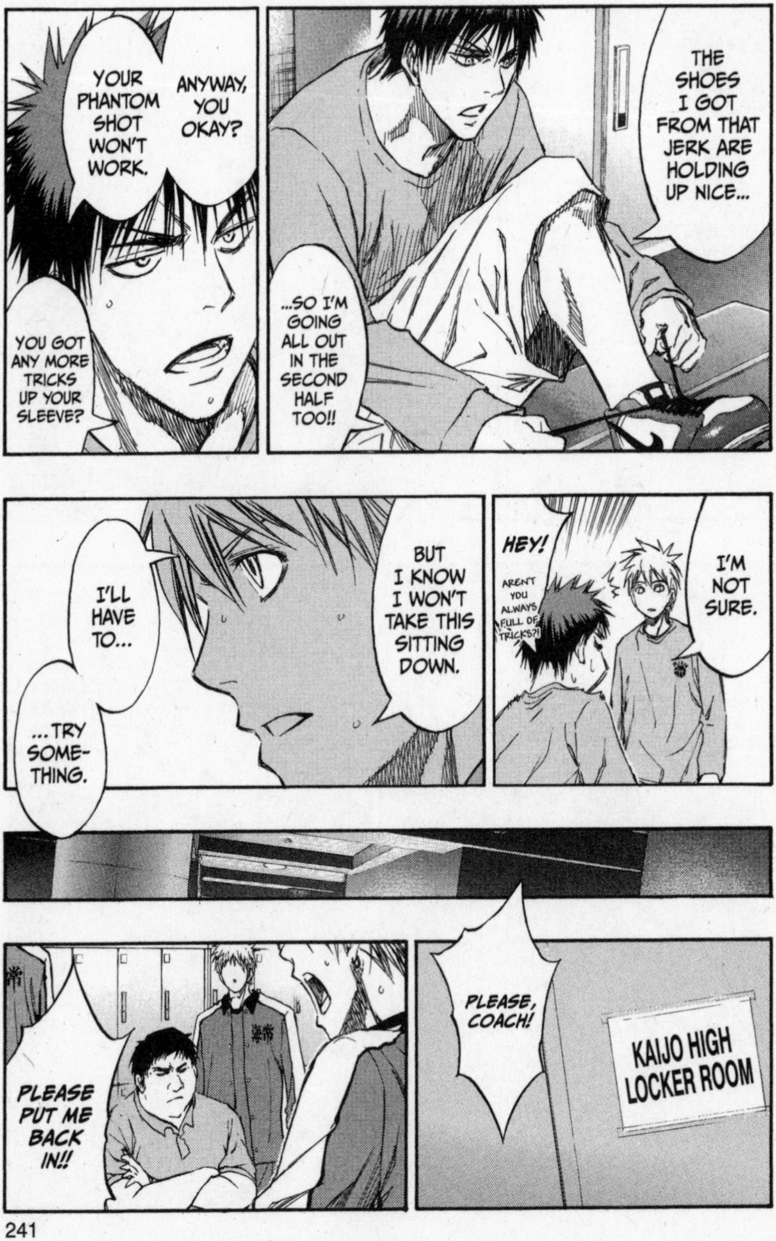
THE SHOES I GOT FROM THAT JERK ARE HOLDING UP NICE...
...SO I'M GOING ALL OUT IN THE SECOND HALF TOO!!
ANYWAY, YOU OKAY?
YOUR PHANTOM SHOT WON'T WORK.
YOU GOT ANY MORE TRICKS UP YOUR SLEEVE?
I'M NOT SURE.
HEY!
AREN'T YOU ALWAYS FULL OF TRICKS?!
BUT I KNOW I WON'T TAKE THIS SITTING DOWN.
I'LL HAVE TO...
...TRY SOMETHING.
PLEASE, COACH!
KAIJO HIGH LOCKER ROOM
PLEASE PUT ME BACK IN!!

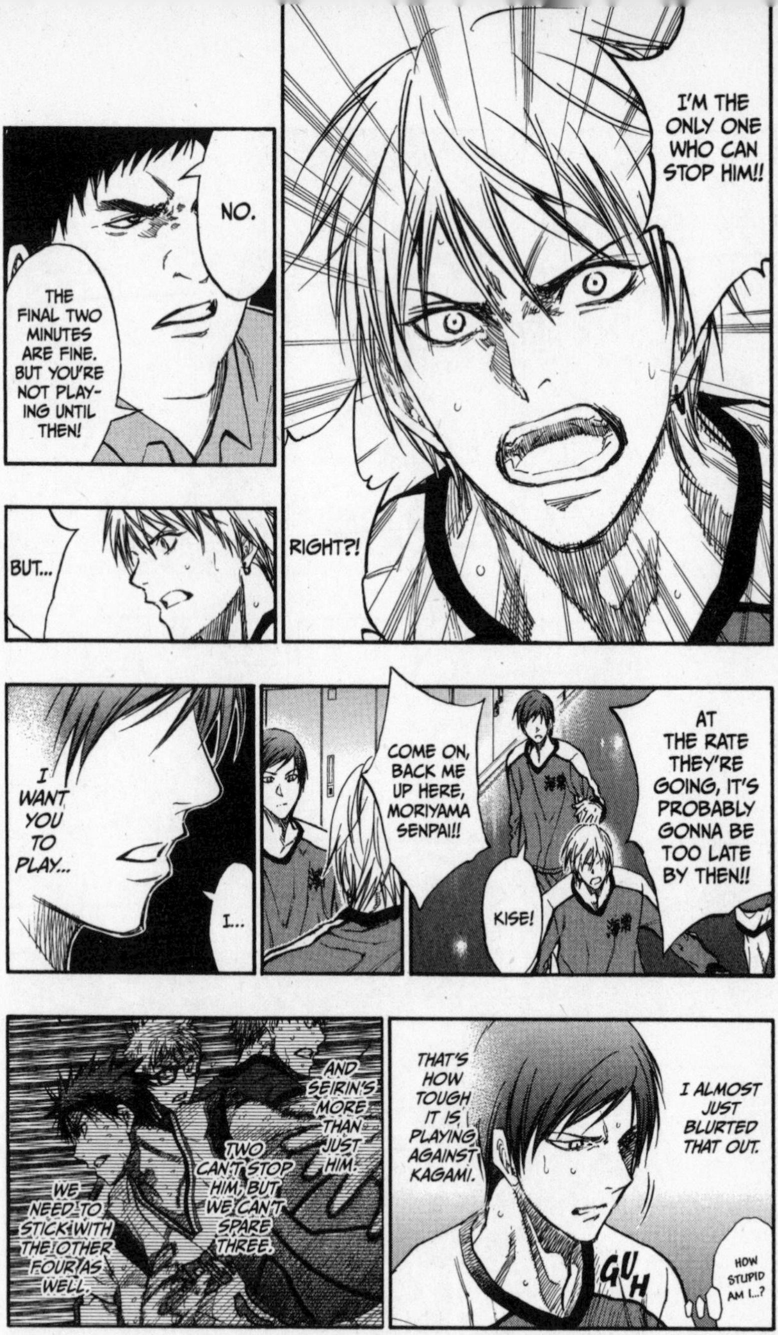
I'M THE ONLY ONE WHO CAN STOP HIM!!
RIGHT?!
NO.
THE FINAL TWO MINUTES ARE FINE. BUT YOU'RE NOT PLAYING UNTIL THEN!
BUT...
AT THE RATE THEY'RE GOING, IT'S PROBABLY GONNA BE TOO LATE BY THEN!!
COME ON, BACK ME UP HERE, MORIYAMA SENPAI!!
KISE!
I...
I WANT YOU TO PLAY...
I ALMOST JUST BLURTED THAT OUT.
THAT'S HOW TOUGH IT IS PLAYING AGAINST KAGAMI.
GUH
HOW STUPID AM I...?
AND SEIRIN'S MORE THAN JUST HIM.
TWO CAN'T STOP HIM, BUT WE CAN'T SPARE THREE.
WE NEED TO STICK WITH THE OTHER FOUR AS WELL.

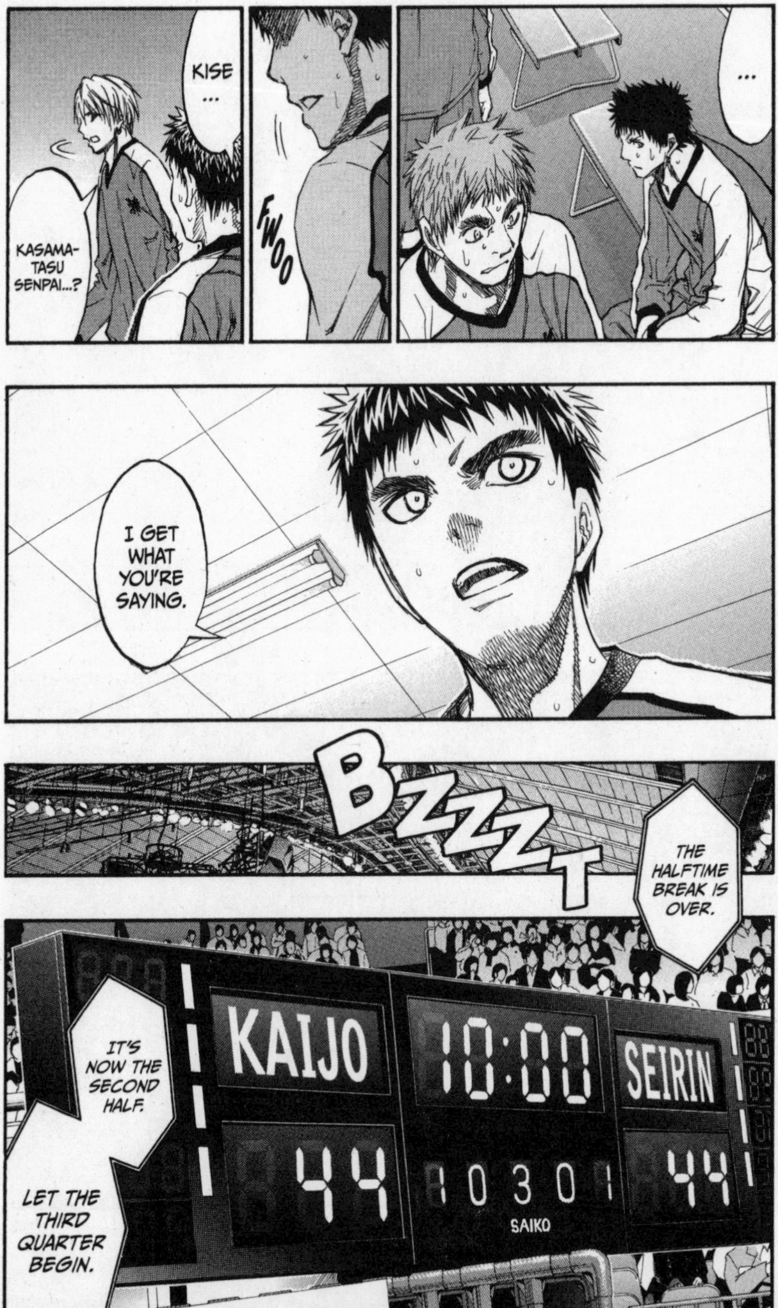
...
FWOO
KISE ...
KASAMA-TASU SENPAI...?
I GET WHAT YOU'RE SAYING.
BZZZT
THE HALFTIME BREAK IS OVER.
IT'S NOW THE SECOND HALF.
KAIJO
10:00
SEIRIN
44
44
SAIKO
LET THE THIRD QUARTER BEGIN.

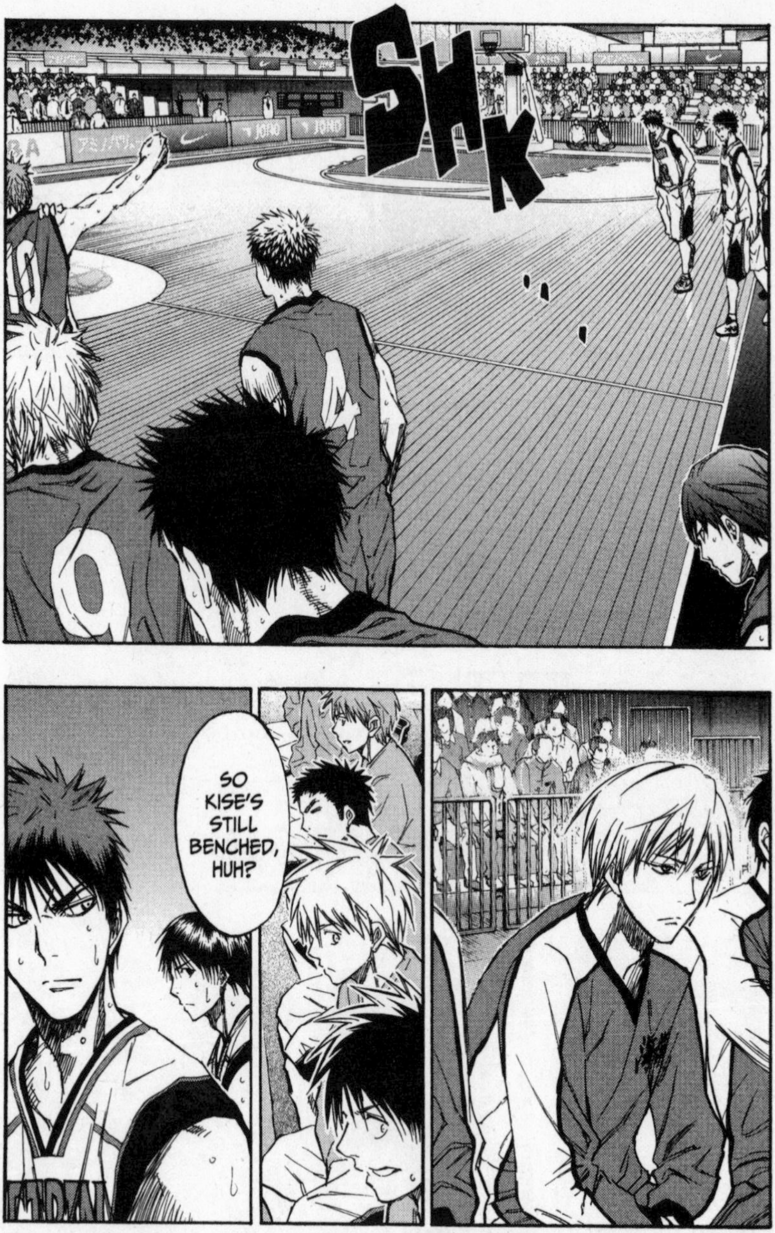
SHK
SO KISE'S STILL BENCHED, HUH?

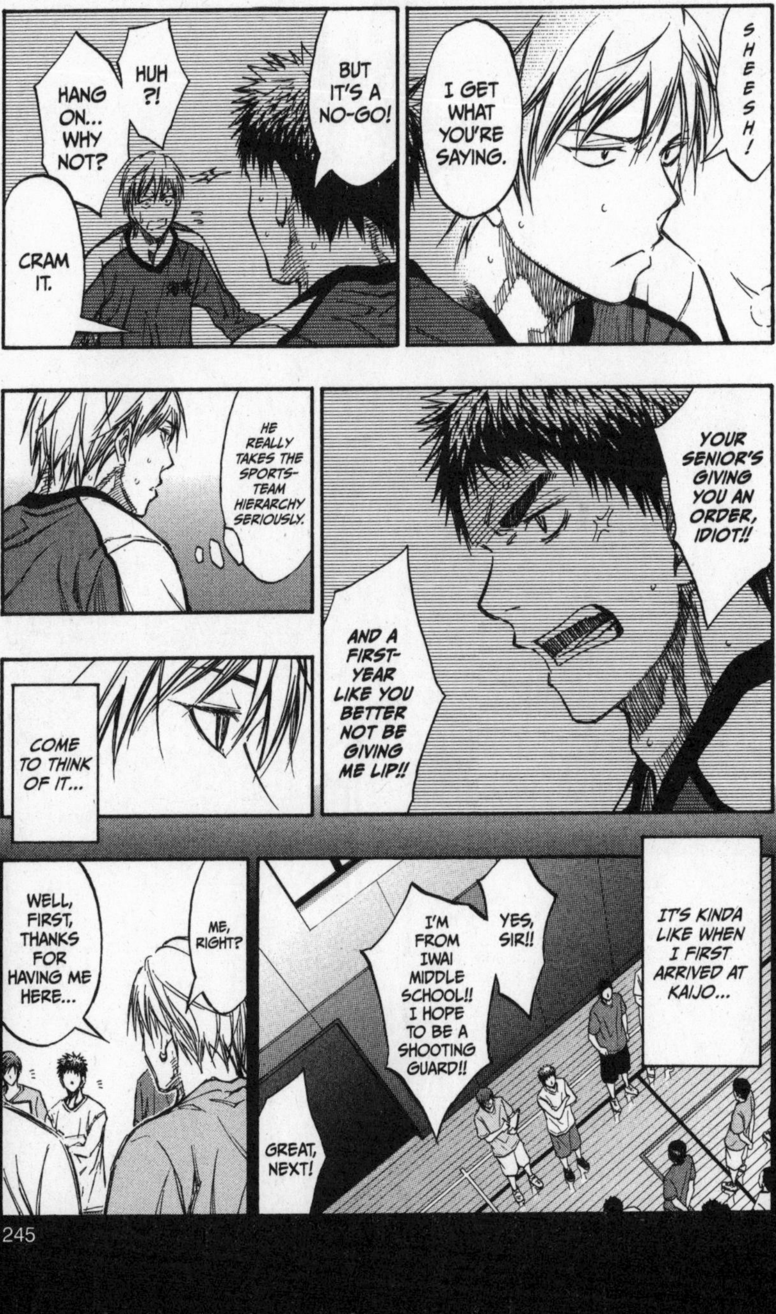
SHEESH!
I GET WHAT YOU'RE SAYING.
BUT IT'S A NO-GO!
HUH?!
HANG ON... WHY NOT?
CRAM IT.
YOUR SENIOR'S GIVING YOU AN ORDER, IDIOT!!
AND A FIRST-YEAR LIKE YOU BETTER NOT BE GIVING ME LIP!!
HE REALLY TAKES THE SPORTS-TEAM HIERARCHY SERIOUSLY.
COME TO THINK OF IT...
IT'S KINDA LIKE WHEN I FIRST ARRIVED AT KAIJO...
YES, SIR!!
I'M FROM IWAI MIDDLE SCHOOL!! I HOPE TO BE A SHOOTING GUARD!!
GREAT, NEXT!
ME, RIGHT?
WELL, FIRST, THANKS FOR HAVING ME HERE...

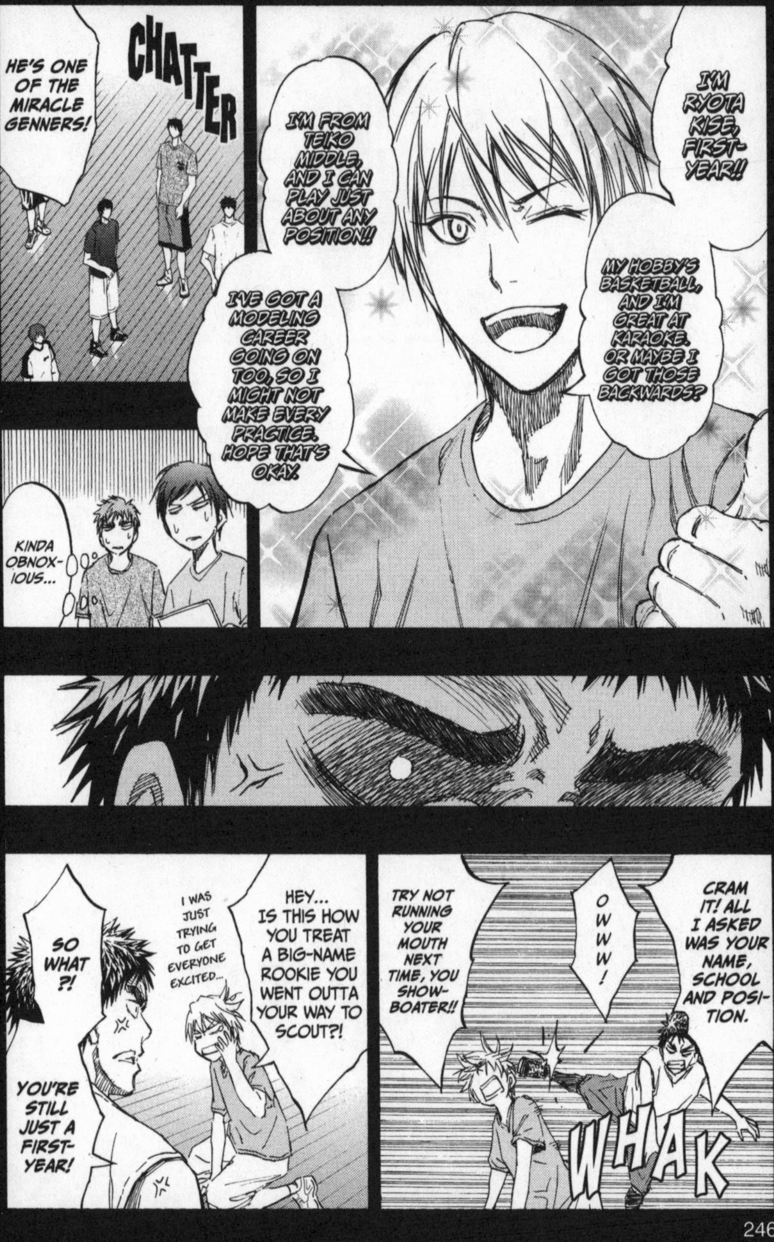
I'M RYOTA KISE, FIRST-YEAR!!
I'M FROM TEIKO MIDDLE, AND I CAN PLAY JUST ABOUT ANY POSITION!!
MY HOBBY'S BASKETBALL, AND I'M GREAT AT KARAOKE. OR MAYBE I GOT THOSE BACKWARDS?
I'VE GOT A MODELING CAREER GOING ON TOO, SO I MIGHT NOT MAKE EVERY PRACTICE. HOPE THAT'S OKAY.
CHATTER
HE'S ONE OF THE MIRACLE GENNERS!
KINDA OBNOXIOUS...
CRAM IT! ALL I ASKED WAS YOUR NAME, SCHOOL AND POSITION.
OWWW!
TRY NOT RUNNING YOUR MOUTH NEXT TIME, YOU SHOWBOATER!!
WHAK
HEY... IS THIS HOW YOU TREAT A BIG-NAME ROOKIE YOU WENT OUTTA YOUR WAY TO SCOUT?!
I WAS JUST TRYING TO GET EVERYONE EXCITED...
SO WHAT?!
YOU'RE STILL JUST A FIRST-YEAR!

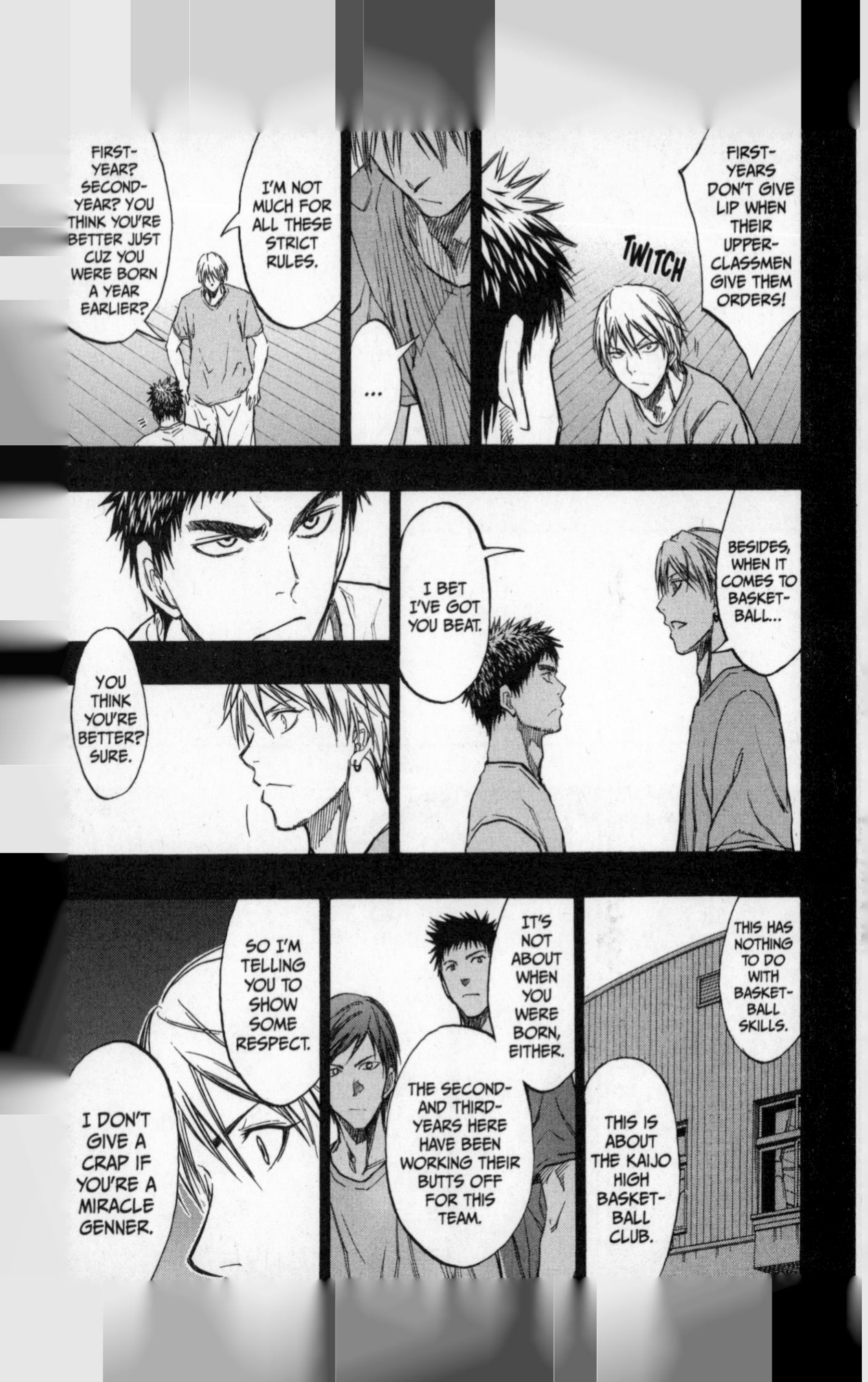
FIRST-YEARS DON'T GIVE LIP WHEN THEIR UPPERCLASSMEN GIVE THEM ORDERS!
TWITCH
...
I'M NOT MUCH FOR ALL THESE STRICT RULES.
FIRST-YEAR? SECOND-YEAR? YOU THINK YOU'RE BETTER JUST CUZ YOU WERE BORN A YEAR EARLIER?
BESIDES, WHEN IT COMES TO BASKETBALL...
I BET I'VE GOT YOU BEAT.
YOU THINK YOU'RE BETTER? SURE.
THIS HAS NOTHING TO DO WITH BASKETBALL SKILLS.
THIS IS ABOUT THE KAIJO HIGH BASKETBALL CLUB.
IT'S NOT ABOUT WHEN YOU WERE BORN, EITHER.
THE SECOND- AND THIRD-YEARS HERE HAVE BEEN WORKING THEIR BUTTS OFF FOR THIS TEAM.
SO I'M TELLING YOU TO SHOW SOME RESPECT.
I DON'T GIVE A CRAP IF YOU'RE A MIRACLE GENNER.

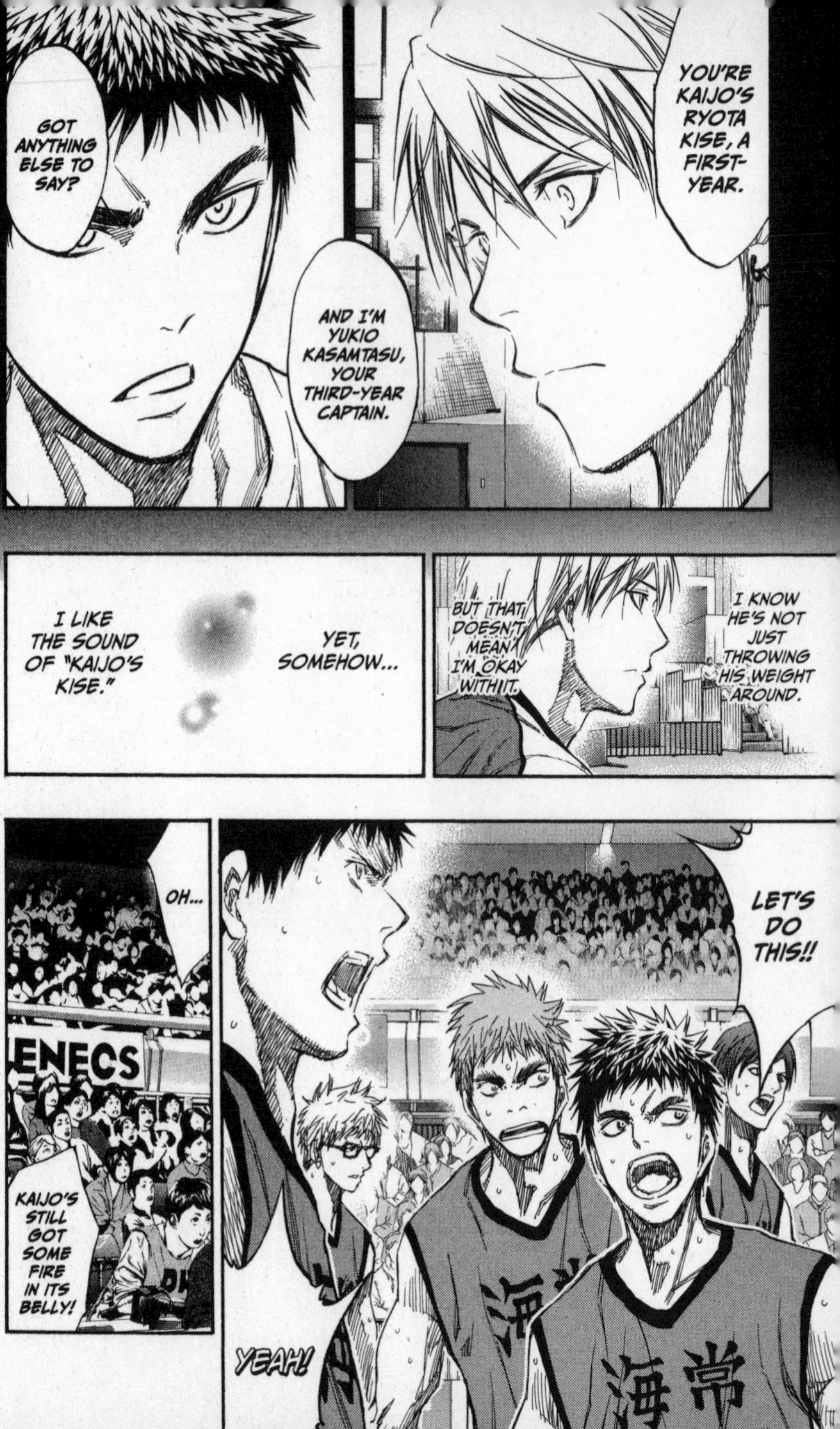
YOU'RE KAIJO'S RYOTA KISE, A FIRST-YEAR.
AND I'M YUKIO KASAMTASU, YOUR THIRD-YEAR CAPTAIN.
GOT ANYTHING ELSE TO SAY?
I KNOW HE'S NOT JUST THROWING HIS WEIGHT AROUND.
BUT THAT DOESN'T MEAN I'M OKAY WITH IT.
YET, SOMEHOW...
I LIKE THE SOUND OF "KAIJO'S KISE."
LET'S DO THIS!!
海常
YEAH!
OH...
ENECS
KAIJO'S STILL GOT SOME FIRE IN ITS BELLY!

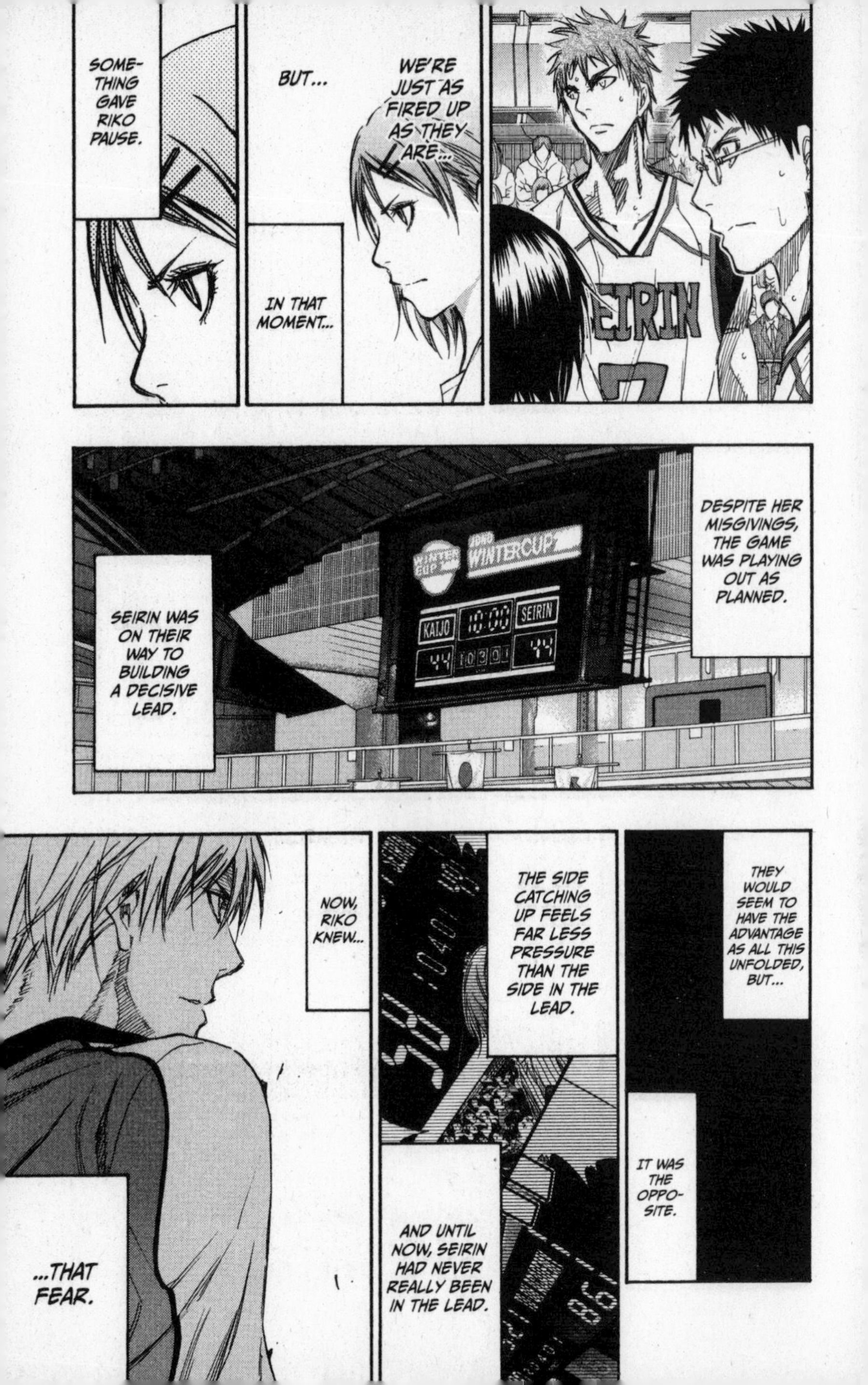
WE'RE JUST AS FIRED UP AS THEY ARE...
BUT...
IN THAT MOMENT...
SOME-THING GAVE RIKO PAUSE.
DESPITE HER MISGIVINGS, THE GAME WAS PLAYING OUT AS PLANNED.
WINTERCUP
KAIJO
10:00
SEIRIN
44
44
SEIRIN WAS ON THEIR WAY TO BUILDING A DECISIVE LEAD.
THEY WOULD SEEM TO HAVE THE ADVANTAGE AS ALL THIS UNFOLDED, BUT...
IT WAS THE OPPO-SITE.
THE SIDE CATCHING UP FEELS FAR LESS PRESSURE THAN THE SIDE IN THE LEAD.
AND UNTIL NOW, SEIRIN HAD NEVER REALLY BEEN IN THE LEAD.
NOW, RIKO KNEW...
...THAT FEAR.

KUROKO'S BASKETBALL BLOOPERS TAKE 4

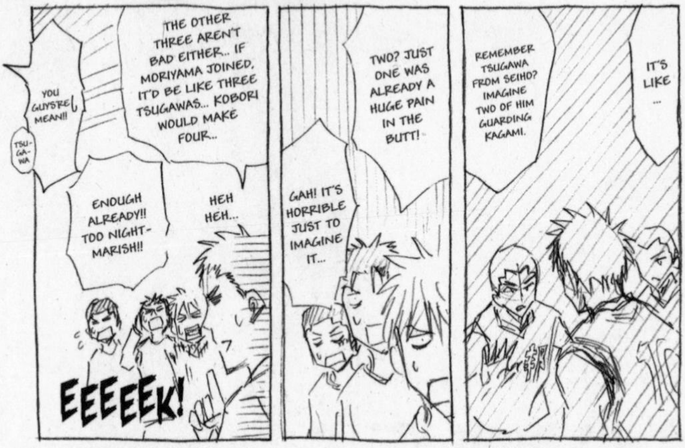
IT'S LIKE...
REMEMBER TSUGAWA FROM SEIHO? IMAGINE TWO OF HIM GUARDING KAGAMI.
TWO? JUST ONE WAS ALREADY A HUGE PAIN IN THE BUTT!
GAH! IT'S HORRIBLE JUST TO IMAGINE IT...
THE OTHER THREE AREN'T BAD EITHER... IF MORIYAMA JOINED, IT'D BE LIKE THREE TSUGAWAS... KOBORI WOULD MAKE FOUR...
YOU GUYS'RE MEAN!!
TSU-GA-WA
HEH HEH...
ENOUGH ALREADY!! TOO NIGHT-MARISH!!
EEEEEK!

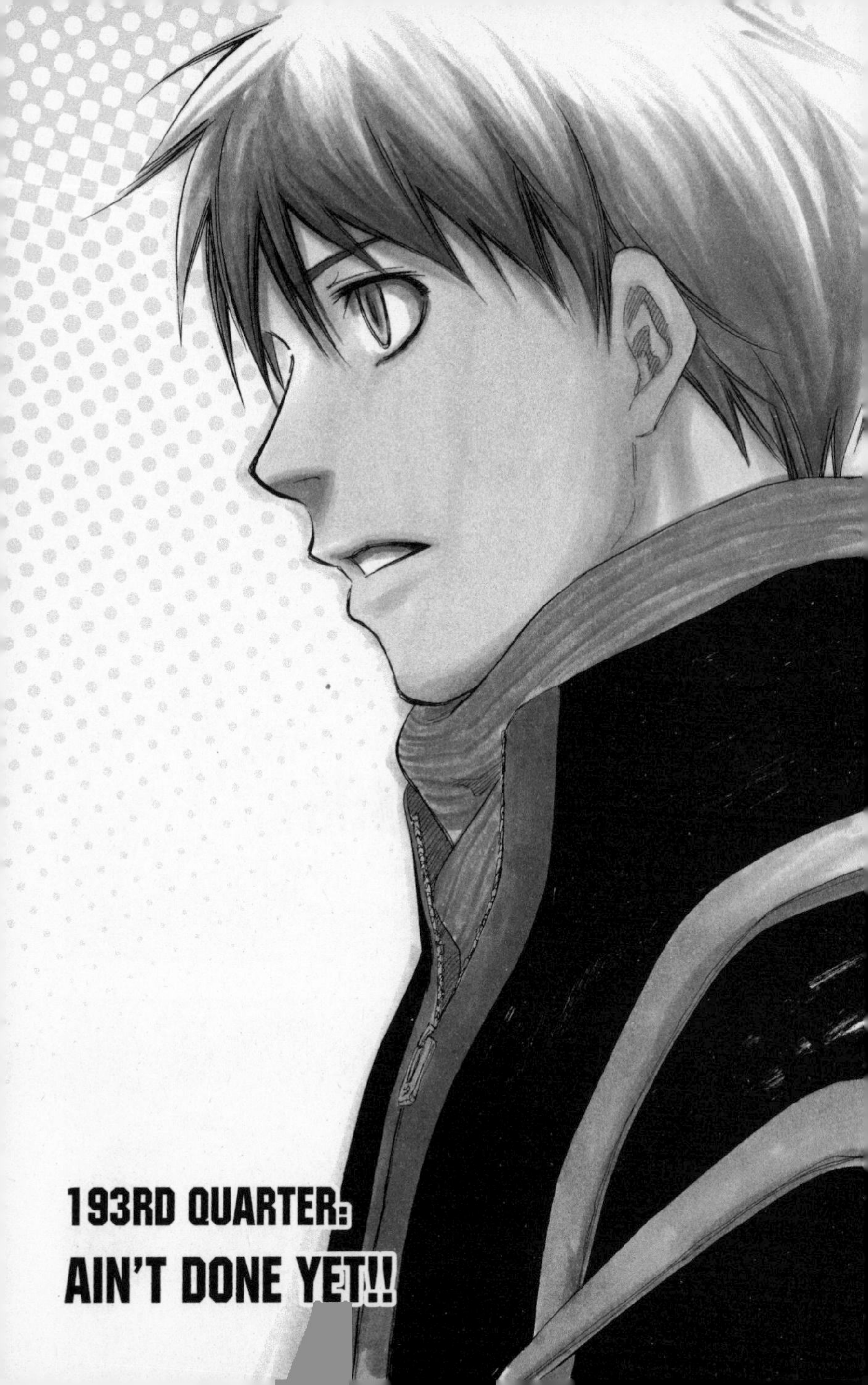
193RD QUARTER:
AIN'T DONE YET!!

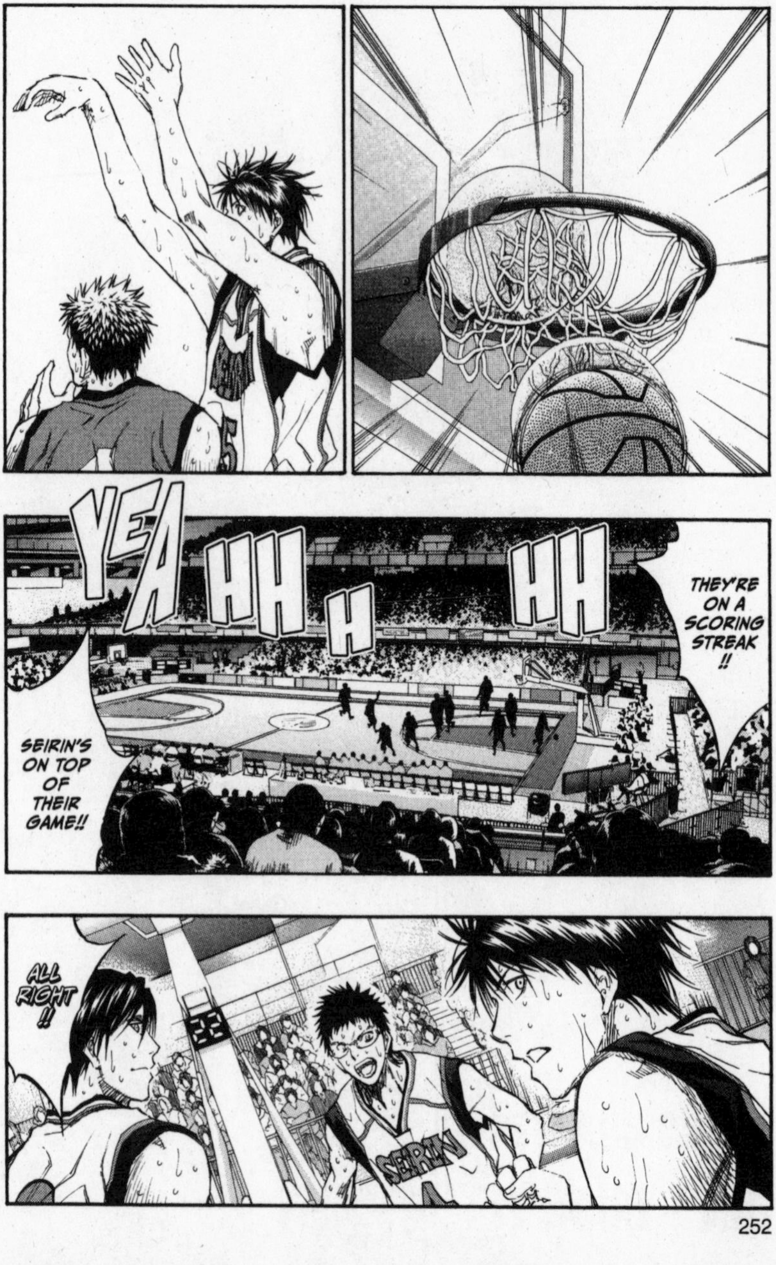
YEAHHHHHH
THEY'RE ON A SCORING STREAK!!
SEIRIN'S ON TOP OF THEIR GAME!!
ALL RIGHT!!
SEIRIN

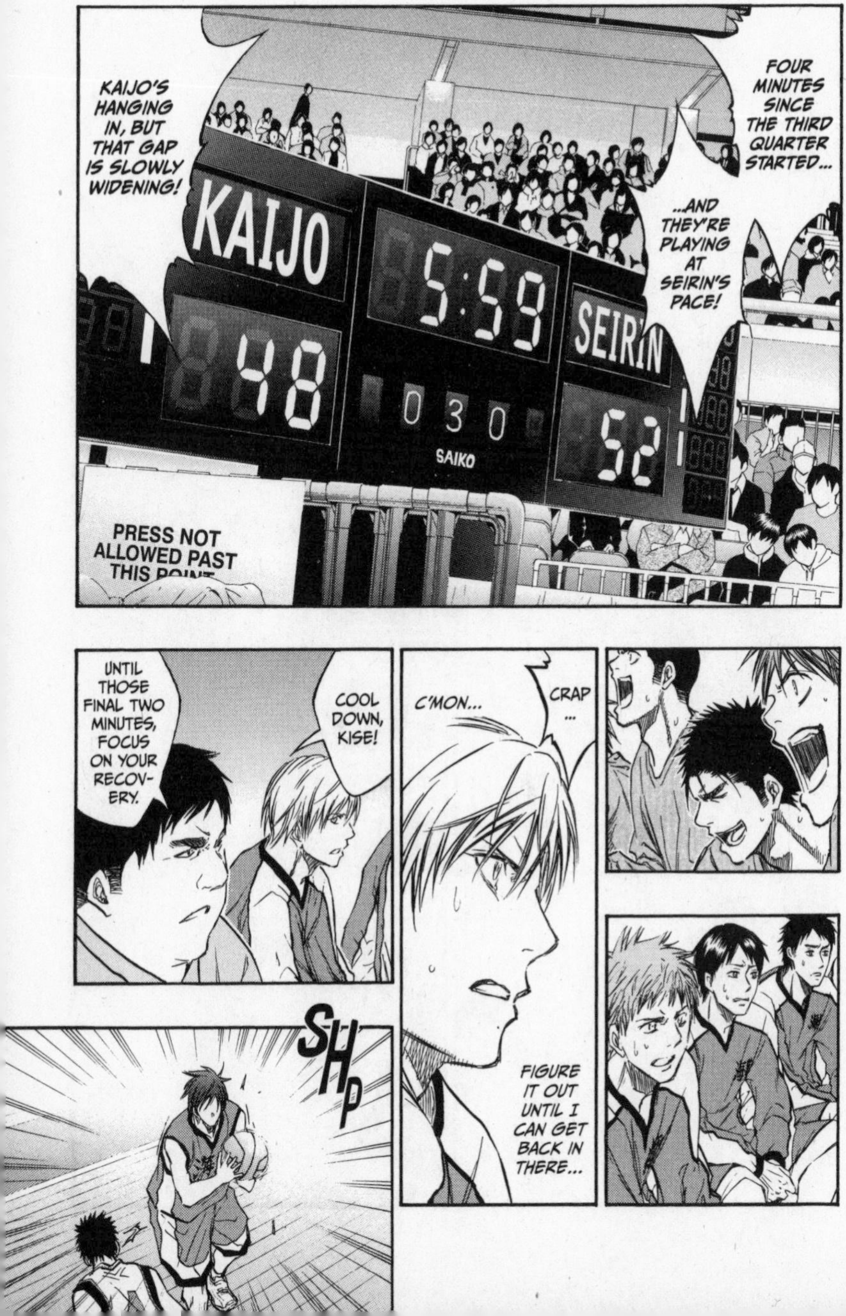
FOUR MINUTES SINCE THE THIRD QUARTER STARTED...
...AND THEY'RE PLAYING AT SEIRIN'S PACE!
KAIJO'S HANGING IN, BUT THAT GAP IS SLOWLY WIDENING!
KAIJO
5:59
SEIRIN
48
030
52
SAIKO
PRESS NOT ALLOWED PAST
CRAP ...
C'MON...
FIGURE IT OUT UNTIL I CAN GET BACK IN THERE...
COOL DOWN, KISE!
UNTIL THOSE FINAL TWO MINUTES, FOCUS ON YOUR RECOV- ERY.
SHP

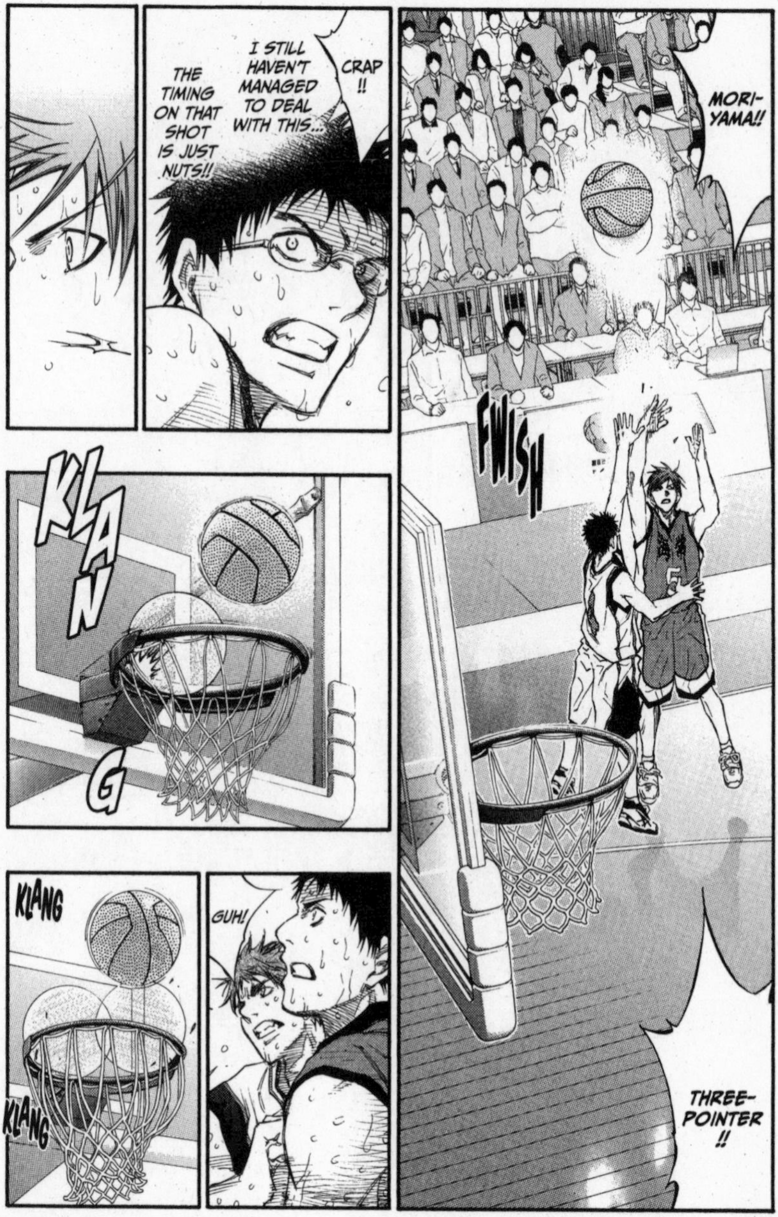
MORI-YAMA!!
FWISH
THREE-POINTER!!
CRAP!!
I STILL HAVEN'T MANAGED TO DEAL WITH THIS...
THE TIMING ON THAT SHOT IS JUST NUTS!!
KLAN
G
GUH!
KLANG
KLANG

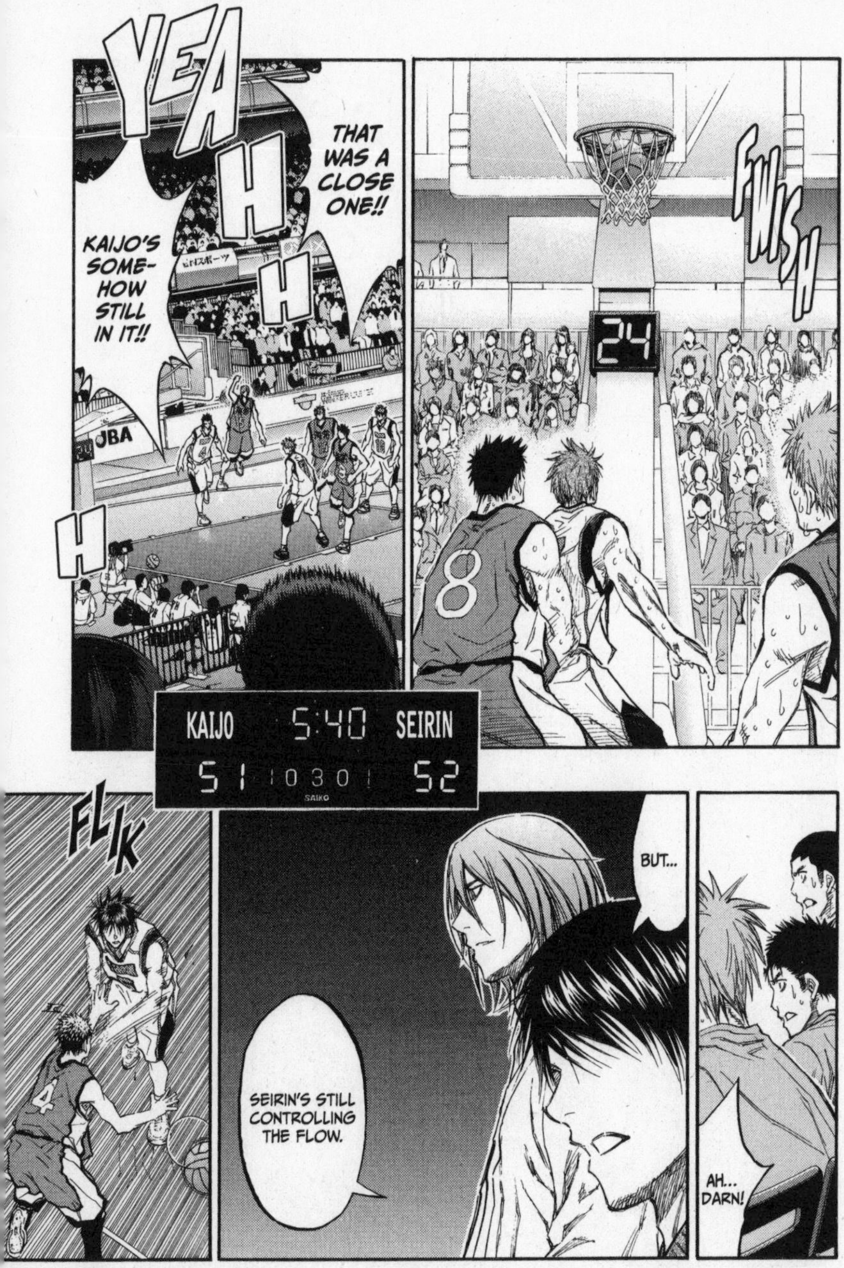
FWISH
24
YEAH
THAT WAS A CLOSE ONE!!
KAIJO'S SOME-HOW STILL IN IT!!
KAIJO 5:40 SEIRIN
51 030 52
SAIKO
AH... DARN!
BUT...
SEIRIN'S STILL CONTROLLING THE FLOW.
FLIK

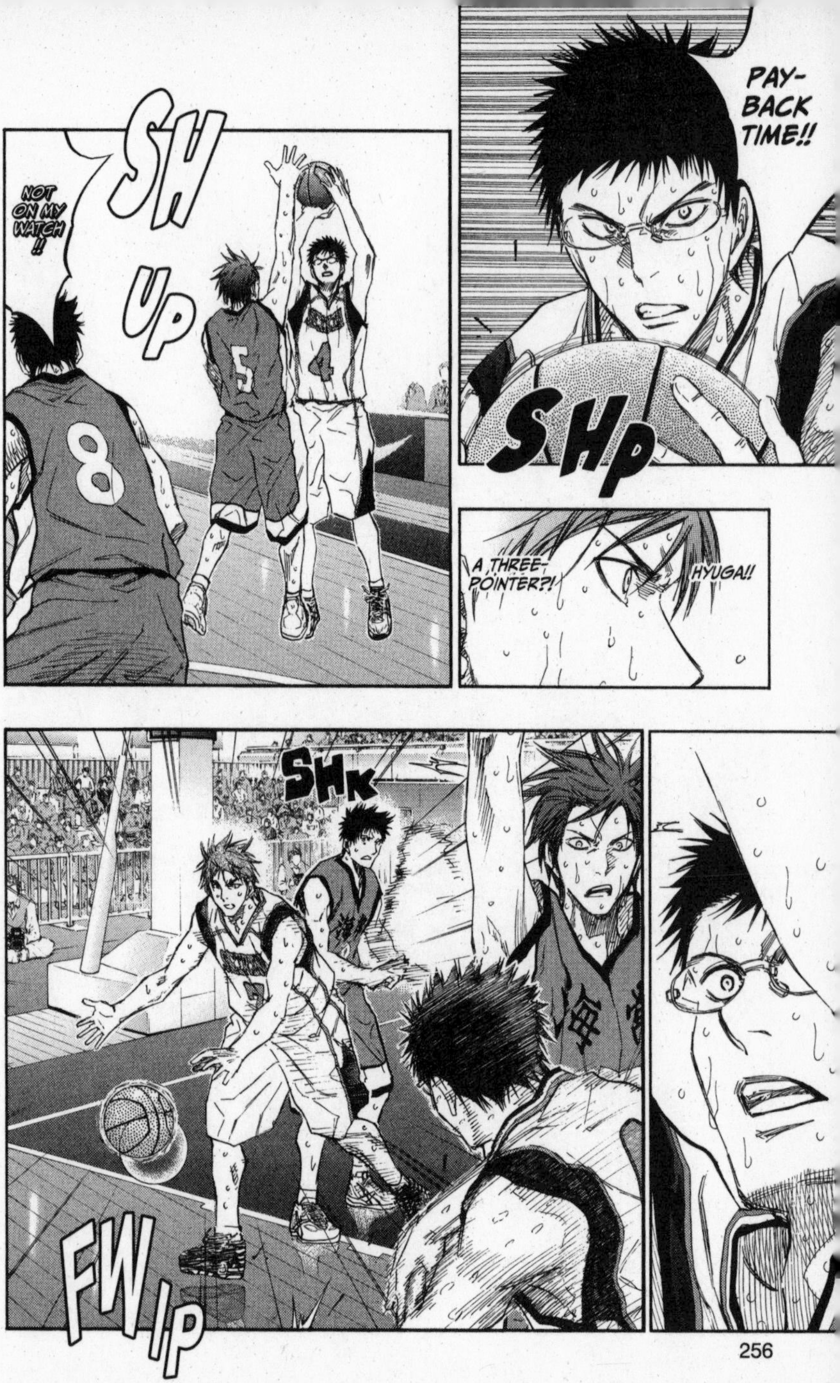
PAY-BACK TIME!!
SHP
HYUGA!!
A THREE-POINTER?!
SH UP
NOT ON MY WATCH!!
SHK
FWIP

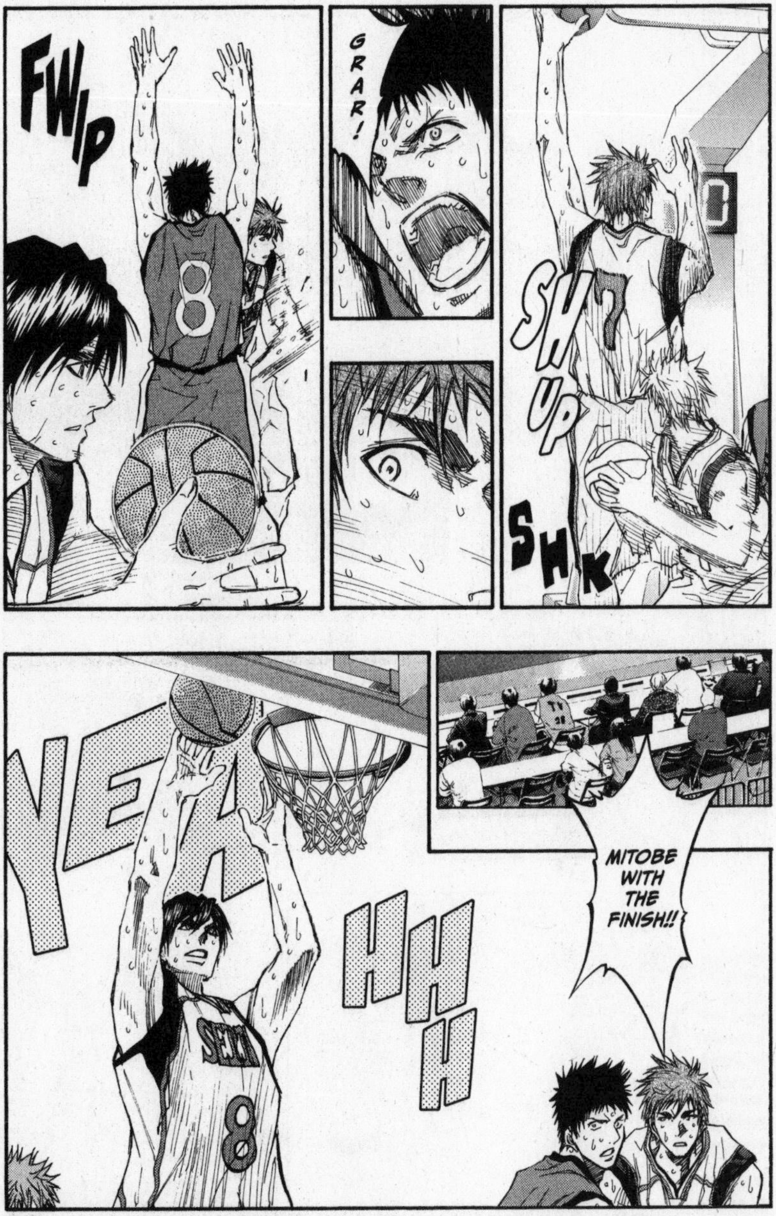
SHUP
SHK
GRAR!
FWIP
MITOBE WITH THE FINISH!!
YEAHHHH

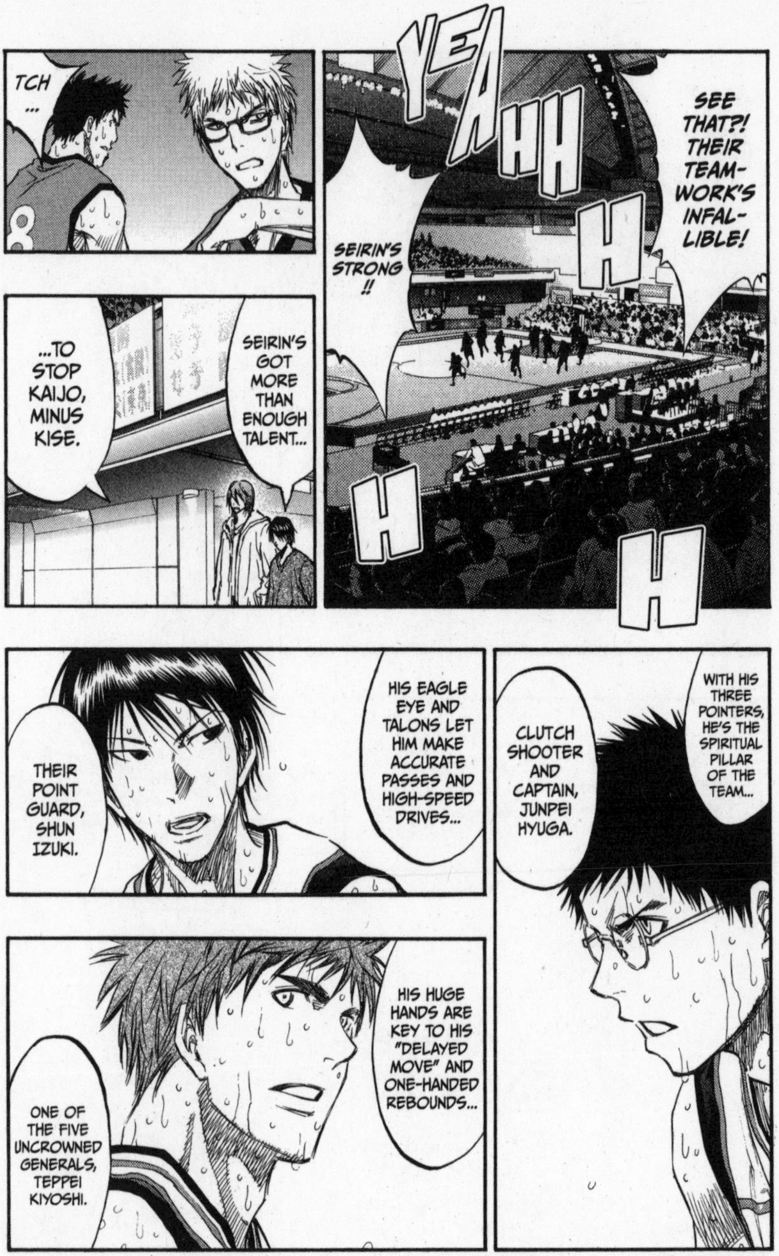
YEAHHHHHH
SEE THAT?! THEIR TEAM-WORK'S INFAL-LIBLE!
SEIRIN'S STRONG!!
TCH ...
SEIRIN'S GOT MORE THAN ENOUGH TALENT...
...TO STOP KAIJO, MINUS KISE.
WITH HIS THREE POINTERS, HE'S THE SPIRITUAL PILLAR OF THE TEAM...
CLUTCH SHOOTER AND CAPTAIN, JUNPEI HYUGA.
HIS EAGLE EYE AND TALONS LET HIM MAKE ACCURATE PASSES AND HIGH-SPEED DRIVES...
THEIR POINT GUARD, SHUN IZUKI.
HIS HUGE HANDS ARE KEY TO HIS "DELAYED MOVE" AND ONE-HANDED REBOUNDS...
ONE OF THE FIVE UNCROWNED GENERALS, TEPPEI KIYOSHI.

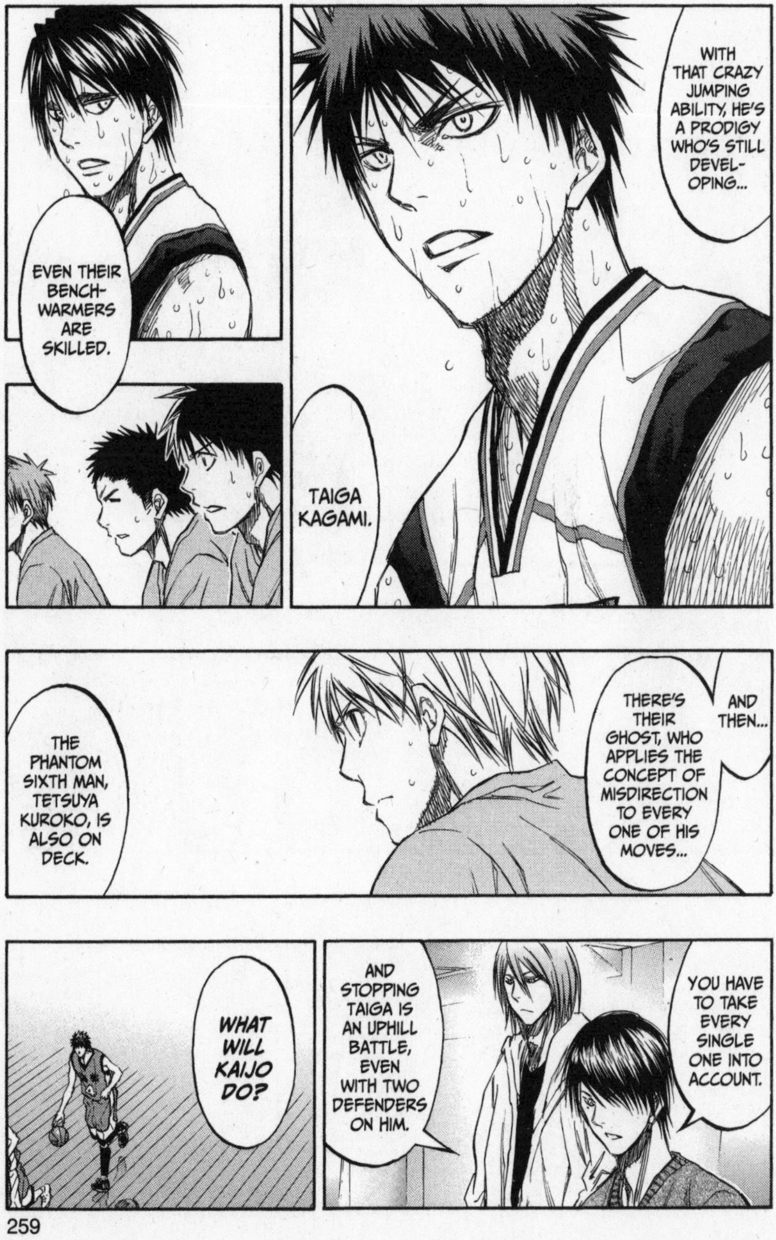
WITH THAT CRAZY JUMPING ABILITY, HE'S A PRODIGY WHO'S STILL DEVEL-OPING...
TAIGA KAGAMI.
EVEN THEIR BENCH-WARMERS ARE SKILLED.
AND THEN...
THERE'S THEIR GHOST, WHO APPLIES THE CONCEPT OF MISDIRECTION TO EVERY ONE OF HIS MOVES...
THE PHANTOM SIXTH MAN, TETSUYA KUROKO, IS ALSO ON DECK.
YOU HAVE TO TAKE EVERY SINGLE ONE INTO ACCOUNT.
AND STOPPING TAIGA IS AN UPHILL BATTLE, EVEN WITH TWO DEFENDERS ON HIM.
WHAT WILL KAIJO DO?

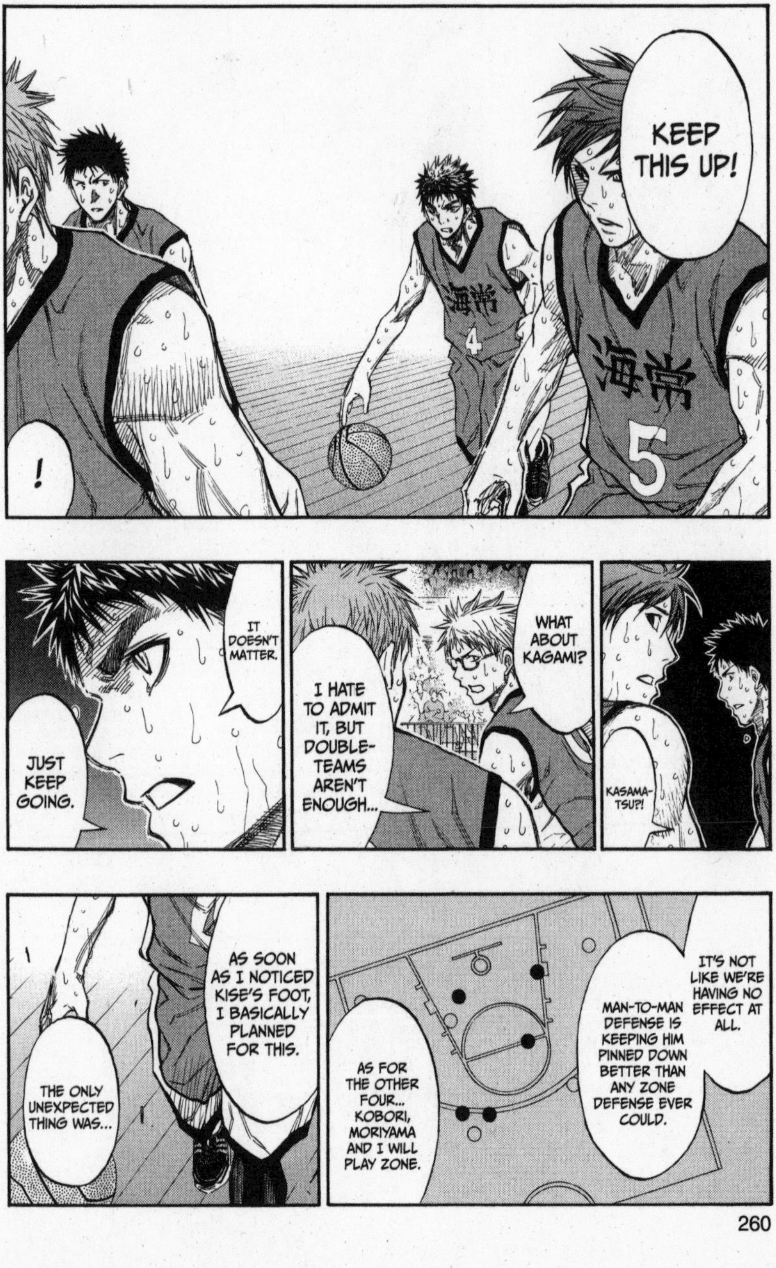
KEEP THIS UP!
!
KASAMA-TSU?!
WHAT ABOUT KAGAMI?
I HATE TO ADMIT IT, BUT DOUBLE-TEAMS AREN'T ENOUGH...
IT DOESN'T MATTER.
JUST KEEP GOING.
IT'S NOT LIKE WE'RE HAVING NO EFFECT AT ALL.
MAN-TO-MAN DEFENSE IS KEEPING HIM PINNED DOWN BETTER THAN ANY ZONE DEFENSE EVER COULD.
AS FOR THE OTHER FOUR... KOBORI, MORIYAMA AND I WILL PLAY ZONE.
AS SOON AS I NOTICED KISE'S FOOT, I BASICALLY PLANNED FOR THIS.
THE ONLY UNEXPECTED THING WAS...

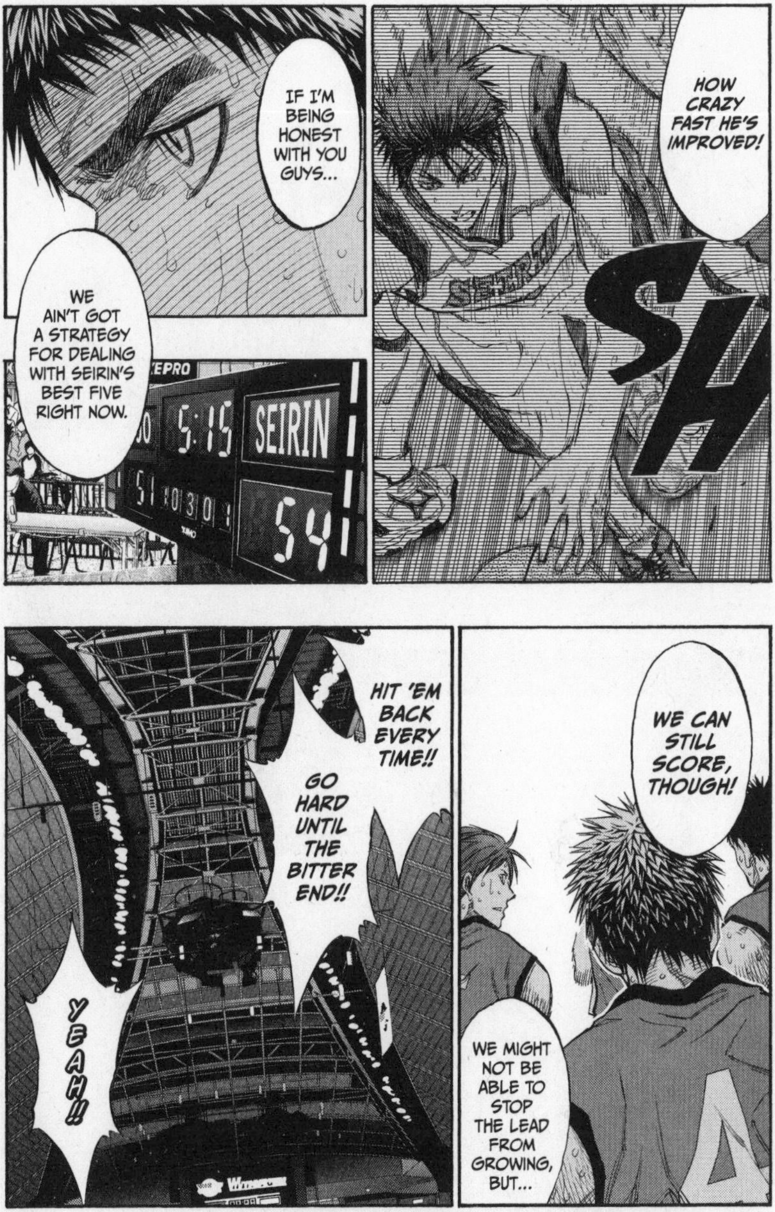
HOW CRAZY FAST HE'S IMPROVED!
SH
IF I'M BEING HONEST WITH YOU GUYS...
WE AIN'T GOT A STRATEGY FOR DEALING WITH SEIRIN'S BEST FIVE RIGHT NOW.
5:15
SEIRIN
54
WE CAN STILL SCORE, THOUGH!
WE MIGHT NOT BE ABLE TO STOP THE LEAD FROM GROWING, BUT...
HIT 'EM BACK EVERY TIME!!
GO HARD UNTIL THE BITTER END!!
YEAH!!

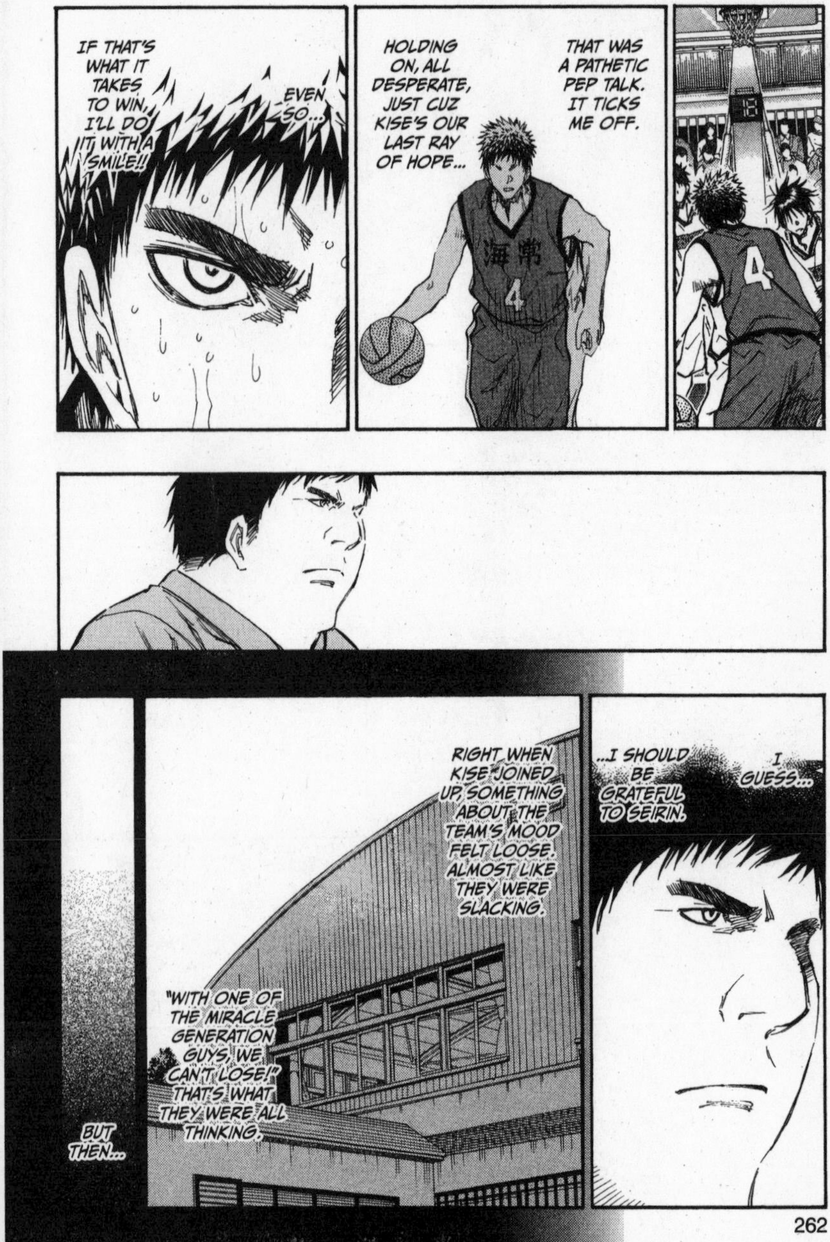
THAT WAS A PATHETIC PEP TALK. IT TICKS ME OFF.
HOLDING ON, ALL DESPERATE, JUST CUZ KISE'S OUR LAST RAY OF HOPE...
EVEN SO...
IF THAT'S WHAT IT TAKES TO WIN, I'LL DO IT WITH A SMILE!!
I GUESS...
...I SHOULD BE GRATEFUL TO SEIRIN.
RIGHT WHEN KISE JOINED UP, SOMETHING ABOUT THE TEAM'S MOOD FELT LOOSE. ALMOST LIKE THEY WERE SLACKING.
"WITH ONE OF THE MIRACLE GENERATION GUYS, WE CAN'T LOSE!" THAT'S WHAT THEY WERE ALL THINKING.
BUT THEN...

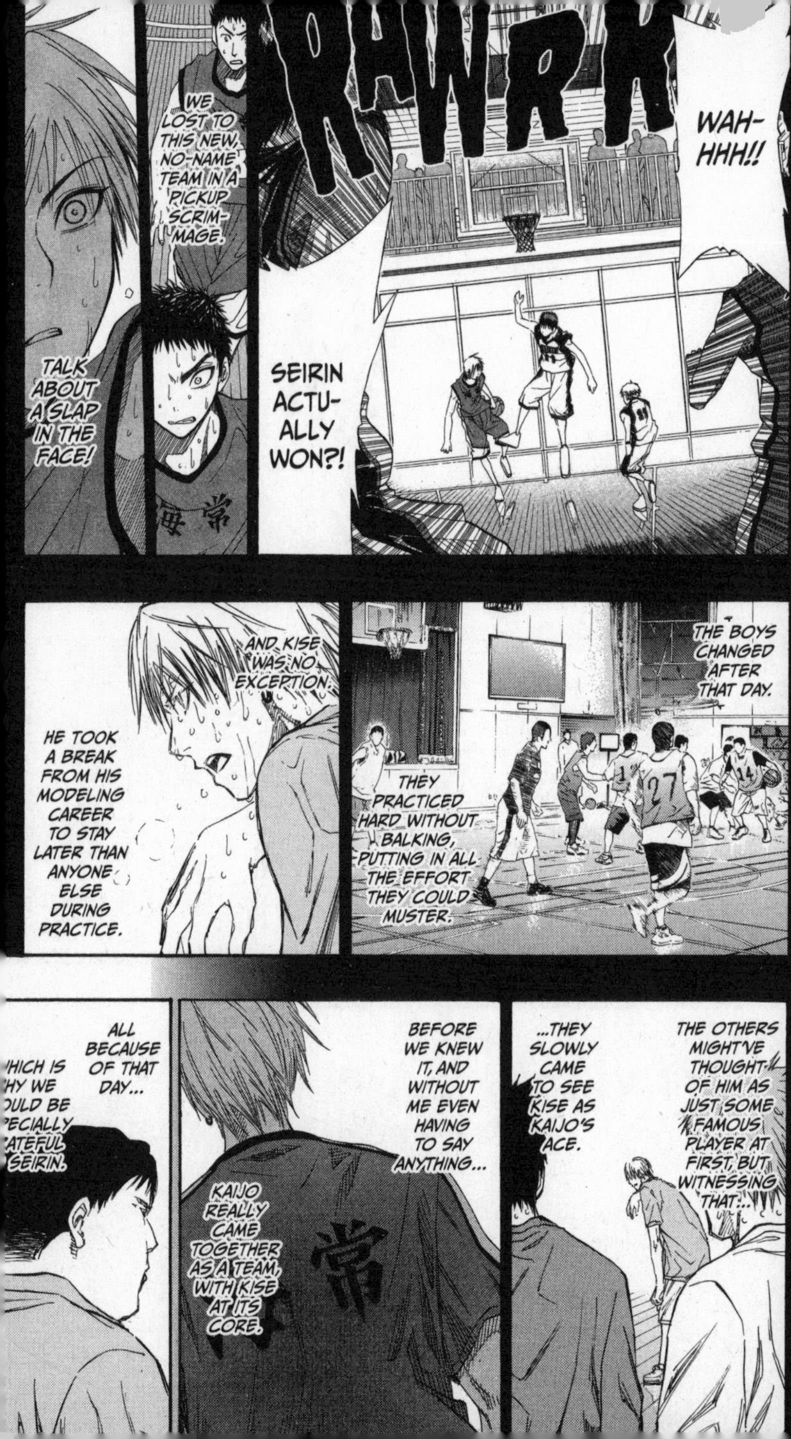
WAH-HHH!!
SEIRIN ACTU-ALLY WON?!
WE LOST TO THIS NEW, NO-NAME TEAM IN A PICKUP SCRIM-MAGE.
TALK ABOUT A SLAP IN THE FACE!
THE BOYS CHANGED AFTER THAT DAY.
THEY PRACTICED HARD WITHOUT BALKING, PUTTING IN ALL THE EFFORT THEY COULD MUSTER.
AND KISE WAS NO EXCEPTION.
HE TOOK A BREAK FROM HIS MODELING CAREER TO STAY LATER THAN ANYONE ELSE DURING PRACTICE.
THE OTHERS MIGHT'VE THOUGHT OF HIM AS JUST SOME FAMOUS PLAYER AT FIRST, BUT WITNESSING THAT...
...THEY SLOWLY CAME TO SEE KISE AS KAIJO'S ACE.
BEFORE WE KNEW IT, AND WITHOUT ME EVEN HAVING TO SAY ANYTHING...
KAIJO REALLY CAME TOGETHER AS A TEAM, WITH KISE AT ITS CORE.
ALL BECAUSE OF THAT DAY...
HICH IS HY WE OULD BE PECIALLY ATEFUL SEIRIN.

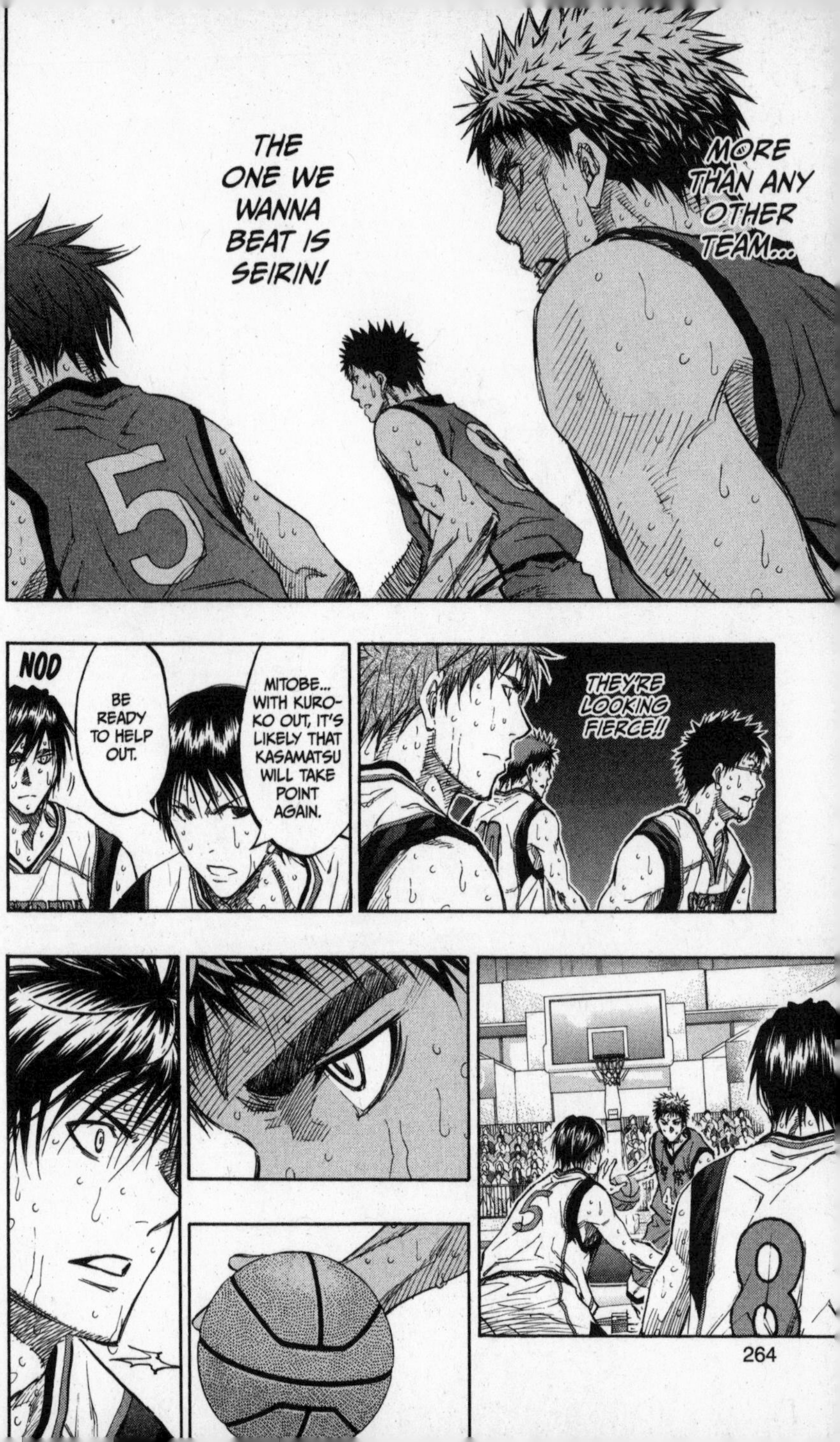
MORE THAN ANY OTHER TEAM...
THE ONE WE WANNA BEAT IS SEIRIN!
THEY'RE LOOKING FIERCE!!
MITOBE... WITH KUROKO OUT, IT'S LIKELY THAT KASAMATSU WILL TAKE POINT AGAIN.
BE READY TO HELP OUT.
NOD

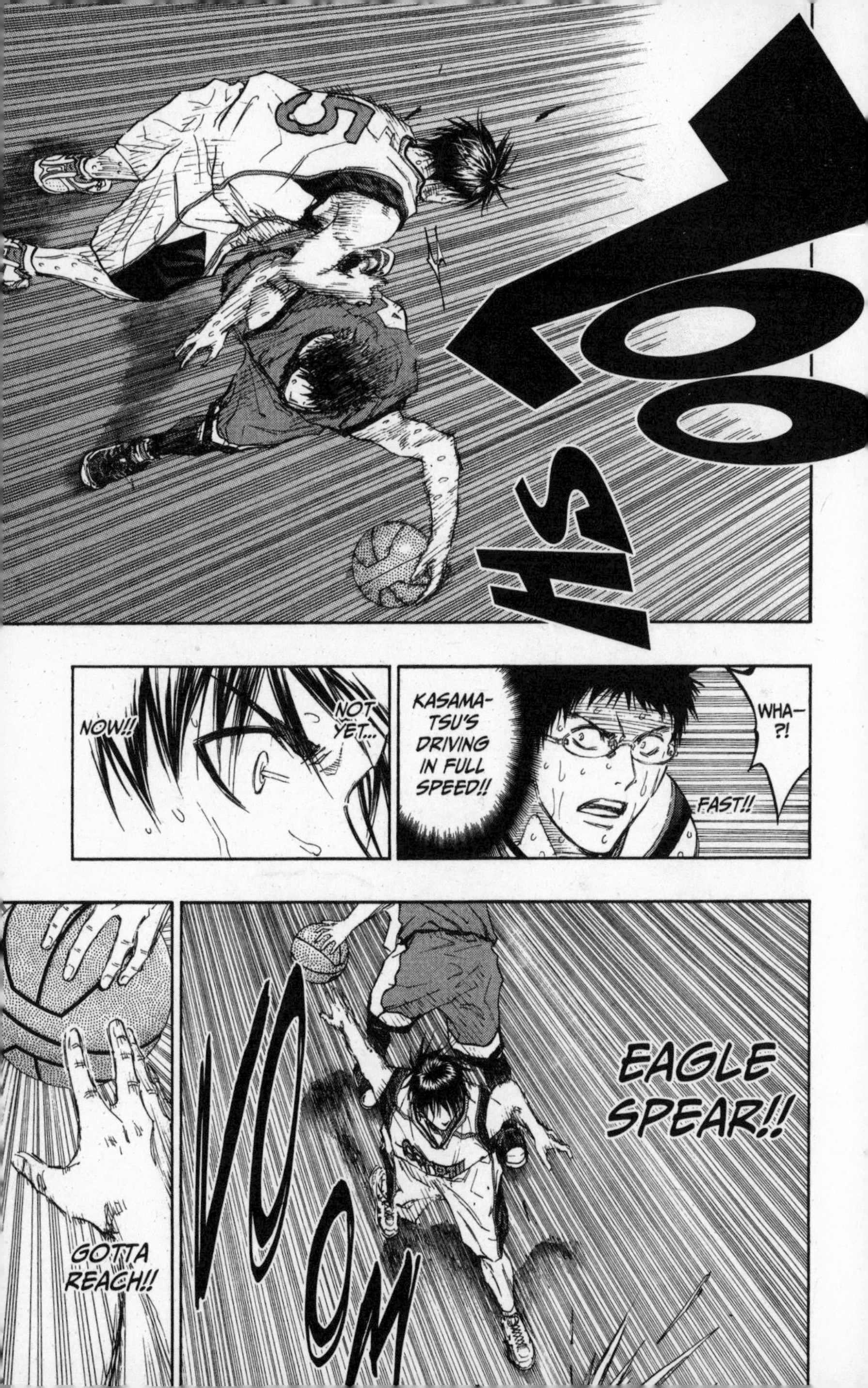
WHA—?!
FAST!!
KASAMA-TSU'S DRIVING IN FULL SPEED!!
NOT YET...
NOW!!
EAGLE SPEAR!!
VOOM
GOTTA REACH!!

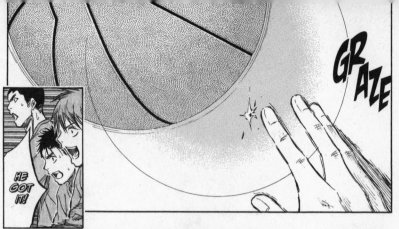

GR AZE

HE GOT IT!

RAHHH!

KASAMA-
TSU!!

GR R

SEN-
PAI!!

266

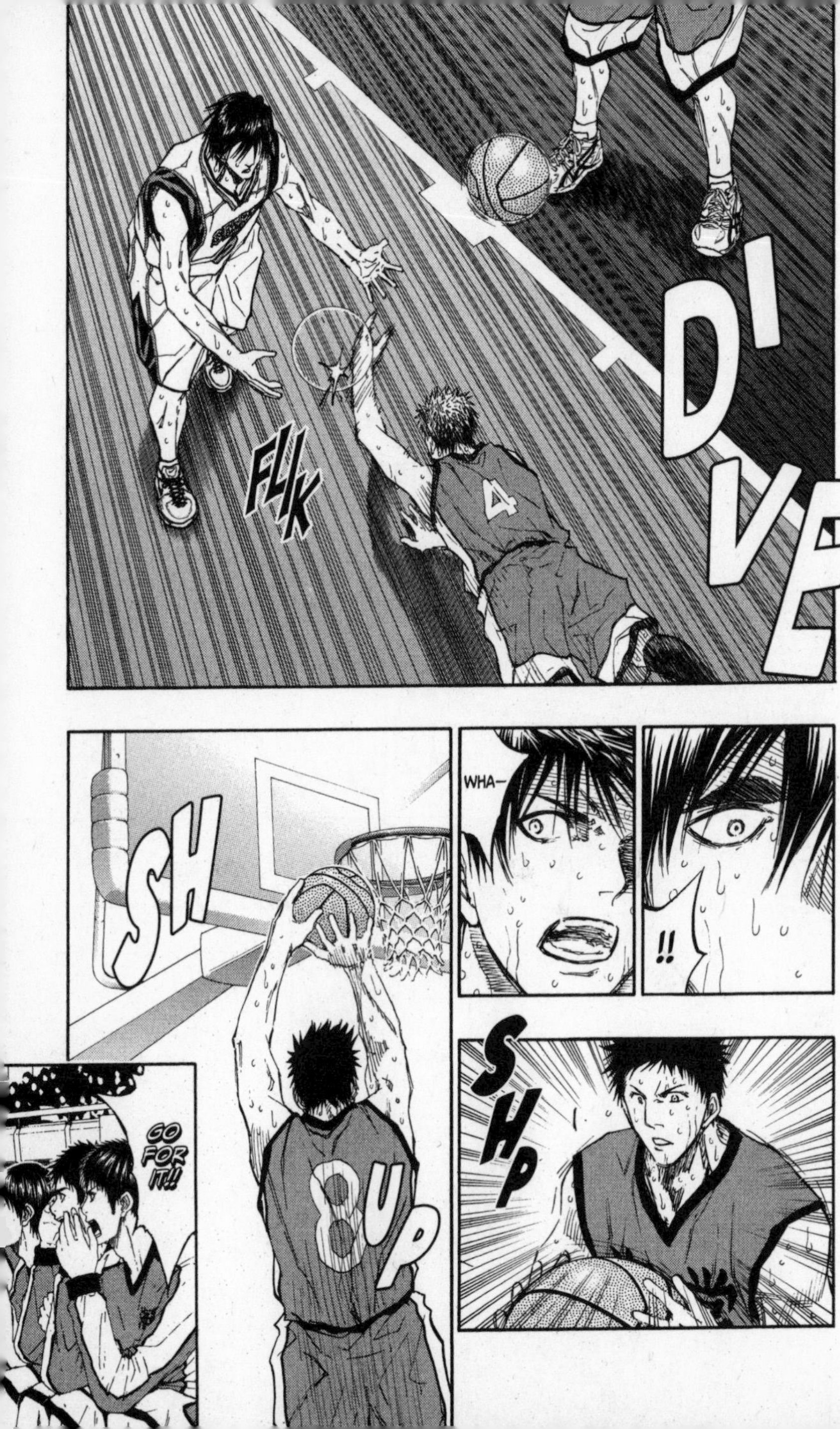
DIVE
FLIK
!!
WHA-
SHP
SH
UP
GO FOR IT!!

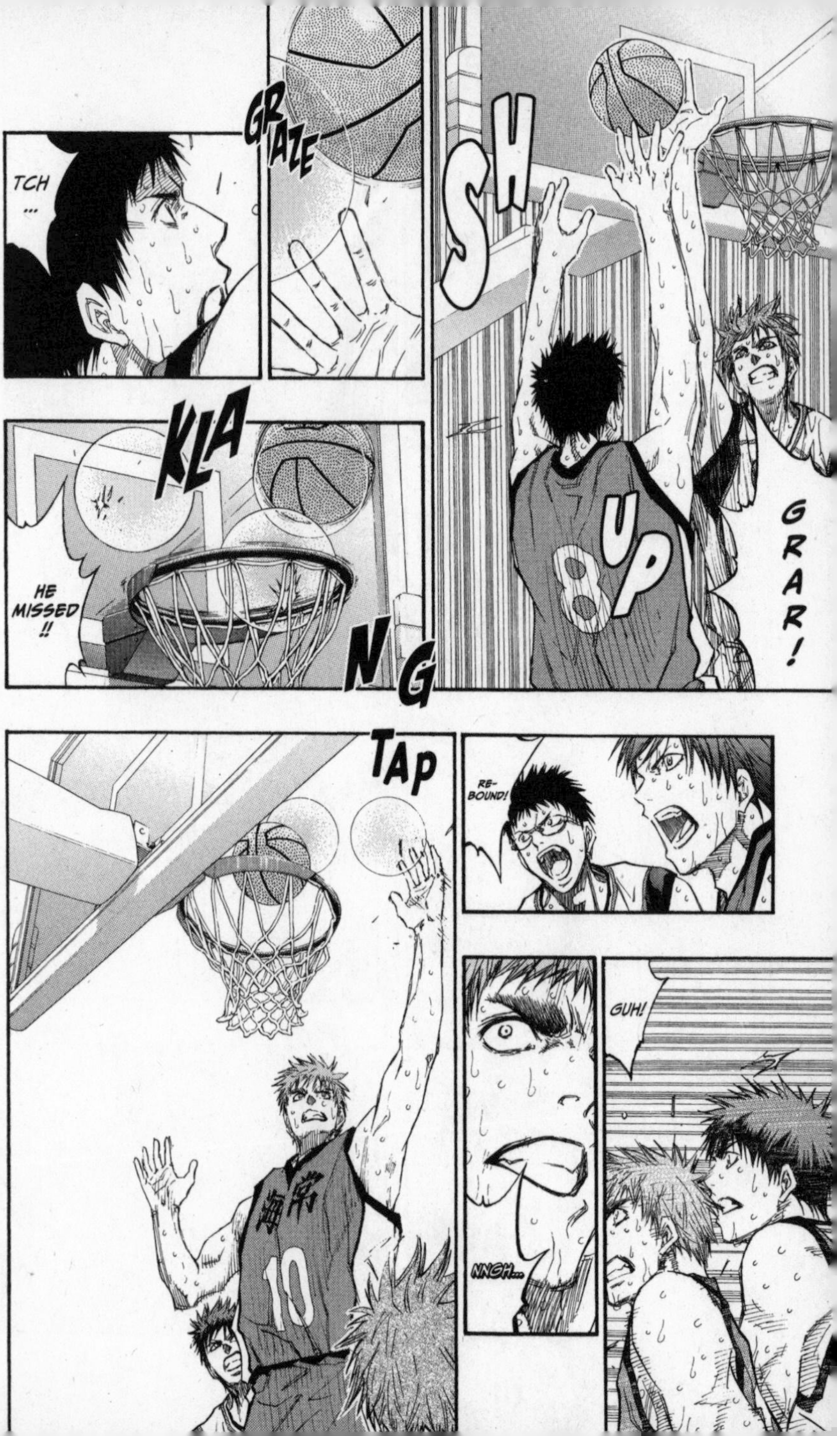
SH
UP
GRAR!
GRAZE
TCH ...
KLANG
HE MISSED !!
TAP
REBOUND!
GUH!
NNGH...

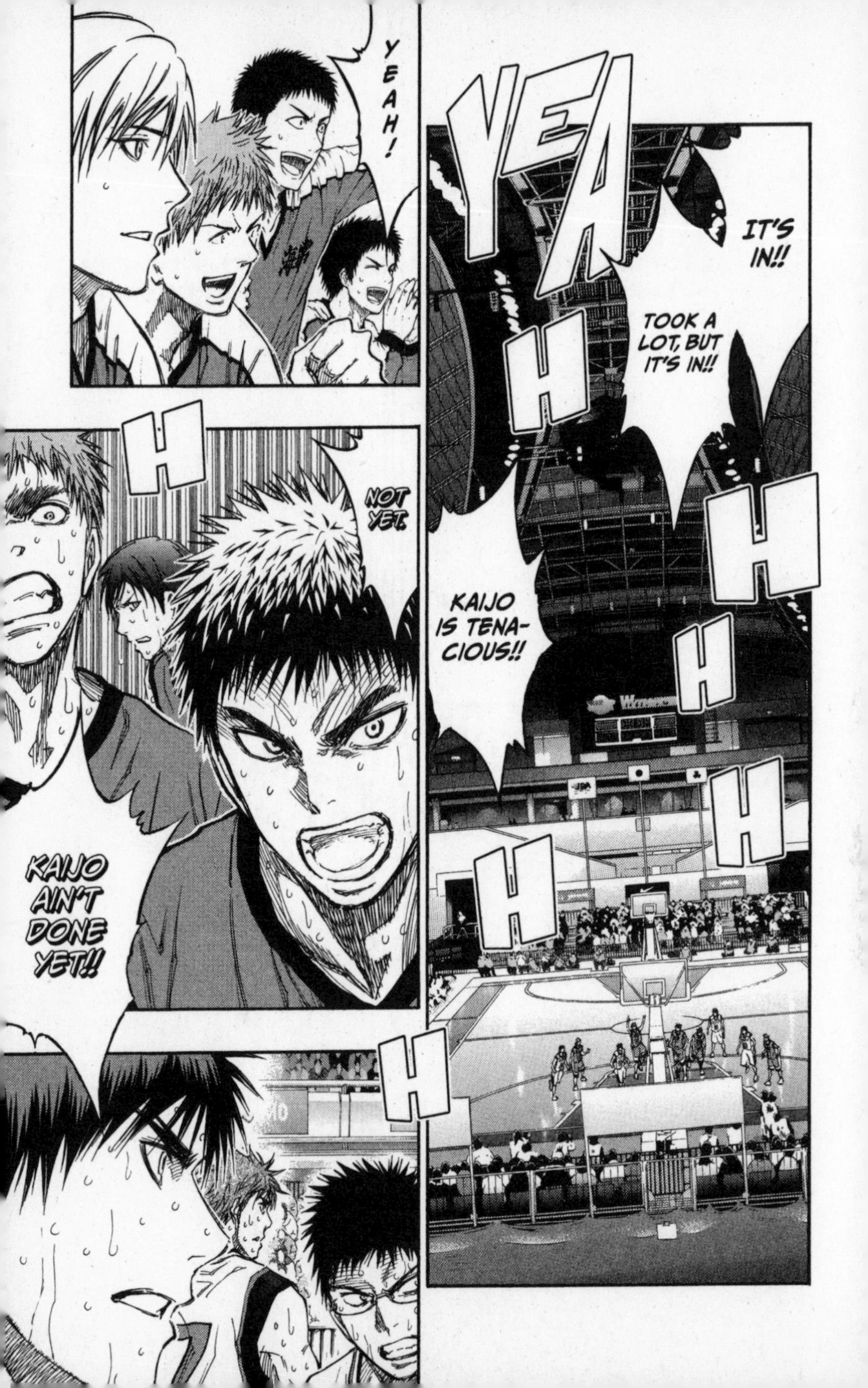
YEAHHHHHHH
IT'S IN!!
TOOK A LOT, BUT IT'S IN!!
KAIJO IS TENA-CIOUS!!
YEAH!
NOT YET.
KAIJO AIN'T DONE YET!!

KUROKO'S BASKETBALL

Q&A

W/ HALFWAY-DECENT ANSWERS

Q. ACCORDING TO HAIZAKI, HIMURO IS A BETTER FIGHTER THAN HE LOOKS. HOW STRONG IS HIMURO, REALLY?
(YOSHIZO from ISHIKAWA PREFECTURE)

A. DEFINITELY IN THE TOP FIVE OF ALL THE CHARACTERS WE'VE SEEN.

KUROKO'S BASKETBALL BLOOPERS

TAKE 1

EAGLE SPEAR!!
VOOM
SEIRIN
PO
KE

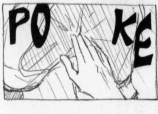

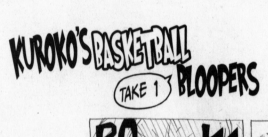

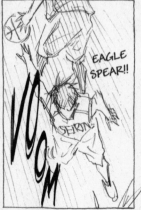

194TH QUARTER: IN ORDER TO WIN

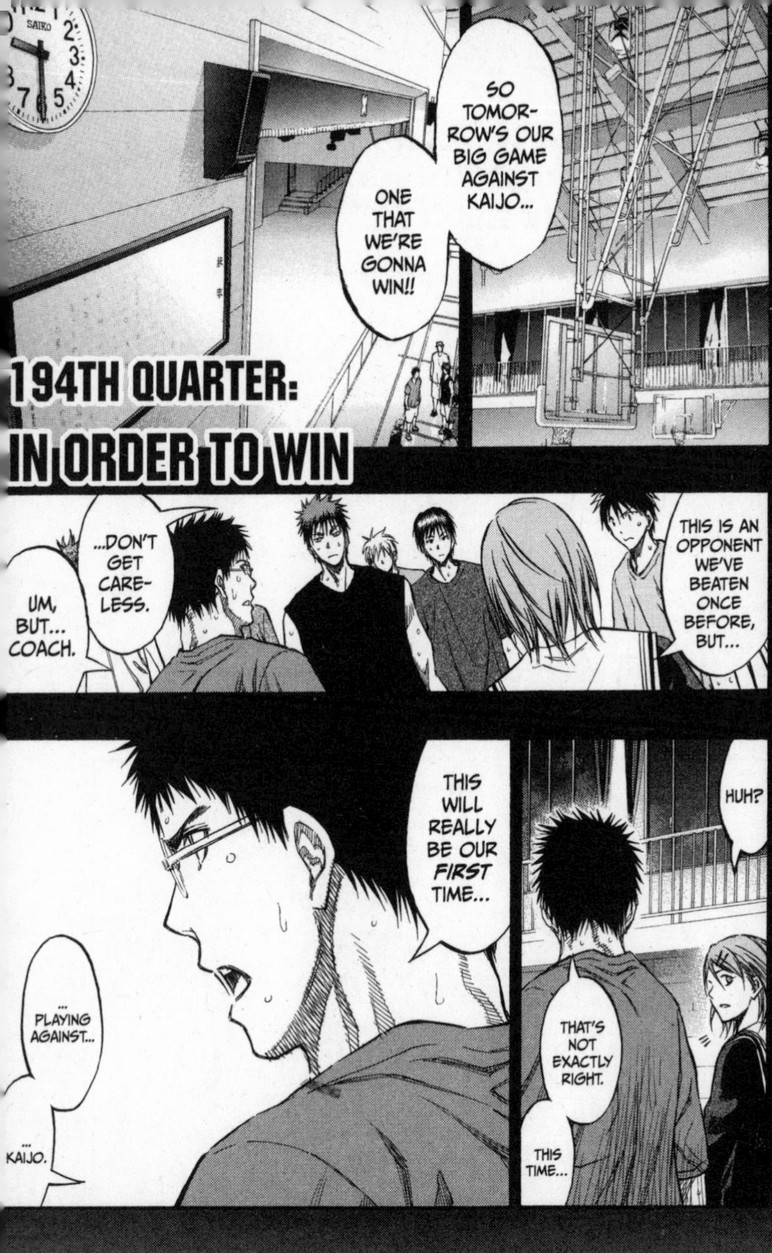

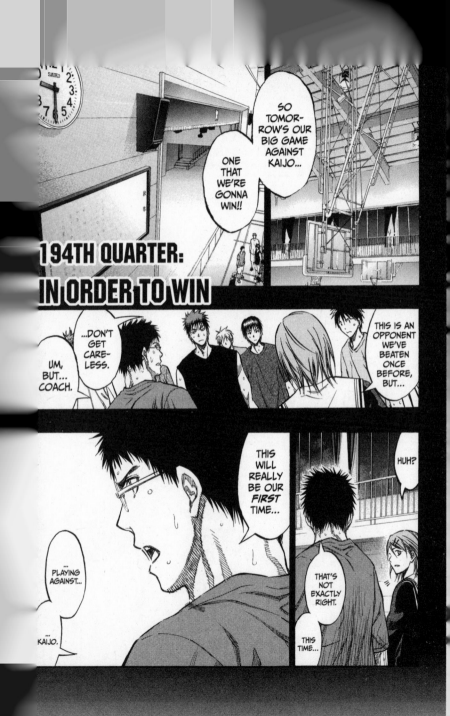

SO TOMORROW'S OUR BIG GAME AGAINST KAIJO...
ONE THAT WE'RE GONNA WIN!!
THIS IS AN OPPONENT WE'VE BEATEN ONCE BEFORE, BUT...
...DON'T GET CARELESS.
UM, BUT... COACH.
HUH?
THAT'S NOT EXACTLY RIGHT.
THIS TIME...
THIS WILL REALLY BE OUR *FIRST* TIME...
...PLAYING AGAINST...
...KAIJO.

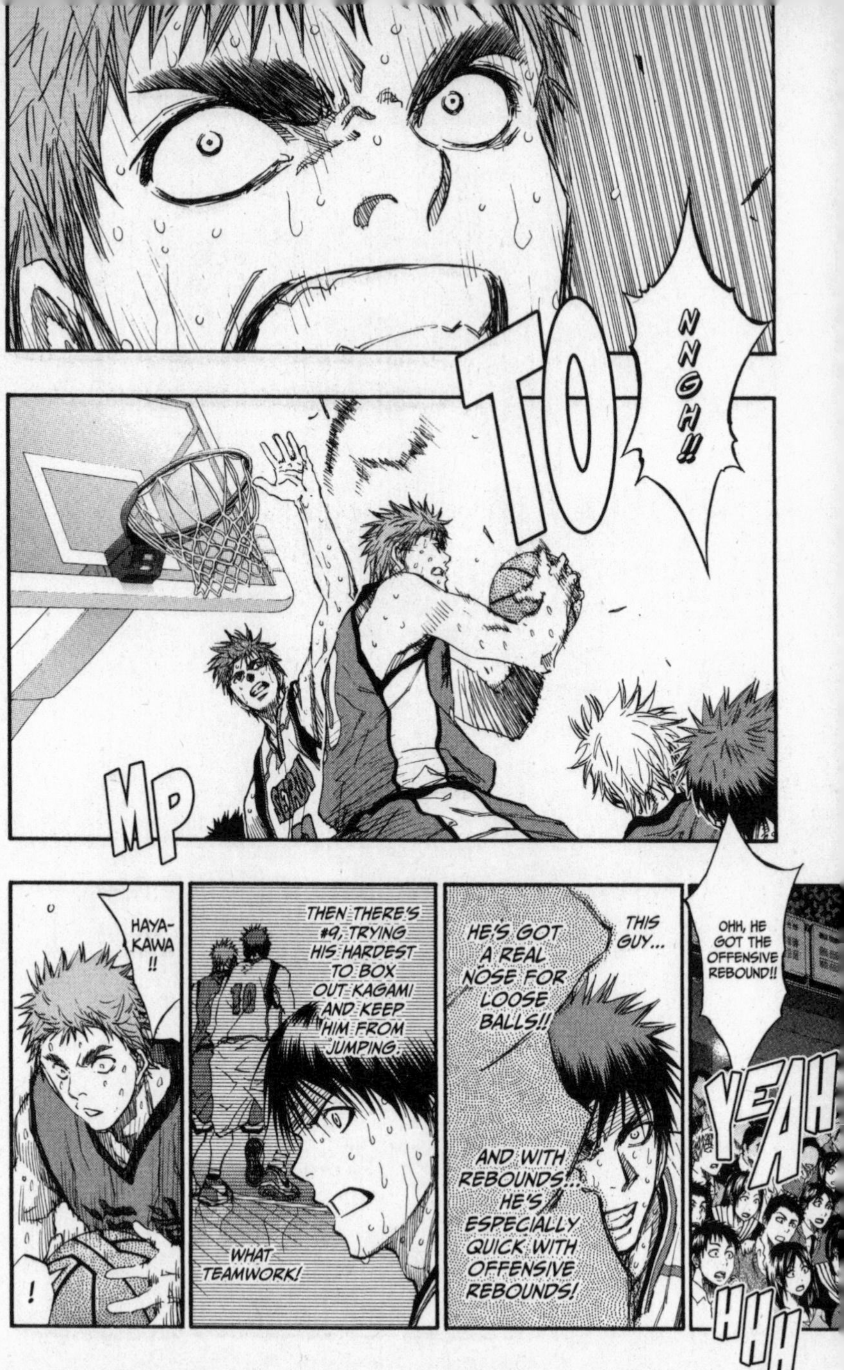
NNGH!!
TO
MP
OHH, HE GOT THE OFFENSIVE REBOUND!!
YEAHHH
THIS GUY...
HE'S GOT A REAL NOSE FOR LOOSE BALLS!!
AND WITH REBOUNDS... HE'S ESPECIALLY QUICK WITH OFFENSIVE REBOUNDS!
THEN THERE'S #9, TRYING HIS HARDEST TO BOX OUT KAGAMI AND KEEP HIM FROM JUMPING.
WHAT TEAMWORK!
HAYA-KAWA!!
!

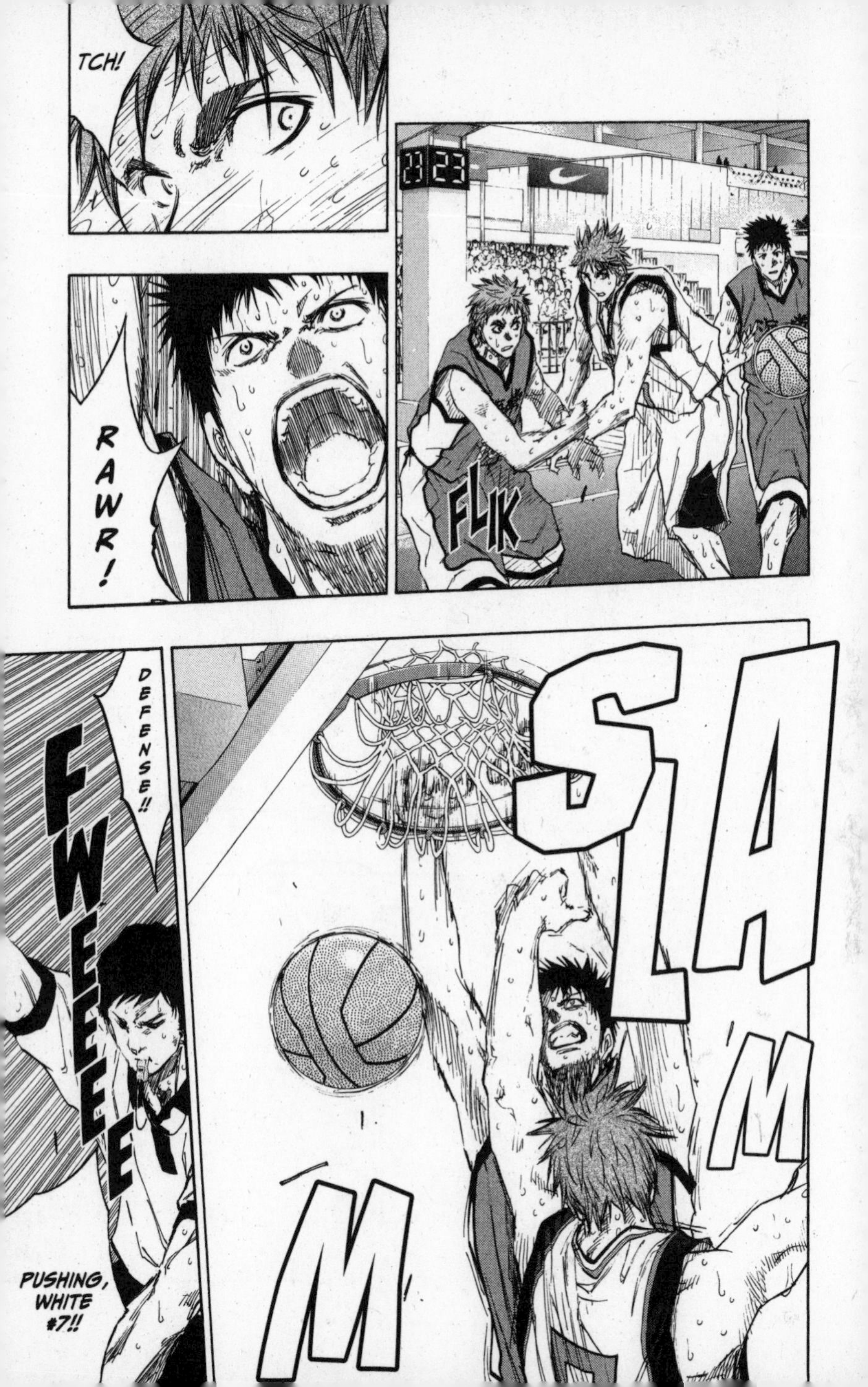
FLIK
TCH!
RAWR!
SLAMM
DEFENSE!!
FWEEEEE
PUSHING, WHITE #7!!

WHAT DETERMINATION !!

THAT DUNK WAS FIERCE !!

AND HE GOT FOULED, TOO...

THE BASKET COUNTS!

AND ONE!!

KAIJO	3:19	SEIRIN
57	10 3 0 1	59

SAIKO

YES!!

TEPPEI KIYOSHI...

CRAP...

...

YOU'VE ALWAYS BEEN A BETTER PLAYER THAN ME.

SHK

SCREWED UP AGAIN.

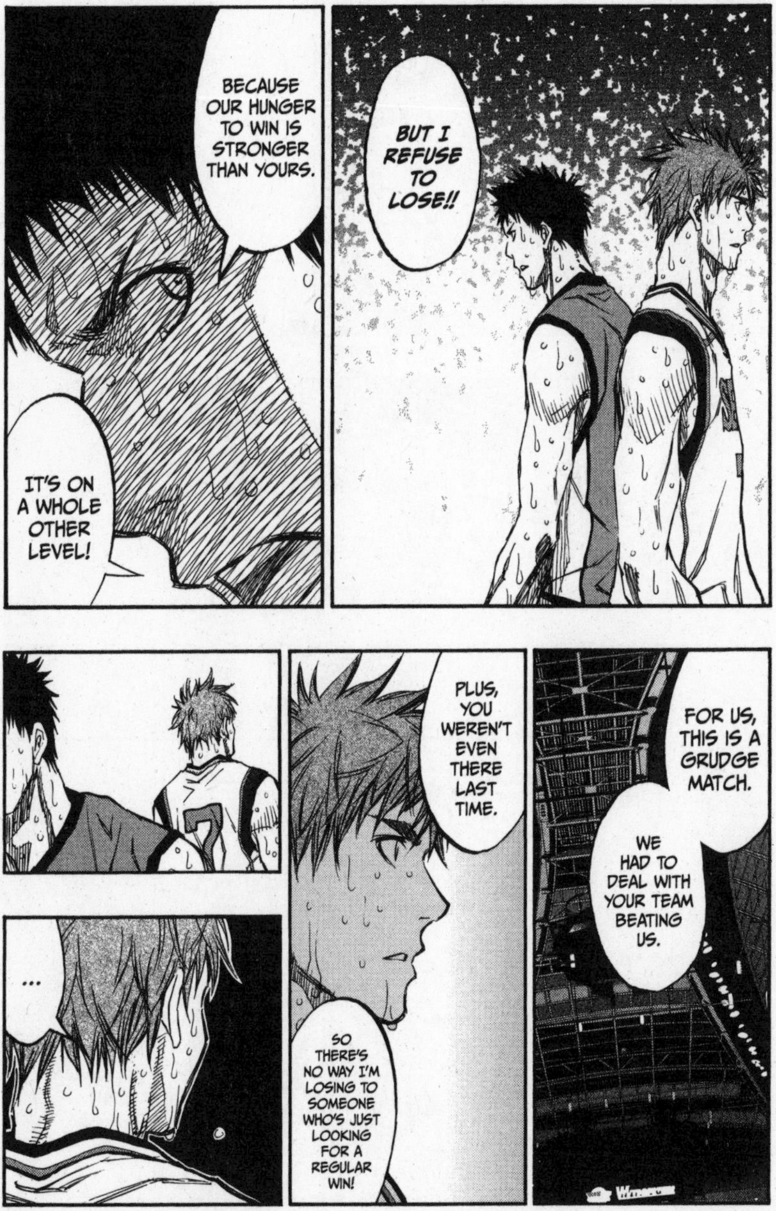
BUT I REFUSE TO LOSE!!
BECAUSE OUR HUNGER TO WIN IS STRONGER THAN YOURS.
IT'S ON A WHOLE OTHER LEVEL!
FOR US, THIS IS A GRUDGE MATCH.
WE HAD TO DEAL WITH YOUR TEAM BEATING US.
PLUS, YOU WEREN'T EVEN THERE LAST TIME.
SO THERE'S NO WAY I'M LOSING TO SOMEONE WHO'S JUST LOOKING FOR A REGULAR WIN!
...

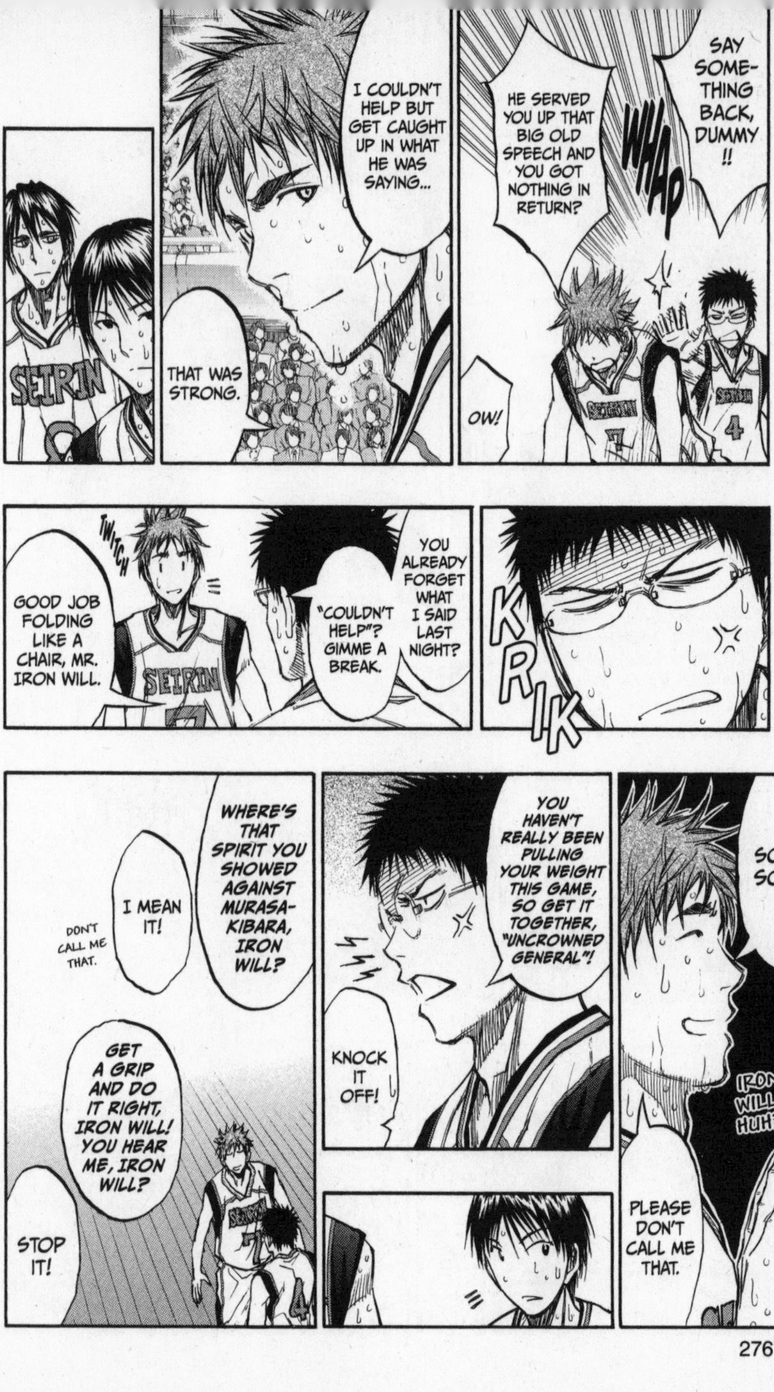
SAY SOMETHING BACK, DUMMY!!
WHAP
HE SERVED YOU UP THAT BIG OLD SPEECH AND YOU GOT NOTHING IN RETURN?
OW!
I COULDN'T HELP BUT GET CAUGHT UP IN WHAT HE WAS SAYING...
THAT WAS STRONG.
KRIK
YOU ALREADY FORGET WHAT I SAID LAST NIGHT?
"COULDN'T HELP"? GIMME A BREAK.
TWITCH
GOOD JOB FOLDING LIKE A CHAIR, MR. IRON WILL.
SORRY, SORRY.
IRON WILL, HUH?
PLEASE DON'T CALL ME THAT.
YOU HAVEN'T REALLY BEEN PULLING YOUR WEIGHT THIS GAME, SO GET IT TOGETHER, "UNCROWNED GENERAL"!
KNOCK IT OFF!
WHERE'S THAT SPIRIT YOU SHOWED AGAINST MURASAKIBARA, IRON WILL?
I MEAN IT!
DON'T CALL ME THAT.
GET A GRIP AND DO IT RIGHT, IRON WILL! YOU HEAR ME, IRON WILL?
STOP IT!

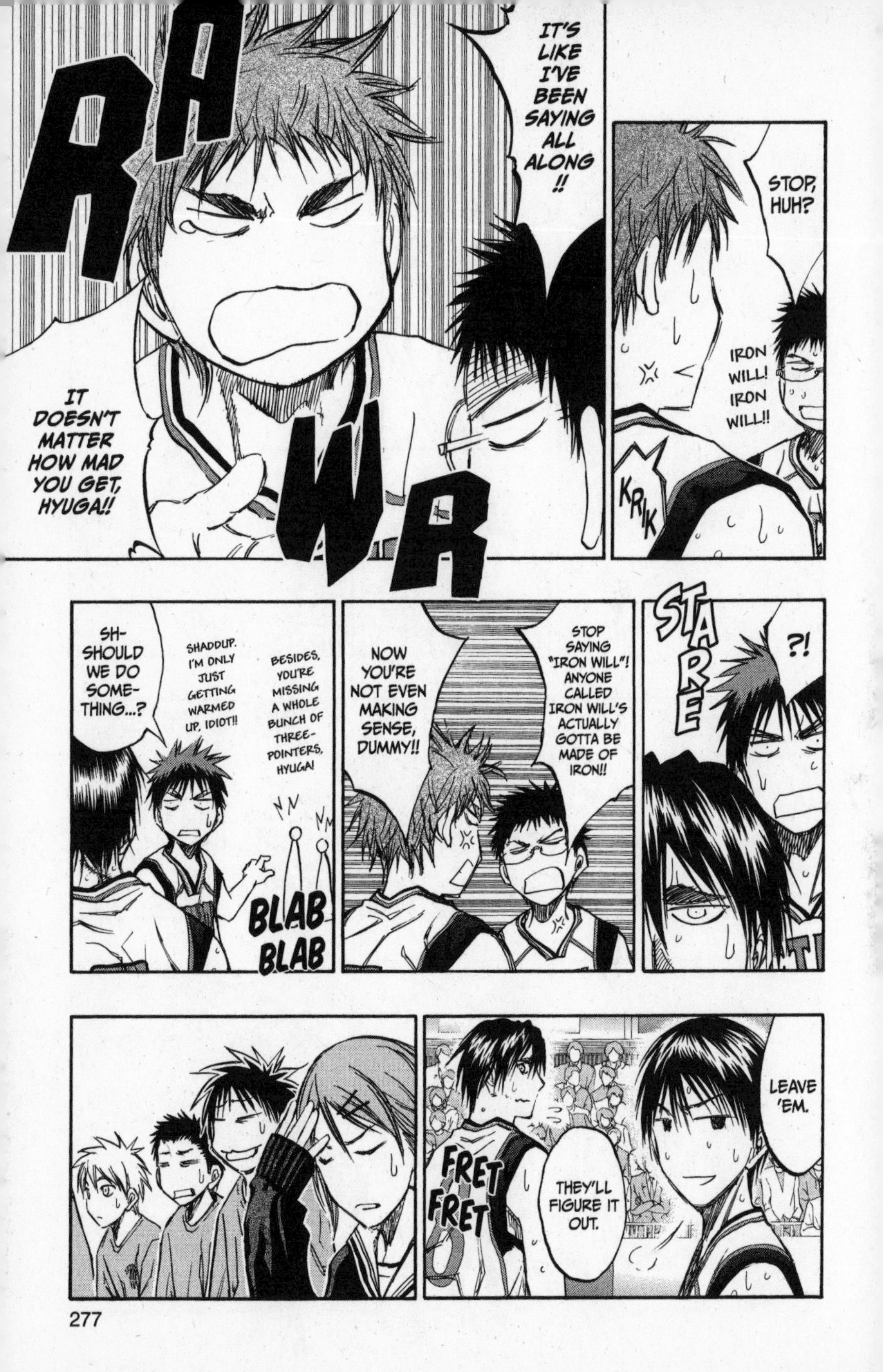
STOP, HUH?
IRON WILL! IRON WILL!!
KRIK
IT'S LIKE I'VE BEEN SAYING ALL ALONG!!
RAAWR
IT DOESN'T MATTER HOW MAD YOU GET, HYUGA!!
STARE
?!
STOP SAYING "IRON WILL"! ANYONE CALLED IRON WILL'S ACTUALLY GOTTA BE MADE OF IRON!!
NOW YOU'RE NOT EVEN MAKING SENSE, DUMMY!!
BESIDES, YOU'RE MISSING A WHOLE BUNCH OF THREE-POINTERS, HYUGA!
SHADDUP. I'M ONLY JUST GETTING WARMED UP, IDIOT!!
SH-SHOULD WE DO SOME-THING...?
BLAB BLAB
LEAVE 'EM.
THEY'LL FIGURE IT OUT.
FRET FRET

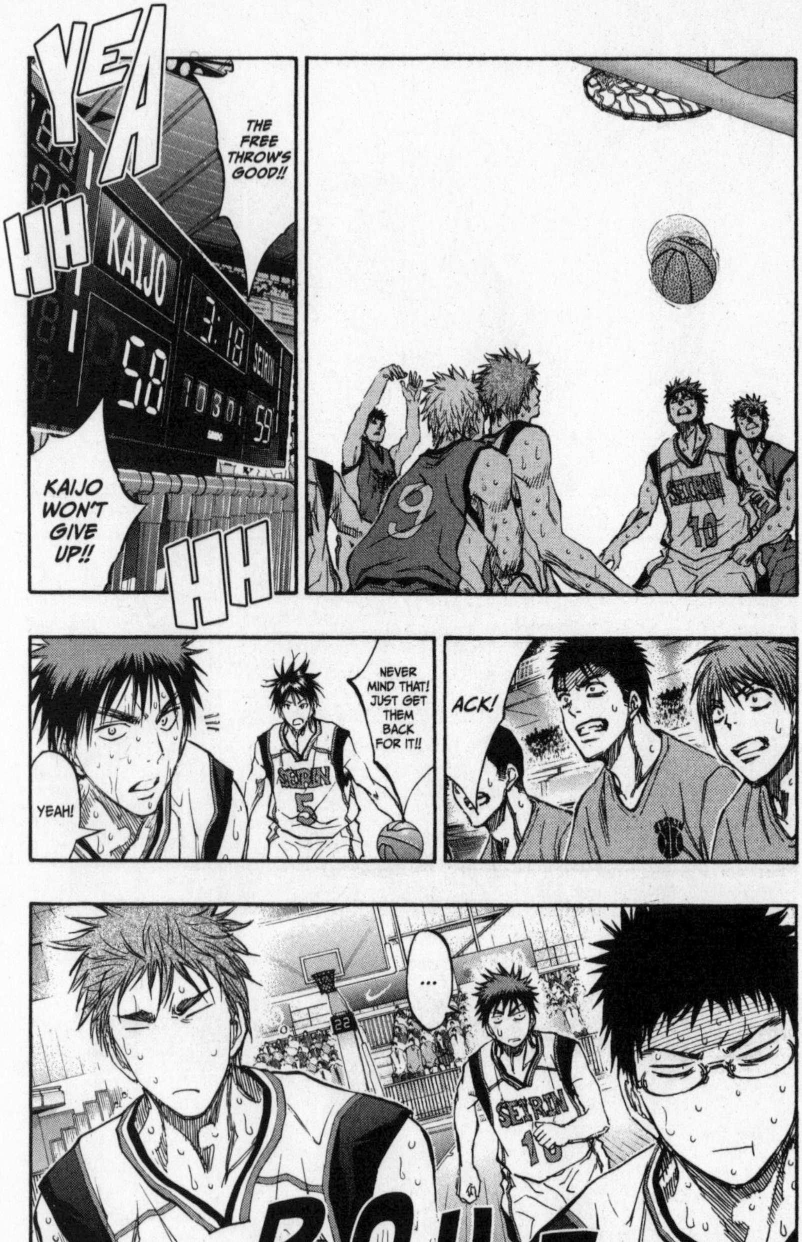
THE FREE THROW'S GOOD!!
YEAHHHH
KAIJO
3:18
SEIRIN
58
59
KAIJO WON'T GIVE UP!!
ACK!
NEVER MIND THAT! JUST GET THEM BACK FOR IT!!
YEAH!
...
POUT

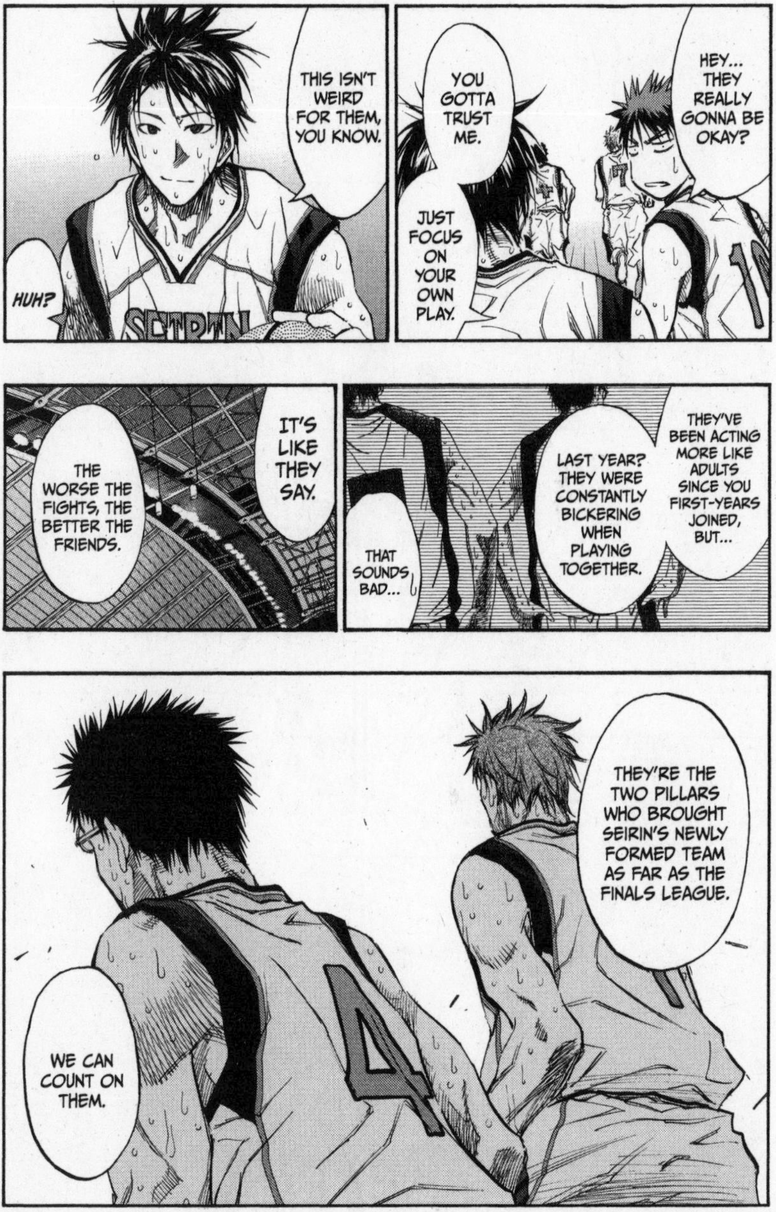
HEY... THEY REALLY GONNA BE OKAY?
YOU GOTTA TRUST ME.
JUST FOCUS ON YOUR OWN PLAY.
THIS ISN'T WEIRD FOR THEM, YOU KNOW.
HUH?
THEY'VE BEEN ACTING MORE LIKE ADULTS SINCE YOU FIRST-YEARS JOINED, BUT...
LAST YEAR? THEY WERE CONSTANTLY BICKERING WHEN PLAYING TOGETHER.
THAT SOUNDS BAD...
IT'S LIKE THEY SAY.
THE WORSE THE FIGHTS, THE BETTER THE FRIENDS.
THEY'RE THE TWO PILLARS WHO BROUGHT SEIRIN'S NEWLY FORMED TEAM AS FAR AS THE FINALS LEAGUE.
WE CAN COUNT ON THEM.

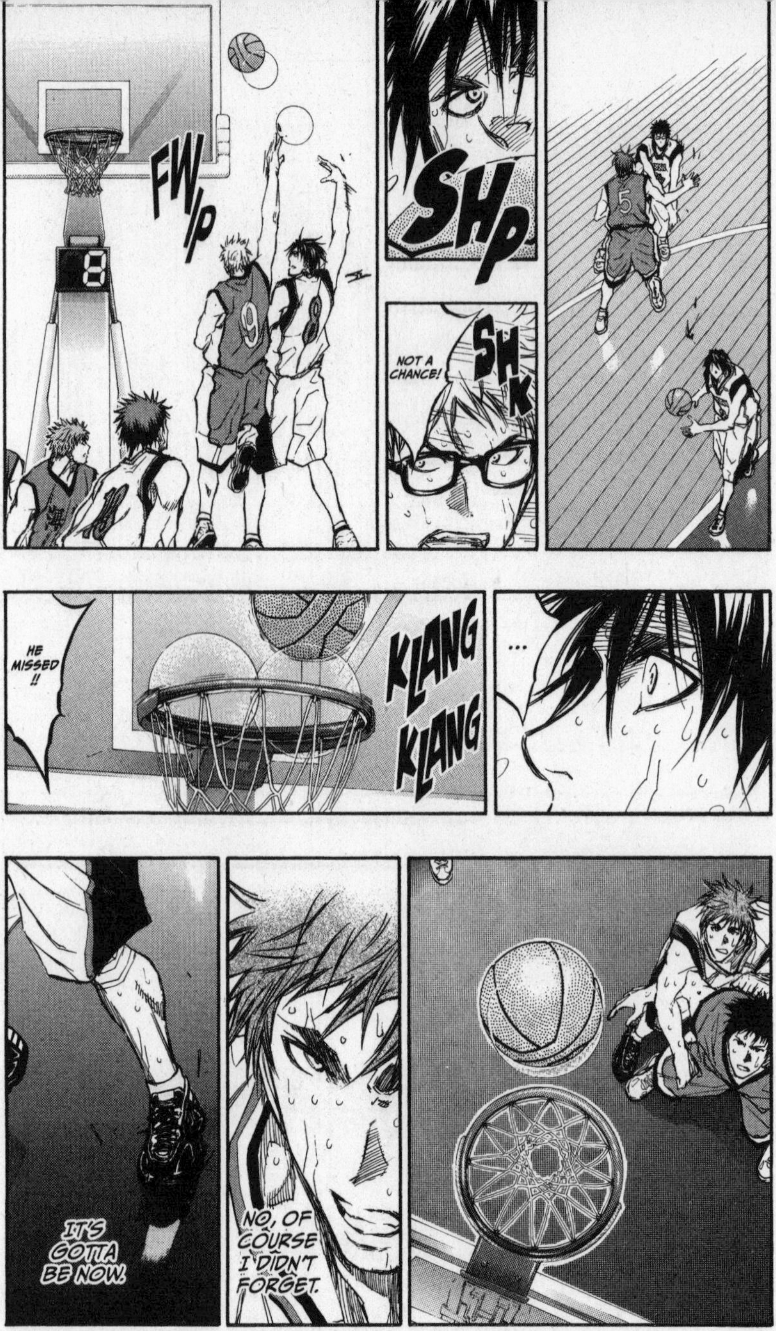
SHP
SHK
NOT A CHANCE!
FWIP
...
KLANG
KLANG
HE MISSED!!
NO, OF COURSE I DIDN'T FORGET.
IT'S GOTTA BE NOW.

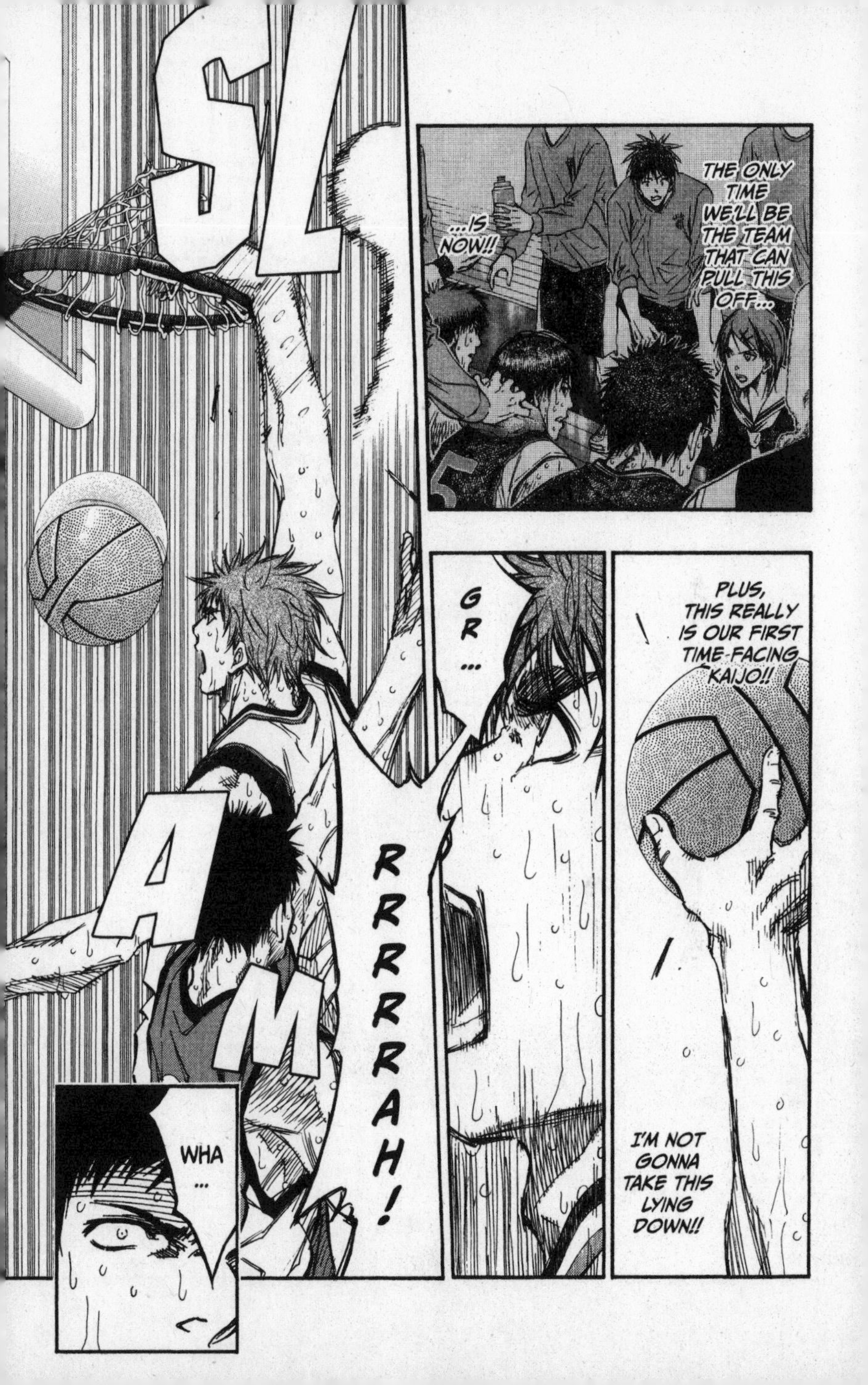
THE ONLY TIME WE'LL BE THE TEAM THAT CAN PULL THIS OFF...
...IS NOW!!
PLUS, THIS REALLY IS OUR FIRST TIME FACING KAIJO!!
I'M NOT GONNA TAKE THIS LYING DOWN!!
GR...
RRRRRAH!
SLAM
WHA...

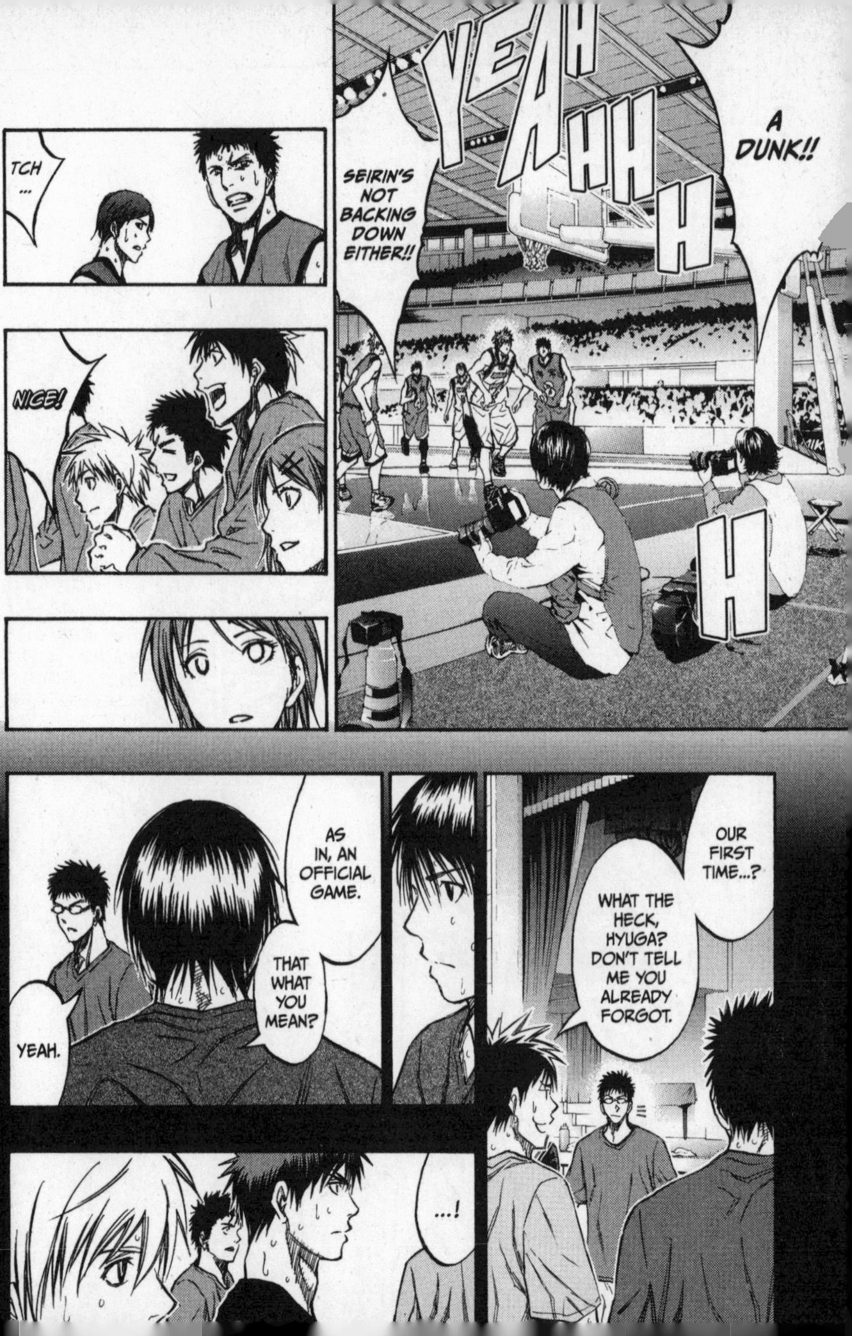
YEAHHHHHH
A DUNK!!
SEIRIN'S NOT BACKING DOWN EITHER!!
TCH...
NICE!
OUR FIRST TIME...?
WHAT THE HECK, HYUGA? DON'T TELL ME YOU ALREADY FORGOT.
AS IN, AN OFFICIAL GAME.
THAT WHAT YOU MEAN?
YEAH.
...!

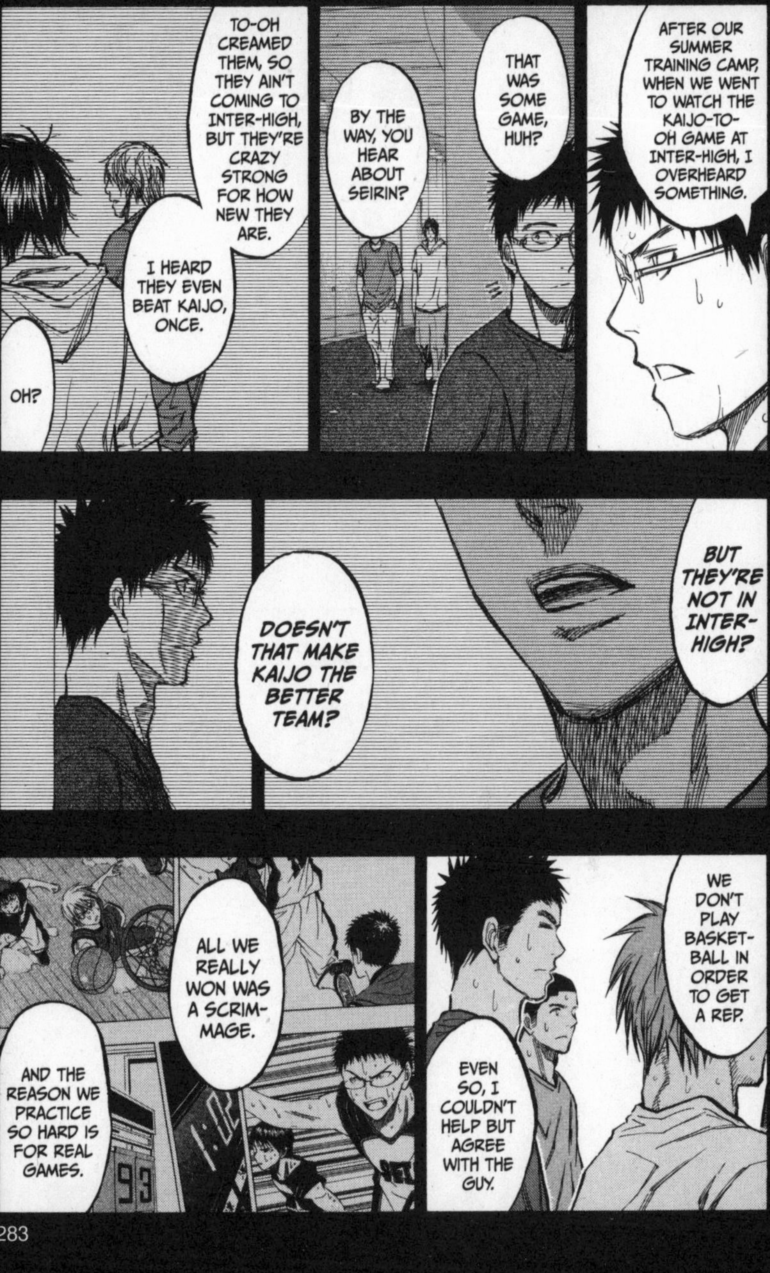
AFTER OUR SUMMER TRAINING CAMP, WHEN WE WENT TO WATCH THE KAIJO-TO-OH GAME AT INTER-HIGH, I OVERHEARD SOMETHING.
THAT WAS SOME GAME, HUH?
BY THE WAY, YOU HEAR ABOUT SEIRIN?
TO-OH CREAMED THEM, SO THEY AIN'T COMING TO INTER-HIGH, BUT THEY'RE CRAZY STRONG FOR HOW NEW THEY ARE.
I HEARD THEY EVEN BEAT KAIJO, ONCE.
OH?
BUT THEY'RE NOT IN INTER-HIGH?
DOESN'T THAT MAKE KAIJO THE BETTER TEAM?
WE DON'T PLAY BASKET-BALL IN ORDER TO GET A REP.
EVEN SO, I COULDN'T HELP BUT AGREE WITH THE GUY.
ALL WE REALLY WON WAS A SCRIM-MAGE.
AND THE REASON WE PRACTICE SO HARD IS FOR REAL GAMES.

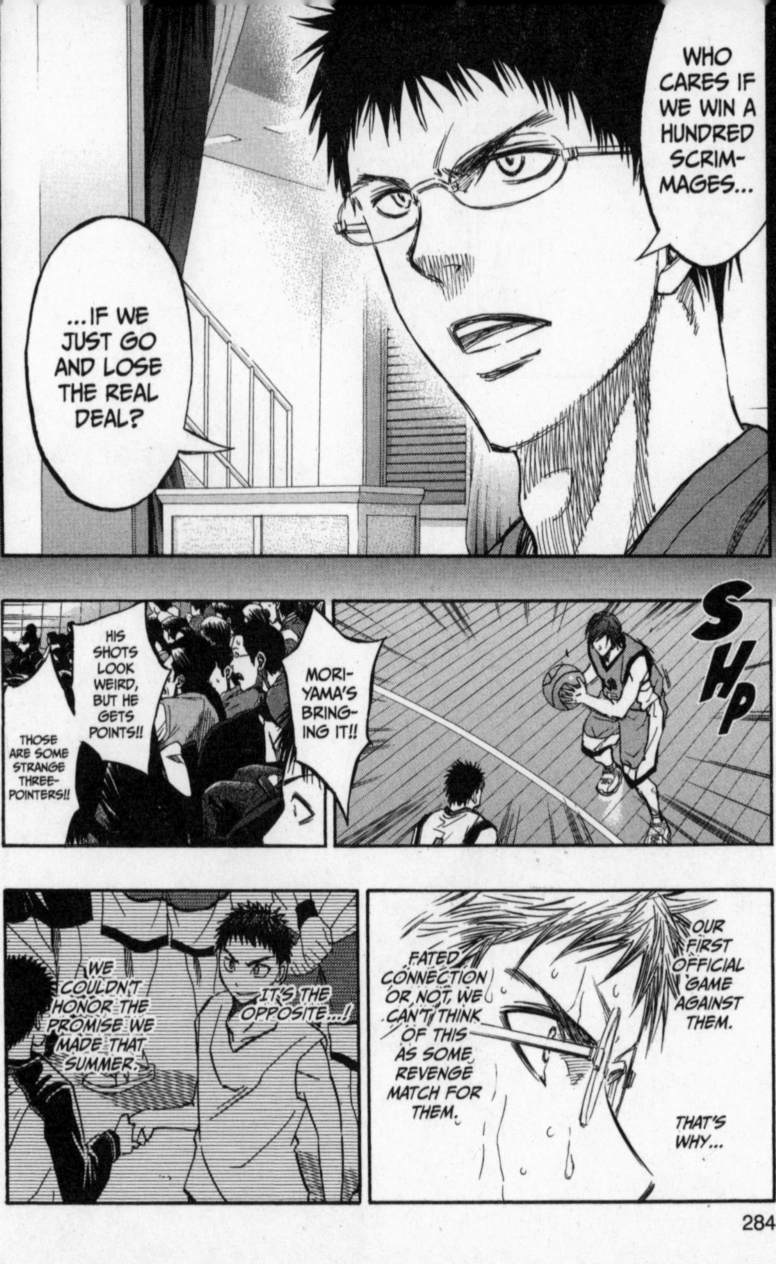
WHO CARES IF WE WIN A HUNDRED SCRIM-MAGES...
...IF WE JUST GO AND LOSE THE REAL DEAL?
SHP
MORI-YAMA'S BRING-ING IT!!
HIS SHOTS LOOK WEIRD, BUT HE GETS POINTS!!
THOSE ARE SOME STRANGE THREE-POINTERS!!
OUR FIRST OFFICIAL GAME AGAINST THEM.
FATED CONNECTION OR NOT, WE CAN'T THINK OF THIS AS SOME REVENGE MATCH FOR THEM.
THAT'S WHY...
IT'S THE OPPOSITE...!
...WE COULDN'T HONOR THE PROMISE WE MADE THAT SUMMER.

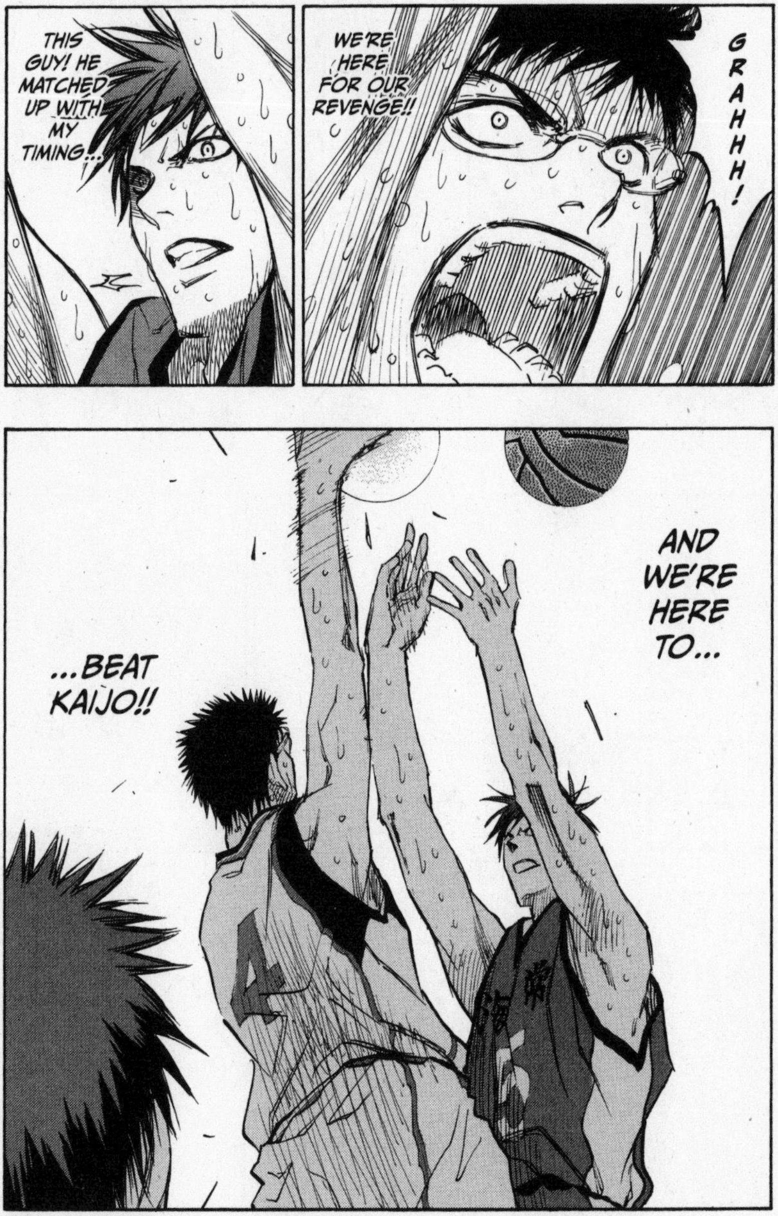
WE'RE HERE FOR OUR REVENGE!!
GRAHHH!
THIS GUY! HE MATCHED UP WITH MY TIMING...
AND WE'RE HERE TO...
...BEAT KAIJO!!

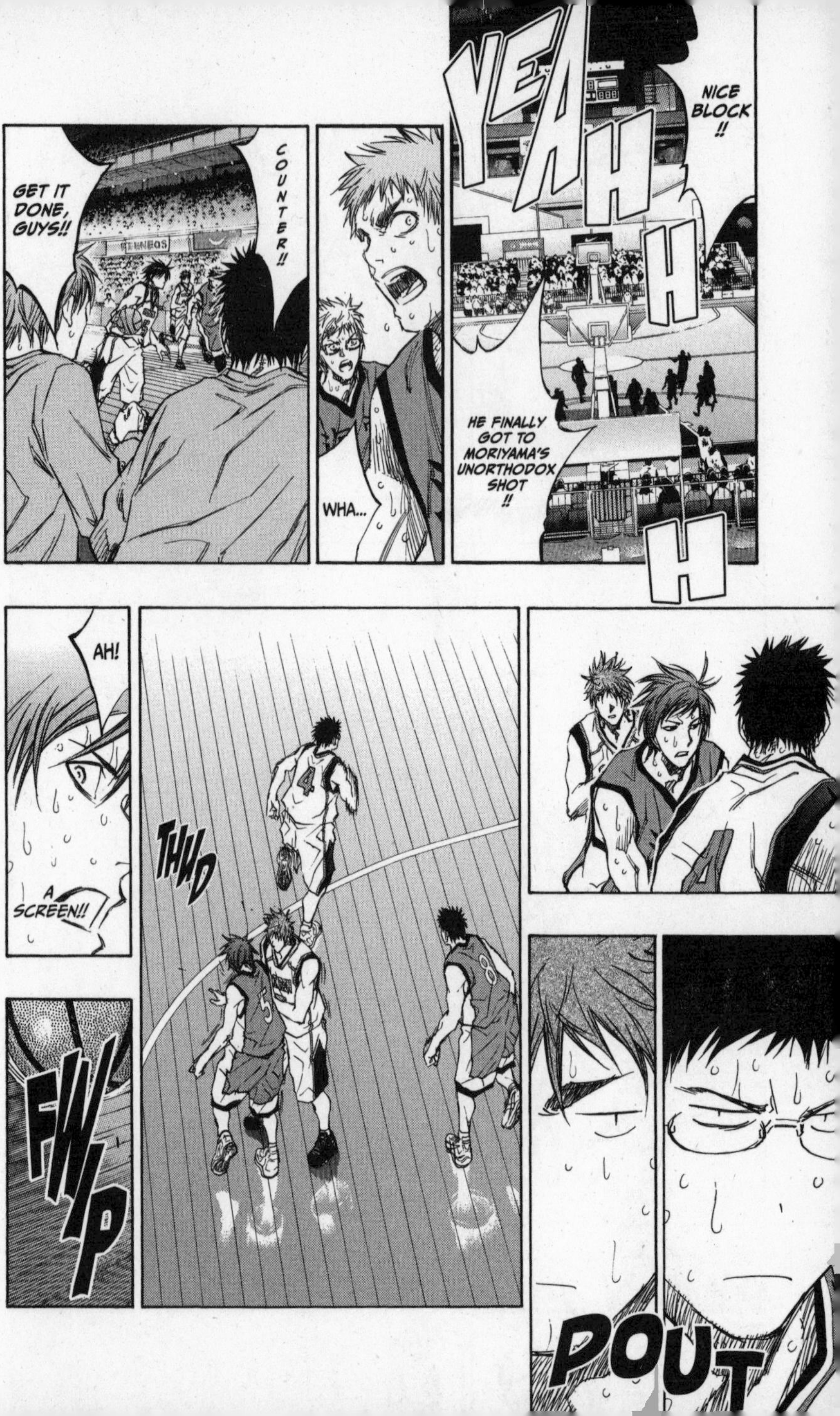
YEAHHHH
NICE BLOCK!!
HE FINALLY GOT TO MORIYAMA'S UNORTHODOX SHOT!!
WHA...
COUNTER!!
GET IT DONE, GUYS!!
POUT
THUD
AH!
A SCREEN!!
FWIP

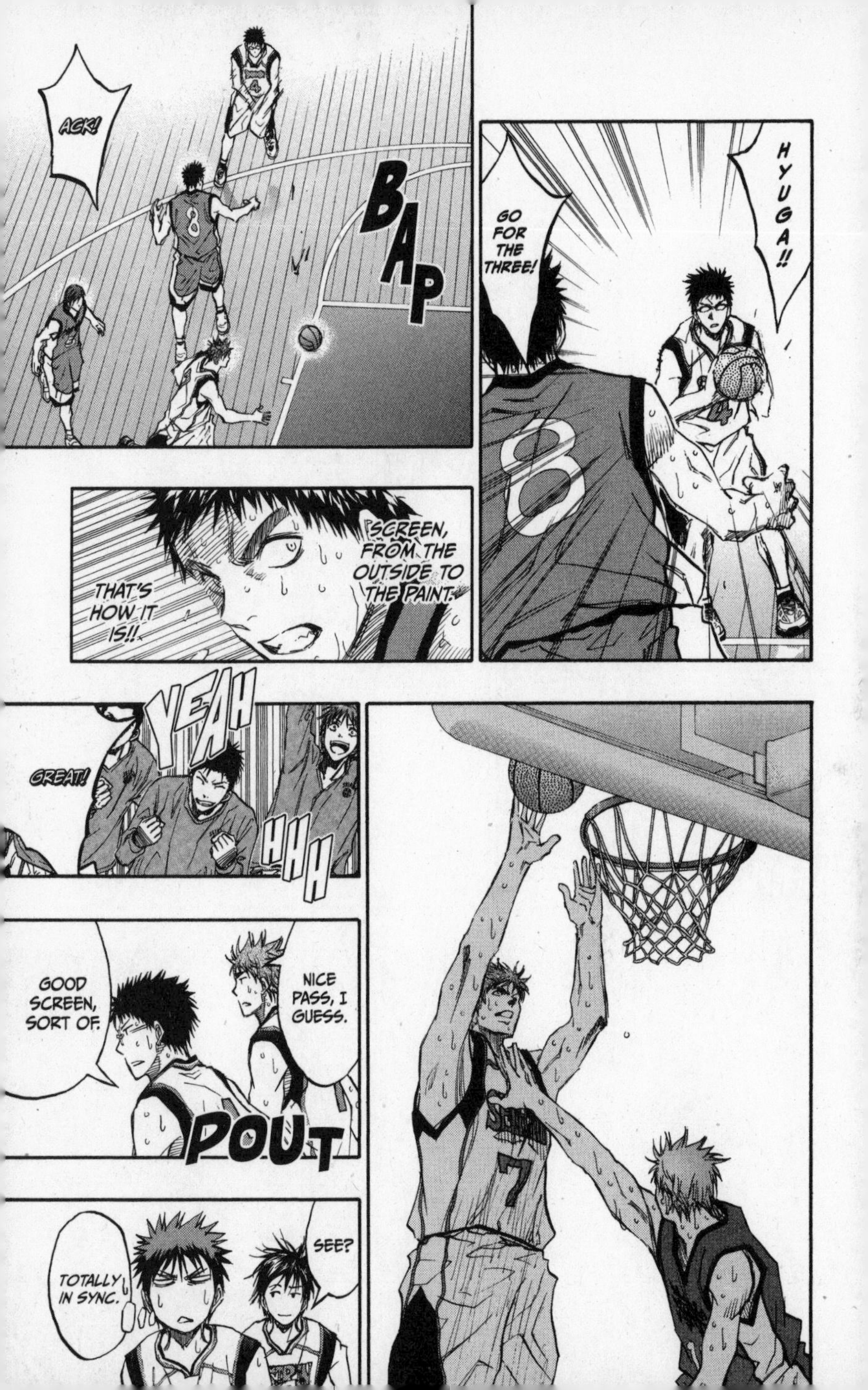
ACK!
BAP
HYUGA!!
GO FOR THE THREE!
SCREEN, FROM THE OUTSIDE TO THE PAINT.
THAT'S HOW IT IS!!
YEAHHHH
GREAT!
NICE PASS, I GUESS.
GOOD SCREEN, SORT OF.
POUT
SEE?
TOTALLY IN SYNC.

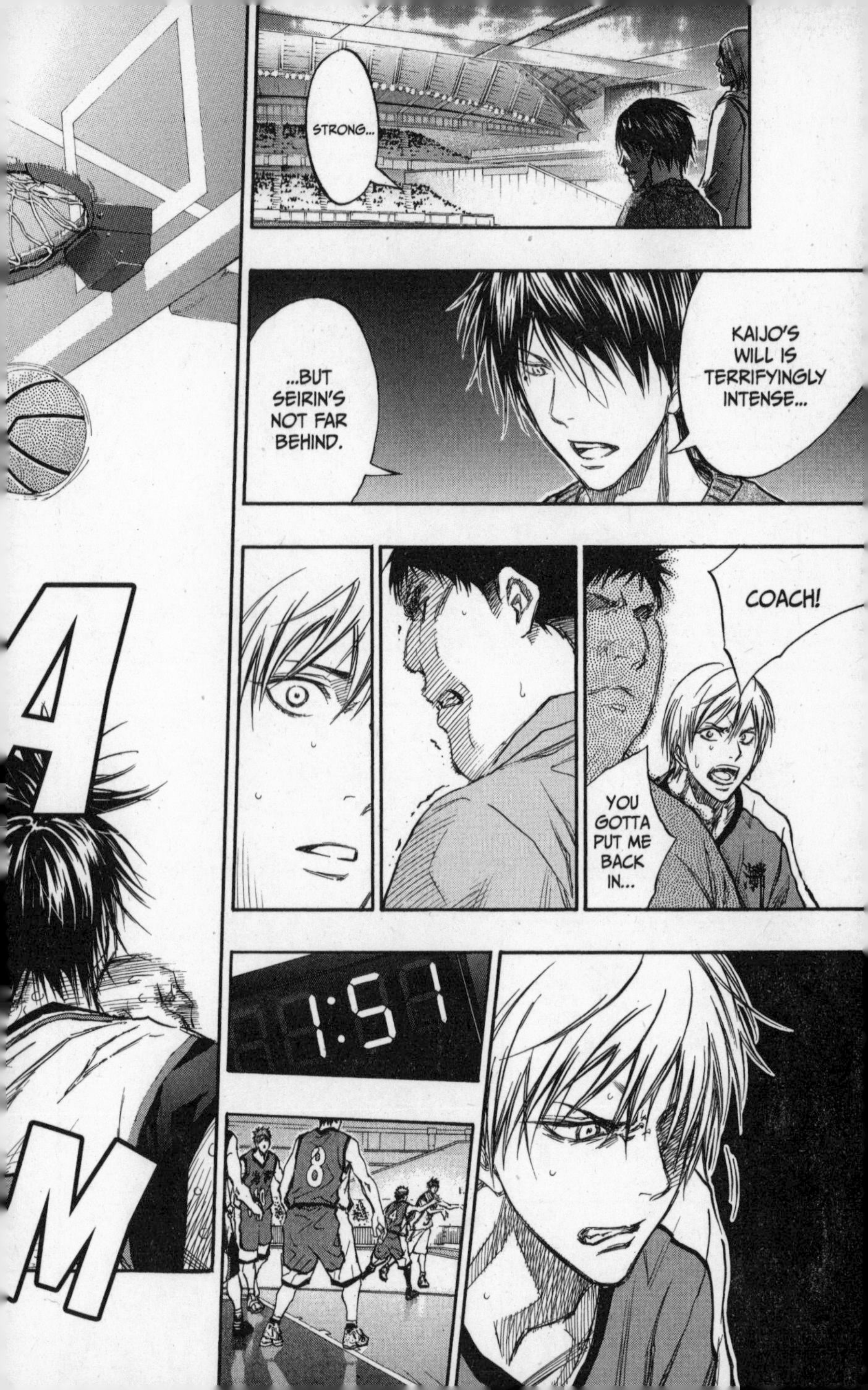
STRONG...
KAIJO'S WILL IS TERRIFYINGLY INTENSE...
...BUT SEIRIN'S NOT FAR BEHIND.
COACH!
YOU GOTTA PUT ME BACK IN...
1:57

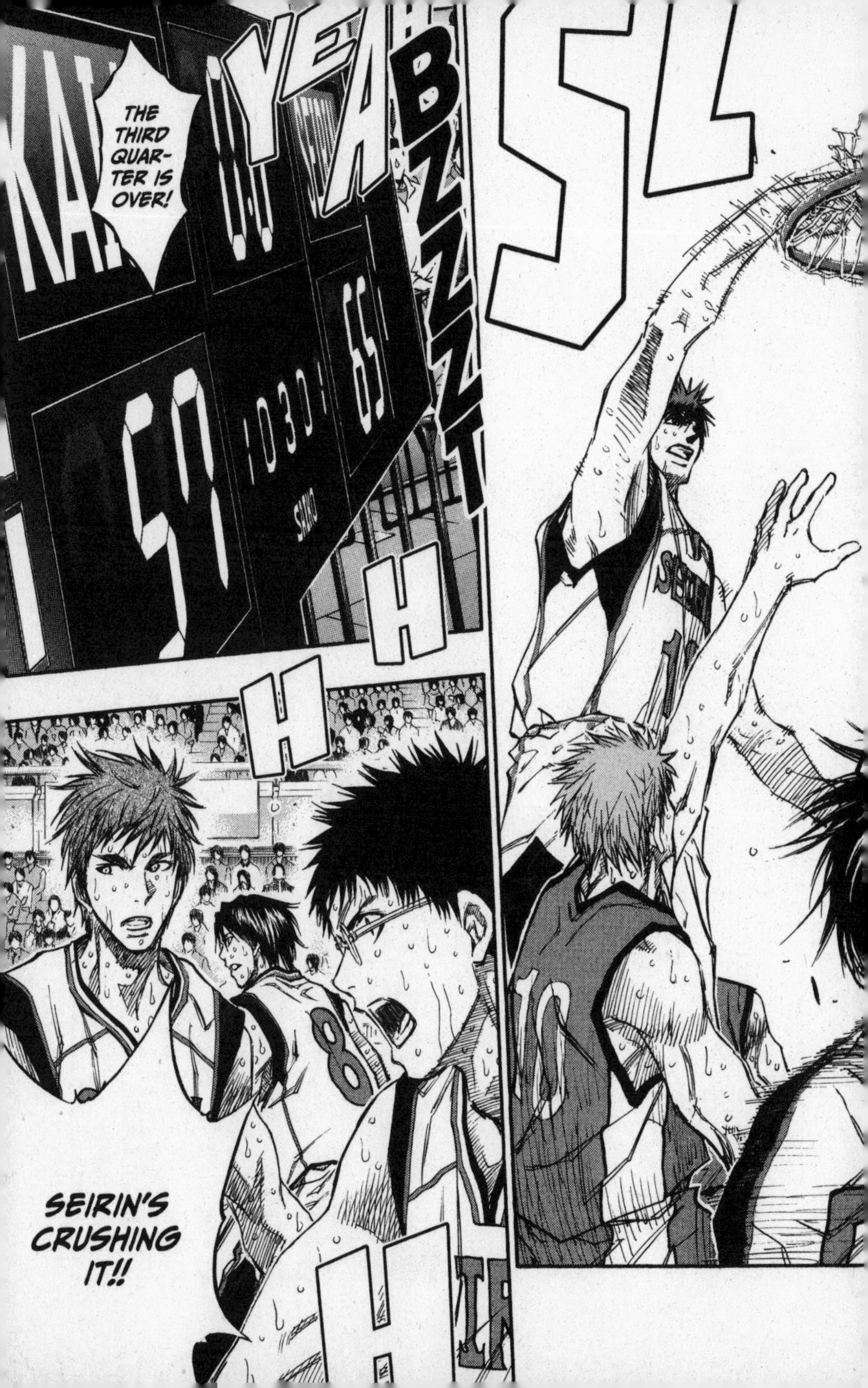
SL
YEAH
BZZZT
THE THIRD QUARTER IS OVER!
HHH
SEIRIN'S CRUSHING IT!!

KUROKO'S BASKETBALL BLOOPERS

TAKE 5

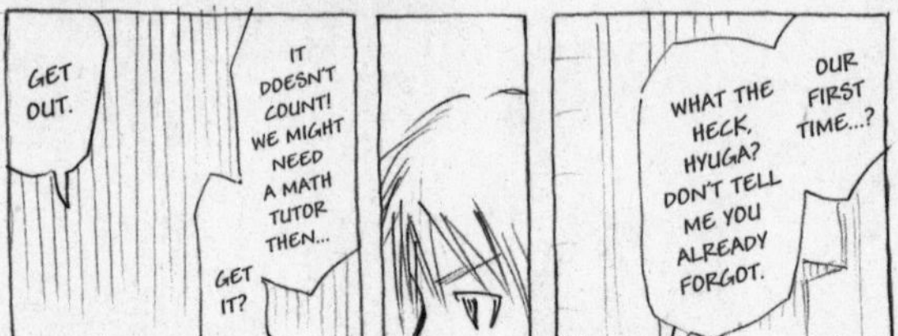
OUR FIRST TIME...?
WHAT THE HECK, HYUGA? DON'T TELL ME YOU ALREADY FORGOT.
IT DOESN'T COUNT! WE MIGHT NEED A MATH TUTOR THEN...
GET IT?
GET OUT.
THAT'S NOT WHAT I MEANT!

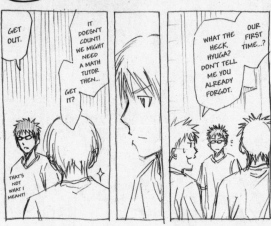

195TH QUARTER: CLIMAX!

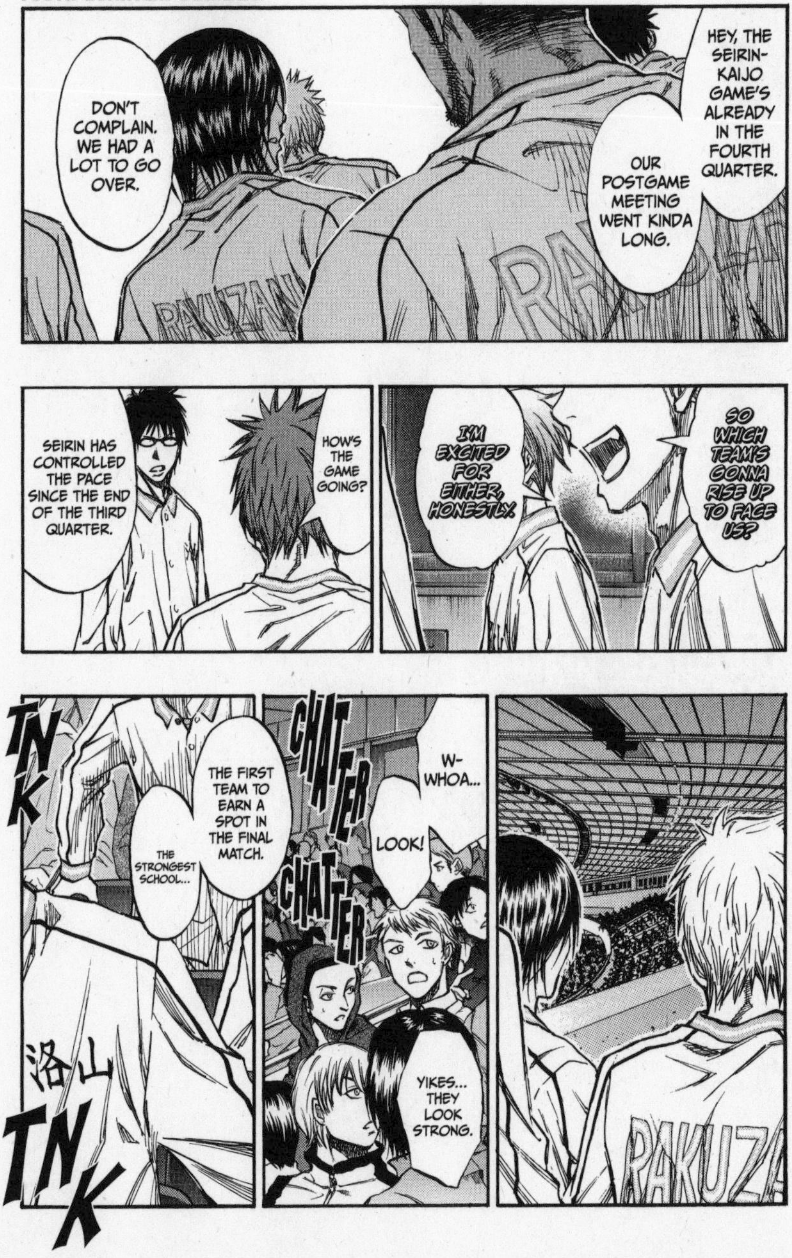
HEY, THE SEIRIN-KAIJO GAME'S ALREADY IN THE FOURTH QUARTER.
OUR POSTGAME MEETING WENT KINDA LONG.
DON'T COMPLAIN. WE HAD A LOT TO GO OVER.
SO WHICH TEAM'S GONNA RISE UP TO FACE US?
I'M EXCITED FOR EITHER, HONESTLY.
HOW'S THE GAME GOING?
SEIRIN HAS CONTROLLED THE PACE SINCE THE END OF THE THIRD QUARTER.
W-WHOA...
CHATTER
LOOK!
CHATTER
YIKES... THEY LOOK STRONG.
TNK
THE FIRST TEAM TO EARN A SPOT IN THE FINAL MATCH.
THE STRONGEST SCHOOL...
洛山
TNK

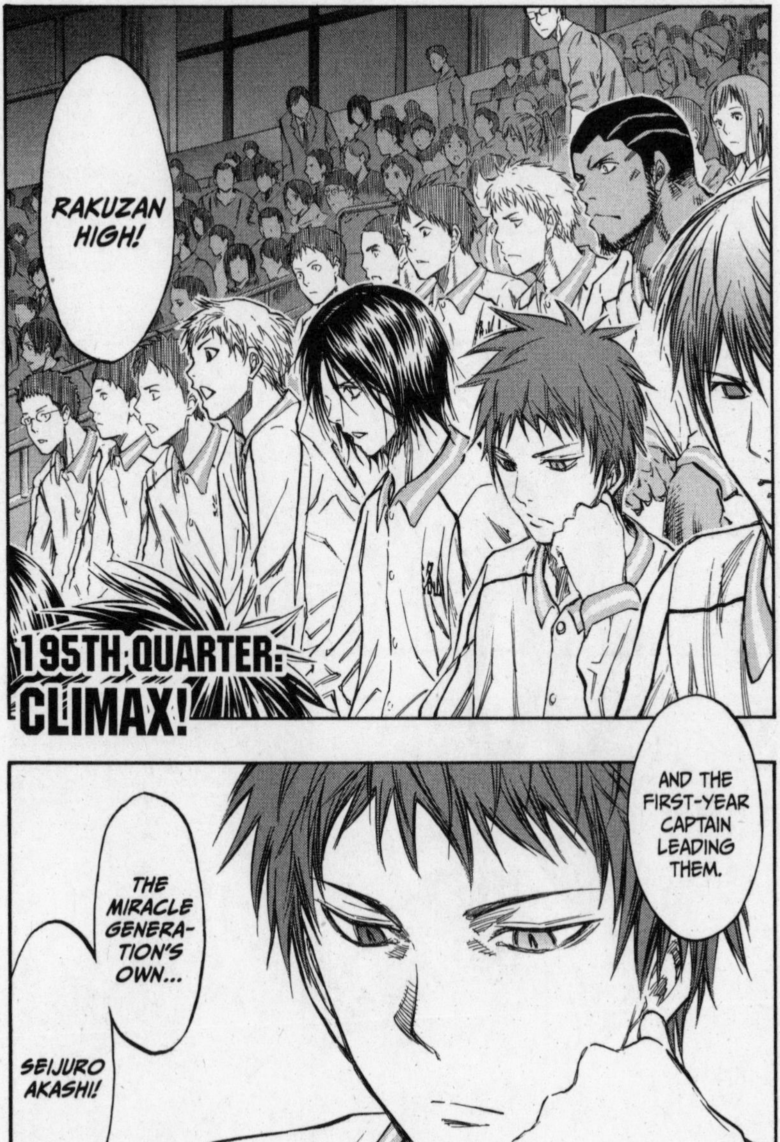
RAKUZAN HIGH!
195TH QUARTER: CLIMAX!
AND THE FIRST-YEAR CAPTAIN LEADING THEM.
THE MIRACLE GENERATION'S OWN...
SEIJURO AKASHI!

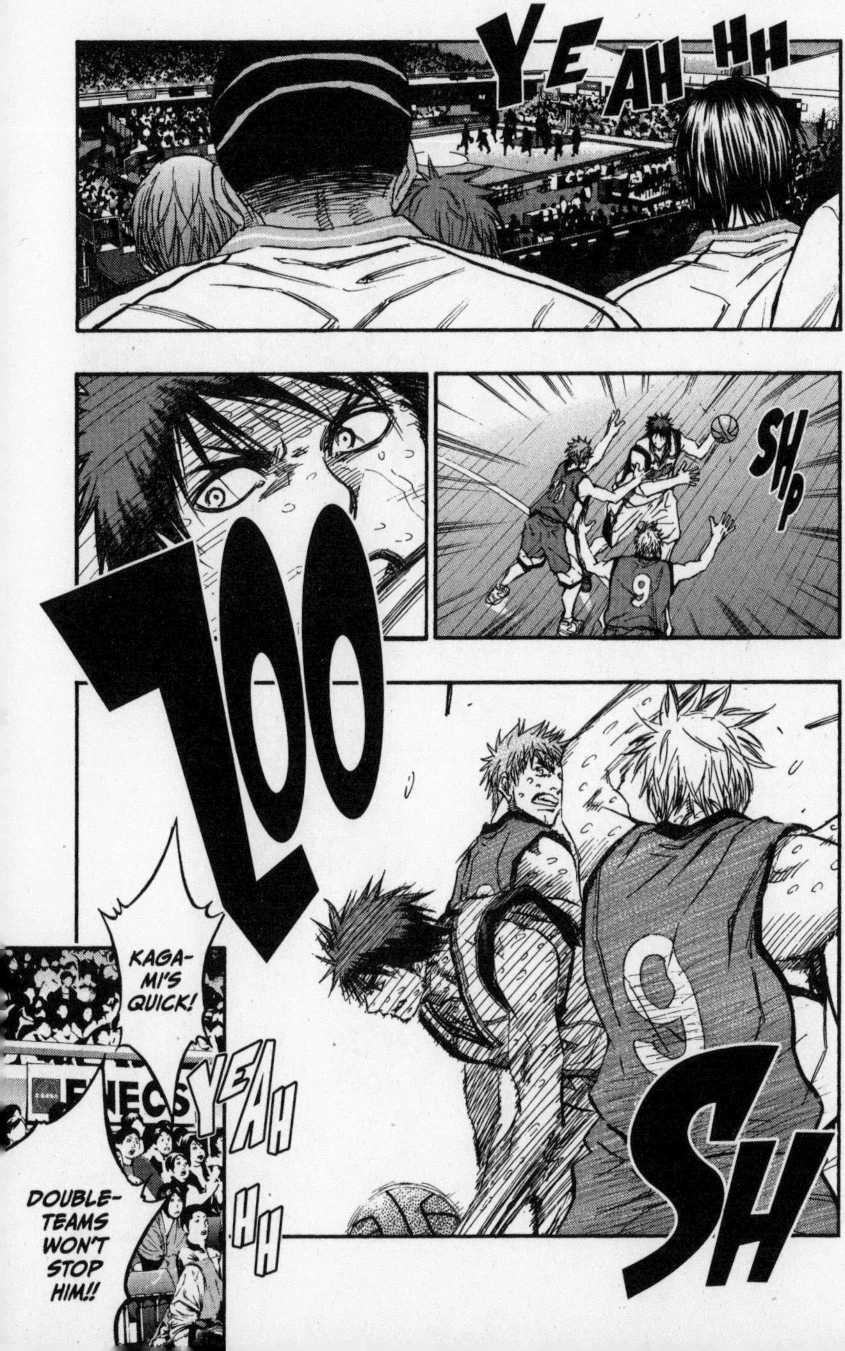
YEAHHH
SHP
ZOOM
SH
KAGA-MI'S QUICK!
YEAHHH
DOUBLE-TEAMS WON'T STOP HIM!!

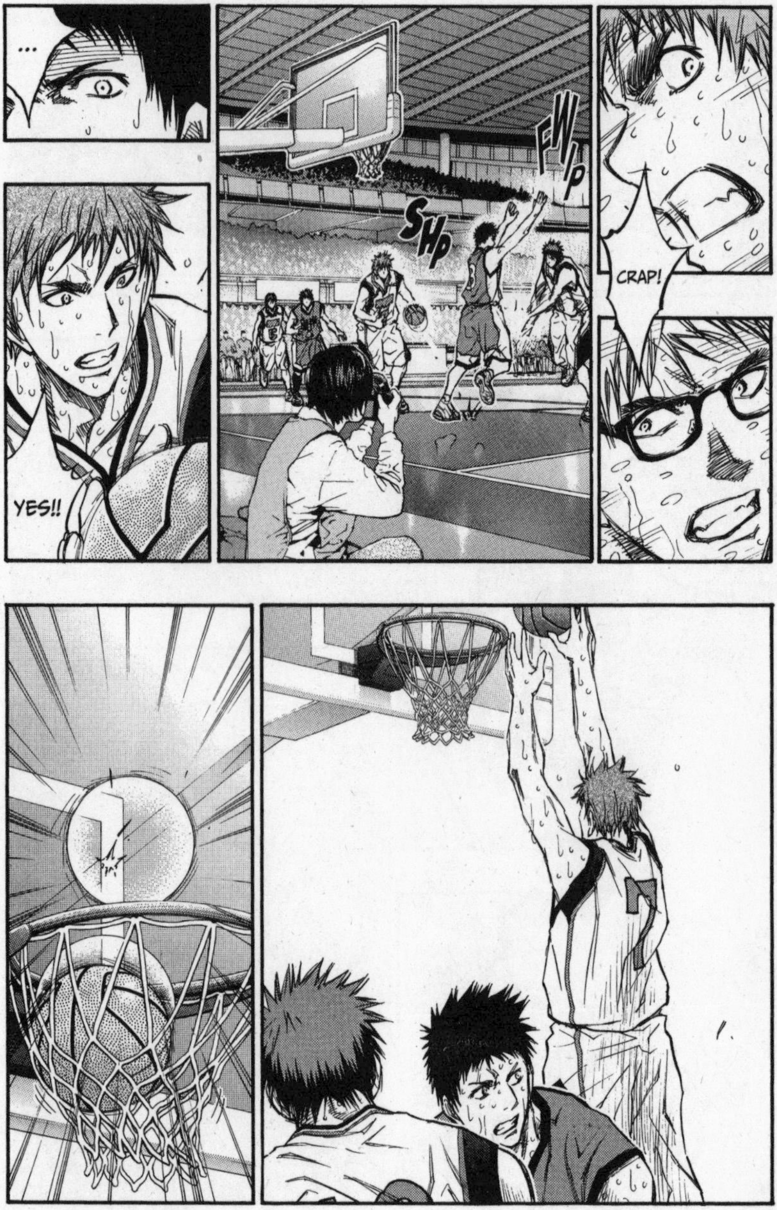
CRAP!
FWIP
SHP
...
YES!!

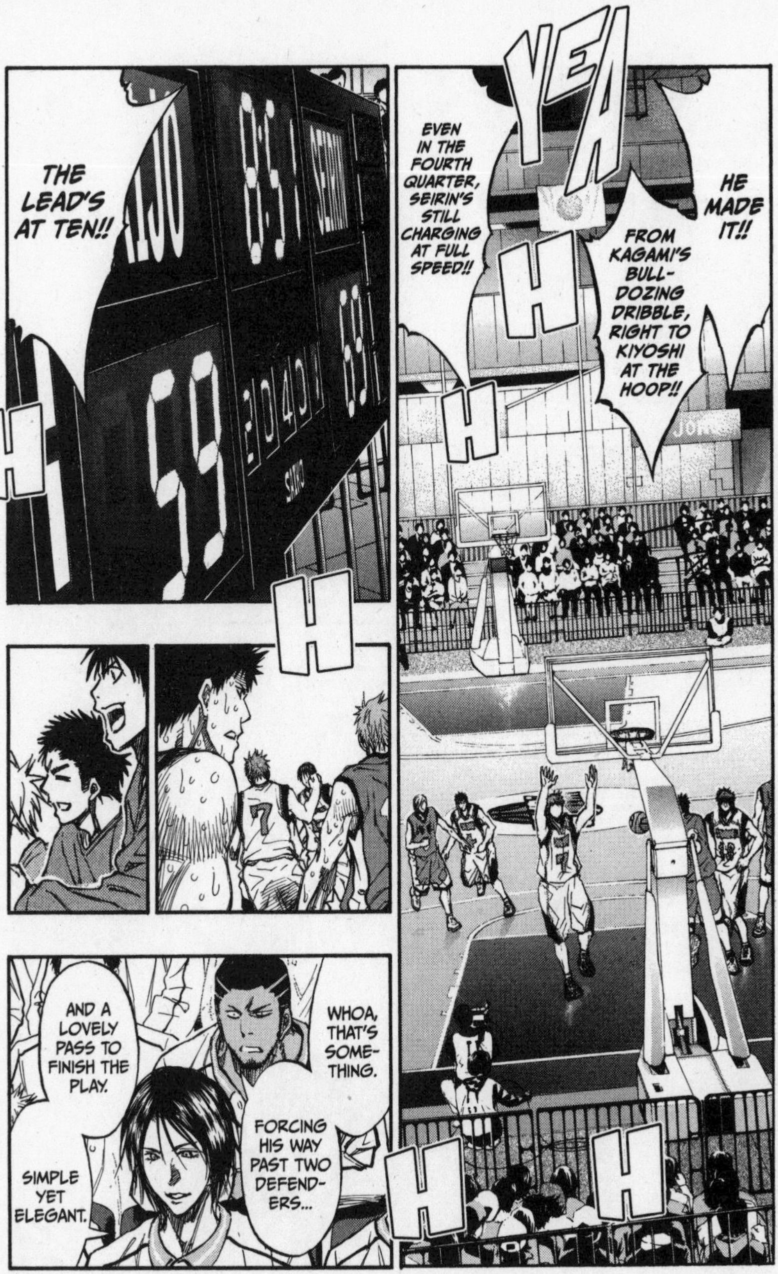
YEAHHHHHHH
HE MADE IT!!
FROM KAGAMI'S BULLDOZING DRIBBLE, RIGHT TO KIYOSHI AT THE HOOP!!
EVEN IN THE FOURTH QUARTER, SEIRIN'S STILL CHARGING AT FULL SPEED!!
THE LEAD'S AT TEN!!
WHOA, THAT'S SOMETHING.
FORCING HIS WAY PAST TWO DEFENDERS...
AND A LOVELY PASS TO FINISH THE PLAY.
SIMPLE YET ELEGANT.

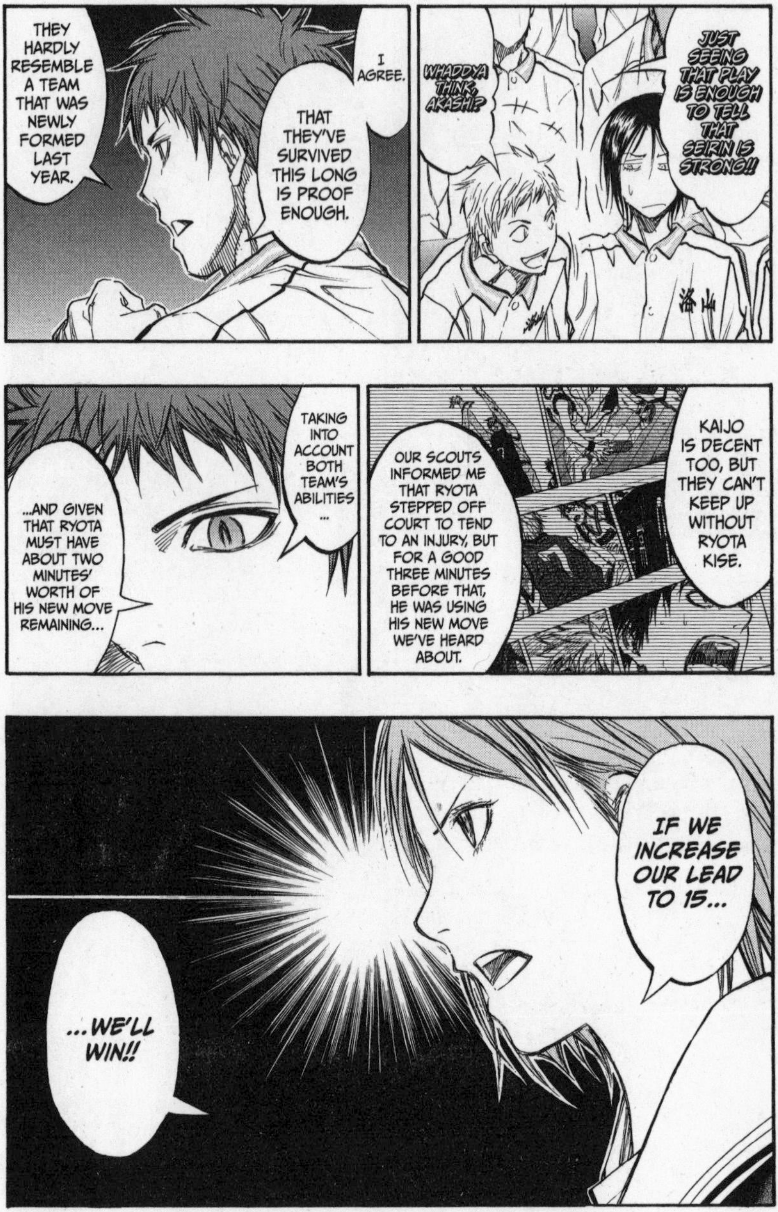
JUST SEEING THAT PLAY IS ENOUGH TO TELL THAT SEIRIN IS STRONG!!
WHADDYA THINK, AKASHI?
I AGREE.
THAT THEY'VE SURVIVED THIS LONG IS PROOF ENOUGH.
THEY HARDLY RESEMBLE A TEAM THAT WAS NEWLY FORMED LAST YEAR.
KAIJO IS DECENT TOO, BUT THEY CAN'T KEEP UP WITHOUT RYOTA KISE.
OUR SCOUTS INFORMED ME THAT RYOTA STEPPED OFF COURT TO TEND TO AN INJURY, BUT FOR A GOOD THREE MINUTES BEFORE THAT, HE WAS USING HIS NEW MOVE WE'VE HEARD ABOUT.
TAKING INTO ACCOUNT BOTH TEAM'S ABILITIES ...
...AND GIVEN THAT RYOTA MUST HAVE ABOUT TWO MINUTES' WORTH OF HIS NEW MOVE REMAINING...
IF WE INCREASE OUR LEAD TO 15...
...WE'LL WIN!!

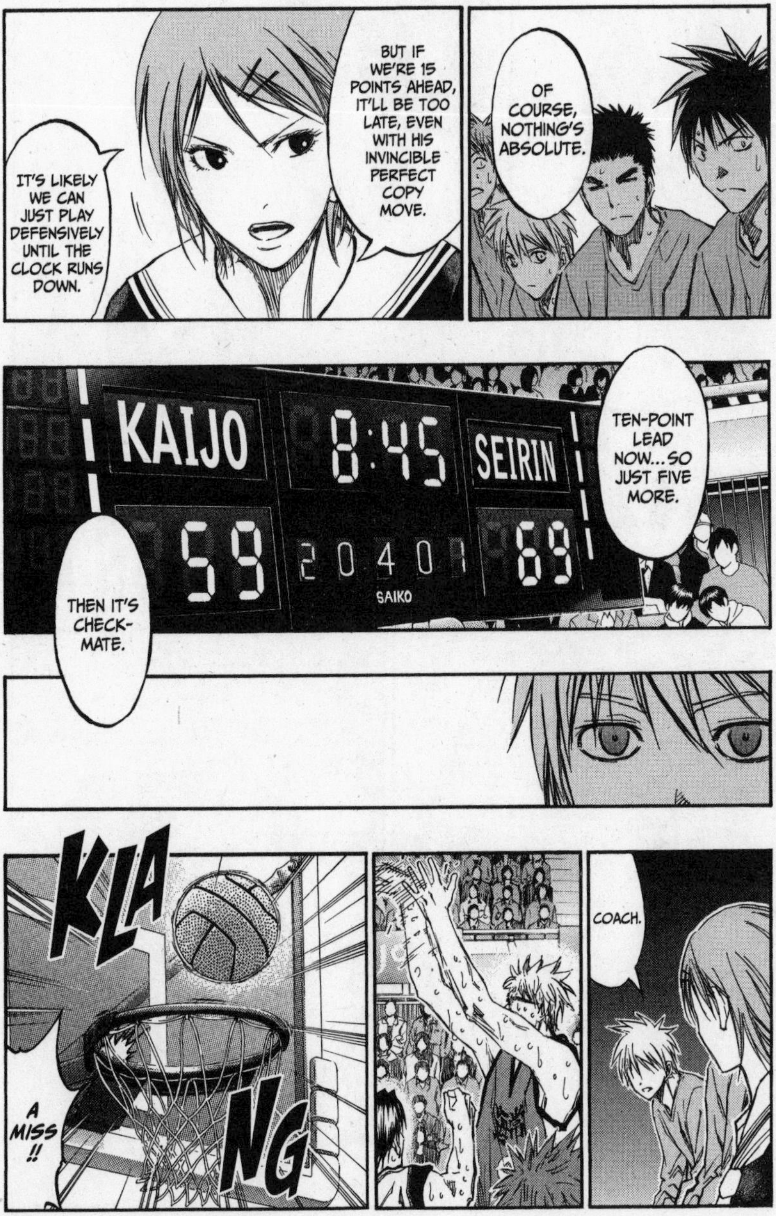
OF COURSE, NOTHING'S ABSOLUTE.
BUT IF WE'RE 15 POINTS AHEAD, IT'LL BE TOO LATE, EVEN WITH HIS INVINCIBLE PERFECT COPY MOVE.
IT'S LIKELY WE CAN JUST PLAY DEFENSIVELY UNTIL THE CLOCK RUNS DOWN.
TEN-POINT LEAD NOW... SO JUST FIVE MORE.
KAIJO
8:45
SEIRIN
59
20401
69
SAIKO
THEN IT'S CHECKMATE.
COACH.
KLANG
A MISS!!

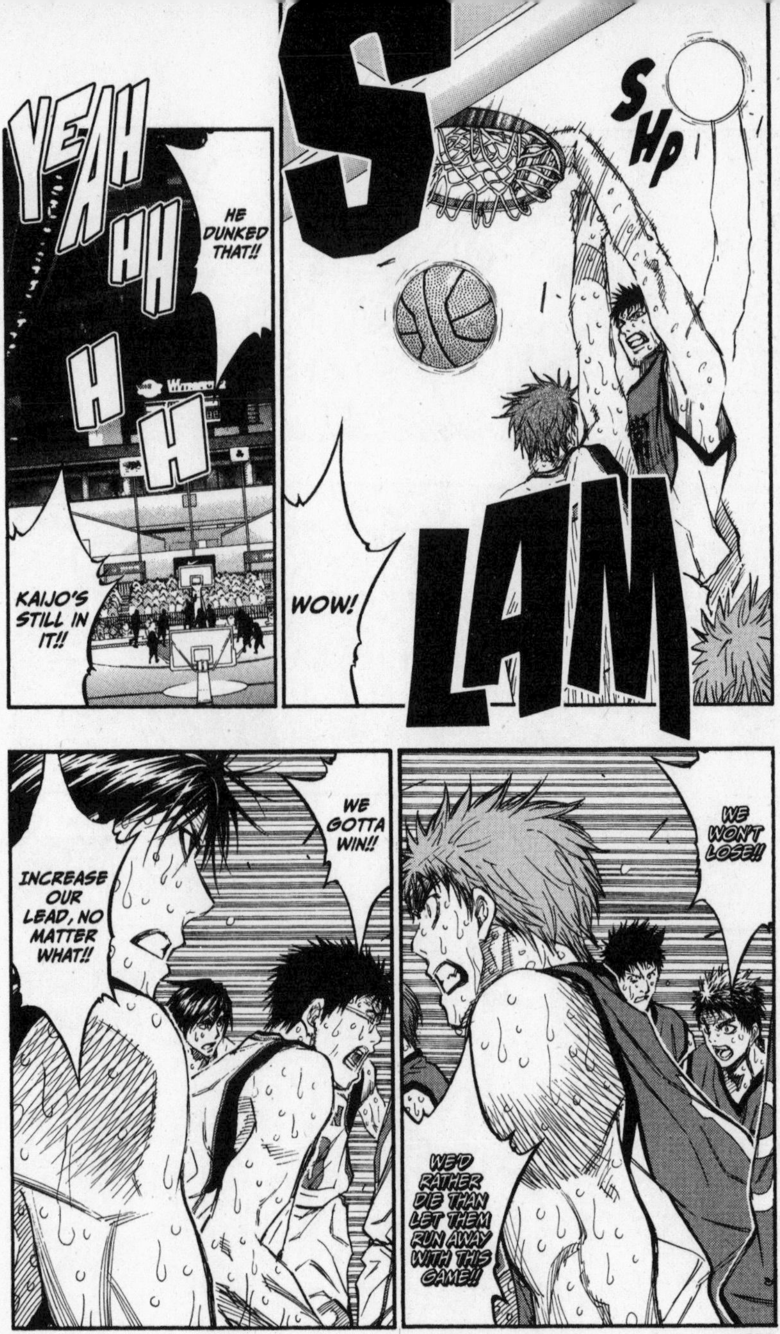
S
SHP
WOW!
LAM
YEAHHHHHH
HE DUNKED THAT!!
KAIJO'S STILL IN IT!!
WE WON'T LOSE!!
WE'D RATHER DIE THAN LET THEM RUN AWAY WITH THIS GAME!!
WE GOTTA WIN!!
INCREASE OUR LEAD, NO MATTER WHAT!!

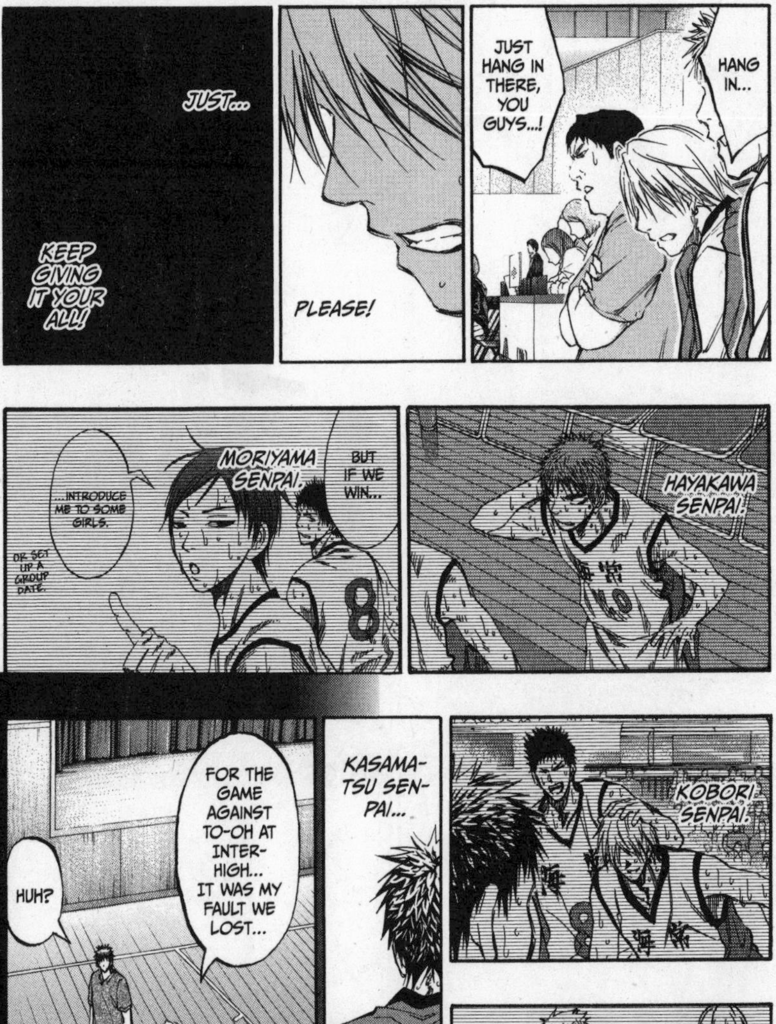

HANG IN...
JUST HANG IN THERE, YOU GUYS...!
PLEASE!
JUST...
KEEP GIVING IT YOUR ALL!
HAYAKAWA SENPAI!
BUT IF WE WIN...
MORIYAMA SENPAI!
...INTRODUCE ME TO SOME GIRLS.
OR SET UP A GROUP DATE.
KOBORI SENPAI!
KASAMATSU SENPAI...
FOR THE GAME AGAINST TO-OH AT INTER-HIGH... IT WAS MY FAULT WE LOST...
HUH?
NAKAMURA SENPAI!

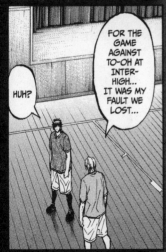

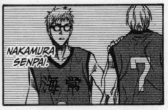

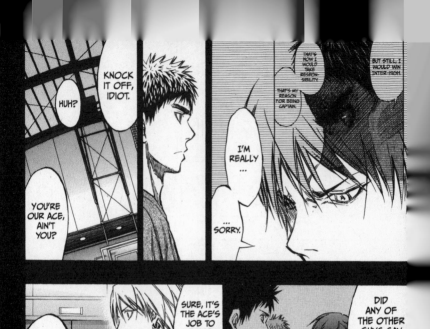

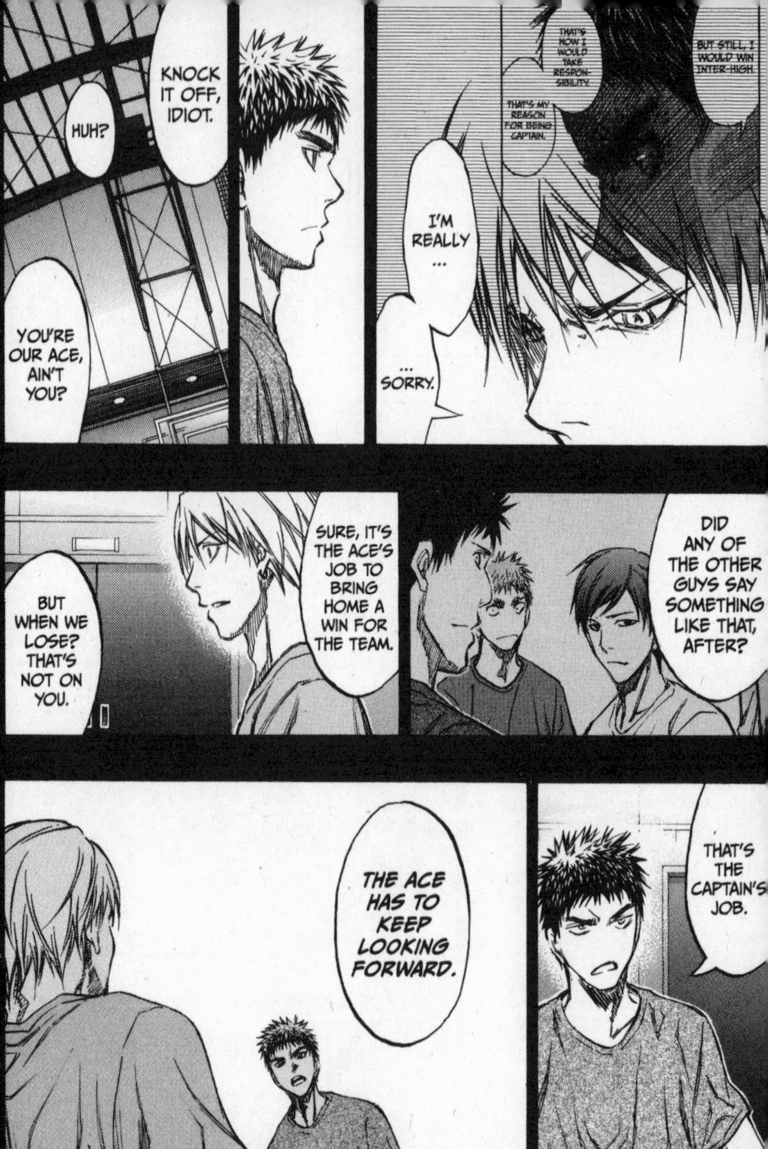
BUT STILL, I WOULD WIN INTER-HIGH.
THAT'S HOW I WOULD TAKE RESPON-SIBILITY.
THAT'S MY REASON FOR BEING CAPTAIN.
I'M REALLY ...
... SORRY.
KNOCK IT OFF, IDIOT.
HUH?
YOU'RE OUR ACE, AIN'T YOU?
DID ANY OF THE OTHER GUYS SAY SOMETHING LIKE THAT, AFTER?
SURE, IT'S THE ACE'S JOB TO BRING HOME A WIN FOR THE TEAM.
BUT WHEN WE LOSE? THAT'S NOT ON YOU.
THAT'S THE CAPTAIN'S JOB.
THE ACE HAS TO KEEP LOOKING FORWARD.

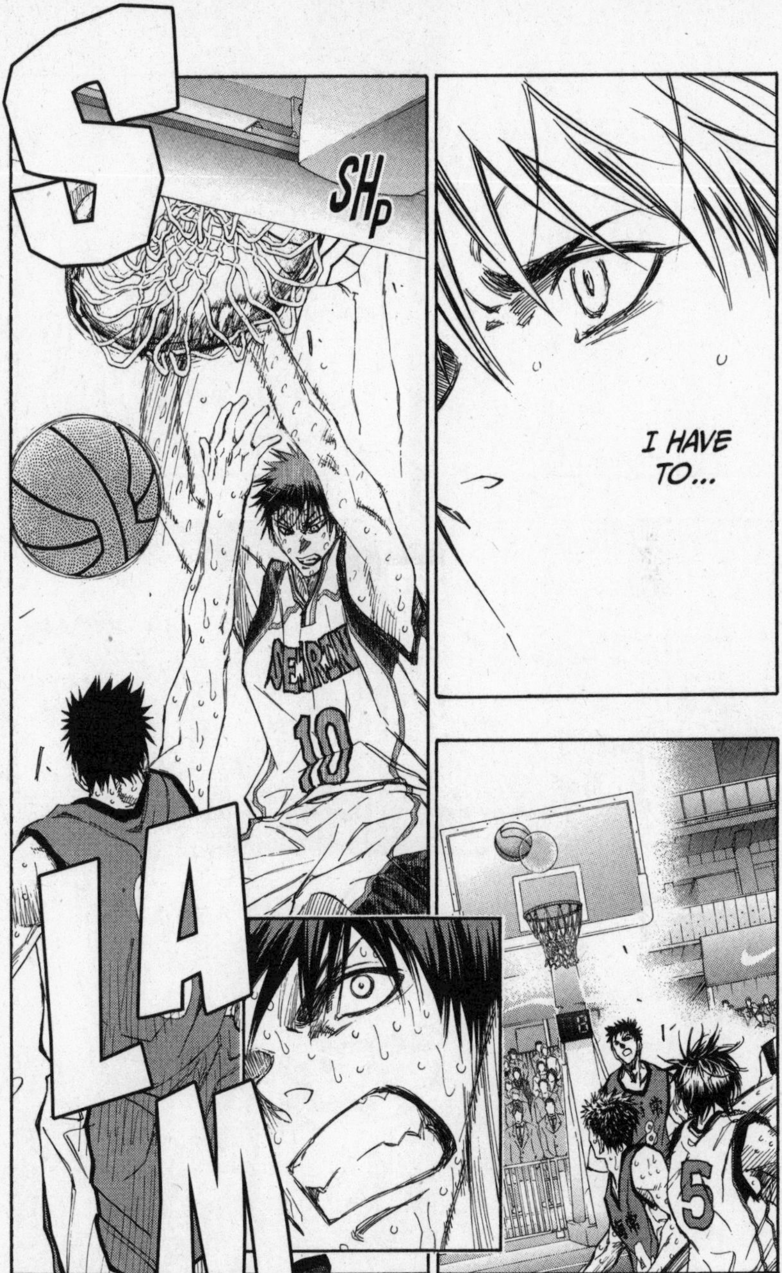
I HAVE TO...
SHP
SLAM

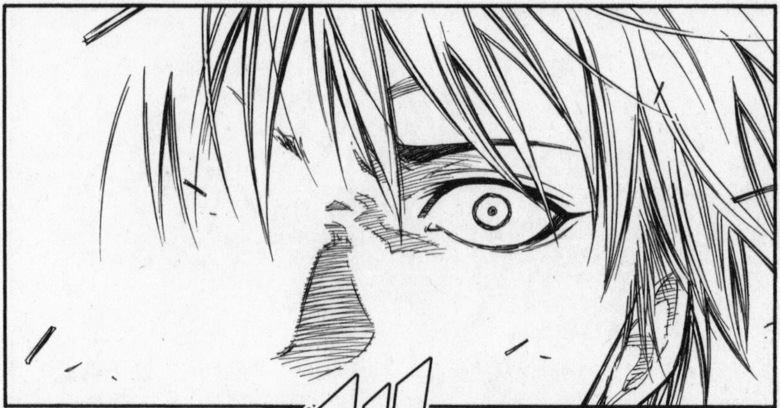

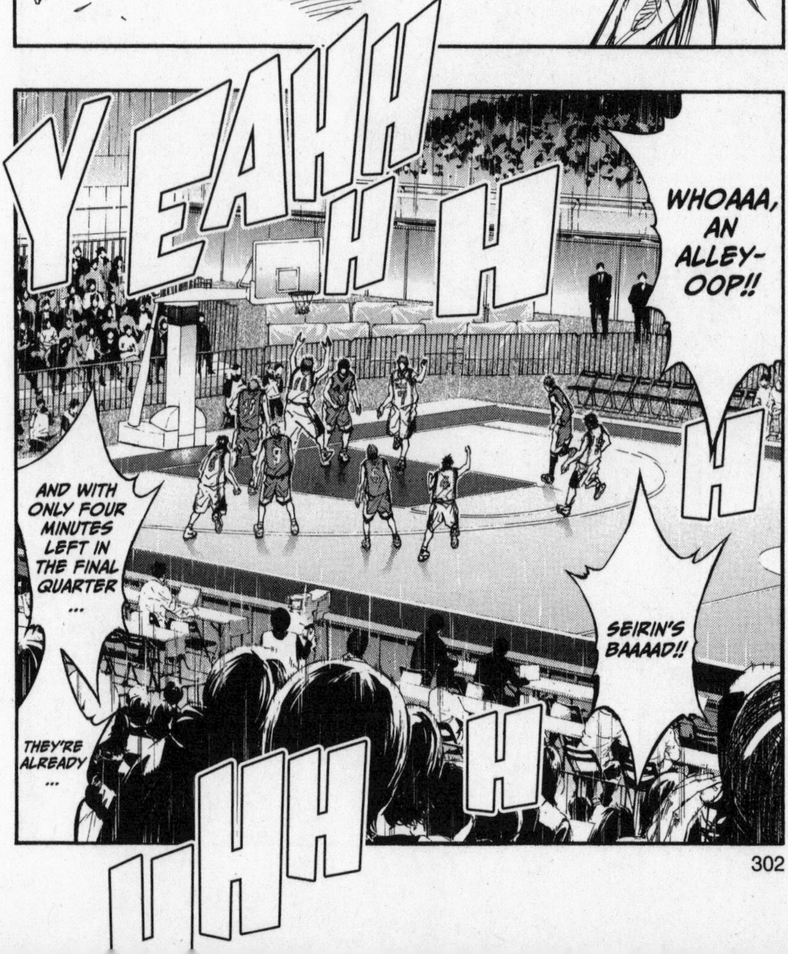
YEAHHHHHHHH
WHOAAA, AN ALLEY-OOP!!
SEIRIN'S BAAAAD!!
AND WITH ONLY FOUR MINUTES LEFT IN THE FINAL QUARTER ...
THEY'RE ALREADY ...

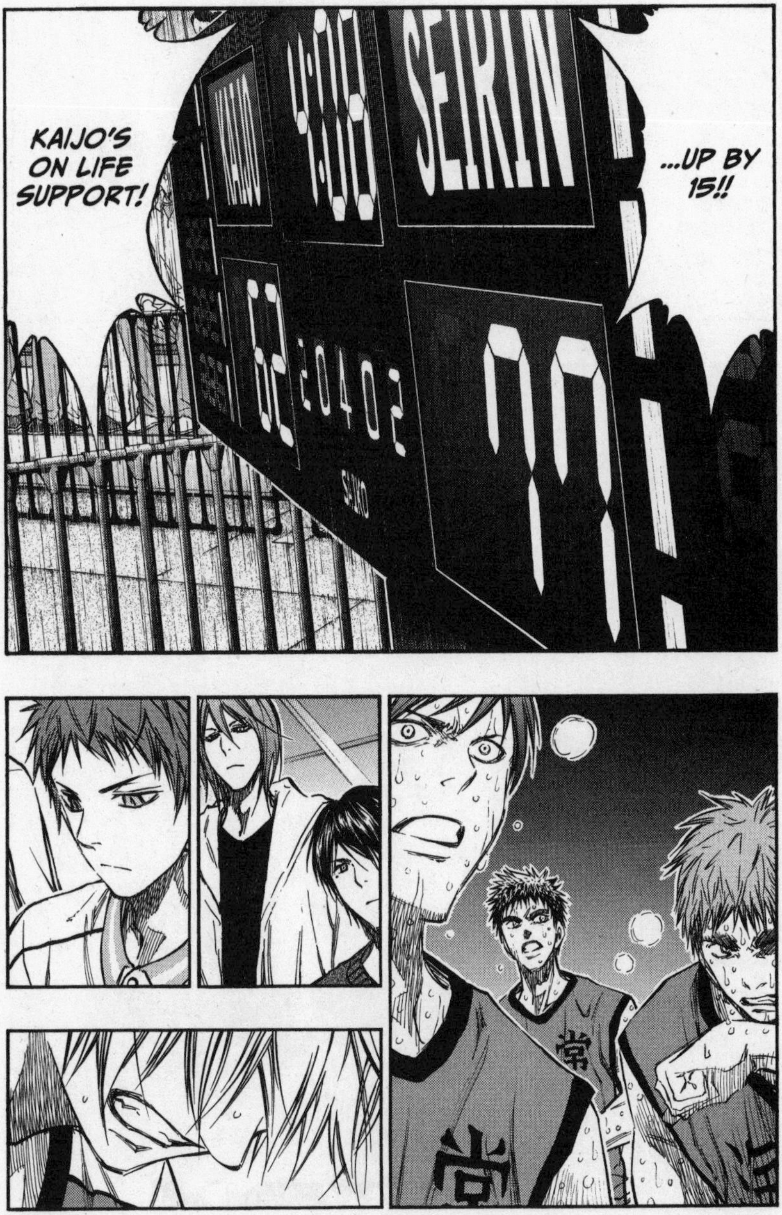
...UP BY 15!!
KAIJO'S ON LIFE SUPPORT!

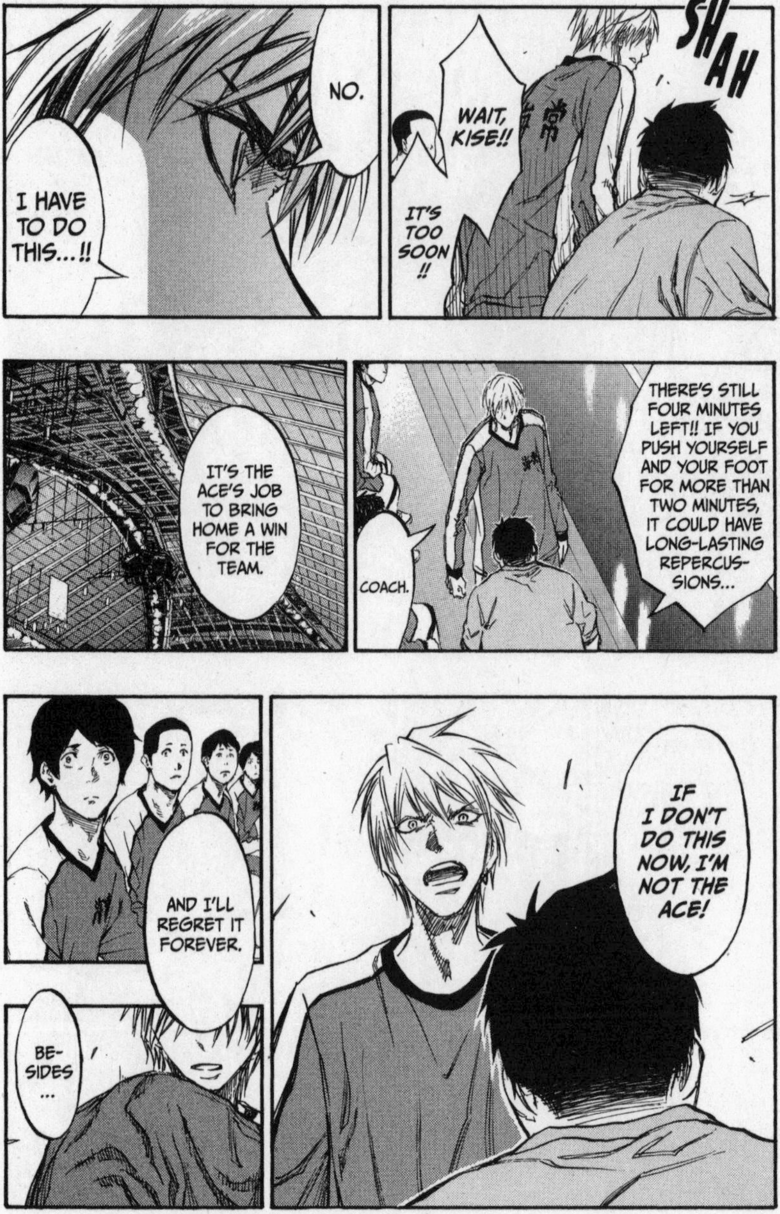
SHAH
WAIT, KISE!!
IT'S TOO SOON!!
NO.
I HAVE TO DO THIS...!!
THERE'S STILL FOUR MINUTES LEFT!! IF YOU PUSH YOURSELF AND YOUR FOOT FOR MORE THAN TWO MINUTES, IT COULD HAVE LONG-LASTING REPERCUSSIONS...
COACH.
IT'S THE ACE'S JOB TO BRING HOME A WIN FOR THE TEAM.
IF I DON'T DO THIS NOW, I'M NOT THE ACE!
AND I'LL REGRET IT FOREVER.
BESIDES...

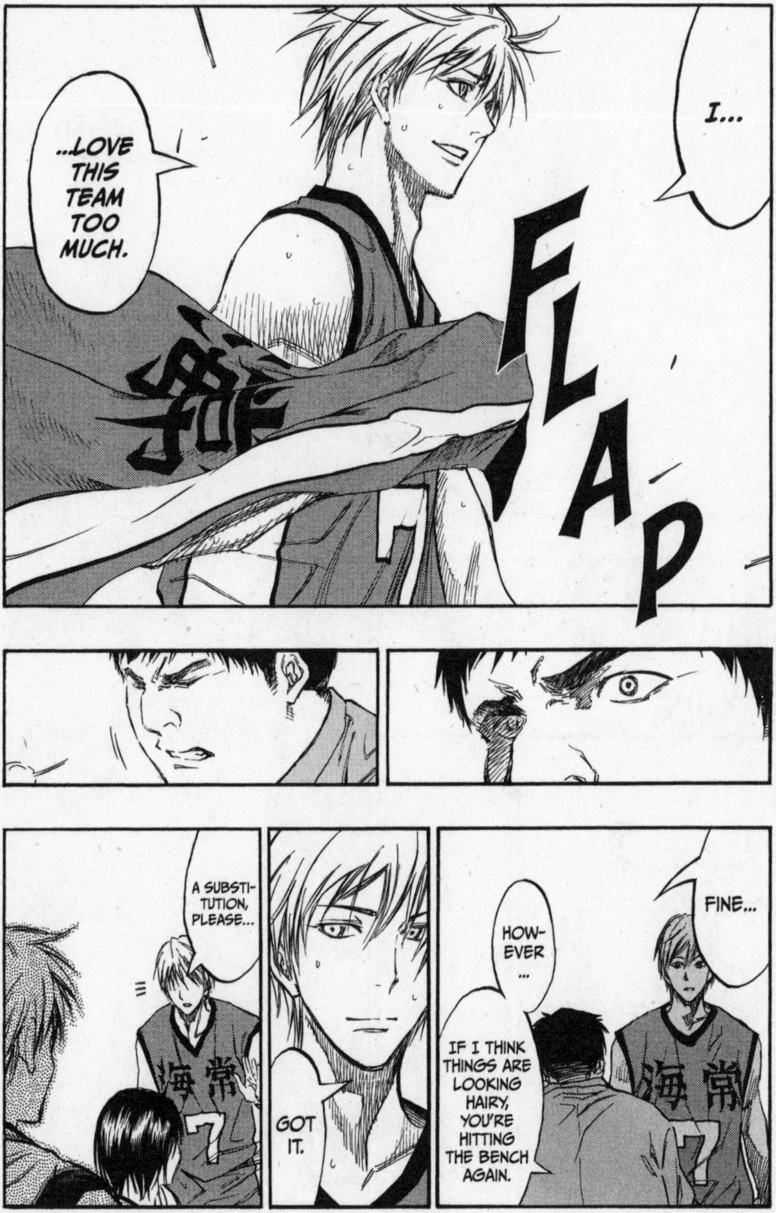

I...
...LOVE THIS TEAM TOO MUCH.
FLAP
FINE...
HOW-EVER...
IF I THINK THINGS ARE LOOKING HAIRY, YOU'RE HITTING THE BENCH AGAIN.
GOT IT.
A SUBSTI-TUTION, PLEASE...

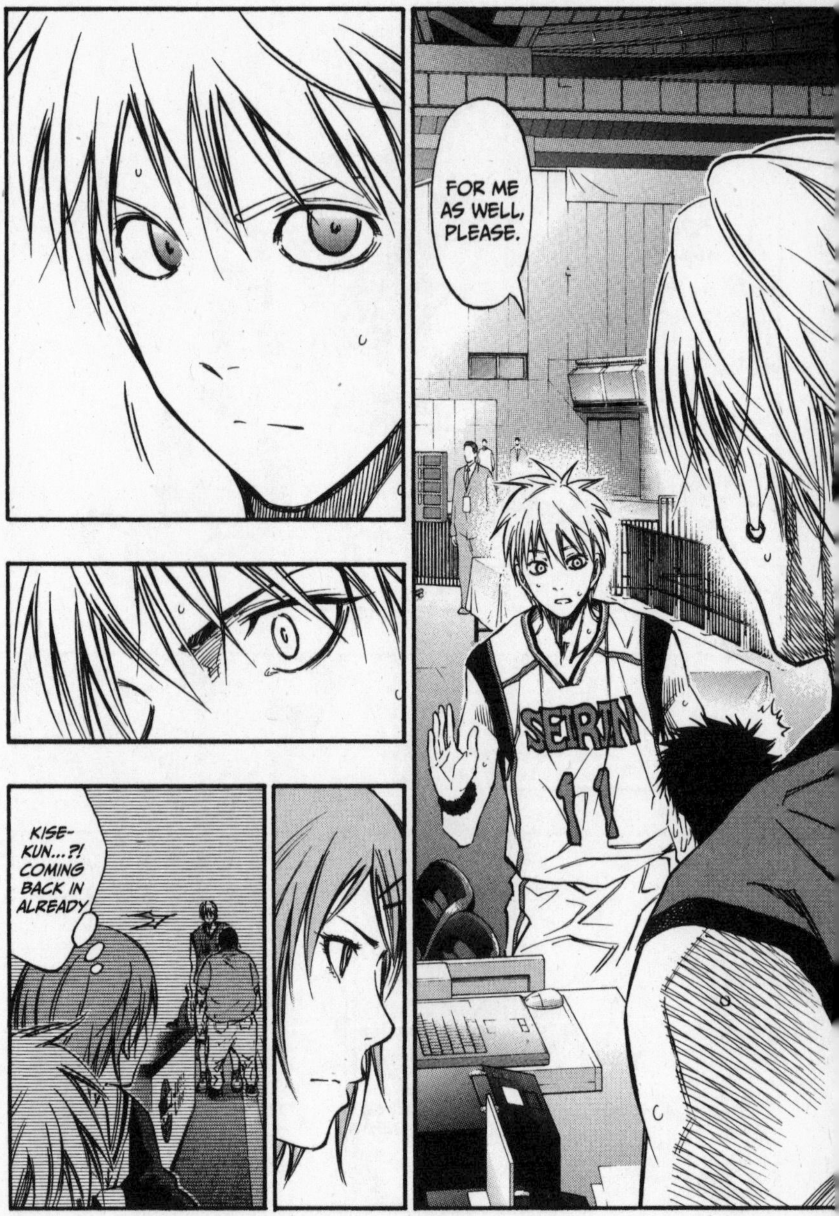
FOR ME AS WELL, PLEASE.
KISE-KUN...?! COMING BACK IN ALREADY

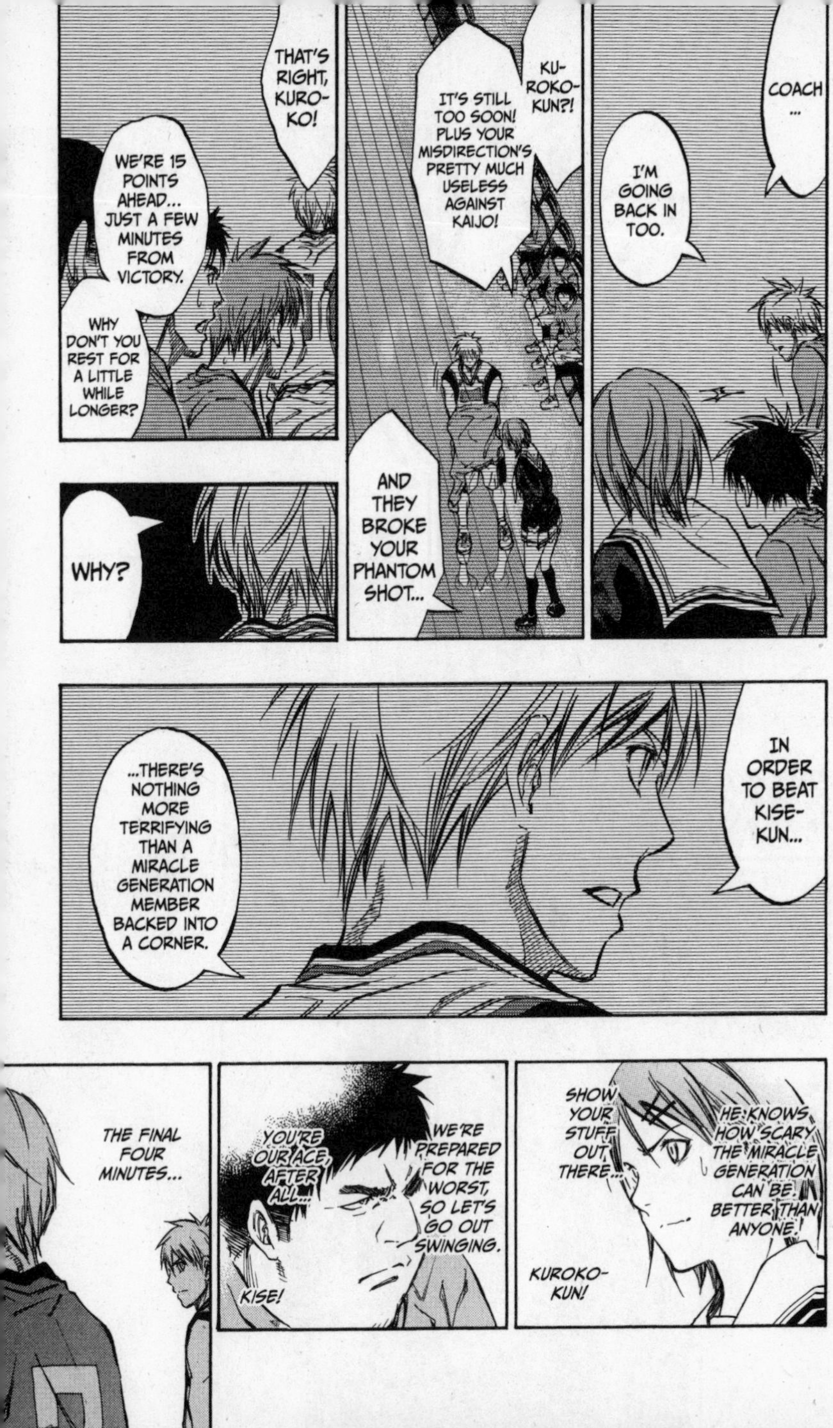
COACH ...
I'M GOING BACK IN TOO.
KUROKO-KUN?!
IT'S STILL TOO SOON! PLUS YOUR MISDIRECTION'S PRETTY MUCH USELESS AGAINST KAIJO!
AND THEY BROKE YOUR PHANTOM SHOT...
THAT'S RIGHT, KUROKO!
WE'RE 15 POINTS AHEAD... JUST A FEW MINUTES FROM VICTORY.
WHY DON'T YOU REST FOR A LITTLE WHILE LONGER?
WHY?
IN ORDER TO BEAT KISE-KUN...
...THERE'S NOTHING MORE TERRIFYING THAN A MIRACLE GENERATION MEMBER BACKED INTO A CORNER.
HE KNOWS HOW SCARY THE MIRACLE GENERATION CAN BE. BETTER THAN ANYONE.
SHOW YOUR STUFF OUT THERE...
KUROKO-KUN!
WE'RE PREPARED FOR THE WORST, SO LET'S GO OUT SWINGING.
YOU'RE OUR ACE, AFTER ALL...
KISE!
THE FINAL FOUR MINUTES...

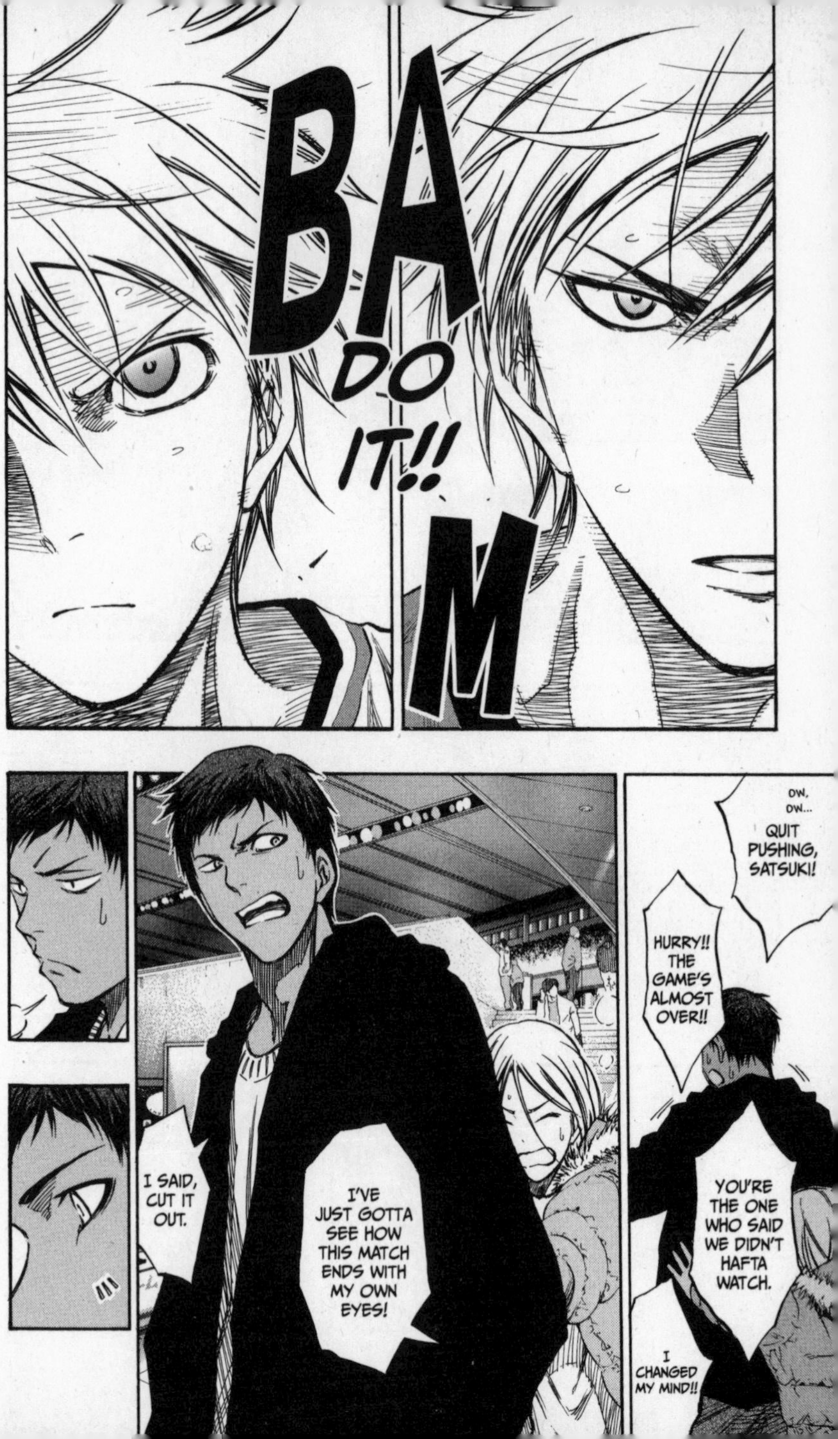
BA
DO IT!!
M
OW, OW... QUIT PUSHING, SATSUKI!
HURRY!! THE GAME'S ALMOST OVER!!
YOU'RE THE ONE WHO SAID WE DIDN'T HAFTA WATCH.
I CHANGED MY MIND!!
I'VE JUST GOTTA SEE HOW THIS MATCH ENDS WITH MY OWN EYES!
I SAID, CUT IT OUT.

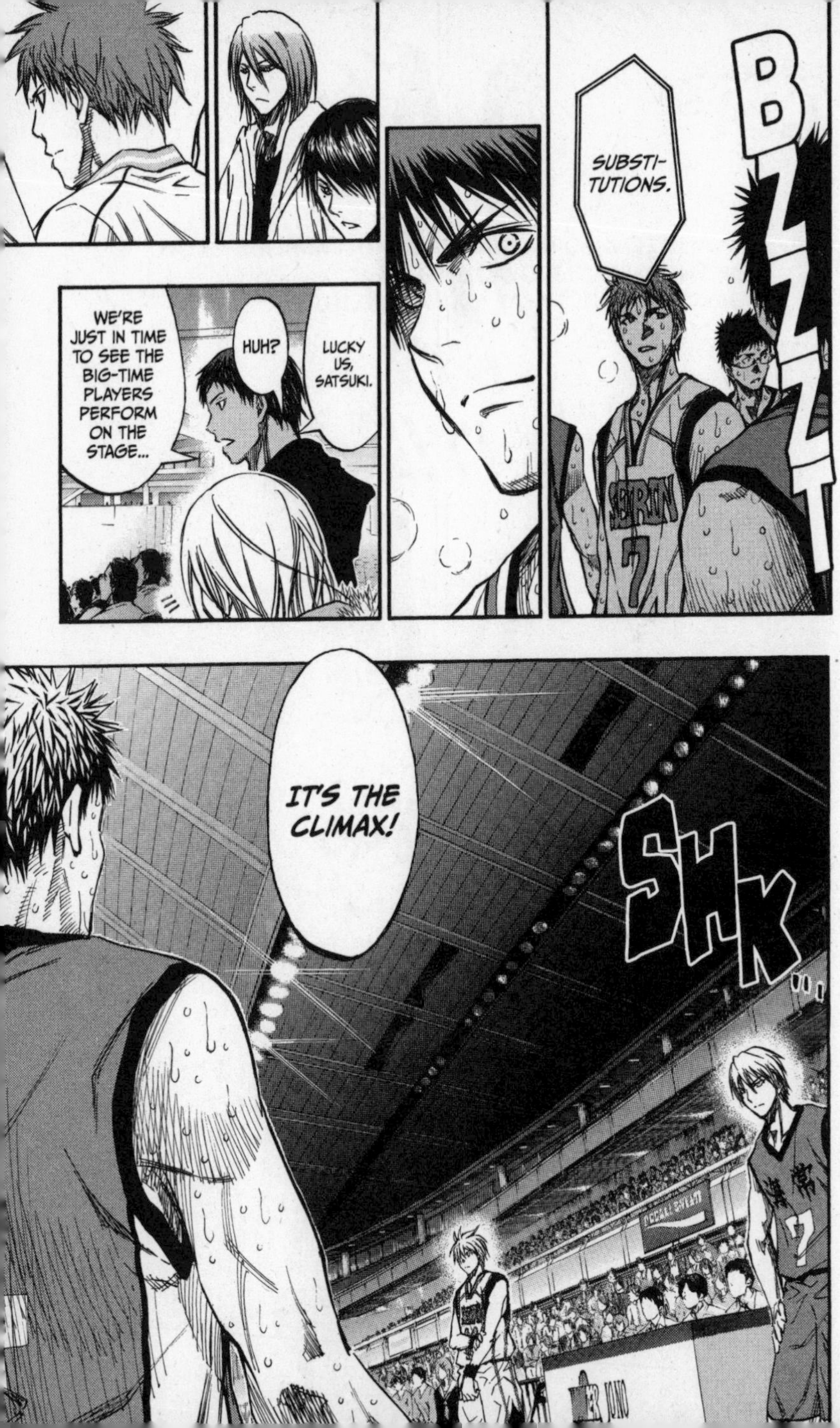
BZZZT
SUBSTI-TUTIONS.
LUCKY US, SATSUKI.
HUH?
WE'RE JUST IN TIME TO SEE THE BIG-TIME PLAYERS PERFORM ON THE STAGE...
IT'S THE CLIMAX!
SHK...

KUROKO'S BASKETBALL Q&A
W/ HALFWAY-DECENT ANSWERS

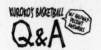

Q. **I WANT TO KNOW WHAT SORT OF FAMILIES EACH OF THE MIRACLE GENNERS HAVE.**
(SAKURAKO FROM SAITAMA PREFECTURE)

A. AKASHI-> SINGLE FATHER
KISE-> FATHER, MOTHER, TWO OLDER SISTERS
MURASAKIBARA-> FATHER, MOTHER, THREE OLDER BROTHERS, ONE OLDER SISTER
MOMOI-> FATHER, MOTHER
AOMINE-> FATHER, MOTHER
MIDORIMA-> FATHER, MOTHER, ONE YOUNGER SISTER
KUROKO-> FATHER, MOTHER, GRANDMOTHER
HAIZAKI-> SINGLE MOTHER, ONE OLDER BROTHER

KUROKO'S BASKETBALL BLOOPERS
TAKE 2

I'VE JUST GOTTA SEE HOW THIS MATCH ENDS WITH MY OWN EYES!
I SAID, CUT IT OUT.
OW... HEY!
HUH?
YOU TRYIN' TO NAIL ME INTO THIS WALL, SATSU-KI?!
OH.
COULDN'T SEE WHERE WE WERE GOING.

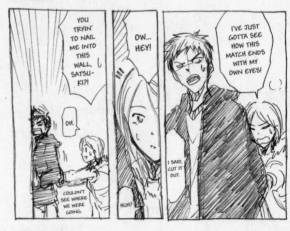

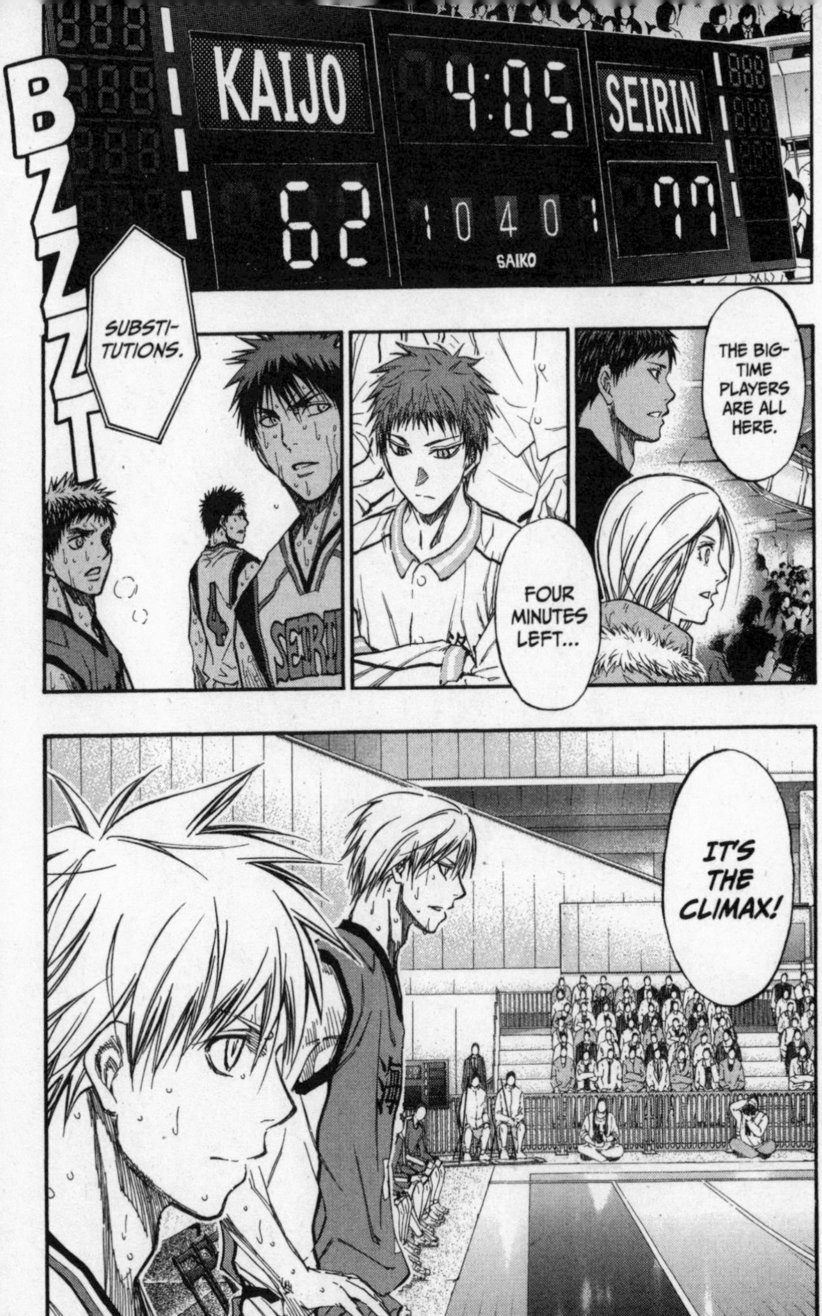
BZZZT
KAIJO
4:05
SEIRIN
62
77
SAIKO
SUBSTI-TUTIONS.
THE BIG-TIME PLAYERS ARE ALL HERE.
FOUR MINUTES LEFT...
IT'S THE CLIMAX!

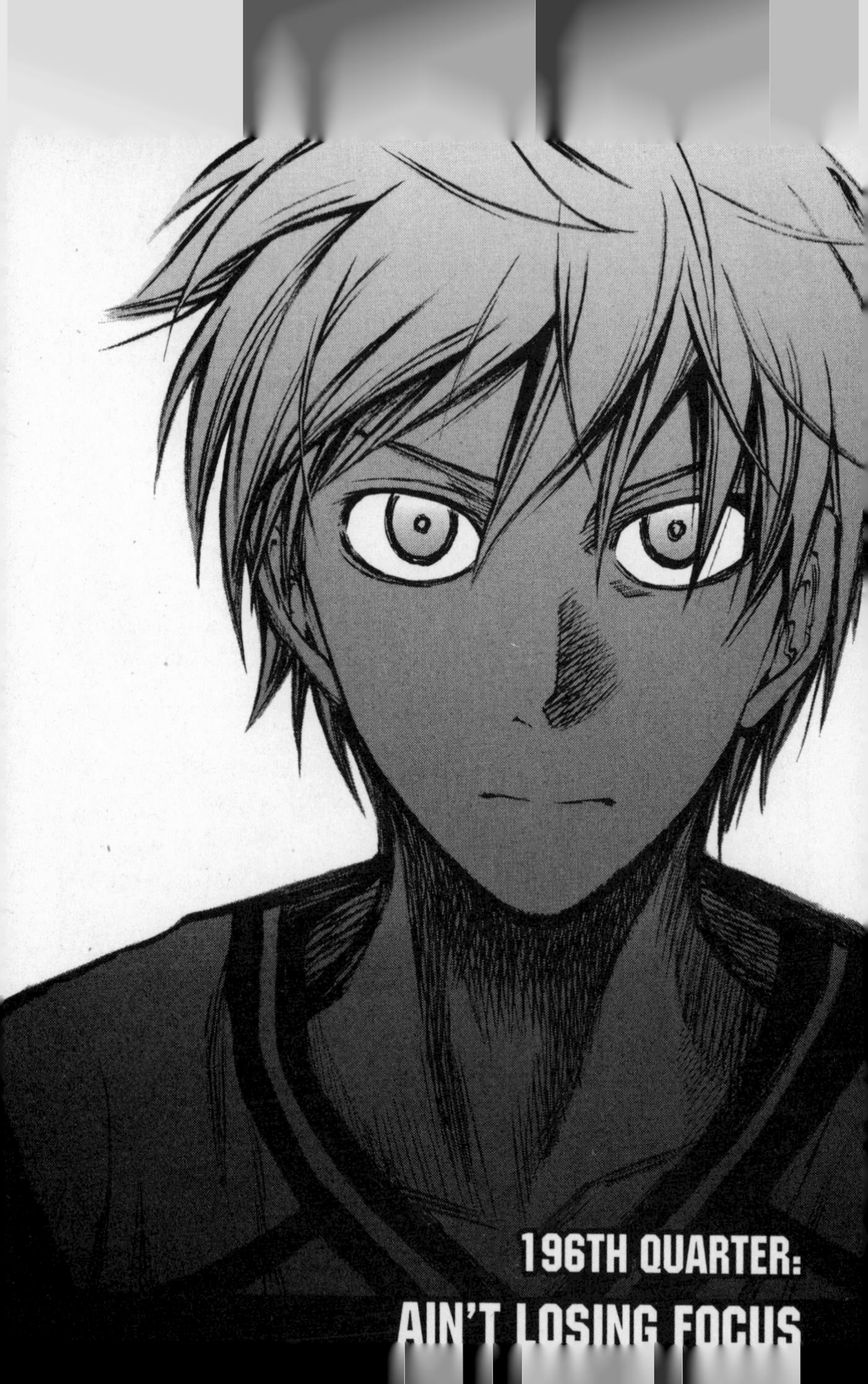
196TH QUARTER:
AIN'T LOSING FOCUS

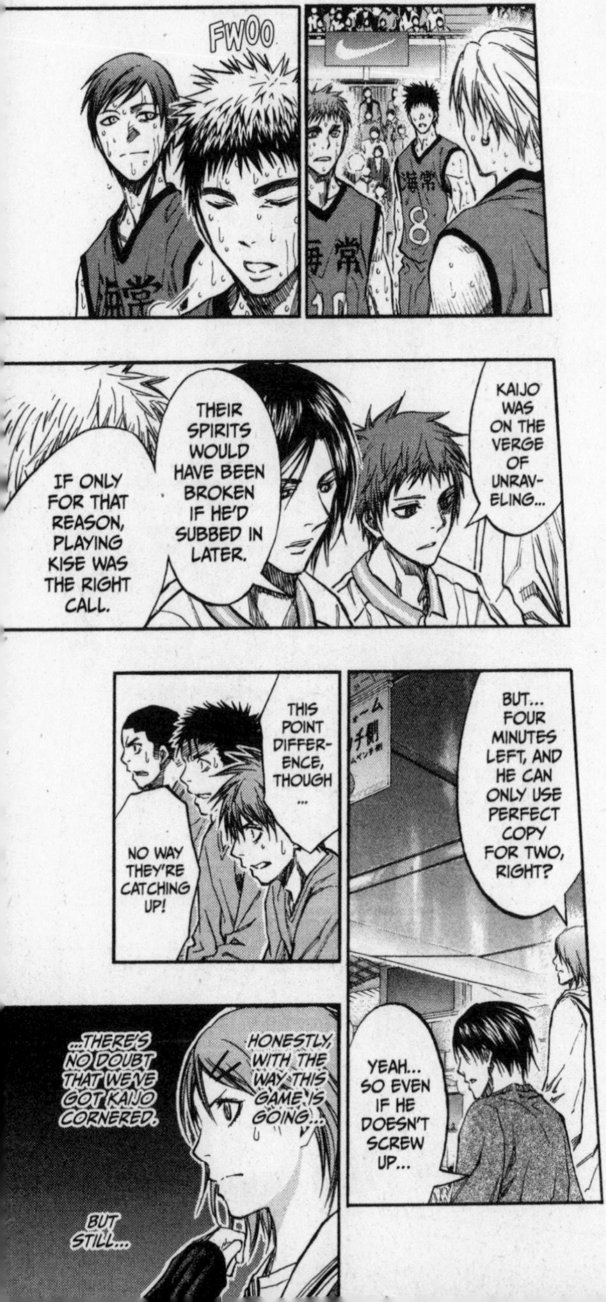
FWOO
KAIJO WAS ON THE VERGE OF UNRAVELING...
THEIR SPIRITS WOULD HAVE BEEN BROKEN IF HE'D SUBBED IN LATER.
IF ONLY FOR THAT REASON, PLAYING KISE WAS THE RIGHT CALL.
BUT... FOUR MINUTES LEFT, AND HE CAN ONLY USE PERFECT COPY FOR TWO, RIGHT?
YEAH... SO EVEN IF HE DOESN'T SCREW UP...
THIS POINT DIFFERENCE, THOUGH...
NO WAY THEY'RE CATCHING UP!
HONESTLY, WITH THE WAY THIS GAME IS GOING...
...THERE'S NO DOUBT THAT WE'VE GOT KAIJO CORNERED.
BUT STILL...

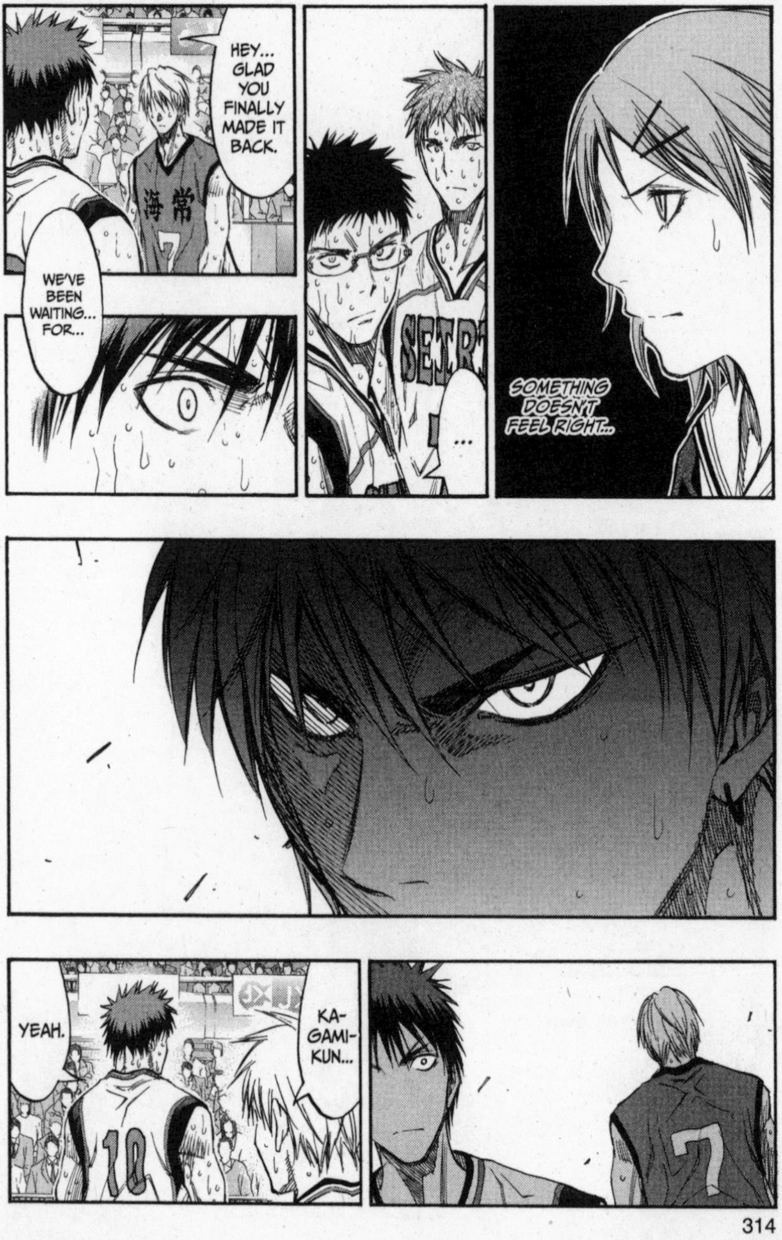
SOMETHING DOESN'T FEEL RIGHT...
...
HEY... GLAD YOU FINALLY MADE IT BACK.
WE'VE BEEN WAITING... FOR...
KA-GAMI-KUN...
YEAH.

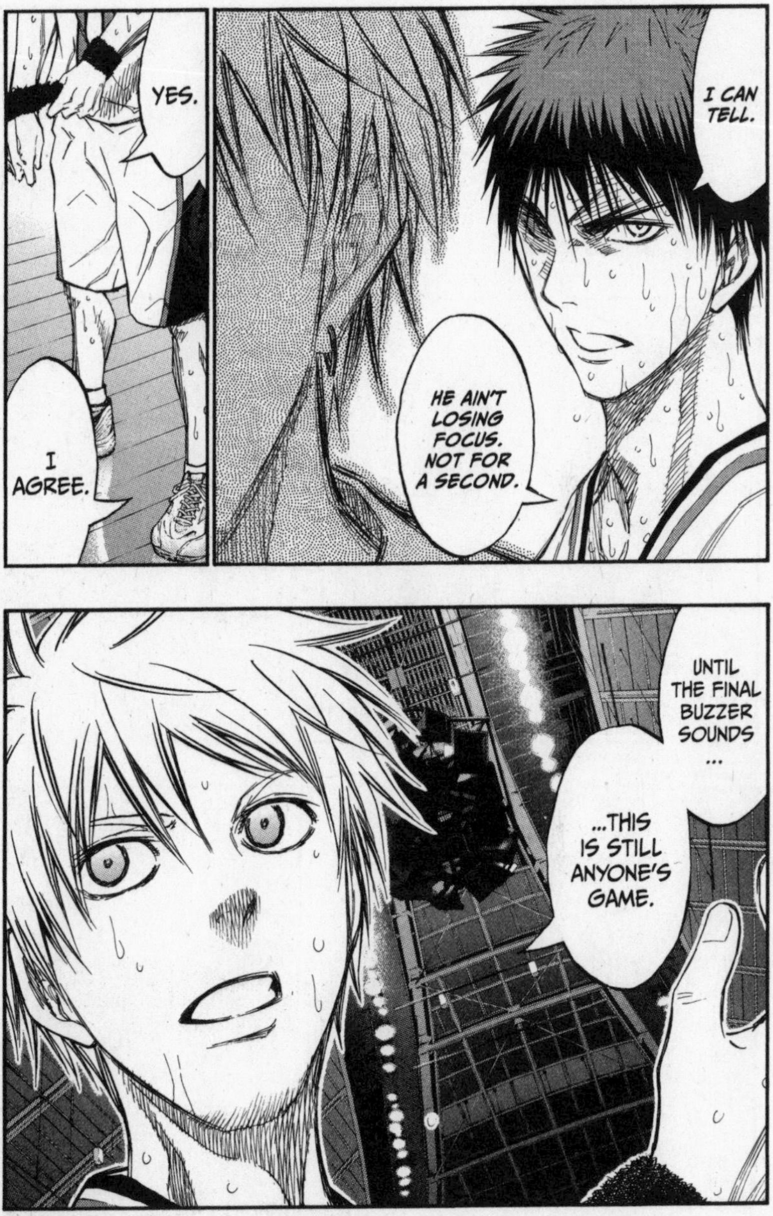
I CAN TELL.
HE AIN'T LOSING FOCUS. NOT FOR A SECOND.
YES.
I AGREE.
UNTIL THE FINAL BUZZER SOUNDS...
...THIS IS STILL ANYONE'S GAME.

SHK

RIGHT!

SHK

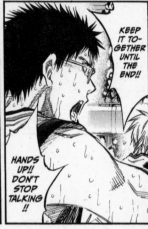

KEEP IT TO- GETHER UNTIL THE END!!

HANDS UP!! DON'T STOP TALKING !!

YEAH

I KNEW IT...

ALL OF KAIJO'S HOPES REST WITH HIM!!

FWIP

HEY !!

TCH!

GUH ...

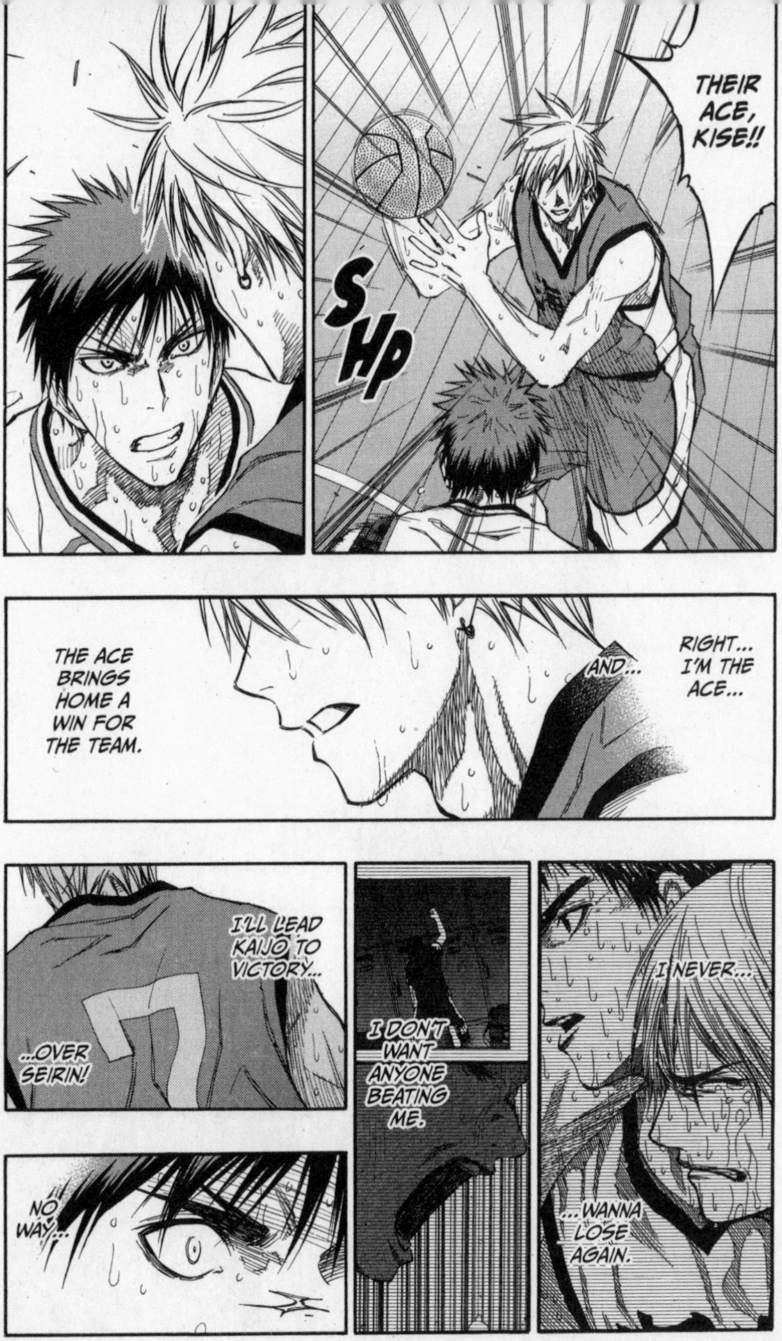
THEIR ACE, KISE!!
SHP
RIGHT... I'M THE ACE...
AND...
THE ACE BRINGS HOME A WIN FOR THE TEAM.
I NEVER...
...WANNA LOSE AGAIN.
I DON'T WANT ANYONE BEATING ME.
I'LL LEAD KAIJO TO VICTORY...
...OVER SEIRIN!
NO WAY...

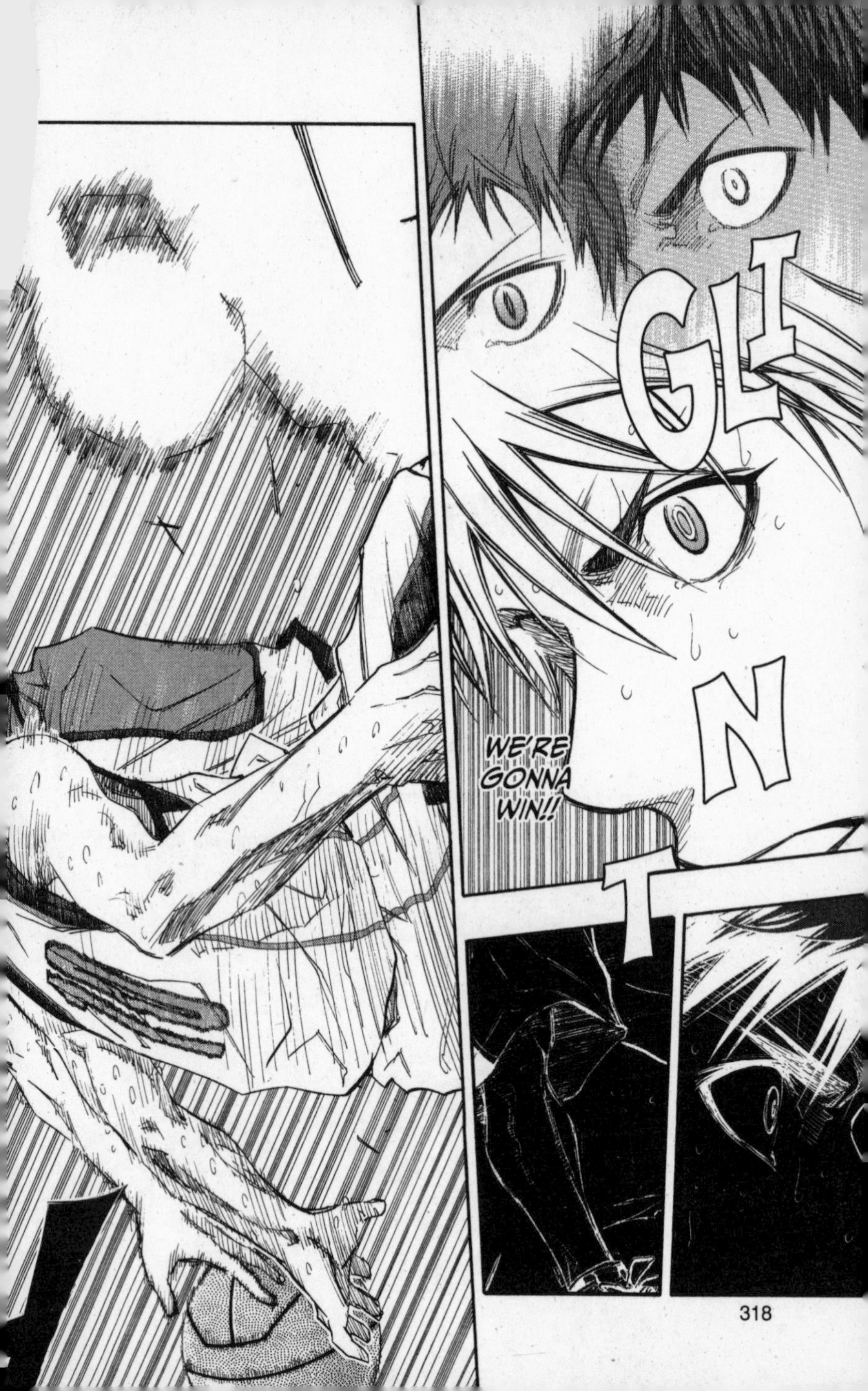
GLINT
WE'RE GONNA WIN!!

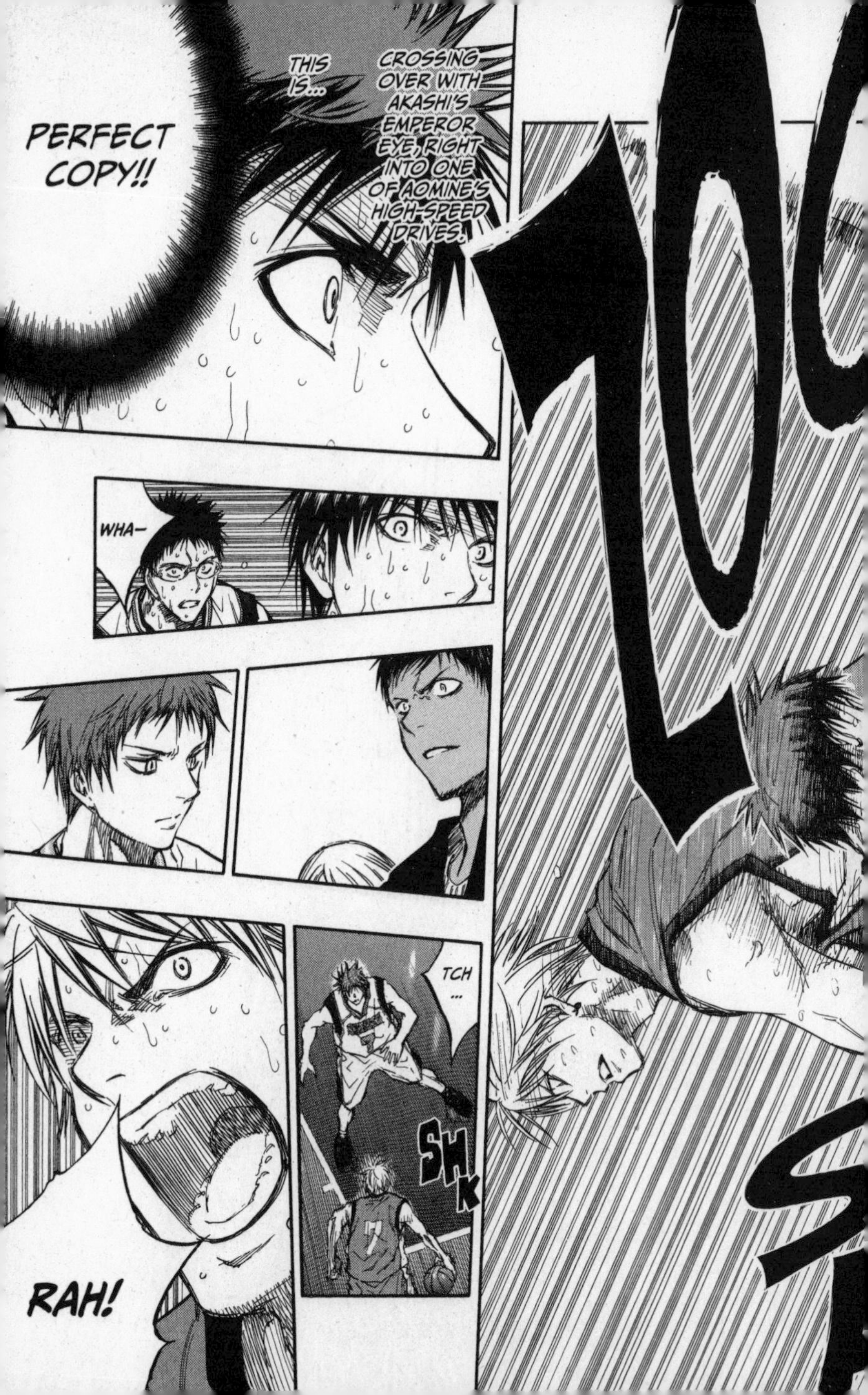
THIS IS...
CROSSING OVER WITH AKASHI'S EMPEROR EYE, RIGHT INTO ONE OF AOMINE'S HIGH-SPEED DRIVES.
PERFECT COPY!!
WHA-
TCH...
SHK
RAH!

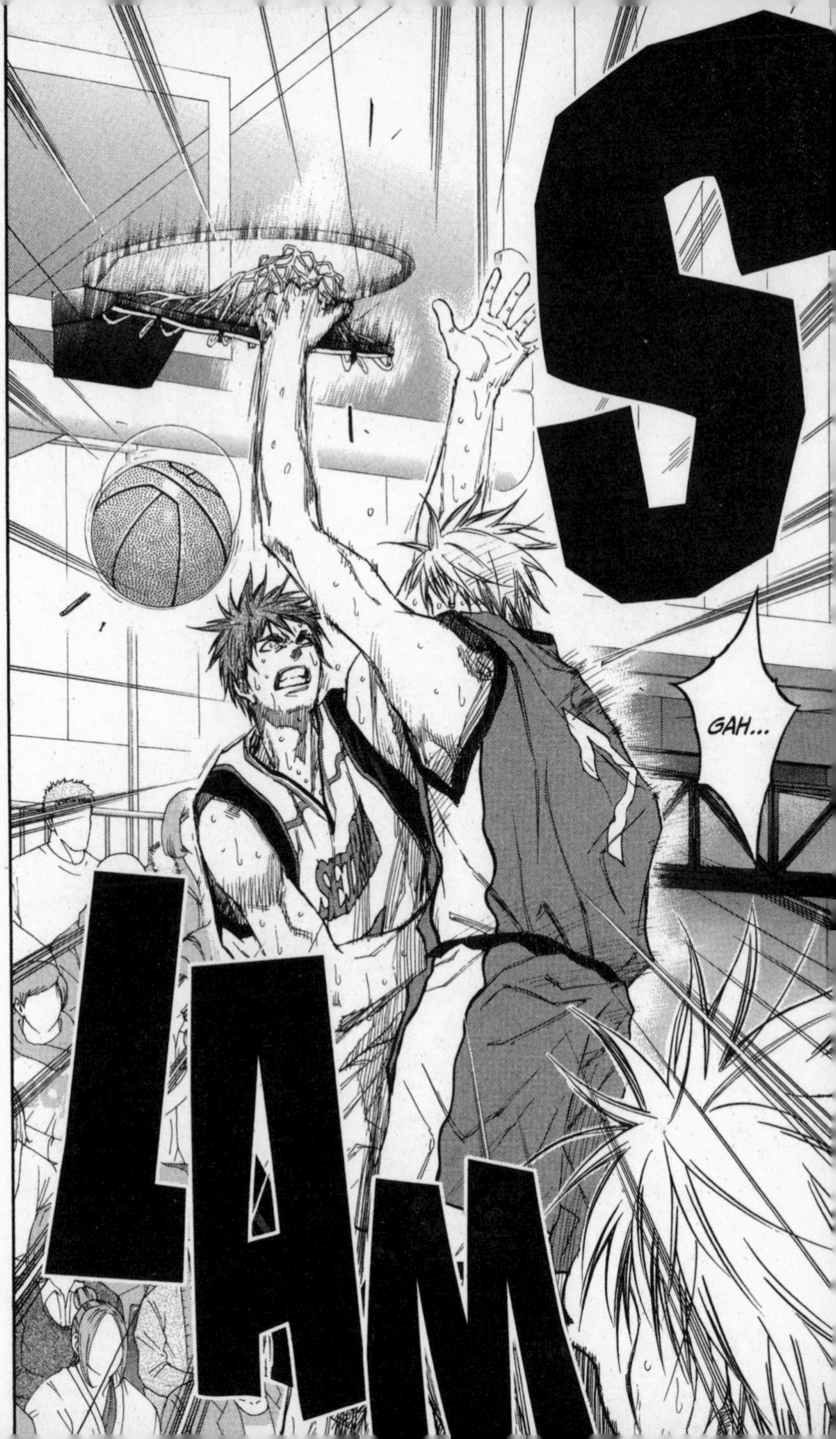
S
GAH...
LAM

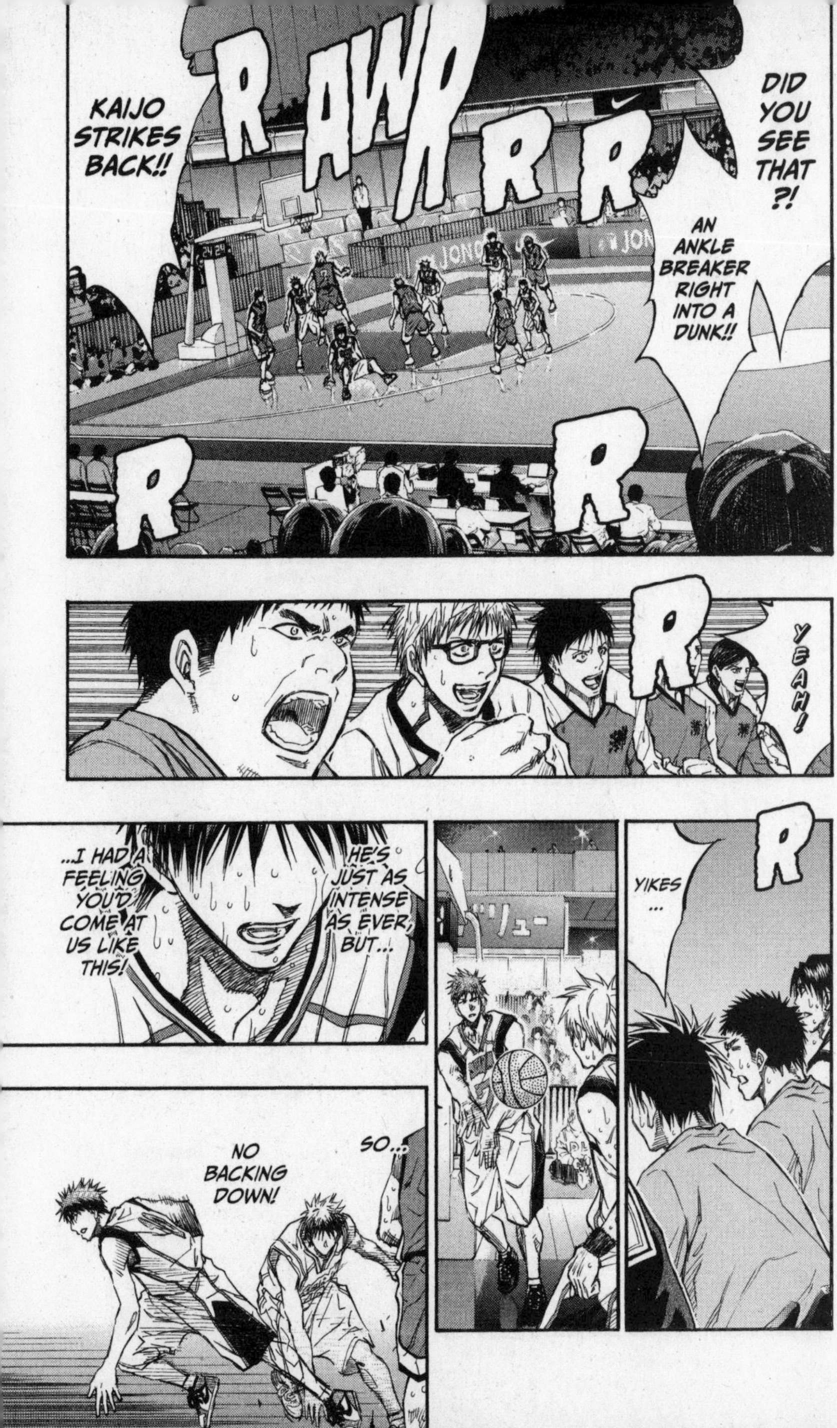
DID YOU SEE THAT?!
AN ANKLE BREAKER RIGHT INTO A DUNK!!
RAWRRRR
KAIJO STRIKES BACK!!
R
YEAH!
R
YIKES...
HE'S JUST AS INTENSE AS EVER, BUT...
...I HAD A FEELING YOU'D COME AT US LIKE THIS!
SO...
NO BACKING DOWN!

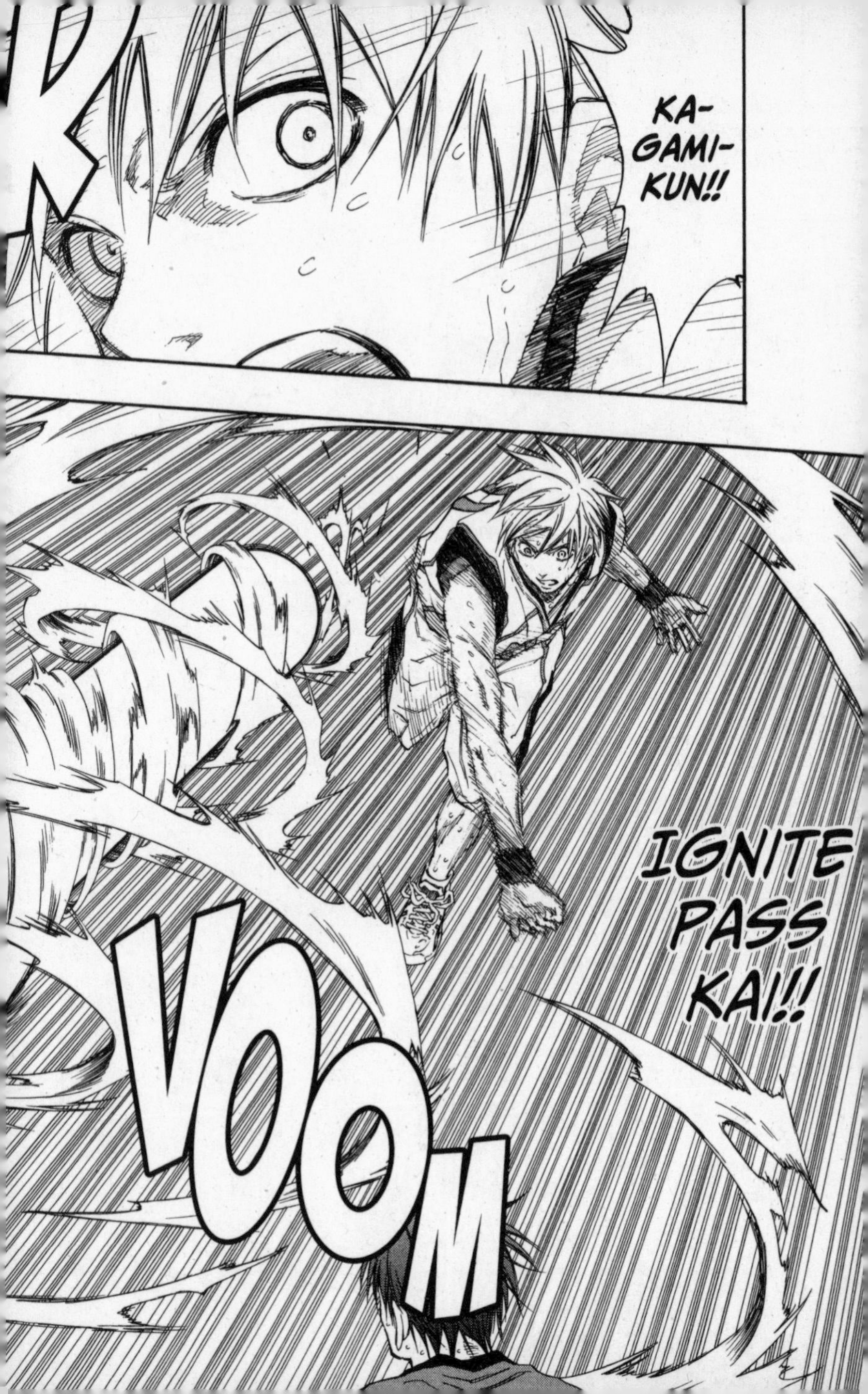
KA-
GAMI-
KUN!!
IGNITE
PASS
KAI!!
VOOM

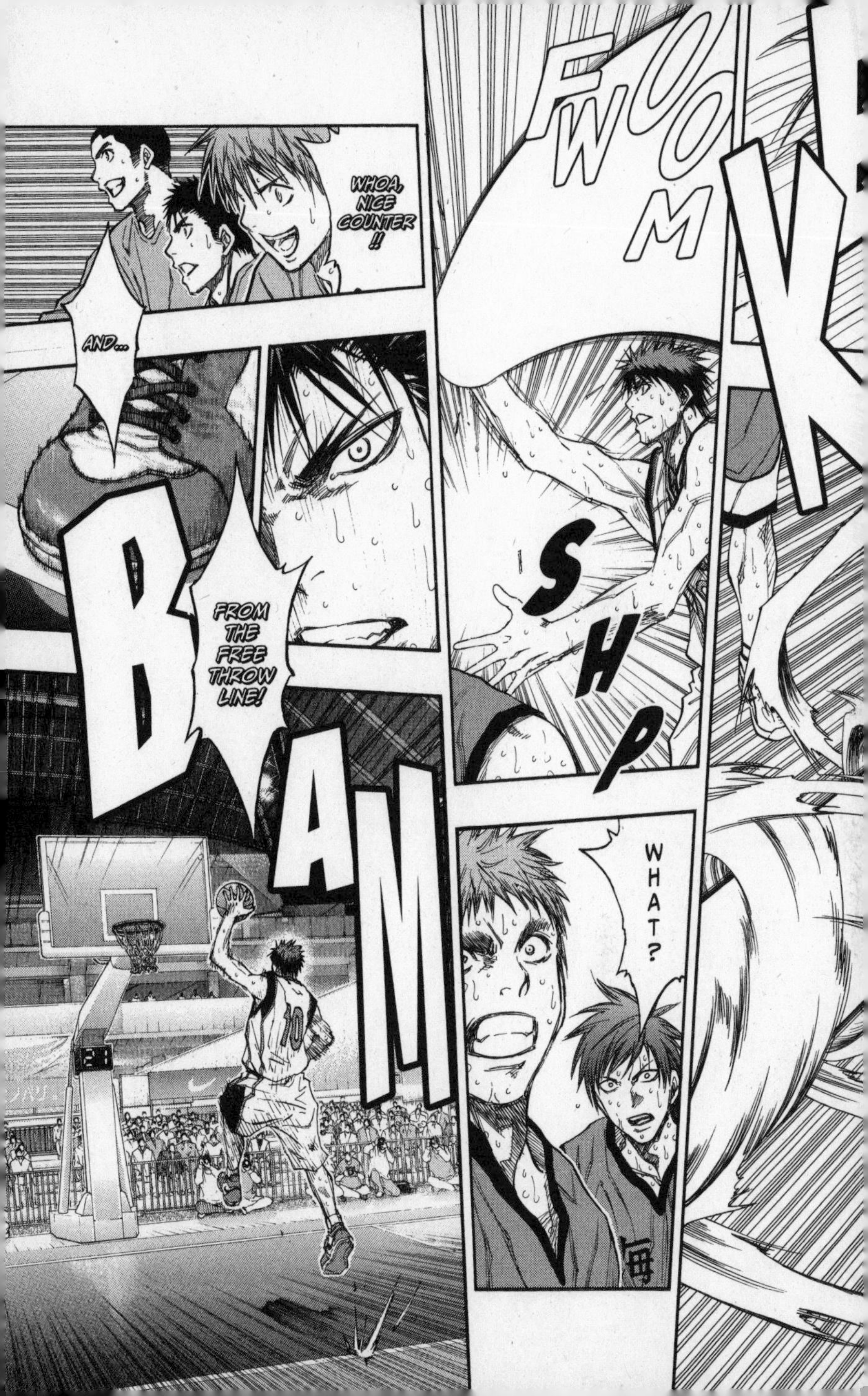
FWOOOM
SHP
WHAT?
WHOA, NICE COUNTER!!
AND...
FROM THE FREE THROW LINE!
BAM

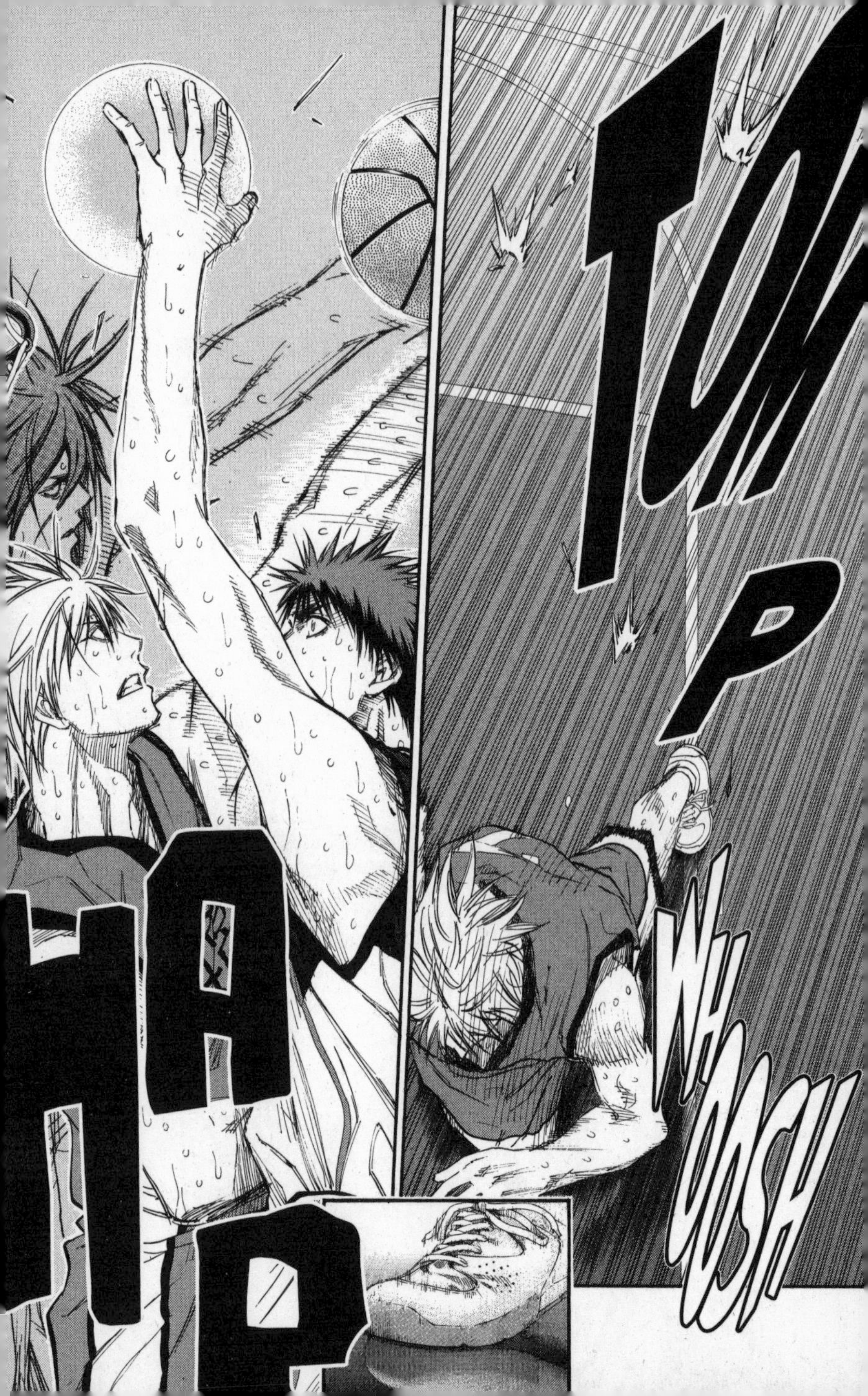
TUMP
WHOOSH
HAP

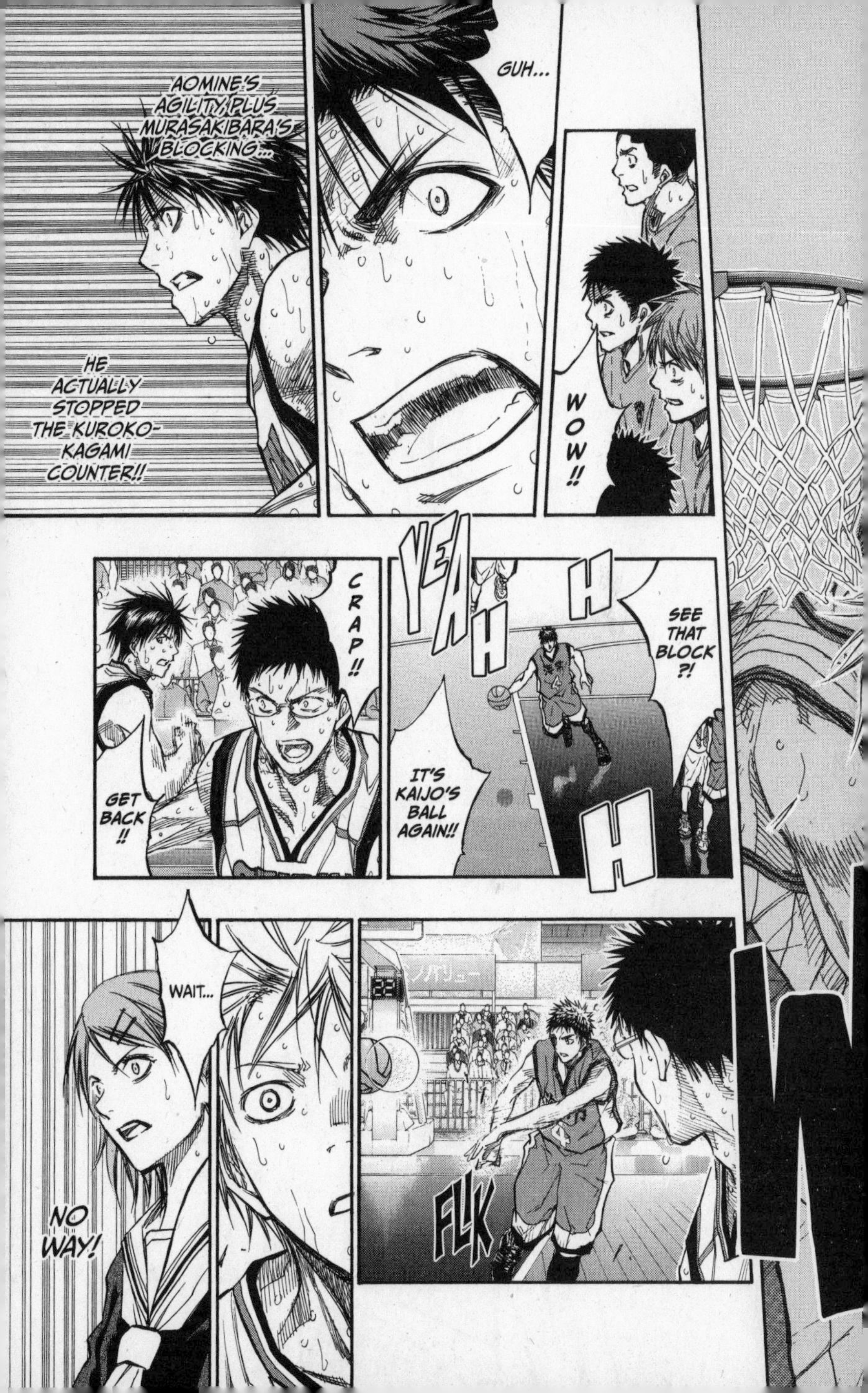
WOW!!
GUH...
AOMINE'S AGILITY PLUS MURASAKIBARA'S BLOCKING...
HE ACTUALLY STOPPED THE KUROKO-KAGAMI COUNTER!!
YEAHHHH
SEE THAT BLOCK?!
IT'S KAIJO'S BALL AGAIN!!
CRAP!!
GET BACK!!
FLIK
WAIT...
NO WAY!

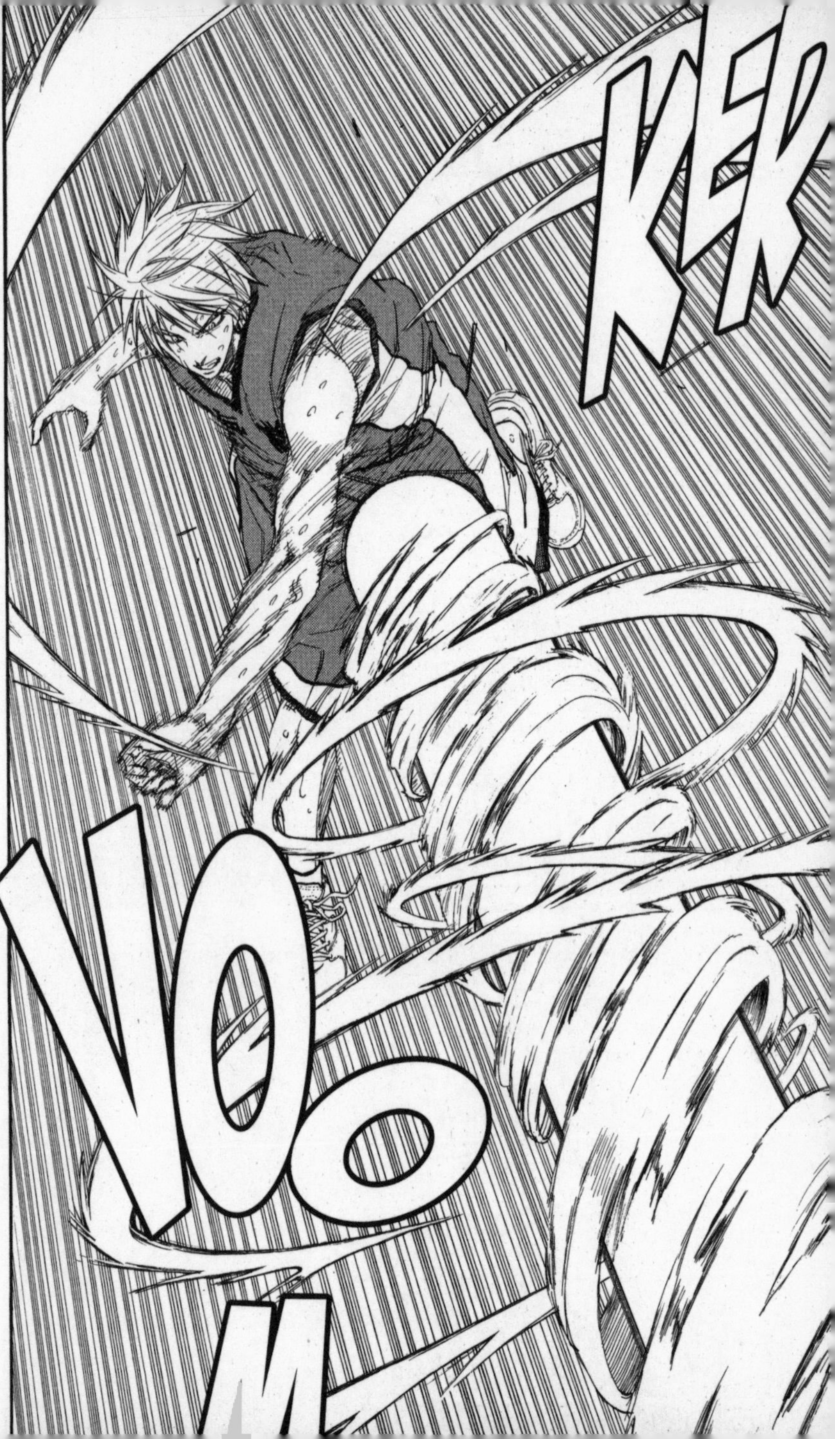
VOOM

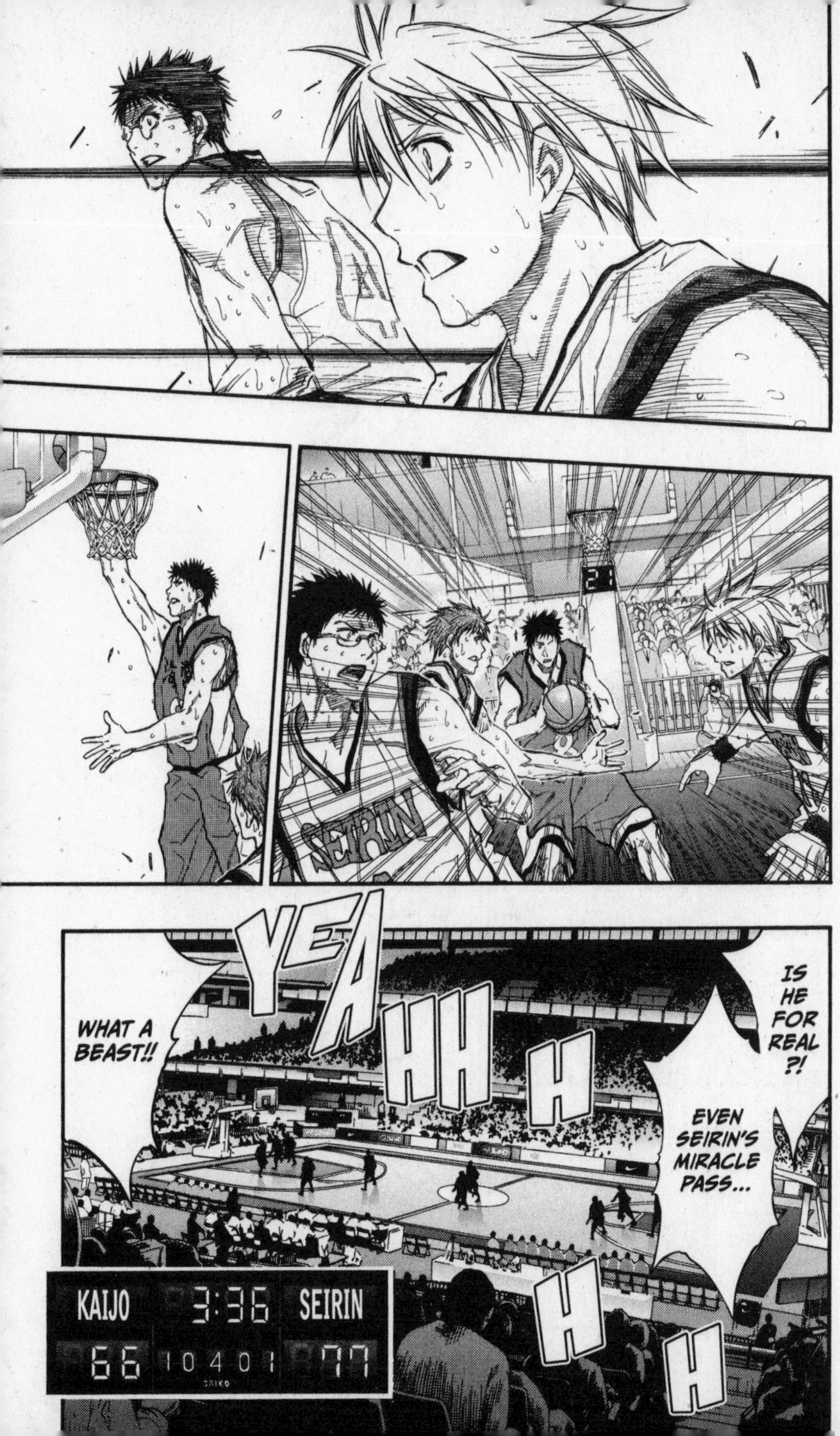
SEIRIN
IS HE FOR REAL?!
YEAHHHHH
WHAT A BEAST!!
EVEN SEIRIN'S MIRACLE PASS...
KAIJO 3:36 SEIRIN
66 10401 77

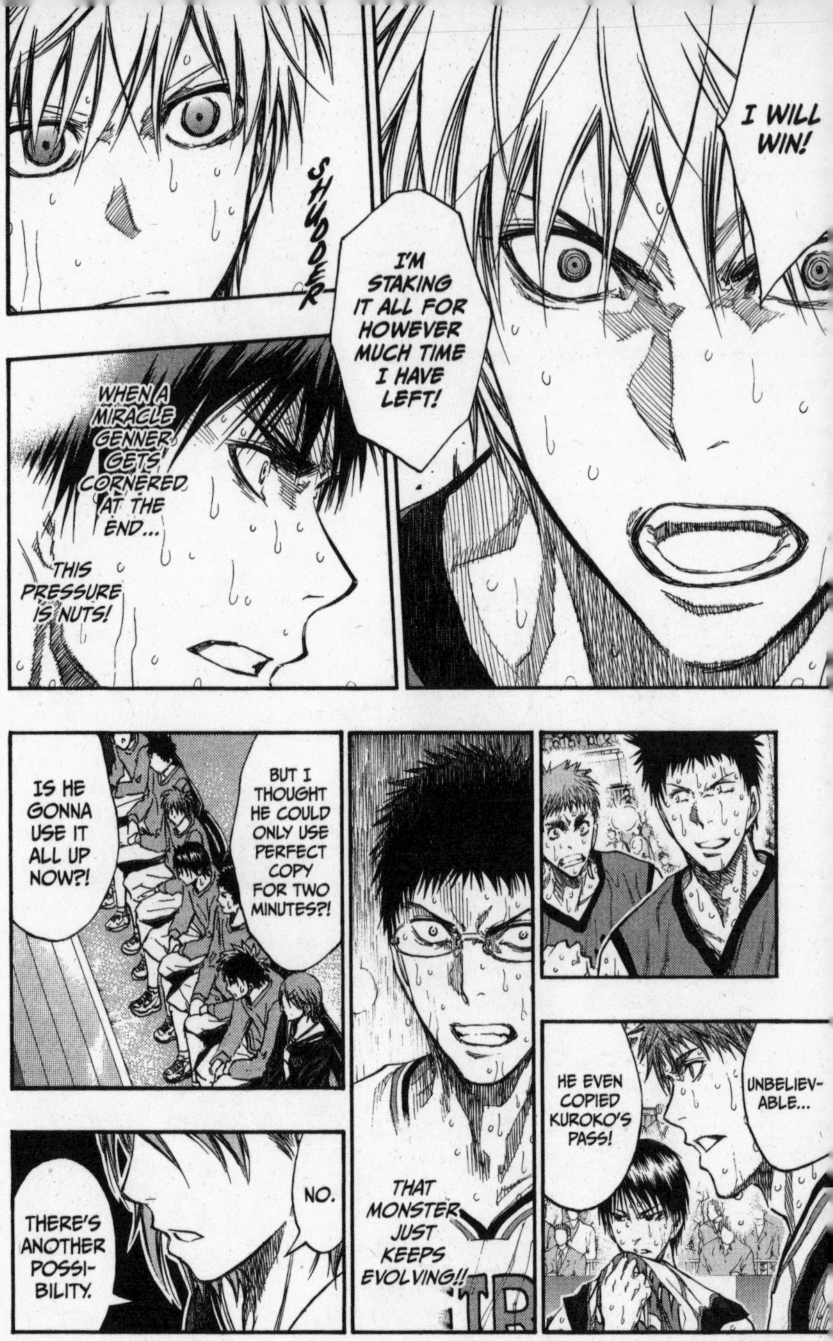
I WILL WIN!
I'M STAKING IT ALL FOR HOWEVER MUCH TIME I HAVE LEFT!
SHUDDER
WHEN A MIRACLE GENNER GETS CORNERED AT THE END...
THIS PRESSURE IS NUTS!
UNBELIEVABLE...
HE EVEN COPIED KUROKO'S PASS!
THAT MONSTER JUST KEEPS EVOLVING!!
BUT I THOUGHT HE COULD ONLY USE PERFECT COPY FOR TWO MINUTES?!
IS HE GONNA USE IT ALL UP NOW?!
NO.
THERE'S ANOTHER POSSIBILITY.

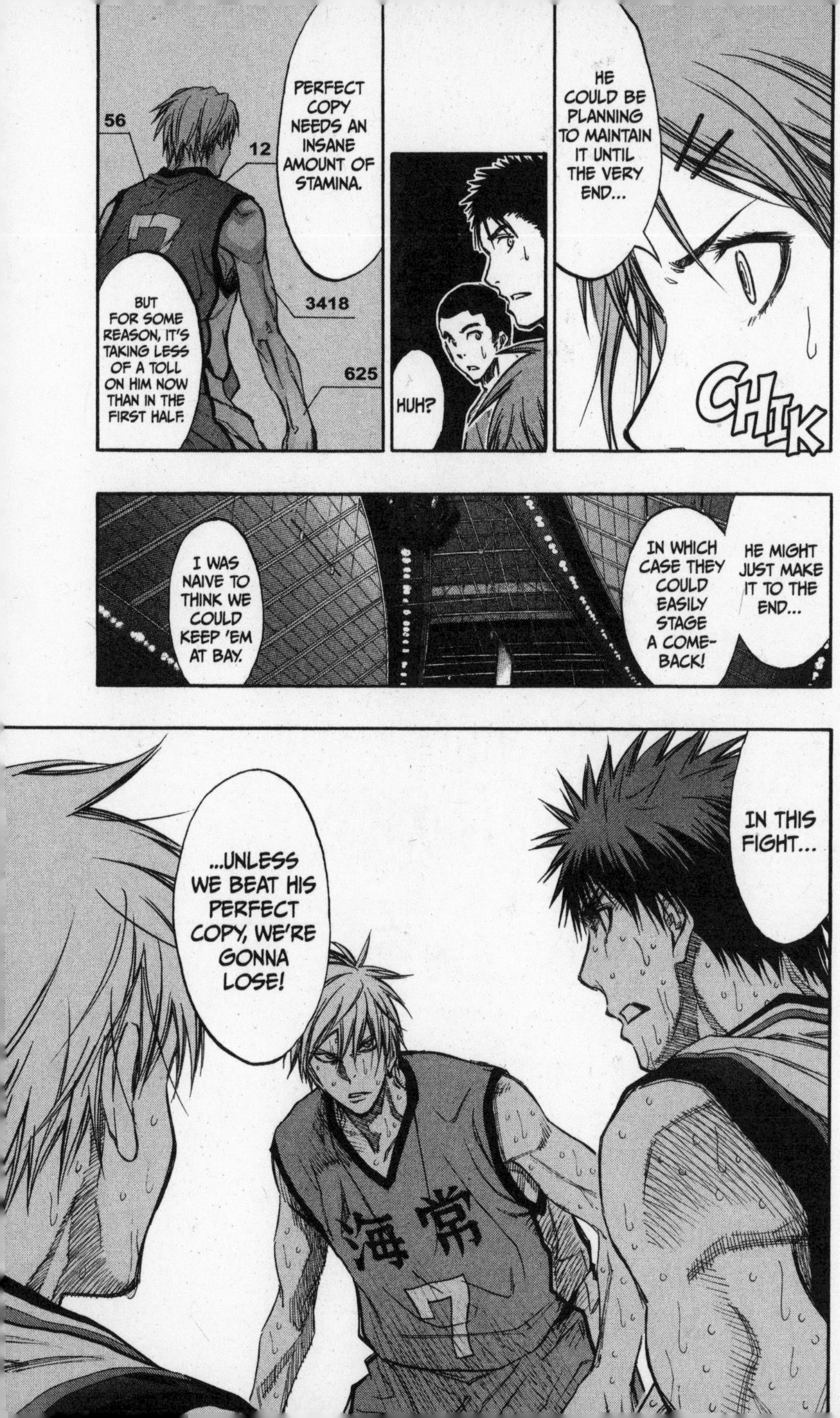
HE COULD BE PLANNING TO MAINTAIN IT UNTIL THE VERY END...
CHIK
HUH?
PERFECT COPY NEEDS AN INSANE AMOUNT OF STAMINA.
56
12
3418
625
BUT FOR SOME REASON, IT'S TAKING LESS OF A TOLL ON HIM NOW THAN IN THE FIRST HALF.
HE MIGHT JUST MAKE IT TO THE END...
IN WHICH CASE THEY COULD EASILY STAGE A COME-BACK!
I WAS NAIVE TO THINK WE COULD KEEP 'EM AT BAY.
IN THIS FIGHT...
...UNLESS WE BEAT HIS PERFECT COPY, WE'RE GONNA LOSE!
海常
7

KUROKO'S BASKETBALL BLOOPERS

TAKE 6

WAIT... I JUST CAUGHT AN IGNITE PASS FROM KISE AT FULL STRENGTH? I'M AMAZING!! COULD I ALSO BE ON PAR WITH THE MIRACLE GENERATION?!
JUST SHOOT ALREADY !!
KOBORI SENPAI!!
KISE
WHOAAA

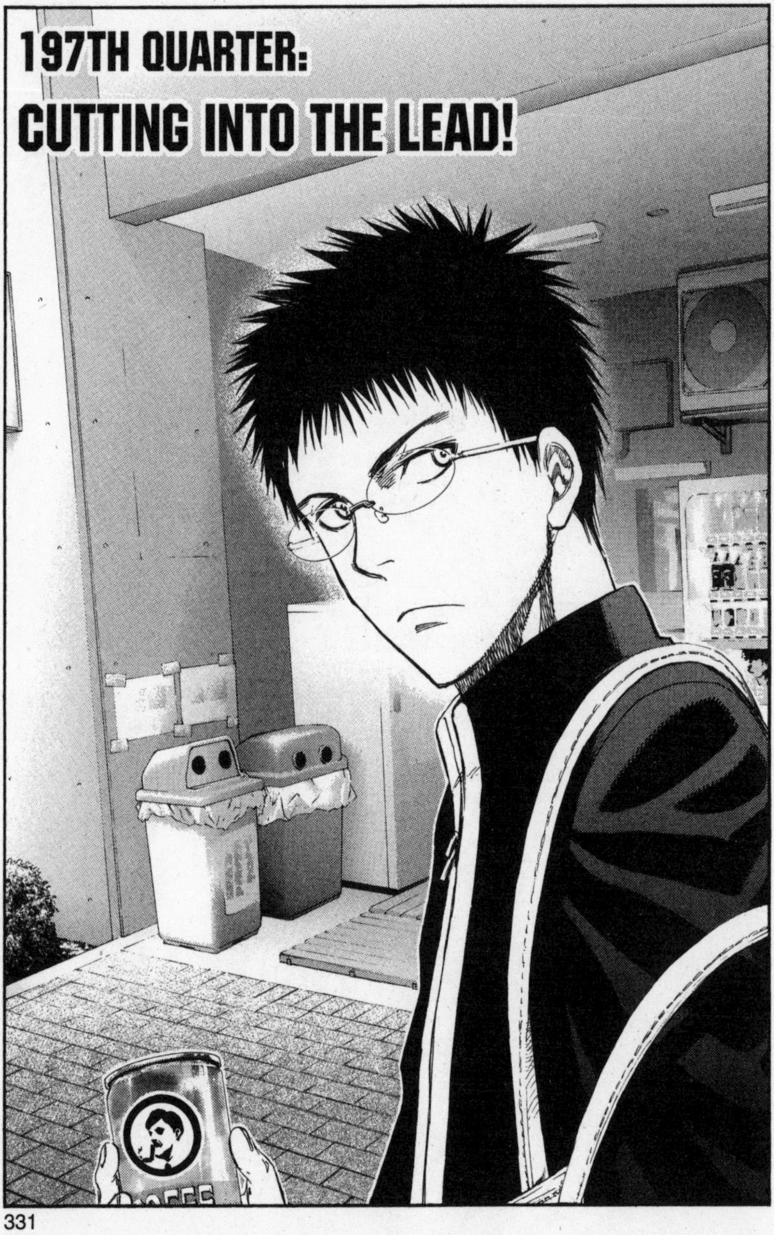
197TH QUARTER:
CUTTING INTO THE LEAD!

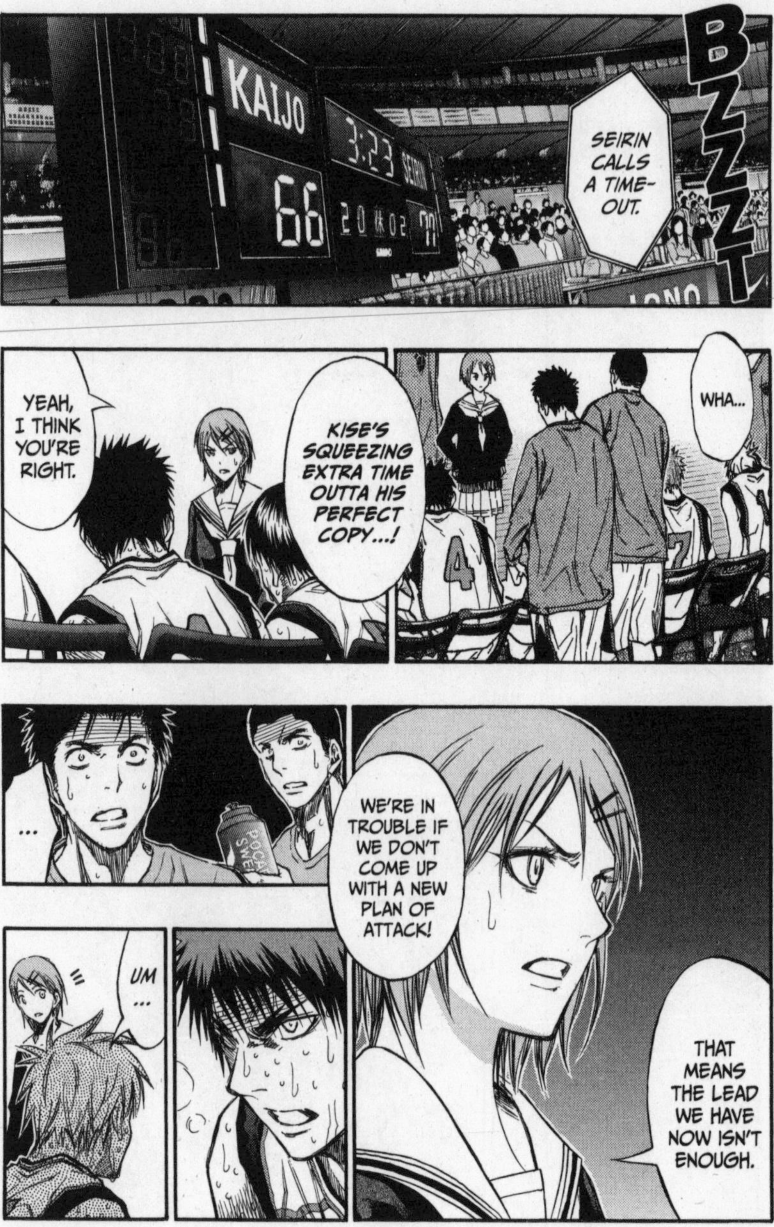
BZZZT
SEIRIN CALLS A TIME-OUT.
KAIJO
3:23
66
WHA...
KISE'S SQUEEZING EXTRA TIME OUTTA HIS PERFECT COPY...!
YEAH, I THINK YOU'RE RIGHT.
WE'RE IN TROUBLE IF WE DON'T COME UP WITH A NEW PLAN OF ATTACK!
THAT MEANS THE LEAD WE HAVE NOW ISN'T ENOUGH.
...
UM ...

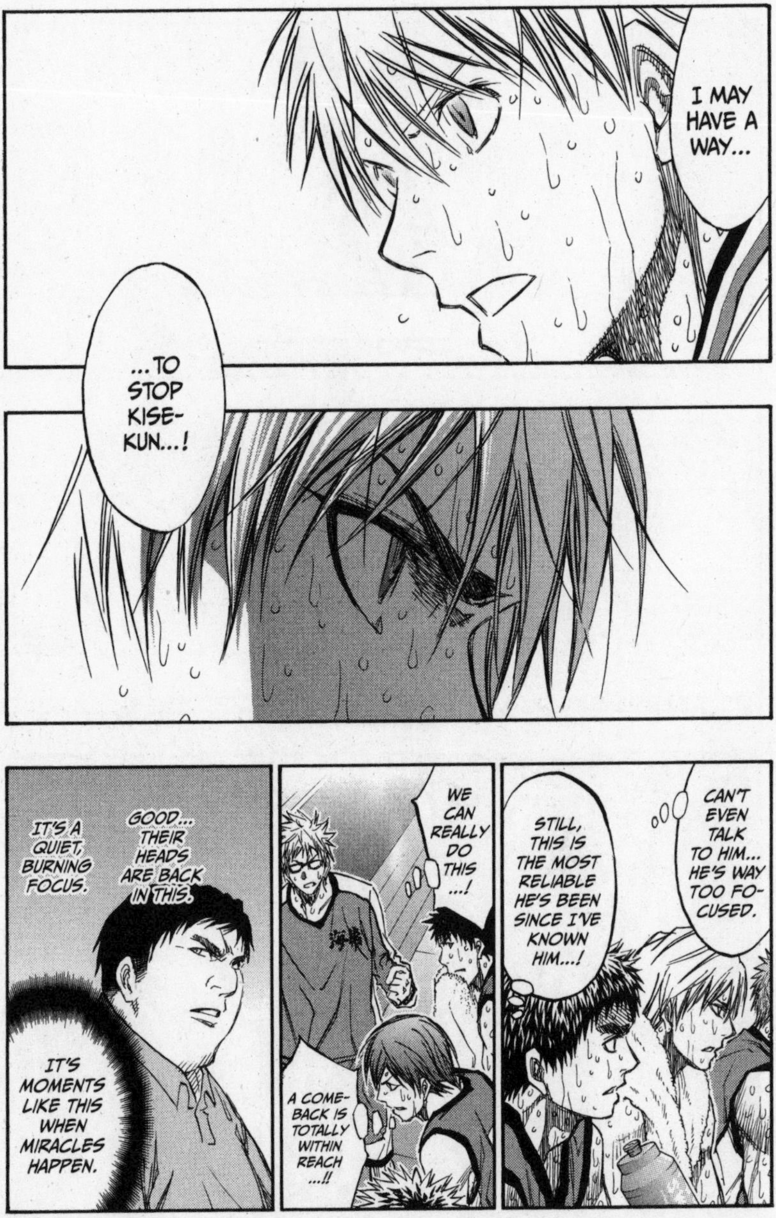
I MAY HAVE A WAY...
...TO STOP KISE-KUN...!
CAN'T EVEN TALK TO HIM... HE'S WAY TOO FO-CUSED.
STILL, THIS IS THE MOST RELIABLE HE'S BEEN SINCE I'VE KNOWN HIM...!
WE CAN REALLY DO THIS ...!
A COME-BACK IS TOTALLY WITHIN REACH ...!!
GOOD... THEIR HEADS ARE BACK IN THIS.
IT'S A QUIET, BURNING FOCUS.
IT'S MOMENTS LIKE THIS WHEN MIRACLES HAPPEN.

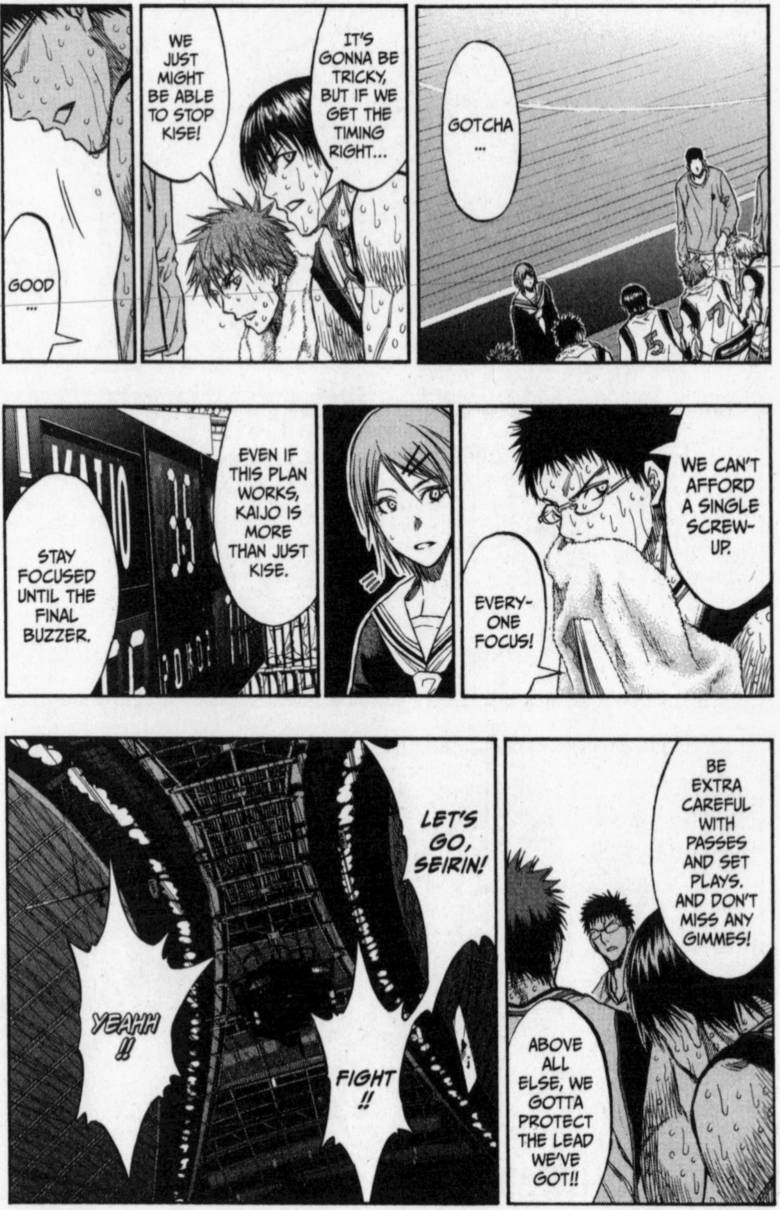
GOTCHA ...
IT'S GONNA BE TRICKY, BUT IF WE GET THE TIMING RIGHT...
WE JUST MIGHT BE ABLE TO STOP KISE!
GOOD ...
WE CAN'T AFFORD A SINGLE SCREW-UP.
EVERY-ONE FOCUS!
EVEN IF THIS PLAN WORKS, KAIJO IS MORE THAN JUST KISE.
STAY FOCUSED UNTIL THE FINAL BUZZER.
BE EXTRA CAREFUL WITH PASSES AND SET PLAYS. AND DON'T MISS ANY GIMMES!
ABOVE ALL ELSE, WE GOTTA PROTECT THE LEAD WE'VE GOT!!
LET'S GO, SEIRIN!
FIGHT !!
YEAHH !!

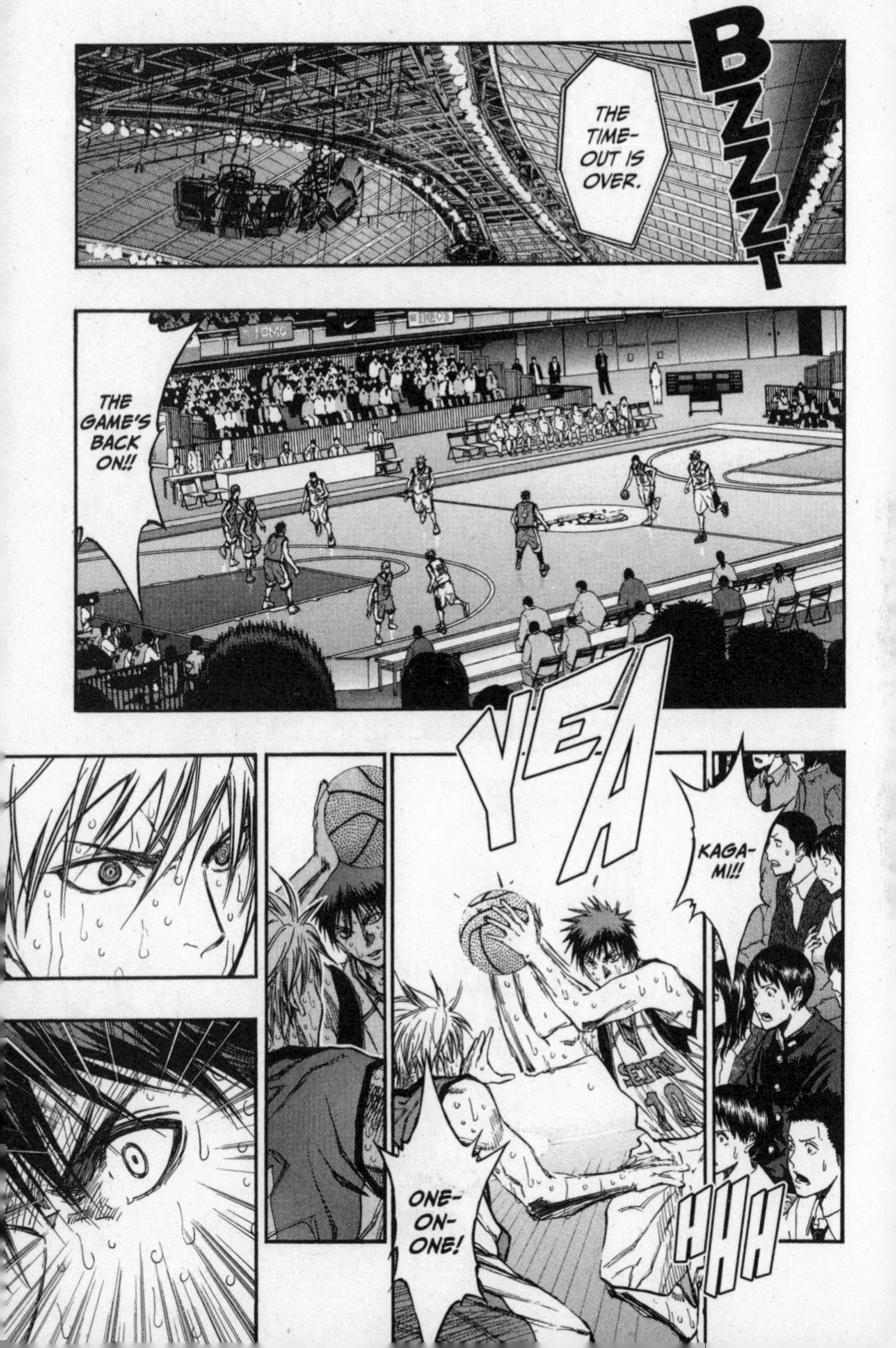
BZZZT
THE TIME-OUT IS OVER.
THE GAME'S BACK ON!!
YEAHHH
KAGAMI!!
ONE-ON-ONE!

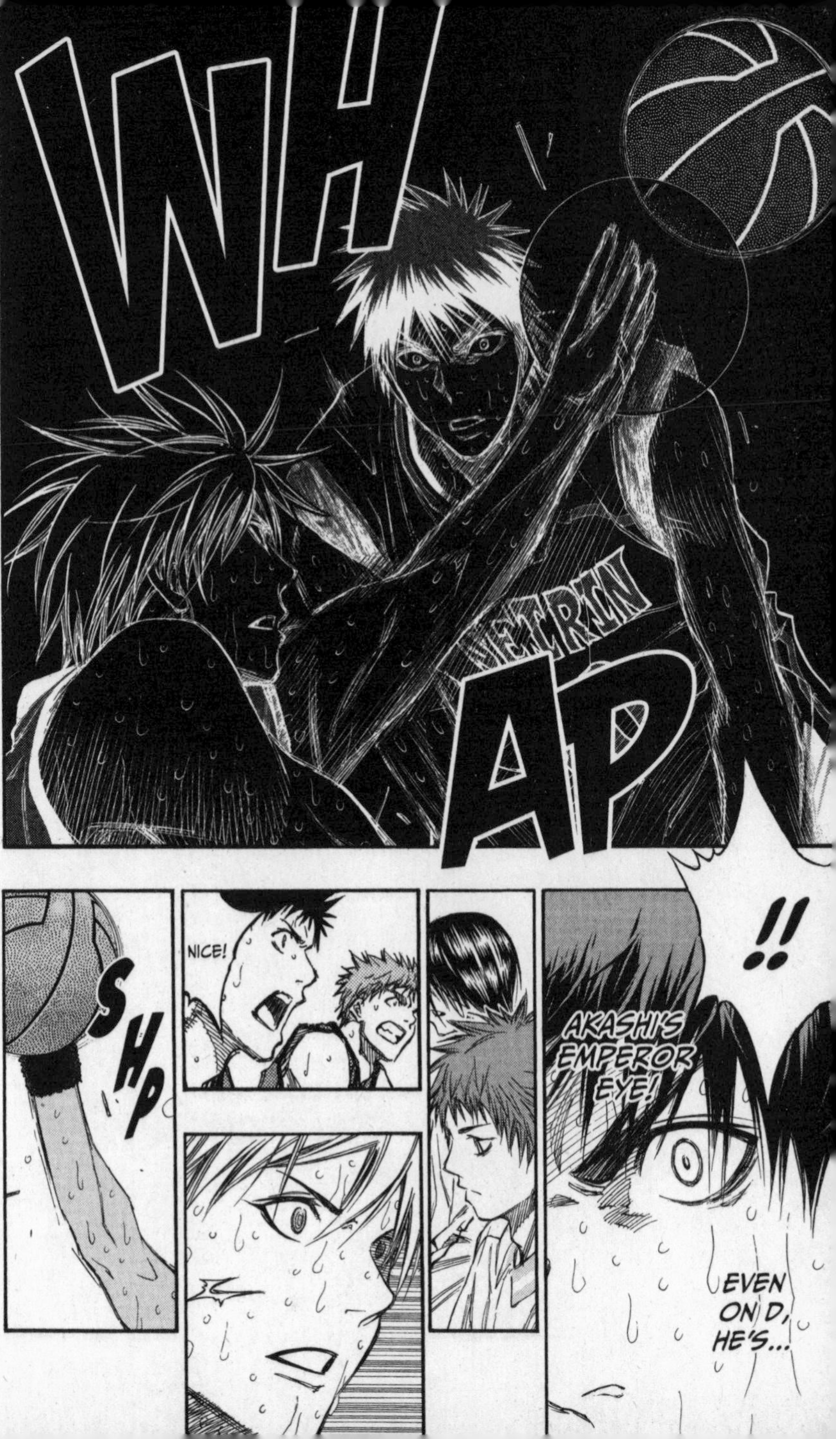
WHAP
!!
AKASHI'S EMPEROR EYE!
EVEN ON D, HE'S...
NICE!
SHP

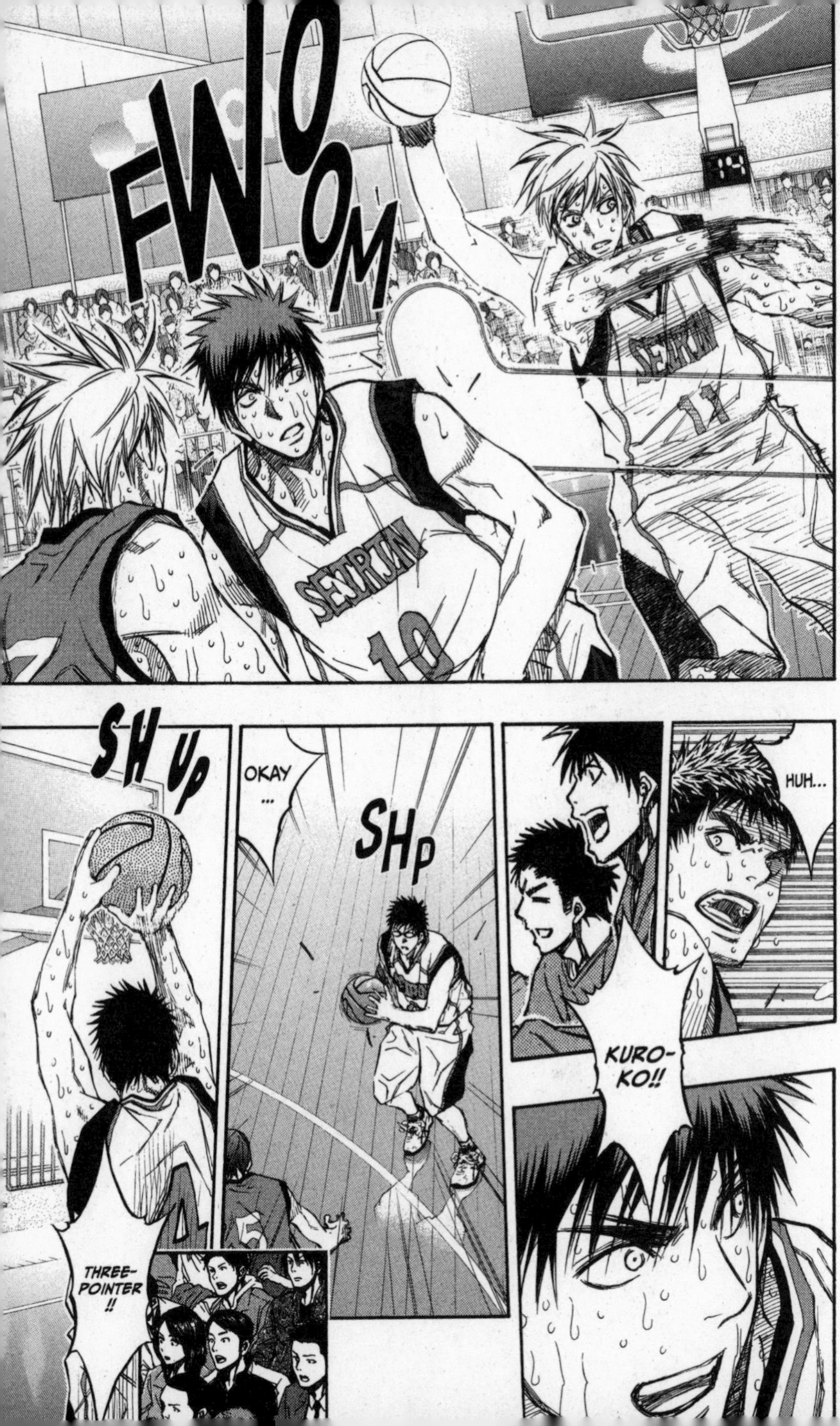
FWOOM
HUH...
KURO-KO!!
OKAY ...
SHP
SHUP
THREE-POINTER !!

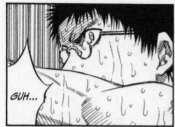

GUH...

GRAZE

ARGHHH!

AHHH!

IT MISSED!!

KLANG

DARN IT!

SHK

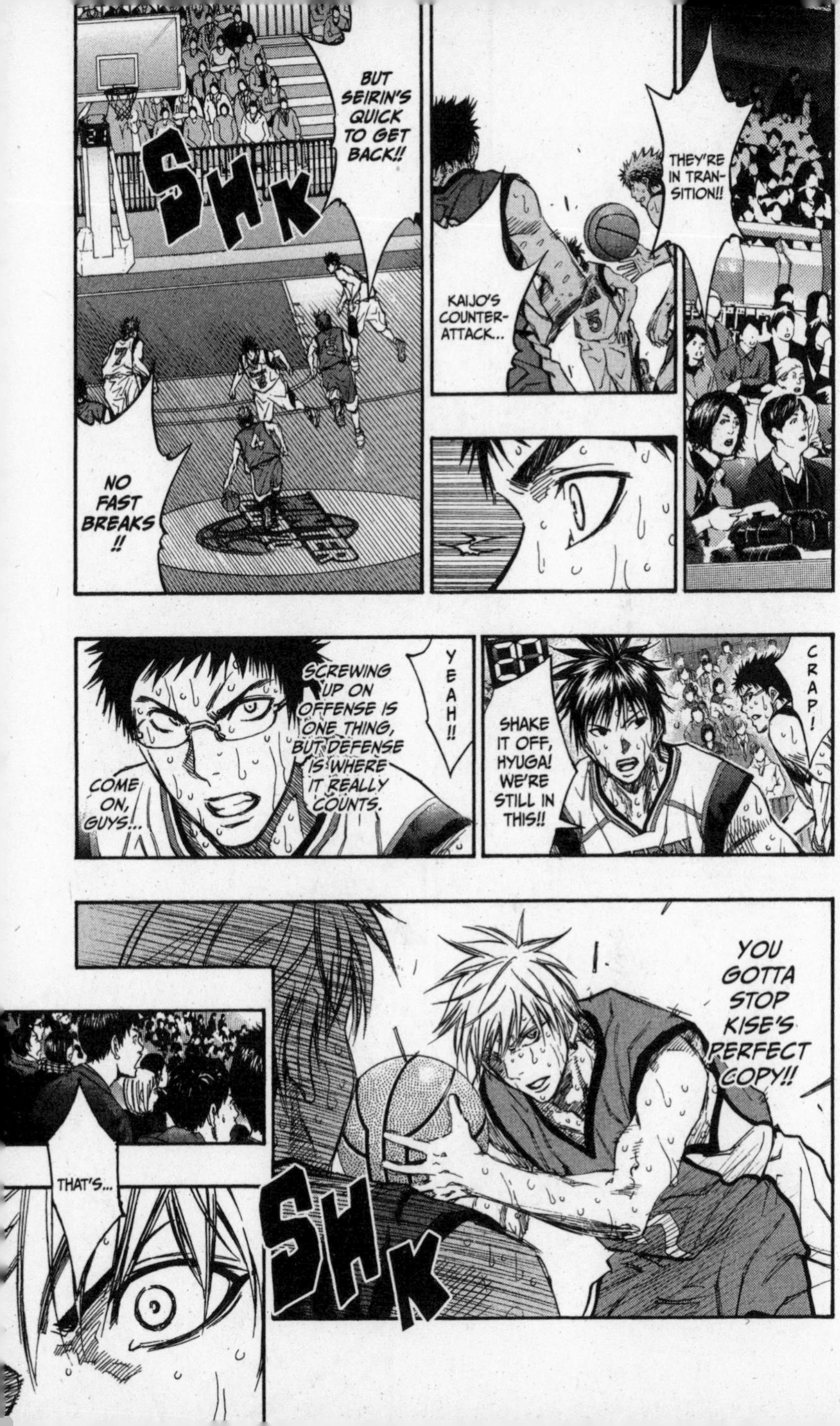
THEY'RE IN TRAN-SITION!!
KAIJO'S COUNTER-ATTACK...
BUT SEIRIN'S QUICK TO GET BACK!!
SHK
NO FAST BREAKS!!
CRAP!
SHAKE IT OFF, HYUGA! WE'RE STILL IN THIS!!
YEAH!!
SCREWING UP ON OFFENSE IS ONE THING, BUT DEFENSE IS WHERE IT REALLY COUNTS.
COME ON, GUYS...
YOU GOTTA STOP KISE'S PERFECT COPY!!
SHK
THAT'S...

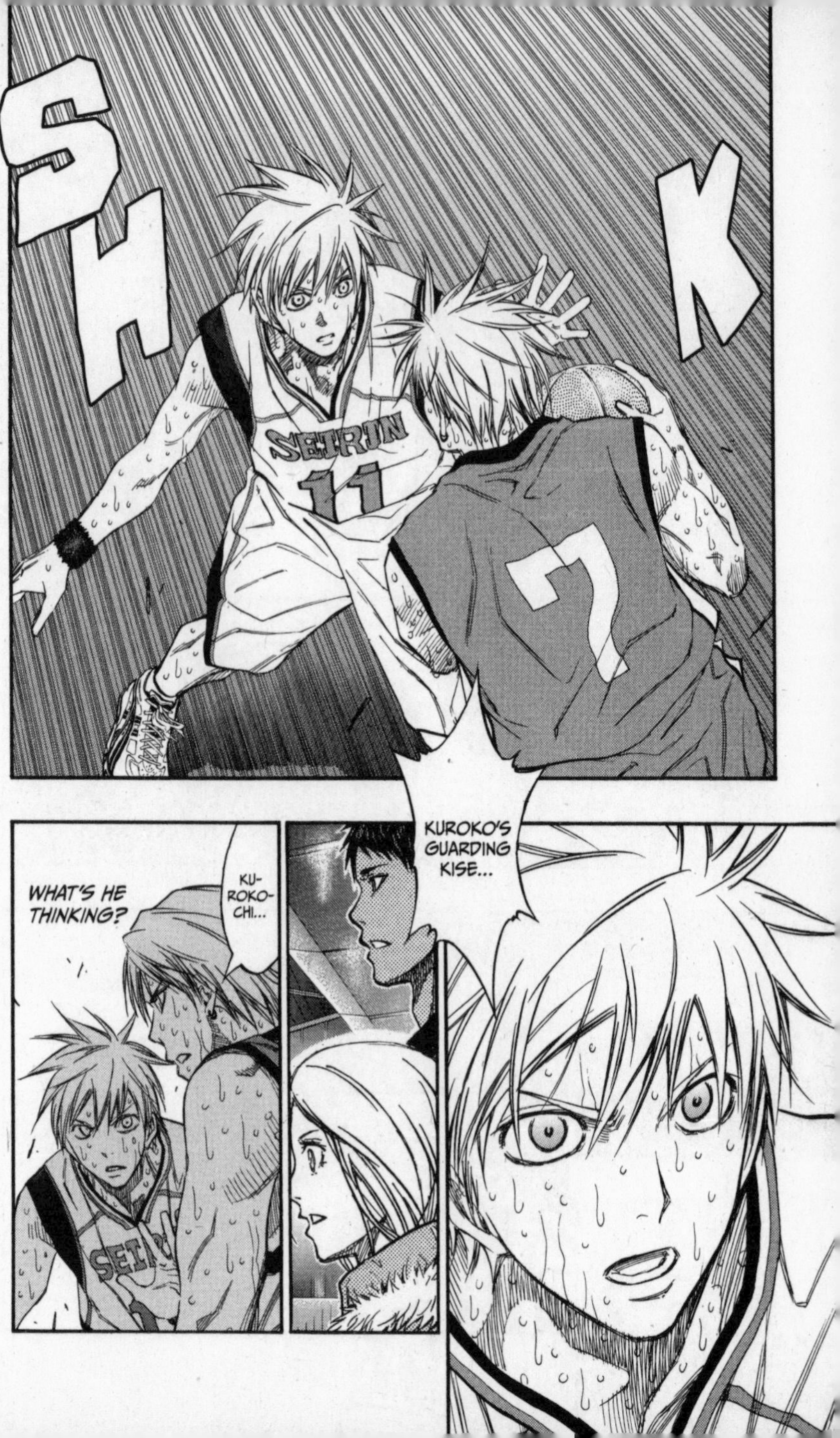
SHK
KUROKO'S GUARDING KISE...
KU-ROKO-CHI...
WHAT'S HE THINKING?

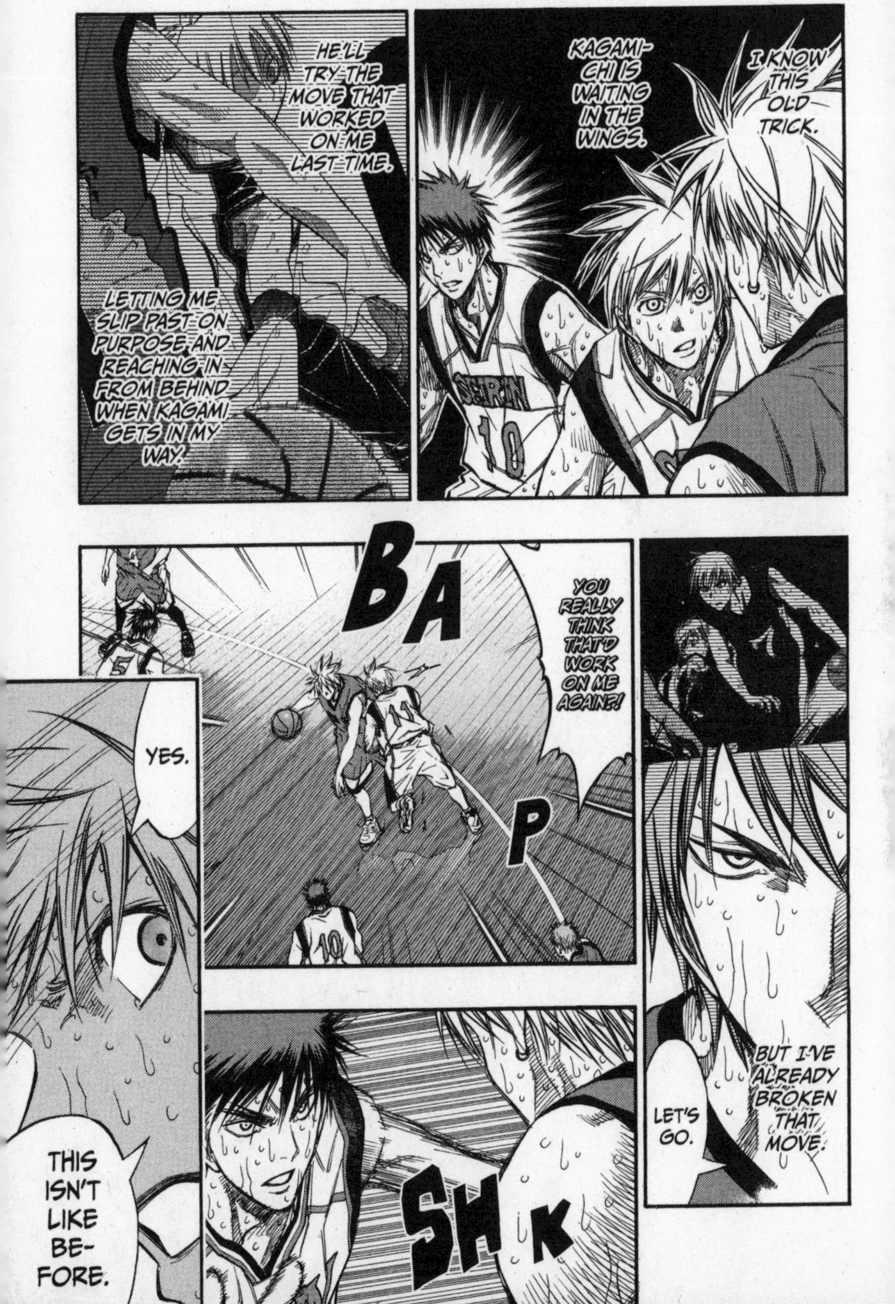
I KNOW THIS OLD TRICK.
KAGAMI-CHI IS WAITING IN THE WINGS.
HE'LL TRY THE MOVE THAT WORKED ON ME LAST TIME.
LETTING ME SLIP PAST ON PURPOSE AND REACHING IN FROM BEHIND WHEN KAGAMI GETS IN MY WAY.
BUT I'VE ALREADY BROKEN THAT MOVE.
LET'S GO.
BAP
YOU REALLY THINK THAT'D WORK ON ME AGAIN?!
YES.
SHK
THIS ISN'T LIKE BEFORE.

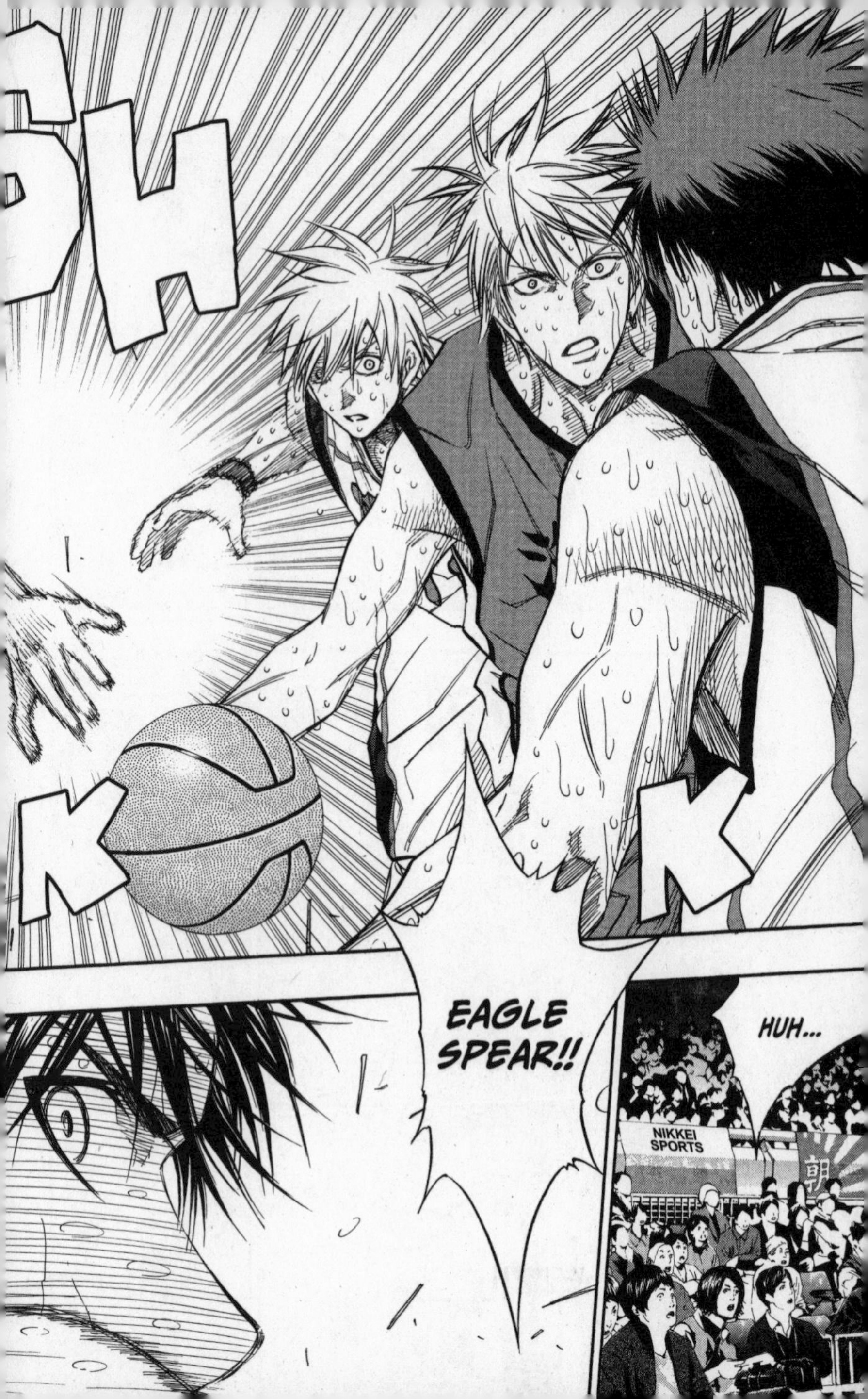
HUH...
NIKKEI SPORTS
朝
EAGLE SPEAR!!

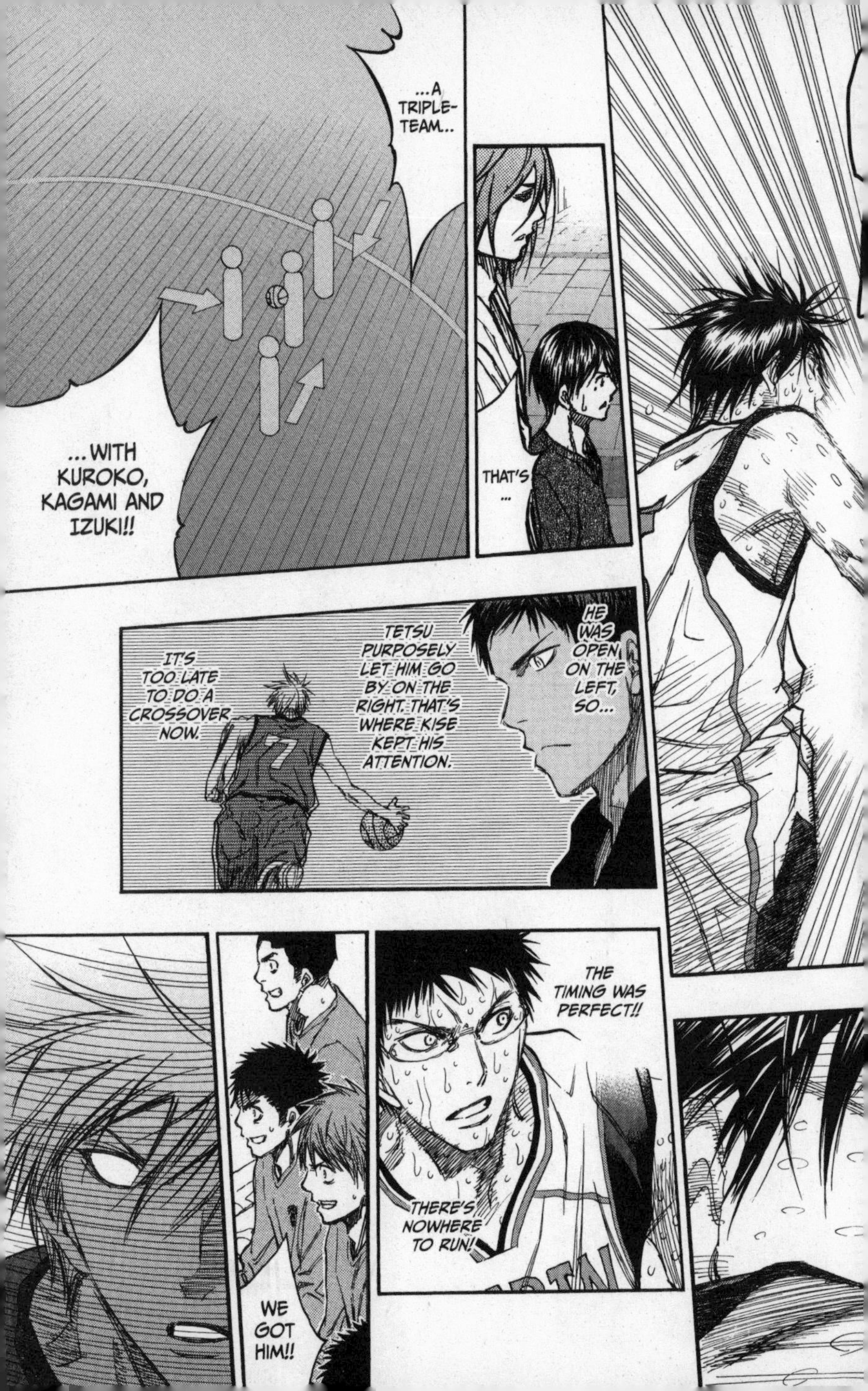
THAT'S ...
...A TRIPLE-TEAM...
...WITH KUROKO, KAGAMI AND IZUKI!!
HE WAS OPEN ON THE LEFT, SO...
TETSU PURPOSELY LET HIM GO BY ON THE RIGHT. THAT'S WHERE KISE KEPT HIS ATTENTION.
IT'S TOO LATE TO DO A CROSSOVER NOW.
7
THE TIMING WAS PERFECT!!
THERE'S NOWHERE TO RUN!
WE GOT HIM!!

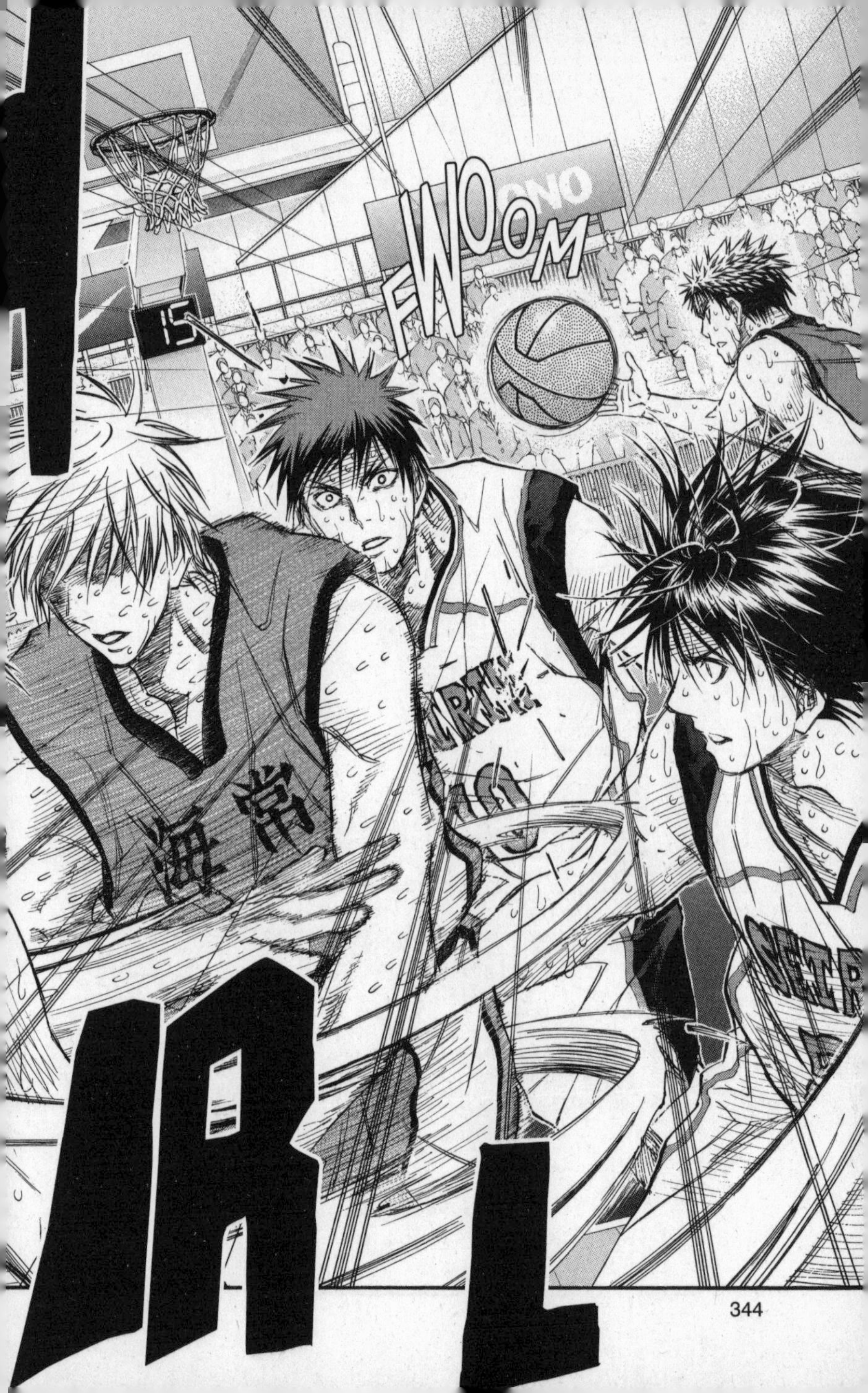
FWOOM

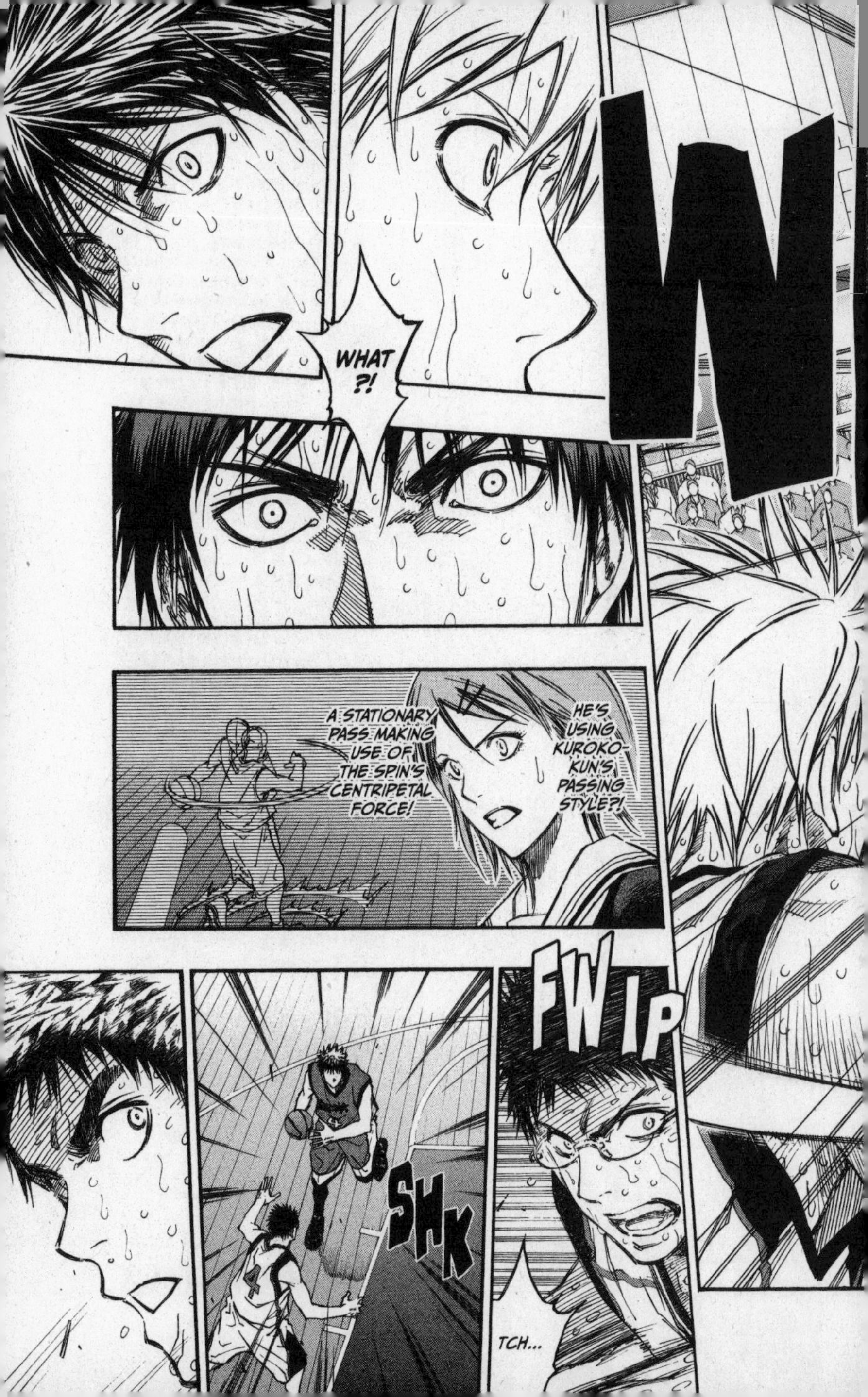
W
WHAT ?!
HE'S USING KUROKO-KUN'S PASSING STYLE?!
A STATIONARY PASS MAKING USE OF THE SPIN'S CENTRIPETAL FORCE!
FWIP
TCH...
SHK

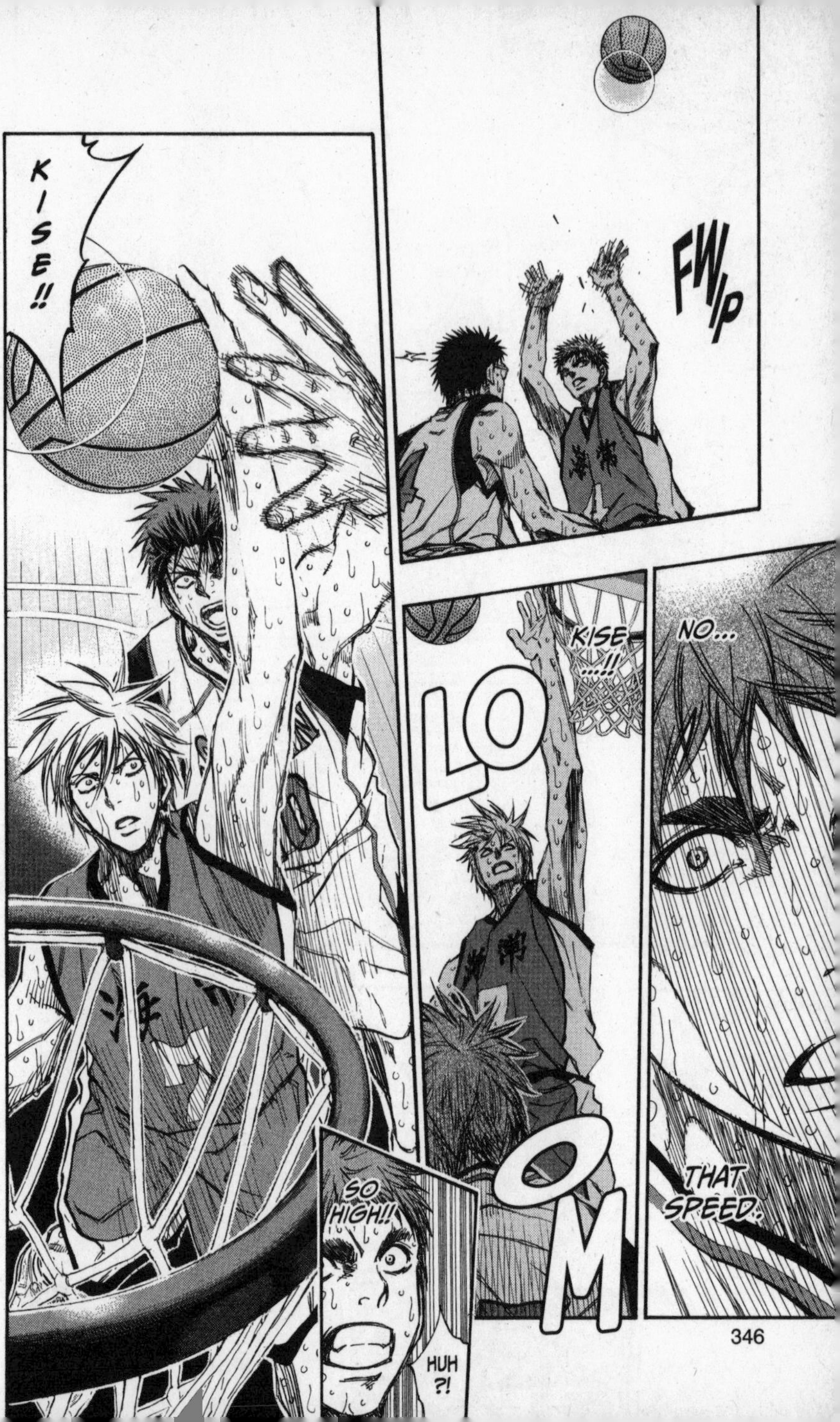
FWIP
NO...
THAT SPEED..
KISE ...!!
LOOM
SO HIGH!!
HUH ?!
KISE!!

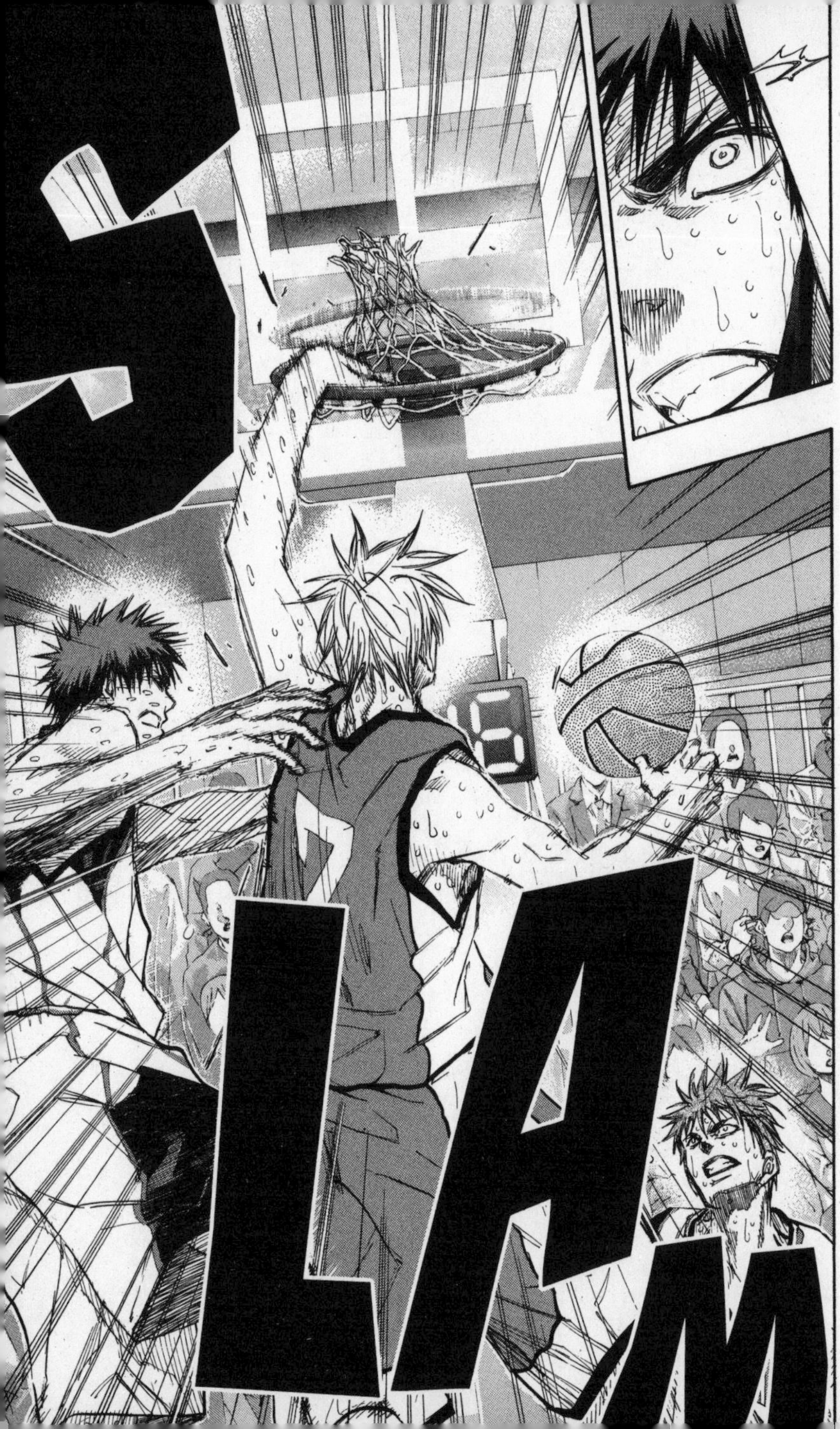
SLAM

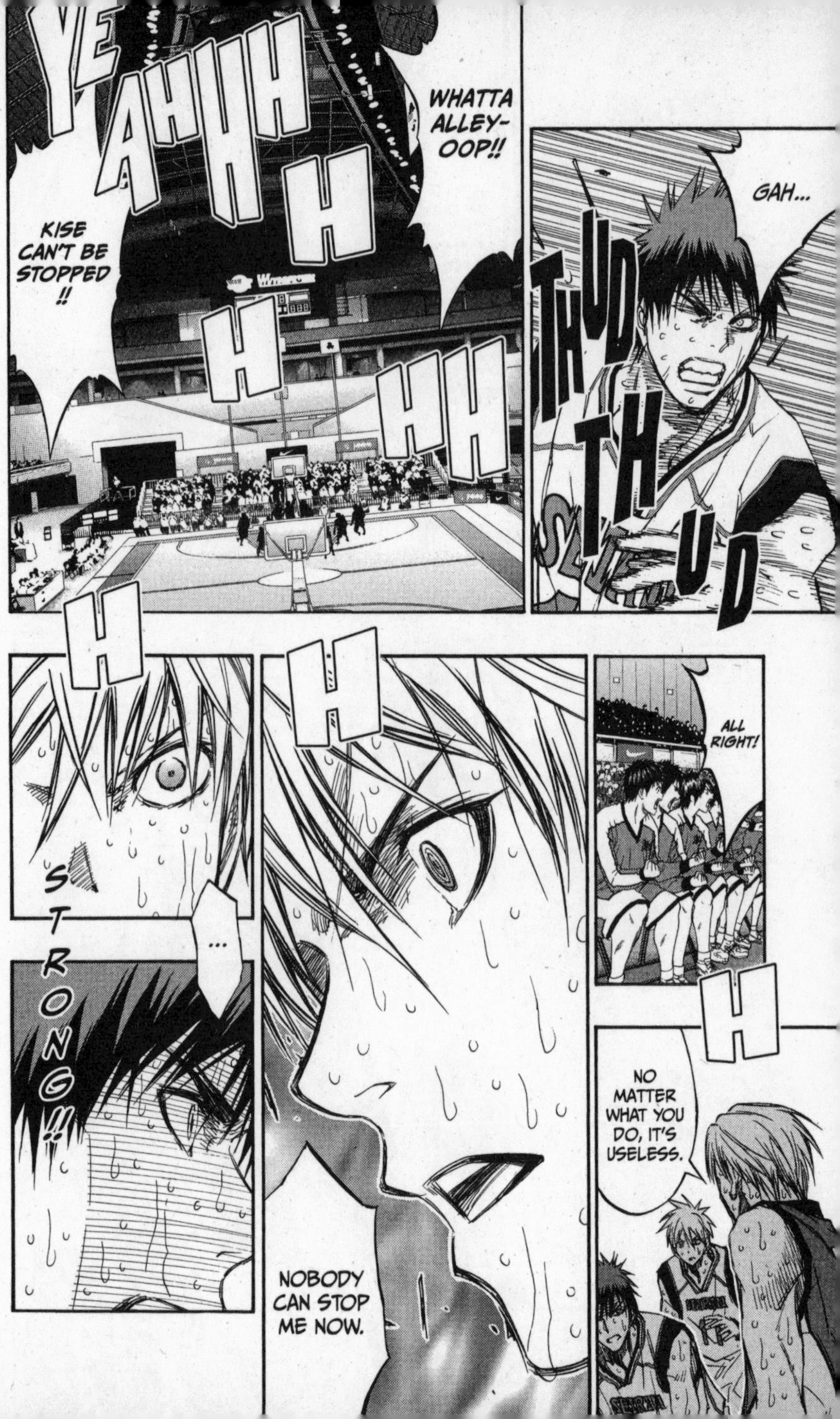
GAH...
THUD
THUD
WHATTA ALLEY-OOP!!
KISE CAN'T BE STOPPED!!
YEAHHHHHHHHHHHHH
ALL RIGHT!
NO MATTER WHAT YOU DO, IT'S USELESS.
NOBODY CAN STOP ME NOW.
...
STRONG!!

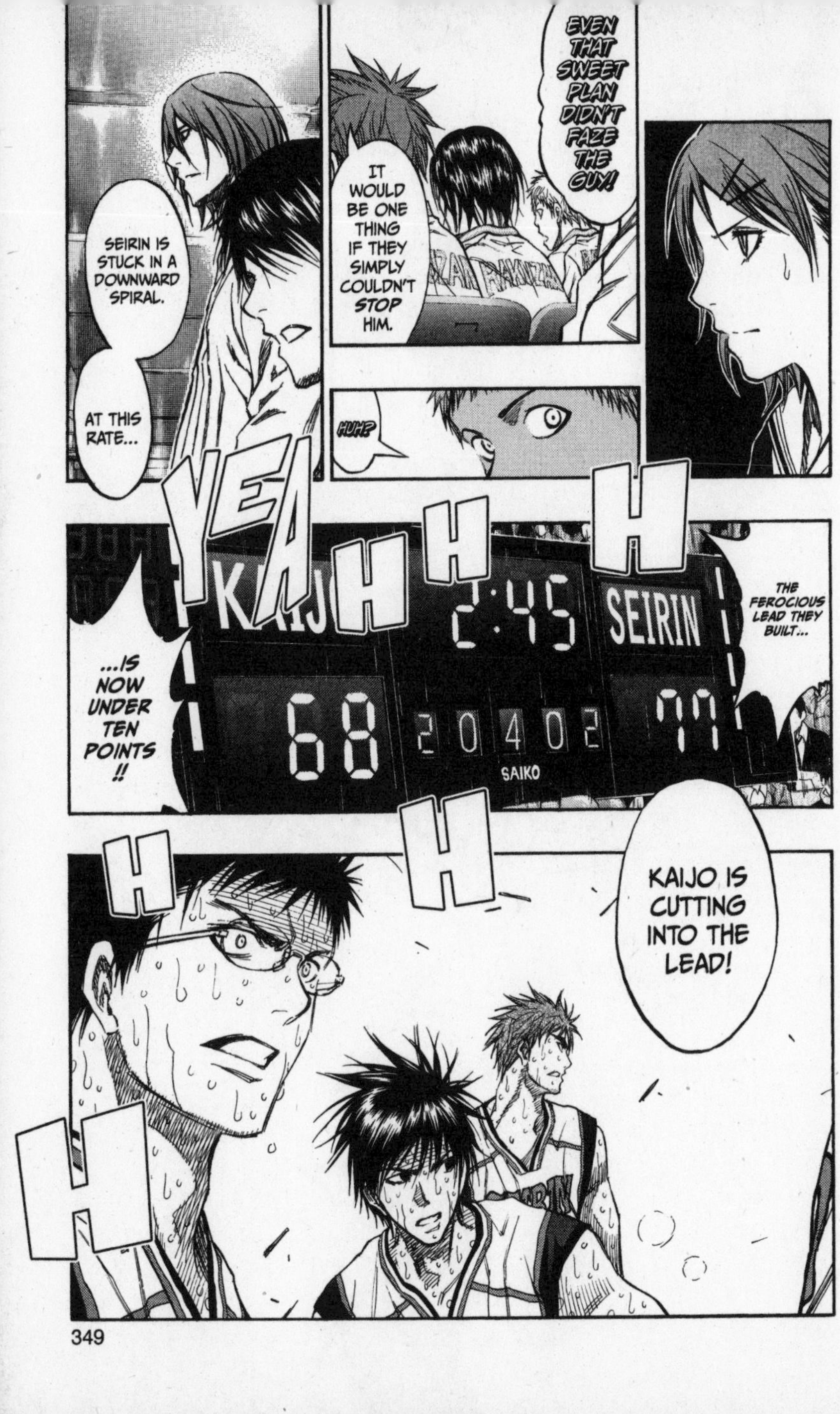
EVEN THAT SWEET PLAN DIDN'T FAZE THE GUY!
IT WOULD BE ONE THING IF THEY SIMPLY COULDN'T STOP HIM.
HUH?
SEIRIN IS STUCK IN A DOWNWARD SPIRAL.
AT THIS RATE...
YEAHHHHHH
THE FEROCIOUS LEAD THEY BUILT...
SEIRIN
2:45
KAIJ
77
68
SAIKO
...IS NOW UNDER TEN POINTS!!
KAIJO IS CUTTING INTO THE LEAD!

KUROKO'S BASKETBALL Q&A
W/ HALFWAY-DECENT ANSWERS

Q. WHAT'S ALEX'S CUP SIZE?
(DONGURI from HIROSHIMA PREFECTURE)

A. G.

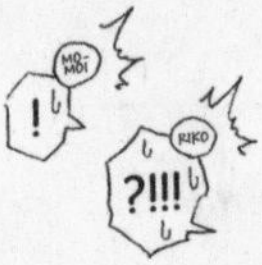
MOMOI
!
RIKO
?!!!

KUROKO'S BASKETBALL BLOOPERS
TAKE 1

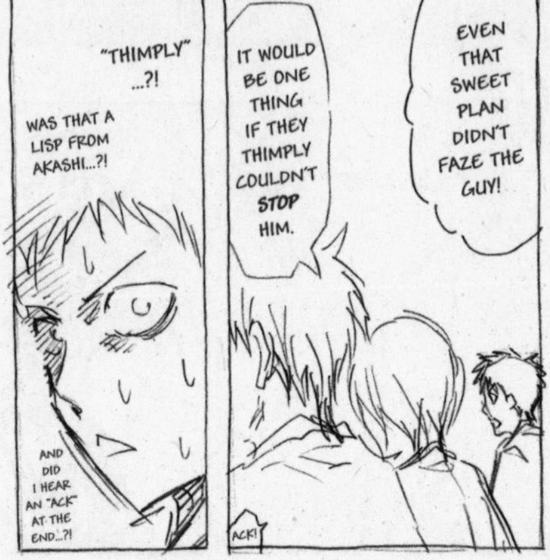
EVEN THAT SWEET PLAN DIDN'T FAZE THE GUY!
IT WOULD BE ONE THING IF THEY THIMPLY COULDN'T STOP HIM.
ACK!
"THIMPLY" ...?!
WAS THAT A LISP FROM AKASHI...?!
AND DID I HEAR AN "ACK" AT THE END...?!

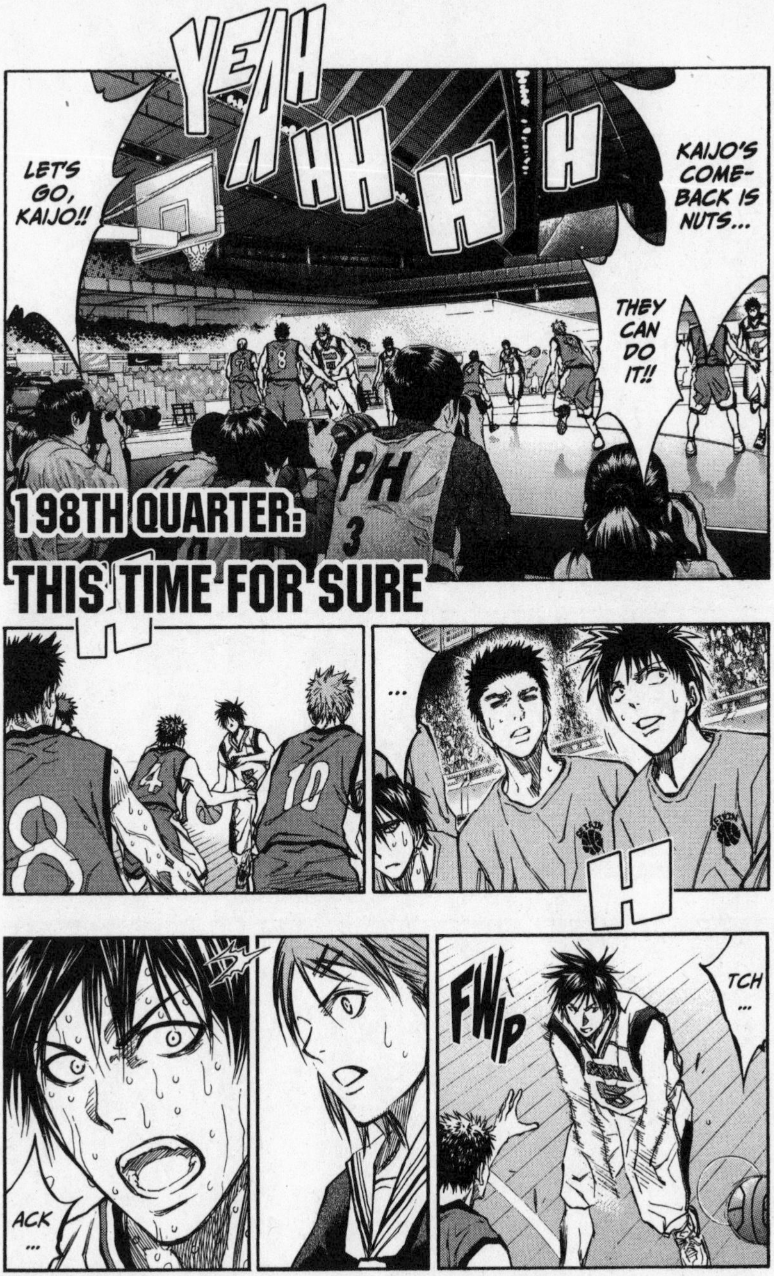
YEAHHHHHH
KAIJO'S COME-BACK IS NUTS...
LET'S GO, KAIJO!!
THEY CAN DO IT!!
198TH QUARTER:
THIS TIME FOR SURE
...
H
TCH ...
FWIP
ACK ...

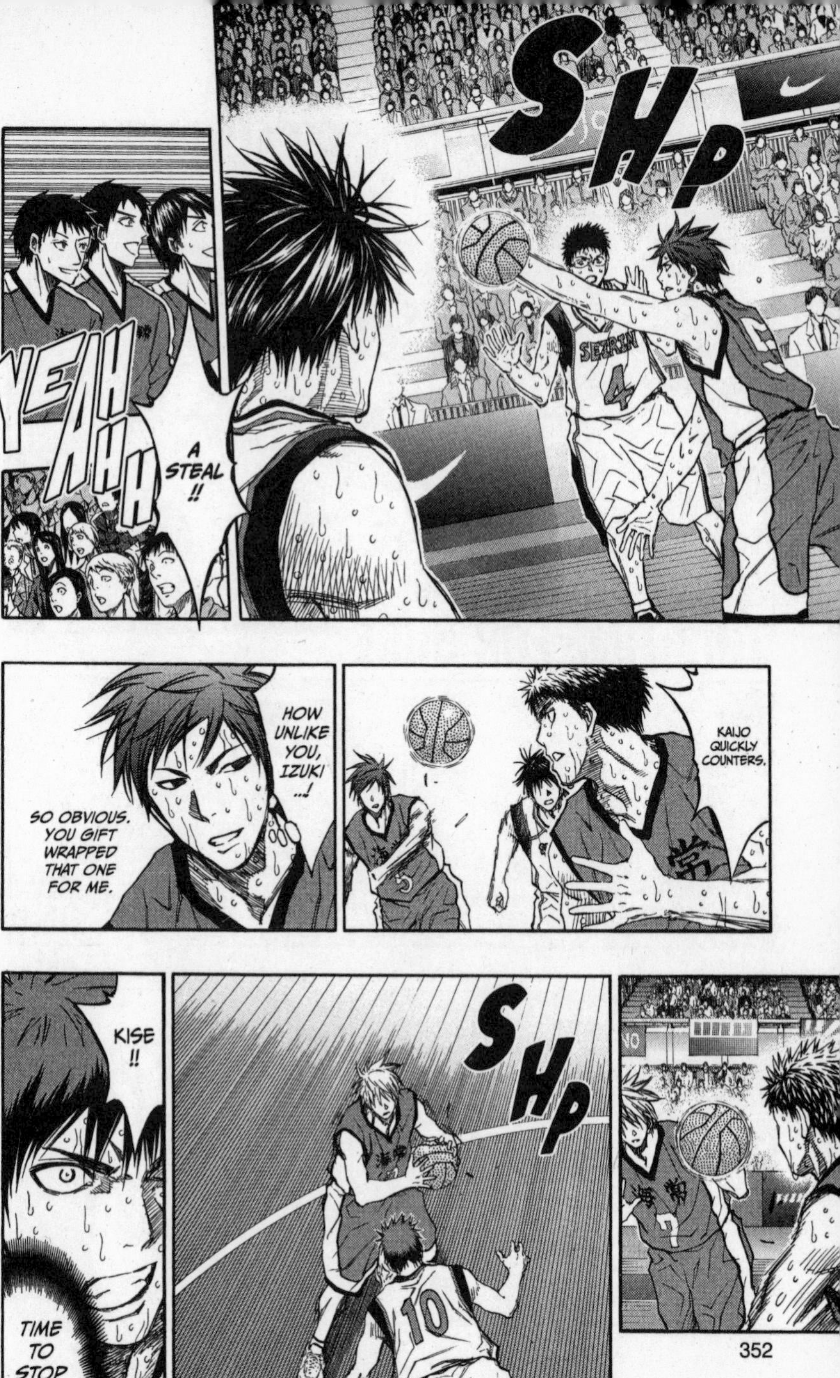
SHP
A STEAL!!
YEAHHHH
KAIJO QUICKLY COUNTERS.
HOW UNLIKE YOU, IZUKI...!
SO OBVIOUS. YOU GIFT WRAPPED THAT ONE FOR ME.
SHP
KISE!!
TIME TO STOP YOU!

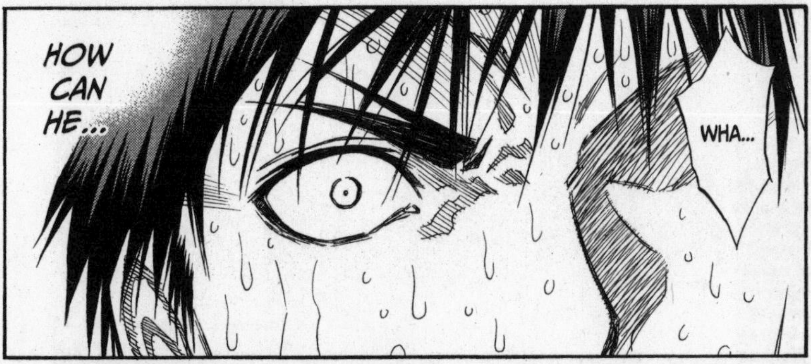
WHA...
HOW CAN HE...
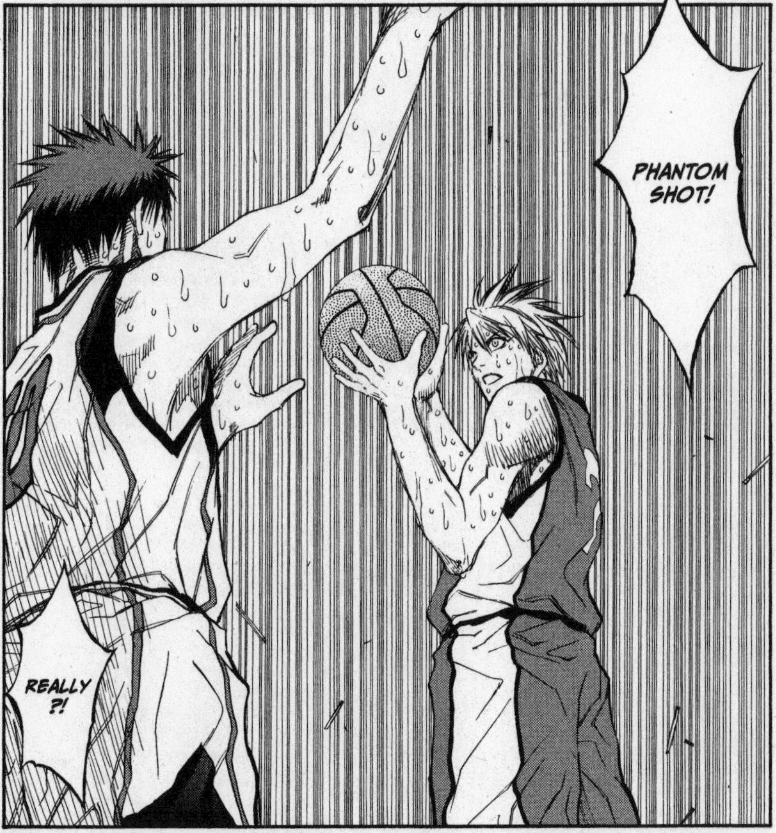
PHANTOM SHOT!
REALLY ?!

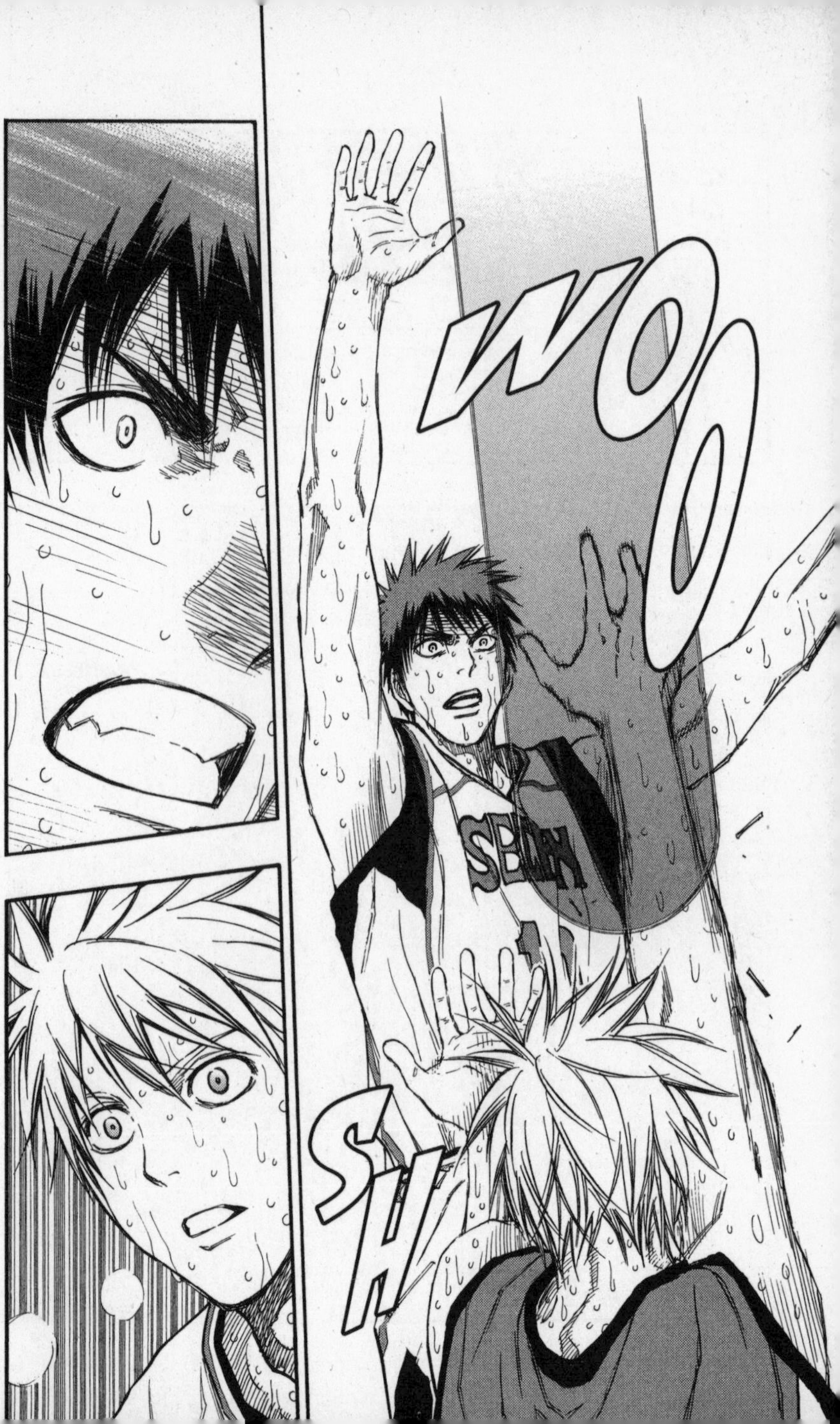
WOOO
SH

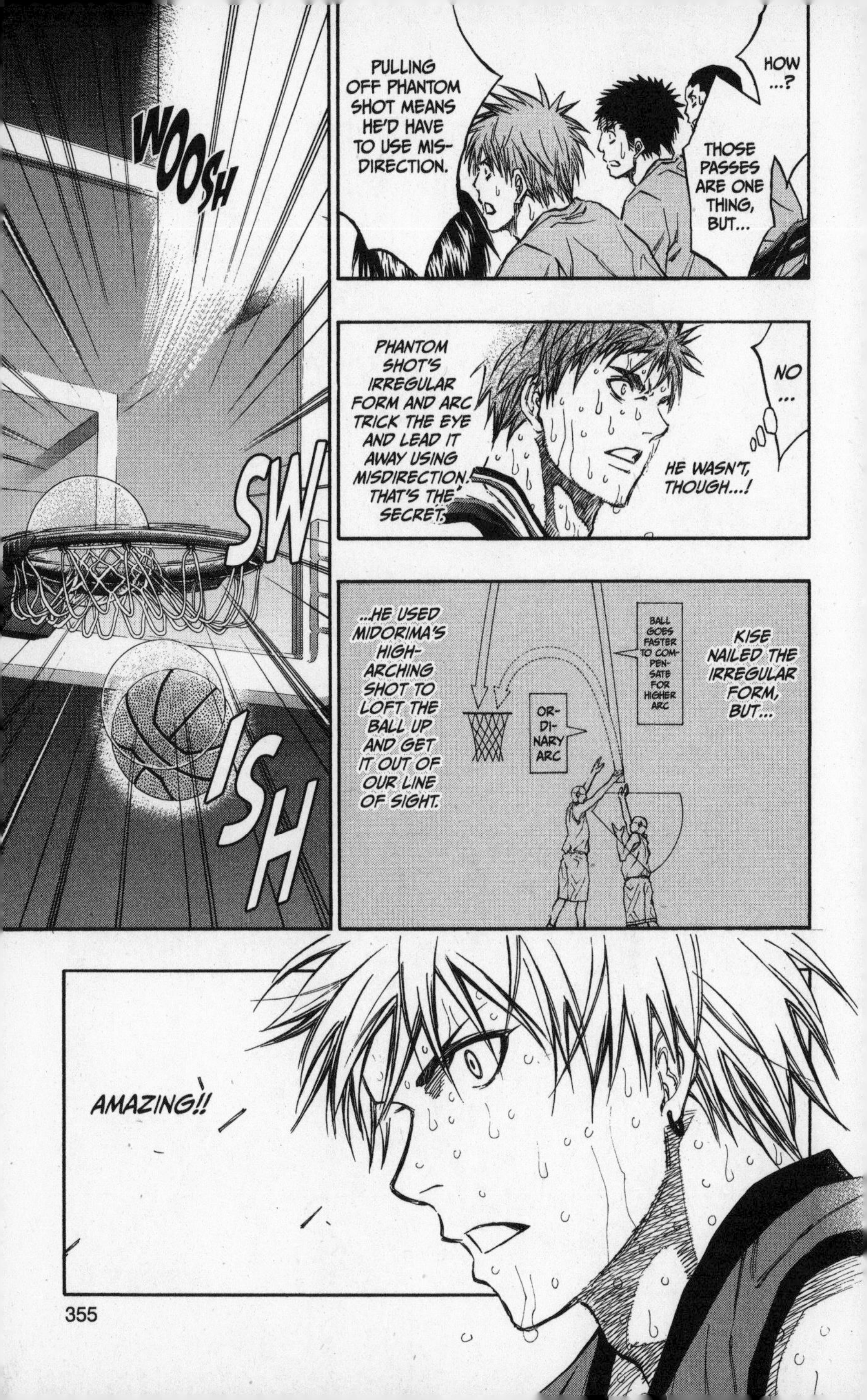
HOW ...?
THOSE PASSES ARE ONE THING, BUT...
PULLING OFF PHANTOM SHOT MEANS HE'D HAVE TO USE MIS-DIRECTION.
NO ...
HE WASN'T, THOUGH...!
PHANTOM SHOT'S IRREGULAR FORM AND ARC TRICK THE EYE AND LEAD IT AWAY USING MISDIRECTION. THAT'S THE SECRET.
KISE NAILED THE IRREGULAR FORM, BUT...
BALL GOES FASTER TO COM-PEN-SATE FOR HIGHER ARC
OR-DI-NARY ARC
...HE USED MIDORIMA'S HIGH-ARCHING SHOT TO LOFT THE BALL UP AND GET IT OUT OF OUR LINE OF SIGHT.
WOOSH
SWISH
AMAZING!!

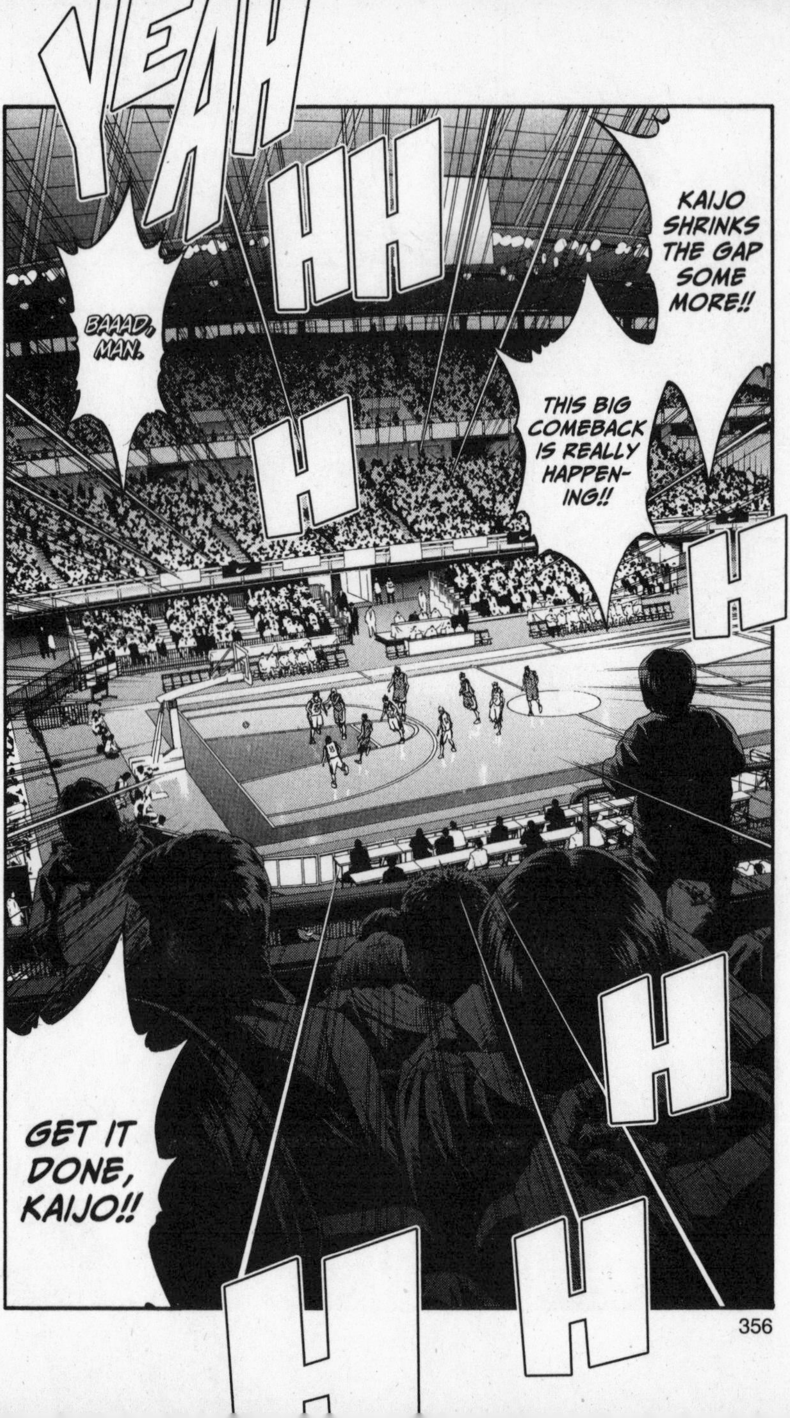
YEAHHHHHHH
KAIJO SHRINKS THE GAP SOME MORE!!
BAAAD, MAN.
THIS BIG COMEBACK IS REALLY HAPPEN-ING!!
GET IT DONE, KAIJO!!

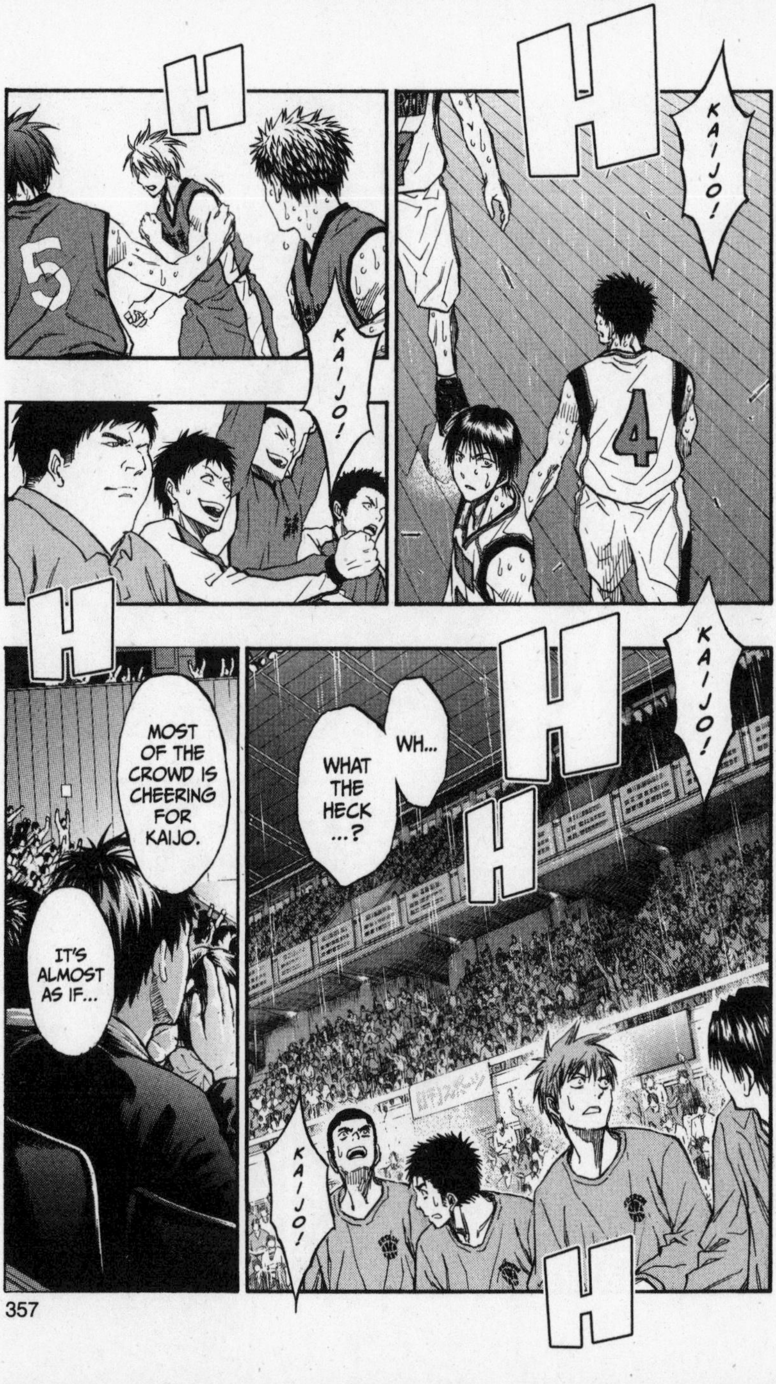
H
KAIJO!
H
KAIJO!
KAIJO!
H
H
WH...
WHAT THE HECK ...?
KAIJO!
H
H
MOST OF THE CROWD IS CHEERING FOR KAIJO.
IT'S ALMOST AS IF...

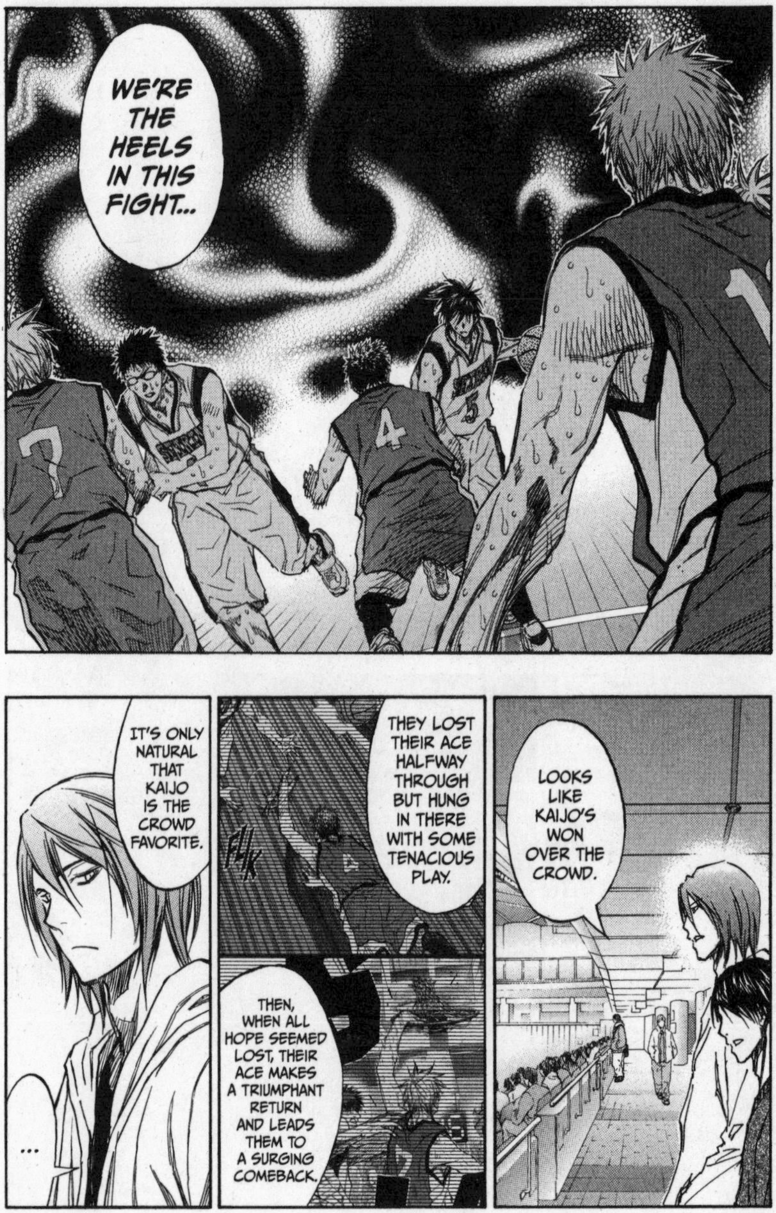
WE'RE THE HEELS IN THIS FIGHT...
LOOKS LIKE KAIJO'S WON OVER THE CROWD.
THEY LOST THEIR ACE HALFWAY THROUGH BUT HUNG IN THERE WITH SOME TENACIOUS PLAY.
FLIK
THEN, WHEN ALL HOPE SEEMED LOST, THEIR ACE MAKES A TRIUMPHANT RETURN AND LEADS THEM TO A SURGING COMEBACK.
IT'S ONLY NATURAL THAT KAIJO IS THE CROWD FAVORITE.
...

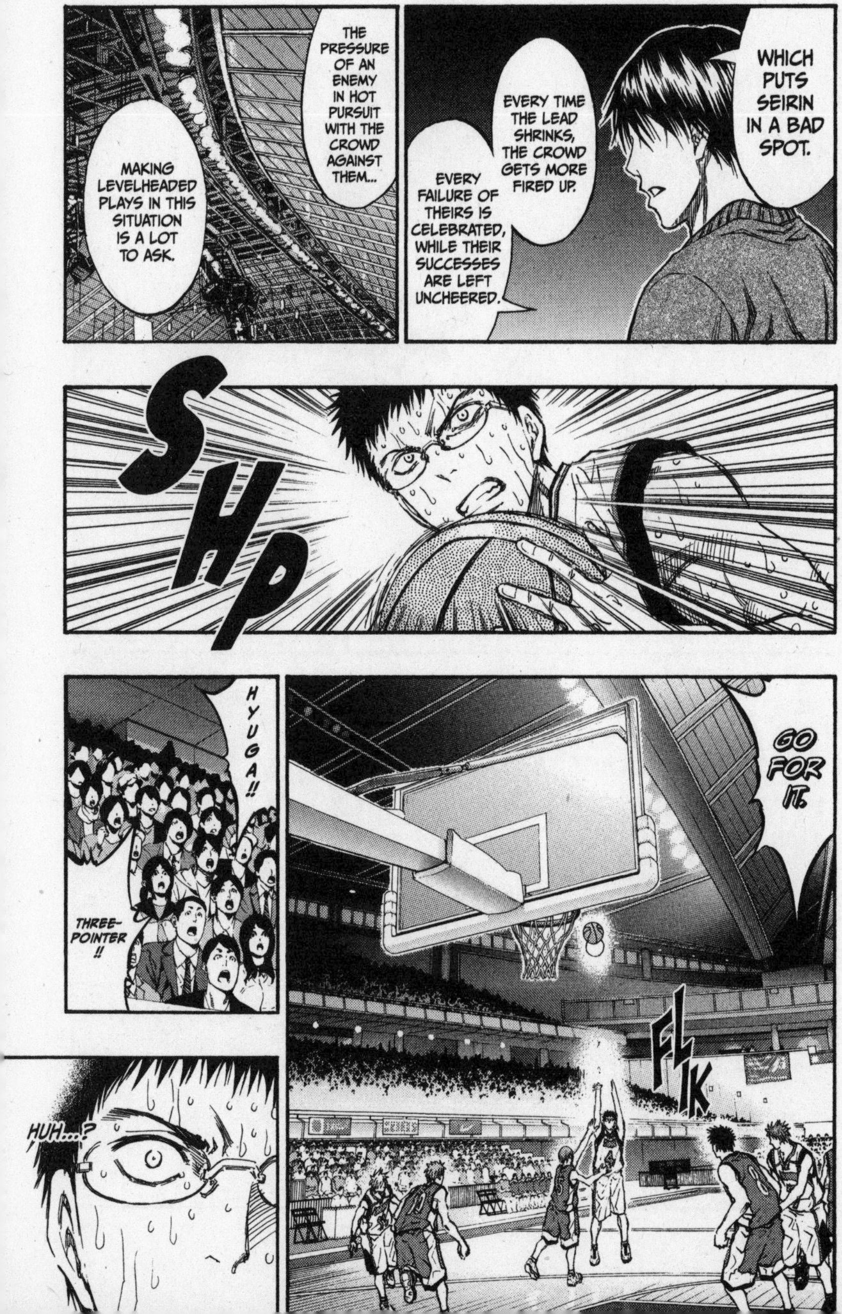
WHICH PUTS SEIRIN IN A BAD SPOT.
EVERY TIME THE LEAD SHRINKS, THE CROWD GETS MORE FIRED UP.
EVERY FAILURE OF THEIRS IS CELEBRATED, WHILE THEIR SUCCESSES ARE LEFT UNCHEERED.
THE PRESSURE OF AN ENEMY IN HOT PURSUIT WITH THE CROWD AGAINST THEM...
MAKING LEVELHEADED PLAYS IN THIS SITUATION IS A LOT TO ASK.
SHP
GO FOR IT.
FLIK
HYUGA!!
THREE-POINTER!!
HUH...?

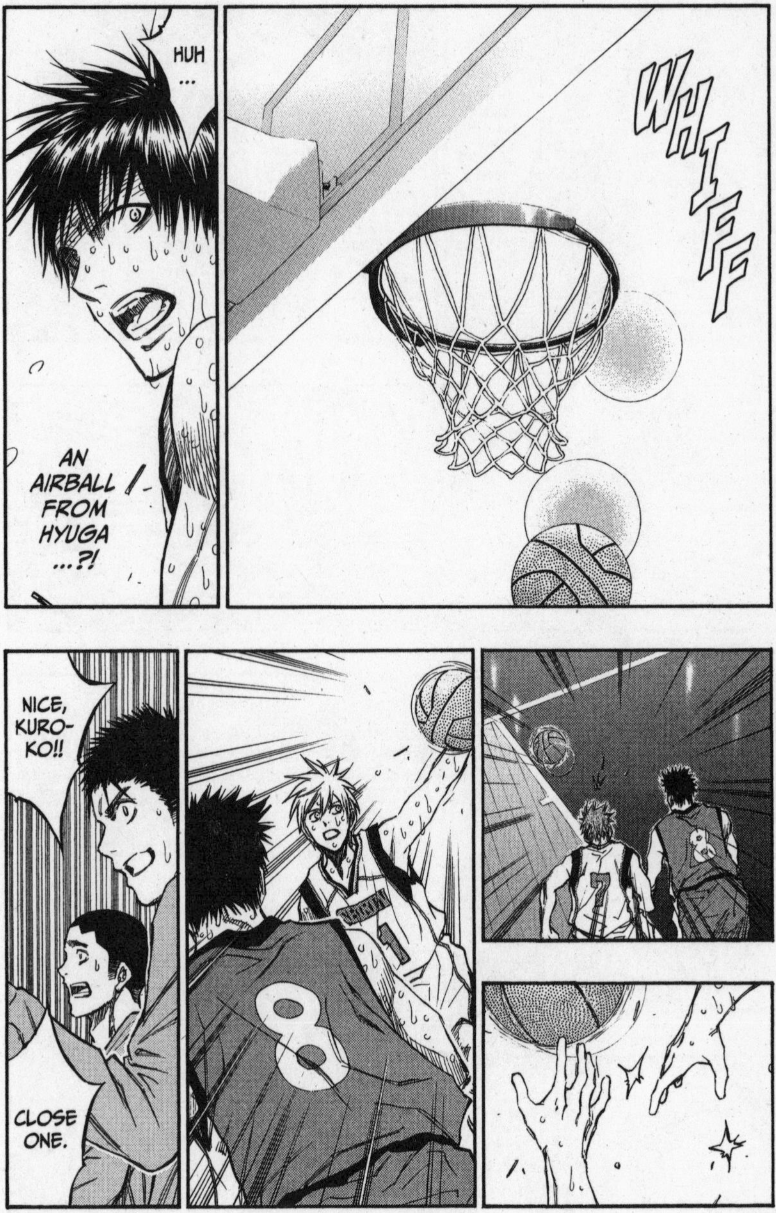
WHIFF
HUH ...
AN AIRBALL FROM HYUGA ...?!
NICE, KURO-KO!!
CLOSE ONE.

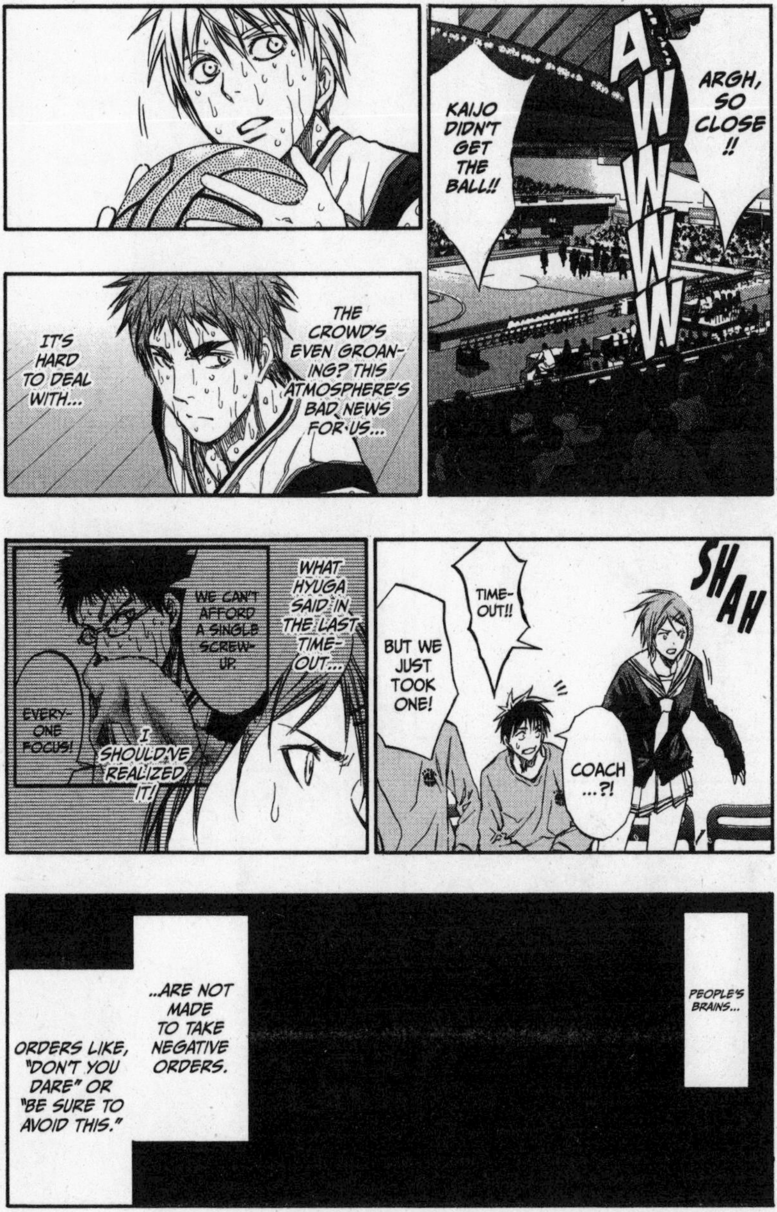
ARGH, SO CLOSE!!
AWWWWW
KAIJO DIDN'T GET THE BALL!!
THE CROWD'S EVEN GROANING? THIS ATMOSPHERE'S BAD NEWS FOR US...
IT'S HARD TO DEAL WITH...
SHAH
TIME-OUT!!
BUT WE JUST TOOK ONE!
COACH ...?!
WHAT HYUGA SAID IN THE LAST TIME-OUT...
WE CAN'T AFFORD A SINGLE SCREW-UP.
EVERYONE FOCUS!
I SHOULD'VE REALIZED IT!
PEOPLE'S BRAINS...
...ARE NOT MADE TO TAKE NEGATIVE ORDERS.
ORDERS LIKE, "DON'T YOU DARE" OR "BE SURE TO AVOID THIS."

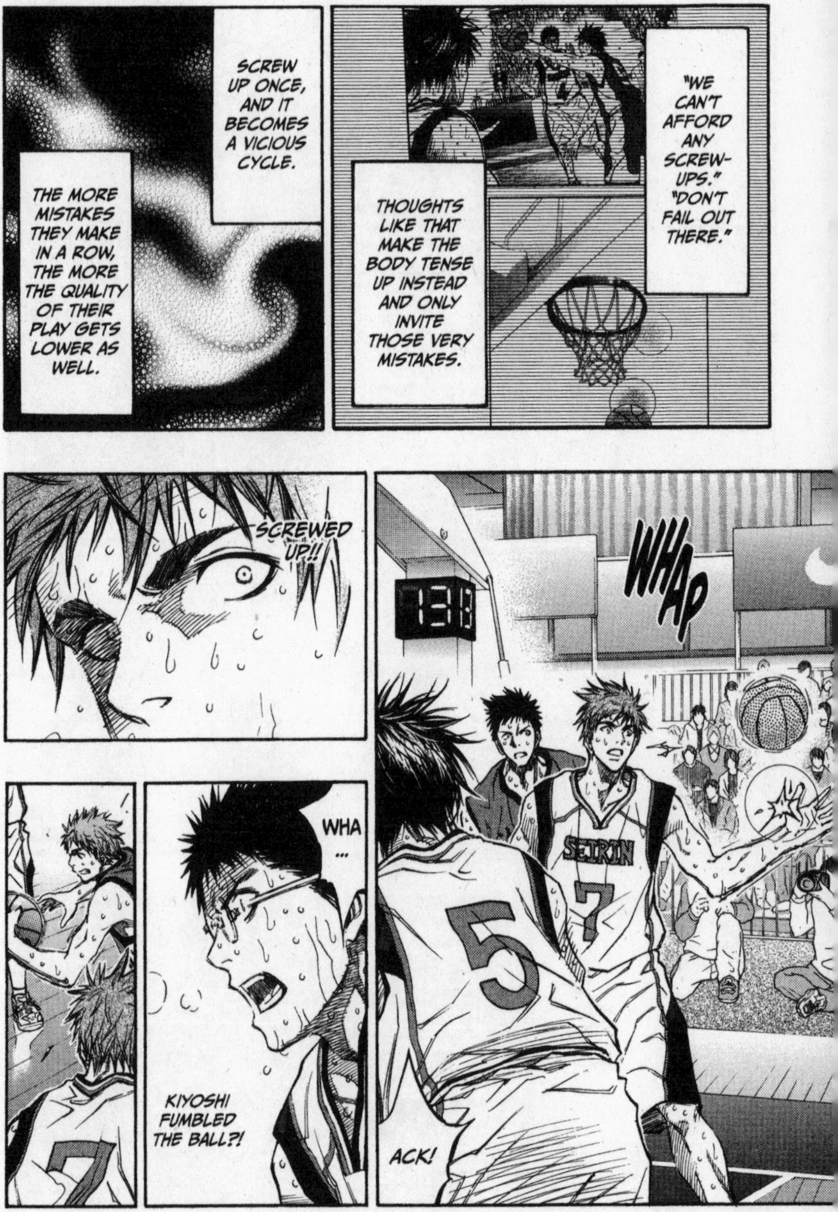
"WE CAN'T AFFORD ANY SCREW-UPS." "DON'T FAIL OUT THERE."
THOUGHTS LIKE THAT MAKE THE BODY TENSE UP INSTEAD AND ONLY INVITE THOSE VERY MISTAKES.
SCREW UP ONCE, AND IT BECOMES A VICIOUS CYCLE.
THE MORE MISTAKES THEY MAKE IN A ROW, THE MORE THE QUALITY OF THEIR PLAY GETS LOWER AS WELL.
WHAP
ACK!
SEIRIN
SCREWED UP!!
WHA...
KIYOSHI FUMBLED THE BALL?!

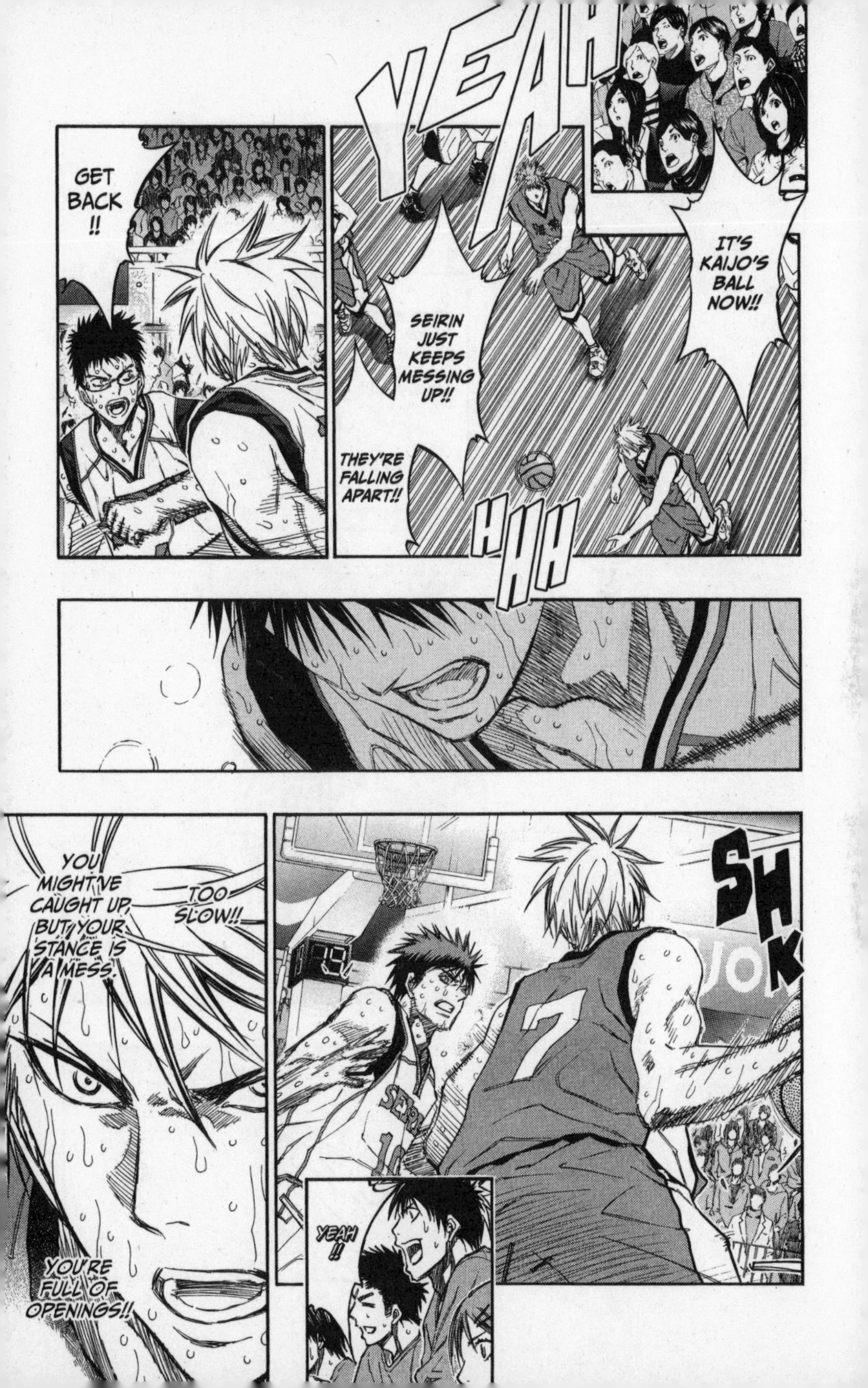
YEAH
IT'S KAIJO'S BALL NOW!!
SEIRIN JUST KEEPS MESSING UP!!
THEY'RE FALLING APART!!
HHH
GET BACK!!
SHK
YEAH!!
TOO SLOW!!
YOU MIGHT'VE CAUGHT UP, BUT YOUR STANCE IS A MESS.
YOU'RE FULL OF OPENINGS!!

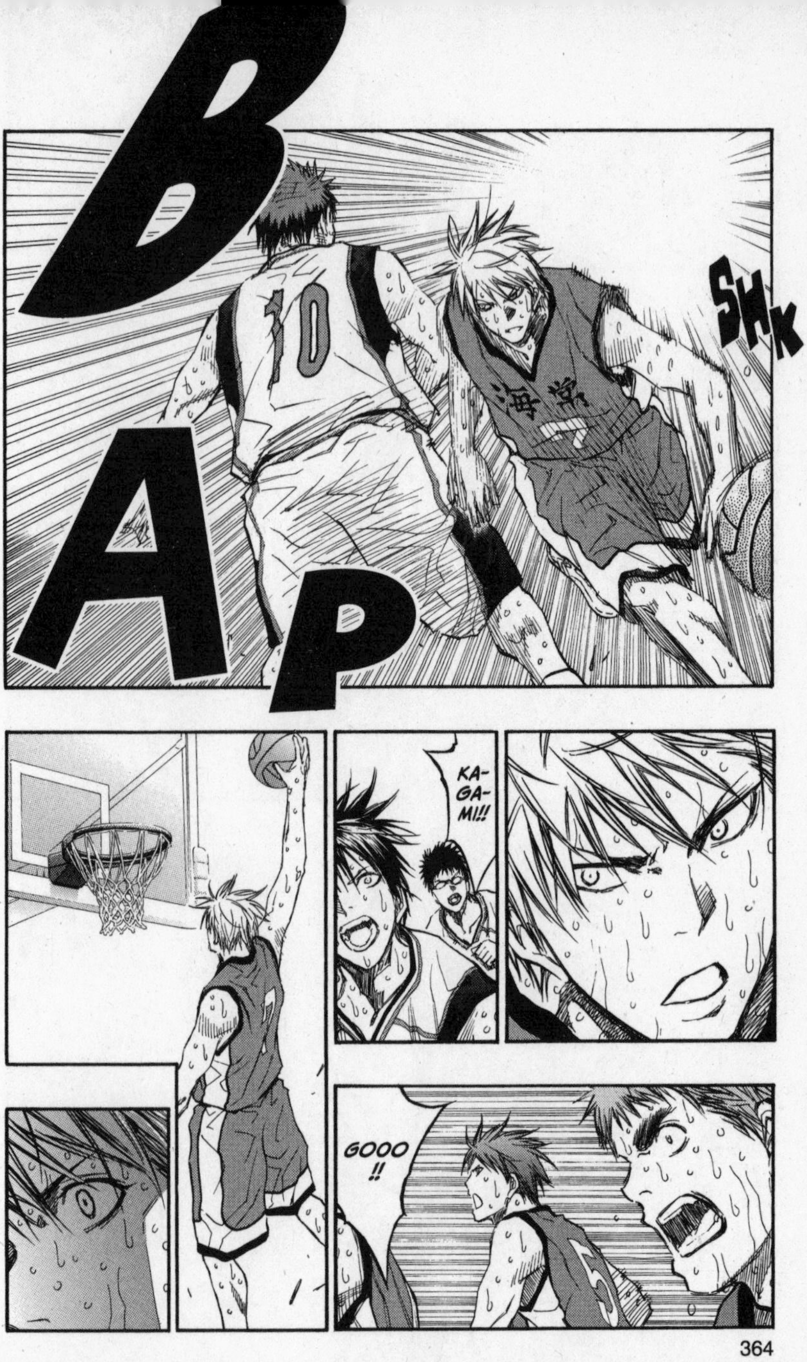
SHK
BAP
KA-GA-MI!!
GOOO!!

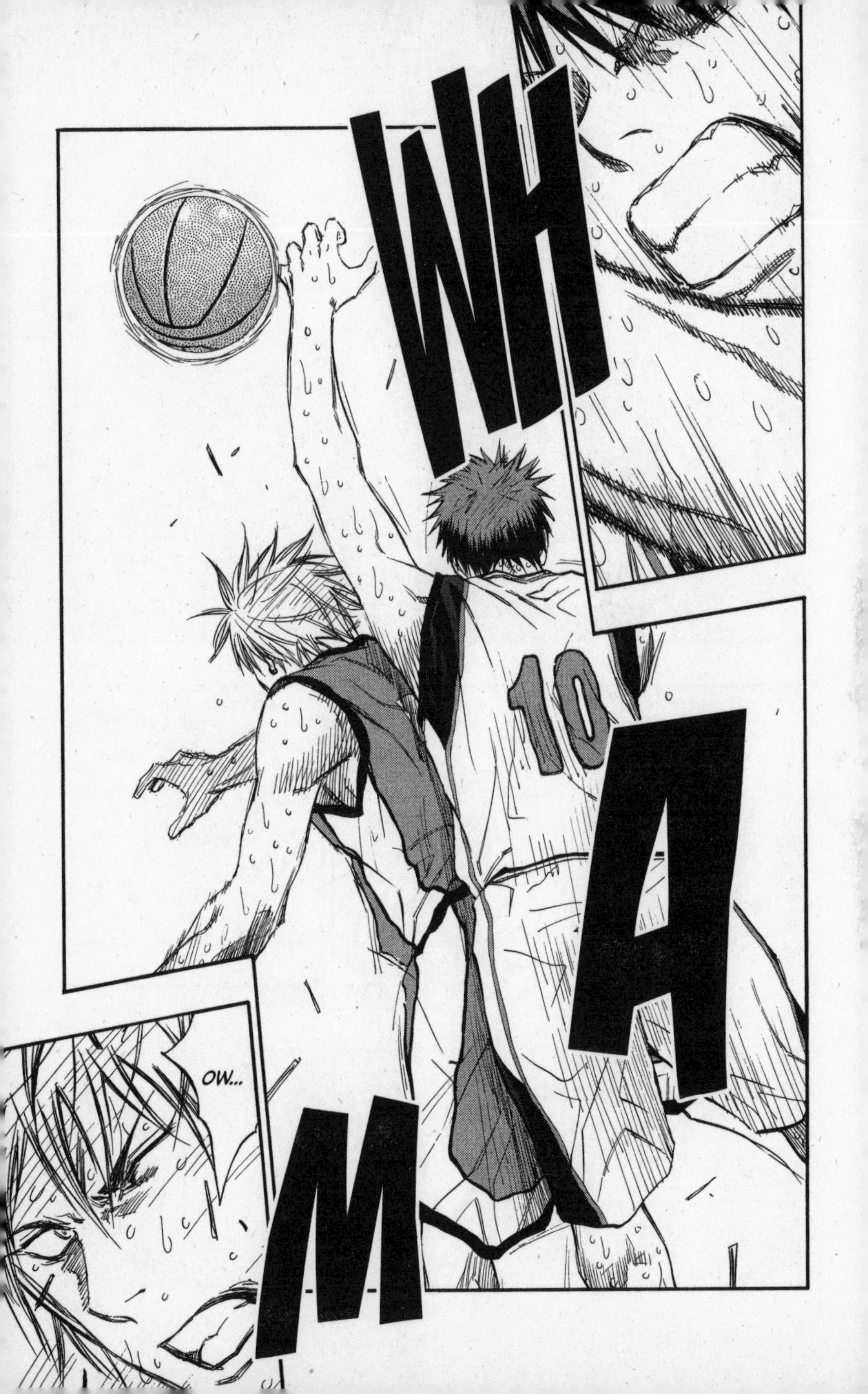
WHAM
OW...

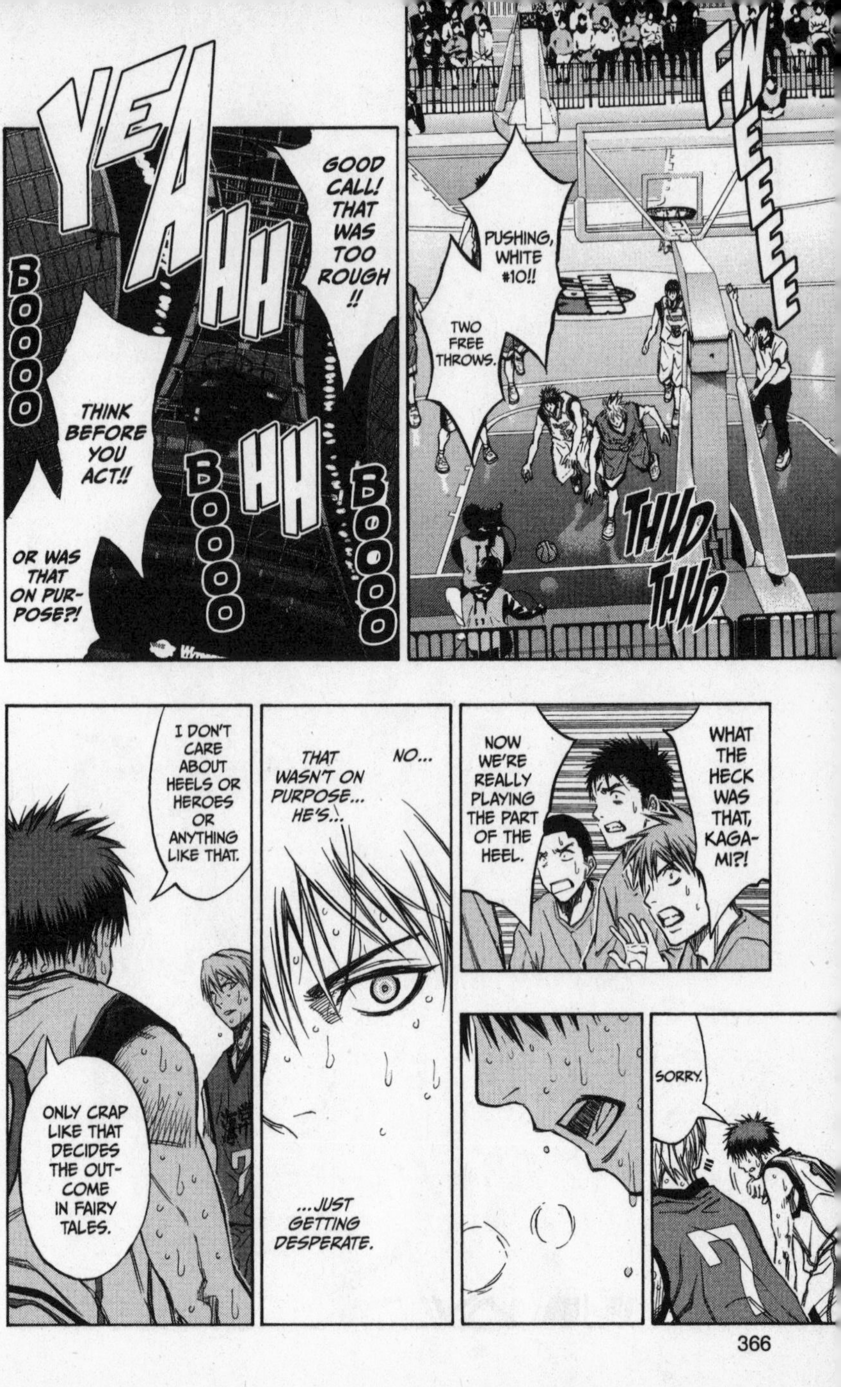
FWEEEEE
PUSHING, WHITE #10!!
TWO FREE THROWS.
THUD THUD
YEAHHHH
GOOD CALL! THAT WAS TOO ROUGH!!
BOOOOO
THINK BEFORE YOU ACT!!
OR WAS THAT ON PURPOSE?!
BOOOOO
BOOOOO
WHAT THE HECK WAS THAT, KAGAMI?!
NOW WE'RE REALLY PLAYING THE PART OF THE HEEL.
SORRY.
NO...
THAT WASN'T ON PURPOSE... HE'S...
...JUST GETTING DESPERATE.
I DON'T CARE ABOUT HEELS OR HEROES OR ANYTHING LIKE THAT.
ONLY CRAP LIKE THAT DECIDES THE OUTCOME IN FAIRY TALES.

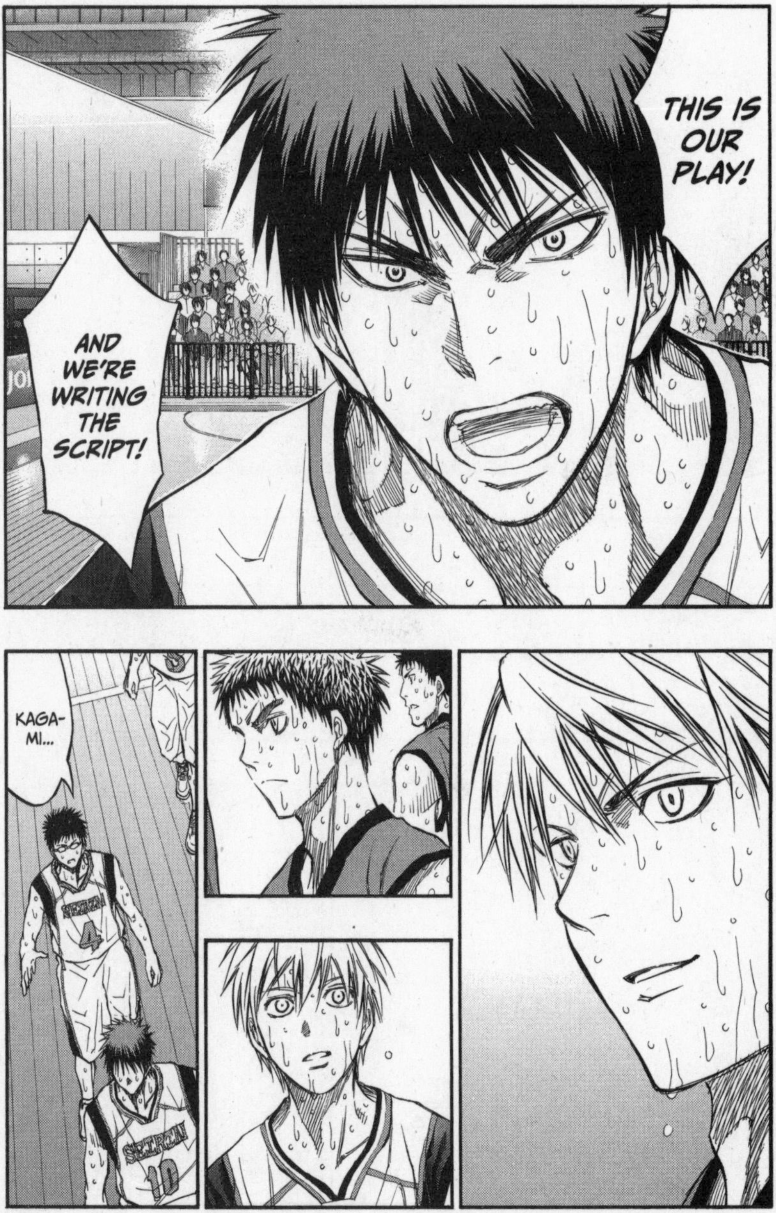
THIS IS OUR PLAY!
AND WE'RE WRITING THE SCRIPT!
KAGAMI...

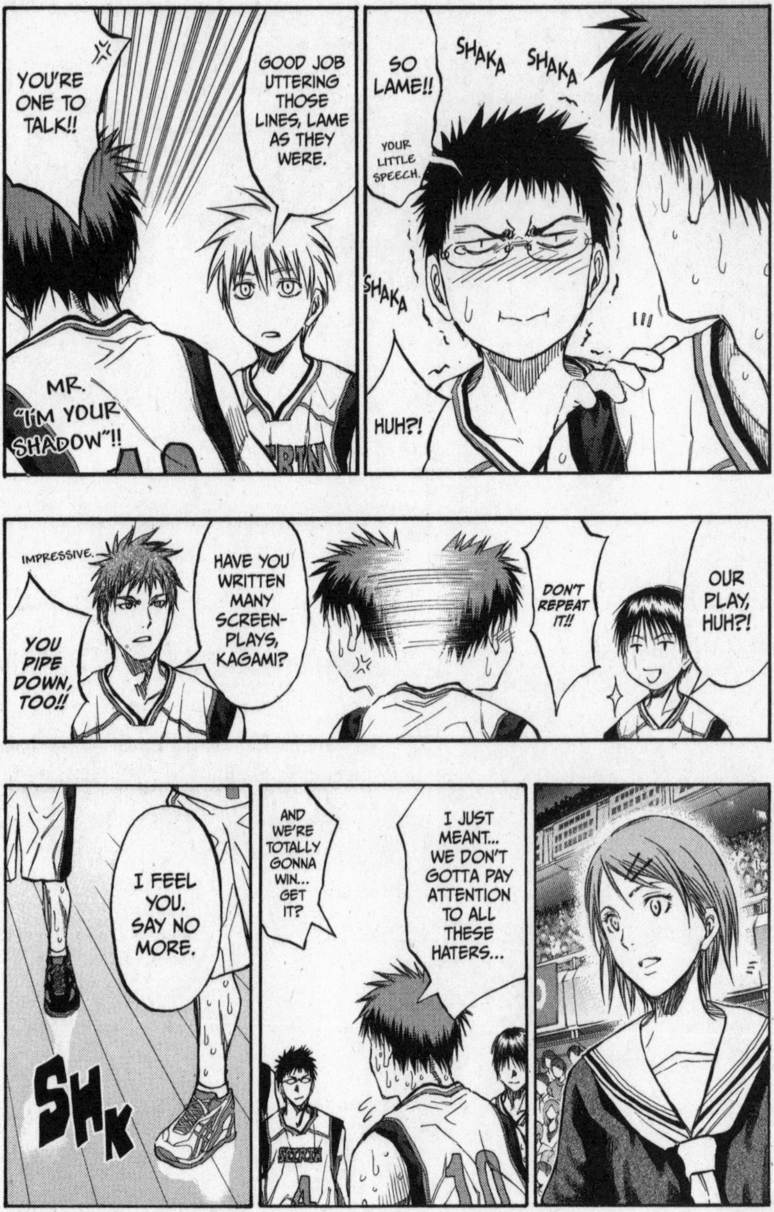
SO LAME!!
SHAKA SHAKA
YOUR LITTLE SPEECH.
SHAKA
HUH?!
GOOD JOB UTTERING THOSE LINES, LAME AS THEY WERE.
YOU'RE ONE TO TALK!!
MR. "I'M YOUR SHADOW"!!
OUR PLAY, HUH?!
DON'T REPEAT IT!!
HAVE YOU WRITTEN MANY SCREEN-PLAYS, KAGAMI?
IMPRESSIVE.
YOU PIPE DOWN, TOO!!
I JUST MEANT... WE DON'T GOTTA PAY ATTENTION TO ALL THESE HATERS...
AND WE'RE TOTALLY GONNA WIN... GET IT?
I FEEL YOU. SAY NO MORE.
SHK

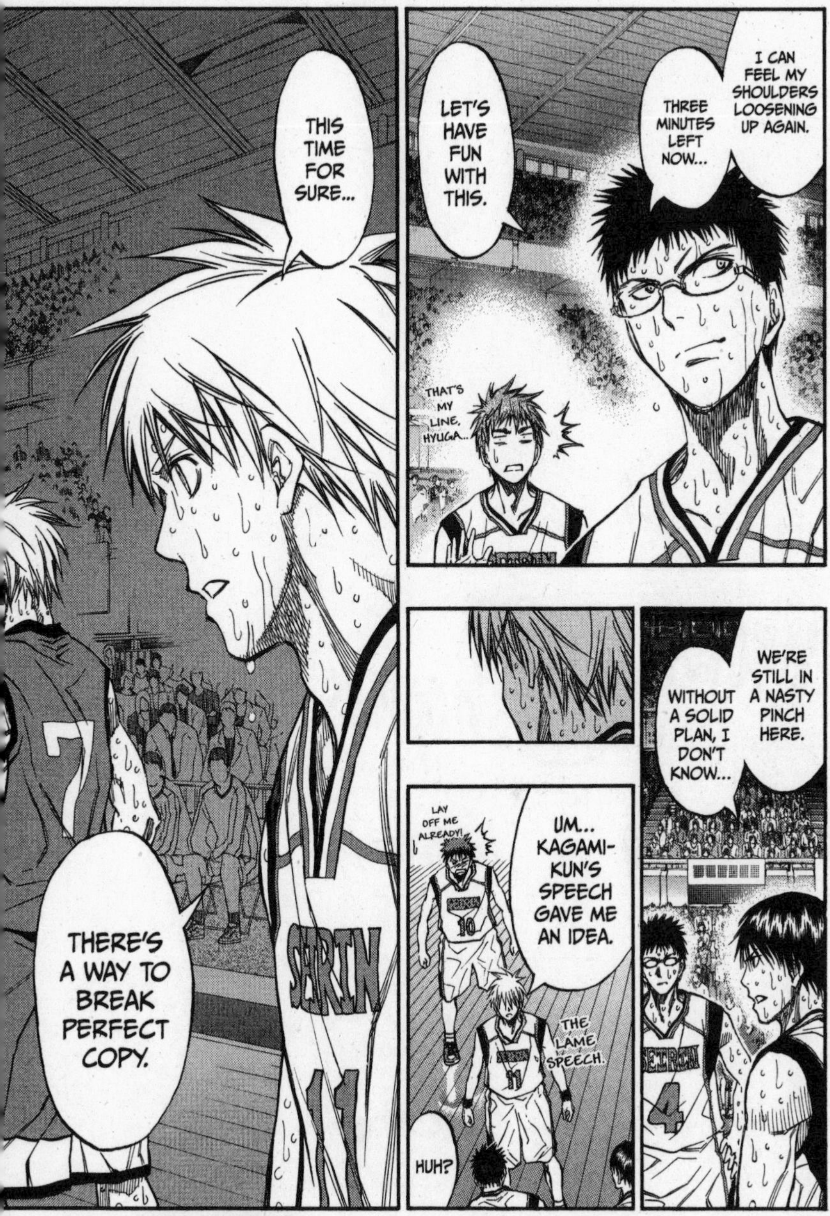
I CAN FEEL MY SHOULDERS LOOSENING UP AGAIN.
THREE MINUTES LEFT NOW...
LET'S HAVE FUN WITH THIS.
THAT'S MY LINE, HYUGA...
WE'RE STILL IN A NASTY PINCH HERE.
WITHOUT A SOLID PLAN, I DON'T KNOW...
UM... KAGAMI-KUN'S SPEECH GAVE ME AN IDEA.
LAY OFF ME ALREADY!
THE LAME SPEECH.
HUH?
THIS TIME FOR SURE...
THERE'S A WAY TO BREAK PERFECT COPY.

TO BE CONTINUED

KUROKO'S BASKETBALL BLOOPERS

TAKE 7

WHAP
ACK!
SCREWED UP!!
BAM
I'VE SAID THAT A FEW TOO MANY TIMES THIS GAME.
JUST REAL-IZED!!
AH!

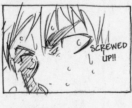

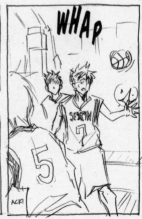

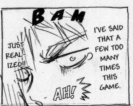

KUROKO'S BASKETBALL: SIDE STORY

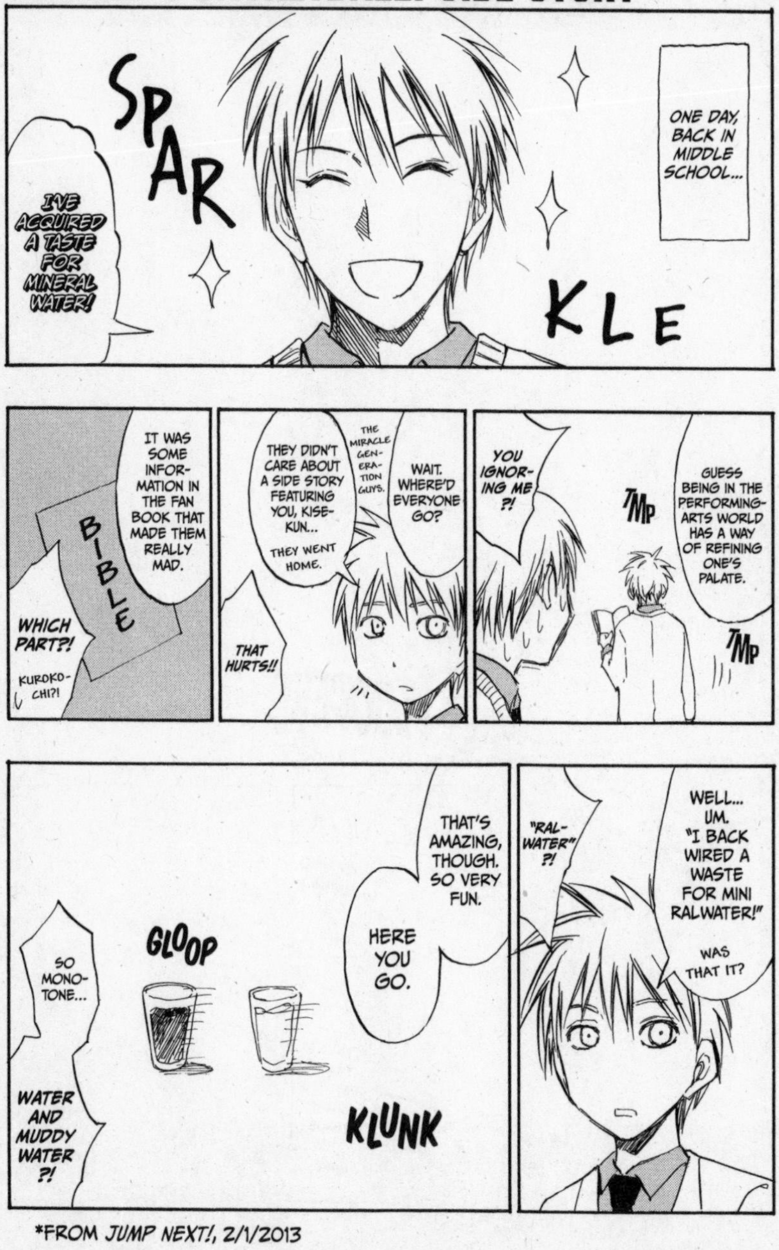
ONE DAY, BACK IN MIDDLE SCHOOL...
SPARKLE
I'VE ACQUIRED A TASTE FOR MINERAL WATER!
GUESS BEING IN THE PERFORMING-ARTS WORLD HAS A WAY OF REFINING ONE'S PALATE.
TMP
TMP
YOU IGNORING ME?!
WAIT. WHERE'D EVERYONE GO?
THE MIRACLE GENERATION GUYS.
THEY DIDN'T CARE ABOUT A SIDE STORY FEATURING YOU, KISE-KUN... THEY WENT HOME.
THAT HURTS!!
IT WAS SOME INFORMATION IN THE FAN BOOK THAT MADE THEM REALLY MAD.
BIBLE
WHICH PART?!
KUROKO-CHI?!
WELL... UM. "I BACK WIRED A WASTE FOR MINI RALWATER!" WAS THAT IT?
"RAL-WATER"?!
THAT'S AMAZING, THOUGH. SO VERY FUN.
HERE YOU GO.
GLOOP
KLUNK
SO MONOTONE...
WATER AND MUDDY WATER?!

*FROM *JUMP NEXT!*, 2/1/2013

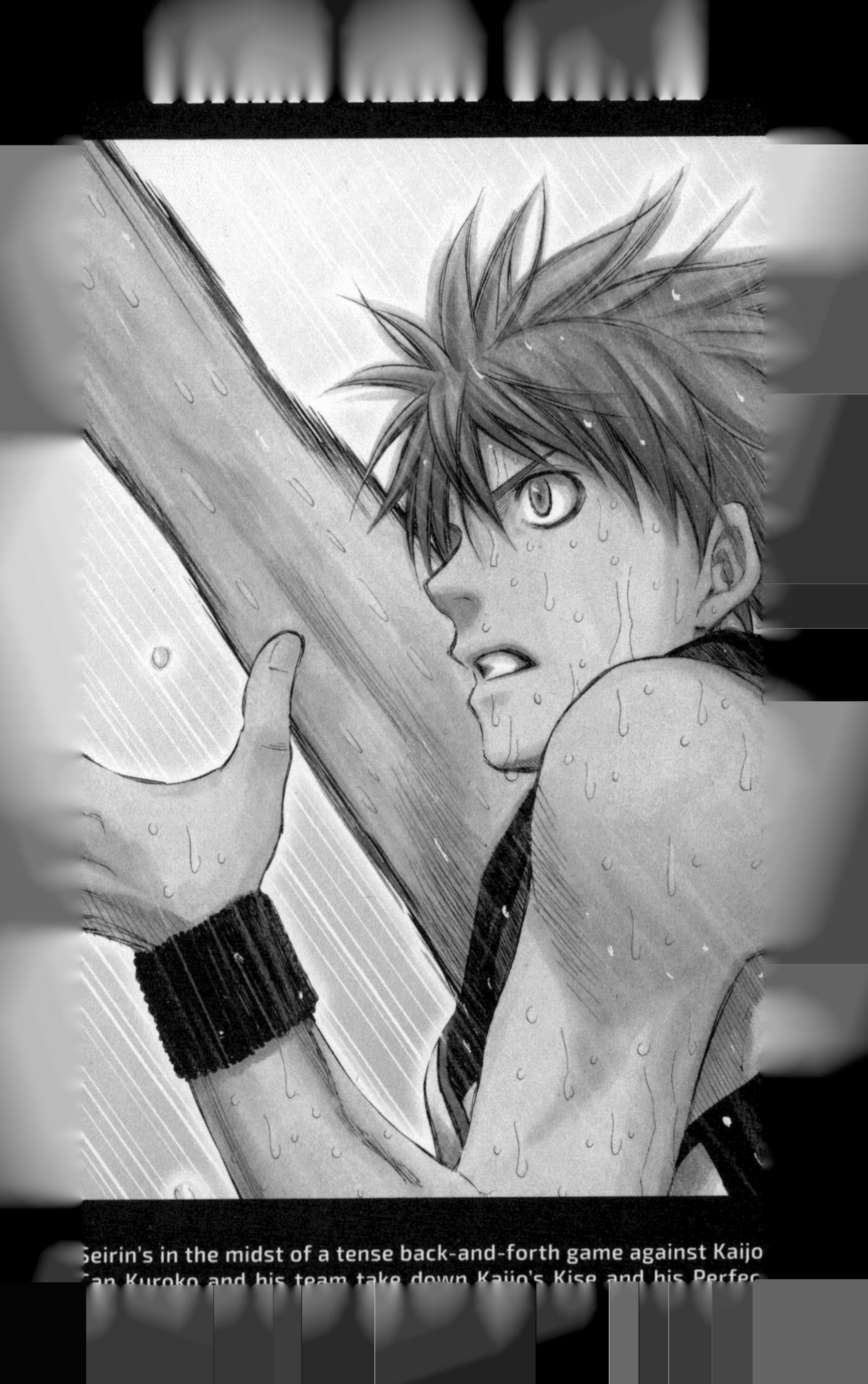

Seirin's in the midst of a tense back-and-forth game against Kaijo. Can Kuroko and his team take down Kaijo's Kise and his Perfec

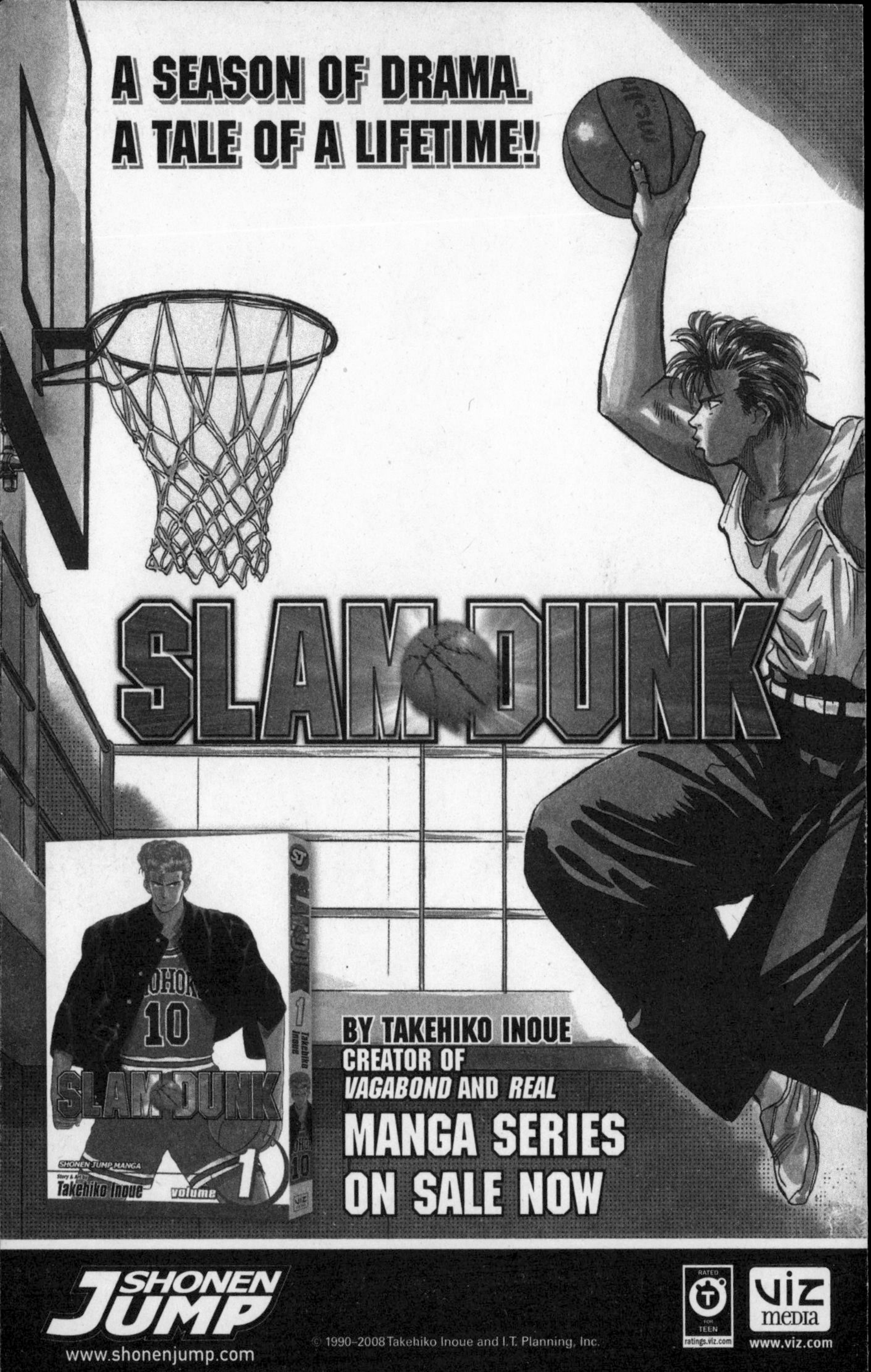
A SEASON OF DRAMA.
A TALE OF A LIFETIME!
SLAM DUNK
SHOHOKU
10
SLAM DUNK
SHONEN JUMP MANGA
Takehiko Inoue
volume 1
BY TAKEHIKO INOUE
CREATOR OF
VAGABOND AND *REAL*
MANGA SERIES
ON SALE NOW
SHONEN JUMP
www.shonenjump.com
© 1990–2008 Takehiko Inoue and I.T. Planning, Inc.
RATED T FOR TEEN
ratings.viz.com
VIZ media
www.viz.com

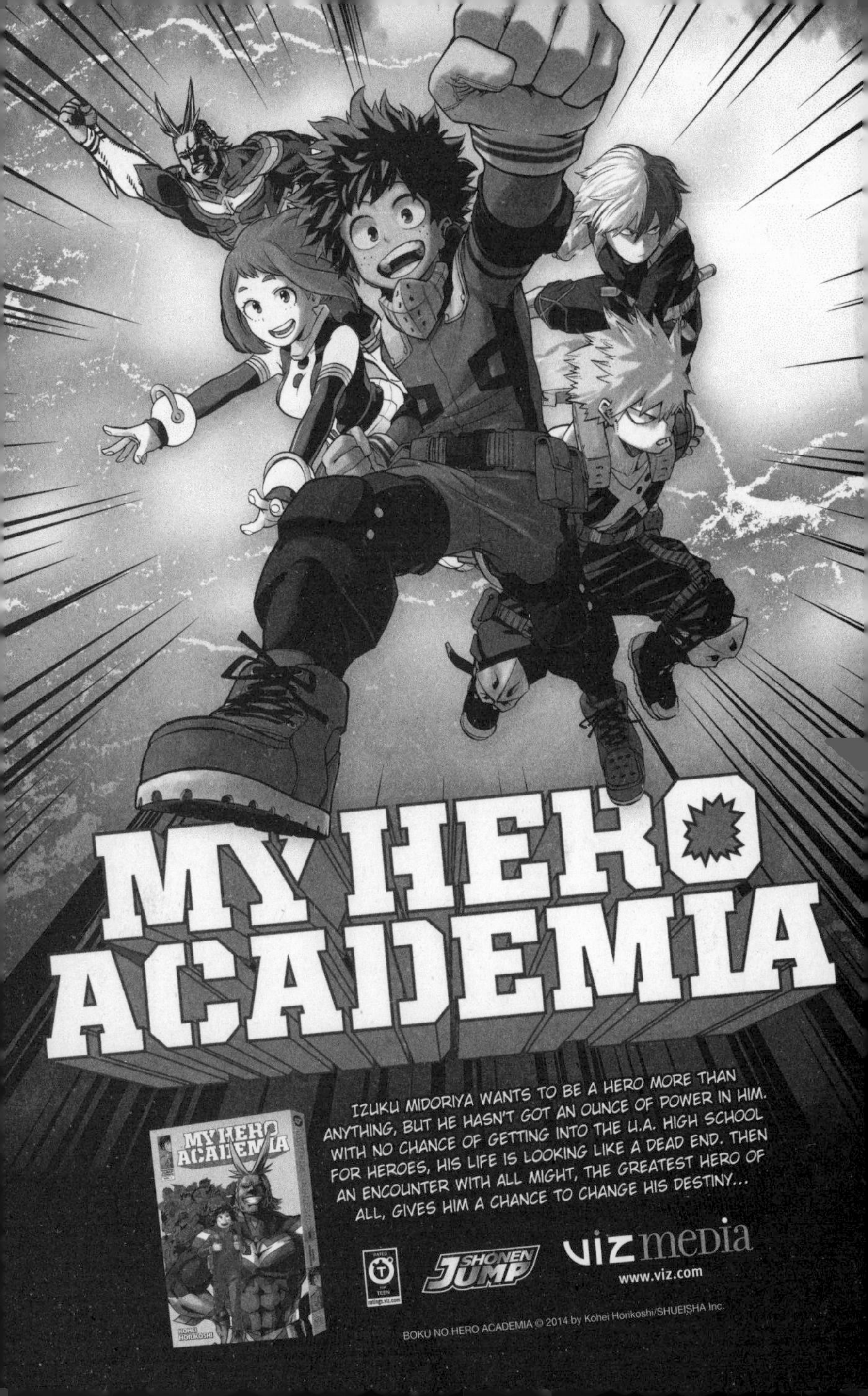
MY HERO ACADEMIA
IZUKU MIDORIYA WANTS TO BE A HERO MORE THAN ANYTHING, BUT HE HASN'T GOT AN OUNCE OF POWER IN HIM. WITH NO CHANCE OF GETTING INTO THE U.A. HIGH SCHOOL FOR HEROES, HIS LIFE IS LOOKING LIKE A DEAD END. THEN AN ENCOUNTER WITH ALL MIGHT, THE GREATEST HERO OF ALL, GIVES HIM A CHANCE TO CHANGE HIS DESTINY...
MY HERO ACADEMIA
KOHEI HORIKOSHI
RATED T TEEN
ratings.viz.com
SHONEN JUMP
VIZ media
www.viz.com
BOKU NO HERO ACADEMIA © 2014 by Kohei Horikoshi/SHUEISHA Inc.

YOU'RE READING THE
WRONG WAY!

KUROKO'S BASKETBALL reads from right to left, starting in the upper-right corner. Japanese is read from right to left, meaning that action, sound effects and word-balloon order are completely reversed from English order.

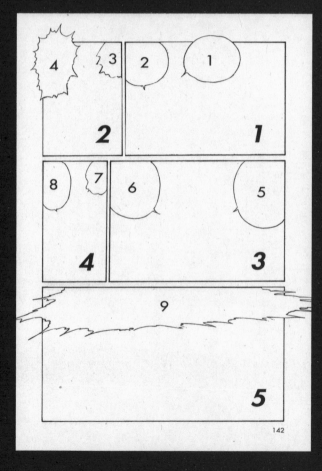

142

FLIP IT OVER TO GET STARTED!

Kuroko's BASKETBALL

21 & 22

SHONEN JUMP Manga Edition
BY TADATOSHI FUJIMAKI

Translation/Caleb Cook
Touch-Up Art & Lettering/Snir Aharon
Design/Julian [JR] Robinson
Editor/John Bae

Printed in the U.S.A.

Published by VIZ Media, LLC
P.O. Box 77010
San Francisco, CA 94107

10 9 8 7 6 5 4 3 2 1
First printing, April 2018

TADATOSHI FUJIMAKI

I can't seem to remember the kanji for "coach" many times I write it out.

You'd think I would, given how often it shows u

Tadatoshi Fujimaki was born on June 9, 1982, in his debut in 2007 in *Akamaru Jump* with *Kuro* which was later serialized in *Weekly Shonen Basketball* quickly gained popularity and beca